D1457301

YALE STUDIES IN ENGLISH

Yale Studies in English publishes books on English, American, and Anglophone literature developed in and by the Yale University community. Founded in 1898 by Albert Stanburrough Cook, the original series continued into the 1970s, producing such titles as *The Poetry of Meditation* by Louis Martz, *Shelley's Mythmaking* by Harold Bloom, *The Cankered Muse* by Alvin Kernan, *The Hero of the Waverley Novels* by Alexander Welsh, *John Skelton's Poetry* by Stanley Fish, and *Sir Walter Raleigh: The Renaissance Man and His Roles* by Stephen Greenblatt. With the goal of encouraging publications by emerging scholars alongside the work of established colleagues, the series has been revived for the twenty-first century with the support of a grant from the Andrew W. Mellon Foundation and in partnership with Yale University Press.

THE VIRTUE
OF SYMPATHY

Magic, Philosophy, and Literature in Seventeenth-Century England

Seth Lobis

Yale

UNIVERSITY

PRESS

New Haven and London

Published with assistance from the Mary Cady Tew Memorial Fund.

Yale University Press books may be purchased in quantity for educational, business, or promotional use. For information, please e-mail sales.press@yale.edu (U.S. office) or sales@yaleup.co.uk (U.K. office).

Set in Electra type by IDS Infotech Ltd., Chandigarh, India.
Printed in the United States of America.

Library of Congress Cataloging-in-Publication Data
Lobis, Seth.
The virtue of sympathy : magic, philosophy, and literature in seventeenth-century England / Seth Lobis.
Pages cm. — (Yale studies in English)
Includes bibliographical references and index.
ISBN 978-0-300-19203-2 (hardback)
1. English literature—Early modern, 1500–1700—History and criticism. 2. Literature and society—England—History—17th century. 3. Sympathy—England—History—17th century. 4. Sympathy in literature. 5. Social ethics—England—History— 17th century. 6. England—social life and customs—17th century. I. Title.
PR438.S63L63 2014
820.9'004—dc23
2014031335

A catalogue record for this book is available from the British Library.

The nature of a relationship is enigmatic.

—*Walter Benjamin, from "Analogy and Relationship"*

In what great distance, secret sympathy,
Through ayre or spirits thou act'st on things remote,
I cannot say with perspicuitie,
Nor how thy impertitions are begot.

Distempers and conceits doe verifie,
Strong fancied objects outwardly appeare,
Paying in opticall realitie,
The intromissions of the impregnat Ayre.

Worke then my faith by thy great energy,
Faith upon others warme with charitie,
The coldnesse of the times to fructifie,
By its diffusive vertuous qualitie;
    Rise Lord and sympathetically encline
    To turne to thee, thy enemies and mine.

—*Dudley North, third Baron North, from* A Forest of Varieties *(1645)*

CONTENTS

ACKNOWLEDGMENTS

I am immensely grateful to the many people whose assistance and encouragement made the completion of this book possible. I would like to acknowledge first David Quint and John Rogers, who advised the project in its initial stages and continued to support it thereafter. At a later stage David Quint very generously read and commented on the manuscript as a whole. I wish to thank the following as well for their long-standing support: Harold Bloom, Marie Borroff, Leslie Brisman, the late Thomas M. Greene, the late John Hollander, Lawrence Manley, Annabel Patterson, and Joseph Roach. William Carroll, Geoffrey Hill, Erin Murphy, Rosanna Warren, and James Winn received me warmly during the two years spent working on this book at Boston University, and I am especially glad to have had the benefit of Michael Prince's advice and conversation at a time when I was thinking and writing about the eighteenth century. I completed this book at Claremont McKenna College and deeply appreciate the support of all my colleagues in the Department of Literature: Audrey Bilger, Leland de la Durantaye, Robert Faggen, John Farrell, James Morrison, Ellen Rentz, Robert von Hallberg, and Nicholas Warner. John Farrell read a version of the entire manuscript and offered many clarifying comments. Leslie Elias-Volz, Cindi Guimond, Gregory Hess, and Nicholas Warner provided much-appreciated institutional support. I am indebted to my research assistants—Chris Ferrer, Carl Peaslee, and Kathryn Punsly—for their timely help. For various kinds of advice and assistance I also wish to acknowledge the following people: Eugenie Birch, Dave Bjerk, Adam Bradley, Jenny Davidson, Kathy Eden, Mordechai Feingold, Angus Fletcher, Lily Geismer, Victoria Kahn, Jamaica Kincaid, Laura Knoppers, Anthea Kraut, Sarah Larson, Aaron Matz, Molly Murray, Mark Oppenheimer, George and Fernande Raine, M. A. Sancho II, Debora Shuger, Phyllis Thompson, Eden Werring, Judy

Wolfe, Marta Zamora, and Katja Zelljadt. I am grateful to Rob Haskell for commenting on a portion of the manuscript at a critical point.

The research for this book was made possible by the support of a Whiting Fellowship in the Humanities, a John F. Enders Fellowship, a Beinecke Library Fellowship, a Yale Center for British Art research grant, and a fellowship from the Gould Center for Humanistic Studies at Claremont McKenna College. The staffs of the Beinecke Rare Book and Manuscript Library and the Medical Historical Library at Yale, the British Library, the National Archives (U.K.), the Wellcome Library, the Huntington Library, and Special Collections at the Honnold/Mudd Library, of the Claremont Colleges provided valuable assistance. Parts of the book were presented at meetings of the Modern Language Association, the Renaissance Society of America, and the International Milton Symposium, and I am grateful for the helpful responses received in those settings. A version of chapter 1 appeared as "Sir Kenelm Digby and the Power of Sympathy," *Huntington Library Quarterly* 74 (2011): 243–260.

I also wish to thank Otto Bohlmann, Eric Brandt, Laura Davulis, Erica Hanson, and Margaret Otzel at Yale University Press for their attention to and support of this book.

For their lasting encouragement I am deeply grateful to Judith, Robert, and Samantha Lobis. It was a great joy to finish this book in the presence of Claudia Lobis. Finally, I wish to thank Victoria Sancho Lobis, whose love, wisdom, forbearance, and companionship have sustained me.

INTRODUCTION:
TOWARD A NEW HISTORY
OF SYMPATHY

The world of *The Tempest*, a remote island somewhere between Naples and Tunis, variously associated with the New World, the Golden Age, and the Garden of Eden, is a sympathetic animal, a spirit world where the winds sigh back to the sighing, the wood weeps with the weeping, and the air carries "sweet airs."[1] Prospero gets revenge on his old enemies by taking strategic advantage of the vital connection between heaven and earth. As he explains to Miranda,

> Know thus far forth:
> By accident most strange, bountiful Fortune
> (Now my dear lady) hath mine enemies
> Brought to this shore; and by my prescience
> I find my zenith doth depend upon
> A most auspicious star, whose influence
> If now I court not, but omit, my fortunes
> Will ever after droop.
>
> (1.2.177–184)

Prospero's art here is that of "constellation"; he works a charm by concentrating the virtue flowing from a particular star.[2] Through extensive study and self-discipline Prospero has learned how to control the natural world. He creates the "enmity" in the elements that his storm-tossed enemies try in desperation and in vain to resist (2.1.117).

As the play unfolds, an analogy emerges between the disturbance that disrupts the nuptial masque for Ferdinand and Miranda and the disturbance that brings Ferdinand to the island in the first place; Prospero's sudden apoplexy, a tempest of the mind, recalls the sudden tempest, an apoplexy of the elements, that opens the play.[3] This analogy is furthered by a mode of sympathetic wordplay linking the play's title to a group of words with which the word "tempest" is cognate: "time," "tempered," "temperate," and "distempered." Miranda marvels at her father's unprecedented loss of composure: "Never till this day / Saw I him touch'd with anger, so distemper'd" (4.1.144–145). Prospero's "passion," as Ferdinand refers to it, is particularly jarring in relation to the masque itself, where Iris convokes "temperate nymphs" to join in the celebration of the young lovers' love (4.1.132). Iconographically, the circle is broken; the reapers and nymphs cannot conclude their festive dance. It is only after Prospero's enemies, charmed into submission, stand in a circle before him at the beginning of act 5 that harmony is restored. Having just renounced his art, Prospero can forgive his enemies through a compensatory "passion" transmuted, as if by the power he has forsworn, from distemper into temperance.

When Prospero weeps with the weeping Gonzalo, we see a sympathetic effect in the little world of man. "Holy Gonzalo, honorable man," Prospero begins, "Mine eyes, ev'n sociable to the show of thine, / Fall fellowly drops. The charm dissolves apace" (5.1.62–64). This sympathy, Shakespeare suggests, is not magical but moral; it is preceded by Prospero's subordination of "vengeance" to "virtue" (5.1.28). His tears recall those shed by Miranda in the opening act of the play, when — in a scene evoking the famous opening to book 2 of Lucretius's *De rerum natura*[4] — she sympathizes with the sailors she views from a distance:

> If by your art, my dearest father, you have
> Put the wild waters in this roar, allay them.
> The sky it seems would pour down stinking pitch,
> But that the sea, mounting to th' welkin's cheek,
> Dashes the fire out. O! I have suffered
> With those that I saw suffer.
>
>   (1.2.1–6)

Miranda's tears, while ever on the verge of running over, provide a living model for an education, too long neglected, that cannot be found in books.[5] What immediately prompts Prospero's tears is not Miranda's "compassion" (1.2.27), as he calls it, but Ariel's spritely approximation of sympathy, the merest "touch" of tenderness in his airy being (5.1.21). Once Prospero regains a feeling for his own humanity, realizing first that he can feel as his enemies and all his kind do, he can decide to feel *with* them. Subject to the influence of others, he no longer needs to rely on the influence of the stars. At the end of the play, as he prepares to leave the island, Prospero looks ahead to the wedding of his daughter, so solidifying a new familial network that can be seen to replace the cosmic network to which he has been wedded.

This is a book about sympathy in seventeenth-century England and more specifically about the relationship between two major concepts of sympathy in the period, one universal and magical, the other interpersonal and moral. The first concept refers to connections among a totality of objects, the second to connections between subjects, sympathy in the modern sense of "fellow feeling," or "the fact or capacity of entering into or sharing the feelings of another or others."[6] This distinction is necessarily schematic, but it may serve for the moment to clarify my motive and method. Literary and intellectual historians have tended to treat the two concepts in isolation, as if they belonged to entirely separate historical traditions, and previous literary studies of sympathy in particular have been limited by an almost exclusive focus on British and American writing after 1700.[7] In taking a more integrative approach, this study aims to fill a significant historiographical gap.

The seventeenth century represents a critical period of transition in conceptions of sympathy. Especially from the middle of the century, sympathy was increasingly conceived as a matter of moral, social, and psychological experience rather than one of broadly natural or cosmological speculation. Long understood as an external reality, sympathy underwent a gradual process of internalization. The movement away from Prospero's island, initiated by Prospero himself, can be seen to allegorize a historical shift from a predominantly natural-philosophical or natural-magical concept of sympathy to one that subordinates cosmic relations to human relations. The play's initial concern with what Antonio terms "consent" (2.1.203), magical affinity or connection, gives way to a new emphasis on "compassion." In following this broad historical movement from natural to moral philosophy, I have not attempted to write a teleological history, nor have I attempted to produce a comprehensive prehistory of sympathy in "the age of sensibility." Rather, I have taken a specific angle of approach, using sympathy as a way into broader debates about magic and science in the seventeenth century, in which it figured as a central topic. The core of my analysis centers on the period from the accession of Charles I to the death of Charles II, a period of intense social, cultural, and political ferment. It was also, I demonstrate, a period of intense concern about the nature, scope, and status of sympathy, a period defined in part by far-reaching and wide-ranging attempts among the intellectual elite to come to terms with sympathy. I analyze the various ways in which an intellectually heterogeneous group of

authors write about sympathy in a generically diverse group of literary and philosophical texts. Literary discussions of sympathy have tended to focus on two
literary kinds—drama and the novel. There are good reasons for this dual
emphasis, but a fuller historical understanding of sympathy requires attending
to and taking into account a wider range of forms, literary as well as nonliterary.
My analysis establishes the intimate interconnection, both positive and negative, between sympathy and magic in the seventeenth century. In so doing, it
opens up a new perspective on representations of sympathy in the eighteenth
and nineteenth centuries, which, in a number of significant cases, show far
greater continuity with earlier representations than has been previously recognized. We need to appreciate that the dialogue between magic and sympathy
was both long-standing and ongoing. The magical idea of action at a distance
persisted long after debates about magnetism, gravitation, and other seemingly
"occult" phenomena receded from the forefront of natural-philosophical speculation. We need to think of sympathy less in narrowly sentimental terms and
more in broadly spatial terms. Distance and difference are its preconditions,
and it acts to attract and connect, to bridge spatial gaps. Standardly affiliated
with ethics, sympathy, I want to argue, needs to be understood more generally
in terms of *dynamics*, as a principle of mobility, communication, and exchange,
of matter and spirit as well as of thought and feeling.

The study of sympathy as a matter of literary and intellectual history presents
a distinct methodological challenge, what might be called the word-thing
problem. In his rather Baconian critique of the history of ideas, first published
in 1969, Quentin Skinner cautioned the intellectual historian against treating
an idea as either a "hypostasized . . . entity" or a "growing organism," things cut
off from the contexts and conditions of writing.[8] "There can be no histories of
concepts as such," Skinner has written more recently; "there can only be histories of their uses in argument."[9] Early modern writers frequently relied on and
appealed to a distinction between *res* and *verba*, words and things, whether
concrete or abstract.[10] I have approached my subject as a matter of both, which
is to say that my method has been both what Leo Spitzer called "semasiological" and "onamasiological." The follower of the former method begins with a
particular word and studies its meaning or range of meanings over time in
various "cultural stylizations," whereas the follower of the latter begins with a
particular concept or thing and studies "the variety of word-material" it has
"attracted."[11] The word "sympathy" does not appear in *The Tempest*, which was
produced in 1611, and in the sense of "entering into or sharing the feelings of
another" it does not become part of a wider cultural vocabulary—it does not
become a "keyword" in Raymond Williams's sense—until after the Restoration.[12]

But I think we can see in Shakespeare's play an emerging concept of sympathy in emphatically positioned "word-material" like "piteous," "compassion," "tender," "sociable," "fellowly."[13]

Yet to neglect the semasiological approach is to court the "mythological," as Skinner puts it, to risk considerable hermeneutical and historical distortion. In his influential study of sympathy in the eighteenth and nineteenth centuries, David Marshall undertakes a brief lexical analysis of "sympathy" and its French counterpart "sympathie," but then quickly shies away from it: "I should emphasize that I am concerned here with the category, concept, and conditions of sympathy in certain key eighteenth-century texts, not with particular words."[14] In a more recent study of sympathy, Rachel Ablow makes a similar point: "I . . . am interested less in the term 'sympathy' than in the wide variety of ways in which the encounter between minds—whether of husband and wife, or of reader and text—was imagined in the nineteenth century."[15] The anxiety, it seems to me, behind these methodological stipulations is that a study overtly concerned with a word necessarily limits its reach and significance, declaring itself for a benighted literal-mindedness. But by divorcing *res* from *verba*, or neglecting the latter in favor of the former, one robs texts of their literary richness and their rhetorical complexity. Semantic lumping—treating "pity," "compassion," and "sympathy," among others terms, as virtual fungibles—can yield a false sense of conceptual coherence.[16] It has been suggested that the Latin word *compassio*, traced back to Tertullian, and rendering the Greek etymon of "sympathy," *sympatheia* (literally, "feeling or suffering with"), was formed in part to fill the semantic space opened up as the primary sense of the older term *misericordia* shifted from "pity" to "charity" in the patristic tradition.[17] Compassion would come to figure centrally in medieval meditative writing about the Passion, as Sarah McNamer has recently shown.[18] Sympathy and compassion are close cousins, both etymologically and conceptually, but we do a certain historical violence by collapsing their histories into one. Compassion was not, as sympathy was, fully embedded in the discourses of natural philosophy and natural magic, and it is the complex relationship between the histories of magic and science and the history of affect that is my primary concern in this book. "Sympathy" was a particularly charged and volatile signifier throughout the seventeenth century, and the authors I consider often deployed it at their peril.

Challenging "the linguistic approach to the history of ideas," and Skinner in particular, Kevin Sharpe has argued that to treat ideology "entirely in discursive terms" is "to ignore the picture and the building, the public procession and religious ritual, the games and pastimes in all of which the meaning a society identifies for itself is embodied and represented."[19] The present book is indeed subject to this limitation, but since sympathy was so often addressed and attacked as a linguistic matter in this period, the orientation of my approach has been necessarily linguistic. A full survey of a semantic field that in mid-seventeenth-century England was something more like a battleground requires a broad historical perspective, stretching back to classical antiquity. In taking this longer view, we can better understand sympathy's rich and diverse philo-sophical legacy and the dynamic interplay at its core between the world of the body and the body of the world.

FROM THE STOICS TO THE NATURALISTS

"Conflux one, conspiration one [sumpnoia mia], all things in sympathy [sumpathea panta]; all its parts as forming a whole, and severally the parts in each part, with reference to the work."[20] In this aphorism from the Hippocratic treatise *On Nutriment* the body emerges as a perfectly interconnected system. By the account of Alexander of Aphrodisias, it was the Stoic Chrysippus (fl. 3c. B.C.E.) who translated this "medical notion" of sympathy from physiology to cosmology, although it has been suggested that a cosmic conception of sympathy originated with the founder of Stoicism, Zeno of Citium, in the fourth century B.C.E.[21] Like the body, the cosmos was filled with, and quickened by, a material *pneuma* whose tension secured the sympathy and coherence of the whole. In his account of Stoic philosophy, published in 1656, Thomas Stanley empha-sizes pneumatic plenitude: "In the World there is no vacuity, but it is compleatly one, for that necessitates a conspiration and harmony, betwixt Celestials and Terrestrials."[22] There is no gap between heaven and earth, microcosm and macrocosm; the world is a single, sympathetic whole.[23] Although it was broadly diffused throughout the ancient world, the idea of sympathy came to be associ-ated particularly with the Stoics.[24] In Cicero's *De natura deorum* the Stoic Balbus appeals to "the sympathetic agreement, interconnexion and affinity of things [rerum consentiens conspirans continuata cognatio]" and "the musical harmony of all the parts of the world [omnibus inter se concinentibus mundi partibus]" as proof that "a single divine and all-pervading spirit" governs the world.[25] In *De divinatione* Cicero refers to the Stoics' emphasis on "the natural connection of distant things [distantium rerum cognatio naturalis]," glossing what "the Greeks call 'sympathy' [sumpatheian Graeci appellant]" as "harmony and consent [concentu atque consensu]."[26] Here it is likely that Cicero had Posidonius, whom he had encountered at Rhodes, particularly in mind.[27] Yet Cicero's use of the generic term "Graeci" can be taken to suggest that sympathy was not an exclusive Stoic property. His use of the terms *concentus* and *concinens* indeed points to a Pythagorean connection. Far more unexpectedly, the Stoics' great rival Epicurus also incorporated the concept of sympathy into his physics, using *sympatheia* to denote the coherence of atoms — "an instance," according to Myrto Garani, "in which Epicurus refutes a rival theory by appropriating its formal name into a new context."[28]

In addition to its Stoic, Pythagorean, and Epicurean associations, sympathy emerged in the Aristotelian tradition through the work of Theophrastus, who, as Ludwig Edelstein has claimed, "gives sympathy its place in natural science."[29] Building on the botanical work of Androtion and the so-called root-cutters, in addition to Aristotle, Theophrastus undertook a comprehensive inquiry into the natural world, noting, for example, the sympathies between olive and myrtle trees, goats and goatskins, and grapes and wine.[30] Theophrastus's botanical writings likely exerted an influence on Bolus of Mendes, who under the name of Democritus wrote a treatise entitled *Peri sumpathōn kai antipathōn*, and to whom Richard Gordon credits the "invention of the idea of natural magic," the idea, as he puts it, that "there is in Nature an inherent, marvelous power, which may be used for healing, exorcizing, divining, becoming rich, and many other purposes."[31] The emphasis of Bolus and the pseudo-Democritean tradition more generally on antipathies — enmities, contrarieties — as well as sympathies in the natural world suggests a possible link to Empedocles, whose cosmology was founded on the dual principles of Love (*philia*) and Strife (*neikos*).[32] Behind, then, what Gordon calls "the emergence in the Hellenistic period of a strong view of magic," to which ideas of sympathy and antipathy were fundamental, lies a complex network of influences and associations: Stoic, Pythagorean, Peripatetic, Democritean, Empedoclean.

But it is the Platonic tradition that is arguably of greatest significance to natural-philosophical conceptions of sympathy from the fifteenth through the seventeenth centuries. The Neoplatonists retained the Stoic emphasis on sympathy as a universal principle but reconceived the substrate; it was not *pneuma* but an immaterial world soul that bound all things. In *The Immortality of the Soul* (1659), Henry More (1614–1687) refers to "that *Magick Sympathy* that is seated in the Unity of the Spirit of the World. . . . The Universe in some sense being, as the Stoicks and Platonists define it, one vast entire *Animal*."[33] In the writings of Plotinus, Iamblichus, Synesius, and Proclus the link between sympathy and magic was strongly reinforced.[34] Plotinus predicates the efficacy of magic on the reality of cosmic sympathy: "But how do magic spells work? By sympathy [sumpatheiai] and by the fact that there is a natural concord [sumphōnian] of things that are alike [homoiōn] and opposition of things that are different. . . .

[T]he true magic is the 'Love' [philia] and also the 'Strife' [neikos] in the All."[35]
For Plotinus, the principle of sympathy accounts not only for magic spells but
also for answered prayers, astral divination, and sympathetic vibrations between
lyres. In his comment on the "true magic" the evocation of Empedocles is more
direct, but the discussion as a whole suggests connections not only to the Stoic
and pseudo-Democritean traditions but also to Plato himself. Diotima associates
love and magic in the *Symposium,* and the animistic worldview presented in the
Timaeus informed Plotinus's cosmology on a foundational level.[36]

What Brian Copenhaver has called the "remarkable rebirth" of magic in the
late fifteenth century depended in part on the revival of Neoplatonism initiated
by Marsilio Ficino (1433–1499), who saw the Neoplatonists as carrying forward
the "ancient theology" (*prisca theologia*), thought to originate with Hermes
Trismegistus, Zoroaster, Orpheus, and Pythagoras and culminating in Plato.[37]
In his *Commentary* on the *Symposium* (1489), Ficino proceeds from sympathy
to love to magic:

> But the parts of this world, like the parts of a single animal, all deriving from
> a single author, are joined to each other by the communion [communione]
> of a single nature. Therefore just as in us the brain, lungs, heart, liver, and
> the rest of the parts draw something from each other, and help each other,
> and sympathize with [compatiuntur] any one of them when it suffers, so the
> parts of this great animal, that is all the bodies of the world, similarly joined
> together, borrow and lend natures to and from each other. From this com-
> mon relationship [cognatione] is born a common love; from love, a com-
> mon attraction. And this is the true magic. . . . Thus . . . the lodestone draws
> iron, amber draws chaff, and sulphur, fire; the sun turns many flowers and
> leaves toward itself, and the moon, the waters.[38]

Here Ficino draws the ancient analogy between the sympathetic microcosm
and the sympathetic macrocosm, which rests on "the communion of a single
nature." The examples he gives of sympathetic attractions, emphasizing the
connections between the celestial and the terrestrial, underline the fact that
sympathy is a force inherent in nature. Ficino's use of the figure anadiplosis—
"From this common relationship is born a common love; from love, a common
attraction"—enacts on the rhetorical level the connectedness that he is asserting
on the ontological level. Ficino developed his sympathetic theory of magic most
extensively in the third book of his *De vita libri tres* (1489), a work whose widespread influence is well attested by its publication history; by the middle of the
seventeenth century, nearly thirty editions had appeared.[39] In articulating his
enchanted worldview, Ficino characteristically passes between east and west:

"Everywhere nature is a sorceress, as Plotinus and Synesius say, in that she every-where entices particular things by particular foods, just as she attracts heavy things by the power of the earth's center, light things by the power of the Moon's sphere, . . . and so on. By means of this attraction, the wise men of India testify, the world binds itself together [secum . . . devinciri]; and they say that the world is an animal . . . and that it everywhere links with itself in the mutual love of its members [mutuoque membrorum suorum amore] and so holds together."[40] Ficino empha-sizes the perfect coherence of the cosmos, which is "bound" and "held together" and completely "linked with itself." The world is both ensouled and "enamored." It is a spiritualized whole bound together by the magical principle of sympathy.

Along with Ficino, Giovanni Pico della Mirandola (1463–1494) was instru-mental in establishing "a new idea of magic," one that emphasized both the spiritual and the natural.[41] For Pico, the true magic was divine. In the *Oration on the Dignity of Man* (composed around 1486), he distinguishes demonic magic, or *goēteia*, from divine *mageia*, or theurgy, including references to a host of sources: Plato, Porphyry, and Plotinus as well as Pythagoras, Empedocles, Democritus, Zoroaster, al-Kindi, Roger Bacon, and others. Of the divine magi-cians, he writes:

> The latter, having more searchingly examined into the harmony of the uni-verse [universi consensum], which the Greeks with greater significance call *sumpatheia*, and having clearly perceived the reciprocal affinity of natures [mutuam naturarum cognitionem], and applying to each single thing the suitable and peculiar inducements (which are called the *iugges* of the magi-cians) brings forth into the open the miracles concealed in the recesses of the world, in the depths of nature, and in the storehouses and mysteries of God, just as if she herself were their maker; and, as the farmer weds his elms to vines, even so does the *magus* wed earth to heaven, that is, he weds lower things to the endowments and powers of higher things.[42]

The reference to the farmer's work underlines the link between magic and nature; indeed, for Pico true magic is "the utter perfection of natural philos-ophy."[43] Pico's mage, a kind of cosmic matchmaker, approaches God through the admiration and contemplation of His works, and so the magic he practices is justly called both natural and divine. In looking back to the wisdom of the ancients, Pico was not just consecrating magic but also articulating a philosophy of nature. In his classic case for the importance of Pico's *"Universal Vitalism"* in Renaissance natural philosophy, Ernst Cassirer writes, "In accordance with this conception any *knowing* of nature can mean only, and can be directed toward nothing higher than, to sympathize with this universal order of Life; all the notions we form of nature must, if they are not to remain mere abstractions, grow out of this feeling."[44] Pico's articulation of a natural philosophy predicated on "an original and thoroughgoing 'sympathy,'" Cassirer argues, exerted a significant influence on Heinrich Cornelius Agrippa von Nettesheim (1486–1535) and Paracelsus (1493–1541).

In Agrippa's treatment of magic, the impact of Pico's and Ficino's theories is widely felt.[45] Agrippa defines "Naturall Magick," to cite a seventeenth-century translation, as "that which contemplates the powers of all naturall and celestiall things, and searching curiously into their Sympathy [sympathiam], doth produce occult powers in nature into publique view, so coupling inferiour things as allurements to the gifts of superiour things, by their mutuall application."[46] The mutual attraction of inferior and superior things in the cosmos depends on the pervasiveness of sympathy. Ontological likeness is not the exception but the rule. Natural magic is possible because of "the mutuall correspondency [convenientiam] of things amongst themselves," which "the Grecians called *sumpatheian*," because of "the attracting of like by like [similium per similia], and of sutable things by sutable."[47] In the work of Paracelsus, sympathy becomes, in effect, a broad principle of homeopathy: "Each like thing understands its like [ein ietlichs simile verstehet sein simile]."[48] Highlighting "the medical dimension of Neoplatonism," Paracelsus conceived the art of healing in terms of the interplay between the macrocosm and the *klein welt* of man; for Paracelsus, as Charles Webster explains, "'Anatomy' was the science of the correspondences and sympathies between humans and the outer world."[49] Paracelsus's iatrochemistry was rooted in, and driven by, his sympathetic worldview. Nor were Agrippa and Paracelsus alone in this philosophical orientation toward the world. What Cassirer calls "the 'fact' of universal sympathy" was a guiding premise for a range of inquiries throughout the sixteenth century and into the seventeenth, from the *De subtilitate* (1550) and *De rerum varietate* (1557) of Girolamo Cardano (1501–1576) to the *De rerum natura . . . libri ix* (1586) of Bernardino Telesio (1509–1588) to the widely popular *Magiae naturalis* (1558, expanded to twenty books in 1589) of Giambattista della Porta (1535?–1615) to the *De sensu rerum et magia* (1620) of Tommaso Campanella (1568–1639).[50] Sympathy was a crucial conceptual nexus between natural philosophy and natural magic.

FROM BACON TO BOYLE

Francis Bacon (1561–1626) advanced his system of learning partly in response to a number of philosophers who maintained sympathy as an organizing principle, including Paracelsus, Telesio, and William Gilbert (1544–1603), whose treatise *De Magnete* appeared in 1600.[51] Gilbert not only rigorously described the process of magnetism but also passionately defended an animistic world-view. The ensoulment of things ensured a universal sympathy: "Therefore the bodies of the globes, as being the foremost parts of the universe, to the end they might be in themselves and in their state endure, had need of souls to be conjoined to them, for else there were neither life, nor prime act, nor movement, nor union, nor order, nor coherence, nor *conactus*, nor sympathy [compassio], nor any generation, nor alternation of seasons, and no propagation; but all were in confusion and the entire world lapse into chaos, and, in fine, the earth were void and dead and without any use."[52] Bacon challenged Gilbert's view of the earth as a great magnet and more generally distanced himself from the natural magicians. In Bacon's view the rudimentary natural philosophy of the pre-Socratics was more scientific than that of Aristotle, his followers, and many of Bacon's contemporaries. Natural magic had lost its divine calling and devolved into sorcery and superstition:

> We must turn all our attention to seeking and noting the resemblances and analogies of things [rerum similitudines et analoga], both in wholes and in parts. For those are the things which unite nature, and begin to constitute the sciences.
>
> But in all this one has to be strict, and very cautious, and accept as resembling and *analogous* only those *instances* which denote physical similarities . . . that is, real and substantial similarities which are founded in nature, not accidental and apparent similarities; much less the sort of superstitious or curious resemblances constantly featured by writers on natural magic (light-minded men and hardly worth mentioning in such serious matters as we are now discussing) when with much vanity and foolishness they describe, and even sometimes invent, empty similarities and sympathies in things [inanes similitudines et sympathias rerum].[53]

Bacon rejects an analogical worldview in the interest of a more "intimate view of nature"; only real, physical analogies can instruct us in God's creation. Bacon did not, however, reject the concept of universal sympathy so much as he sought to purify and clarify it. In *Thema Coeli* (1612) he posited a motion that "echoes through the universe of movable things, and penetrates from the stellar heaven all the way to the bowels and insides of the Earth, not by some violent or vexatious compulsion, but by constant consent [consensu perpetuo]."[54] For Bacon "sympathy," unlike "consent," had become a corrupt term. He demoted it in the *Novum Organum* (1620): "The interior agreements and aversions of bodies, or friendships and conflicts (for I am quite tired

of the words 'sympathies' and 'antipathies' because of superstitions and stupidi-
ties [taedet enim nos fere vocabulorum sympathiae et antipathiae, propter
superstitiones et inania]), are falsely associated, or tainted with fables [fabulis
conspersae], or little known because ignored."[55] Bacon prefers his own terms
("consensus et fugae") and even those of Empedocles ("amicitiae et lites") to
those of his mystified and mystifying contemporaries. With his lofty ambitions
for the advancement of learning, Bacon could not ignore the misguided natural
magicians and their "countless fables [innumeris fabulis]"; still, he believed it
was "an undeniable fact [verissimum est] that bodies do entice certain other
bodies (and do this so that they may be united with them) but, on the other
hand, keep and drive certain others away from them."[56] Sympathies and antipathies were real but needed to be carefully discriminated.

Bacon's commitment to pursuing sympathies and antipathies in nature—
according to a purer, proper method—continued right up until the end of his
life. He set out to write, but never completed, a "Historia Sympathiae et
Antipathiae Rerum," in the preface to which he laments, "this part of Philosophy,
namely of the Sympathy and Antipathy of things [Sympathia et Antipathia
rerum] is most impure [impura], which also they call Natural Magick." The
subject was not inherently "impure"—indeed, Bacon straightforwardly considers
it a "pars philosophiae"—but it had become so because of the intellectual lazi-
ness of natural magicians. "For the Precepts of Natural Magick are such," Bacon
writes, "as if men should be confident that they could subdue the earth, and eat
their bread without the sweat of their Brow, and to have power over things by
idle and easie applications of bodies," whereas, in truth, "God hath appointed
the best of things to be enquired out and be wrought by labours and endeavours.
We will be a little more carefull [diligentiores] in searching out the law of
Nature, and the mutual Contracts of things [rerum foederibus], neither
favouring Miracles, nor making too lowly and straightned an Inquisition."[57]
Bacon's reformation of natural magic depended on the virtue of hard work. The
sympathetic and antipathetic relationships of things were not to be merely relied
or speculated on but rather to be "searched out" and studied. Bacon's *Sylva
Sylvarum*, which he was working on in his last years, and which was published
posthumously in 1626, was a vast and eclectic collection of "experiments" in
natural history and in a sense a partial fulfillment of his planned history of
sympathy and antipathy.[58] In it he extends his critique of natural magic: "Some
of the Ancients, and likewise divers of the Moderne Writers, that have laboured
in *Naturall Magicke*, have noted a *Sympathy*, between the *Sunne, Moone*, and
some Principall *Starres*; And certaine *Herbs*, and *Plants*. And so they have
denominated some *Herbs Solar*, and some *Lunar*; And such like Toyes put into

great Words."[59] Such "labour," more verbal than practical, was hardly of the sort Bacon had in mind. But, in spite of this condemnation of terms, he does not reject "sympathy." In the tenth "Century" of *Sylva*, which suggests a considerable familiarity with Della Porta's *Magia naturalis*, Bacon refers to "the *Universall Configuration*, and *Sympathy* of the *World*" and goes on to assert, "There be many *Things*, that worke upon the *Spirits* of *Man*, by *Secret Sympathy*, and *Antipathy*."[60] These claims both for and against a sympathetic view of the world reached a relatively wide audience; the most frequently reprinted of Bacon's natural-philosophical works in the seventeenth century, *Sylva* was, in Graham Rees's characterization, "one of the great engines of seventeenth-century Baconianism."[61]

In the latter part of the seventeenth century Bacon's critique of the fables of analogy and sympathy contributed to a wider attack on a sympathetic world-view. Robert Boyle (1627–1691), who referred to "the four sorts of Idols . . . that mislead the studiers of Philosophy" conceived by "our excellent *Verulam*," sought to establish a more rigorous ontological division between the animate and the inanimate realms than had his misled scholastic predecessors.[62] "To say that the ascent of the Water . . . proceeds from Natures Detestation of a Vacuity," Boyle writes, "supposes that there is a kinde of *Anima Mundi*, furnished with various Passions, which watchfully provides for the safety of the Universe; or that a Brute and Inanimate Creature, as Water, . . . has a power to move its heavy Body upwards, contrary (to speak in their Language) to the tendency of its particular Nature."[63] For Boyle, careful experimentation obviated animistic "supposition."[64] To universalize such endowments as passion and motion was to ignore and collapse the scale of nature. In a later treatise on "the Chymists Philosophy," Boyle writes,

> I am dissatisfied with the very fundamental Notion of this Doctrine, namely a supposed Hostility between the tribe of Acids and that of Alkalies, accompanied, if you will have it so, with a friendship or sympathy with bodies belonging to the same tribe or Family. For I look upon Amity and Enmity as Affections of Intelligent Beings, and I have not yet found it explained by any, how those Appetites can be placed in Bodies Inanimate and devoid of knowledge, or of so much as Sense. And I elsewhere endeavour to shew, that what is called Sympathy and Antipathy between such bodies does in great part depend upon the actings of our own Intellect.[65]

Boyle draws a firm distinction here between "Intelligent Beings" and "Bodies Inanimate and devoid of knowledge"; "Amity and Enmity" were not common to both, as the Scholastic and Neoplatonic philosophers maintained, but the unique possession of the former. In limiting "Affections" to "Intelligent Beings," ultimately Boyle was not only undermining an animistic worldview but also promoting a much narrower sphere of activity for sympathy, one in which it was not an idol of the "Intellect" but an empirical fact. Sympathy was above all a human "Affection," and the sympathies of inanimate objects were not intrinsic to them but imposed on them by errant minds.

Similarly challenging a universal idea of sympathy, John Spencer used a long epigraph from Bacon's *Advancement of Learning* to authorize his *Discourse concerning Prodigies* (1663, 2nd ed. 1665). In the course of arguing against prodigies, Spencer argued against the animistic premise underlying them. He cites an anonymous true believer:

> Others again seem to me to apprehend the World, as a kind of *Great Animal*, informed by a very subtil and apprehensive Spirit, which . . . in its several parts suffers mighty emotions and disturbances. But this notion will perhaps look more temptingly, when presented to us as the Parents thereof are pleased to dress it forth: *There is* (saith a late Writer) *that sympathy and fellow-feeling which God hath put in his whole Creation, whereby each part hath a care of the whole. . . . As when our Savior died, the Sun was darkned,* the Rocks were rent, the Earth shook, *by a kind of natural sympathy and compassionate horror, at so dreadful and amazing a spectacle* . . . .
>
> The pretty Allegories and Allusions of which Discourse (but the watering of weak and worthless stuff) might possibly shew not unhandsomly in an Oration, but are too airy and thin for a Sermon.[66]

By the author's fanciful logic God made the universe sympathetic as a condition of the Fall. Spencer does not deny "those direful and amazing alterations in the whole frame of the World, which attended our Saviors Passion, and the fates of *Jerusalem*," but he considers them exceptional and miraculous.[67] To generalize from these few instances is merely to allegorize. Spencer conceives sympathy tropologically. An audience might well be entertained by stories of sympathetic effects, but certainly not instructed or illuminated by them. For those who credit the idea of universal sympathy, Spencer claims, the classical *auctores* are merely a crutch, shoring up their own wild fancies. He cites Cicero, who provides "the Patrons of such kind of Divinations" with the notion that "there was *Cognatio Naturae, Concentus & sumpatheia rerum*, a kind of common sense in Nature, a secret consent and sympathy between the parts of this Great Animal, the World; and that therefore nothing could happen in one part, without some touch and passion in another," and these "Patrons" thereby "procure reputation to their Opinion." The view does not warrant credit in and of itself; it must be trumped up. Spencer then cites Synesius, who "prefers Dreams and portentous Events to the regards of men . . . because there is (saith He) . . . a great affinity and common feeling between the several parts of the World; and that in the World . . . one thing draws and affects through another, carrying the present pledges, voices, figures and images of most distant objects." For Spencer, however, Synesian oneiromancy is nothing more than an "antick notion," ascribing "not onely sense to the World, but Prophecy," such that the world becomes "one great Oracle," Delphi, in effect, writ large.

This absurdity, a relic of the benighted past, thrives not because it accurately describes reality but because it answers a habit of mind. Spencer lectures his readers in a Baconian vein on the psychological origin of a sympathetic worldview:

> It is the nature of the Soul to be greatly impressive to a Perswasion of Parallels, Equalities, Similitudes, in the frame and Government of the World: and that (indeed) so far, as to make them (by the poesie of Fancy) where it cannot really discover them; that so it may please and solace it self in some supposed lines and figures of its own uniform and harmonious nature portray'd upon the World. . . . To this among the rest, that there is a very rigid and strict analogy and conformity between the Macrocosm and the Microcosm, the World and Man, that he is a kind of *Terella*, containing lines, natures, conditions and necessities correspondent to those which display themselves in the World with greater pomp and observation, (a conceit as dear to some Ancient and Modern Writers as their very eyes:).[68]

Here again in Spencer's attack the concept of universal sympathy, with its correlates animism and microcosmism, is dismissed as a "conceit." By quoting him at length, however, I hope to have suggested what such a dismissal required— a painstaking argument, an extensive series of propositions and objections—so that we might begin to understand just how "dear" the conceit was, even after the Restoration, to Spencer's opponents.

Yet it is equally important to recognize that the concept of cosmic sympathy was treated as a conceit well before the Restoration. The speaker of Donne's *First Anniversary*, published in 1611, identifies Elizabeth Drury with the world soul, "she which did inanimate and fill / The world."[69] In an extravagant hyperbole, she dies, and the world dies with her. Donne describes precisely the "confusion" and "chaos" that Gilbert a decade earlier had imagined as the consequences of a world without soul.[70] In Donne's poem the natural magicians that Bacon defied have simply disappeared:

What artist now dares boast that he can bring
Heaven hither, or constellate anything,
So as the influence of those stars may be
Imprisoned in an herb, or charm, or tree,
And do by touch, all which those stars could do?
The art is lost, and correspondence too.

(391–396)

The art of sympathy is lost, because sympathy is lost. Donne lets the hemistich "and correspondence too" hang as if to underline the point. In *The Tempest*, which appeared during the same year as *The First Anniversary*, Shakespeare made Donne's lost artist his protagonist. And yet Prospero, an exile on a remote island, is lost in another sense; he is not nowhere but elsewhere. What we get with *The Tempest* is not the death of the world but, quite literally, the isolation, the marginalization, of the sympathetic universe. The sympathetic effects of the island, repeatedly described as "strange," point to a larger estrangement. It is only by giving up his art and rejoining the world of humankind that Prospero ceases to be a "stranger" (1.2.76).

FOUCAULT AND THE "FORGETTING" OF SYMPATHY

This selective historical account of macrocosmic conceptions of sympathy is meant in part as a modification of Foucault's "irruptive" history of similitude in *The Order of Things*.[71] As the critiques of Bacon, Boyle, and Spencer suggest, over the course of the seventeenth century a sympathetic worldview was increasingly called into question, but it did not suddenly disappear.[72] Foucault's well-known constructive history of the sixteenth and seventeenth centuries has been challenged from a number of angles, but not his account of sympathy in particular, which is in many ways the conceptual crux and pivot of his history of the period as a whole.[73] Against his insistence on total rupture, this book makes a case for a more continuous history of sympathy. In "The Prose of the World," his analysis of the sixteenth-century episteme, Foucault begins by identifying four forms of similitude or resemblance: "convenientia," "aemulatio," "analogy," and "sympathy." In the sixteenth century to know something was to see it as adjacent to, reflective of, parallel to, or drawn to something else. What distinguishes sympathy is its kinetic energy: "But such is its power that sympathy is not content to spring from a single contact and speed through space; it excites the things of the world to movement and can draw even the most distant of them together." In Foucault's largely nontheological account, sympathy is a kind of prime mover. But if it has God's power, so to speak, it also has Satan's ambition:

"Sympathy is an instance of the *Same* so strong and so insistent that it will not rest content to be merely one of the forms of likeness."[74] Sympathy ultimately threatens to level the world, to divest it of all particularity. It is the "twin" force of antipathy that guarantees the proper being of all things; as one object repels another, the integrity of both is secured. The cosmic cycle of generation and corruption plays out according to the cosmic dynamics of sympathy and antipathy.

Foucault concludes his opening analysis by making sympathy, along with antipathy, the master form of similitude. The other three forms are subsumed by it: "Because of the movement and the dispersion created by its laws, the sovereignty of the sympathy-antipathy pair gives rise to all the forms of resemblance. The first three similitudes are thus all resumed and explained by it. The whole volume of the world, all the adjacencies of 'convenience,' all the echoes of emulation, all the linkages of analogy, are supported, maintained, and doubled by this space governed by sympathy and antipathy, which are ceaselessly drawing things together and holding them apart. By means of this interplay, the world remains identical." Sympathy is not only a form of similitude but also the force field behind similitude itself. Once he goes on to discuss the "signatures" by which the manifold similitudes of the world can be recognized, however, Foucault appears to modify the hierarchical structure of his scheme: "It is sympathies and emulations that indicate analogies."[75] With this apparent confusion of terms and structures, it is as though sympathy has taken over the argument, reducing Foucault's "semantic web of resemblance" to a "homogeneous mass." Just as the world of the sixteenth century "must fold in upon itself," so must the set of terms used to describe it.[76] For Foucault the knowledge accumulated in such a world was convoluted to the point of opacity. Conceived as a book, it was nothing but a vast collection, and a vast confusion, of cross-references.

At the beginning of the seventeenth century, Foucault insists, the book of knowledge became altogether new. In a moment of profound "discontinuity," knowledge and resemblance parted ways; knowledge was ordered—untangled, unfolded—and rationalized. Analysis replaced analogy, and assimilation yielded to discrimination. "From then on," Foucault writes, "the noble, rigorous, and restrictive figures of similitude were to be forgotten."[77] The dawn of Foucault's "classical age" corresponds to the demise of sympathy as a cosmic principle. The world was no longer known by studying the "play of sympathies"; it was known by establishing identities and differences. And those who did study the play of sympathies were no longer "artists," in Donne's sense, but visionaries and madmen. Sympathy was increasingly associated with imagination on one hand and with pathology on the other, with what Foucault calls "alienation in analogy."[78] This analysis is supported by a work like Spencer's, where prodigies are repudiated as fables, invented "by the poesie of Fancy." But what finds less support—even within his own analysis—is Foucault's claim for a sudden and total rupture. Three of the four quotations he uses to illustrate the status of sympathy in the sixteenth-century episteme appear in mid-seventeenth-century French translations. And although Foucault explains that his mode of archaeo-logical history subordinates "individuals" to "rules," he leans heavily on the work of Descartes.[79] By contrast, he locates Bacon on the far side of the epistemic divide, as if Bacon's critique of idols were but a ripple in the pool, leading up to the sea change that was Cartesian rationalism. But just as we can see signs of "classical" discrimination in Bacon, so we can see signs of preclassical assimila-tion in Descartes.

In considering the place of sympathy in seventeenth-century natural-philosophical writing more closely, we find not an absence but an active pres-ence. For natural philosophers, sympathy was an important subject of reflection and site of contestation. Sympathy's presence in this period has been illumi-nated in part by the revisionist account of "occult qualities" undertaken by historians of science beginning in the 1980s. Occult qualities, with which sympathy was associated, were distinguished in the sensationalist epistemology of the schools from manifest qualities, which could be sensed and so under-stood. In a characteristic statement of the older whiggish view, Marie Boas writes of Boyle's experimental achievements, "From this time forward, most competent scientists accepted the pressure of the atmosphere as the cause of suction. . . . In this way, 'attraction,' 'sympathy,' 'abhorrence' and similar terms were banished forever from pneumatics."[80] Keith Hutchison, John Henry, and others argued on the contrary that occult qualities were not "banished" to make way for the new philosophies but rather were incorporated into them.[81] In the seventeenth century mechanical philosophers like Walter Charleton (1620–1707) challenged "the presumption of the *Aristotelean*" that insensibility entailed unintelligibility.[82] The attraction of iron to the lodestone—the occult quality par excellence, at least until the controversy over Newtonian gravita-tion—no longer needed to be viewed as a mystical unknowable but rather could be analyzed and understood in terms of matter in motion. The develop-ment of mechanistic theory held out the promise of a new philosophical under-standing of sympathy, of a proper *res* behind an abused *verbum*. "And certainly," Descartes wrote with heroic confidence, "there are, in rocks or plants, no forces so secret [occultas], no marvels of sympathy and antipathy [nulla sympathiae vel antipathiae miracula] so astounding" that their causes could not be "deduced" from "principles known and accepted by all (namely, from the figure, magnitude, situation, and motion of particles of matter)."[83] Far from rejecting the "marvels of sympathy and antipathy," Descartes promised to reveal them. After condemning "Secret *Sympathies* and *Antipathies*" as "no less a Refuge for the Idle and Ignorant, than that of Occult Proprieties," Charleton accepted the terms in a nonmystical sense, defining "*Sympathy*" as "a certain *Consent*, and *Antipathy* a certain *Dissent* betwixt Two Natures, from one, or both of which there usually ariseth some such Effect, as may seem to deserve our limited Admiration."[84] He refused to accept that the action of sympathy differed in kind from "Gross and *Mechanique* operations," concluding that in "those finer performances of Nature, called *Sympathies* and *Antipathies*" there exist "certain slender Hooks, Lines, Chains, or the like intercedent Instruments, continued from the Attrahent to the Attracted."[85] Charleton treats sympathy not as an unaccountable marvel but rather as one of many "performances of Nature" explicable in mechanistic terms. Sympathy was not suddenly being "forgotten"; as part of the broader philosophical problem of the "occult," it was, rather, a focus of scientific attention.

In "The Prose of the World," Foucault gives sympathy pride of place; it is marked relative to the other forms of similitude. In his account of the classical age, by contrast, it is itself assimilated, lumped in with the other "noble, rigorous, and restrictive figures of similitude" and tossed into the epistemological dustbin. But sympathy had a life, and a history, of its own. Where Foucault sees thoroughgoing rejection I see varied reconception. Subject to mechanization, sympathy was over time increasingly given to moralization. Foucault's account teaches us a still-important lesson—that sympathy is at base a principle of power. But even as it entered more fully into the sphere of moral philosophy, that power, we need to recognize, remained active and undiminished.

SYMPATHY AND SENSIBILITY

If Foucault's "history of resemblance" leaves out later moral conceptions of sympathy, genealogies of sensibility, variously coupled with sympathy and sentimentality, have tended to leave out earlier natural conceptions, as if sympathy were always already moral.[86] In a lastingly influential—and controversial—essay published in 1934, R. S. Crane argued that the conception of man as a "sympathetic creature," essential to the "mid-eighteenth-century cult of the 'man of feeling,'" emerged not in the drawing rooms of the third Earl of Shaftesbury (1671–1713) and his readers but rather after the Restoration in the pulpits of "the anti-Puritan, anti-Stoic, and anti-Hobbesian divines of the Latitudinarian school."[87] Puritanism, Stoicism, and Hobbism all promoted a negative view of human nature and of the passions. Asserting a positive view, these divines raised up fallen man, whose instinct was not to sin or to struggle, they argued, but to sympathize. Literary and intellectual historians have identified this concept of sympathy with various texts: Henry More's *Enchiridion Ethicum* (1667), Richard Cumberland's *De legibus naturae* (1672), Isaac Barrow's sermons from the 1670s, and Ralph Cudworth's drafts of a treatise on free will, composed at some point between the 1650s and '80s.[88] With varying emphases, these accounts, generally following Crane's, draw a historical line from the Cambridge Platonists to Latitudinarian divines to Shaftesbury to Francis Hutcheson, David Hume, and Adam Smith. And yet More's natural-philosophical engagement with the "*Magick Sympathy*" of "the Stoicks and Platonists" has played little or no part in such accounts.[89] Even as critics have challenged and sought to expand Crane's focus by suggesting that sympathy was not a unique "latitudinarian" possession but a topic that figured significantly in Puritan and Presbyterian discursive traditions as well, the basic assumption that sympathy is solely a phenomenon of human, moral experience has remained firmly settled.[90] Rather than identifying a textual smoking gun for the "rise" of sympathy in the moral sense, we need to adopt a wider historical purview and a broader disciplinary approach. In so doing, we see that the moral and the natural were not rigidly divided but importantly interconnected and overlapping.

In antiquity sympathy was moralized in both theological and political-theoretical terms. Variants of *sympatheia*, applied in the sense of fellow feeling between and among human beings, appear in the New Testament, if infrequently.[91] Peter exhorts his audience to "be ye all of one mind, having compassion one of another [sumpatheis], love as brethren, be pitiful, be courteous" (1 Pet. 3:8). The classical concept emerges most clearly and emphatically in Paul's figure of the body in 1 Corinthians 12, which, like Menenius Agrippa's famous fable of the belly, turns on the "organic analogy" between the body natural and the body politic or ecclesiastic.[92] Likely influenced by aspects of Roman Stoicism, Paul's insistence on bodily sympathy strengthens his appeal to ecclesial unity: "That there should be no schism in the body; but that the members should have the same care one for another. And whether one member suffer, all the members suffer with it; or one member be honoured, all the members rejoice with it" (1 Cor. 12:25–26).[93] Sympathy is a spiritual principle prior to and antithetical to schism. However diverse the parts of the body may be in terms of function, they are united in terms of feeling. Of the original Pauline context, Wayne Meeks writes, "The Corinthian congregations have experienced a process that is normal in groups or social movements: the differentiation of roles, with some accorded higher prestige than others, and consequently the rise of competitiveness, jealousy, and the other shocks that threaten group life," but "Paul's emphasis on the 'one Spirit,' his stress on the inversion of prestige ('honor') in the divine economy of the body . . ., indicate that he is concerned to limit if possible the developing stratification and above all to reinforce the cohesion of the group."[94] In Paul's discourse, the trope of the body functions to encourage social coherence and to discourage division and factionalism. Carrying the weight of spiritual as well as textual authority, Paul's call for sympathetic unity could be readily adapted and applied to a variety of social contexts and contingencies. Most prominently, it could be called on to authorize a particular view of political organization.[95]

This move assumed a new urgency with what Jonathan Gil Harris calls "the movement from the religious body of Catholic Europe to the largely secular body of the English nation-state."[96] In his *Mervailous Combat of Contrarieties*, published in the year that the Spanish Armada was defeated, William Averell posits "a continuall *Sympathie*" in the "whole course of natural things" and then proceeds from the body cosmic to the body natural to the body politic: "This consent hath God left in nature betweene the heavens with their elements, and our humane members, that wee might learne what agreement ought to bee among our selves, that are tied together in a politique state."[97] Averell appeals to both the macrocosm and the microcosm to reinforce the Elizabethan sociopolitical order. And what Averell was attempting on behalf of Elizabeth I, Edward Forset attempted on behalf of James I. In his *Comparative Discourse of the Bodies Natural and Politique*, which appeared in 1606, Forset pressed the analogy between head and king: "We see the head naturally endued with a fellow feeling of any of the griefes in the whole bodie, in so much as there is scant any disease so weake or small in any part, as doth not affect and disturbe the head also; yea, it holdeth such a sympathie with the verie foot, as that a little wet or cold taken in that remotest place, hath forthwith a readie passage to the head. Gracious Soveraignes have the like compassions and compunctions in the distresses of their subiects, and be in the same sort deeply peirced & perplexed with any wrong or distemperatures, hapning to the meanest of their people."[98] In making a claim for James as a sympathetic sovereign, in touch with all parts of the body politic, Forset nevertheless reinforces a sense of hierarchical distance; between the king and the "meanest" people lies a gap far greater than that measured between the head and the feet. The organic analogy, as Kevin Sharpe argues, "not only unified a fragile state; it elevated and incorporated the person of the king into that larger body of the common weal at a time when the monarch as personal overlord was becoming a monarch as ruler of the nation."[99]

But even as the analogy was called upon to do ideological work in a new national context, it continued to thrive in the religious domain, and beyond. In a sermon delivered in 1636, Charles FitzGeffry invokes the Pauline analogy in the context of Turkish piracy off the coasts of Devon and Cornwall, which had reduced a number of his countrymen to captivity.[100] FitzGeffry departs from Paul, however, in extending the analogy from the sympathy of the body natural not to that of the body politic but rather to the idea of a sympathy "in our mindes":

> But the more to move us to compassionate these our barbarously oppressed brethren, let us . . . lay to your hearts, these few among many forcible incentives.
>
> First, Nature it selfe incites us to this *Sympathy*. This naturall instinct we finde in our own bodies. Whence is it that one in a company yawning or gaping, the rest doe so likewise unlesse they prevent it? . . . Is there such a *Sympathy* in our bodies? Why not much more in our mindes?
>
> From our selves desend we to bruite beasts. Wee finde in them a kinde of compassion towards their kinde. The wild buls doe bellow in the fields or woods if they finde one of their fellowes slaine, and by kinde obsequies doe celebrate their brothers funerals. . . .
>
> Come we unto senseles Creatures. As in some things there is an *Antipathy*, so there is a *Sympathy* in others. Touch but one string in a lute, and another soundeth though not neare unto it. I omit the *Sympathy* betweene the *loadstone* and the *iron*, between *Amber* and *straw*, *jet* and an *hayre*, rare secrets in nature, common in triall. Out of the premises I argue thus: If our owne *naturall bodies*, if brute creatures, which are led only by sence, yea if senselesse creatures by an occult quality be thus affected one towards another, then what ought *Christians* to doe who are endued with *reason*, enlightned with *religion*, and led or rather drawne with naturall affection? Now if nature doe teach us this compassion, how much more *Grace*, and that sundry waies. As first by that argument that we are all members of one mysticall body, and fellow-members one with another, which hath beene formerly urged.
>
> Of this *body* the *Head* is *Christ*, who hath shewed this *sympathy* by his owne example.[101]

FitzGeffry's concept of a sympathy "in our mindes" finds a double authority in God and nature. As Christ suffered with man, so Christians should follow Him in suffering with other Christians. Introducing a citation of 1 Corinthians 12, FitzGeffry asserts, "The Apostle presents us with a sound reason why there should be a *Sympathy* among Christians. We are all members of one body."[102] In his examples of natural sympathy FitzGeffry evokes a long tradition of natural-philosophical speculation. Thales, as Diogenes Laertius reported, saw life in the magnet and amber; Theon of Smyrna described the phenomenon of sympathetic vibration in his propaedeutic work on Plato; and the seventh chapter of the pseudo-Aristotelian *Problems* opens with a reflection on sympathetic yawning.[103] But FitzGeffry's authority in these matters, as his marginal citations show, was Girolamo Fracastoro's *De sympathia et antipathia rerum*, published at Venice in 1546. FitzGeffry uses Fracastoro's natural philosophy to make a moral point. It is not only the "naturall instinct" of human beings but also the duty of Christians to sympathize with those who suffer.

A student of Pietro Pomponazzi (1462–1525), who sought a purified Aristotelianism, Fracastoro (1478–1553) maintained that reason and experience, rather than recourse to occult qualities, should guide philosophical inquiry. The marvels of nature—magnetism and resonance, but also enmities between such animals as the lion and the cock—required natural explanations, not verbal dodges. Fracastoro posited a "spiritual species" emitted by objects that enabled them to act on other objects; all of these interactions together produced a stable and harmonious whole. Although his model of action by contact was indebted to the ancient atomists, Fracastoro's concept of sympathy as a "universal consent of all things [consensus . . . rerum omnium in universo]" points back to the Stoics and Neoplatonists. All parts of the universe sympathize, in his formulation, "just as in a living being the parts hold among themselves no little consent and affinity [sicut enim in animali partes inter se consensum & relationem non parvam habent]."[104] And although Fracastoro did not adhere to the principles of what would later be called the mechanical philosophy, his natural philosophy cannot be easily assimilated to Foucault's rigid epistemological categories.[105] In his discussion of "Occult Qualities made Manifest," which includes his mechanistic account of sympathy, Charleton praises "the method of the no less Acute than Judicious *Fracastorius*."[106]

Nevertheless, as a project like Fracastoro's became increasingly marginal toward the end of the seventeenth century, one like FitzGeffry's—naturalizing and generalizing human sympathy—became increasingly central. The latter project assumed a particular urgency in England in the middle of the seventeenth century, when the need for social, political, and religious coherence was intensely magnified. The assertion of a fundamental sympathy in human nature could underwrite nothing less than a new unity in church and society. I have been suggesting that representations of sympathy in this period bear a significant relation to an extraordinarily vital philosophical culture, with the new prominence of Neoplatonic, magical theories, the advancement of mechanistic theories, and the complex and ambivalent reception of both. But an understanding of that culture requires taking into account the sociopolitical conditions and circumstances in which, and in response to which, those theories took shape. The social upheaval of the Civil Wars gave the broader philosophical debate about sympathy a new seriousness and a new sense of purpose. The question of if and how God's creatures connected became especially critical in the face of enormous disconnection in the nation as a whole. The Civil Wars exposed significant differences and enforced significant distances, physical as well as emotional, and for those faced with adversity, whether isolation or persecution or imprisonment, the idea of sympathetic action, or interaction, at a distance provided a significant means of consolation and reconnection.

The conflicts of the mid-seventeenth century extended and intensified new approaches to, and emphases on, the question of human motivation—in rhetorical theory, in political theory, in natural law theory. At the very beginning of his *De jure belli ac pacis* (1625), to take one important example, Hugo Grotius (1583–1645) makes a strong claim for natural sociability, according to which infants show "a Propensity to do Good to others, before they are capable of Instruction," and "Compassion [misericordia] likewise discovers itself upon every Occasion in that tender Age."[107] We do not learn to concern ourselves in the lives of others, Grotius insists; we do so naturally and instinctively. We are fellow feelers by nature. Albert Hirschman's influential claim for a general shift in attitudes toward the passions in the seventeenth and eighteenth centuries emphasizes, like Crane's, a reaction against a negative view of human nature, ultimately giving rise to sentimentalist ethics. Hirschman's historical point of departure, however, is not Restoration theology but sixteenth-century political theory. As the aristocratic ideal of glory lost its prestige, seventeenth-century thinkers confronted "the overwhelming reality of restless, passionate, driven man" and responded with a "principle of countervailing passion," of treating or curing passion with passion.[108] "But gradually, toward the end of the seventeenth century and more fully in the course of the eighteenth century," he argues, "the passions were rehabilitated as the essence of life and as a potentially creative force." This process of rehabilitation depended on "the rejection, by the Enlightenment, of the tragic and pessimistic view of man and society that was so characteristic of the seventeenth century."[109] Such a claim runs the risk of double overstatement—that is, of exaggerating both the extent of rejection in the eighteenth century and the extent of pessimism in the seventeenth— but Hirschman's emphasis on politics represents a critical supplement to Crane's emphasis on theology. Reading English royalist romances of the 1650s, Victoria Kahn has built on Hirschman's work by shifting attention to the category of aesthetic interest. She argues that the "achievement" of these romances ultimately "is to refigure the public interest as a matter not only of Hobbesian calculation but also of aesthetic interest, affection, and sympathy."[110] Over time, Crane's suggestion of a monolithic anti-Hobbesianism has come to seem less and less tenable. An important achievement of Kahn's argument is to challenge the consensus driven by Crane's genealogy that sympathy emerged as a distinctive formation of the Restoration. In its emphasis on magical and natural-philosophical traditions, my approach to representations of sympathy in the mid-seventeenth century differs from Kahn's, but it shares her commitment to a more complex and textured understanding of how the passions were conceived and converted to use in this period.

In an essay that appeared the year before Hirschman's *The Passions and the Interests*, one strongly influenced by the deep historical "decoding" of Thomas Kuhn and Foucault, G. S. Rousseau supplemented Crane's genealogy of sensibility by emphasizing the "paradigmatic" achievement of Thomas Willis (1621–1675) in the fields of anatomy and physiology.[111] Willis's "mere or naked Doctrine of the *Nerves*," developed in the 1660s and '70s, led ultimately to the conception of a sympathetic nervous system.[112] His neurological conception of sympathy does not specifically enter into Rousseau's account, but subsequent studies by Christopher Lawrence, John Mullan, Ann Van Sant, and others have brought to light the historical interrelations among sympathy, sensibility, and physiology.[113] By limiting the soul to the brain, Rousseau argues, Willis established the neural basis of all higher human functioning; this anatomical idea not only made possible the sensationalist epistemology of Locke, "in the course of time Willis' best student," but also "greatly enhanced the doctrines of anti-Stoic and anti-Puritan divines of the Latitudinarian school."[114] Rousseau draws a genealogical line from Willis to Adam Smith: "From pure anatomy, it was one step to an integrated physiology of man and just another to a theory of sensory perception, learning, and the further association of ideas. Locke . . . took these steps perhaps not visibly in the written *Essay* but in the stages that may be construed as the preformation of the *Essay*; and the schools of moral thinkers he in turn deflected—Shaftesbury, Hutcheson, Hume, Adam Smith, and many others—carried his brilliant act of integration to its fullest possible conclusion." The medical writings of George Cheyne, the sentimental novels of Samuel Richardson, and the neurological inquiries of Robert Whytt and William Cullen can all be understood ultimately in terms of the new "*science* of man," which Willis's doctrine of the nerves underpinned.[115]

But if the "deep structure" of sensibility is to be exposed, Willis's science itself needs to be "decoded." "But that so many nerves," Willis writes, "being destinated to so many several members, and remote from one another, yet arising together, are collected as it were into one bundle, the reason is, that in all the parts to which those Nerves belong, a certain Sympathy and consent of actions might be conserved: to wit, the communion of those Nerves is the cause why the sight and smell move spittle and please the Palate."[116] His neurophysiological understanding of sympathy came out of the medical tradition of Galen and the Hippocratic writers but was inflected by a broader natural tradition that included Joan Baptista van Helmont (1580–1644), who was "palpably indebted" to Paracelsus, and whose chemical discourse of "sense," "fermentation," and "irradiation," as well as "sympathy," Willis adopted and adapted in his various works.[117] Discussing a particular remedy, Willis rehearses "the Aetiology of *Helmontius*," according to which "the application terrifying the *Archaens*, compels the blood being astonished, either to go back, or desist from its inordinate excursion." Like sympathy itself, for Paracelsus and Van Helmont the "archeus" was a fundamental organizing principle.[118] To get the full resonance of sympathy in Willis's science we might also consider a passage from his early treatise "Of Feavers": "For the Air, which we necessarily draw in for the continuance of Life, consists of an heap of Vapors and Fumes, which are perpetually breathed forth from the Earth; in which the exhalations of Salt and Sulphur, being mingled with the atomical vaporous little Bodies, constitute here as it were a thick cloud: the motions of these are swift and unquiet, they are of a manifold figure, and very much diverse, wherefore some continually meet against others, and according to their various Configurations, they cohere with these, and are mutually combined one with another, and from those they are driven, and fly away: from hence the reasons of the Sympathy and Antipathy of every thing, depend."[119] Willis's theory of the nerves did not rest on a theory of the cosmos, but it carried mystical associations that went far beyond the borders of the body. The history of sympathy did not begin with a new science of man, nor did it begin with a new religion of man; it began, rather, with the old system of the world.

SYMPATHY AND THE DISENCHANTMENT OF THE WORLD

In the fall of 1667 John Dryden and Sir William Davenant's adaptation of *The Tempest* appeared on the stage. The Prologue that Dryden wrote some three years later for publication assumed an enlightened audience:

That innocence and beauty which did smile
In Fletcher, *grew on* this *Enchanted Isle.*
But Shakespeare's *Magick could not copy'd be,*
Within that Circle none durst walk but he.

I must confess 'twas bold, nor would you now,
That liberty to vulgar Wits allow,
Which works by Magick supernatural things:
But Shakespeare's *pow'r is sacred as a King's.*
Those Legends from old Priest-hood were receiv'd,
And he then writ, as people then believ'd.[120]

Prospero's magic, in other words, was really Shakespeare's, and whereas Shakespeare's audience took Prospero's magic to be real, Dryden and Davenant's audience know it to have been feigned. In this sense, the Restoration *Tempest* marks the progress of the process that Weber memorably referred to as "die Entzauberung der Welt," the "demagification" or "disenchantment of the world."[121] For Weber, the disenchantment of the world was not an "archaeological" event, in Foucault's sense, but a longitudinal trend. Referring to the Calvinist doctrine of predestination, Weber writes, "That great historic process in the development of religions, the elimination of magic from the world [Entzauberung der Welt] which had begun with the old Hebrew prophets and, in conjunction with Hellenistic scientific thought, had repudiated all magical means to salvation as superstition and sin, came here to its logical conclusion."[122] Puritanism in particular, and Protestantism in general, represents the climax of a teleological narrative. While the process of disenchantment continued in the Catholic Church, it was limited and halted by the magical culture presided over by the priest, "a magician who performed the miracle of transubstantiation, and who held the key to eternal life in his hand," and whereas the Catholic could turn to him for "atonement, hope of grace, certainty of forgiveness," the Calvinist found no "release from that tremendous tension to which [he] was doomed by an inexorable fate, admitting of no mitigation."[123] In its historically intimate relationship with magic, sympathy is importantly bound up in this process—one that has been the subject of sustained and energetic debate for social and intellectual historians. Over the course of the seventeenth century, as the status of magic was increasingly called into question among the intellectual elite, so were all-encompassing, magical concepts of sympathy.

In the English context, Keith Thomas influentially reinforced the idea of a "decline of magic" over the course of the sixteenth and seventeenth centuries, though he made a more qualified and balanced claim for the role of the Reformation in the decline. "In this revolution," he writes, "the dogmas of Protestantism played some part." Thomas tentatively correlates the decline of magic to "the growth of urban living, the rise of science, and the spread of an ideology of self-help."[124] The first of these promoted a wider exposure to new ideas and undermined the kinds of intimate social networks in which magical practices flourished; the second promoted a mechanistic conception of the world that was inimical to magical beliefs and explanations; and the third promoted the development of new technologies and discouraged appeals to supernatural aid. In Charles Taylor's more recent argument that the development of a new idea of the "buffered" self, "not open and porous and vulnerable to a world of spirits and powers," depended on disenchantment and a "confidence in our own powers of moral ordering" we can see a parallel to, and an extension of, Thomas's claim for "the emergence of a new faith in the potentialities of human initiative."[125] Nevertheless, although the extremity of Thomas's assertion of decline has been exaggerated, the idea of what he calls a "revolution" has been widely challenged.[126] Social and intellectual historians have impugned the view that the rise of Protestantism on one hand and the rise of the new philosophies on the other conspired to produce the disenchantment of the world.

The revisionist aim of historians of early modern science has indeed extended far beyond the problem of occult qualities.[127] In an influential study setting out to remove the "wedge between the cultures of Paracelsus and Newton," Charles Webster inveighed against the "distorting element . . . introduced into accounts of the rise of modern science through underestimation of the degree to which authors like Paracelsus, or authors belonging to the tradition of Neoplatonism or hermeticism, remained an integral part of the intellectual resources of the educated elite into the late seventeenth century."[128] Among this group, "the conceptual infrastructure of magic" endured even as judicial astrology and the performance of magical rituals increasingly fell into disfavor. "From the historical point of view," Webster concludes, "it is impossible to disregard the sources of evidence suggesting that non-mechanistic modes of scientific expression remained intellectually challenging to natural philosophers of all degrees of ability into the age supposedly dominated by the mechanical philosophy. It is therefore questionable whether the rise of science was associated with a total decline of magic as it was understood in Western society in the sixteenth and seventeenth centuries."[129] B. J. T. Dobbs, Michael Hunter, and others have demonstrated the considerable interest that Boyle and Newton took in magic and alchemy.[130] Hunter suggests that although such matters "had ceased to be acceptable in the public sphere," Boyle and those of his mindset engaged with the occult in private while maintaining a public distance from it. Of the age of Boyle, he claims, "in some respects we need to think less in terms of a 'decline of magic' than of a 'rise of schizophrenia' in this period."[131] Where Hunter sees "schizophrenia," John Henry detects "fragmentation," a process by which over the course of the seventeenth century a more unified magical tradition was broken up into useful, absorbable elements and dangerous, dismissible ones.[132] In a subsequent study Webster has made a parallel claim for "a change in the balance of enchantment" rather than "a general disenchantment of the worldview."[133]

Even as occultism was increasingly drawn into the closet, in its printed forms it was increasingly available to the reading public. Referring to a "democratisation" of magic in the 1640s and '50s, Thomas noted that the period between 1650 and 1680 represented the high-water mark for the publication of books on alchemical subjects, and Webster observes that the "tide of translations of Paracelsian and alchemical works which began in the 1650s continued uninterruptedly after the Restoration."[134] Lauren Kassell has confirmed these findings, referring to a "tenfold" increase in the production of alchemical books in the 1650s and arguing that "alchemists were creatures of the library as much as the laboratory."[135] In his study of "books of secrets," William Eamon narrowed the gap between magic and science further, arguing that such books "were bearers of attitudes and values that proved instrumental in shaping scientific culture in the early modern era" and, with their practical heritage and orientation, "were the 'missing link' between medieval 'secrets' and Baconian experiments."[136] Magic did not exactly become science, but continuities between the two suggest that science did not exactly do away with magic. Nor did Protestantism do away with magic. In shifting the focus of historical attention to "popular magic" and "popular Protestantism," Robert Scribner's influential work directly challenged Weber's thesis, which Scribner saw as the result of "nineteenth-century concerns . . . projected onto historical understanding of religion in the Reformation."[137] Scribner concedes that "the Reformation, both in its first and second generations, could be said to have drawn a firmer line between magic and religion by its changed understanding of the sacraments, and its repudiation of Catholic sacramentals," but the movement away from sacred objects "did not remove the popular desire for some kind of instrumental application of sacred power to deal with the exigencies of daily life, and Protestants often turned to distinctively 'Protestant' remedies, using Bibles, hymnals, and prayer books for their healing and protective power." In "'scripturally-based' spells and charms" Scribner identifies "what was, in effect, a Protestant form of magic." Protestantism did not disenchant the world; it "was as caught up as Catholicism in the same dilemmas about the instrumental application of sacred power to secular life because it was positioned in the same force-field of sacrality."[138] Alexandra Walsham has both reaffirmed and extended Scribner's work, referring to "a new historical consensus that Protestantism played a less decisive part" in the disenchantment of the world and arguing that although Protestantism "presented itself as intent upon shearing away the magical and miraculous elements from religion, it never denied that divine and demonic forces could and did intrude into the earthly realm."[139] Walsham refers to a "rhetoric of 'disenchantment'" on the part of the reformers that "paradoxically acquired much of its urgency from a heightened sense that supernatural or preternatural forces were at work in the world," and over time a "degree of slippage between souvenir and sacramental, sign and receptacle of supernatural virtue . . . seems if anything to have increased."[140] Against a "linear paradigm of disenchantment" Walsham proposes a "perennial process," comprising the Reformation as well as the Enlightenment, "by which the boundaries between 'religion' and 'magic' were readjusted and the malleable category of 'superstition' was redefined, as successive loops in a perpetual spiral of desacralization and resacralization" and "cycles of . . . disenchantment and re-enchantment."[141] According to this view, the history of magic in England is marked not by a single, straightforward decline but by multiple, recurrent declines—and ascents.

In making a case for an energetic confrontation and coming to terms with sympathy in seventeenth-century England, the present book reinforces the "continualist" trend in the historiography of magic. But it also aims to record and recognize what Walsham refers to as "the fact of long-term change."[142] In this sense, I think, Weber's argument—like Foucault's—continues to be heuristically useful. In view of the longer-term fortunes of sympathy, moreover, Weber's analysis of disenchantment yields what I take to be an especially valuable suggestion. Addressing an audience of German students in 1918, Weber wrote,

> The fate of our times is characterized by rationalization and intellectualization and, above all, by the "disenchantment of the world." Precisely the ultimate and most sublime values have retreated from public life either into the transcendental realm of mystic life or into the brotherliness of direct and personal human relations. It is not accidental that our greatest art is intimate and not monumental, nor is it accidental that today only within the smallest and intimate circles, in personal human situations, in *pianissimo*, that something is pulsating that corresponds to the prophetic *pneuma*, which in former times swept through the great communities like a firebrand, welding them together.[143]

Weber posits a translation of value from the cosmic network to the "circles" of social relation. The social sphere holds out the promise of a "fullness," to use Taylor's term, that the world as a whole can no longer provide.[144] This sociological reading of history suggests a compensatory model for the history of sympathy—moral, social, and psychological conceptions of sympathy carried the potential to restore a sense of coherence that the decline in status and credit of cosmic conceptions had undermined. In what can be considered a parallel analysis of metaphysical loss, Spitzer interprets "the 'sympathy' between the cosmos and man" as "a kind of loving milieu round about him," and the disappearance of the "world-embracing, metaphysical cupola that once enfolded mankind," he suggests, led to crass materialism, a compulsion to fill space with "Things."[145] This claim resonates with Horkheimer and Adorno's analysis of the Enlightenment, in which the "manifold affinities between existing things are supplanted by the single relationship between the subject who confers meaning and the meaningless object, between rational significance and its accidental bearer."[146] The disenchantment of the world, Weber intimates, was remedied not by acquiring objects but by relating to other subjects—by establishing sympathies between human beings.

Describing the context for Weber's lecture, entitled "Science as a Vocation," Anne Harrington writes, "Since the 1890s, an intensifying stream of German-language articles and monographs had been identifying the rise of a certain kind of mechanistic thinking in the natural sciences as a chief culprit in a variety of failed or crisis-ridden cultural and political experiments. Science had declared humanity's life and soul a senseless product of mechanism, so people now treated one another as mere machines."[147] Harrington claims that a number of German-speaking scientists shared Weber's pessimistic view of science and elegiac view of disenchantment; they responded, however, not by abandoning science but by setting out to reform it: "Under the banner of Wholeness, these scientists argued, in varying ways, that a transformed biology and psychology—one that viewed phenomena less atomistically and more 'holistically,' less mechanistically and more 'intuitively'—could lead to the rediscovery of a nurturing relationship with the natural world."[148] In looking back more than two centuries earlier to the rise of the mechanical philosophy, when the place of humanity and of God in the world was newly in doubt, we can see the type of crisis to which that in the age of Weber stands as an antitype. In the seventeenth century the new emphasis on sympathy as an organizing principle, I argue, needs to be understood in part as a response to the renewed interest in, and threat of, Epicureanism, which, in the eyes of its opponents, reduced the world to a godless heap of random, disconnected matter. Sympathy emerged as a keynote of anti-Epicurean writing of various kinds. Associating atheism with the denial of "all *Natural Charity* and *Benevolence*," Cudworth saw it as a certainty "that there could be no *Faith* nor *Hope* neither, in these *Sensless Atoms*, both *Necessarily* and *Fortuitously* moved, no more than there could be Faith and Hope in a Whirlwind, or in a Tempestuous Sea, whose merciless waves are *Inexorable*, and deaf to all *Cries* and *Supplications*."[149] This was the view of the world against which a sympathetic Miranda raised her voice. The project of Harrington's scientists can serve not only as further evidence in support of Walsham's helical scheme but also as a helpful caution. The rise of the mechanical philosophy did not simply force sympathy from the domain of natural philosophy into the domain of moral philosophy. Alternative modes of description and explanation remained viable and, indeed, vital. And as the balance shifted to the moral, as sympathy was increasingly conceived in human terms, it remained significantly in contact with natural and magical traditions. Long after the heyday of Neoplatonic and Paracelsian thought in seventeenth-century England, sympathy retained its aura of enchantment. In this sense sympathy represents what Jane Bennett calls a "fugitive from rationalization."[150] As it was rationalized over time, this book ultimately demonstrates, sympathy also exposed the *limits* of rationalization.

I have omitted Weber's emphasis on "mystic life," but before summarizing the contents of the book, I want to comment briefly on his emphasis on art, not least because of my own orientation as a scholar. Elsewhere Weber claims that art "provides a *salvation* from the routines of everyday life, and especially from the increasing pressures of theoretical and practical rationalism."[151] Art, too, then, represents a kind of fugitive. In Foucault's formulation, literature is a "'counter-discourse,'" in which "the being of language shines once more on the frontiers of Western culture—at its centre—for it is what has been most foreign to that culture since the sixteenth century; but it has also, since this same century, been at the very centre of what Western culture has overlain."[152] Literature is in effect a process and a product of re-enchantment; it resists the new orders and reifies the old resemblances. "The poet," Foucault writes, "brings similitude to the signs that speak it." Epistemologically obliterated, or so he claims, sympathy survives—and thrives—in the "separated state" of litera-ture.[153] There whatever claims are made for it cannot possibly be counterfac-tual. We can understand Adorno's epigram in this light: "Art is magic delivered from the lie of being truth."[154] In accord with these suggestions, I show toward the end of the book that in the eighteenth century a sympathetic worldview was increasingly subject to aestheticization. As magic and the supernatural were, in Walsham's formulation, "very slowly migrating into the sphere of art and the imagination," so, I suggest, were magical conceptions of sympathy.[155] Yet at the core of my analysis is the idea that literature can serve as a vehicle not only of enchantment or re-enchantment but also of disenchantment. Milton repre-sented sympathy in his epic, one both "monumental" and "intimate," in Weber's terms, not to animate it but to rationalize and contain it. Only then could the power of sympathy be put to virtuous use.

The focus of my first chapter is the most noted and extensive attempt to account for sympathy in mechanistic terms in the seventeenth century, Sir Kenelm Digby's treatise on sympathetic cures, a now peculiar-seeming pharmacopoeia of salves and powders alleged to heal wounds though applied at a distance from the patient. Dissociating his account of the "powder of sympathy" from the magical explanations of his Paracelsian predecessors, Digby ultimately pursues a more ambitious aim, the mechanization of the sympathetic world picture. I go on to examine the reception of Digby's treatise and suggest that the declining status of sympathetic cures in the late seventeenth and early eighteenth centuries serves as an index to a broader decline in the status of a sympathetic worldview. That Digby's powder seemed to fail as often as it worked undermined the credibility of his claim that sympathy was a fundamental principle of the natural world. Yet, in its extended treatment of the power of the imagination and in its implicit elevation of the stoic ideal of impassivity, Digby's treatise also suggests that sympathy was a problem in the social domain, where the contagion of the passions resisted containment. Digby's distrust and depreciation of human sympathy, I go on to show, emerge particularly clearly in his response to Sir Thomas Browne's *Religio Medici*, in which charity is significantly defined not only in terms of virtuous action but also, and emphatically, in terms of fellow feeling. The precarious balance of science, sociability, and Hobbesian philosophy is the subject of my second chapter, centered on the wide-ranging writings of Margaret Cavendish. Cavendish largely shared Hobbes's vision of society, but her natural philosophy underlay and informed a very different view of sympathy. She ultimately projected a vision of nature as a vital, material whole, held together by sympathetic, and antipathetic, forces largely subject to the will. In the literary milieu of her *Sociable Letters*, sympathy emerges as a moral virtue, as Cavendish models the idea of compassionate interest that she describes. But throughout the work her speaker struggles to reconcile this ideal with the grim social and political realities of a nation warring with itself. Returning to Crane's genealogy of sensibility, I provide a more complex and nuanced account of the reception of Hobbes's psychology as it pertains to the history of sympathy.

My third and fourth chapters are devoted to the poetry and prose of John Milton, whose active and sustained engagement with sympathy as a philosophical idea serves particularly clearly to support the revisionist history of sympathy that is a central motive of this book as a whole. Milton's moral conceptions of sympathy emerge out of, and develop in relation to, his natural conceptions, which are influenced by a range of classical and contemporary sources. I begin chapter 3 by analyzing the varied representations of sympathy in Milton's early poetry and prose and argue that he expresses a deep ambivalence about the idea of cosmic sympathy; associating that idea with the distant past, he articulates both a desire to make it a present reality and a doubt that it is recoverable. I go on to claim that in his first divorce tract Milton conceives of sympathy in a new way, translating it from the macrocosm to the microcosm of the modern home. He discusses sympathy not as the binding force of the universe but rather as the bonding force of marriage. Yet in grounding this new concept in a sympathetic view of nature with the same magical and occult associations that Digby and Cavendish sought to dispel, Milton's argument lapses into rhetorical uncertainty. In *Paradise Lost* Milton appears to abandon the moral, marital ideal he had left in suspense in the divorce tracts by associating sympathy with Ovidian error on one hand and occultist error on the other. In the middle books of the poem, he depicts a thoroughgoing cosmic sympathy before the Fall and then uses the narrative of the Fall in book 9 to suggest the breakdown of the sympathetic universe. Adam falls through sympathy with Eve, and the world falls with them. In chapter 4 I argue that Milton rehabilitates the moral ideal of the divorce tracts in the final movement of *Paradise Lost*. Purged of its magical associations, sympathy emerges at the center of postlapsarian experience. The reconciliation of Adam and Eve hinges on the ability of the fallen couple to sympathize with each other. Once they can look beyond their own individual miseries, they can come together and create a new sympathetic society in a new world. Human sympathy, Milton suggests, compensates for the loss of universal sympathy. I go on to argue that, in the last two books of the epic, Milton moves sympathy further into the realm of moral philosophy by extending his analysis from "economics," in the classical sense, to ethics and politics—that is, from the family to the individual and the polity. Milton's final achievement is an epic vision of intimacy without enchantment.

In chapter 5 I turn to the Cambridge Platonists Ralph Cudworth, Henry More, and Benjamin Whichcote, who against Hobbes advanced not only a natural view of morality but also a broadly nonmechanistic, magical worldview. If Paracelsus and Fludd suggest one course out of the Florentine Academy, the font of Renaissance Neoplatonism, the Cambridge Platonists represent a more classicizing alternative. For More and Cudworth in particular, the sympathetic universe was not an irrecoverable prelapsarian ideal, as it was for Milton, but a vitally present reality. Extending my narrative beyond the age of Milton, I proceed to set the philosophical writings of the third Earl of Shaftesbury, long a central and controversial figure in histories of sensibility, not only in the context of the moral-philosophical tradition that he deeply influenced but also in relation to the natural-magical and natural-philosophical traditions analyzed in previous chapters. Deeply influenced himself by the Cambridge Platonists, Shaftesbury aimed not to demystify sympathy—a core project for Digby, Cavendish, and Milton—but in essence to re-enchant it. Shaftesbury, I claim, represents a critical transitional figure between a broadly natural culture of sympathy and a broadly moral one.

Shaftesbury's moralization of sympathy went hand in hand with an aestheticization of sympathy. His sympathetic worldview was at once moral, magical, and beautiful. I examine the complex and ambivalent legacy of Shaftesburianism in chapters 6 and 7, which demonstrate the enduring vitality of natural and magical conceptions of sympathy well into the eighteenth century. In so doing, I revise the standard model of treating sympathy in eighteenth-century studies. In a series of readings of eighteenth-century literary and philosophical texts, from James Thomson's *Seasons* to Hume's *Treatise*, I argue that the advancement of moral ideas of sympathy functioned both to counter skeptical and empirical challenges to universal natural ideas and to restore a sense of order in the human sphere that had become more and more uncertain in the world as a whole. Shaftesbury's poetic vision of the world informed and imprinted not only eighteenth-century moral philosophy but also eighteenth-century poetry. The aesthetic was an increasingly hospitable environment, I suggest in chapter 6, for a universal conception of sympathy that was increasingly out of place in mainstream scientific accounts of the natural world. In chapter 7 I turn to Hume's engagement with, and critique of, Shaftesbury and show that Hume aimed to disenchant and to redefine sympathy in the interest of a rigorous moral science. In various works and from multiple angles Hume undertook a thoroughgoing critique of totalizing principles, claiming that the whole was utterly unavailable, except to fancy. That critique worked together with Hume's elevation of sympathy as a fundamental organizing principle of society—one not enchanted but experienced—to provide a solution to the problem of coherence that was a crucial inheritance from the seventeenth century. Hume's debunking of false imaginings of the whole did not, however, fully succeed in rendering Shaftesburianism obsolete, as I go on to suggest in a reading of Samuel Jackson Pratt's late eighteenth-century poem *Sympathy*. In the persistence of a Shaftesburian sort of sympathetic worldview, we can see a longing for magical presence that lingered into the nineteenth century and beyond.

In *We Have Never Been Modern*, Bruno Latour asks, "Haven't we shed enough tears over the disenchantment of the world?"[156] Perhaps so, but the more compelling question, it seems to me, is why we have shed so many. This book does not attempt or provide a direct answer. What it does do is to suggest that the complex process of coming to terms with sympathy in the seventeenth century reached no simple or straightforward conclusion—and that it enriched and enlivened a remarkable and diverse body of writing.

—————————∞∞◆◆◆◆∞∞—————————

SIR KENELM DIGBY AND THE
MATTER OF SYMPATHY

"Stout *Orsin*," as Samuel Butler punningly suggests in the first part of *Hudibras* (1st ed., 1663), is both a soldier and a "solderer"—that is, one who heals and closes, or "solders," wounds. The wonder is that he does so at a startling distance from the wounded:

> Learned he was in Medc'nal Lore,
> For by his side a Pouch he wore
> Replete with strange Hermetick Powder,
> That wounds nine miles point-blank would solder.[1]

Of Butler the anonymous annotator of the 1704 edition of *Hudibras* writes, "He here ... Sarcastically derides those who were great Admirers of the Sympathetick Powder and Weapon Salve; which were in great Repute in those Days, and much promoted by the Great Sir *Kenelm Digby*, who wrote a Treatise *ex professo* on that Subject, and I believe thought what he wrote to be true; which since has been almost exploded out of the World."[2] Courtier, privateer, virtuoso, Sir Kenelm Digby (1603–1665) claimed to have introduced the "Sympathetick Powder" to the West in *A Late Discourse made in a Solemne Assembly of Nobles and Learned Men at Montpellier in France. . . . Touching the Cure of Wounds by the Powder of Sympathy* (1658), which went through more than forty editions in French, English, Latin, Dutch, and German.[3] That the treatise continued to appear in print after the turn of the eighteenth century suggests that the annotator's slight hedging—"almost exploded"—was justified, and indeed sympathetic powders continued to be advertised well into the eighteenth century.[4] Nevertheless, during the half century between the first edition of *A Late Discourse* and the 1704 edition of *Hudibras*, a new emphasis on the experimental establishment of fact undermined the status of sympathetic cures and began to relegate them to the margins of natural philosophy. Over time, discussions of sympathetic cures came to center less on *how* they worked and more on *if* they worked at all; that is, medical and philosophical attention shifted from the principle behind sympathetic cures—sympathy itself—to the question of their efficacy.

A *Late Discourse* was the most widely known natural-philosophical treatment of sympathy in the seventeenth century. In its active engagement with earlier treatments and in its extensive reception by contemporaries and successors, it offers a particularly clear and significant insight into the contest over, and confrontation with, sympathy during this period. I use the case of Digby's treatise to suggest that the decline in the philosophical status of sympathetic cures paralleled and contributed to a decline in the philosophical status of a sympathetic worldview more generally. Digby's own version of this worldview occupied a kind of middle ground between the animistic and the mechanistic. His avowed master was Aristotle, whose system he saw as ultimately consistent with the mechanical philosophy of Gassendi and others. At the same time, he learned and drew from the work of chymical philosophers like Nicaise Le Fèvre, who posited a universal spirit at work in the world. Digby's larger project in *A Late Discourse* can be summed up as an attempt to redraw a sympathetic world picture according to new scientific principles. On the evidence of its reception, that attempt ultimately failed.

Yet, contrary to Foucault's claim for epistemological rupture, Digby's treatise does not attest to the sudden impotence of sympathy at the dawn of the classical age. For Digby, sympathy was not, as Foucault puts it, a "spent force, outside the realm of knowledge," but still a vitally—and dangerously—active one.[5] The guiding concern of *A Late Discourse*, I argue, is not the powder of sympathy but the *power* of sympathy. This power can be perceived most clearly in the sprawling, anecdotal middle of *A Late Discourse*, where Digby broaches the subject of human sympathy, beginning with the sympathy between mothers and children and generalizing from there. He links sympathetic effects to the power of the imagination, a topic of long-standing philosophical interest, particularly among sixteenth- and seventeenth-century "searchers out of secrets," in Della Porta's phrase. In his discussion of the *vis imaginativa*, both in *A Late Discourse* and in his earlier, more comprehensive *Two Treatises* (1644), Digby extends the usual bounds of the topic by discussing not only monstrous births and marvelous birthmarks but also more mundane phenomena like rhetorical persuasion and emotional "contagion." For the most part Digby has received attention from historians of science and medicine, who have shed light on his early articulation of a mechanical philosophy as well as on the broader, international debate about sympathetic cures. But the significant, and complex, relationship between Digby's mechanical philosophy and his moral philosophy has yet to be illuminated. In the social sphere, Digby suggests, sympathy threatens reason; it impedes the assertion of the rational self. In pathologizing human sympathy in A *Late Discourse*, Digby opens up a gap between medicine and morals. Whereas the sympathetic cure heals, the sympathetic imagination harms. At the same time that he describes healing matter in motion, Digby seems ultimately to prescribe an ethics of immovability—that is, of impassivity. He elevates an implicitly stoic subject whose imaginative and intellectual strength prevents him from falling under the sway of others. Digby's opposition to sharing affection suggests both a recognition of and a response to the power of sympathy. He aimed to commodify that power chemically as well as to contain it psychologically. In so doing, he stood to enhance his gentlemanly status and so to expand his social power.

Throughout his various writings, Digby conceived sympathy as a universal principle. Insofar as it was advanced on behalf of a cure that was unreliable at best, his claim that sympathy possessed a seemingly endless sphere of activity became over time increasingly dubious and untenable. But Digby's innovative, if unsystematic, philosophical analysis of human interaction suggests an approach to sympathy that would become increasingly resonant and prevalent in the decades after his death. In the realm of human nature, if not nature at large, sympathy continued to be perceived and conceived as an active force. I begin this chapter with a brief history of the controversy over sympathetic cures, emphasizing the account of Robert Fludd (1574–1637) and showing that the controversy was as much about the nature and structure of the world as it was about the action of a cure. It brought to the fore questions not only about natural philosophy and the authority of Aristotle but also about theology and the power of God and Satan. In the controversy we can see the intimate association between sympathy and magic in the sixteenth and seventeenth centuries. To many of the cure's critics, "sympathy" was no more than a mystifying occultist term of art. In the next section I analyze Digby's mechanistic account of the powder of sympathy. His opponents were all those who had preceded him in writing about sympathetic cures, but the energy of his opposition is at first directed at more abstract antagonists: magic and rhetoric. Digby treats both of these as problems of the imagination. Magic is what the unenlightened imagine to be behind the marvelous, and rhetoric works on the imagination to persuade them that this is so. Digby aims to demonstrate that sympathy is not a magical principle but a natural, material one. Yet ultimately he does not succeed in banishing from his own account traces of the very mysticism that he censured in the accounts of others. In the following section I consider the reception of *A Late Discourse* and show that Digby's attempt to mechanize a sympathetic worldview, while widely acknowledged, was not widely confirmed or accepted. It was received as an impressive hypothesis, but not a fully persuasive one. Increasingly, I demonstrate, practitioners cast aside the cosmic framework within and according to which sympathetic cures had been understood to work. No longer a topic of urgent philosophical and theological debate, the powder of sympathy ultimately became just another remedy, part of the practitioner's stock-in-trade.

In the next section, I examine Digby's analysis of the imagination and focus on the problem of sympathy in the social sphere. I bring to light the disjunction in his thought between sympathy as a principle of universal coherence and sympathy as a threat to social and psychological well-being. Digby strongly subordinated emotion and imagination to reason and logic, casting human sympathy in pathological terms, as the catching of contagious passions by weak minds. In the final section of the chapter I set Digby's generally negative account of human sympathy against the more positive account of Sir Thomas Browne (1605–1682) in *Religio Medici* (1642, 1643), a work of considerable fame in the seventeenth century. Digby's *Observations* on Browne's work, written in 1642, were bound into copies of the 1659 edition of *Religio Medici* and were formally incorporated into the 1669 edition as well as subsequent editions.[6] Taken together, the two works present a dialogue and debate about the nature and value of human sympathy, one that enables us to get a clearer sense of sympathy's shifting place in natural and moral discourses of the period. Although he was responding primarily to Browne's metaphysics, Digby also took aim at Browne's ethics and in particular his view of charity as an act of sympathetic connection between and among human beings. Whereas Digby aligned himself first and foremost with Aristotle in matters of natural philosophy, the *Observations* reveals that in matters of moral philosophy he aligned himself with the Stoics; Digby endorsed their view that human sympathy was harmful in and of itself and ethically significant only insofar as it motivated one to act. Influenced in part by his experiences as a Catholic and a royalist in the 1640s, when he was imprisoned in England and exiled to France, Digby retreated from human sympathy, affectively conceived, and took refuge not only in Stoic apathy but also in a concept of sympathy between souls, which enabled him to maintain nonaffective connections at a greater distance. This concept represents a potent model of social and political allegiance in a time of crisis; sympathy suggests not only a psychic bond but also a way out of a political bind, by which the hardship of imprisonment or exile could be mystically transcended. Directed beyond the here and now, Digby's philosophical vision was fundamentally concerned with, and oriented toward, the eternal. His body of work as a whole represents one of the last mainstream attempts to cast a sympathetic worldview in broadly natural-philosophical terms. Whereas the moral was subordinate to, and at odds with, the natural in his view of sympathy, that hierarchy would be reversed in the next age, when sympathy was increasingly understood as a principle not of moral confusion but of moral order.

THE PARACELSIAN MILIEU

Credit for the discovery of the weapon salve, a "sympathetic" ointment applied not to a wound but to the weapon that caused it, was frequently given to Paracelsus.[7] An account of the weapon salve appears in the pseudo-Paracelsian *Archidoxis magica* (1570), which ranges widely among such diverse subjects as metals, diseases, planets, and pygmies.[8] Before the author discusses the cure, he sets out the cosmic principle underlying its efficacy: "Simpathy, or Compassion, hath a very great power to operate in humane things [Die sympathia oder mitleidenheit bringt vil in den menschlichen dingen]."[9] This "operation" depends on the vital and intimate connection between macrocosm and micro-cosm.[10] The author of the *Archidoxis magica* does not explain how the ointment works, leaving the reader to ponder its specific sympathetic course of action, but he does go into great detail about how it is made. The recipe begins with "Moss that groweth upon a Scull, or Bone of a dead body that hath lain in the Air," to which are added "Man's Grease," "Mummy," "Man's Blood," "Linseed Oyl," "Oyl of Roses," and "Bole-Armoniack." Once the ingredients have been collected and measured out, the synthesis is straightforward: "Let them be all beat together in a Morter so long, until they come to a most pure and subtil Oyntment; then keep it in a Box. And when any wound happens, dip a stick of wood in the blood, that it may be bloody; which being dryed, thrust it quite into the aforesaid Oyntment, and leave it therein; afterwards binde up the wound with a new Linen Rowler, every morning washing it with the Patients own Urine; and it shall be healed, be it never so great, without any Plaister, or Pain. After this manner, you may Cure any one that is wounded, though he be ten miles distant from you, if you have but his blood."[11] If the weapon that caused the wound can be found, the practitioner should add an ounce of honey and ox fat to the mixture before anointing the weapon, and "the said wounds shall be cured without pain."[12]

The distant action of the cure raised challenging philosophical and theolog-ical questions. By producing an effect without contact, the cure appeared to violate what Walter Charleton referred to as the "no less manifest than general Axiome," backed by Aristotelian tradition, that "*Nihil agere in rem distantem.*"[13] If the cure was not natural, it could then be concluded, it was either diabolical or divine. In a treatise published in 1581, Matthias Mairhofer, a Jesuit professor at the University of Ingolstadt, claimed the cure to be "the work of demons."[14] Thirteen years later, his countryman Andreas Libavius argued that the real demon was Paracelsus himself, who had perpetrated this "imposture" against so many.[15] But supporters of the cure were just as emphatic, and in the early years of the seventeenth century its fame grew. The most influential early champion of the weapon salve was Della Porta, whose *Magiae naturalis* was an exhaustive attempt to distinguish true magic from sorcery. Della Porta includes Paracelsus's recipe for making the unguent, relating that it was provided by a "noble man" in the court of Emperor Maximilian I, to whom Paracelsus had given it, that it was "experimented by him," and that it was "always very much accounted of by him while he lived."[16] Rudolphus Goclenius echoed Della Porta's approval in a work published in 1608, and when Goclenius was charged with necromancy and other sins, Van Helmont wrote a treatise arguing that the problem was not the cure, which was purely natural, but Goclenius, who was too "weak" a philosopher to defend it with any kind of rigor.[17]

In 1639, Henri de Mohy wrote about a similar cure, but referred to it as "pulvis sympatheticus," a designation that, according to Lynn Thorndike, "seems to have given a further impetus to its popularity."[18] Soon thereafter another French natural philosopher, Nicolas Papin, produced a work on "sympathy powder" entitled *De Pulvere sympathetico dissertatio*, which was published in 1647 and translated into French in 1650. Although Paracelsus appeared to distinguish between the "Sympatheticall Oyntment" and the "Weapon-Salve," some writers equated the two, and the distinction remained blurry. In his *Physiologia Epicuro-Gassendo-Charltoniana* (1654), Charleton wrote of the "Armarie or Magnetic Unguent, and its Cousin German, the Sympathetic Powder or Roman Vitriol calcined."[19] It was Charleton who, five years earlier, had brought out an English translation of Van Helmont's treatise, along with two others, under the title *A Ternary of Paradoxes*. Up to that point, the debate about sympathetic cures had been largely confined to universities and urban centers in Germany, Belgium, and France. The faculties of Cologne, Louvain, and Reims all censured Van Helmont's defense of magnetic cures, as did the college of physicians at Lyon, and in 1626, the book was banned by the Inquisition.[20] Challenging the traditional scholastic understanding of the natural world, and so by extension of God's role in it, the cure excited an especially strong reaction among Jesuits. By the time Van Helmont weighed in on the question, the pamphlet war between Goclenius and the Belgian Jesuit Jean Roberti had entered its third decade.[21]

Roberti's religious affiliation lay behind the first significant debate about the weapon salve to appear in print in England, which began in 1631 with the publication of William Foster's *Hoplocrisma-spongus: or, A Sponge to wipe away the Weapon-Salve.*[22] Although Foster's treatise is mostly a vitriolic attack on the views of Robert Fludd, who wrote approvingly of the weapon salve in his *Anatomiae amphitheatrum* (1623), Foster was initially responding to Roberti's charge that supporters of the weapon salve were "Magi-Calvinists."[23] For Foster, a proud English clergyman, Roberti's term was an outrageous oxymoron. Foster countered that such cures "are more frequent amongst Papists," who had yet to cast off the yoke of superstition. "Wee of the Church of *England*," Foster solemnly declares, "detest any superstitious and magicall Cures."[24] As this exchange suggests, however, the problem of magic bedeviled both churches. For Fludd, who would go on to accuse Foster himself of serving "papisticall Masters" like Mersenne and Gassendi, the cure involved nothing less than the magical structure of the world.[25]

Fludd's account of the weapon salve, elaborated in *Doctor Fludds answer unto M. Foster: Or, The squeesing of Parson Fosters sponge, ordained by him for the wiping away of the weapon-salve* (1631), shows how closely his physiology was bound up with his cosmology.[26] In defending the cure, he was also defending a particular worldview. For Fludd, the action of the weapon salve depended on the diffusion of the universal spirit, which unified the cosmos and guaranteed a direct correspondence between microcosm and macrocosm. "The party wounded," Fludd writes, "may rightly be compared to the world, and therefore is called a little world: he is composed of heaven and earth; namely, of spirit and body," and "the incorruptible Spirit," which "is in all things," is "most abundantly (next unto the great world) in the little world called man."[27] The universal spirit, which he explains as an extension of the Holy Spirit, "requireth a spirituall vehicle like it selfe" and so is carried "in the hidden spirit of the blood."[28] Fludd compares the relationship between the anointed weapon and the wound to that between two identically tuned lutes at a distance from each other.[29] This analogy is more than merely didactic; it reflects the larger analogical structure of the universe, where sympathy functions, in Foucault's phrase, as "the vast syntax of the world," bringing together the diverse kinds of creation into complex and multifarious apposition.[30] Fludd insists on "an admirable sympathy, betwixt the vegetable, mineral and Animall, and the parts of mans body."[31] This universal sympathy translates into a universal symphony. "Therefore without doubt," Fludd boldly begins, "there is the selfe-same relation of unison betwixt this ointment with the blood in it and the wounded mans nature; as is between the string of one lute, that is proportioned unto the other in the same tone: And for this cause will be apt to vibrate and quaver forth one mutuall consent of simpatheticall harmony, if that the spirits of both, by the vertuall contact of one anothers nature, be made by conveying the individuall spirit of the one into the body of the other, that the lively balsamick vertue of the one, may comfort and stir up the dull and deadly languishment of the other, no otherwise then the activity of one lute string struck, doth stirre up the other to move, which was before still and without life."[32] Resemblance, or "consent," makes a virtual contact possible. The weapon and the wound vibrate sympathetically, though at a distance from each other, harmonized by spirit in the blood and in all things.

For Foster, this "unison" is nothing more than a far-fetched conceit. He objects to the weapon salve both as a theologian and as a philosopher. The cure is not authorized by Scripture and cannot be considered indirectly authorized by God, because it goes against the laws of nature. Citing the authority of Aristotle, Foster denies action at a distance: *"Nullum agens agit in distans."*[33] There is no corporeal contact between the weapon and the wound, and there can be no virtual contact between them, as between the iron and the lodestone, because virtual contact works only at a small distance, and the proponents of the weapon salve claim for it an unlimited "sphere of activitie." "Certainely the Angels of heaven cannot worke at such a distance," Foster replies; only God, "whose Essence is infinite, and is *Omnia in omnibus*, all in all, can worke thus." Those who accept the weapon salve, therefore, need fear for their souls. Foster dismisses the cure as "the new invention of the divell, an old impostor," and its bane is spread by his agent in the world, Paracelsus, who is nothing but "a Witch and Conjurer."[34] In the final analysis, Fludd and the other "Unguentaries" mistake rhetoric, that devilish art, for philosophical and physiological truth. "Mans life is his soule," Foster writes; "Farre be it from us that we should thinke the blood of man his soule. . . . When we say the blood is the life, it is a figurative speech, *Metonomia subjecti*, The Thing containing is put for the thing contained." When a murdered body begins bleeding again in the presence of the murderer, the phenomenon should be attributed not to the life of blood but rather to "a supernaturall motion proceeding from the just judgement of God, who gives the blood a wonderfull and supernaturall motion to come forth and meet the murtherer, and accuse him to his face." The blood has a "voice," as the Paracelsians claim, but "onely by *prosopopeia*."[35] The sympathetic universe becomes a rhetorical displacement of the divine universe, God's creation. The devil can use natural forces to his advantage, but only God can do the supernatural.[36]

Foster denies the cosmic basis of Fludd's argument. He does not reject sympathy, however defined, but wants to limit it to its proper sense; only sensible substances are subject to sympathetic interaction, and even when this "co-affection" exists, it exists only because a relative proximity makes it possible. Foster scoffs at the idea that "the smearing of a Weapon here below, can call the Starres above, at any time when we will, to give an influence which they gave not before, nor had not given at all, had not the Weapon been smeared at all."[37] His rejection of the weapon salve entails the rejection of an animistic cosmos. He takes on not only Fludd and Paracelsus but the Florentine Neoplatonic tradition as well: "When *Marsilius Ficino* can perswade mee that the Starres have the senses of seeing and hearing, and do heare mens prayers; then *Paracelsians* shal perswade me that the Loadstone hath life sense and fantasie."[38] God gave sense to some of His creatures, but not to all creation. Animated by their lies and false persuasions, the world of Fludd and Paracelsus and Ficino was a blasphemous trope. The Fludd-Foster debate was one of three such pamphlet wars to take place over a fifty-year period.[39] Behind this lack of consent, as Foster's skeptical star-gazing suggests, lay a new uncertainty about the consent of the cosmos. Fludd's physics might have seemed extravagant, but in the early decades of the seventeenth century it was not irrelevant. With or without a clearly articulated alternative, Foster could not sermonize the sympathetic worldview out of existence.

Fludd shared with, and inherited from, Paracelsus a strong and abiding commitment to magic, with which both closely associated sympathy. Paracelsus had attempted nothing less than a "bold conflation of medicine and magic," and, as Charles Webster explains, "at every stage of his career and in writings of every kind, the term magic was favored as the label for both the speculative and utilitarian aspects of his engagements with nature."[40] On the defensive, Fludd advanced a kind of "bad apple" view of magic, rejecting Foster's conclusion "that all Magick in generall is damnable and diabolicall, because one *species* or member of it, is justly to be banished from Christian mens remembrance: as if there were not a naturall magick, by which Salomon did know all the mysteries in nature, and the operations thereof." Fludd goes on to refer to "the three wise Kings of the East," a historical appeal frequently made by Paracelsus, who believed that the scriptural exaltation of the Magi placed magic on a secure theological foundation.[41] Fludd looks further back in the Bible, appealing to the authority of Solomon to justify his commitment to magic, which he represents as inseparable from, even tantamount to, his commitment to knowledge. If magic was not only licit but also sacred, by extension so, too, was sympathy.

SYMPATHY MECHANIZED

I turn now to *A Late Discourse* and Digby's attempt to disenchant sympathy by incorporating it into his mechanical philosophy. Digby aimed both to sever the tie between sympathy and magic and to resolve the long-standing debate about sympathetic cures once and for all. At the beginning of the treatise, he preempts an attack along the lines of Foster's, with which he was likely familiar.[42] He explicitly denies that magic will play a part in his account of sympathy powder and roundly refuses to admit rhetorical distortions into his natural philosophy. Where magicians and rhetoricians masquerading as philosophers have obscured the truth, Digby promises to uncover it, endeavoring "to make clear, how the Powder, which they commonly call the Powder of Sympathy, doth naturally, and without any Magick, cure wounds without touching them."[43] By 1657, when Digby traveled to Montpellier to give his lecture, the designation "Powder of Sympathy" had already become well established. Attributing that designation to anonymous others, Digby keeps the word "sympathy" at arm's length until he can reclaim it from the magicians. He goes on to advance a concept of sympathy based on matter in motion that accounts for the sympathetic action of the cure and ultimately for all sympathetic activity in nature. The ground for this philosophical project is a curious composite world picture, in which the old sympathies are retained but fundamentally reconfigured. Digby's account of sympathy powder was, according to Dobbs, "impeccable by the best pre-Newtonian standards."[44] Dobbs's compliment is not backhanded, as it might be in a Whig history of science, and yet it is not clear in the end that Digby's account measures up to his own stringent standards. Setting out to disenchant the cure, he does not ultimately release it from an enchanted world.

In his *Two Treatises*, published in Paris in 1644, Digby devotes three chapter sections to the sympathies and antipathies of animals, but he proceeds cautiously and hesitantly, as if he would rather not use those words at all. Having noted general enmities between the weasel and the toad, the lion and the cock, and the toad and the spider, Digby is determined to explain the matter as clearly and precisely as possible, without recourse to mystifying terms and phrases: "All which are caused in them, not by secret instincts, and antipathies, and sympathies, whereof we can give no account; (with the bare sound of which wordes, most men do pay themselves, without examining what they meane;) but by downe right materiall qualities, that are of contrary natures (as fire and water are)."[45] In his discussion of sympathy powder, Digby repeats this critique almost verbatim. By the end of the seventeenth century, the attack on sympathies and antipathies as well as occult qualities had become an anti-Scholastic commonplace. Inveighing against the natural philosophy of "The Schools," Thomas Hobbes wrote, "And in many occasions they put for cause of Naturall events, their own Ignorance; but disguised in other words: As when . . . they attribute many Effects . . . to *Sympathy, Antipathy, Antiperistasis, Specificall Qualities*, and other like Termes, which signifie neither the Agent that produceth them, nor the Operation by which they are produced."[46] Robert Boyle, too, remarked on "those numerous abstrusities of Nature, which 'tis well known that the *Aristoteleans* are wont to refer to Sympathy, Antipathy, or Occult Qualities, and strive to put off Men with empty Names, whereby they do not so much lessen our Ignorance, as betray their own."[47] As part of his systematic attempt to remedy the defects of speech, Locke made "sympathy" a case in point: "A Man should take care *to use no word without a signification*, no Name without an *Idea* for which he makes it stand. This Rule will not seem altogether needless, to any one who shall take the pains to recollect how often he has met with such Words; as *Instinct, Sympathy*, and *Antipathy*, etc. in the Discourse of others, so made use of, as he might easily conclude, that those that used them, had no *Ideas* in their Minds to which they applied them; but spoke them only as Sounds, which usually served instead of Reasons, on the like occasions."[48] For Digby, as for Hobbes, Boyle, Locke, and others, "sympathy" and "antipathy" were semantic blanks, smokescreens designed to conceal the Schoolman's ignorance.

The sense in which sympathy has become, or at least has come to be seen as, an empty signifier supports the mainspring of Foucault's analysis, but so long as the critique remained on the level of pragmatics—that is, a matter of the terms of use and the use of terms—the idea of sympathy was not simply nullified. At Montpellier, before an audience of *savants*, Digby endeavored to deliver on Descartes's promise to reduce the "marvels of sympathy and antipathy" to mechanical principles and so to reunite *res* and *verbum*. Building on the corpuscular theory he worked out in the 1640s, often with Descartes in mind, Digby approaches the subject of sympathetic cures in such a way that he can "give an account," a rational, mechanical explanation. For that account to succeed, it would have to rise above the hollow and mystical rhetoric marring all previous attempts. At the beginning of the treatise, Digby recalls Bacon in opposing "*perswasions*," which "do rather tickle the imagination, than satisfie the understanding," and "*Demonstrations*," which "are built upon certain and approved principles" and which "draw after them necessary conclusions" (17). While acknowledging that its aims were "noble," as we have seen, Bacon had identified "Natural Magic" as one of the three "sciences . . . which have had better intelligence and confederacy with the imagination of man than with his reason."[49] Digby aligns his science firmly with the latter. Hoping to secure for his account a "geometrical" rigor, he assures his listeners that he will persuade them "otherwise than by words" (18, 16). This grand, and seemingly paradoxical, claim follows the introduction of his test case, which Digby manufactured, according to Elizabeth Hedrick, in the interest of claiming the powder as his "intellectual property."[50]

At some point in the 1620s, Digby relates, his friend James Howell came between two friends engaged in a duel and, in the process, suffered a serious wound to his hand. In great pain, Howell visited Digby, knowing that his friend was highly skilled in the medical arts. Digby fetched a basin of water and proceeded to dissolve a small quantity of "Powder of Vitriol" in it, while the garter with which Howell's wounded hand had been first wrapped was retrieved. He then placed the garter into the basin and waited for Howell's response. Digby notes that Howell, talking to someone else in a far-off corner of the room, was not paying attention to what he did. As Thomas Fuller put it, "conceit is very contributive to the well working of Physick," but Digby, putting matter over mind, takes pains to deny that Howell's imagination played a part in the cure; its healing power, Digby insists, is independent of the power of the imagination.[51] Soon after the garter was immersed, Howell felt "a pleasing kind of freshnesse" in his hand (9). After dinner, Digby removed the garter from the water and hung it up to dry in front of a fire. Howell's servant came back immediately, announcing that his master was in as much pain as before, "for the heat was such as if his hand were twixt coales of fire" (10). Digby then returned the garter to the basin and noted that Howell's pain subsided once again. This operation, he suggests, demonstrates that the powder is the efficient cause of healing.

Building up to a strict philosophical explanation of Howell's case, Digby outlines a series of seven natural principles that make the cure possible. Digby's first principle is that the atmosphere is filled with light, which he defines as "a materiall and corporall substance, and not an imaginary and incomprehensible quality, as many Schoolmen averre" (19). Taking issue with the philosophy of the "Schoolmen," Digby appears to position himself against the Aristotelian tradition, but in reality his theory of matter and material dynamics depends heavily on it. That theory is best classified, to adapt Antonio Clericuzio's phrase, as "Aristotelian atomism."[52] Although Ernest Gilman has referred to Digby's "assiduous application of neo-Democratean atomic theory,"[53] Digby's atomism comes more clearly out of the *minima naturalia* tradition, which originated not with the classical atomists but with Aristotle, whose notion that substantial forms have essential limits, existing *ad maximum* and *ad minimum*, was developed by medieval commentators on his *Physics*, and emerged as a corpuscular philosophy in the sixteenth century. Scaliger and Sennert came to interpret *minima* not as physical limits but rather as material particles with distinct qualities.[54] Digby retains the Aristotelian elements; his atoms are "composed of the four Elements, (as all bodies are)" (22). They are not indivisible and are not defined by size, shape, and motion, as the classical atomists maintained.

Digby asserts that all bodies are infinitely divisible and emphasizes the corpuscular nature of light. He claims in his fourth principle that reflected light carries with it "some small particles or atomes" of the reflecting surface (21), which it loosens in bombardment. This loosening caused by the light is actually the result of "some small incisions proportionable to her rarity and subtility" (22), and once loosened, as Digby goes on to explain in an elaborate simile, with perhaps a hint of royalist mythmaking, "These Atomes then are like Cavaliers mounted on winged coursers, who go very far, untill that the Sun setting, takes from them their Pegasus, and leaves them unmounted; and then they precipitate themselves in crowds to the earth, whence they sprung, the greatest part of them, and the most heavy fall upon the first retreating of the Sun" (23). Here the idea of action by contact begins to seem hardly less fanciful than that of action at a distance, but the point of Digby's figure is to reinforce his claim that matter is potentiated by light.[55] Light represents a rushing stream of atoms, the wind is nothing but agitated atoms, and air, in the third principle, "is no other than a mixture, or confusion of such atomes, wherein the aereall parts do predominate" (35). Digby substantiates this principle by relating that vipers were seen to grow in a large, covered gourd with nothing but air to nourish them and that a certain Monsieur Ferrier synthesized oil of tartar that took on the scent of rose because "it was then in the season of Roses" (37). The air is full of atoms deriving from bodies off which light has reflected.

These atoms move in linear currents unless they are attracted away from their natural course, which can happen in several different ways. Digby considers suction, siphoning, magnetic attraction, "electrick" attraction, as between "straws" and "the Jett-stone" (54), the attraction of fire, and filtration. The last provides him with an opportunity to revisit his point about those who bandy about the word "sympathy" without understanding the concept or the mechanism:

> *Filtration* may seem to him who hath not attentively considered it, nor examined by what circumstances so hidden a secret of nature comes to passe, and to a person of a mean and limited understanding, to be done by some occult virtue, or property, and will perswade himself, that within the Filtre, or strayning Instrument, there is some secret Sympathy, which makes water to mount up contrary to its naturall motion.
>
> But he who will examine the business as it ought to be, observing all that is done, without omitting any circumstance, will find there is nothing more naturall, and that it is impossible it should be otherwise. And we must make the same judgement of all the profound and most hidden mysteries of nature, if one would take the pains to discover them, and search into them with judgement. (54–55)

Digby's atomistic theory allows him to posit a new and more rigorous theory of natural sympathy. Whereas those of "a mean and limited understanding" imagine in the marvels of nature "some occult virtue" or "secret Sympathy," Digby would "take the pains to discover them," denying that sympathy is "secret" or "occult," and thus outside the realm of understanding. He denounces the occultist as lazy and injudicious, a mere philosophaster, who takes refuge in mysticism to make up for his lack of diligence and discernment. The true philosopher penetrates the marvels of attraction and accounts for them clearly and rationally.

Weight, quantity, and figure—all natural charactcristics that can be clearly understood—underlie the attraction of bodies and their various sympathies. Homogeneity is crucial to Digby's theory:

> My sixth Principle shall be, that when fire, or some hot body attracts the aire, and that which is within the air, if it happens that within that air there be found some dispersed atoms of the same nature with the body which draws them, the attraction of such atoms is made more powerfully, then if they were bodies of a different nature, and these atoms doe stay, stick, and mingle with more willingnesse with the body which draws them. The reason hereof is the resemblance and Sympathy they have one with the other. (68)

Digby elaborates this theory several pages later, explaining "that the bodies which draw the atomes dispersed in the aire, attract unto themselves with a greater power and energy such as are of their own nature, then such as are heterogeneous, and of a strange nature" (110). Like, in short, powerfully attracts like. Having emptied out its mystical connotations and imbued it with matter, Digby now admits the term "sympathy" into his philosophy. The sixth principle is understood to account for a vast array of phenomena. Digby's audience learns of the Roman nun whose devotional activities made her body so hot that her bones dried up, after which she excreted more than two hundred pounds of water every day. Such a prodigious occurrence, which Digby claims to have found in the writings of Petrus Servius, physician to Urban VIII, can be explained in terms of the attraction of air to the heat inside the nun's body; once inside, it turned to liquid in her bladder. Digby emphasizes and variously illustrates the "power and energy" of sympathy but aims to show that it is contained by the explanatory power of his materialist philosophy.

When Digby returns to the story of Howell's cure and to the dynamics of atomic flow involved, all of his principles are firmly in place. The blood atoms on the garter are attracted to those of the wound, where they are more plentiful. When the powder is added to the garter, light, which enables the cure, carries both the blood atoms and those of the vitriol in the powder and diffuses them in the air, where they are borne directly to the wound, which "is immediately solac'd and eased, and consequently comes to be healed by the spirits of the Vitriol, which is of a Balsamicall virtue" (146). The aeration of the vitriol concentrates this virtue, and so the powder is more effective when applied at a distance than when it is administered directly. The vitriol, varieties and preparations of which Digby spends some time discussing, is a very special substance indeed:

> The *Chymists* do assure us that it is no other then a corporification of the universall spirit which animates and perfects all that hath existence in the sublunary World, which is drawn in that abundance by a Lover so appropriated, by meanes whereof I my self have in a short time, by exposing it onely unto the open aire, made an attraction of a celestiall Vitriol ten times more in weight, which was of a marvelous purenesse and vertue; a priviledge which hath not been given but to it, and to pure virgin salt-peter. (142)

It is not clear which "Chymists" Digby has in mind, but he might well be referring to Nicaise Le Fèvre, whose "course of *Chymistrie*" Digby—and, according to Evelyn, "divers Curious Persons of Learning & quality"—attended in Paris in 1651.[56] Apothecary in Ordinary and "Chymical Distiller" to Charles II, Le Fèvre begins his *Compendious Body of Chymistry*, published in 1662, by defining the "Universal Spirit" as "the spring and root of all things . . . a spiritual substance, homogeneous and like unto itself, to which ancient and modern Philosophers have attributed several names, calling it a *Vital substance, a Spirit of life, Light, Balsom of life, Vital Mummy, Natural heat, Universal Spirit, Mercury of life*; and many more names."[57] The chymist studies the transformations of this vital substance, showing "not only . . . how a body may be spiritualized, but how a spirit also may be fixt to become a body." Thus the vitriol represents a "corporification" of a noncorporeal substance.[58] Such an assertion, while relying on recent work in chymical theory, is nevertheless consistent with the mode of Fludd, who was determined to show that sympathetic cures both participate in and concretely demonstrate the sympathetic structure of the cosmos. In the first chapter of his compendium, Le Fèvre appeals to the authority of Paracelsus, "our *German Trismegistus*," who identified "the strength of Nature" not with the body but with "that seminal spirit which it contains."[59]

Influenced by Paracelsus and Van Helmont, Le Fèvre was, according to Dobbs, "the last major representative of the older science."[60] Referring in various places to Galileo and Gassendi, Digby seemed to have little interest in associating himself with such a science, and his desire to separate himself from any scientific activity that evoked the occult can be seen to underlie the hedging and shifting that immediately follow his chymical account of vitriol: "But to anatomise as we ought the nature of this transcendent individuall, which never-thelesse in some fashion may be said to be universall, and fundamentall to all bodies, it would require a Discourse far more ample then I have yet made" (142). Such a discourse never appeared. Instead of continuing in this vein, Digby sums up the mechanism of his sympathetic cure and relates it to that of the weapon salve, which works "because the subtil spirits of blood do penetrate the substance of the blade, as far as the extent which the sword made within the body of the wounded party, where they use to make their residence, there being nothing to chase them away, unless it be the fire" (149). Digby leaves open the possibility that a universal spirit exists and is at work, but he will make no defi-nite statements about it, preferring to project his sympathetic universe according to more concrete atomistic principles.

Still, the mechanistic system that Digby unfolds cannot fully contain the "marvel" of the cure. The sprawling, anecdotal middle of the treatise, straining his distinction between demonstration and persuasion with its uncertain "sympathetic" logic, extends this problem of containment into the very form of the argument, as we shall see. In his peroration, Digby moves hastily from the cosmos back to the cure: "I am perswaded my Discourse hath convincingly shewed you, that in this Sympatheticall cure, there is no need to admit of an action distant from the Patient. I have traced unto you a real Communication twixt the one and the other, *viz.* of a Balsamicall substance, which corporally mingleth with the wound" (151). The strong phrase "real Communication" sets up a marked contrast with "any effects of Charme or Magick" (151) in the next paragraph. Digby's vehement antimagical stance thus bookends the treatise. To the end he stays true to his muse, maintaining the Aristotelian theory of action and integrating it into his own theory of matter. Yet the theory of spirit he chose not to articulate suggests the ambivalence of his allegiance to the animists and to a worldview that he could neither fully abandon nor fully embrace.

"SOLID SATISFACTION"

In this section I examine contemporary responses to *A Late Discourse* and consider the subsequent fortunes of sympathetic cures. From this wider historical perspective we can see a gradual decline in status both of the cures themselves and of the sympathetic worldview that Digby set out to revise and to reinforce. For Digby, the efficacy of sympathy powder was a crucial, concrete example of a sympathetic nature at work in the world. Over time, however, it was increasingly recognized that, if the cure worked at all, it did so only when applied directly, and claims about its efficacy were more and more subject to falsification. What might be called the indexical function of sympathetic cures was gradually voided. They did not reveal or reflect truths about the world; rather, they were only as good as, and effectively no more than, their active ingredient. In 1659, the year after Digby's treatise appeared, Henry More published a comprehensive theory of spirit under the title *The Immortality of the Soul*. Praising Digby's "witty and eloquent *Discourse of the Cure of Wounds by the powder of Sympathy*,"[61] More, it seems, was more impressed by Digby's persuasions than by his demonstrations. This gentlemanly compliment appears in a chapter that clarifies More's use of the term "the Spirit of Nature," which he defines as a *"substance incorporeal, but without Sense and Animadversion, pervading the whole Matter of the Universe, and exercising a plastical power therein according to the sundry predispositions and occasions in the parts it works upon, raising such Phænomena in the World, by directing the parts of the Matter and their Motion, as cannot be resolved into meer Mechanical powers."* Against Cartesianism, of which he had been an early evangelist in England, More posits "some more mysticall Principle then what is meerly Mechanical."[62] He insists that the human soul cannot be localized anatomically but rather is diffused throughout the body. And as "in every partic-ular world, such as Man is especially," so in the greater world, or macrocosm. Like Fludd's, More's psychic "mysticism" allows him to link the general to the particular, and vice versa:

> From this Principle, I conceive that not onely the *Sympathy of parts* in one particular Subject, but of *different and distant Subjects*, may be understood: such as is betwixt the party wounded, and the Knife or Sword that wounded him, besmeared with the Weapon-salve, and kept in a due temper: Which certainly is not purely Mechanical, but Magical, though not in an unlawful sense; that is to say, it is not to be resolved into meer Matter, of what thinness or subtility soever you please, but into the *Unity* of the *Soul of the Universe*, and *Continuity of the subtile Matter*, which answers to our *Animal Spirits*. And in this sense it is that *Plotinus* sayes, that the World is . . . *the grand Magus* or *Enchanter*.[63]

Digby, whom More cites later in the work, is undoubtedly the silent interlocutor here. More is unpersuaded that the "agency of emissary Atoms" can simply account for "*Sympathetick* Cures, Pains and Asswagements," because the size of the particles "argues the suddainness of their extinction, as the smallest wires made red hot soonest cool." He appeals instead to the Neoplatonic world soul to save the phenomena.[64] Unlike Digby, More embraced magic as a matter of ancient authority. Whereas Digby saw himself continuing the true Aristotelian tradition, More saw himself continuing the true Platonic tradition. Neither considered his chosen tradition incompatible with recent discoveries. More cites Digby's example of the "woman of *Carcassona*," whose imaginative engagement with an ape during her pregnancy led to the monstrous birth of an ape-child, but relies on the authority of "that judicious Naturalist Dr. *Harvey*" to free the mother's soul of blame. "What remains therefore," More asks, "but the *universal Soule of the World* or *Spirit of Nature* that can doe these feats?" Ockham's razor seems here a rather blunt instrument. More gives a more detailed account of resonance, but comes inevitably to the same conclusion: "If it were the meer Vibration of the Aire that caused this tremor in the Unison string, the effect would not be considerable, unless both the strings lay well-nigh in the same Plane, and that the Vibration of the string that is struck be made in that Plane they both lie in. . . . All which things do clearly shew, that pure *corporeal* causes cannot produce this effect: and that therefore we must suppose, that both the strings are united with some one *incorporeal* Being, which has a different *Unity* and *Activity* from *Matter*, but yet a *Sympathy* therewith."[65] For Digby, More's spiritual principle was too airy a premise from which to build a rigorous philosophical account. Yet, as we have seen, the philosophical premise behind Digby's iatrochemistry was hardly rock-solid.

Digby's mechanistic account of sympathy was more favorably received two years later by Joseph Glanvill (1636–1680), who asserts in the *The Vanity of Dogmatizing* (1661) that the cure of wounds "by the *Sympathetick medicine . . .* is for matter of fact put out of doubt by the Noble Sir *K. Digby*, and the proof he gives in his ingenious discourse on the subject, is unexceptionable."[66] Here Glanvill affirms Digby's demonstrations, his "proof." But Glanvill's subsequent discussion moves out in a new direction. Of the virtuous particles of vitriol, he writes,

> The particular way of their conveyance, and their regular direction is handsomly explicated by that learned *Knight*, and recommended to the Ingenious by most witty and becoming illustrations. It is out of my way here to enquire whether the *Anima Mundi* be not a better account, then any *Mechanical* Solutions. The former is more desperate; the later hath more of ingenuity, then solid satisfaction. It is enough for me that *de facto* there is such an entercourse between the *Magnetick unguent* and the *vulnerated* body, and I need not be solicitous of the Cause.[67]

Counterpoising the two major world systems of the age in a single sentence, Glanvill in effect makes a case for the irrelevance of both; what matters is not how the wound heals, or why it heals, but *that* it heals. Once the cure can be conceived without reference to the cosmos, the controversy has reached a new

stage, perhaps even its final stage. In Glanvill's remarks we can see the beginning of the breakup of the ontological continuum weapon-wound-world.

When Robert Boyle discussed sympathy powder in his *Two Essays Concerning
the Unsuccessfulness of Experiments*, also published in 1661, he made no appeal
to the world beyond the bounds of the body. He treats the powder as one
example of a more general problem in the realm of physic:

> But besides the general uncertainty to which most remedies are subject,
> there are some few that seem obnoxious to Contingencies of a peculiar
> nature: such is the Sympathetick Powder, of which not onely divers Physicians
> and other sober persons have assur'd me they had successfully made trial, but
> we ourselves have thought that we were Eye-witnesses of the operation of it;
> and yet not onely many that have try'd it have not found it answer Expectation,
> but we our selves trying some of our own preparing on our selves, have found
> it ineffectual, and unable to stop so much as a bleeding at the Nose, though
> upon Application of it a little before we had seen such a bleeding, though
> violent, suddenly stopt in a person, who was so far from contributing by his
> Imagination to the effect of the Powder, that he derided those that he saw
> apply it to some of the drops of his blood. Wherefore that the Sympathetick
> Powder and the Weapon-salve are never of any efficacy at all, I dare not
> affirm; but that they constantly perform what is promised of them, I must
> leave others to believe.[68]

Like Glanvill, Boyle refuses to dogmatize, but he also challenges the fact
itself. The crux is "constancy." Experimentally unreliable, the cures pose a
problem of credit.[69] In an essay published two years later under the title
"Proposing some Particulars wherein Natural Philosophy may be useful to the
Therapeutical part of Physick," Boyle writes, "I have seen sometimes something
follow upon the use of the Sympathetick Powder, that did incline me to think,
that sometimes it might work Cures." The utterance is thick with qualifiers.
Charting a course between "never" and "constantly," Boyle builds a creditable
claim around "sometimes." He enjoins neither belief nor disbelief but rather
further trial, "especially," as he argues, "since these sympathetical wayes of cure
are most of them so safe and innocent, that, though, if they be real, they may do
much good, if they prove fictions they can do no harme."[70] In July 1668, the first
Earl of Shaftesbury, under the medical care of John Locke, was treated on three
consecutive days with sympathy powder. That Shaftesbury recovered from the
mysterious illness, apparently hydatid disease, was no doubt due to the surgical
drainage of the abscess rather than to the application of the powder, but Locke
and others were evidently willing to consider both interventions on the same

footing.[71] Both he and Boyle approached sympathetic cures as physicians rather than as metaphysicians. What mattered was not that the cures acted sympathetically but that they worked safely and effectively.

Over time it became more widely acknowledged that sympathy powder—as a distance cure—did not work, or if it did, that it worked only sporadically. Scientific attention was increasingly focused on the active ingredient rather than on the theory of application. The history of sympathy powder merges with the history of English vitriol in the pharmacological literature.[72] In 1682, George Hartman published Digby's recipe for sympathy powder, but with a significant difference—the powder was to be applied directly to the wound.[73] Digby had been quite explicit about this "grosser Application"; it was not nearly so effective as the distance method he had taken great pains to describe.[74] A recipe similar to Hartman's, with similar directions for application, appeared in George Wilson's *Compleat Course of Chymistry* (1698) and then again in William Lewis's *Course of Practical Chemistry* (1746). The treatment described by Wilson and Lewis, styptic in nature, is sympathetic only in name. By the late eighteenth century sympathy powder no longer had a place in the major British pharmacopoeias.[75]

Digby's name—attached to his theory—greatly enhanced the status of sympathy in the seventeenth century. The Latin translation of Digby's discourse appears to have been the impetus for the publication of a *Theatrum Sympatheticum* in 1660. That edition, published at Nuremberg, was followed by another the next year in Amsterdam, and then in 1662 a greatly enlarged revised edition, containing twenty-six treatises instead of four, appeared in Nuremberg. This new *Theatrum* included not only Digby's treatise and those of de Mohy, Papin, and Van Helmont but also Fracastoro's *De sympathia et antipathia rerum*. The collection was translated into Flemish for an edition that came out in 1665.[76] But when the action of the powder was isolated from the various actors on behalf of it, it increasingly failed to persuade. Digby worked hard to rationalize his cure, but also to authorize it. In *A Late Discourse* we can see sympathy powder functioning as a kind of political capital, which Digby used to strengthen his ties to king and court. In a single page toward the beginning of the treatise, Digby notes that his patient was "illustrious," that "the hands . . . through which the whole businesse passed" were "above the *Vulgar*," that "the circumstances were examined, and sounded to the bottom," by none other than King James himself, and that "all was registred among the observations of great *Chancelor Bacon*, to adde by way of Appendix, unto his Naturall History" (5).[77] Digby affirms Howell's status and then appeals to the highest authority in the land. When the king learned of Howell's cure, Digby relates, "his Majesty . . . drolled with me first (which he could do with a very good grace) about a Magitian and a Sorcerer" (11). Given the cure's origins as a "secret . . . learnt in the oriental parts" (12), the very cradle of magic itself, Digby's mention of the king's joke functions to certify the cure and, in a sense, to purify it, to free it from its associations with occultness and otherness.[78] Digby then uses Bacon's authority to enhance the credit of the cure even further. But the "registration" of "great *Chancelor Bacon*" is nowhere in evidence. Before going on to give Oswald Crollius's recipe for the weapon salve, Bacon writes, "It is constantly Received, and Avouched, that the *Anointing* of the *Weapon*, that maketh the *Wound*, will heale the *Wound* it selfe. In this *Experiment*, upon the Relation of *Men* of *Credit*, (though my selfe, as yet, am not fully inclined to beleeve it,) you shall note the *Points* following."[79] Exemplifying the cautious, skeptical attitude for which he was to become famous, Bacon refuses to accept the efficacy of the cure solely on the basis of report, however creditable.

In the end, neither the ingenuity of Digby's mechanical account nor the authority of those who vouched for it could make the powder work. As John Henry has suggested, Glanvill's strictly factual take on sympathetic cures, in its subordination of etiology to phenomenology, operates according to the same logic as Newton's position on gravity: "And to us it is enough that gravity does really exist and act according to the laws which we have explained, and abundantly serves to account for all the motions of the celestial bodies and of our sea."[80] The fact could be established experimentally even if the cause remained unknown. In the Cartesian mode, however, Digby enlisted mechanism in the pursuit of what he referred to as "true causes" (15). While praising Digby's ingenuity, Glanvill acknowledged that his solution lacked "solid satisfaction." And although Glanvill attested that the cure really worked, there is evidence to suggest that his certitude on the matter was not airtight. Whereas in *The Vanity of Dogmatizing* Glanvill claims the question of the cure "is for matter of fact put out of doubt" by Digby, in a subsequent revision of that work, given the title *Scepsis Scientifica* (1664), Glanvill writes that the question "as to matter of fact is with circumstances of good evidence asserted" by Digby.[81] This rhetorical adjustment renews the possibility of doubt, and as we have seen, Boyle, like Bacon, "left others to believe" that the cure was universally effective. To use Newton's language, it came to seem ever less certain that sympathy, as a universal force, did "really exist." When in Thomas Shadwell's comedy *The Virtuoso* (1676) his protagonist, Sir Nicholas Gimcrack, discusses the tarantula's apparent affinity for music and exclaims, "There's your phenomenon of sympathy!" the audience is convinced of nothing more than Gimcrack's fatuity.[82] Digby, whom Walter E. Houghton Jr. long ago identified as the seventeenth-century virtuoso par excellence, could not ultimately persuade others that, when it came to healing wounds at a distance, the "phenomenon of sympathy" was real.[83]

CONTAGION AND THE SYMPATHETIC IMAGINATION

Centered on a sham cure, Digby's project of a scientific sympathy was doomed to fail, and yet his exploration of sympathy beyond the immediate context of the cure suggests not a dead end but a significant development, one whose promise would increasingly be fulfilled in the decades after his death. In shifting his analysis of sympathetic interaction from powders and wounds to parents and children and more broadly to persons, Digby applied his materialist philosophy to a realm in which the factual basis of sympathy was ultimately far more secure. I want now to return to *A Late Discourse* and to look closely at the digressive middle of the treatise, where Digby narrows his focus to the imagination and human sympathy. The formal excess of the digression undermines the sense of methodological containment, as if sympathy were taking over and overflowing the argument. By this point the audience, whose learned members Digby would have likely supposed to share his bias from the outset, has been further conditioned to see the imagination not as a simple faculty of mind but rather as a dangerous source of error.

Digby begins by discussing birthmarks caused by the longing of pregnant mothers, which attest to "the force of the imagination" (108). In the English translation of his expanded *Magiae naturalis*, which appeared, like *A Late Discourse*, in 1658, Della Porta begins his chapter "Of the wonderful force of imagination" with a list of authorities on the subject. "*Empedocles*," he writes, "held that an infant is formed according to that which the mother looks upon at the time of conception," an idea also maintained by Hippocrates, Quintilian, St. John Damascene—who relates that a mother gave birth to a hairy child after gazing at an image of John the Baptist—and Heliodorus—who relates that the Queen of Ethiopia gave birth to a "fair daughter" after looking at a picture of Andromeda.[84] These and other such anecdotes attesting to the *vis imaginativa* appear in a wide range of sixteenth- and seventeenth-century texts addressing themselves to the marvelous and the monstrous.[85] Digby treats "longing marks" as "marvailous effects" whose causes he aims "to penetrate" using the same materialist principles applied to the sympathetic cure (85). Endeavoring to account for the berry-shaped birthmark on the neck of a "Lady of high condition" (83), Digby seems at first to go against the grain of his discourse in that he does not pathologize the imagination but rather pays it tribute.[86] In a curious double trope he pictures the imagination on the field of battle and in the home: "The great Architect of nature in the fabrick of human body, the master-peece of corporal nature, hath placed there some intern spirits, to serve as centinells, to bring their discoveries to their General, *viz.* to the imagination, who is as it were the Mistresse of the whole family" (89). The master of the family, in the familiar sense, relies on the "Mistresse" of the familial body, in Digby's sense, for survival. The imagination thus assumes a positive supervisory role, but Digby's proliferating tropology suggests a crisis of containment on the rhetorical and categorical levels that reinforces the sense in which sympathy poses a threat to the order and integrity of the body.

Some pages earlier, Digby adduces the example of a lady who "hath upon her neck the figure of a Mulberry, as exactly as any Painter, or Sculptor can possibly represent one, for it bears not onely the colour, but the just proportion of a Mulberry" (84). Digby here treats a natural marvel as an aesthetic one, a virtual work of art produced by the imagination.[87] But if the artistry of the imagination, its mimetic exactitude, is admired, it is quickly called into question; in "Mulbery-season," Digby relates, "this impression, or rather excrescence of flesh did swell, grow big, and itch" (84). The shift from "impression," with its suggestions of printing and engraving, to "excrescence" turns the imagination's sculpture into a kind of tumor. This pejorative redescription is reinforced by Digby's next example, a woman whose strawberry-shaped birthmark "broke like an Impostume" and needed to be cauterized by a surgeon. Associated with pathological growth, the imagination's art seems finally to mar the "master-peece" of the body, the creation of the true artist, the "great Architect of nature."

In the social sphere, Digby suggests, interaction, mediated by the morbid imagination, becomes infection. His most focused account of human sympathy uncovers a powerful, and dangerous, imaginative mechanism:

> Now lets consider how the strong imagination of one man doth marvailously act upon another man, who hath it more feeble and passive. We see dayly, that if a person gape, those who see him gaping, are excited to do the same. If one come perchance to converse with persons that are subject to excesse of laughter, one can hardly forbear laughing, although one doth not know the cause why they laugh. If one should enter into a house, where all the World is sad, he becomes melancholy, for as one said, *Si vis me flere dolendum est primum ipsi tibi*, Women and Children being very moist and passive, are most susceptible of this unpleasing contagion of the imagination. (93)

Whereas sympathized atoms move in the direction of greater quantity, sympathized imaginations act in the direction of greater susceptibility. Digby traces a downward trajectory of imaginative "strength"—from the strong male mind to the relatively weak male mind to the minds of women and children, which are considered essentially weak—and at the same time a widening arc of sympathetic effect. He notes the phenomenon of sympathetic "gaping," or yawning, and then passes from laughter not to crying but to sadness—that is, from an action to a state or mood, as if the "melancholy" have the power to transfuse their own humoral "excesse." At this point Digby quotes Horace's *Ars poetica*, but the epigram ("If you would have me weep, you must first feel grief yourself") jars somewhat with the discussion.[88] It suggests not only artfulness, whereas Digby is emphasizing natural reflex, but also control, whereas Digby is emphasizing passivity. The preceding line and a half of Horace's analysis of affect and effect seems more apposite: "Ut ridentibus arrident, ita flentibus adsunt / humani voltus [As men's faces smile on those who smile, so they respond to those who weep]."[89] Digby treats Horace not as a theorist of poetry but rather as an observer of human nature. Sympathy is represented here as automatic and irresistible.

All human beings are subject to sympathy, but some are more subject than others: this observation would be widely repeated and variously moralized by theorists of sensibility in the next century, when the responsiveness of women in particular was understood not in terms of humoral physiology ("moisture") but according to the new science of neurophysiology.[90] For Digby, greater susceptibility does not suggest superior sensibility; rather, it suggests constitutional weakness, or "feebleness." A significant contrast develops at this point in the treatise between the sympathetic healing of wounds and the sympathetic infection of minds, between the "pleasing kind of freshnesse" Howell feels in his treated hand and the "unpleasing contagion of the imagination." The pejorative force of the word "contagion" here depends in part on Digby's earlier references to plague and physical disease, the "time of contagion, or universal infection of the air" (65), and again the "time of common contagion," when "they use to carry about them the powder of a toad, and sometimes a living toad or spider shut up in a box; or else they carry arsnick, . . . which draws unto it the contagious air" (77). To suggest that Digby transforms "contagion" into a metaphor is to miss his point that catching another's infection and catching another's affection are analogous atomic processes; while others commonly understood the former in terms of sympathy, he understood both as involving the same mechanism.[91] In the case of the latter, the individual cannot rely on an apotropaic box to ward off infection; he must rely on the strength of his mind. Digby's discussion of the *vis imaginativa* at points recalls Bacon's in *Sylva Sylvarum*, which reads, "For as in *Infection*, and *Contagion* from *Body* to *Body* . . . it is most certaine, that the *Infection* is received (many times) by the *Body Passive*, but yet is by the *Strength*, and good *Disposition* thereof, Repulsed . . . ; So much more in *Impressions* from *Minde* to *Minde* . . . the *Impression* taketh, but is Encountred, and Overcome, by the *Minde* and *Spirit* . . . before it worke any manifest *Effect*.

And therefore, they worke most upon *Weake Mindes*."[92] Digby amplified Bacon's concern with "weak minds." Digby begins *A Late Discourse* with Howell's wound and the success of the "vulnerary powder," but in his discussion of imaginative contagion he gives us the sense of a deeper vulnerability in human nature, of the trauma of sympathy.

Within the larger discussion, Digby's account of imaginative contagion functions to set up an argument *a fortiori*. If sympathy has the power to affect all, it affects the infant above all because of its proximity to the mother. Since two persons could not be closer than those two, "one may thence conclude, That all the effects of a strong and vehement imagination working upon another more feeble, passive, and tender, ought to be more efficacious in the Mother acting upon her son, then when the imaginations of other persons act upon them who are nothing to them" (95–96). The atoms of the mulberry or strawberry, released by light, pass through the eyes into the mother's imagination and thence to the child, "who hath his parts also tuned in an harmonious consonance with the mothers" (97). The atoms of the fruit then move from the child's imagination to his skin, where they make a mark. A birthmark is thus a kind of sympathetic vibration, and the effect of Digby's wide-ranging discussion is of a larger world in tune. But, on the microcosmic level, the "longing mark" is also a "lasting mark," a signature, of human passivity and weakness. In an anecdote that was later retold by Nicolas Malebranche, who twice refers to Digby in his discussion of the imagination in the second book of *De la recherche de la vérité* (1674–1675), Digby goes on to trace King James's "strange antipathy . . . to a naked sword" to a tragic event that occurred while he was in the womb: his mother, Mary Stuart, saw before her eyes the brutal stabbing of her secretary, and her distress impressed itself on her son in the form not of a birthmark but rather of a fear of swords, such "that he could not see one without a great emotion of the spirits, although otherwise couragious enough, yet he could not over-master his passions in this particular" (105).[93] The power of the maternal imagination precludes the complete stoic self-mastery of the king, whose body natural was not immune to the power of sympathy.

The child's imagination sympathizes with the mother's, the consonant string sympathizes with the principal string, the expressionless sympathize with the yawning or laughing, and the audience sympathizes with the orator or poet—in narrower compass Digby had presented a similar conjunction of analogous passive-active pairs in *Two Treatises*. Having done so, he drew a wider conclusion about human nature: "All these effects, do proceed out of the action of the seene object upon the fantasy of the looker on. . . . And hence it is, that when we heare one speake with love and tendernesse of an absent person, we are also inclined to love that person, though we never saw him, nor heard of him before: and that whatsoever a good oratour delivereth well, (that is, with a semblance of passion agreeable to his wordes) rayseth of its owne nature, like affection in the hearers: and that generally men learne and imitate (without designe) the customes and manners of the company they much haunt."[94] Although Digby attaches no explicit moral value to the sympathetic love that he describes, he does not reject it, nor does he analyze sympathetic behavior in general according to the same gendered dynamic of strength and weakness. Digby adopts a more neutral attitude toward "the fantasy" and toward human sympathy. Yet in the chapter *"Of Discoursing,"* toward the beginning of the second treatise, "of mans soule," we can hear the more negative tone echoed in *A Late Discourse.* Digby repeated in the latter elements of the two chapters from *Two Treatises.* In the earlier work, the Horatian epigram provides a kind of climax to Digby's discursive definition of rhetoric:

> Her rules instruct us . . . how to give life and motion to what we say, by our action and gesture; that so we may persuade our Auditory, such passions raigne in us, as we seeke to stirre up in them: for as we may observe, that one who yawneth, maketh an other likewise yawne; and as our seeing others laugh, provoketh laughing also in us . . . after the same manner, what passion soever we exhibit in ourselves, the same stealeth insensibly upon those we speake unto; whiles their mind attending to the wordes they heare, is not aware of the subtile spirits motions, that by a kind of contagion rise and swell in their hartes: according to which naturall inclination in all men, the Master of Poets and excellent observer of mens humours said passing well:
>
> > *Si vis me flere, dolendum est*
> > *Primùm ipsi tibi.*
>
> Hence grow those encreases by metaphores, hyperboles, and other tropes and figures . . . which when they are fittely placed, they carry the Auditor even against his will.[95]

Digby's epitome of the art is largely conventional; he identifies rhetoric with persuasion, groups it with logic and grammar, and analyzes it into invention, disposition, elocution, and action, but what he emphasizes disproportionately— taking Horace as his original—is the affective side of rhetoric. Digby describes persuasive language as a kind of decoy that allows a sympathetic exchange of emotion to occur without the auditor's awareness. By referring to the auditor's sympathetic response as "a kind of contagion," a phrase that becomes more strongly pejorative in *A Late Discourse,* Digby subtly pathologizes rhetoric, which exploits our predisposition to sympathy, a "naturall inclination in all men." He does not single out women and children but rather reflects more generally on human nature, following the lead of "the Master of Poets and excellent observer of mens humours." He adheres to Horace's account of *poemata* more closely here than he does in *A Late Discourse*; his reference to sympathetic laughter recalls Horace's phrase "ut ridentibus arrident," and his idea of tropes and figures "fittely placed" answers Horace's "male . . . mandata."[96] The presence, then, of "contagion," for which there is no equivalent in Horace, is especially striking. In immediate context, Horace's concern is not the infection of an audience but its derision when the poet breaks with decorum.

Digby expresses in the treatise on sympathy powder his anxiety about the power of rhetoric to deceive and to manipulate others. Behind this power, he suggests, is the power of sympathy. It moves the patient "even against his will." The synthesizing of sympathy powder, which Digby describes at the end of *A Late Discourse*, can be seen to represent the harnessing of that power; reduced to tangible form, or "corporified," that power could itself be manipulated. But what could be mastered and measured in the laboratory or in the circles of the elite could not be so managed in society at large. In the social sphere the vulgar majority continually fell victim to the contagion of sympathy. It might have been the case, as Digby laments early in the treatise, "that now there is scarce any Country Barber but knows" the secret of sympathy powder (14), but the capacity to resist the contagion of sympathy was not so easily learned; it was in large part a matter of birth and breeding. Highlighted in his final sentence, with its condemnation of "pusillanimity" (151) — the traditional ethical ill of small-mindedness — Digby's response was to address himself only to an ideal audience of *savants*, syllogists, and rationalists, those whose strong and seeking minds could discover the true nature and true causes of things. In his discussion "*Of Discoursing*," Digby begins with the subject of the syllogism, "whose end and effect is to gaine the knowledge of something, before hidden and unknowne," and goes on to exalt *homo logicus*, a man of reason rather than of imagination or emotion: "Now these Syllogismes, being, as it were interlaced and woven one within an other, (so that many of them do make a long chaine, whereof each of them is a linke) do breede, or rather are all the variety of mans life: . . . man as he is man, doth nothing else but weave such chaines: whatsoever he doth, swarving from this worke, he doth as deficient from the nature of man."[97] Digby's sage was "unswerving," acting rather than being acted upon, pursuing the "hidden and unknowne" and demonstrating it to the world of his peers. He acted truly by acting on his true nature, which was not passionate but rational and logical. Whereas passion and imagination tended toward chaos, both internal and social, reason promoted and preserved order. The rational world, constituted syllogistically, was summed up by what became for Digby a favored and frequent figure—the well-linked "chaine."

DIGBY, SIR THOMAS BROWNE, AND PSYCHIC SYMPATHY

Late in 1642, while imprisoned in Winchester House for his Catholic and royalist affiliations, Digby acquired a copy of Sir Thomas Browne's *Religio Medici*, which had been recommended to him by the fourth Earl of Dorset, and which would go on, in its various editions, to reach an unusually large readership in the seventeenth century. Digby claimed to have written his *Observations upon Religio Medici* in a mere day, and the work appeared in print the next year, ultimately achieving wide diffusion by virtue of its inclusion in editions of *Religio Medici* from 1659.[98] Digby's remarks on the second part of *Religio Medici*, whose "intended *Theame*," as he puts it, is charity, make clear the stoic cast of Digby's ethics and anticipate as well as illuminate the negative stance toward human sympathy that he adopts in *A Late Discourse*. Although his mechanization of the passions there and in *Two Treatises* aligned him with the moderns, his depreciation of the passions associated him with the ancients. In moral matters, Browne, too, characteristically looked back to the ancients, but in his particular and peculiar fusion of classical and Christian values he developed an innovative conception of charity predicated on the sympathetic communication of emotion. Emphasizing affect over conduct, Browne effectively transformed charity into the virtue of sympathy. For Digby, this redefinition was an impious distortion, the reduction of the heavenly to the earthly, the divine to the human. Digby ultimately bypassed the problem of human sympathy by conceiving interpersonal connection as a meeting of minds and, in particular, of souls. In so doing, he effectively drove a wedge between his moral and "psychological" views of sympathy on one hand and his natural, material view on the other. Denying the possibility of action at a distance in his natural philosophy, he found consolation in it in his psychology, by means of which the grim realities of war and exile could be remedied and transcended.

In the *Observations* Digby criticizes Browne not only for his openness to the passions but also for his this-worldly perspective. He challenges Browne's narrow view of charity: "And I doubt he mistaketh the lowest *Orbe* or *Lembe* of that high *Seraphicke* vertue, for the top and perfection of it; and maketh a kind of humane compassion to bee divine *Charity*. Hee will have it to bee a generall way of doing good."[99] By emphasizing "humane compassion," according to Digby, Browne makes a sacred virtue a secular one; divine charity is redefined as, and narrowed

to, human sympathy. In this sense Digby's Browne anticipates the broader secu-
larizing trend of British moral philosophy over the next century, according to
which sympathy was increasingly elevated as a source of moral value and coherence without reference to any kind of overarching religious order. It seems quite
unlikely, however, that Browne would have accepted Digby's summation of his
position on charity. With a broader historical perspective in mind, Basil Willey
calls attention to Browne's dictum "that vertue is her owne reward, is but a cold
principle" before going on to note that "by the beginning of the eighteenth
century this 'cold principle' had become the mainstay of moralists of the enlightenment."[100] Browne is not easily recast as an "Enlightenment moralist," nor,
returning to Digby's critique, as one who simply subordinated the human to the
divine. Nevertheless, the emphasis on "humane compassion" in Browne's
account of charity enables us to understand more fully the transitional and, to
use one of Browne's own terms, "amphibious" status of sympathy in the seventeenth century. In *Religio Medici* Browne defines "compassion" as the process
by which "we make anothers misery our own" and then in the passage to which
Digby is responding elaborates on his own compassionate nature:

> There is, I thinke, no man that apprehends his owne miseries lesse than my
> selfe, and no man that so neerely apprehends anothers. I could lose an arme
> without a teare, and with few groans, mee thinkes, be quartered into pieces;
> yet can I weepe most seriously at a Play, and receive with a true passion, the
> counterfeit griefes of those knowne and professed Impostors. It is a barbarous
> part of inhumanity to adde unto any afflicted parties misery. . . . It is not the
> teares of our owne eyes onely, but of our friends also, that doe exhaust the
> current of our sorrowes, which falling . . . into many streames, runs more
> peaceably . . . , and is contented with a narrower channel. It is an act within
> the power of charity, to translate a passion out of one breast into another, and
> to divide a sorrow almost out of it selfe.[101]

This passage, which begins the fifth section of the second part, recalls the
beginning of the first section, where Browne declares, "I am of a constitution so
generall, that it consorts and sympathizeth with all things."[102] All nations, all
animals, and even all foods agree with him, he goes on to point out there, and
here he asserts his sympathy with all humanity. Charity represents the manifestation of "the secret Sympathies of things"—a Paracelsian reference from the first
part—in the social realm.[103] Browne's emphasis on "secret" and mysterious
connection suffuses *Religio Medici*, bridging the natural and the moral, from
the "natural charity of the Sunne" to the "*Aenigmaes*, mysteries and riddles" of
"true affection," from the macrocosm to the microcosm and all the "middle and

participating natures" in between.[104] Browne sees himself not as narrowing the scope of charity, as Digby claims, but rather as widening it.[105] He advances a concept of sympathetic "translation" whereby the spectator, to follow his example of the theater, is not infected by the actor—as Digby will go on to suggest in *A Late Discourse*—but rather helps to cure him of his pain. Browne describes, in effect, an affective mode of sympathetic healing. Whereas Digby inveighed against the power of sympathy in moral and social experience, here Browne exalts and embraces the "power of charity." For Browne, the two powers are mystically one. The schism between medicine and morals that we have seen in *A Late Discourse* does not obtain in *Religio Medici*, where Browne repeatedly insists on a "common harmony" between the natural and moral orders of things.[106]

For Digby, Browne's sympathetic form of charity harms the fellow feeler more than it helps the sufferer. He counters Browne's emotionalism with Stoicism: "I may safely produce *Epictetus* to contradict him when he letteth his kindnesse engulfe him in deep afflictions for a friend: For hee will not allow his wise man to have an inward relenting, a troubled feeling, or compassion of anothers misfortunes. That disordereth the one, without any good to the other. Let him afford all the assistances and relievings in his power; but without intermingling himselfe in the others *Woe*. As *Angels* that doe us good, but have no passion for us."[107] Digby is referring here to chapter 16 of Epictetus's *Encheiridion*, of which the end reads, in John Healey's popular early seventeenth-century translation, "Thus resolved, doe not doubt to minister the best counsel that thou canst affoorde to asswage his passion, to which end thou maist lawfully put on a forme of teares to associate his teares. But bee sure thy minde bee not any way molested, looke to that above all things."[108] Epictetus allows his follower to "groan with [sunepistenazai]" another, but not to groan "within himself [esōthen]," a process that A. A. Long has referred to as "controlled empathy."[109] Digby does not preserve this complex distinction, simply enjoining action, "assistances and relievings," and rejecting passion, "intermingling . . . in the others *Woe*." Seneca, too, had urged his wise man not to pity but to help others ("non miserebitur sapiens, sed succurret") before going on to associate sympathetic weeping, laughing, and yawning with disease ("morbum")—an association that might well have inspired or encouraged Digby's own.[110]

In the upheaval of the mid-seventeenth century, Seneca's view of passion and action was affirmed but also contested. At the end of his *De l'usage des Passions*, which was published in 1641 and translated into English by the Duke of Monmouth in 1649, J. F. Senault quotes from Seneca's discussion of pity in the *De clementia* only to condemn it. Of mercy he writes, "The *Stoicks* calumnies will not be able to banish her from off the Earth; the weaknesses which men impute to her, will not stain her glory."[111] Against the views of "these inhumane Philosophers," Senault exalts mercy as "the best employment we can make of Sorrow," and, he goes on, "Though she be accused of Weakness, she stirs our desires; and interesting us in the afflictions of the miserable, she endues us with strength to assist them: After she hath witnessed her fellow-feeling of them by her Sorrow, she gives them testimony of her power by the Effects." In urgent rhetorical terms, Senault breaks down the moral barrier erected by the Stoics between passion and action, weakness and strength. He reverses the thrust of Seneca's etymological play on "misericordia" and "miseria"; it is not that pity participates in and produces misery but rather that "Misery teacheth us Mercy." In a phrase that approaches Browne's description of charity, and embodies the very antithesis of Digby's position, Senault writes, "Mercy is a sanctified Contagion, which makes us sensible of our Neighbors sufferings." It is "sanctified" in part because the "Vertue" of "Compassion" is one that Christ "hath pleased to consecrate in his own Person."[112] Senault's "sanctified Contagion" is Digby's debilitating disease. For Browne, the Stoics had much good to teach us, but their philosophy was in need of sanctification. In his *Christian Morals*, on which he was working toward the end of his life, and which did not appear in print until 1716, Browne denounced those who would be "Rocks unto the Cries of charitable Commiserators" before concluding, "Look beyond Antoninus, and terminate not thy Morals in Seneca or Epictetus. . . . Be a moralist of the Mount, an Epictetus in the Faith, and Christianize thy Notions."[113] In his response to *Religio Medici*, Digby opens himself up to the objection on the part of anti-Stoics that the sage is inhuman, but he puts a different spin on the matter of *apatheia*; in Digby's "Christianization" of the "Notion" of charity, the sage is less human than angelic. Digby sanctifies and, in effect, celestializes action without passion.

In rejecting Browne's view of charity, and its valorization of compassion, Digby offers his own view, one that is directed not out into the world but, again, up above it. He subordinates horizontal relations to vertical: "*Whereas*, perfect *Charity*, is that vehement love of God for his own sake . . . that carrieth all the motions of our Soule directly and violently to him. . . . And that face of it that looketh toward mankind with whom we live, & warmeth us to doe others good, is but like the overflowings of the maine streame, that swelling above its bankes runneth over in a multitude of little Channels."[114] Digby here picks up Browne's language of "streames" and "channels," but rather than talking about sympathetic tears and the division of sorrows, Digby approves "doing," not feeling, and makes clear that even the beneficent "face" of charity must be understood as merely secondary. Moreover, by using the figure of "overflowings," Digby suggests that even this positive mode is ever in danger of becoming excessive, literally superfluous; the life-giving stream can become a dangerous flood, and, for Digby, Browne's compassionate tears are not, as he claims, irrigating the plains of human experience more widely but are instead flooding the banks.

This account of charity in the *Observations* as a love that moves the soul "directly and violently" to God subtly, but compellingly, recalls the opening of the work, where Digby writes to Dorset, "I will . . . endeavour, in the way of *Duty* and observance, to let you see how the little needle of my Soule is thoroughly touched at the great loadstone of yours, and followeth sudainely and strongly which way soever you becken it."[115] Here Digby is, in effect, showing us "the overflowings of the maine streame." His love of God flows into the channel that is his love of Dorset. Given Digby's "restraint," as he calls it, this expression of social sympathy—part rhetorical ornament, part philosophical consolation— seems particularly apt; imprisoned and so constrained to be at a distance from others, he could remain invisibly connected to them. In a pamphlet published in 1641, Digby relates that at a dinner in France a French nobleman defamed Charles in a toast, and the next night Digby invited the nobleman to dinner and proceeded to toast "the health of the bravest King in the world, which is the King of England my royall Master, for although my body bee banished from him, yet is my heart loyally linckt."[116] Digby affirmed "links"—to God, to Charles, to Dorset—that transcended distance, but he conceived of them in primarily psychic, rather than emotional, terms. He refers to "the motions of our Soule," "the little needle of my Soule," and even his reference to "heart" suggests soul (*OED* 6a).[117] Digby opposed human sympathy as a form of emotional contagion, as a sign of constitutional debility, and as a potential distraction from true charity, but we can see in the broader context of his various writings a more positive view rooted in his psychology, his carefully considered view of the soul.

In *A Discourse Concerning Infallibility in Religion*, addressed to his kinsman Lord George Digby and published in 1652, Digby wrote that the soul, once it has been separated from the body, "shall . . . see the connexion that every one hath with every one: how the severall linkes of this admirable chaine that containeth all that is in the world, from highest to lowest, are so fitted to one an other, that if any one of them were but broken or in disorder, all would fall in pieces; and withall, are made with such powerfull art, that every one of them is a support and a strengthning to all the rest."[118] Digby's natural philosophy, accounting for the action of the sympathetic cure as well as a great deal else, was predicated on this sympathetic, or catenary, worldview. He believed that he could surpass all previous theorists of the cure because he believed that he could clearly and definitively identify the "concatenation of naturall causes" behind it (15). Although the complete connectedness of the world was visible only after death, in life the sage could gain a powerful insight into its intricate, interlinked structure. With its syllogistic chains, *A Late Discourse*, properly conceived, was the world in epitome.

Yet as the status of sympathetic cures gradually declined, so did the status of a sympathetic worldview. The cosmic significance of the cures was increasingly in danger of becoming merely comic. In the *Encyclopédie* (1751–1772) we find the following account of *A Late Discourse:* "The work that this Englishman brought to light to justify the natural possibility of sympathetic cures, and then the famous imposture of Jacques Aymar with his divining rod, were the reason that in the last century some people revived the ridiculous system of sympathies [le système ridicule des sympathies]."[119] Digby, one imagines, would have rather had his name set beside Descartes's than that of Jacques Aymar-Vernay, an exposed charlatan. It was, however, not only after his lifetime that Digby's vision of a perfectly interconnected, sympathetic universe was fundamentally called into question. Thinking not of the soul's ascent but of man's fall, Sir Richard Barckley wrote around the turn of the seventeenth century,

> And where all the meane causes of things, even from the uppermost heaven unto the lowest part of the earth, depended each upon other in such an exact order and uniformitie to the production of things in their most perfection and beauty, so as it might well bee likened to that *Aurea Catena*, as *Homer* calleth it, by the grievous displeasure, which God conceived against man, hee withdrew the vertue which at the first hee had given to things in these lower parts, and now through his curse the face of the earth and all this elementarie world, doth so much degenerate from his former estate, that it resembleth a chaine rent in peeces, whose links are many lost and broken, and the rest so slightly fastened as they will hardly hang together.[120]

Barckley was not alone among his contemporaries in seeing the subject of the seventeenth-century world picture as the story of man's fall—for Milton, as we shall see, the Fall "rent" the sympathetic universe once and for all. Digby did not deny "that humane nature hath bin corrupted," but he chose to emphasize the melioristic soul, "enriching her selfe with knowledge."[121] By communicating his knowledge to others, by "weaving" his syllogisms together, Digby was not only advancing the mechanistic cause; he was also trying to keep the great chain of being intact.

2

The "Self-Themes" of Margaret Cavendish and Thomas Hobbes

In a letter written from Paris and dated 9 June 1657, Sir Kenelm Digby expresses his gratitude to Margaret Cavendish (1623?–1673), the Marchioness—later Duchess—of Newcastle, for the gift of one of her books: "The worthy present which your Excellency hath been pleased to make me by Mr. *Slaughter*, hath strucken me into new admiration of your goodness and knowledge."[1] Praising its "abundant matter," Digby does not refer to the book by title, but given the date of the letter and the works by Cavendish listed in the *Bibliotheca Digbeiana*, it was probably either her *Poems, and Fancies* (1653) or her *Philosophical and Physical Opinions* (1655).[2] Both books variously outline Cavendish's idiosyncratic natural philosophy, which Digby engages neither in the letter nor elsewhere in his writings.[3] He came into contact with Cavendish through her husband, William, to whom he duly pays his respects in a postscript to the letter, and through her brother-in-law, Charles, at whose lodgings in Paris Digby, Walter Charleton, and Thomas Hobbes (1588–1679) discussed scientific ideas in the 1640s.[4] The lack of substance in Digby's letter is one sign that he did not take the wife of the marquess seriously as a natural philosopher; his praise of her "goodness" before her "knowledge" is another.[5]

Although her conception of matter ultimately differed from his, Cavendish shared with Digby a commitment to rationalizing an older sympathetic view of the world through a new theory of material dynamics. In *Poems, and Fancies*, the first of her published works, the universal balance of things is justly conveyed by a single couplet: "And *Sympathies*, which keep the *world unite*, / *Aversions* otherwise would ruine quite."[6] Several of her poems explore the theoretical possibility that atomic motion, the attraction and repulsion of matter, establishes that balance.[7] After moving away from a mechanistic-atomistic physics, Cavendish continued to pursue a unified theory of nature, and the idea of sympathy—whose significance in her body of work as a whole has yet to be fully recognized— remained a constant in her system.[8] In a characteristic formulation, she describes sympathies and antipathies in the natural world as "nothing else but ordinary Passions and Appetites amongst several Creatures, which Passions are made by the rational animate Matter, and the Appetites by the sensitive."[9] All things are made up of self-moving matter, which exists in rational, sensitive, and inanimate degrees. Like motions produce sympathy, and unlike, or "cross," motions produce antipathy. Motion is for the most part voluntary; sympathetic motions proceed by imitation, not by compulsion. In resisting the idea of compulsion, Cavendish was engaging with and challenging the mechanistic theory of Hobbes. She proposed a nondeterministic view of interaction according to which an agent did not automatically and necessarily force a reaction by a patient; rather, the patient could exert his or her will against or in accord with the action. The natural world, as Cavendish understood it, was vital and free. In its sustained emphasis on sympathy, her natural-philosophical writing yields an important insight into the broader intellectual debate about sympathy in the seventeenth century; it enables us to see that sympathy functioned as a crucial conceptual intervention in the new philosophical debate about Epicurean physics. The advancement of sympathy in a natural-philosophical system served to contest and correct some of the more troubling aspects of Epicureanism—a topic to which I return in chapter 5. Against a vision of dead and dispersed atoms randomly colliding with one another, Cavendish insisted on sympathy as a principle of vital connection and coherence.

Cavendish opposed Hobbes's mechanics of pressure and force, but she found much to agree with in his view of society. In the Civil Wars and their aftermath, Cavendish, who suffered on the king's side, saw man in Hobbes's "naturall condition," caring only for himself and attacking others as enemies. As she surveyed the social world of the mid-century, she found not universal sympathy but widespread enmity. In spite of this fact, however, and in part because of it, she held up a sympathetic society as an ideal, one that could become a reality if only the warring passions of the people could be pacified. She made the moderation of passion an important point of emphasis throughout her various writings. Similarly suggesting that for Cavendish "virtue consists in actions which promote peace and social stability," Deborah Boyle has argued that Cavendish's view of virtue and honor is consistent with the ethical positions of Justus Lipsius.[10] But to whatever extent she might have been influenced by Neostoicism, Cavendish also made a strong claim for the positive ethical significance of the passions, a claim that distances her from Digby and his critique of Browne. For

Cavendish, sympathy—that is, fellow feeling between and among individuals—was a virtue. Moving from Digby to Cavendish, and focusing more directly on the crises of the Civil Wars, we gain a fuller sense of the difficulty of developing a unified conception of sympathy that bridges the natural and moral spheres. In Cavendish's case, however, we find a more extensive attempt to make sympathy a principle of moral and social order.

I suggested in the Introduction that R. S. Crane's influential "genealogy of 'the man of feeling'" has had the effect of narrowing and distorting the history of sympathy. Crane's account emphasized a new religion of man after the Restoration, an account reinforced and supplemented by subsequent accounts emphasizing a new science of man. In leaving out the older science of the world, however, these accounts have left us with a significant gap in our historical understanding of sympathy. To fill in that gap, I have proposed, we need to recognize the importance of natural-philosophical and natural-magical traditions in the history of sympathy. Cavendish's writing about sympathy supports the larger argument of this book in two principal ways. First, it supports my case for conceiving the history of sympathy in terms of a broader interplay between the natural and the moral. Cavendish's moral view of sympathy, I demonstrate, was deeply bound up with her natural view. By a habit of thought that she shared with a number of her intellectual contemporaries, she understood the world in which human beings moved and interacted not apart from the natural world but in close and complex relation to it.[11] Second, in casting doubt on the idea of sympathy as a natural human instinct and elevating it as a moral, social ideal, Cavendish's writing about sympathy poses a significant challenge to Crane's claim that a straightforward and sweeping anti-Hobbesianism prevailed among those who theorized and moralized human sympathy in the years following the Restoration.[12] The reaction against Hobbes's "egoistic psychology" has rightly been associated with the rise of sentimentalist ethics in later decades, but Cavendish's writing about sympathy suggests that we need to understand the contemporary reception of Hobbes not as a uniform, monolithic "reaction" but as a rhetorically and ideologically diverse set of individual responses. We need, in other words, to take a finer-grained and more complex view of Hobbes's place in the history of sympathy.

In the opening section of this chapter, I suggest that discourse provides a material link between Cavendish's moral and natural thought.[13] Cavendish's most sustained reflections on what she calls "the Humors of Mankind" come in *Sociable Letters* (1664), a volume of letters written for the most part by one anonymous lady to an anonymous correspondent.[14] Appearing at a time when power was increasingly linked to sociability, and when an emerging culture of politeness was increasingly expressed in social visits, the volume exposes a world of expansive discourse, of conversation and controversy.[15] In relating or creating miniature social dramas that turn on competing modes of discourse, Cavendish moralizes the dynamic of sympathy and antipathy that she theorizes in her scientific writing. In *Sociable Letters* she prescribes the process of sympathetic imitation that she describes elsewhere. The letter writer (hereafter "the author") uses rhetoric to establish and to reestablish sympathetic relations; in so doing, she represents Cavendish's social and discursive ideal, a rhetorically adept "woman of feeling." As we have seen, Digby, critical of the rhetorical movement of the passions, formulates that ideal quite differently. Cavendish gives her readers an image of female sympathy defined not by a stereotypical lack of emotional regulation but by an exemplary combination of concern and control.

Reading *Sociable Letters*, we can more fully grasp the intimate relationship between sympathy and rhetoric — as a means of both stirring up and sharing affection — as well as the intimate relationship between sympathy and genre. Cavendish habitually viewed both relationships through the lens of gender. In *Sociable Letters* she uses the epistolary form not only to moralize the dynamic of sympathy and antipathy but also, in effect, to actualize it. Her prescription of sympathy as a virtue is enacted in the unfolding relationship between author and addressee, a social form of action at a distance. "Though its content does not radically vary from that of her other writings," Henry Ten Eyck Perry wrote almost a century ago of *Sociable Letters*, "its form and its avowed intention, dimly, gropingly, but surely, foreshadow the later letter-novels."[16] Rather than drawing a "dim" historical line from Cavendish's use of the epistolary form to Richardson's, I want instead to suggest that *Sociable Letters* serves to challenge the widely held assumption that sympathy was first and foremost an eighteenth-century novelistic concern. The epistolary production and solicitation of sympathy, or "technology of affect," had a longer and more varied history, as a number of scholars have shown.[17] For Cavendish, the form of the letter allowed her not only to express ideas clearly and concisely but also to model in spatial and emotional terms the idea of sympathy in particular. The forms of Digby's philosophical prose, with its emphasis on syllogistic concatenation and perspicuous demonstration, generally worked to reinforce his aim to rationalize and materialize sympathy. Although Cavendish largely shared that aim, her prismatic genres worked to reinforce her representation of sympathy as a principle of unity in diversity. The extraordinary generic diversity of Cavendish's writing, with which Lisa Sarasohn has argued she "contested the new rhetorical orthodoxy of the Royal Society,"[18] embodies the emphasis Cavendish places throughout on variety, as a way of keeping an audience engaged and entertained, but also more broadly as a way of defining the vitality of nature. While Cavendish celebrated that variety in nature as a whole, however, she struggled with it as it played out in the social world, where she found mostly difference and discord.

Again and again the socialites encountered in *Sociable Letters* fall far short of Cavendish's social and discursive ideal. Rhetoric emerges in the volume, I show, as a principle of socialization; it has the power to repair the broken chain of social being. In Cavendish's natural philosophy, the greater chain of being remains intact; it is not only unbroken but also unbreakable. Cavendish clearly distinguishes the order of "Man" from the order of nature: "though Man did fall, yet Nature never did, nor cannot fall, being Infinite."[19] Whereas in the natural world the movements of sympathy and antipathy balance each other out, producing a universal order or equilibrium, in the world of "Man" imbalance obtains, and Cavendish proposes rhetoric as the proper corrective. Rhetoric holds out the promise of unifying her views of the social world and of the natural world, of bringing a disconnected, antipathetic society in line with a coherent, sympathetic Nature. As I demonstrate in the next section, however, this promise is never quite fulfilled, and a disjunction remains between her natural and moral thought. Over the course of *Sociable Letters*, Cavendish's rhetorical solution seems increasingly like a fantasy. "I wish my Speech were like a Loadstone," the character Poor Virtue writes in one of Cavendish's plays, "to draw the iron hearts of men to pity and compassion, to charity and devotion."[20] The power of sympathy in the moral world seems to fall woefully short of that in the natural world; whereas magnetic attraction is a reliable natural phenomenon, its moral equivalent is capricious and uncertain, more a matter of "wish" than of fact. The epistolary sympathy between the author and addressee in *Sociable Letters* begins to seem less mimetic and archetypal than anomalous. In spite of her sociable discourse, the author's visitors, who function as a synecdoche for the masses, remain willfully unmoved, willfully unsociable.[21] Of the "Generality" the author writes, "Every One is against Another; indeed, every One is against All, and All against every One" (61). This formulation strongly recalls Hobbes's description of the state of nature as war, "every one against every one."[22] Correlating the Hobbesian social world of *Sociable Letters* with Cavendish's experience and representation of the Civil Wars, I show that the trials of the Cavendish family in the mid-century made it painfully clear to her that sympathy was not the rule but the exception. Persuasion for her implied a willingness to be moved; the freedom to sympathize went hand in hand with the freedom not to.

In the next section I focus on Cavendish's complex conception of the self in relation to society and argue that she ultimately turned within to solve the problem of sympathy in the moral and social spheres. As she understood it, the self was its own sympathetic society, with all the parts communicating and working together. At the same time that it functioned sympathetically, the self could also create a sympathetic society by means of the imagination, a society independent of and untouched by the tragic and violent drama beyond it. I analyze this radical subjectivization of a sympathetic worldview in Cavendish's utopian fiction *The Blazing World* (1666), in which, I argue, she counters a Hobbesian worldview with a modified Platonic one. Cavendish labored to assert volition over necessity, but, in conceiving sympathy in terms of deep psychic connection, she was effectively substituting one determinism for another. Translated into the social sphere, her enduring sense of the fragility of matter moved her in the direction of a deterministic immaterialism. Like Digby— though to a much greater extent and in a manner very much her own— Cavendish took refuge in a concept of sympathy between souls as a way of solving the problem of sympathy in society. This strategy, as the case of Cavendish more clearly suggests, held a particular appeal to those on the losing side of the Civil Wars, who, given the realities of loss, exile, and constraint, could find a kind of comfort and consolation in the idea of spiritual interaction at a distance. Yet ultimately Cavendish's development of a moral idea of sympathy ends up not in altruism—or "benevolence," a keyword of late seventeenth-century and early eighteenth-century moral philosophy—but in egoism, one might even say autism.[23]

Scholarly attention has focused for the most part on Cavendish the natural philosopher, and by widening that focus to include her moral and social thought, we gain a fuller sense of the complex "sympathies" connecting the enormously varied topics that she addressed and the enormously varied modes and genres in which she addressed them. In the last section of the chapter I consider Cavendish's finally disunited view of sympathy in the light of Crane's genealogy of sensibility; its villain, Hobbes; and its hero, Isaac Barrow (1630–1677), whose insistence on the sympathetic nature of humankind provides a pointed and instructive contrast to Cavendish's and Hobbes's claims about human nature. In valorizing sympathy and sharing rather than shunning Hobbes's social vision, I argue, Cavendish not only complicates the received genealogy of sensibility but also reveals what might be called its dark side. Later theorists of a universal moral sympathy struggled to account for the antipathies, the factiousness and fractiousness, of those around them. Cavendish's writing about sympathy makes clear that this struggle was not endemic to eighteenth-century moral philosophy but rather had broader and deeper cultural roots.

SYMPATHETIC RHETORIC AND
SOCIABLE LETTERS

The idea of sympathetic communication provides a crucial point of connection between Cavendish's natural and moral philosophies. She theorized communication in *Philosophical and Physical Opinions*, which she published in three versions; the first edition appeared in 1655, the second in 1663, and the final version, carrying the title *Grounds of Natural Philosophy*, in 1668. In the first two editions, Cavendish devotes a chapter to what she calls "the Sympathies and Antipathies of Sound to the Mind and Actions." The discussion begins with an anatomical description of the ear followed by an account of the relationship between the tension of the eardrum and the quality of sound perceived by the hearer. The brain has its own natural motions, and when a particular sound, as she puts it, "moves cross" to those motions, the sensitive part of the brain responds with pain, and the rational part responds with anger or hatred. Other sounds, whose motions agree, have the opposite effect:

> And as these or the like External Objects may Disorder by the Irregular and Antipathetical motions, the Health and Understanding, which are the Interior motions, so Regularity and Sympathy of the Verbal or Vocal motions brought through the Ear, may Compose the Differences and Disorder of the Natural Interior motions, as Health, Reason, Understanding, Affection, or Reconcilement; as for Example, a Timely, Kind, Discreet discourse may Compose a Disquiet mind; for the Motions of Wise, Sober, Kind, Gentle or Eloquent words may turn the motion of Troubled or Extravagant thoughts into a Smooth and Calm temper, or Regular order; Likewise Unkind, and Indiscreet, Double, False, Malicious, Hasty, Sudden, Sad, or Frightfull discourses, may Discompose and Disorder a Quiet and Well-tempered mind, Disordering the Regular motions, by Mis-placing the Thoughts, making a War in the Mind. . . . The like with Vocal Sounds, As for Musick, the Notes in Musick agree with the Motions of the Passions, and the Motions of several Thoughts, as some Notes Sympathize with Passions . . . and Move the Actions accordingly, so others Discompose the Mind.[24]

Cavendish treats discourse and music as analogous exterior motions; both can have either sympathetic or antipathetic effects on the hearer. She opposes "a Smooth and Calm temper" to "a War in the Mind," a figure that seems to register the trauma of recent political history. But the physiology of response remains somewhat obscure here. She explains that sounds enter into the ear, approach the eardrum, and then "Beat thereon"; an especially violent sound, she writes, "many times Breaks that Skin."[25] At other moments Cavendish seems to imply that the tension of the eardrum causes a sound to be perceived in a certain way without the concussion of the exterior motion.

In the final version of this discussion, which appears as part of a chapter entitled "Of the Effects of Forrein Objects, on the Human Mind," Cavendish makes it clear that a "foreign," or external, object does not directly motivate an internal response. "As there is often Antipathy of the Parts of a Human Creature, to Forrein Objects," she writes, "so there are often Sympathetical Effects produced from Forrein Objects, with the Parts of a Human Creature. As for example, A timely, kind, and discreet Discourse from a Friend, will compose or quiet his troubled Mind: Likewise, an untimely, unkind, hasty, malicious, false, or sudden Discourse, will often disorder a well-temper'd, or Regular Mind, the Mind imitating the smooth or harsh strains of the Object: and the same Effects hath Musick, on the Minds of many Human Creatures."[26] According to Cavendish's mature physical theory, an object derives its form and figure from its internal motions. Since motion is constitutive, an object cannot transfer any of its motion to another object without changing figure. A sound does not, then, beat on the eardrum; rather, the eardrum imitates the motion of the sound, so that the overall figure of the sound remains intact. The process of causation is indirect or, more precisely, occasional.[27] As she refined her theory of perception, Cavendish retained the analogy between discourse and music and continued to use both as master examples of sympathetic and antipathetic relations between bodies.

In the first two editions of *Philosophical and Physical Opinions*, Cavendish concludes the chapter on verbal and vocal motions with what can be read as an affected modesty topos, and here we can begin to appreciate the centrality of rhetoric in her body of work. Having claimed that thoughts, like musical notes, are composed "in Crotchets, Quavers, Semibriefs, &c," she goes on to consider her own text, the very text she is producing, as a verbal-vocal composition: "If I have not matched my Strains and Notes, with Words and Thoughts properly, let those that Understand Musick and Rhetorick mend it, for I Understand neither, having neither Fed at the Full Table, nor Drunk at the Full Head of Learning, but Lived always upon Scattered Crums."[28] In her *Sociable Letters*, which appeared a year after the second edition of *Philosophical and Physical Opinions*, Cavendish imagines a female author, bearing a distinct but uncertain resemblance to herself, with all the rhetorical skills she feared she lacked. Several of the letters fall into a particular narrative pattern. Certain persons of quality pay a visit to the author, begin to discuss a particular topic, disagree with increasing rancor, reach a dangerous impasse, and then eventually make up when the author steps in and effectively "sympathizes" them with her "timely discourse."

The author gives us the rhetorician as heroine, rushing in to restore the peace that her quarreling peers have disturbed. Rhetoric, Cavendish suggests, has the power to transform discord into concord, antipathy into sympathy.

In one letter exemplifying this pattern the author recounts an argument between two visitors, "the Lady *D.C.* and the Lady *G.B.*" The two ladies get into a discussion of good and bad wives in history, disagreeing about the case of Lucretia—which Cavendish seems to have viewed less in terms of state politics than in terms of gender politics—and, in so doing, appearing to ignore their hostess altogether. By the time the author gets involved, the situation has become almost improbably dire; the two ladies, would-be paragons of politeness and sociability, are on the verge of slaughtering each other like wild animals. The author has no choice but to intervene:

> But these two Ladies arguing whether *Lucretia* Kill'd her self for her Husband's Honour or for her Own, at last grew so Earnest in their Discourse, as they fell to Quarrel with each other, & in such a Fury they were, as they were ready to Beat one another, nay, I was afraid they would have Kill'd each other, and for fear of that Mischief, I was forced to be a Defender of both, standing between them, and making Orations to the one and then to the other; at last I intreated them to Temper their Passions, and to Allay their Anger; and give me leave Ladies, said I, to ask you what *Lucretia* was to either of you? (110)

The author's rhetorical question suggestively echoes Hamlet's, a locus classicus in the early modern literature of sympathy: "What's Hecuba to him, or he to Hecuba, / That he should weep for her?" (2.2.559–560).[29] Hamlet marvels at the actor's ability to sympathize with a shadowy figure from the distant past, which particularizes his sense of his own inability to sympathize with a shadowy figure from the very near past, his father. Cavendish shifts from soliloquy to colloquy and sets up a contrast between the actor's sympathy and the ladies' antipathy; "arguing," they sympathize neither with Lucretia nor with each other. The author entreats them to "leave *Lucretia* to live and dye in History," and, as she explains, "Thus talking to them, at last I calmed their Passions, and made them Friends again, but making Peace between them, I spent more Breath and Spirits, than the Peace of two Foolish, at least, Cholerick Ladies was worth" (65–66). Cavendish here makes the act of producing sympathy emphatic: "at last I intreated them to Temper their Passions"; "therefore Allay your Passions"; "at last I calmed their Passions." The author tunes her words to the ladies' murderous affections and reduces them to stillness, or, as the natural philosopher would put it, the ladies' vital interior parts pattern out the smooth strains of the author's "orations" and then resume their regular motions. As in her philosophical accounts, Cavendish balances sympathetic and antipathetic motions, here the destructive discourse of the ladies and the sympathetic rhetoric that saves them from destruction. The effect of this hyperbole is to magnify our perception of the social power of rhetoric. Cavendish valorizes a mode of discourse that promotes social harmony while at the same time she criticizes one that tends toward division and enmity. Ringing with the wrong sort of discourse, she goes so far as to suggest, the sitting room is no more civilized than the slaughterhouse, or, as we shall see, the battlefield. Elsewhere Cavendish denounced disputation as an "enemy to society," one "which makes men become Tigers and Vultures to one another, when otherwise they would be like the society of Angels."[30] Well-tempered words, she suggests, produce a well-tempered society.

Cavendish's frequent analogy between discourse and music turns into identity in a subsequent letter, in which the author yet again uses a sympathetic rhetoric to produce sympathy. "Yesterday a Consort of Learning and Wit came to Visit me," she relates, "but they became at last to be a Discord; This Consort was Natural Philosophers, Theological Scholars, and Poets, and their Discourse was their Musick" (153). After an increasingly heated discussion on the nature of the soul, the author again fears a bloodbath: "At last the Theologers and Philosophers became so Violent and Loud, as I did fear they would have Fought, if they had had any other Wounding Weapons than their Tongues, but Heaven be praised, they had no Killing Swords, and so they did no harm to each other" (154–155). This account again underlines the power of discourse—to wound, but also to heal. The author intervenes "after the Violence of their Dispute was past" and implores the men to "leave the Foolish Custom of Disputing, and bring in a Devout Custom of Praying, leaving your Souls to Gods disposing, without troubling them with Idle Arguments; and hearing me talk Simply, they laught at my Innocency, and in their Mirth became Good Friends and Sociable Companions, and after some time they took their leave" (155). The author's "simple talk" is deceptively simple; it is a well-orchestrated rhetorical performance, marked by careful formal patterning and strategic self-presentation. She adopts the role of the naïve in order to charm the men down from their top of speculation, when in fact Cavendish had devoted much of her adult life to scaling the same heights. The author vindicates Cavendish's piety and her unwillingness, as she puts it in *Philosophical Letters*, "to mingle Divinity and Natural Philosophy together, to the great disadvantage and prejudice of either."[31]

At the same time that the author's behavior calls to mind the state of philosophical "Innocency" to which women were generally condemned—and the derision to which they were subject when they tried, as Cavendish did, to present themselves otherwise—it also suggests a positive performative response to that state, one that puts the author in a position of social power. The men may be performing the various vocal parts, but in the end the author-hostess is conducting the chorus. Earlier in the volume she expresses her doubts about the ability of women to persuade: "I find in my self an Envy, or rather an Emulation towards Men, for their Courage, Prudence, Wit, and Eloquence, as not to Fear Death, to Rule Commonwealths, and to Speak in a Friend's behalf, or to Pacifie a Friend's Grief, to Plead for his own Right, or to Defend his own Cause by the Eloquence of Speech; . . . all which I fear Women are not Capable of, and the Despair thereof makes me Envy or Emulate Men," and, she goes on, "though I love Justice Best, and trust to Valour Most, yet I Admire Eloquence, and would choose Wit for my Pastime. Indeed Natural Orators that can speak on a Sudden and Extempore upon any Subject, are Nature's Musicians, moving the Passions to Harmony, making Concords out of Discords, Playing on the Soul with Delight" (51–52). The emphasis on eloquence here is striking even before the author singles it out; she sets up a syntactic pattern linking each of the qualities for which she envies men to a clarifying infinitive phrase, but the one-to-one correspondence breaks down when she glosses eloquence, and the phrases begin to proliferate. Moving beyond the formal scheme that she has imposed, and thus allowing her own eloquence freer rein, the author identifies the power of rhetoric with its sympathetic effects, "moving the Passions to Harmony, making Concords out of Discords." By making a concord out of the discord produced by the philosophers and theologians, the author overcomes her doubt about the possibility of female eloquence. Cavendish refers to her own contribution to the male-dominated rhetorical tradition in the preface, where she describes her *Orations of Divers Sorts* as a collection of "Declamations, wherein I speak *Pro* and *Con*, and Determine nothing" (C2r).[32] Cavendish defends the classical practice of argument *in utramque partem* as socially appropriate; if she presents both sides of a question, she leaves it open and so cannot be justly accused of "speaking too Freely, and Patronizing Vice too much" (C2v). In the letters that follow this defense, the author's rhetoric, whether she "determines nothing" or offers a strong opinion, is clearly productive; it moves the wayward passions of her audience to harmony and restores proper sociability. Having analyzed the mechanics of sociability in her earlier treatises, Cavendish explores the ethics of sociability in her letters. She invests sympathetic discourse with a high moral value.

In the moral scenes I have discussed so far, the author's own passions barely register. Her relative impassiveness allows her more effectively to manage the passions of others. This strategic detachment is abandoned when "the Lady

M.L.," overwhelmed by grief, reveals to the author that her tyrannical husband, as she explains, "Tortured me, nay Threatned Death to me, to Force me to Serve his Concubines" (319). After disburdening herself, the author continues, "she Wept, as if her Eyes had been two Perpetual Springs, and mean'd to make a Deluge of their Tears, and with seeing her, my Eyes began to Drop too" (320). Moments later, after both women have collected themselves, the author tries to reassure the Lady M.L. that her husband would never in the end prefer a wanton mistress to a chaste wife. The author's discourse, that of the "Natural" rather than the "Formal Orator," still follows set rhetorical patterns: "and though he loved a Wanton Mistress, yet certainly he was not so Unjust, or Unwise, as to Hate a Chast Wife, or to Part from a Virtuous Wife, for the sake of a Lewd Mistress, . . . for though her Husband was an Independent to Amour, yet he was an Orthodox to Honour" (320–321). The author carefully measures and balances her clauses using antithesis and antimetabole ("Wanton Mistress" [A] — "Chast Wife" [B] — "Virtuous Wife" [B] — "Lewd Mistress" [A]). Pacified and relieved, the Lady M.L. smiles before expressing her gratitude and taking her leave. Two letters later, she reappears, visiting the author with the news that her husband's misbehavior was only an elaborate ruse designed to test her virtue: "The truth is," the author gushes, "her Joy was so much, as I may say it was Contagious and Infectious, for it Affected me with Joy, to See, and Observe her" (325). Here Cavendish imagines a scene in which the author not only sympathizes the passions of others but also sympathizes *with* them. As the Lady M.L. grieves, the author grieves; as the Lady M.L. rejoices, the author rejoices. The author's responsiveness should put us in mind of the observation Digby twice borrowed from Horace — "ut ridentibus arrident, ita flentibus adsunt"[33] — but it has another important counterpart in Paul's injunction to the Romans: "Rejoice with those who rejoice, weep with those who weep [gaudete cum gaudentibus, flete cum flentibus]" (Rom. 12:15). Cavendish uses the author of *Sociable Letters* to model this imitative idea, and ideal, of moral and social sympathy for her readership, and this modeling is vividly reinforced by the epistolary framing of the work.

The sympathetic relationship between the author and the Lady M.L. parallels that between the author and the addressee, and both promote a sympathetic relationship between Cavendish and the reader. In her preface to *Sociable Letters* Cavendish explains the nature of the work: "The truth is, they are rather Scenes than Letters, for I have Endeavoured under the Cover of Letters to Express the Humors of Mankind, and the Actions of Man's Life by the Correspondence of two Ladies, living at some Short Distance from each other, which make it not only their Chief Delight and Pastime, but their Tye in Friendship, to Discourse by Letters, as they would do if they were Personally together, so that these Letters are an Imitation of a Personal Visitation and Conversation" (Dıv). In identifying her "Letters" with "Scenes," Cavendish pairs two forms, epistolary and dramatic, that particularly emphasize the relationship between author and audience and are particularly conducive to the communication of affect between the two. She sets out to represent "the Actions of Man's Life" in terms of emotional *interaction*. Cavendish develops a pointed contrast between physical "Distance" and emotional connection, the two ladies' "Tye in Friendship." The effect of epistolary correspondence is virtual presence; the two ladies act "as they would do if they were Personally together." The problem of absence is effectively solved both in and by writing. Communication by letter is an "Imitation" of communication in person, a kind of sympathetic proxy.[34] For Cavendish, the "Delightful" sympathetic interaction at a distance of her two characters furnishes an imitative as well as imitable model for her readers. Her desire to connect with and delight her audience from afar is emphasized when she goes on to explain why she decided on "the Form of Letters, and not of Playes"; having already written a number of plays, she "saw that Variety of Forms did Please the Readers best, and that lastly they would be more taken with the Brevity of Letters, than the Formality of Scenes." As epistolary communication pleases her two characters, so the epistolary form is meant "to Please the Readers," ultimately providing "a Full Satisfaction of what they Read." In *Sociable Letters* Cavendish provides her readers not only with a "satisfying" sense of narrative completion, which is effectively deferred in the longer running time of a play, but also with a reassuring sense of virtual compassion and companionship. In having her characters provide for each other emotionally, Cavendish attempts to provide for her readers emotionally. Earlier in the volume the author writes, "You were pleased to tell me in your Letter how much out of Countenance you were, being Surprised with a Visit you Expected not; Truly, Madam, I am very Sensible of your Pain, insomuch as methinks I Feel what you Suffered, for I my self have been, and am still, so Troubled with that Imperfection" (280–281). This account of the author's sympathetic response, "insomuch as methinks I Feel what you Suffered," emphasizes the idea not only of virtual presence but also of what might be called virtual "Pain." The author has, to borrow the especially vivid language of Adam Smith, "entered as it were into the body" of the addressee and "become in some measure the same person with" her. For her most congenial audience, those in the same social and cultural milieu, passing the time in "Personal Visitation and Conversation," Cavendish provides, by extension, an opportunity to enter into the bodies of like-minded characters, facing the same kinds of challenges, suffering the same kinds of indignities, and finding the same kinds of satisfactions. Yet, as the preface makes clear, Cavendish intended the sympathetic reach of her work to extend far beyond women of similar status and situation; her aim was, in effect, morally universal, her subject nothing less than "the Humors of Mankind" and "the Actions of Man's Life." This universalizing aspiration underlies and informs Cavendish's attempt to square her moral and natural thought as part of a unified worldview expressed in a "Variety of Forms."

We can clearly see this kind of crossover in Cavendish's *Philosophical Letters*, whose formal design exactly parallels that of *Sociable Letters*. For her, sympathy was a universal principle to the extent that it applied not only to nature and society but also to genre, unifying the "various forms" of her writing. In a letter prefaced to the 1668 edition of *The Blazing World*, which had been first published two years earlier together with her *Observations upon Experimental Philosophy*, Cavendish explains that the two works, "*having some Sympathy and Coherence with each other, were joined together as Two several Worlds, at their Two Poles.*"[35] The book not only expresses her worldview (or *worlds*-view) but also embodies it. In a philosophical letter devoted to the subject of sympathy and antipathy, and particularly engaged with the natural philosophy of Van Helmont, Cavendish assimilates the relationship between author and addressee to her natural theory of the passions.[36] The letter concludes, "and as without an object a Pattern cannot be, so without inherent or natural Passions and Appetites there can be no Sympathy or Antipathy: And there being also such Sympathy betwixt your Ladiship and me, I think myself the happiest Creature for it, and shall make it my whole study to imitate your Ladiship, and conform all my actions to the rule and pattern of yours."[37] The scientific register quickly shifts to the social. The ideas of patterning out and imitation, crucial to Cavendish's natural philosophy, assume a moral dimension; the addressee is a "pattern" of virtue to be imitated by all. And, indeed, sympathy undergoes a parallel movement of moralization and valorization. Human sympathy promotes "happiness" as well as goodness. Cavendish's universal vitalism makes this a fluidly natural movement; as "the Loadstone draws Iron, and the Needle turns toward the North" whether "for nourishment, or refreshment, or love and desire of association," so the author moves toward the addressee.[38] The affective "contagion" or "infection" to which the author of *Sociable Letters* refers in her interaction with the Lady M.L. is not merely figurative, and here again we should recall Digby. It represents the moral manifestation of a natural idea that Cavendish expresses elsewhere in scientific terms. In the same philosophical letter that we have been considering, the author explains the dynamics of sympathy between two human beings: "But a sympathetical inclination in a Man towards another, is made either by sight, or hearing; either present, or absent: the like of infectious Diseases. I grant, that if both Parties do mutually affect each other, and their motions be equally agree-able; then the sympathy is the stronger, and will last longer, and then there is a Union, Likeness, or Conformableness, of their Actions, Appetites, and Passions; For this kind of Sympathy works no other effects, but a conforming of the actions of one party, to the actions of the other, as by way of Imitation, proceeding from an internal sympathetical love."[39] The communication of human sympathy is analogous to that of "infectious Diseases." But Cavendish does not use this analogy, as we saw Digby do, to pathologize human sympathy. For her, sympa-thetic passions are not passive; they are emotions, or more properly "in-motions." Passions do not happen to the patient; the patient, rather, actively imitates the passions of the passionate, just as the hearer actively imitates the sounds, or words, of the source. Cavendish emphasizes the "internal" motions that produce an external response rather than the external motions that produce an internal response. Sympathy, she insists, is constituted by voluntary motions. The author sees the sadness and joy of the Lady M.L. and "moves"; she is moved in the figurative sense but not moved in the physical sense—Cavendish's imitative theory of perception requires an active construction.

This same theory accounts for the transmission of infectious diseases like the plague, an important and recurrent topic in the science of sympathy, as Cavendish's treatment of it in *The Blazing World* suggests. At the beginning of that work, to which we shall return later in the chapter, romance is hybridized with utopian fiction. The protagonist survives a shipwreck, passes into a new world from the North Pole, and marries the Emperor of that world. She goes on to interrogate representatives of each of the disciplines about their respective views of things. The Empress asks her "Galenic physicians" to explain to her the nature and cause of the "plaguey-gangrene": "The Gangrene of the Plague, infects not onely the adjoining parts of one particular Creature, but also those that are distant; that is, one particular body infects another, and so breeds a Universal Contagion." The Empress proceeds to inquire about the process of transmission, and they explain that there is a dispute between those who favor a model of "expiration and inspiration" and those who favor a model of "imita-tion." "Some Experimental Philosophers," the physicians say, "will make us believe, that by the help of their Microscopes, they have observed the Plague to be a body of little Flyes like Atomes, which go out of one body into another, through the sensitive passages; but the most experienced and wisest of our society, have rejected this opinion as a ridiculous fancy, and do for the most part believe, that it is caused by an imitation of Parts, so that the motions of some parts which are sound, do imitate the motions of those that are infected, and that by this means, the Plague becomes contagious and spreading."[40] Cavendish shores up the authority of her own account of imitative perception—not to mention her critique of experimental philosophy—by attributing it to "the most experienced and wisest of our society."[41] She dismisses a more mechanistic—we might say Digbeian—theory of atomic motion between bodies in favor of a vitalistic theory of self-motion *within* bodies. Just as the author's internal motions imitate the emotions of the Lady M.L., so the internal motions of the Lady M.L. imitate the rhetorical motions of the author. These "equally agreeable" motions constitute a mutual sympathy. Digby's account of communication, whether verbal or emotional, is, as we have seen, significantly different. The skillful rhetorician persuades his audience "even against his will," and the grieving communicate their grief by an "unpleasing contagion of the imagination." Digby's qualifier makes it clear that we are to understand this contagion in negative terms. Not positing, as Digby does, a gendered notion of "susceptibility," Cavendish allows greater freedom on the part of women and men to feel what they wish to feel.

By insisting in her scientific writing that "natural self-motions are free and voluntary," Cavendish was responding primarily not to Digby, however, but to Hobbes.[42] "Thoughts are not like *Water upon a plain Table, which is drawn and guided by the finger this or that way,*" the author of *Philosophical Letters* argues, citing *Leviathan,*

> for every Part of self-moving matter is not always forced, perswaded or directed, for if all the Parts of Sense and Reason were ruled by force or perswasion, not any wounded Creature would fail to be healed, or any disease to be cured by outward Applications, for outward Applications to Wounds and Diseases might have more force, then any Object to the Eye: But though there is great affinity and sympathy between parts, yet there is also great difference and antipathy betwixt them, which is the cause that many objects cannot with all their endeavours work such effects upon the Interiour parts, although they are closely press'd, for Impressions of objects do not always affect those parts they press. Wherefore, I am not of your Author's opinion, that all Parts of Matter press one another.[43]

Pressures, or "Impressions," do not of necessity cause reactions because antipathies to those same pressures exist in—some, but not all—bodies. Here Cavendish predicates her theory of perception on the existence of sympathy and antipathy; one body perceives another and reacts on the basis of sympathy or antipathy, imitating and agreeing or resisting and disagreeing.[44] But in spite of the strong suggestion here she does not fully or systematically integrate her theory of perception with her view of sympathy and antipathy. She later quotes

Henry More on what he perceived to be the fallacy of an autokinetic theory of perception. Of matter he writes, *"For if it had any such perception, it would, by vertue of its self-motion withdraw its self from under the knocks of hammers, or fury of the fire; or of its own accord approach to such things as are most agreeable to it."* Cavendish's author goes on to acknowledge that some bodies "may over-power others, as the fire, hammer and hand doth over-power a Horse-shooe, which cannot prevail over so much odds of power and strength," but she is unwilling to generalize from that one example. Some bodies do have the power to resist the force of others. The letter ends with a rather unrigorous restatement of her theory: "And as for what your *Author* says, That every thing would approach to that, which is agreeable and pleasant; I think I need no demonstration to prove it; for we may plainly see it in all effects of Nature, that there is Sympathy and Antipathy, and what is this else, but approaching to things agreeable and pleasant, and withdrawing it self from things disagreeable, and hurtful or offensive?"[45] Again Cavendish associates the resistibility of matter with antipathy in matter, but in this case the association is attenuated.

If More used impact as a counterexample, Hobbes used it as his master example; one body strikes another, and the less powerful reacts. Cavendish envisioned a benevolent alternative to the Hobbesian account of impact. After denying that opposite actions are necessarily warring, she writes, "For example, two men may meet each other contrary ways, and one may not only stop the other from going forward, but even draw him back again the same way he came; and this may be done with love and kindness, and with his good will, and not violently, by power and force. The like may be in some actions of nature."[46] Here Cavendish translates the idea of occasional and voluntary reaction into human terms. It is not that the second man lacks the antipathetic power to resist the impact of the first, but rather that he has the sympathetic (will)power to imitate it. This distinction may seem rather arbitrary, but Cavendish's point is clear: the majority of actions in nature, if not all, are voluntary. Hobbes had a blinkered view of the natural world. In a philosophical letter addressing his natural philosophy, she writes, "Nature moveth not by force, but freely. 'Tis true, 'tis the freedom in Nature for one man to give another a box on the Ear, or to trip up his heels, or for one or more men to fight with each other; yet these actions are not like the actions of loving Imbraces and Kissing each other."[47] The epistolary form of *Philosophical Letters* and *Sociable Letters* functioned to reinforce Cavendish's project of contesting Hobbes's philosophy and correcting it by means of an emphasis on "loving" and sympathetic "actions" rather than violent and malevolent ones, connections rather than collisions. Her theory of mechanics was better suited to a nonimpactive case like emotional contagion;

the question of force never enters into the encounter between the author and the Lady M.L. The author's sympathy is purely a matter of will, of "love and kindness."

Conceived as a principle of harmonious interaction, sympathy was at the center of Cavendish's vitalist alternative to Epicurean atomism, Hobbesian or otherwise. Against the Epicurean vision of dead matter she maintained a worldview predicated on active, living matter; she could not understand how the movement of lifeless particles could eventuate in anything other than confusion—a recurrent term in her account of Epicurean philosophy—rather than the coherent whole that she perceived. "Matter, if it were all Inanimate and void of Motion," she writes, answering Hobbes, "would lie as a dull, dead and senseless heap"—a favored anti-Epicurean image, or, in a sense, anti-image, since the point is that such a homogeneous mass of matter offers to the mind no particularity with which or from which to generate a distinct, visible form. As we shall see, Cudworth, too, made use of this figure of figurelessness against his opponents. Cavendish continues, "If sensitive and rational perceptions, which are sensitive and rational motions, in the body, and in the mind, were made by the pressure of outward objects, pressing the sensitive organs, and so the brain or interior parts of the Body, they would cause such dents and holes therein, as to make them sore and patched in a short time; Besides, what was represented in this manner, would always remain, or at least not so soon be dissolved, and then those pressures would make a strange and horrid confusion of Figures, for not any figure would be distinct."[48] Such a view of interaction led not only to injury and violent discontinuity, "dents and holes," but also to a chaos of indistinctness, mere "confusion." The "Natural Philosophers," a synecdoche for the Epicurean atomists, "do so stuff [Nature] with dull, dead, senceless *minima's*, like as a sack with meal, or sand, by which they raise such a dust as quite blinds Nature and natural reason."[49] The figure of "a sack with meal, or sand" conveys the very antithesis of Cavendish's view of nature as a teeming variety of dynamic figures, organized by sympathy and antipathy. As she concludes her discussion "*Of* Epicurus *his Principles of Philosophy*," "his Chance is but an uncertain God, and his *Vacuum* an empty God; and if all natural effects were grounded upon such principles, Nature would rather be a confused Chaos, then an orderly and harmonical Universe."[50] Cavendish's anti-Epicurean universe was overarchingly sympathetic; it was not ruled by "Chance" but guided by free will.

By conceiving imitation in terms of volition, however, Cavendish also had to acknowledge that women as well as men were free not to sympathize. They could choose, in effect, not to be moved by certain pressures, but also not to be moved by less forceful impetuses like the sight of a stranger's tears or the sound of a friend's words. Unlike the Lady M.L., who, faultless and suffering, becomes a distant antitype of Lucretia, the "onely true and honest Wife," the Ladies D.C. and G.B. willfully bring disorder and dissension on themselves.[51] In a previous letter the author laments, "in my Opinion, there is no better Argument for Free Will, than to Observe how Opposite Constraint and Inforcement is to the Nature of Mankind; But when I Consider, that Mankind for the most part Will what is Worst, and most Hurtful for themselves, or their Kind, I then am apt to think Mankind are Predestinated so to do, otherwise it were strange that Mankind should Wilfully Hurt themselves, when they have that which is call'd Reason, which informs them, that that which they Will, is Hurtful for them, or to them" (273). Cavendish resisted a Hobbesian philosophy of constraint, but, as we shall see, she struggled to find an empirically true—as opposed to a theoretically compelling—alternative. Experience and observation made her, in the moment at least, a Calvinist—and, more enduringly, a social Hobbist. She would rather, it seems, consider a philosophical and theological doctrine inimical to her theory of nature than deny the immanence of reason in humankind.

Cavendish was unwilling to argue that rationality entailed benevolence; reason inhered in all matter, and all matter was free. But she was also unwilling to foreclose the possibility that benevolence was within the power of all. It is in this sense that we can understand the moral impetus of *Sociable Letters*. When the author catches by contagion the joy of the Lady M.L., she adds to the account of her own response an expression of hope for a wider communal response: "If all her Neighbours were the like Affected, she might do as the man, that call'd his Neighbours and Friends, to Rejoyce at the Finding his Lost Sheep" (325). Cavendish's model society is one in which each member acts as a neighbor and friend, and each responds in like fashion. A feeling rhetoric, she suggests, can be the occasional cause of a general fellow feeling. The benevolent rhetorician—part orator, part motivator, part therapist—cannot compel others to sympathize, but she can provide an ethical pattern for them to imitate.

"WHEN SYMPATHY JOYNS NOT"

We have seen that in *Sociable Letters* Cavendish moralizes sympathetic discourse by dramatizing it, by making it part of a didactic "Scene," but when the volume is conceived as a whole, the scenes of sympathetic imitation represent a fringe of idealism. The general contagion of her age was not sympathy but, as she increasingly makes clear, antipathy. In this section I demonstrate more fully Cavendish's social Hobbism and interpret it in contemporary political terms. I will argue that she appealed to a more deterministic, Platonic conception of sympathy as a way of securing ties that rhetoric alone could not guarantee. Having related that the Lady G.P. conveyed a letter she received from Mrs. O.B. "from Company to Company to Jest at, because it was not Indited after the Courtly Phrase," containing more "Friendly and Kind Expressions" than "Courtly Complements," the author laments, "Indeed, one may say, that in this Age there is a malignant Contagion of Gossiping, for not onely one Woman Infects another, but the Women Infect the Men, and then one Man Infects another, nay, it Spreads so much, as it takes hold even on Young Children, so strong and Infectious is this Malignity; . . . for there is nothing more Dangerous in all Malignant Diseases, than Throngs or Crowds of People" (179, 180–181). This gossip model of sociability, according to which relationships are reinforced negatively, is sustained by ill will. Cavendish describes a dark social contagion, communicated both within and between groups. If these are Cavendish's neighbors, they are certainly not her friends; they are neighbors only in name. The ultimate result of this "Malignity" of malevolence is widespread disaffection.

Over the course of *Sociable Letters* Cavendish describes antipathy across a range of social and familial relationships. The author is repeatedly critical of her own gender.[52] In one such critical passage, Cavendish introduces a challenging new concept of sympathy: "But, Madam, I have often Observed," she writes, "that Women with Women seldom Agree, for our Sex is so Self-loving, as we cannot Indure a Competitor, much less a Superiour, especially for Beauty, Wit, and Worth . . . and therefore the less Acquaintance we have with each other, the better, unless they be Chosen by an Immaculate, and Pure Sympathy, and Honour Knit the Knot of Friendship, otherwise the more Acquaintance we have, the more Enemies we have; wherefore to Live Quietly, Peaceably, and Easily, is to be Strangers to our own Sex" (331). The author's cynical view of female association not only suggests a prevailing antipathy but also calls into question the idea of volitional sympathy that Cavendish theorizes in her natural-philosophical writing. In such a construction the possibility of a rhetorically occasioned sympathy is occluded. Women agree not because they choose to imitate each other but because they are "Chosen by an Immaculate, and Pure Sympathy." The tension between voluntary self-motion and what sounds like external determination, or "predestination," is exposed in the very next letter, where the author discusses sympathy and antipathy as a universal natural phenomenon. Moving from moral to natural philosophy, the letter glosses Cavendish's own "Condemning Treatise of Atomes," which had appeared before the first edition of *Philosophical and Physical Opinions*. The author, as she explains, maintained that "every Atome must have . . . Passions and Appetites that Sympathize and Antipathize, as not only to Create, but to Dissolve the Self-creating Figures," and this "Sympathy and Antipathy might cause the Continuation of the World, for if they did alwayes Agree, there would be no Change, and if they did alwayes Disagree, there would be a Confusion" (333). Here Cavendish returns to an active conception of sympathetic and antipathetic passions; in the natural world sympathies and antipathies produce a dynamic equilibrium. Whereas the general result of sympathy and antipathy in society is difference and disturbance, in nature as a whole it is "variety." Although "there be a unity in the nature of Infinite Matter, yet there are divisions also in the Infinite parts of Infinite Matter, which causes Antipathy as much as Sympathy," she argues in one of her philosophical letters, "but they being equal in assistance as well as in resistance, it causes a conformity in the whole nature of Infinite Matter; for if there were not contrary, or rather, I may say, different effects proceeding from the onely cause, which is the onely matter, there could not possibly be any, or at least, so much variety in Nature, as humane sense and reason perceives there is."[53] These statements of Cavendish's natural philosophy represent a freer and more frequent sympathy than what she allows in the world of women. There is a dissonance, if not a strict inconsistency, between her "Self-creating Figures" and her immaculate acquaintances, which suggest not variety so much as invariability, and which occur not in general but only in rare cases. "There are Infinite sorts of Figures or Creatures that have Sympathy," Cavendish writes in her revised *Philosophical and Physical Opinions*, "and Infinite sorts of Figures that have Antipathies, both by their Exterior and Interior Motions, and some Exterior Sympathize with some Interior, and some Interior with some Exteriors, and some Exteriors with Exteriors, and Interiors with Interiors, both in one and the same Figure, and with one and the same Kind, and with different Kinds, and with several Sorts, which works Various Effects."[54] The repetition of "some" underlines the sense of variety that becomes explicit at the end of this extravagantly paratactic sentence, as she proceeds from "different" to "several" to "Various." Among the women in the author's orbit, however, the number of sympathetic relationships appears to have been decidedly — and, it seems, deter-minedly — finite. Whereas the various figures of nature generally agree but do not "always Agree," "Women with Women seldom agree." Whereas the natural world is balanced by equal but opposite forces, the social world seems funda-mentally imbalanced, with antipathies radically outnumbering sympathies.

In the social world, antipathies between men and women were no less prev-alent and were even more dire. As Cavendish describes it, the state of society closely approximates the Hobbesian state of nature. In an earlier work she deemed "the society of men and women . . . much more inconvenient, then men with men, and women with women; for women with women can do little inconvenience, but spights, and effeminate quarrels, . . . but of the society of men and women comes many great inconveniencies, as defamations of womens honours, and begets great jealousies, from fathers, brothers, and husbands, those jealousies beget quarrels, murthers, and at the best discontent."[55] The example of Lucretia lurks behind this reflection like a phantom. In the crisis of the Lady M.L. the author provides her own example of the misery to which a married woman could be exposed. But although the Lady M.L. found joy in reconciliation, in another letter the author suggests that not all marital crises have happy endings. This is the first instance in *Sociable Letters* where Cavendish appeals to a more deterministic idea of sympathy:

> I Am sorry to hear there is such a Difference betwixt the Lady *F.O.* and her Husband, as they are upon Parting, I wish their Humours and Dispositions were more Agreeable, and their Froward Passions less Violent; I cannot Condemn Either, nor Excuse Both, for if they anger each Other, they have Both cause to be Angry . . . : But Marriage is a very Unhappy Life when Sympathy Joyns not the Married Couple, for otherwise it were better to be Barr'd up within the Gates of a Monastery, than to be Bound in the Bonds of Matrimony; but whenas Sympathy Joyns Souls and Bodies in Marriage, then those Bonds are like Diamond-Chains to Adorn, not to Inslave them. (123–124)

In spite of her good intentions, the author cannot sympathize the estranged couple; she can only express compassion for them at a distance. In this passage her rhetoric, her musical variation of "both" and "each," amounts to little more than surface noise. A happy marriage depends on a sympathetic bond deeper than the matrimonial bond, and without the former, the latter merely binds the couple together, depriving "Souls and Bodies" of their freedom. Again our sense is that the author is powerless to join what "Sympathy" has not already determined to join. Broadly Platonic, Cavendish's discourse of the soul sits uneasily with her characteristic materialist emphasis. Sympathy seems here not a motion so much as a kind of disembodied mover.

Cavendish's deterministic expressions of human sympathy might reasonably be explained as unremarkable examples of a Platonic dialect to which she was introduced as a young woman at court. As such, they need not be squared with the decidedly un-Platonic cast of her natural philosophy. But I do think that, like Cavendish's Platonism itself, the salience of conjunction and disjunction in the language and imagery of *Sociable Letters* warrants further explanation. Determinism, I would suggest, serves a protective function in Cavendish's conception of human relations. Just as the author invokes the idea of predestination to safeguard reason, so she speaks of "choice" or election to protect her attachments. If sympathetic bonds are determinate, they cannot be simply created, but nor can they be easily destroyed. The author describes a world in which antipathetic forces pose a constant threat to the resistive strength of sympathetic bonds. In a typical account, the reality of "neighborly" behavior clashes with the ideal that we identified earlier: "I Am Glad to hear the Lady U.S. and her Husband live so Happily, as only to Themselves, and Love so well One Another, as seldome to be Sunder'd by Each others Absence, and I am Glad that She and He are so Wise as not to be perswaded from a Loving and Agreeable Course of Life. But I perceive by your Letter, that their Neighbours and Acquaintance Indeavour by their Little and Petty Flouts, Jeeres, and the like, to Disunite them" (220). Knowing only a hateful and disagreeable course of life, the others mock what they do not have, "wherefore it is out of Envy, that the Lady U.Ss. Neighbours and Acquaintance Dispraise or Undervalue her Husband, and his Birth and Breeding, and Laugh at their United Associating, and not out of Love, for true Love Commends true Worth, and Honest Unity: But as Women Envy Women for Beauty, Bravery, Courtships and Place, So Men Envy Men for Power, Authority, Honour and Offices. Wherefore leaving the Generality to Envy and Spite, and the Lady U.S. and her Husband to Love and Happiness, I rest" (222). The privileged couple represents a notable exception to the Hobbesian "Generality." The Cavendishes suffered an analogous impediment during their courtship, when rumors were spread at court about the illegitimacy of Margaret's oldest brother. As she related to William in the spring of 1645, "I fear others foresee we shall be unfortunat, tho we see it not our seleves, or elles ther would not be such paynes takeing to unty the knot of our affecion. . . . but tis the natur of thos that can not be happy to dessir non elles should be so, as I shall be in having you, and will be so, in spit of all malles."[56] In response to the malicious maneuverings of others and the tumult of the times, Cavendish imagined a knot that could not be untied, a bond that could not be broken. Gerard Langbaine paid tribute to that bond some two decades after their deaths. "Her Soul sympathising with his in all things," he writes, Margaret was "a fit Consort for so Great a Wit, as the Duke of *Newcastle*."[57]

We need not take a psychobiographical approach to uncover the trauma behind Cavendish's deterministic drive, since in *Sociable Letters* the author has, in effect, given us that psychobiography. The volume is full of references to the Civil Wars, through which Cavendish suffered on the losing side. As "the Generality" came into conflict with itself, the bonds of kinship came under unprecedented attack. After relating that the addressee has been asked by once wealthy acquaintances for financial support, "by which we may know, that neither Riches nor Peace is Permanent," the author describes the devastation "of these last Civil Wars": "and many are not only Ruin'd in their Estates, and Banished their Native Country, but Forsaken of their Friends, which is a terrible Misery; but Misery and Friends seldom keep together, and it is to be observed, that a Civil War doth not only Abolish Laws, Dissolve Government, and Destroy the Plenty of a Kingdom, but it doth Unknit the Knot of Friendship, and Dissolve Natural Affections, for in Civil War, Brothers against Brothers, Fathers against Sons, and Sons against Fathers, become Enemies, and Spill each others Blood, Triumphing on their Graves" (240). Cavendish puts the greatest emphasis here on the destruction and dissolution of fundamental sympathies—what Milton called "Relations dear"—between "Brothers" and between "Fathers" and "Sons." War rages both within and without: "When a Kingdom is Inflamed with Civil War, the Minds of all the People are in a Fever of Fury, or a Furious Fever of Cruelty, which, by nothing, but Letting Blood by the Surgeon of War, can be Cured," and "Vices Increase in a Civil War . . . all the Evil Passions and Debauch'd Appetites are let Loose, to take their Liberty" (240–241). Cavendish could not forget the ravages of war; there could be no mental act of oblivion. Behind the author's reference to "triumphing on graves" lay a horrific historical act. Soldiers on the side of Parliament dug up Cavendish's family tomb in St. John's Abbey. Hesitant again to impugn the rationality of humankind, the author associates such inhumanity with disease, with a kind of temporary insanity, but the emotional consequences were permanent. Once the knot of natural affection came undone, it was not clear that it could be "re-knit." The agent of undoing is "Civil War" itself, which seems to represent an irresistible force. In the author's Hobbesian account, no central power constrains the warring masses from doing their worst. Her repetition of the word "civil" in this extended passage ("Civil War . . . Civil Government . . . Civil Magistrates . . . Civil Laws . . . Civil Manners") traces an arc from literal or merely descriptive to moral. The effect is antiphrastic; Cavendish painfully underlines the radical *incivility* of civil war.

In her memoir Cavendish describes the outbreak of war while giving an account of her family's extraordinary civility and sociability—the model of a sympathetic community. "As for the pastimes of my Sisters when they were in the country," she explains, "it was to reade, work, walk, and discourse with each other," and in London her siblings "were dispersed into several houses of their own, yet for the most part they met every day, feasting each other like Job's Children. But this unnatural War came like a whirlwind, which fell'd down their Houses, where some in the Wars were crusht to death, as my youngest brother Sir Charls Lucas, and my Brother Sir Thomas Lucas." Quite jarringly, Cavendish then returns to her siblings' "Recreations," riding in their coaches in winter, in boats in summer, which "they would pass their time away with; for I observed, they did seldom make Visits, nor never went abroad with Strangers in their Company, but onely themselves in a Flock together agreeing so well, that there seemed but one Minde amongst them: And not onely my own Brothers and Sisters agreed so, but my Brothers and Sisters in law, and their Children, although but young, had the like agreeable natures, and affectionate disposi- tions; for to my best remembrance I do not know that ever they did fall out, or had any angry or unkind disputes."[58] The account as a whole reads like a utopian narrative with an apocalyptic middle. The deaths of Cavendish's siblings in the Civil Wars necessarily challenged her view of her extended family as a perfect "monistic" system, "one Minde amongst them." Especially before the war her family embodied the ideal of sociability that the author struggles to realize in *Sociable Letters*, where visits are frequent and frivolous and where conversa- tions quickly devolve into disputes, the opposite of "a Flock together agreeing so well." Later relating of her mother that "they" — a menacing blank pronoun — "plundered her and my Brothers of all their Goods, Plate, Jewels, Money, Corn, Cattle, and the like, cut down their Woods, pull'd down their Houses, and sequestered them from their Lands and Livings," Cavendish completes her modern "brief epic" in reverse, but unlike Job, her family did not in the end get back what they had lost, much less in double supply.[59]

When Cavendish returned to England to lay claim to a portion of her husband's estate, she encountered an immovable antipathy. The Committee for Compounding rebuffed her. In a letter she displaces the experience onto the addressee: "Fortune ... yet hath had more Pity and Compassion of your Sufferings, than they who keep you from the Extremity of Misery they have Exposed you to; yet those who have your Estate, cannot be much Happier, although you never have it again, for they cannot Enjoy it Long, the Longest Life being but Short" (291–292). Against the malice of the Parliamentarians the author can manage only a mawkish platitude. Their unnatural acts, she suggests, spring from unnatural affections. In *Natures Pictures* (1st ed., 1656) Cavendish had referred to the incident under allegorical cover in verse:

> SHE said, I over Sea to *Lapland* went,
> My Husband being then in banishment:
> His Estate gone, and being very poor,
> I thought some means Compassion might restore:
> But when I ask'd, no pity could I find;
> Hard were their Hearts, and cruel every Mind.[60]

The initial trochee in the last line puts assaulting emphasis on "Hard," amplified by "Hearts." In a more idealizing vein Cavendish had written, "Civil behaviour . . . begets compassion in the cruel, it moves pity in misery, it begets love in prosperity."[61] But civil war was the very antithesis of civil behavior. In the closing couplet of the previous verse scherzo, Cavendish expresses a grim generalization: "Calamity doth find no Pity; for / All Pity's buri'd in a Civil-Warr."[62] The war dead are buried, and with them the best affections of the living. Finding no pity or compassion in the world at large, Cavendish and her various alter egos are left to seek it on the wheel of Fortune, a notoriously false friend. The "cruel minds" of those from whom she sought sympathy—and failed to get it—suggest a striking contrast to the unified sympathetic mind she attributed to her family. These lines relate a momentous rhetorical failure. To recall the physiology of communication with which we began, Cavendish's words fall on deaf ears. Her "timely discourse" does not occasion sympathetic imitations, because her auditors exert their will against it. With this failure in mind, we can now better understand not only Cavendish's fictions of persuasion but also her fictions of audience, on which her complex view of sympathy depends.

EGOISTIC SOCIABILITY

Cavendish's more permanent solution to the problem of sympathy in the social world was to theorize a sympathetic self and to create a social world within. She imagined the constitution of a social world without by means of a sympathetic rhetoric, but this mode of idealism, shearing against harsher realities, could go only so far. By introjecting a sympathetic worldview, Cavendish could insulate herself from and against those realities. The author writes approvingly of "Retirement from the publick Concourse and Army of the World, and Regiments of Acquaintance" (62). It is no wonder that, conceiving of her visitors as enemy soldiers, she did not easily sympathize with them. Years after it ended, even after the monarchy was restored, the Civil Wars, in effect, raged on—in the petty disputes and violent quarrels of "civilized" society. The value of privacy is eloquently and energetically defended throughout the volume. "But this Retired Life is so Pleasing to me," the author writes, "as I would not change it for all the Pleasures of the Publick World, nay, not to be Mistress of the World, for I should not desire to be Mistress of that which is too Big to be Commanded, too Self-willed to be Ruled, too factious to be Govern'd, too Turbulent to live in Peace, and Wars would Fright, at least Grieve me, that mankind should be so Ill-natur'd and Cruel to Destroy each other" (61–62). The repetition of the adverbial "too" here, leading to a summary "so," emphasizes the structural and emotional imbalance that Cavendish saw in the social world. A lasting peace, she concluded, could be found only in the private world of the self. The author takes pains to point out that although she prefers retirement, she does not seek, as she puts it, "to bar my self from the Company of my good Friends" (61). In the letter in which she celebrates "an Immaculate, and Pure Sympathy," the author makes a similar distinction between intimates and others when she advocates retirement only "from those we call Strangers, such as we have no Relation to, or Obligation from" (331–332). But as the earlier letter draws to a close, the sense that emerges is that her ideal company is not her family, not even her husband, but her own thoughts: "I am more Happy in my Home-retirement, than I believe the Lady S.P. is in her Publick Frequentments, having a Noble and Kind Husband, who is Witty and Wise Company, a Peaceable and Quiet Mind, and Recreative Thoughts, that take harmless Liberty" (62). At home the author finds refuge from the world, but her retirement, she suggests, is deeper still.[63]

Home ultimately becomes a figure for the mind, a self-enclosed sympathetic space that is open to endless imaginative possibility. Expressions like the following abound in *Sociable Letters*: "I by this Retirement live in a calm Silence, wherein I have my Contemplations free from Disturbance, and my Mind lives in Peace, and my Thoughts in Pleasure, they Sport and Play, they are not Vext with Cares nor worldly Desires, they are not Covetous of worldly Wealth, nor Ambitious of empty Titles; . . . they have no quarrelling Disputes amongst them; they live Friendly and Sociably together" (56–57). Within, the author enjoys a true and lasting sociability. She emphasizes the freedom of the mind, a freedom that even a woman with "a Noble and Kind Husband," like Cavendish, was denied in a world of male mastery. Toward the end of the volume the author laments that wives are either "Slaves" or "Servants" before concluding, in a stoic fashion, "the Best is to be Mistress of your self, which in a Single Life you are" (427). As Cavendish conceived it, self-mastery involved not the elimination of passion but its liberation. The ego was at its freest and strongest in isolation.

Cavendish laid the foundation for the idea of an egoistic sociability in her natural-philosophical writing. She maintained that the natural self constituted a sociable society in and of itself. "But, in a Regular Society," she writes, "every Part and Particle of the Body, is Regularly agreeable, and Sympathetical," and then shortly thereafter, "Wherefore, if the Society be Regular, the Sensitive and Rational Parts are agreeable and sociable."[64] In her memoir Cavendish writes that from as early as she can remember she has been "addicted . . . to contemplation rather than conversation, to solitariness rather than society."[65] In her natural-philosophical theory, however, these are false binaries; contemplation is "a Conversation amongst some of the Rational Parts of the Human Mind," and the solitary self, with its "*Sympathetical Endeavours amongst the Associate Parts,*" enjoys society.[66] Only within could Cavendish find lasting refuge from the Hobbesian world of antipathetic endeavor. The sympathetic self, as she explains, is organized for resistance: "There is a strong Sympathy between the Rational and Sensitive Parts, in one and the same Society, or Creature: not only for their Consistency, Subsistency, Use, Ease, Pleasure, and Delight; but, for their Safety, Guard, and Defence: as for example, When one Creature assaults another, then all the Powers, Faculties, Properties, Ingenuities, Agilities, Proportions, and Shape, of the Parts of the Assaulted, unite against the Assaulter, in the defence of every particular Part of their whole Society; in which Encounter, the Rational advises, and the Sensitive labours."[67] The mustering of nouns in this passage has the effect of turning the tables on the "assaulting creature," who, rather than having the upper hand, is outnumbered by the "Powers, Faculties, Properties, Ingenuities, Agilities, Proportions, and Shape, of the Parts of the Assaulted." We have seen that Cavendish opposed Hobbes by adumbrating a theory of resistance based on antipathy; here she outlines a vision of self-defense by sympathy. The society of the self sympathizes its motions to generate a counterforce, which may or may not represent an antipathy; Cavendish did not fully work out this crucial point.

For Cavendish, Hobbes's theory of matter, as we have seen, amounted to a theory of violence. In *The Blazing World*, after the Empress consults with the various learned creatures around her, she proceeds to meet with and interrogate the spirits of her new world, who reinforce a Hobbist view of humankind: "You men are more cruel to another, then evil Spirits are to you."[68] When the Empress decides that she wants "to make a Cabbala," an esoteric religious system, the spirits encourage her to take "the Duchess of Newcastle" as her spiritual "scribe" and then ultimately encourage both women to turn away from the outside world and create worlds of their own. Before doing so, the Duchess tries out the worlds of others. Cavendish's account of the "Opinion of *Epicurus*," which creates a "confusion" of "Atoms" and leads to "a Chaos" in the Duchess's mind, "sympathizes" with her earlier discussion of Epicurus's philosophy in *Observations*, which, we recall, was published together with *The Blazing World*. A parallel textual sympathy is occasioned by the Duchess's encounter with "*Hobbs's* Opinion."[69] When she holds the Hobbesian worldview in her mind, she is assaulted by it: "But when all the parts of this Imaginary World came to press and drive each other, they seemed like a company of Wolves that worry Sheep, or like so many Dogs that hunt after Hares; and when she found a reaction equal to those pressures, her mind was so squeesed together, that her thoughts could move neither forward nor backward, which caused such an horrible pain in her head, that . . . she could not, without much difficulty, settle her mind, and free it from that pain which those pressures and reactions had caused in it."[70] Entitling one of her fictions "Assaulted and Pursued Chastity," Cavendish, like Hobbes, generally conceived of human relations in terms of "the Assaulted" and "the Assaulter," but by limiting the scope of "pressure and reaction" in the mechanics of nature, she was, in effect, protecting the assaulted from the assaulter.[71] In this case, a witty if far-fetched conceit, the "pressure" comes from Hobbes's theory of pressure. The sympathetic motions of the Duchess's mind unite to produce an equal but opposite reaction to the pressure of "*Hobbs's* Opinion." Her mind is not invulnerable—she ends up with a "horrible" Hobbesian migraine—but it causes no lasting damage. This episode translates into narrative terms a point that Cavendish makes earlier in the volume in *Observations*: "We do not deny but there is many times force and power used between particular parts of nature, so that some do overpower others; but this causes no disturbance in nature."[72] Like nature in its entirety, the mind as a whole has an infinite power and resilience not granted to its parts.

The pain of "*Hobbs's* Opinion" in *The Blazing World* occasions not only a reaction but also an original imaginative action, a turn within. "At last," Cavendish writes, "when the Duchess saw that no patterns would do her any good in the framing of her World; she was resolved to make a World of her own invention, and this World was composed of sensitive and rational self-moving Matter."[73] The invention follows no pattern but Cavendish's own; in other words, the Duchess patterns out Cavendish's opinion. Then, struggling to create worlds of her own, the Empress patterns out the Duchess's world by means of her own "rational corporeal motions."[74] This sequence of sympathetic imitations represents a peculiar feedback loop. "I delight my self with my Self" (58), the author of *Sociable Letters* writes. Cavendish, more precisely, delighted her self with her *selves*; the author and the addressee, the Empress and the Duchess, are all patterns of their creator. Douglas Grant has speculated that the addressee of *Sociable Letters* was Cavendish's sometime maid Elizabeth Topp, to whom she addressed an "Epistle" prefaced to *Poems, and Fancies*. The identity cannot be established definitively, he acknowledges, but he maintains that Cavendish's sociable letters "were not simply self-communings."[75] And yet there is compelling internal evidence that the letters are just that. In a poem prefaced to *Sociable Letters*, "Upon Her Excellency the Authoress," the anonymous poet—could it be Cavendish herself?—describes a closed system:

> *This Lady only to her self she Writes,*
> *And all her Letters to her self Indites;*
> *For in her self so many Creatures be,*
> *Like many Commonwealths, yet all Agree.*

(D1r)

The broader political sympathy, or "agreement," whose absence Cavendish lamented in the world without is present in the world within. The position of the poem encourages the identification of "Authoress" with Cavendish, and Cavendish with "This Lady," so that once the letters begin there is an immediate confusion between the unnamed author of the letters and the "Authoress." That the addressee's experiences occasionally mirror Cavendish's only adds to the subjective confusion and complexity. The sympathy that we noted earlier between the author and the "Bashful" addressee who was "much out of Countenance" when she was "Surprised with" an unexpected visit can be interpreted as Cavendish's sympathy with herself: "Truly, Madam, I am very Sensible of your Pain, insomuch as methinks I Feel what you Suffered, for I my self have been, and am still, so Troubled with that Imperfection, (if it may be call'd one) that I have been often … out of Countenance, … and the Thoughts that Bashfulness leaves in the Mind, are as great an Affliction as the Mind can have for a Crimeless Defect" (280–281). As Cavendish effectively doubles herself, her bashfulness, which represents a constrictive rather than a creative inwardness, seems to disappear. In one of her natural-philosophical works Cavendish raises the question of whether a perfect or complete sympathy with another person is possible—a recurrent doubt in the history of sympathy that, as we shall see, only intensified over time: "If the Mind was not joyn'd and mix'd with the Sensitive and Inanimate Parts, and had not interior, as well as exterior Parts, the whole Mind of one Man, might perceive the whole Mind of another Man; but, that being not possible, one whole Mind cannot perceive another whole Mind."[76] If, however, that other mind were really the same mind "under the Cover" of another, no such problem of perception arose.

In the prefatory poem to *Sociable Letters* these versions of the self become "Creatures" within, and thus creations of, the self. The character and tone of this kind of "self-sympathy" are established in the opening letter, where the author rhapsodizes about epistolary communion. Her emphasis on the soul, as in her explicit references to sympathy, has the immediate effect of distancing Cavendish the natural philosopher, in whose materialist system the "natural soul of man" was marginal.[77] "Truly, Madam," the author writes, "I take so much delight in your wise, witty, and virtuous Conversation, as I could not pass my life more pleasing and delightfully; wherefore I am never better pleased, than when I am reading your Letters, and when I am writing Letters to you; for my mind and thoughts are all that while in your Company: the truth is, my mind and thoughts live always with you, although my person is at distance from you; insomuch, as, if Souls die not as Bodies do, my Soul will attend you when my Body lies in the grave; and when we are both dead, we may hope to have a Conversation of Souls, where yours and mine will be doubly united, first in Life, and then in Death" (1–2). "Company" is defined here as essentially a state of mind. The mind is invested with the power of action at a distance; the "mind and thoughts" of the author can be with the addressee even though her "person is at distance." Over the course of the letter the sense of "conversation" shifts from social intercourse to a more mystical psychic connection.[78] Cavendish associated the latter with the "Platonicks."

Having considered the tensions in, and between, Cavendish's social and scientific discourse, I think we can now make better sense of her complex and ambivalent Platonism. More often than not in Cavendish's writing the term "Platonick" is dyslogistic. "Or if they be in years," she writes of women, "they strive to be thought Wits, and all their Discourse is of Love, justifying Loving Friendships by the Conversation of Souls."[79] So strives "Mrs. R.E.," whose "Wit is a *Platonick* Wit, as loving Friendships, and the conversation of Souls, but take her from the *Platonicks*, and she is gone, both from Wit and Understanding, or those are gone from her" (93). Cavendish was likely exposed to the doctrine of Platonic love in the court of Henrietta Maria, whom she served as maid of honor.[80] In a well-known letter written in 1634 James Howell described the fashion: "The Court affords little news at present, but that there is a Love call'd *Platonick* love, which much swayes there of late; It is a love abstracted from all corporeall gross impressions, and sensual appetit, but consists in contemplation and Ideas of the mind, not in any carnall fruition: This love sets the wits of the Town on work; and they say there will be a Maske shortly of it, whereof Her Majestie, and her Maids of Honour will be part."[81] Cavendish did not join the Queen until 1643, by which time the court had removed to Oxford. There Cavendish, paralyzed by her bashfulness, formed no friendships, Platonic or otherwise; with its intrigues and entanglements, it was an environment inimical to her sensibilities.[82] Ever skeptical of the "Mode," Cavendish saw behind the doctrine of Platonic love the potential for deceit and corruption. "I am no Platonick," the author writes; "for this opinion is dangerous, especially for married Women, by reason the conversation of Souls may be a great temptation, and a means to bring Platonick Lovers to a neerer acquaintance, not allowable by the Laws of Marriage, although by the sympathy of the Souls."[83] Elsewhere Cavendish put the matter more bluntly: "Platonick Love is a Bawd to Adultery."[84] The spirituality of the "Platonicks" was nothing more than a dressed-up carnality.[85]

By contrast, the Duchess's friendship with the Empress, like the author's with the addressee, preserves the Platonic doctrine in a pristine state. "Conversation," closely associated with sympathy in the Platonic dialect, is a keyword in *The Blazing World*. Early in the work the idea of connection is represented in straightforward structural terms, as the Empress organizes "conferences" with the various hybrid animal-men of her new world and then moves on to the local "Spirits": "After this, and several other Conferences, which the Emperess held with the Worm-men, she dismissed them. . . . Then she made a convocation of her Chymists, the Ape-men"; "Lastly, her Majesty had some Conferences with the Galenick Physicians about several Diseases"; "wherefore she made a Convocation of the most learned, witty and ingenious of all the forementioned sorts of men"; "at last, after a great many conferences and particular intelligences, which the Spirits gave the Emperess, to her great satisfaction and content, she enquired after the most famous Students, Writers, and Experimental Philosophers in that World."[86] But after the Empress sets out to make her "Cabbala" and encounters the Duchess, the romance and utopian dimensions of the work receive a distinct Platonic overlay, and the philosophical "conferences" give way to mystical "conversations." The "meeting" of the Empress and the Duchess "truly. . . did produce such an intimate friendship between them, that they became Platonick Lovers, although they were both Females." Sympathetic friendship is associated with and transformed into "Platonick Love."

Even as this account emphasizes a kind of sympathetic presence, it also calls attention to a particular absence. Indeed, at one point "the Duchess's soul grew very Melancholy" because "she had an extreme desire to converse with the soul of her noble Lord and dear Husband." This "desire" leads to the formation of "a Platonick Seraglio": "But the Dukes soul being wise, honest, witty, complaisant and noble, afforded such delight and pleasure to the Emperess's soul by his conversation, that these two souls became enamoured of each other; which the Duchess's soul perceiving, grew jealous at first, but then considering that no Adultery could be committed amongst Platonick Lovers, and that Platonism was Divine, as being derived from Divine *Plato*, cast forth of her mind that Idea of Jealousie. Then the Conversation of these three souls was so pleasant, that it cannot be expressed." Cavendish seems here to be working through her anxiety that Platonic love, with its fantasy of sympathetic souls, was a fashionable screen for lustful bodies, whose "conversation" had potentially divisive and ruinous consequences. What she ends up with is the fantasy of an ineffable sympathetic rapture among unimpeachably virtuous souls. This curious "Platonick Seraglio" emerges as the model for a utopian "World" configured "as one united Family, without divisions; nay, like God, and his Blessed Saints and Angels."[87] In the utopian mode, sympathetic friendship is extended to the whole of society, figured in terms of the one plural structure that was reliably positive in Cavendish's mind, the family—it is notable here that she passes almost immediately from earth to heaven, from people to God and "his Blessed Saints and

Angels." As the first part of *The Blazing World* ends, Cavendish strongly reasserts the more exclusive idea of sympathetic conversation that is her major emphasis in the work: "The Emperess's Soul embraced and kiss'd the Duchess's soul with an immaterial kiss, and shed immaterial tears, that she was forced to part from her, finding her not a flattering Parasite, but a true friend; and, in truth, such was their Platonick Friendship, as these two loving Souls did often meet and rejoice in each others Conversation."[88] "Chosen" by Cavendish herself, to recall the deterministic Platonic language I considered earlier in the chapter, this sympathy is subject neither to infection, as by a "Parasite," nor to dissolution. "And as for this Age we live in now," the author writes to her Platonic correspondent, "'tis Prodigal to their Enemies, and Ungrateful to their Friends; but, Madam, though this Age be so Infected in the Generality, yet some Particulars escape this Infection, for You and I are as Constant in Friendship as the Light to the Sun" (165). Platonism provided Cavendish with a theoretical framework for "escape." It provided imaginative access to a world far above the fray and impervious to it. The repetition of the word "immaterial" in the account of the Duchess's and Empress's parting is striking; removed from matter, the friendship was protected from the assaults of the Hobbesian generality, assaults that could be parried only partially and imperfectly by her theory of matter. In the mind of its creator the friendship was secure.

Within—and only within—could Cavendish find a sympathetic society; she had to found it imaginatively. "I did imagine my self Empress of the whole World," the author writes, anticipating *The Blazing World*, "which World was to be Governed by my Fancy, Opinion and Approvement; and first, I would have my Counsel-Ministers of State, and Magistrates, Philosophers, both Natural and Moral, and my Court-Officers and Attendants, Poets of all sorts, so should I Govern Wisely, and Live Pleasantly, by which I Imagined the World of Men would be so United in Peace, Concord, and Tranquillity, as it would be Harmonious" (411). This larger sympathy, like the particular Platonic sympathy between author and addressee, is not a material reality but "a Fiction of the Mind."[89] The natural and moral philosophers of the author's imaginary world are united in concord, but insofar as she conceived a social sympathy beyond the "gross material world," Cavendish's natural and moral philosophies remained divided.[90] Claiming in a natural-philosophical context, we recall, that "one whole Mind cannot perceive another whole Mind," she concluded, "By which Observation we may perceive, there are no *Platonick Lovers* in Nature."[91] There was fantasy, and there was reality. Cavendish peopled her imaginary worlds with versions of the one person with whom she shared a perfect sympathy, herself. In its intricacy and insistency, this "self-theme" (18)—Cavendish's neologism—runs the risk of committing her to what Catherine Gallagher calls "total self-referentiality."[92] At the extreme of subjectivity, or one might say of "intrasubjectivity," true intersubjectivity ceases to be possible. In identifying herself with her fictions and ultimately with herself, Cavendish was potentially compromising her ability to identify with others. If in *The Blazing World* the Duchess's soul, like the Empress's, could enter into the Duke's soul, what need did the real duchess have of the real duke? The world of the self did not lead back to the world of others; it led to other selves and to other worlds.

At the same time that it drew her within, however, writing provided Cavendish with a solution to the problem of infinite interiority, of "the thoughts left in the mind." She describes her literary and philosophical output as a process of externalization, as a return to the outside world. The thoughts and ideas her "Mind likes best, it sends them forth to the Senses to write them down, and then to send them out to the publick view of the World" (57). The creations of her private self are made public, moving from her brain to her hand to paper to the printer and thence to the larger world. Publication for Cavendish is thus the opposite of retirement. In the preface to *Natures Pictures* she expresses high hopes for the volume: "I hope, that this Work will rather quench Passion, then enflame it; will beget chast Thoughts, nourish the love of Virtue, kindle Human Pity, warm Charity, encrease Civility, strengthen fainting Patience, encourage noble Industry, crown Merit, and instruct Life: will damn Vices, kill Follies, prevent Errors, forewarn Youth, and arm the Mind against Misfortunes; and in a word, will admonish, direct, and perswade to that which is best in all kinds."[93] If Cavendish could not herself bring the social world into sympathy, perhaps her "Work" could; it could "kindle Human Pity" and "warm Charity."

This process of civilizing, of emotional "kindling," depends on persuasion— "perswade" is the climactic verb in a characteristically drawn-out series—but for Cavendish, as we have seen, persuasion could not be constrained. Having converted the Blazing World with her "Sermons of Terror" and "Sermons of Comfort," the Empress, another of Cavendish's ideal female rhetoricians, "knew well, that belief was a thing not to be forced or pressed upon the people, but to be instilled into their minds by gentle perswasions."[94] The will of the audience was to move—to be moved, not forced—to sympathetic imitations. Cavendish does not begin *Sociable Letters* with such a lofty statement of purpose, but in her prefatory letter to William, she offers a prayer for her fellow "Man": "O Lord God, I do beseech thee of thy infinite Mercy, to make Man so, and order his Mind, Thoughts, Passions, and Appetites, like Beasts, that they may be Temperate, Sociable, Laborious, Patient, Prudent, Provident, Brotherly-loving and Neighbourly-kind, all which Beasts are, but most Men not" (B2v).[95] Beyond the curiously porous boundaries of Cavendish's text we return to the moral and social sympathy, the "neighborliness," that flickers only dimly within. But here it is not to words but to the Word that she appeals. Perhaps in the end the solution to the problem of antipathy was a simple Protestant one—faith.

CAVENDISH AND "THE MAN OF FEELING"

Cavendish's diverse output—literary, philosophical, rhetorical—has been widely and variously contextualized over the past two decades. I want finally to consider Cavendish's work in a new light, by setting her writing on sympathy in the broader context of the history of sensibility, a history in which Hobbes's work has long figured centrally.[96] To do so I will return to R. S. Crane's "Suggestions toward a Genealogy of the 'Man of Feeling'" and contrast the representation of human sympathy in the sermons of Isaac Barrow, who emerges as a kind of protagonist in Crane's account, to those of Cavendish and Hobbes.[97] Crane names Barrow first in his list of Latitudinarian divines, refers to his sermons as "particularly rich" in their treatment of benevolence as a "theme," and singles Barrow out as "one of the most important" of "the anti-Hobbesian preachers of 'natural goodness' in the years immediately following the Restoration." Crane rightly emphasizes the negative stimulus to a benevolist ethics provided by Hobbes, but in suggesting that there was something like an "anti-Hobbesian" consensus, Crane's account has promoted a simplified and whitewashed view of the histories of sympathy and sensibility.[98] An important historical point to be drawn from Cavendish's work is that moral concepts of sympathy were developed not exclusively against Hobbes but also with and aslant him. Barrow's sermons enable us to see sympathy at the center of an ideological movement—in which Cavendish participated—toward community and coherence in the wake of the Civil Wars. In locating Cavendish in the history of sensibility, we gain a clearer sense of the history of sympathy as an ongoing clash and competition between ideals and realities, desired aims and stubborn facts.

In a sermon on Romans 12:18, published in 1680, Barrow affirms the usual hierarchy of men and beasts, reversed in Cavendish's prayer. Cavendish did not have his pulpit—and, indeed, we should acknowledge significant differences of occasion and genre—but Barrow's representation of human sympathy is, by contrast with hers, untroubled and unequivocal. Of "the offices of humanity" he writes,

> We are indispensably obliged to these duties, because the best of our natural
> inclinations prompt us to the performance of them; especially those of pity

and benignity, which are manifestly discernible in all, but most powerfull and vigorous in the best natures; and which questionless by the most wise, and good Authour of our beings were implanted therein both as monitors to direct, and as spurrs to incite us to the performance of our duty. For the same bowels, that in our want of necessary sustenance, do by a lively sense of pain informe us thereof, and instigate us to provide against it; do in like manner grievously resent the distresses of another, and thereby admonish us of our duty, and provoke us to relieve them. Even the stories of calamities, that in ages long since past have happencd to persons, no-wise related to us, yea the fabulous reports of tragical events, do (even against the bent of our wills, and all resistance of reason) melt our hearts with compassion, and draw tears from our eyes: and thereby evidently signify that general sympathy which naturally intercedes between all men, since we can neither see, nor hear of, nor imagine anothers grief, without being afflicted ourselves. Antipathies may be natural to wild beasts; but to rational creatures they are wholly unnatural.[99]

Cavendish's experiences in the middle of the century taught her otherwise. The antiroyalists had plain evidence of her grief and distress and yet pitilessly turned away. Walter Pope relates that when Barrow was a student at Trinity College, Cambridge, in the mid-1640s the master defended the young royalist in spite of their ideological differences on account of Barrow's virtues; his "irresistible merits" were such that they could "make a Presbyterian kind to a Cavalier."[100] The sense of Barrow's social power, transcending ideology, is enhanced in a more elaborate anecdote—almost a parable—from after the Restoration, when John Wilkins asked Barrow to give a sermon. Barrow, it seems, showed up attired not unlike Petruchio on his wedding day, prompting the congregants to flee. A number of them confronted Wilkins "in full Cry, saying, they wonderd he should permit such a Man to Preach before them, who lookt like a starvd Cavalier who had been long Sequesterd, and out of his Living for Delinquency, and came up to *London* to beg, now the King was restord." Wilkins attested to, and vouched for, Barrow's virtue as the master of Trinity had done years before. One of the few congregants who had stayed to hear Barrow's sermon was Richard Baxter, "that Eminent Non-conformist," who reportedly said that "*Dr.* Barrow *Preachd so well, that he could willingly have been his Auditor all day long.*" Hearing Baxter's testimony, Barrow's enemies "were prickt in their hearts," revealed that they had paid no attention to the sermon itself, and "earnestly desird Dr. *Wilkins* to procure Dr. *Barrow* to Preach again, engaging their selves to make amends, *by bringing to his Sermon their Wives and Children, Man-servants, and Maid-servants, in a word, their whole Families.*"[101] Barrow was able to move others to sympathy, to community, in a way that Cavendish could not.

Her theory of the will implied that people were free to sympathize, but also free not to. Like Digby, but in a very different spirit, Barrow bypassed the problem of the will by asserting a sympathetic instinct; we sympathize "even against the bent of our wills." This instinct comes close to the "moral sense" elaborately theorized in the 1720s by Francis Hutcheson: for Barrow, "the practice of benignity, of courtesy, of clemency do at first sight, without aid of any discursive reflection, obtain approbation and applause from men; being acceptable and amiable to the mind, as beauty to their sight, harmony to their hearing, fragrancy to their smell and sweetness to their taste."[102] We are naturally moved not only to sympathize with others but also to approve of others' sympathies. Cavendish, by contrast, exploited the paradox that most men and women were more beastly, more *antipathetic*, than beasts, with which she felt a deep and abiding sympathy. "I wish Men were as Harmless as most Beasts are," she writes, "then surely the World would be more Quiet and Happy than it is, for then there would not be such Pride, Vanity, Ambition, Covetousness, Faction, Treachery, and Treason, as is now" (B2v). Cavendish's "World" was far closer to Hobbes's than to Barrow's.

Unlike Cavendish, Barrow wholeheartedly opposed the Hobbist view of human nature. Not needing to name his enemy, he sermonized against the "monstrous paradox, crossing the common sense of men, which in this loose and vain world hath lately got such vogue, that all men naturally are enemies one to another."[103] Hobbism was nothing more than a fashionable distortion. Barrow invests in the "common sense of men," a term that would have great significance in the moral scheme of Shaftesbury, and stops short of implying that the world was "loose and vain" because Hobbes made it so. Sympathy, not enmity, Barrow countered, was natural to men. Yet if it seemed that Hobbes had distorted the nature of things, it was also the case that Hobbes's enemies frequently distorted Hobbes, undertaking, in Jon Parkin's summation, "deliberate reductions" of his positions and branding them with "undesirable social and political signifiers such as atheism and immorality."[104] Hobbes did indeed argue in *Leviathan* that the natural equality of men led to "diffidence," or distrust, of one another, that diffidence led to war, and that "men have no pleasure, (but on the contrary a great deale of griefe) in keeping company, where there is no power able to over-aw them all. For every man looketh that his companion should value him, at the same rate he sets upon himself." Cavendish sympathized with Hobbes's conviction that the absence of a central power led to chaos in the social world. But although he argued that first among "the Passions that encline men to Peace" was "Feare of Death," in his account of the passions Hobbes also recognized "*Desire* of good to another, BENEVOLENCE, GOOD WILL, CHARITY. If to man generally, GOOD NATURE."[105]

Hobbes's formulation of the idea emphasized by many of his opponents that concern for others was at root concern for oneself was not unequivocal or unqualified.[106] In a scenic dialogue so pertinent as to be almost suspicious, John Aubrey, considering Hobbes "very charitable (pro suo modulo)"—not the kind of qualification Barrow would have been inclined to make—relates that he and Hobbes encountered "in the Strand, a poor and infirme old man [who] craved his almes." Hobbes, "beholding him with eies of pitty and compassion, putt his hand in his pocket, and gave him 6d. Sayd a divine . . . that stood by—'Would you have donne this, if it had not been Christ's command?' 'Yea,' sayd he.— 'Why?' quoth the other.— 'Because,' sayd he, 'I was in paine to consider the miserable condition of the old man; and now my almes, giving him some reliefe, doth also ease me.'"[107] Here Hobbes's selfish pleasure seems secondary to that of the other. But his account of pity in *Leviathan* puts fuller weight on the pitier: "*Griefe*, for the Calamity of another, is PITTY; and ariseth from the imagination that the like calamity may befall himselfe; and therefore is called also COMPASSION, and in the phrase of this present time a FELLOW-FEELING: And therefore for Calamity arriving from great wickedness, the best men have the least Pitty; and for the same Calamity, those have least Pitty, that think themselves least obnoxious to the same."[108] Hobbes is not denying "FELLOW-FEELING" here so much as trying to define it clearly. His account is indebted to Aristotle's discussion of pity (*eleos*) in the *Rhetoric*, in which—in Hobbes's translation from *A Briefe of the Art of Rhetorique* (1637)—Aristotle defines "Pitty, or Compassion" as "a perturbation of the mind, arising from the apprehension of hurt, or trouble to another that doth not deserve it, and which he thinkes may happen to himselfe or his."[109] Cavendish differed from Hobbes's Aristotelian account in suggesting that "Pitty, or Compassion" was not an inward "perturbation" but an orderly, organizing motion, with the potential to calm the emotional distresses of others. The Aristotelian account concludes with the observation that "all that men fear in regard to themselves excites their pity when others are the victims."[110] Given exposure to an object of distress, according to this logic, the greater the fear, the greater the pity. As Joseph Butler put it in his sermon "Upon Compassion," which offered perhaps the most detailed attempt to refute Hobbes's account of pity, "Thus Fear and Compassion are the same Idea, and a fearful and a compassionate Man the same Character."[111]

Barrow would not concede to Hobbes the primacy of fear, nor would he concede the authority of Aristotle. After inveighing against the "monstrous paradox" of Hobbism, Barrow writes, "*Aristotle* himself . . . affirmeth the contrary, that all men are friends, and disposed to entertain friendly correspondence with one another." For Barrow, charity is "genuine meekness," but also "true fortitude," the antithesis of fearfulness or weakness.[112] In arguing that "pity and benignity . . . are manifestly discernible in all, but most powerfull and vigorous in the best natures," Barrow counters Hobbes's claim that "the best men have the least Pitty"—although it should be pointed out that Hobbes did not make this as an absolute claim; it applied specifically in the case of "Calamity arriving from great wickedness." Barrow's position on pity was not merely analytical, or covertly critical, but overtly positive. For his valorization of pity Barrow had an important precedent in Descartes, who defined pity in the *Passions de l'âme* less in terms of the self and who claimed that "those who are the most generous and strong-minded, in that they fear no evil for themselves and hold themselves to be beyond the power of fortune, are not free from compassion when they see the infirmities of other men and hear their complaints. For it is a part of generosity to have good will towards everyone." The most generous soul "has the satisfaction of thinking that it is doing its duty in feeling compassion [compatit] for those afflicted."[113] In his *Natural History of the Passions* (1674), Walter Charleton draws heavily on Descartes when discussing "*Pity* or *Commiseration*"; he likens "the *Grief* of . . . *Heroick Commiseration*" to "that which Tragical cases represented in a Theatre produce," asserts that it gives the soul "the satisfaction of thinking that she doth her duty in sympathizing with the afflicted," and praises it only in "men of the most *generous* and Heroick spirits" with "brave resolutions, and habitual magnanimity." The example of the theater, as we saw in the previous chapter, also informed Browne's positive view of human sympathy—and, as we shall see in chapter 4, it assumed even greater significance in Milton's representation of sympathy in *Paradise Lost*. Yet, in supporting Descartes's account of compassion, Charleton did not simply reject Hobbes's, and here we can gain a more concrete sense of the limitations of a history of sympathy in which Hobbes is seen as coming under attack from a unified opposition. Charleton goes on to formulate an account of sympathy that synthesizes those of Descartes and Hobbes. "Manifest it is . . . , that in *some*," Charleton writes, "*Commiseration* is nothing but imagination of future Calamity to our selves, proceeding from the sense of another mans calamity; as it is defined by Mr *Hobbs*," whereas, "in *others*, a species of *Grief*, mixt with *Love* or *Benevolence* toward those whom we observe to suffer under some evil, which we think they have not deserved; as it is defined by *Monsieur des Cartes*."[114] Mediating between his two authorities, Charleton describes sympathy as a complex and variable negotiation between the self and others.

Like Digby—and unlike Cavendish—Charleton, as he explained, wrote of the passions primarily not "as a Moral Philosopher, but . . . as a *Natural* one conversant in *Pathology*." He accordingly rejected Descartes's location of the soul in "so incommodious a closet of the brain, as the *Glandula Pinealis*" and praised the mapping of the "plenty and singular contexture of nerves" by "*Dr. Willis*" and "the most accurate of our Modern Anatomists."[115] Charleton's neurophysiological approach to the passions contributed to the development of "the man of feeling" as well as Barrow's theological approach. Conceiving of sympathy as a distinctly human impulse, "implanted" by God, Barrow split apart the old Greek dyad sympathy-antipathy intact in Cavendish's philosophical system. Sympathy has become in his writing the basis of a *moral* worldview. Unlike Cavendish, Barrow expresses no anxiety or doubt about the pervasiveness and permanence of sympathetic bonds. Whereas for Cavendish conflict, faction, and war threaten to "Dissolve Natural Affections," for Barrow the "bands" of affection are "indissoluble." Of nature he goes on to assert definitively, "with indissoluble bands of mutuall sympathy she hath concatenated our fortunes, and affections together."[116] Antitypes of the "more sacred bands" between Christ and humanity, those between persons partake of his "miraculous power."[117] This "concatenation" is not Digby's chain of being; Barrow, elevating the "affections," describes a space different in kind from Digby's syllogistic universe.

This is not to say that logos has no place in Barrow's system. "The slightest argument, the most simple and unpolished oration, issuing from the mouth of a friend," Barrow writes in one of his many very polished sermons, "is wonderfully more prevalent, than the strongest demonstration, than the most powerful eloquence of an enemy. For obliging usage and courteous speech unlock the affections, and by them insinuate into the reason of men."[118] Leveling the classical hierarchy of reason and emotion, Barrow celebrates what Cavendish calls "natural oratory"—with a strong Christian undertone. Sympathetic words foster sympathetic bonds. For Barrow true rhetoric is "the language of charity," and "charity doth enlarge our minds beyond private considerations, conferring on them an universal interest, and reducing all the world within the verge of their affectionate care; so that a mans self is a very small and inconsiderable portion of his regard."[119] Barrow's formulation reminds us of how large and considerable a portion of Cavendish's regard her self was. In a world without charity, she retreated into her "private considerations"; at times they were, she felt, all she had.

Whiggishly conceived, the history of sympathy was on the side of Barrow, rather than on the side of Cavendish, but to leave her out of that history, who feared she would be left out of all histories, is ultimately to simplify it. In responding affirmatively to the question "Does Cavendish matter?" Lisa Sarasohn has suggested that Cavendish created "her own scientific revolution."[120] In arguing for her place not only in the history of science but also in the histories of sympathy and sensibility, I have made a further claim for Cavendish's significance. Like

Charleton's, but to a considerably greater degree, Cavendish's account of sympathy importantly complicates and challenges the idea of a monolithic anti-Hobbesianism giving rise to a univocal culture of sensibility. Cavendish struggled to generalize and to naturalize her ideal of sympathetic sociability. If the "egoistic psychology" that she developed partly in response to that struggle was unique to her, the struggle itself was not. The problem of sympathy that emerges with such frequency and intensity in her writing—the problem of self versus others, of others versus intimates—was to concern and confound theorists for the next century.

3

MILTON AND THE LINK OF NATURE

This chapter and the next address the various and complex ways in which John Milton (1608–1674) conceived and represented sympathy from his Cambridge orations in the 1620s to the second edition of *Paradise Lost* in 1674.[1] I see Milton, like Digby and Cavendish, as taking part in a broad intellectual conversation in the mid-century about sympathy; for him, as for them, sympathy was a crucial and controversial concern, a force to be reckoned with. Given the extraordinary breadth of his reading and the extraordinary range of his writing, constituting altogether a staggeringly extensive and intensive engagement with a diversity of ancients and moderns, Milton occupies not only a significant place in Anglo-American literary and intellectual history but also a central place in the more integrative history of sympathy for which I have been making a case. In the specific historiographic dead zone that is the seventeenth century, Milton's writing about sympathy was particularly vital.

In book 10 of *Paradise Lost*, Milton has Sin appeal to the idea of occult "sympathy" to account for her distant interaction with, and attraction to, Satan after the Fall. Commenting on this passage in the mid-eighteenth century, Robert Thyer sounded the usual attack but defended poetic license against philosophical error: "The modern philosopher may perhaps take offense at this now exploded notion, but every friend to the Muses will, I doubt not, pardon it for the sake of that fine strain of poetry, which it has given the poet an opportunity of introducing in the following description."[2] In the sequestered domain of the Muses, "sympathy" was not an "empty name" but a melodious one. Yet in associating sympathy with the epic's anti-Trinity, Milton was, if not "exploding" it, exploring it cautiously and critically. The mechanical philosophy, as we have seen, held out the promise of an intelligible *res* behind what Digby and other writers on sympathy considered a corrupt *verbum*. Milton was not clearly of "this

Mechanizing Humour," as Ralph Cudworth put it, but he shared with the mechanists a commitment to coming to terms with the occult, rather than simply
repudiating it.[3] Over the course of his career, Milton approached sympathy in a
number of ways and from a number of angles—poetic, theological, cosmological, natural historical, and moral philosophical—ultimately producing what
Geoffrey Hartman has called the "greatest vision in English of a sympathetic
universe."[4] But Milton's treatment of sympathy, I argue, was not only variable
but also deeply ambivalent. From a wider perspective, it serves to suggest and to
support the idea that, among the mid-century intellectual elite, there was a
broad crisis of coherence on the level of the whole. As the cases of Digby and
Cavendish have further shown, different views of the world were in doubt and
in flux, and Milton's worldview, as much as that of any of his intellectual
contemporaries, was very much his own. This chapter analyzes Milton's varied
responses to the problem of coherence, and the next suggests his solution.

I begin this chapter with the representation of cosmic sympathy in Milton's
second prolusion and show that he characterizes it as an original condition of
things and also as a no longer present one. This diachronic conception of
sympathy anticipates that in *Paradise Lost.* The young Milton wavers between
fantasizing a return to a prefallen state of sympathetic connectedness and recognizing that such a return can be no more than a fantasy. I observe a similar
oscillation in Milton's self-declaratory early poem *On the Morning of Christ's
Nativity,* in which the speaker imagines a kind of running back to the golden
age only to come to terms with the fact that a fully sympathetic universe will not
exist again until the end of time. As for Cavendish, so for Milton sympathy was
a matter not only of definition and investigation but also of imagination and
desire, the world not only as it had been and was but also as it could be and was
wished to be. In a brief discussion of *Il Penseroso,* I demonstrate that Milton
associated the idea of cosmic sympathy not only with the Ciceronian and
Pythagorean traditions evoked in the prolusion but also with Hermetic tradition—an association that over time Milton would set in an increasingly negative
light. In the next section I analyze the philosophical argument of Milton's first
divorce tract, *The Doctrine and Discipline of Divorce* (1643, 2nd ed. 1644).
Attempting to justify a radically new position on divorce in the 1640s, Milton
shifted his attention from world harmony to social and domestic harmony,
developing a concept of consent that went far beyond "compliance" and
"concurrence" (*OED* 1).[5] Having imagined the "true consent" of the world in *Il
Penseroso,* Milton reconceived it in the microcosm of the modern home; there
could be "no true marriage," he wrote emphatically in *Tetrachordon* (1645),
"without a true consent" (*CPW,* 2:610).[6] The reliance of Milton's argument in

the *Doctrine* on the idea of a sympathetic macrocosm, I suggest, leads to the sense of overreaching that I observe in the prolusion and the *Nativity Ode*. In what amounts to a gesture of bad faith, he hangs his vision of domestic consent on a golden chain whose existence he cannot rationalize. The result, as in the prolusion, is rhetorical dissonance; the philosophy of world harmony becomes a rhetoric of world harmony, a verbal tetrachord. The "instability," both rhetorical and conceptual, of Milton's divorce tracts has been observed before; my claim is that this instability is largely produced by the tension between competing concepts of sympathy.[7]

In the next section of the chapter I turn to Milton's representation of a sympathetic universe in *Paradise Lost*. The world before the Fall, in his poetic cosmology, is vitally interactive and interconnected. As Milton proceeds from the creation of the world to the creation of Adam and Eve, he suggests that sympathy is as much a principle of human nature as it is of nature as a whole. In the following section, I examine Milton's representation of human sympathy before the Fall. Adam and Eve participate in a cosmic network; they are intimately connected to each other as all the parts of the world are intimately connected. Yet, as Milton acknowledges and negotiates the claims of likeness and difference in his poetic cosmos, his representation of human sympathy becomes challengingly complex. I show that, beginning with a surprising echo in book 4 of *Paradise Lost*, Milton's elevation of "love and sympathy" in the divorce tract is apparently reversed in the epic. When Eve, associated with Ovid's Narcissus, sympathizes with her own reflection, Milton's divine principle of connection begins to seem disturbingly unstable and even deviant. Eve is revealed, in effect, as the ancestral mother of Margaret Cavendish, fixated on the sympathetic self.[8] I resolve the tension in Milton's account of sympathy in book 4 by suggesting that he ultimately conceives it as an attractive force independent of reason that must serve reason—so as not to serve sin.

I highlight in the next section the demonic appropriation and degradation of sympathy in book 10. I argue that the centrality of the concept in occultist philosophy, as represented by Milton's "Buckinghamshire neighbour" Robert Fludd, forces the term itself to the margins of Miltonic thought.[9] In the early decades of the seventeenth century, as we saw in the first chapter, Fludd described a sympathetic worldview painstakingly and defended it passionately, aligning himself with "the deepe Philosophers and Physicians," like Paracelsus, "which have been conversant in the Mysteries of God and nature."[10] For his critics, Fludd represented a mode of philosophizing inimical to reason as well as to religion, but one that, as the substance and detail of the critiques suggest, could not be dismissed out of hand. For Milton, the claim to be "conversant" with God's secrets implied a dangerous presumption. That Milton himself engaged with Fludd's philosophy is a hypothesis that has been much weighed since Denis Saurat advanced it in the 1920s.[11] Bringing to light an unacknowledged borrowing of Fludd in Patrick Hume's *Annotations on Milton's Paradise Lost* (1695), I do not make my own case for (or against) influence here but rather use Fludd as a principal guide to a complex set of beliefs that Milton was calling into question.[12] If Milton embraced the mystical speculation of "thrice-great Hermes" and others alongside his "Penseroso"—and Fludd—in the 1630s, on the evidence of books 9 and 10 his relationship to it had become strongly critical by the 1660s. The occult philosophy of sympathy provided Milton, as it did Digby, with an opportunity for rationalist critique and revision. Milton aimed to sever the tie between sympathy and magic in the interest of reason and freedom.

In the "notes . . . tragic" of book 9, the focus of the final section, I argue that Milton raised the contemporary critique of occultism to a climactic pitch by making sympathy the very cause of the Fall.[13] Our appreciation of his critique is to a significant extent retrospective; the case of Satan, Sin, and Death after the Fall enables us more clearly and fully to comprehend Adam's sin at the Fall. Like Sin one book later, Adam acts on a sympathetic attraction to his kind— with catastrophic consequences. In a devastating irony, Adam's sympathy with Eve destroys the sympathy of the world. If in the *Doctrine* Milton strategically muted the difference between the postlapsarian and prelapsarian worlds, in *Paradise Lost* the Fall is revealed to be the "great caesura" of world history, one that disrupts and irrevocably changes the order of things.[14] If Cavendish understood nature primarily in terms of variety, Milton did so primarily in terms of change. In ascribing the Fall to sympathy, I suggest, Milton was exposing the dark theological implications of a philosophical principle that ran the risk of diminishing, even displacing, God. In books 9 and 10 Milton sets the power of sympathy against the omnipotence of God as well as against the good of reason and the spirit of love. Adam errs in reducing his spiritual connection to Eve to a purely physical connection and in redescribing a voluntary connection as a necessary one. Like iron to the lodestone, Adam's heart is, as he claims, unavoidably drawn to Eve's. The mindful and heartfelt sympathy that Adam and Eve enjoy before the Fall becomes a mystical, deterministic force that overcomes will and reason. Adam and Eve's "mortal tast" not only brings death "into the World" but also in some sense brings about the death of the world (1.2, 3). To the urgent question raised again and again in the mid-seventeenth century about the nature and structure of the universe Milton provided a clear and indelible poetic response: the sympathy binding all things together in harmony was once, but is no more.

"THIS UNIVERSAL CONCORD"

In his second prolusion, *De Sphaerarum Concentu*, composed in the mid to late 1620s, Milton chose Pythagoras as his muse, both because Pythagoras imagined the world poetically and because he was himself "a true Poem" (2:890). Milton argues that Pythagoras conceived of the harmony of the spheres as a figure of speech, a way of describing "the close interrelation of the orbs [amicissimos orbium complexus]" (1:235). Plato's version of this Pythagorean allegory, which Milton echoed in *Arcades*, showed a harmonious world order that Homer had troped before both: "Homer moreover used the remarkable and apt metaphor of the golden chain suspended by Jove from heaven to represent this universal concord and sweet union of all things [hanc . . . conspirationem rerum universam, & consensum amabilem] which Pythagoras poetically figures as harmony" (1:236). Concent—like concatenation, as we saw with Digby—figures consent.

In the prolusion Milton looks back to the deep structure of Cicero's Pythagoreanism, the idea of world harmony that, in *De natura deorum*, unites Stoics, Epicureans, and Academics alike. In book 2, Balbus expounds Stoic theology, treating the fact of cosmic consent as proof of divine regulation:

> Again, consider the sympathetic agreement, interconnexion and affinity of things [rerum consentiens conspirans continuata cognatio]: whom will this not compel to approve the truth of what I say? Would it be possible . . . for the tides to flow and ebb in the seas and straits with the rising and setting of the moon, or for the different courses of the stars to be maintained by the one revolution of the entire sky? These processes and this musical harmony of all the parts of the world [Haec . . . omnibus inter se concinentibus mundi partibus profecto] assuredly could not go on were they not maintained in unison by a single divine and all-pervading spirit.[15]

In the next book Cotta voices the Academic opposition, approving the basic idea of "sympathetic agreement" but attributing it to nature rather than to divine *pneuma*:

> I fully agreed with the part of your discourse that dealt with nature's punctual regularity [convenientia consensuque naturae], and what you termed its concordant interconnexion and correlation [cognatione continuata conspirare]; but I could not accept your assertion that this could not have come about were it not held together by a single divine breath. On the contrary, the system's coherence and persistence is due to nature's forces and not to divine power; she does possess that "concord" (the Greek term is *sympatheia*) of

which you spoke [iste . . . consensus, quam sumpatheian Graeci vocant], but the greater this is as a spontaneous growth, the less possible is it to suppose that it was created by divine reason.[16]

Through Balbus and Cotta, Cicero implicitly but insistently refutes Aristotle's anti-Pythagoreanism, embracing the idea of universal "concord." In his magisterial study of this cosmic theme, *Classical and Christian Ideas of World Harmony*, Spitzer refers to the proliferation of complex words formed from the prefix *con-* as a "linguistic topos," "'symphonic clusters' . . . insisting, by means of the prefix, on a theme."[17] As if miming the *copia verborum* he sees as characteristic of the Roman philosophical style—as opposed to the Greek preference for "*one* firmly established, circumscribed term at a time"—Spitzer piles up terms for this phenomenon: "'prefixal leitmotivs,'" "the anaphoral *co-*," "the *consonare-harmonia topos*," "the 'prefix of concord.'"[18] Spitzer's variations follow the relative emphasis he places on style and theme, but his larger point is that, starting with Cicero, the two are deeply interfused. When Milton refers to the sympathy of the cosmos as "complexus," "conspiratio," and "consensus," putting the latter two in direct apposition, he makes the Ciceronian topos his own.

After emphasizing the poetic virtue of Pythagoras's idea, Milton goes on in the prolusion to suggest that the blinding and deafening produced by sin should not lead us to conclude, as Aristotle did, that there never was a music of the spheres. It is conceivable that, recognizing his consummate virtue, the gods thought Pythagoras worthy "to partake of the fellowship [consortio] of heaven," "to share the most secret mysteries of nature" (1:238), and so to hear the heavenly chime. In "consortio" Milton punningly unites the ideas of company and symphony. That Pythagoras "alone among men" (1:238) could hear the harmony of the spheres makes him a prototype of the "one just man" of *Paradise Lost* (11.818), anticipating Abdiel, Enoch, and Noah. By his theft of fire, which set in motion a pagan fall, Prometheus introduced sin into the world, putting the music of the spheres out of our range. Milton's suggestion here that a sympathetic, or symphonic, universe is a *prelapsarian* reality would come to assume quasi-doctrinal status. When he appropriates Homer's figure at the end of book 2 of *Paradise Lost*, where the "pendent world" is shown "hanging in a golden chain" (1052, 1051), Milton does so in part to suggest that the sympathetic structure of the world remains intact.

At the end of *De Sphaerarum Concentu*, Milton fantasizes a return to the golden past. "But if our souls were pure, chaste, and white as snow, as was Pythagoras' of old," he speculates, "then indeed our ears would ring and be filled with that exquisite music of the stars in their orbits; then would all things turn back to the Age of Gold, and we ourselves, free from every grief, would pass our lives in a blessed peace which even the gods might envy" (1:239). The mood of Milton's conditional sentence is optative, and by the end of it he seems to have got carried away, as if what might be called the paradise principle has triumphed over the reality principle. Immediately after looking up to the gods, he changes course and perorates abruptly: "At this point time cuts me short in mid career, and luckily too, for I am afraid that by my confused and unmelodious style I have been all this while offending that very harmony of which I speak, and have myself been an obstacle to your hearing it. And so I have done" (1:239). Like a mirage, Milton's vision of timeless primeval perfection vanishes with a sudden glance at the clock; Atropos succeeds Saturn. Milton circles back to where he began, "with open hand, as we say, and rhetorical exuberance" (1:235). His affected modesty topos reverses the narrative thrust of the oration, turning the harmony of the spheres back into a trope, and a rather mechanical one.[19]

This movement of overreaching and hasty retreat is repeated in the elegiac climax of *On the Morning of Christ's Nativity* (composed in 1629), where, in the familiar idiom of world harmony, the poet imagines the Incarnation as a return to the golden age: "For if such holy Song / Enwrap our fancy long, / Time will run back, and fetch the age of gold" (133–135).[20] Ten lines later, the poet catches himself, forcing a dramatic peripety: "But wisest Fate says no, / This must not yet be so" (149–150). Looking back, Milton must instead look ahead; Christ's sympathizing of the cosmos will not be complete until the end of time, "then at last" (165). The "full consort" he imagines in the past is still only partial (132). The prolusion and the *Nativity Ode* both register, I would like to suggest, an ambivalence about the idea of cosmic sympathy—on one hand, a powerful desire to recover a past ideal and, on the other, a rational doubt about the immediate prospect of recovery.[21] Whereas this doubt darkens Milton's portrait of Prometheus in the prolusion, in *Ad Patrem*, composed in the early 1630s, Milton suggests that poetry "retain[s] sacred traces of Promethean fire" (20), as if it could make time run back.

Up to this point I have associated Milton's early idea of cosmic sympathy with the worldviews of Pythagoras and Cicero. That Milton conceived this idea at least in part in Stoic terms is indirectly supported by his mention of two works in *Of Education* (1644): "*Seneca*s naturall questions" and Manilius's *Astronomica* (2:390, 395–396). Seneca maintains against the atomists that "effort can never exist in a body unless the body is held together by unity, since the components need to work in harmony [*consentire*] and to assemble their strength for tension."[22] Manilius's vision of cosmic sympathy, unfolded in a cosmic poem, is especially resonant with Milton's epic in mind. The poet promises to sing "how the entire universe is alive in the mutual concord [alterno consensu] of its elements and is driven by the pulse of reason, since a single spirit [spiritus unus] dwells in all its parts and, speeding through all things, nourishes the world and shapes it like a living creature."[23] Given, however, that in *Of Education* Milton also names Theophrastus, Pliny, and Columella—all important ancient sources for speculation on sympathy and antipathy—we should think of Milton as registering the wide diffusion of sympathy in classical thought rather than associate him exclusively with a single school.[24]

It is clear, indeed, from *Il Penseroso*, likely written in the early 1630s, that the young poet's interest in the "lovely consent [consensus amabilis]" of all things intersected with a more mystical tradition. His lucubrating speaker gives priority to Hermes Trismegistus over Plato:

> Or let my Lamp at midnight hour,
> Be seen in som high lonely Towr,
> Where I may oft out-watch the *Bear*,
> With thrice great *Hermes*, or unsphear
> The spirit of *Plato* to unfold
> What Worlds, or what vast Regions hold
> The immortal mind that hath forsook
> Her mansion in this fleshly nook:
> And of those *Daemons* that are found
> In fire, air, flood, or under ground,
> Whose power hath a true consent
> With Planet, or with Element.
>
> (85–96)

This passage has been frequently cited as evidence of Milton's sympathies with Hermetic tradition.[25] For Hill, the reference to Hermes here, like that in Milton's Cambridge composition *De Idea Platonica*, suggests that Milton "seems to have possessed a copy of the Hermetic writings."[26] Frances Yates hears "a Brunian ring" in these lines, which "brilliantly suggest the atmosphere of the Hermetic trance, when the immortal mind forsakes the body, and religiously consorts with demons, that is to say, gains the experience which gives it miraculous or magical powers."[27] For Thomas M. Greene, *Il Penseroso* represents a kind of Hermetic wish fulfillment: "Whereas Spenser seems genuinely to have been frightened by sorcery, it is clear that Milton was tempted by the myth of the magus and fantasized becoming one. . . . The 'unsphering' of Plato to learn hermetic secrets from his spirit is followed by the invocation of demons (not necessarily evil) whose power the speaker would control through the 'consent,' the harmony of sympathies, binding the cosmos with the four elements."[28] In Greene's paraphrase the speaker, a version of Milton himself, becomes in effect the reincarnation of Prospero. Greene associates Milton's Hermeticism with a "youthful . . . Orphism" that he argues disappears in the mid-1640s.[29] Hill makes a case for a Hermetic influence throughout Milton's career. I would argue, combining the two positions, that the influence of "Hermetic" mysticism becomes increasingly negative in Milton's writing. The *"Daemons"* of *Il Penseroso* "Whose power hath a true consent / With Planet, or with Element" are, as Greene rightly notes, "not necessarily evil," but so long as they remained speculative, they could not be proved necessarily good; speculation and conjuration were always linked in Milton's mind. That ever-crucial Miltonic "or," splitting the line in two, separating the planets from the elements, leaves the matter of "true consent" open to what Belial in *Paradise Lost* calls "Ominous conjecture" (2.123), with which it would be associated for the rest of Milton's career.[30]

LOVE AND SYMPATHY

In the letter prefaced to *The Doctrine and Discipline of Divorce*, Milton links the occasion of his writing to the recent formation of the Westminster Assembly, the "select Assembly" called by Parliament in the early summer of 1643 to help oversee the restructuring of the church. The title page of the first edition, which appeared anonymously around the first of August, refers to the Assembly's mission as nothing less than a "Reformation intended," a phrase that, in the light of what follows, seems to refer as much to Milton's mission as to the Assembly's. Milton undertakes a daring reform both within the church and far beyond it, from hearth to heart, advancing a radically new exegetical position with far-reaching philosophical consequences. It is no wonder, then, that the divorce tracts have given us so many Miltons — Milton the jilted husband, Milton the social reformer, Milton the protonovelist, the monist, the dualist, the prude, the libertine. Behind all of these stands Milton the rhetorician, the writer-strategist whose "reformation intended" is carried forward by the form of his argument. Milton refers to "Callicles the Rhetorician" and "Demetrius the Rhetorician" in the second edition of the *Doctrine*, joining Socrates in refuting the former's subordination of *physis* to *nomos*. Plato becomes one authority among many enlisted to shore up Milton's polemical position, which establishes nature as a sacrosanct first principle against the belated and extraneous mystifications of custom.

In emphasizing this Milton, I do not mean to imply that the rhetoric or rhetorical strategies of the divorce tracts have gone unnoticed; on the contrary, sensitive readings of his modes of argumentation — those of Lana Cable, Stanley

Fish, and James Turner, in particular—have sharpened our understanding of just how adroit Milton's left hand seems to have been.[31] But I do think that once the *Doctrine* is set in a wider philosophical context the main argument begins to seem more and more contingent. Milton's doctrine of divorce relies on an ad hoc theory of nature ostensibly predicated on a worldview that, by the mid-1640s, the evidence of his early poetry suggests he had abandoned, if indeed he ever maintained it at all. The natural world he evokes, "without enchantment," as he promises in his preface (2:241), seems closer to Cicero, to Pliny, and even to Spenser than to the author of *Lycidas*. Milton describes the world of the *Doctrine* most explicitly while arguing that prohibiting divorce goes against nature: "There is indeed a twofold Seminary or stock in nature, from whence are deriv'd the issues of love and hatred distinctly flowing through the whole masse of created things, and that Gods doing ever is to bring the due likenesses and harmonies of his workes together" (2:272). This is the Garden of Adonis writ large, stretched out from pole to pole, but it is also the ancient dyadic cosmos in miniature. At the same time, Milton works to Christianize sympathy here by proclaiming its divine origin; throughout the created universe, like is drawn to like, because God weds them together.

In a note on this passage in the Yale edition of the *Doctrine*, Ernest Sirluck helpfully refers to book 20 of Pliny's encyclopedic *Natural History* (2:272n). I cite the proem in Philemon Holland's translation:

> For in the pursute and discourse of this argument we shall take occasion to enter into a large field as touching the peace and war in Nature; we shall handle (I say) a deep secret, even the naturall hatred and enmitie of dumbe, deafe, and senselesse creatures. And verily, the main point of this theame, and which may ravish us to a greater wonder & admiration of the thing, lieth herin, That this mutuall affection, which the Greeks call sympathie, whereupon the frame of this world dependeth, and whereby the course of all things doth stand, tendeth to the use and benefit of man alone. For to what end else is it, that the element of Water quencheth fire? For what purpose doth the Sun suck and drink up the water, as it were to coole his heat and allay his thirst? . . . But to leave the heaven and those celestiall Bodies in their majestie. What is the cause, that as the Magnet or loadstone draweth iron unto it so there is another stone abhorreth the same, and driveth iron from it? . . . Besides many other secrets in nature, as strange, yea and more miraculous. All which we purpose to reserve unto their severall places, and will speake of them in order.[32]

Pliny's categorizing logic aims to follow that of the cosmos he is describing, where all things exist "in suis locis." Milton, of course, does not set out to write a natural history of the world; his aim is to persuade, not to astonish, and his mode is to marshal quotations, not to catalogue marvels. But his argument rests on a similar premise, a similar dynamics, a similar Greek feeling for the world, which organizes "the whole masse of created things" according to first princi-ples, the sympathies and antipathies that constitute the binary order of nature.

The problem for a reader of Milton, even one who makes allowances for changes of mind over time, and for differences between genres and occasions of writing, is that the natural world of the early poetry seems so disenchanted that, propounding this "Greco-Roman" view of nature in the *Doctrine*, Milton begins to seem like the very enchanter he assures us he is not. The more his natural concept of sympathy can be seen to emerge primarily in response to the dictates of the rhetorical situation, the more it seems not a concept but a conceit, the child of Milton's own "*Penury* or *Loneliness* of the soul" (2:253). His ideal order of "*Love*" and "*Hate*," expounded to "dispell" the epidemic pain and suffering newly "crept into the best part of humane societie," could be, under the cover of its authoritative endorsements, nothing more than an old "spel" (2:241).

Milton's references to Demetrius and Callicles, added in the second edition of the *Doctrine*, can be seen to reflect a revisionary tactic aimed at releasing some of the pressure built up by his strenuous readings of Scripture, which, in apparently inverting the biblical typology articulated in his antiprelatical tracts, left him open to charges of hypocrisy. Milton broadens the base of his argument, focusing more on what Sirluck refers to as "general ideas: reason, nature, and Christian liberty" (2:150n). The brief example of Plato's *Gorgias* allows Milton to claim support for his argument from a remote and uncontested source. The rhetorical payoff is evident in his conclusive ergo: "If therfore divorce may be so natural, and that law and nature are not to goe contrary, then to forbid divorce compulsively, is not only against nature, but against law" (2:346). The subject of the *Doctrine*, divorce, would seem perforce to install a kind of dualism at its very core, but the tract ultimately reveals a monistic drive that provides crucial meta-physical support for the argument. This is not to say that the Milton of the *Doctrine* was a committed monist, but it is to suggest that he was a strategic one, adapting according to his rhetorical needs.[33] The logic of his complex condi-tional suggests a sort of monistic continuum, so that the apparent chiasmus in the sequence divorce-law-nature / divorce-nature-law is only apparent. The terms are syntactically fungible, because they are metaphysically coplanar. Over the course of the *Doctrine*, God enters into that sequence as a fourth term, para-doxically both its end and its beginning. "And that we may further see what a violent and cruell thing it is," Milton writes, "to force the continuing of those together, whom God and nature in the gentlest end of mariage never joyn'd, divers evils and extremities that follow upon such a compulsion shall here be set in view" (2:250). For the purposes of Milton's argument, "God and nature" functions as a hendiadys, the master trope of the *Doctrine* in large part because it enacts on a semantic and syntactic level the idea of unity in duality that underlies the larger argument. Against those crude dualists who predicate marriage and divorce on purely corporeal concerns, Milton grounds both in a unified nature, where body and spirit exist in harmony. By naturalizing divorce, he attempts to remove it from the realm of misguided moral judgment. If a man's affections are "meerly naturall," he cannot be found guilty for wanting a divorce from her whom his nature and—this is the key extension—"God and nature" resist. To convict him is to convict nature and the Spirit in nature, because both participate in the same cosmic network. That network, Milton explains, is regulated by sympathy and antipathy, "two prime statutes . . . to joyn . . . to that which is good and acceptable and friendly; and to turn aside and depart from what is disagreeable, displeasing and unlike" (2:345). The movements of "joyning" and "departing" together produce a higher state of order.

Throughout the *Doctrine* Milton articulates and rearticulates these "prime statutes," a phrase that, given his earlier references to the "statutes & edicts" of the Canon (2:238), reinforces his argument about natural law: Love and Hate, peace and discord, amity and enmity, conversation and "aversation," benevolence and malevolence, sympathy and antipathy. The reader encounters these terms again and again, but rarely as a pair. The positive term is repeatedly expanded by hendiadys. Milton enshrines "love and peace," a coupling that occurs six times, "love and amity," "love and sympathy." The verbal connection emblematizes a spiritual connectedness. "Conversation"—a keyword, as we have seen, for Cavendish as well—becomes Milton's master term for harmonious relation, one that, as Thomas Luxon has shown, goes to the very heart of his rethinking of marriage and divorce.[34] Of Milton's deployment of the term Donald M. Friedman justly writes, "It is typical of his usage to dissolve the boundaries between physical and intellectual interchange, while acknowledging their hypostatic union in the word itself."[35] When "conversation" first appears, in the Preface to the first book, it is itself expanded by an adjectival form of hendiadys, functioning as a kind of agglutinate base in much the same way as the word "nature": "For although God in the first ordaining of marriage, taught us to what end he did it, in words expresly implying the apt and cheerfull conversation of man with woman, to comfort and refresh him against the evill of solitary life, not mentioning the purpose of generation till afterwards" (2:235). The pair of modifiers "apt and cheerfull" glosses the key biblical term "meet," at the heart of the implied and, crucially for Milton's argument, nonprocreative definition of marriage in Genesis 2:18.[36] The phrase "expresly implying" is a revealing oxymoron; in it we see Milton's exegetical pressure at work, pressing a possible implication into a direct revelation. When he cites Genesis 2:18 in the second chapter, "the apt and cheerful conversation" becomes "a meet and happy conversation" (2:246), originating in the mind, "from whence must flow the acts of peace and love, a far more precious mixture then the quintessence of an excrement" (2:248). This comparison, putting the passions and their works on the same plane as reproductive seed, represents a typical unification of the physical and the spiritual. Milton's monistic drive here makes what could easily be dismissed as a proper Erasmian use of rhetorical *copia* — "a fit and matchable conversation" (2:239), "cheerfull and agreeable conversation" (2:248), "free and lightsome conversation" (2:273) — a formal correlative of his great chain of being.

In this light, Milton's "two prime statutes," an antonymic pair that does not unite by hendiadys, would seem to threaten to undermine his ontological scheme. He works hard to negate this apparent dualism, shifting his focus increasingly to the negative term, first named as *"antipathy"* (2:236). Having outlined his view of attractive and repulsive forces, Milton writes, "of the two this latter is the strongest, and most equal to be regarded: for although a man may often be unjust in seeking that which he loves, yet he can never be unjust or blamable in retiring from his endles trouble and distast. . . . Hate is of all things the mightiest divider, nay, is division it self" (2:345). Milton's rhetorical correction emphasizes the priority of hate; it is not a thing but a principle behind things. Milton strips away a level of ontological remove, bringing hate closer to God.

The preponderance of the negative term is graphically enacted in Milton's version of Plato's myth of the birth of Love, the second of what Annabel Patterson has called the *Doctrine*'s "micronarratives."[37] Denied a "meet help," the penurious and lonely man — given dual authority as a type by Plato and Moses — "cannot conceive and bring forth *Love*," and "Then enters *Hate*, not that Hate that sins, but that which onely is naturall dissatisfaction and the turning aside from a mistaken object" (2:253). Milton wants to make it clear that this Hate is natural antipathy, blameless and guiltless, "not that Hate that sins," but more a kind of natural tropism. Plato and Moses have effectively naturalized love, assimilating it to an anthropomorphic pattern of generation, and now Milton can complete their mythopoeic work by naturalizing hate. The work of the tract can be understood as an energetic attempt to persuade his audience that the negative statute is not, in fact, negative. It is "meerly naturall" and so not susceptible of moral judgment, a point that Milton makes again and again in a series of genitival phrases both associating the two — "an uncomplying discord of nature" (2:254), "the sleeping discords and enmities of nature"

(2:272), "the unreducible *antipathies* of nature" (2:342)—and emptying them out—"the faultless proprieties of nature" (2:237), "the reverend secret of nature" (2:270), "the fundamentall law book of nature" (2:272), "the immutable bent of nature" (2:328), "the radical and innocent affections of nature" (2:345), "those deep and serious regresses of nature" (2:346), "the guiltles instinct of nature" (2:346). Nature emerges by a kind of negative grammatology, in its hidden recesses inaccessible to temporal power and regulation and externally imposed moral categories. True society is a natural conversation, a mutual attraction, a turning toward, the "coequal & *homogeneal* fire" that Eros finds with his twin Anteros (2:255). The fallen lexicon necessarily moralizes both love and hate, but neither is anything more than what it is.

Milton's naturalization of hate—not a divisive feeling, nor a divider, but *division*—effectively entails a naturalization of divorce. That a mismatched couple should divorce "God and nature signifies and lectures to us not onely by those recited decrees, but ev'n by the first and last of all his visible works; when by his divorcing command the world first rose out of Chaos" (2:273). Again Milton looks beyond Scripture, "those recited decrees," in relation to which his argument seems more contingent, seeking the support of more incontrovertible evidence—here not in the works of Plato but in the visible works of God, joined with nature once again by hendiadys. Milton's argument runs as follows: just as God divorced the world from Chaos, because there existed a natural antipathy between them, so a man should divorce his wife if they do not sympathize with each other, which is no fault of his own but rather the result of an immutable natural bias. The existence of this deep incompatibility should not deject the husband; in fact, his act of divorce, merely a natural regulation, recreates him in the image of his maker. Divorce becomes not only nonblasphemous but also quasi-divine.

Milton revisits this analogy toward the end of the *Doctrine*, where divorce, "like a divine touch in one moment heals all; and like the word of God, in one instant hushes outrageous tempests into a sudden stilnesse and peacefull calm" (2:333). Evoking Matthew 8, Milton extends the medical theme introduced in the Preface, where he promised to "[undertake] the cure of an inveterate disease crept into the best part of humane societie" (2:241).[38] In a seeming paradox that ultimately has the effect of harmonizing his two "prime statutes," Milton makes divorce, the pious acting on antipathy, an act of sympathy; not itself tempestuous, it stills the storm and leads to what Milton calls "true concord" (2:332). Thus he opens up a complete vision of cosmic sympathy, where like things cleave to like, and unlike things are divorced from unlike, both processes producing peace, order, and harmony. Hate is in a preliminary state of Love, awaiting the touch, the speech act, that can bring it in line with the cosmic network. Divorce is yet again linked both to nature (climate) and to words (Logos). It is as if the original and originating rhetoric of God authorizes not only divorce, being a divorcive act, but also Milton's writing about divorce. The double simile enacts and reenacts in miniature the circulation of the sympathetic universe; like is joined to like both literally and figuratively. This is not simply a case of imitative form but also evidence for the larger participation of words in the vast network of things.

This ultimately "monistic" argument, that antipathy is really a prelude to sympathy, is a highlight in the overall argument. Milton sets it up in chapter 6, where, in a familiar refrain, he exalts "Love and Peace": "And it is a lesse breach of wedlock to part with wise and quiet consent betimes, then still to soile and profane that mystery of joy and union with a polluting sadnes and perpetuall distemper; for it is not the outward continuing of marriage that keeps whole that covnant, but whosoever does most according to peace and love, whether in mariage, or in divorce, he it is that breaks mariage lest" (2:258). Marriage and divorce, as understood by society, are merely formal arrangements; their truth is in nature, or as Milton puts it more forcibly at the beginning of his nomological argument, in the law "character'd in us by nature, of more antiquitie and deeper ground then mariage it selfe" (2:237). Antipathy need not create "distemper" so long as the mismatched spouse acts in the interest of his proper temperament. The divorce he must turn to society to formalize is already within him and within the world.

I have argued that Milton's argument for divorce is grounded in a sympathetic worldview that purges the act of any possible moral slant and proclaims it as not only natural but also divine. Such a premise, however, left Milton in a serious bind. His discomfort becomes explicit in one of the few extended statements of sympathetic philosophy in the *Doctrine*:

> And that there is a hidden efficacie of love and hatred in man as wel as in other kinds, not morall, but naturall, which though not alwayes in the choyce, yet in the successe of mariage wil ever be most predominant, besides daily experience, the author of *Ecclesiasticus* . . . acknowledges, 13.16. A *man*, saith he, *will cleave to his like*. But what might be the cause, whether each ones alotted *Genius* or proper Starre, or whether the supernall influence of Schemes and angular aspects or this elementall *Crasis* here below, whether all these jointly or singly meeting friendly, or unfriendly in either party, I dare not, with the men I am likest to clash, appear so much a Philosopher as to conjecture. (2:271)

In what has by this point already become a familiar move, Milton then shifts to a safe authority—in this case, Homer—far removed from the natural-philosophical debates of the seventeenth century. The last sentence, with its inverted syntax and complex coordination, eloquently proclaims its author's unwillingness to enter into a matter of high conjecture. It also provides the best insight into Milton's attitude toward the heavy freight carried by his argument. He will not commit to a specific causal link between individual dispositions and cosmic positions, but he does commit to a deterministic theory of human relations that would appear to contradict his generally voluntaristic theory of human action. Two people are drawn to, or away from, each other not because they choose to sympathize, or to antipathize, but because the cosmos mystically draws them one way or the other. Milton seems unwilling to leave such a formulation unqualified and unrationalized. Here is his reference to Homer: "The ancient proverb in *Homer* lesse abstruse intitles this worke of leading each like person to his like, peculiarly to God himselfe: which is plain anough also by his naming of a meet or like help in the first espousall instituted" (2:271–272). Milton moves from a more "abstruse" astrological position to a less mystical theological position, but in a sense he is simply trading determinisms, as we have seen Cavendish do.[39] He might well have felt more at ease attributing this claim to the Greek poet than explicitly making it himself.

In the *Doctrine* Milton arrives at the modern-sounding conclusion that spiritual incompatibility is a legitimate ground for divorce, but the radical nature of that conclusion at the time he asserted it necessitated a more comprehensive theory of human relations, and what better theory than one that derived its force and validity from an ancient and authoritative view of the world? The problem, however, was that by 1643 such a worldview was associated as much with Paracelsians and "Hermetic" philosophers as with Pliny and Homer. Milton's synthetic idea of sympathy might have been Heraclitean in spirit, insisting on "a harmony which comprehends strife and antagonism,"[40] but his divorcive view of creation was Paracelsian in emphasis: "The principle . . . of all generation," Paracelsus had written, "was Separation."[41] The word "sympathy" appears three times in the *Doctrine*, once each in *Colasterion* and *The Judgement of Martin Bucer*, and not at all in *Tetrachordon*. It may be no coincidence that Milton used so many different terms for sympathy and antipathy other than those two and that he resorted to creating his own post-Platonic myth to describe them. The nature relied on so heavily in the *Doctrine* has not suffered the "heavy change" mourned in *Lycidas* (37) and does not need the music celebrated in *Arcades* to "steddy" it (70). It is not the lascivious and sumptuously decked-out Nature "Pollute with sinful blame" from the *Nativity Ode* (40). It is, on the contrary, absolutely sinless and blameless, as Milton reminds the reader again and again.

As the Hymn in the *Nativity Ode* opens, Nature in deference to the incarnate Christ "[doffs] her gawdy trim, / With her great Master so to sympathize" (33–34), relying on a snowy rhetoric, "speeches fair" (36), to make herself presentable. But so deformed, she can redeem herself only through the superior sympathizing of Christ, who authorizes the intercession of "meek-eyd Peace"; the sympathetic economy is imperfect, requiring a divine supplement.[42] The only figure in Milton's early poetry who seems to support the view of nature advanced in the *Doctrine* is the Lady in *Comus*, who, answering her tempter's claim that she lives like one of "Natures bastards" (727), counters, "Impostor do not charge most innocent nature" (762). But when she threatens to respond to Comus's "gay Rhetorick" (790), alleging that should she try, "the uncontrouled worth / Of [her] pure cause would kindle [her] rap't spirits / To such a flame of sacred vehemence, / That dumb things would be mov'd to sympathize" (793–796), it is not at all clear that her words have the sympathetic power that, a decade or so later, Milton would claim for the divorcive Logos or, more to the point, even if they do, that nature could sympathize back.[43] When he calls on nature to express a floral sympathy with the drowned Lycidas, Milton's mourning speaker has little confidence that the call will be answered: "For so to interpose a little ease, / Let our frail thoughts dally with false surmise" (152–153). Milton raises the suggestion that universal sympathy may be no more than a "false surmise," produced by and in the service of our own psychological needs. Perhaps the prospect of a reformed and ideal civil order in the years to come moved Milton to a new faith in an old world. But it seems just as likely that he needed that world, which, with its tint of Catholicism and sorcery, he could only partially embrace, to make a new argument. That argument persuaded no one who could translate it into reality. Milton's most significant achievement in the *Doctrine* might well have been an unintended one: to move sympathy into the realm of moral philosophy.

THE BIRTH OF THE SYMPATHETIC UNIVERSE

By 1667, when the first edition of *Paradise Lost* appeared, Milton's faith in the world was much diminished, having turned inward, like the "Celestial light" that had become his only source of vision (3.51). For his sins of the previous decades, the argument for divorce among them, his blindness was widely accounted divine retribution; sneering references to "blind Milton" dot the annals of the early Restoration.[44] Milton interpreted his blindness differently.

The loss of his vision gave him new access to a higher visual power. Nothing less would allow him to tell the story of everything and everywhere, from beginning to end. Milton's suggestion in the second prolusion that universal sympathy was an original condition became in the epic a sublime depiction. In the astonishing variety of its features and effects, the poetry of the prelapsarian books of *Paradise Lost* produces and reinforces a sense of total sympathetic connectedness. In Eden, the birthplace of humankind, Milton found a natural domain where the idealizing argument of the divorce tracts could take root. Yet, as we shall see, he did not exactly transplant it there. Even before he narrates the catastrophe of the Fall in book 9, Milton casts a shadow of doubt on the status of sympathy as a primal fact. In this uncertainty we can sense his ongoing struggle to come to terms with sympathy as a principle and, above all, as a power, a force of attraction.

Before the Fall, Adam and Eve are shown to participate in an all-encompassing network, a sympathetic cosmos in which all things are vitally interactive. As in the second prolusion, Milton emphasizes the affinity between concent and consent:

> The Birds thir quire apply; aires, vernal aires,
> Breathing the smell of field and grove, attune
> The trembling leaves, while Universal *Pan*
> Knit with the *Graces* and the *Hours* in dance
> Led on th' Eternal Spring.
>
> (4.264–268)

Commenting on the meaning of "aires" here, Empson overgoes Milton's early close readers: "The airs attune the leaves because the air itself is as enlivening as an air; the trees and wild flowers that are smelt on the air match, as if they caused, as if they were caused by, the birds and leaves that are heard on the air; nature, because of a pun, becomes a single organism."[45] The poet's use of enjambment in this passage, emphasizing the key words of connection, "attune" and "Knit," reinforces the overall sense of organic unity. For Milton, "Universal *Pan*" functions as a figure for the all-embracing sympathy that defines prelapsarian reality and Adam and Eve's prelapsarian experience.

Of Milton's first couple Samuel Johnson writes, "The weakest of his agents are the highest and noblest human beings, the original parents of mankind; with whose actions the elements consented; on whose rectitude, or deviation of will, depended the state of terrestrial nature, and the condition of all the future inhabitants of the globe."[46] Johnson's description of this original sympathy subtly echoes Milton's own phrasing from *Il Penseroso*, the demons "whose power hath a true consent / With Planet, or with Element." Adam and Eve are in accord with the elements, and the elements are in accord with them. They are married not only to each other but also to the world. In the account of their wedding, Adam leads Eve to the nuptial bower, where the marriage ceremony continues. Everything beyond them participates in their wedded bliss:

> all Heav'n,
> And happie Constellations on that houre
> Shed thir selectest influence; the Earth
> Gave sign of gratulation, and each Hill;
> Joyous the Birds; fresh Gales and gentle Aires
> Whisper'd it to the Woods.
>
> (8.511–516)

These lines echo those in book 4, as the wedding energizes "Universal *Pan*." Milton primarily uses not enjambment but sound patterning here to convey the idea of total consent. He pairs "Heav'n" and "happie"; "selectest," "influence," and "sign"; "Gave" and "gratulation"; "Gales" and "gentle"; and, finally, "Whisper'd" and "Woods." Such phonemic schemes abound in the poem, of course, but in this instance they vividly enhance Milton's representation of a sympathetic whole consisting of underlying sympathetic parts, a cornucopian multiplicity of individual connections and affinities.

Having revealed the sympathetic universe in action in books 4 and 5, Milton proceeds to narrate its birth in book 7. His creation narrative opens in emphatically aural terms, so that concent and consent are not simply associated but, as it appears, causally connected.[47] Peace must prevail before the symphony of the world can strike up: "Silence, ye troubl'd waves, and thou Deep, peace, / Said then th' Omnific Word, your discord end" (7.216–217). With a circular sweep of golden compasses, the Logos initiates the reign of universal concord both physically and symbolically. The account of creation itself is particularly attuned to temperature:

> Thus God the Heav'n created, thus the Earth,
> Matter unform'd and void: Darkness profound
> Cover'd th' Abyss: but on the watrie calme
> His brooding wings the Spirit of God outspred,
> And vital vertue infus'd, and vital warmth
> Throughout the fluid Mass, but downward purg'd
> The black tartareous cold Infernal dregs
> Adverse to life: then founded, then conglob'd
> Like things to like, the rest to several place

Disparted, and between spun out the Air,
And Earth self ballanc't on her Center hung.

(7.232–242)

The relationship between hot and cold produces a kind of cosmogonic convection.[48] In the "conglobing" of "Like things to like," Milton represents divine "love," God's will to sympathize. No less prime is the negative statute, the "disparting" of things unlike, which leads to perfect terrestrial harmony. Here, in epitome, is the earlier argument for divorce, or rather its divine natural-philosophical justification: just as the disparting of unlike elements leads to cosmic balance, so the parting of "unmatchable societies" leads to civil or domestic balance. Antipathy is again folded into a larger sympathy.

Milton reinforces the sense of sympathy between creation and creator by emphasizing not only the responsiveness of particular "creatures" but also the instantaneity of the response. At God's command "*forthwith* Light / Ethereal, first of things, quintessence pure / Sprung from the Deep" (7.243–245); "*Immediately* the Mountains huge appeer" (7.285); the waters "*Hasted* with glad *precipitance*" (7.291); and "He *scarce* had said, when the bare Earth, till then / Desert and bare, unsightly, unadorn'd, / Brought forth the tender Grass" (7.313–315); "Then Herbs of every leaf, that *sudden* flour'd / Op'ning thir various colours" (7.317–318); "*Forthwith* the Sounds and Seas, each Creek and Bay / With Frie innumerable swarme" (7.399–400); "The Earth obey'd, and *strait* / Op'ning her fertile Woomb teem'd at a Birth / Innumerous living Creatures" (7.453–455); "*At once* came forth whatever creeps the ground" (7.475—my emphasis throughout). The infusion of "vital vertue" is strikingly evident in these sympathetic effects.[49] A quieter effect is achieved by the poet's repetition of the verb "conglobe": the waters "uprowld / As drops on dust conglobing from the drie" (7.291–292). Here creature sympathetically echoes creator. The shift from the transitive to the intransitive use of "conglobe" subtly conveys the idea that, having been "sympathized" by God, matter has itself become sympathetic.

As Milton's cosmogonic narrative proceeds, the association between sympathy and symphony is heightened. On the seventh day, the discord of the primordial surges is definitively answered by the sweet-sounding music of the celestial instruments, which "Temper'd soft Tunings, intermixt with Voice / Choral or Unison" (7.598–599).[50] This is not work but a kind of natural play, verging on emanation. Like "consort," "temper" is an extremely rich thematic keyword; both, according to Spitzer, point back to "an ancient semantic texture" that began to unravel into two distinct threads in the seventeenth century, "the ideas of the 'well-tempered mixture' and of the 'harmonious consonance,' which fuse into the

one all-embracing unit of the world harmony."[51] The various senses of "temper"
present a virtual diagram of a sympathetic cosmos, from its primary meaning—
"the due or proportionate mixture or combination of elements or qualities"—to its
secondary designations—"temperament" (*OED* 4), "climate" (6), and "temperature" (7). As a verb, it also takes on a specifically musical sense, "to tune, adjust the
pitch of" (15a), and by extension "to bring into harmony, attune" (16). Fully
tempered, the world is linked in harmony: "the Earth, the Aire / Resounded, . . . /
The Heav'ns and all the Constellations rung" (7.560–562). The phenomenon of
sympathetic resonance occurs here on a macrocosmic scale.

One book later we see the sympathetic union of like things translated into
the little world of man. God allows Adam to discover the order of nature for
himself:

> Among unequals what societie
> Can sort, what harmonie or true delight?
> Which must be mutual, in proportion due
> Giv'n and receiv'd; but in disparitie
> The one intense, the other still remiss
> Cannot well suite with either, but soon prove
> Tedious alike: Of fellowship I speak
> Such as I seek, fit to participate
> All rational delight, wherein the brute
> Cannot be human consort; they rejoyce
> Each with thir kinde, Lion with Lioness;
> So fitly them in pairs thou hast combin'd;
> Much less can Bird with Beast, or Fish with Fowle
> So well converse, nor with the Ox the Ape;
> Wors then can Man with Beast, and least of all.

$$(8.383–397)$$

Music tropes relation or "societie," but it is more than an "allegoria," as Fowler
refers to it.[52] Harmonious relation is itself, as Adam suggests, a distinct mode
of harmony, a special kind of music. The language of this passage is organized
around the word "consort." It begins with the aural pun "Can sort," reinforced
by "harmonie," and leads into an elegant musical progression:

> Can sort . . .
> Cannot well suite . . .
> Cannot be human consort . . . .

The tedium to which Adam refers, the product of mismatching, seems like a
prelapsarian version of the "continuall sorrow and perplexitie" that Milton

inveighs against and sets out to resolve in the *Doctrine*. Adam recognizes a disproportion in the chain of being, born not out of an oversight or error in the divine plan but out of his awareness of his own needs; God, in effect, staggers creation to allow Adam maximal "rational delight."

Although Adam realizes that such delight is not possible with the unreasoning creatures around him, with whom he happily converses in one sense but not in another, he is also aware that he is more like them than he is like God.[53] Adam's desire for "fellowship" is not errant or ungrateful but rational. In his appeal, Milton establishes a crucial connection between cosmic and human sympathy:

> Thou in thy self art perfet, and in thee
> Is no deficience found; not so is Man,
> But in degree, the cause of his desire
> By conversation with his like to help,
> Or solace his defects. No need that thou
> Shouldst propagat, already infinite;
> And through all numbers absolute, though One;
> But Man by number is to manifest
> His single imperfection, and beget
> Like of his like, his Image multipli'd,
> In unitie defective, which requires
> Collateral love, and deerest amitie.
> Thou in thy secresie although alone,
> Best with thyself accompanied, seek'st not
> Social communication, yet so pleas'd,
> Canst raise thy Creature to what highth thou wilt
> Of Union or Communion, deifi'd;
> I by conversing cannot these erect
> From prone, nor in thir wayes complacence find.

(8.415–433)

Conversation here becomes a virtual life-support system; without it man cannot find balance, his order within the cosmos, like the earth "on her center hung." Adam's ad hoc anthropology gives birth to a notion of *homo sympatheticus*. Unlike Adam here or Eve at the pool, God is "Best . . . accompanied" by Himself; He is perfectly consorted in His "secresie." But man requires "Like of his like." Humbly and piously, Adam expresses man's lower position, speaking in succession of "deficience," "defects," and "defective." A series of antiphonal words builds momentum toward the end of the passage, the prefix "co-" (Latin *cum*) chiming through "accompanied," "communication," "Communion,"

"conversing," and "complacence." This is Spitzer's "'prefix of concord,'" the
Ciceronian topos of world harmony extended into the human sphere.[54]

The harmony of humankind depends on "Collateral love, and deerest
amitie." Emphatically placed at the head of its line, "Collateral" primarily
denotes side by side (*OED* 1), but also more figuratively "accompanying" (2a)
and "corresponding" (2c), a typically Miltonic interfusion of physical and metaphysical senses. For the reader of the *Doctrine*, the phrase as a whole has a
familiar ring; it sounds like one of the many instances of hendiadys Milton had
used to express his "prime statute," sympathy by another name. Adam has understood that the lower species sympathize "Each with thir kinde" (8.393), and so
he seeks a consort of his own kind, one who reciprocates his love both in the
sense that she belongs to his kind and in the sense that, so belonging, she feels
as he feels. Only after the Fall does antipathy divide the kinds of nature from the
inside out. Adam's sympathy with Eve before the Fall constitutes an especially
privileged subset of the sympathy that unites all creation. The phrase "Collateral
love, and deerest amitie" is applied to them; the principle applies to all.

Yet unlike the pool in which Eve first discovers herself, to anticipate the
discussion of the next section of this chapter, Milton's representation of a
sympathetic universe before the Fall is not perfectly smooth. Before Adam
discovers his need for sympathy with another human being, he enters into an
apparently sympathetic relationship with the sun. As he recounts in his own
creation narrative, "I found me laid / In Balmie Sweat, which with his Beames
the Sun / Soon dri'd, and on the reaking moisture fed" (8.254–256). Puzzling
out this peculiar act of consumption, Hartman comments that "Milton wished
to emphasize the conjunction of highest and lowest. . . . The meridian sun
participates in creation like an animal tending its newborn."[55] Milton, in other
words, uses Adam's narrative initially to reinforce the sense of cosmic sympathy.
But, as the narrative proceeds, that sense is almost immediately complicated.
Adam's marvelous ability to designate whatever he sees by true names is set
against his inability to comprehend his true estate:

> Thou Sun, said I, faire Light,
> And thou enlight'nd Earth, so fresh and gay,
> Ye Hills and Dales, ye Rivers, Woods, and Plaines,
> And ye that live and move, fair Creatures, tell,
> Tell, if ye saw, how came I thus, how here?
> Not of my self; by some great Maker then,
> In goodness and in power praeeminent;
> Tell me, how may I know him, how adore,
> From whom I have that thus I move and live,

And feel that I am happier than I know.
While thus I call'd, and stray'd I knew not whither,
From where I first drew Aire, and first beheld
This happie Light, when answer none return'd,
On a green shadie Bank profuse of Flours
Pensive I sate me down.

(8.273–287)

Hartman contrasts these lines with Satan's at the beginning of book 4, where the fallen angel bitterly laments his new estate; Hartman's point is that the "same sun, shining to the same spot and seen as if for the first time, yields radically different responses."[56] And yet the final two and a half lines of Adam's speech, which Hartman does not cite, suggest a disturbing conjunction between Adam and the forces of hell, that "dungeon horrible" where, in a typically Miltonic etymological conceit, a combination of suspense, suspension, and pensiveness characterizes the experience of the fallen angels.[57] This cluster of terms, governing a wide variety of referents, conveys a sense of the pervasive fixity and paralysis that is a condition of God's punishment. The strongest echo in Adam's speech is of Sin's account of her mortal liaison with Satan: "Pensive here I sat / Alone, but long I sat not" (2.777–778). This state of metaphysical suspension, heightened by the enjambment of "Alone," is decidedly antisympathetic; it represents the mind isolated in itself. And, ironically, after Sin gives birth, Death brings her not society or sympathy but fierce antipathy, seizing her "in embraces forcible and foule" (2.793). The sun, by contrast, touches Adam with a benevolent lightness.

The participation that Hartman sees in the sun's feeding is, at least initially, one-way. In Adam's account of his first day, he tries to complete a sympathetic circuit that appears to break down in front of him. When he addresses himself to the sun, he gets no response: "answer none return'd." In his analysis of this passage Hartman jumps from the end of Adam's first question "to the synoptic and interanimating metaphor of 'Happy Light,'" leaving out the unresponsiveness that leaves Adam in suspense. "By insisting with great and literal power on his vision of a sympathetic cosmos," Hartman goes on to write, "Milton diverged significantly from the *Divine Weekes* of Du Bartas."[58] But how literal can Milton's insistence be if, in this crucial scene, nature can be seen to abandon Adam?[59] Indeed, returning to book 4, we find that some five hundred lines after celebrating the cosmic round of "Universal *Pan*," Milton effectively blanks him out: "In shadier Bower / More sacred and sequesterd, though but feignd, / *Pan* or *Silvanus* never slept, nor Nymph, / Nor *Faunus* haunted" (4.705–708). In an instant Pan is dismissed as pagan furniture, one pastoral deity among many.

And, ten lines later, having signified the sympathetic connectedness of the universe, the image of "all," he is reduced to a mere syllable, disappearing into the dark suggestiveness of *"Pandora"* (4.714). This instance registers the broader tension in the epic, and in Milton's work as a whole, between pagan and Christian traditions, but it can also be seen more specifically to suggest a discomfort with the pagan character and heritage of cosmic sympathy as an idea. Milton did not depict a sympathetic universe in bad faith, but I do think that we can detect some of the ambivalence about the cosmic idea that we have seen in his earlier writing even before what Satan refers to as "the hateful siege / Of contraries" (9.121–122). This ambivalence adds a significant dimension of complexity to Milton's representation of the sympathetic relationship between Adam and Eve.

SYMPATHY AND LOVE

The first conversation that Adam and Eve have in *Paradise Lost* is the sort of conversation that a fallen reader can imagine them having over and over again, as if playing on a looped tape. What do they have to talk about? Chiefly, it seems, the sole prohibition that God has given them, but talking also gives them a chance to reconfirm the perfection and mutuality of their love and the bliss accompanying it—that is, the deep sympathy they share. In book 4 Milton sets himself the complex task of representing Adam and Eve simultaneously as a couple and as two individuals. This double duty raises challenging questions about the nature of sympathy and its relation to the will. Foucault, we recall, argues that, in its power to assimilate, sympathy threatens to undo and to do away with all individuality. Milton, I suggest, was keenly aware of, and troubled by, this threat and labored to develop a conception of sympathy that took it into account and contained it. For him, sympathy existed as a force outside reason, but not inaccessible to it. The rational mind was capable of approving and disapproving the stirrings of sympathy and choosing to act on them accordingly. Milton shifted the focus of his concern from the individual's feeling or impulse of sympathy to his or her response to and management of it.

The complex matter of assimilation versus difference and differentiation is raised by Adam's first words. In the vocative mode, he exalts Eve: "Sole partner and sole part of all these joyes" (4.411)—an ingenious way of suggesting their mutual participation, the ideal balance of independence and interdependence they enjoy. The word "part" is part of "partner" just as Eve is part of Adam, both in the sense that they are spiritually connected and in the sense that she derives from a physical part of him, his rib. She is wholly his partner but part of the greater whole that is the couple; Adam cannot imagine joy without her, since although her creation entailed a physical deduction, it paradoxically filled, or fulfilled, a spiritual absence in him. Eve dutifully answers Adam in her own terms: "O thou for whom / And from whom I was formd flesh of thy flesh, / And without whom am to no end" (4.440–442). Eve's mode of expression is different from his; it is emphatically "prepositional," which has the effect of suggesting that she is a primarily relational being, defined or individuated in relation to Adam. She puts "for," metaphysical, before "from," physical, highlighting her connection to him. Eve then follows Adam in looking beyond their circuit of bliss to God, who has made it possible. And then, in a sort of prelude to the narrative that turns this first conversation in an entirely unexpected direction, Eve looks at herself: "I chiefly who enjoy / So farr the happier Lot, enjoying thee / Praeeminent by so much odds, while thou / Like consort to thy self canst nowhere find" (4.445–448). Here the poet plays "odds" against "like," "Lot" against "consort," bringing to the surface the etymon *sors*, lot or fate, behind that Miltonic keyword: "and what a solace," Milton writes in the *Doctrine*, "what a fit help such a consort would be through the whole life of a man" (2:250). Eve overvalues her happiness relative to Adam's by underestimating her worth. Although he may be superior in certain respects, they are made equal by their love, by the bliss they share, and by the harmonious life they lead together. In the terms of the divorce tracts, each is the other's perfect consort; they have cast their lots in life together, as the tragic drama of book 9 will make darkly apparent.[60]

Adam does not get the chance to correct Eve's imbalanced equation, but he does not need to, since the narrative she goes on to relate in effect enacts the correction, moving from modest self-regard to an informed mutuality. I cite the passage, which has received particularly intense critical attention, in full:

> That day I oft remember, when from sleep
> I first awak'd, and found my self repos'd
> Under a shade of flours, much wondring where
> And what I was, whence thither brought, and how.
> Not distant far from thence a murmuring sound
> Of waters issu'd from a Cave and spread
> Into a liquid Plain, then stood unmov'd
> Pure as th' expanse of Heav'n; I thither went
> With unexperienc't thought, and laid me downe
> On the green bank, to look into the cleer
> Smooth Lake, that to me seemd another Skie.
> As I bent down to look, just opposite,
> A Shape within the watry gleam appeard

Bending to look on me, I started back,
It started back, but pleas'd I soon returnd,
Pleas'd it returnd as soon with answering looks
Of sympathie and love; there I had fixt
Mine eyes till now, and pin'd with vain desire,
Had not a voice thus warnd me, What thou seest,
What there thou seest fair Creature is thy self,
With thee it came and goes: but follow me,
And I will bring thee where no shadow staies
Thy coming, and thy soft imbraces, hee
Whose image thou art, him thou shall enjoy
Inseparablie thine, to him shalt beare
Multitudes like thy self, and thence be call'd
Mother of human Race: what could I doe,
But follow strait, invisibly thus led?
Till I espi'd thee, fair indeed and tall,
Under a Platan, yet methought less faire,
Less winning soft, less amiablie mild,
Then that smooth watry image; back I turnd,
Thou following cryd'st aloud, Return faire *Eve*,
Whom fli'st thou? Whom thou fli'st, of him thou art,
His flesh, his bone; to give thee being I lent
Out of my side to thee, neerest my heart
Substantial Life, to have thee by my side
Henceforth an individual solace dear;
Part of my Soul I seek thee, and thee claim
My other half: with that thy gentle hand
Seisd mine, I yielded, and from that time see
How beauty is excelld by manly grace
And wisdom, which alone is truly fair.

$$(4.449\text{--}491)$$

Adam's phrase "Part of my Soul I seek thee," which Eve relates, chimes with the address that begins the frame conversation, "Sole partner and sole part of all these joyes." The echo, which is unremarkable, is part of the loop effect. But Eve's implication that she is now somehow "experienc't" relative to the figure in her first memory does have a significant formal correlative. Although Adam and Eve seem to say the same thing in the frame conversation, they say it differently; the mode of expression is personalized, individualized, as though there were two looped tapes rather than one. But in Eve's account of their first conversation, formal blurring takes on thematic significance. Her descriptions of her earliest self, like Adam's, are strongly objective, in the sense that she seems to figure herself as an object: "I . . . found my self repos'd," "I . . . laid me downe," as if she had yet to assimilate her incarnation.[61] Here, though, the reflexivity anticipates in grammatical terms the neo-Ovidian optical drama at the center of the passage.[62] Eve as later narrator is distinguished by her ability to distinguish. She uses a simile to set the scene, likening the body of water to "th' expanse of Heav'n" in terms of its purity; this act of figuration presupposes an awareness of difference ("a" is like, and therefore is not, "b"), but for the "unexperienc't" Eve, the lake "seemd another Skie." This is not a metaphor but a conflation, an errant identification.

The passage is full of formal repetitions denoting different kinds of identities and identifications. Reflection is figured in both visual and aural terms: "I started back" — "It started back," "pleas'd I soon returnd" — "Pleas'd it returnd as soon," "What thou seest" — "What there thou seest," "Whom fli'st thou?" — "Whom thou fli'st." Milton seems especially interested in the word "return" here, suggesting a fine distinction between the two senses of its prefix that serves only to highlight the loss of distinction leading Eve astray; "turning back" is the same as "turning again." Eve bends or turns to the image, and it turns back, but what is really the same turn she construes as taking turns. Although the reflection initially gives her a shock, she turns back to it, and it turns back to her again. When Eve leaves the pool and sees Adam, she gets another shock; she turns back, but here the cycle of "back" and "again" is broken. Adam does not mime her response back to her. Instead, he echoes himself, but it is reflection with a difference; his echo is productive, turning an interrogative into a declarative statement, which clarifies the nature of their relationship. Eve is both "partial" and "individual." Her solidity and her individuality — that is, her integrity in inseparability — save her from being imaged into the abyss.

Before her education in selfhood, Eve is in danger of drowning in a shallow pool, of becoming nothing but an image, like Narcissus, and nothing but a voice, like Echo. The Ovidian account returns again and again to the threat of bodilessness, a variation on the poet's unifying theme, loss of body as change of form, and it is easy to see how Milton might have read it as a kind of metaphysical drama. In this miniature *Ovide moralisé*, dualism is a state of punishment. Milton redeems Echo's disembodied voice, making it not repetitive but profoundly initiative, divine. It leads Eve to what Adam refers to as "Substantial Life," following Porphyry's allegory of the Homeric cave. When Narcissus cannot escape his own gaze, the identity of the image revealed to him not by an external guide but by the momentary unclouding of his inner eye, he must face annihilation. In a tragic, ironic reversal, his body echoes Echo's—"nec corpus remanet."[63] Eve, by contrast, marries her body to Adam's; their hands come together, following their hearts, in a ceremonial union that, in its apparent coerciveness, has long troubled readers of the poem.[64] The narrator emphasizes the matrimonial quality of this scene when, just after she finishes speaking, Eve gazes at Adam, the true image of her love, "with eyes / Of conjugal attraction unreprov'd" (4.492–493). The word "conjugal" recalls the moment of contact she has just narrated; when they join hands, they are "yoked" together both physically and symbolically. In its immediate context, it also recalls an earlier moment in Eve's narrative, when the pool first seemed to reciprocate her pleasure, "with answering looks / Of sympathie and love." With their parallel structure and position, these two phrases point in the direction of a doctrine and discipline of marriage that, like its earlier counterpart, seems to cover up deeper tensions and inconsistencies under a veneer of formal harmony.

After its incremental disappearance from the divorce tracts, the word "sympathy" appears twice in Milton's writing before this scene in *Paradise Lost*, but in neither instance does it concern marital relations. Its appropriateness to the occasion here, where Eve discovers the phenomenon of reflection, seems clear enough. But the reappearance of the word in this context, given what I see as Milton's increasing discomfort with it in the 1640s, strikes me as significant enough to warrant careful consideration beyond assessing its local felicity. The word "sympathy" carries a heavy philosophical burden, as his gingerly handling of it in the *Doctrine* suggested. But its burden in book 4 is heavier still, carrying with it the weight of that doctrine; Eve's phrase "sympathie and love" echoes an important passage toward the end of the *Doctrine*, where Milton's argument about law and nature reaches a climax, circling back to Parliament and its long history of procedural reform. Milton fervently argues there that society has no right "to command love and *sympathy*," which, springing from "the inward and irremediable disposition of man" (2:346), cannot be manufactured at will. By this point the reader of the *Doctrine* has been conditioned to read the phrase "love and *sympathy*" as yet another hendiadys for the positive of the two "prime statutes," but it is more than just an elegant variation.

Here the word "sympathy," italicized like "antipathy" throughout the *Doctrine*, specifically denotes the natural bond that exists between well-matched consorts; it is more forceful and meaningful than "peace," Milton's usual doublet. In its first appearance in the *Doctrine*, where Milton suggests that physical disfigurement can undermine "sympathy in mind," the word simply denotes agreement or harmony, but just a few words later, in the same extended period, its semantic field greatly expands: "Much more will the annoyance and trouble of minde infuse it self into all the faculties and acts of the body, to render them invalid, unkindly, and even unholy against the fundamentall law book of nature; which *Moses* never thwarts, but reverences: therfore he commands us to force nothing against sympathy or naturall order, no not upon the most abject creatures" (2:272). Here it is as though sympathy becomes the prime statute of nature, and "sympathy," in effect, becomes a superordinate term, subsuming itself and "antipathy," its apparent opposite. Milton proclaims the universe sympathetic and, more important, lays the foundation for his new "hendiadystic" doctrine of divorce: if divorce is natural, and nature is sympathetic, then divorce is sympathetic; it is in concert with the universe, because it restores concord to the universe. Milton requires a game reader to work out the elaborate logic of his argument, but it is precisely when he uses the word "sympathy" for the third and final time, in the passage I have been examining, that he spells out that argument explicitly. And when he argues that "to command love and *sympathy* . . . is not within the province of any law to reach," he is echoing himself, reconjuring Moses, who "commands us to force nothing against sympathy or naturall order."

I have widened the echo chamber to suggest just how important the phrase "love and *sympathy*" is to the *Doctrine* and so to suggest just how troubling it is for Milton to repeat it in Eve's narrative of her creation. His carefully constructed concept of love, as a universal bonding force, is, in a moment, recast as an illusion, the product of an unenlightened mind. Sympathy is linked not to "naturall order," much less harmony or conversation, but rather, it seems, to narcissistic projection.[65] Once Eve has left the pool and escaped the fate of her Ovidian ancestors, or descendants, as Milton would have it, she finds true love with Adam, figured as true vision. Now she looks "with eyes / Of conjugal attraction unreprov'd." She does not project her own vision onto the object of her vision, as she did with the pool, mistaking her "looks" for its. Adam, in fact, does not, so far as the reader knows, look back at her; instead of returning coy glances, he smiles and kisses her when she leans into him, a gesture of physical forwardness that goes some way toward correcting, or at least muting, the imbalance implied by his "seizing" hand. Placed at the end of the prepositional phrase, the word "unreprov'd" is an ambiguous modifier, associating itself both with "eyes" and with "attraction." Fowler glosses it as "innocent," and although the form of the adjective suggests action rather than state (hasn't the mysterious voice at the pool just reproved her?), this more absolute sense complements the referential flexibility the word has by virtue of its position.[66] It functions as a kind of moral cleansing agent, purifying any hint of error and guiding the sense in which the phrase as a whole should be taken. Unlike her imagined "sympathie and love," it seems, Eve's "conjugal attraction" is neither suspect nor misguided.

It is as though Milton were detaching *res* from *verbum*, with its shady network of connotations and associations. "Sympathy" differs in status from words like "error" and "wanton," on whose obvious fallen senses the poet plays to make a point about prelapsarian language; its semantic status is more uncertain and less codifiable, sliding more easily between positive and pejorative senses. And yet the word "attraction" would certainly have had some of the same connotations for a seventeenth-century reader, suggesting a mysterious and invisible force like magnetism, to which Gilbert's treatise at the turn of the century had brought renewed philosophical attention. The word first appears in the poem in the voice of Sin before the gates of hell, when she reminds Satan, the being out of whom she was formed, that her "attractive graces won / The most averse, thee chiefly" (2.762). James Turner has argued that attraction is redeemed when, two books later, Eve is described as possessing "sweet attractive Grace" (4.298), ostensibly "to show how human sexuality is poised on a scale between Satan and Adam, Sin and Eve—a necessary stage in realizing its potential for good. This process of discrimination and restitution is also enacted in the language of Paradise, where phrases first associated with Satan and Sin ('dalliance,' 'enamoured,' 'attractive grace') are restored to Adam and Eve."[67] I take this point, but Turner's assertion of the precarious status of human sexuality works against his claim for a clear-cut "restitution." When Sin goes on to cast Satan as a proto-Narcissus and thus apparently as a proto-Eve,[68] the prolepsis undercuts the idea of redemption:

> thee chiefly, who full oft
> Thy self in me thy perfect image viewing
> Becam'st enamour'd, and such joy thou took'st
> With me in secret, that my womb conceiv'd
> A growing burden.
>
> (2.763–767)

From this point forward the idea of specular sympathy is effectively satanized. Sin's attractiveness is surely of the false, magical kind feared and abhorred by Milton the domestic economist; his play on "attractive" and "averse," antonyms masquerading as synonyms, dramatizes in a ludicrous mode of abstraction the sort of torturous, mismatched pairing that he inveighed against so feelingly in the divorce tracts. Here he imagines a scenario never dreamed of, or at least never articulated, there—that a bad (not to mention violent, unnatural, and incestuous) marriage could remain intact if each partner were so radically narcissistic that sympathy and conversation mattered not a whit to their happiness or well-being. This is marriage as zeugma, forced yoking, not hendiadys.

The failure of complete restitution makes a word like "unreprov'd" necessary, or to put it differently, its presence is symptomatic of that failure; attraction remains, to whatever extent, under the spell of Sin.

The application of the word "attraction" to human relationships was a fairly late development; the OED does not record instances of its use to mean "the action of drawing forth interest, affection, or sympathy; the power of so doing" (7) until the middle of the eighteenth century. In this semantic-historical light, reflecting back on Milton's mythography of Sin, the scene in book 4 takes on a more enchanted aura, as if Eve's eyes were magnetically drawing Adam's body to hers. But "unreprov'd" functions to reprove a Circean, or Sinful, reading of her charms. There is something magical about Adam and Eve's love; it is a potent natural force drawing them together, both within them and between them, but also beyond them. Milton, I would suggest, has not simply dismissed the argument he made a decade or two earlier, quickly discarding it by retrojection, consigning it to a metanarrative of past error, but he seems to be struggling to find the right moral grammar with which to express it. Although he conceives sympathy as a natural truth, an aura of uneasiness and uncertainty surrounds it.

I have stressed the importance of "unreprov'd," acting as a kind of semantic buffer, ensuring that the reader does not construe Eve's consorting as spellbinding. But what allows her to remain unreproved is also, it seems to me, what allows Milton to return to the idea of sympathetic attraction with greater confidence. The real correction of Eve's vision precedes the moment when her eyes focus on Adam at the end of her narrative; it comes right after Adam's hand seizes hers, and she relates, "I yielded, and from that time see / How beauty is excelld by manly grace / And wisdom." Eve narrates, in effect, the birth of her mind, the transformation of her consciousness into a faculty of differentiation, however troubling the differences may seem to us. "Seeing" here becomes knowing. Her recognition of wisdom, as a superior quality in Adam, is propaedeutic to the development of this faculty in her; it becomes a kind of wisdom in and of itself.[69] Once Adam and Eve come to an intellectual understanding, they can more safely act on their mutual attraction, the subintellectual force that binds them to each other and to nature. In book 4 sympathy assumes the quality of a natural instinct, one that can lead either to rationalized love or to an irrational and destructive self-love.

SIN, SATAN, AND INTERACTION AT A DISTANCE

Although Eve's naïve self-fascination in book 4 of *Paradise Lost* need not— and I think should not—imply the fall of sympathy, the later uses of the word are unmistakably demonic. In book 10, sympathy comes to seem quite properly

sinful, as Sin is mystically informed of Satan's success in Eden. Milton's representation of the mystical sympathy among Satan, Sin, and Death serves to reveal
and ultimately to refute the irreligious and atheistic implications of an occultist
view of sympathy as an irresistible, deterministic force. In the Argument to book
10 Milton introduces three emotional vectors—from the Son to Adam and Eve,
from Satan to Sin and Death, and from Eve to Adam. Of the three, it is not the
Son's "pity" or Eve's "condolement" that receives qualifying emphasis but rather
the "wondrous sympathie" of Sin and Death "feeling the success of *Satan* in this
new World." Context supplies a warrant for "wondrous" beyond its equivocal
generic propriety (marvels are proper to epic—or, Milton asks, are they?):
whereas the Son expresses pity in proximity to Adam and Eve, Sin and Death
sympathize at a distance from Satan; the marvel is spatial, geographical. The
Aristotelian prohibition against action at a distance, which, as we saw in the first
chapter, Digby worked energetically to uphold in his account of sympathy
powder, was grounded in the view that action presupposed "a spatially continuous set of causes."[70] In his justification of creation *ex deo* in *De Doctrina
Christiana*, Milton operates from a similar premise: "For since 'action' and
'passivity' are relative terms, and since no agent can act externally unless there is
something, and something material, which can be acted upon, it is apparent
that God could not have created the world out of nothing" (6:307). Milton
describes creation here as action by contact.[71] Sin, by contrast, readily embraces
the idea of action at a distance and, in so doing, effectively denies the divine
substrate of the world. Her account of "wondrous sympathie" matters intensely
to the poem not only because it begins the movement by which death is "Brought
. . . into the World" (1.3) but also because it interacts at a textual distance with
two of the poem's central narratives—of the Creation and of the Fall:

> Methinks I feel new strength within me rise,
> Wings growing, and Dominion giv'n me large
> Beyond this Deep; whatever drawes me on,
> Or sympathie, or som connatural force
> Powerful at greatest distance to unite
> With secret amity things of like kinde
> By secretest conveyance. Thou my Shade
> Inseparable must with mee along:
> For Death from Sin no power can separate.
>
> (10.243–251)

Sin's "Wings growing" echoes Adam and Eve's "breeding wings" after their
fall (9.1010), but both are echoes—and mockeries—of the "brooding wings" of

the creative Spirit (7.235). More important, Sin's "connatural force" uniting "things of like kind" eerily recalls the vital cosmogonic potency of the Spirit joining "Like things to like" (7.240). The contrast, however, could not be more pointed; Satan, Sin, and Death ultimately do not create but destroy—or, rather, create to destroy.

Milton casts Sin here in the role of the speculator he had seemed so reluctant to take on in the *Doctrine*, where, we recall, he wondered aloud about the source of sympathetic connection in nature: "But what might be the cause, whether each ones allotted *Genius* or proper *Starre*, or whether the supernall influence of Schemes and angular aspects or this elementall *Crasis* here below, whether all these jointly or singly meeting friendly, or unfriendly in either party, I dare not, with the men I am likest to clash, appear so much a Philosopher as to conjecture" (2:271). Milton anxiously raises the suggestion that the "hidden efficacie" of sympathy and antipathy works independently of God only to revoke it, quickly retreating from the deterministic "conjectures" of contemporary natural philosophers to the safe authority of Homer and the conclusive authority of Genesis. God draws Eve from Adam and draws her to him; "the first espousal" rests on a divine sympathy. Unlike Milton and his unimpeachable authorities, Sin mystifies the source of sympathy: "whatever drawes me on." In hypothesizing "som connatural force," she fails to recognize the unifying power of God. Whereas Milton valorizes the "less abstruse" and the "plain," Sin fetishizes the "hidden," the "secret," the occult, allied for him with the irrational and the irreligious.[72]

By displacing onto Sin in book 10 the very "conjecture" that he dodged in the *Doctrine*, Milton distances himself further from those who vainly and vauntingly "list to try / Conjecture" (8.75–76). It is as though the closer Milton got to the mysteries of sympathy, the closer he felt to the miseries of hell. Sin's "Or . . . or . . ." clause is analogous to a Latin "sive . . . sive . . . , " or "seu . . . seu . . . , " clause and produces an uncertain relationship between the two items joined; the syntax creates the expectation of disjunction ("whether *a* or *b*"), but the second item seems very much like a periphrastic gloss on the first ("*a*—that is, *b*"), as if Sin were clarifying her own definition of "sympathie." Through her speculation Milton gets at both the method and the matter of the occult philosopher. In his posthumously printed summa, *Mosaicall Philosophy* (1659), Robert Fludd attempted to synthesize a staggering range of sources, scriptural and classical, ancient and contemporary, "that each wise man may thereby the better conjecture and guesse at the truth of the business."[73] Far from shying away from "conjecture," Fludd holds it up as the way of the sage. Without any hedging about "this elementall *Crasis*," he defines sympathy as "a consent, union, or concord" deriving from "a secret league or friendship" between things, "even from their

very mixtion in their first creation." Fludd did not attempt to square his explanation of "the secret bowels of . . . Sympathy and Antipathy" with the Aristotelian
prohibition against distant action; he simply accepted action *"ad distans"* as an
empirical reality: "The action of each elementary thing is effected, as well by
disjunction of their bodies, that is to say, *ad distans,* as when they are joined
together by mutuall contact of one another," and the distant interaction of things
"is performed by a fit application, and infusion of their beamy influences unto
each other, which would hardly be believed, by reason of the occultness of the
action, did not experience guide us, by the observation of the Load-stones attraction of Iron unto it at a distance."[74] Terrestrial bodies receive influence not only
from celestial bodies but also from other terrestrial bodies, which similarly emit
"beams." At base Fludd conceives of these influences in spiritual rather than
astrological terms; as we saw in the first chapter, for him all influence, all interrelation, depends on the diffusion of the universal spirit or world soul, the immaterial substrate most closely associated with the Neoplatonists.

Milton's view of matter generally sets him at odds with Fludd's Neoplatonism,
though, in a passage that has exercised critics, Milton seems to refer to the
anima mundi when Adam and Eve hymn the sun, "of this great World both Eye
and Soule" (5.171).[75] Patrick Hume's seventeenth-century gloss on this phrase
aligns Milton with the *prisca theologia*:

> The most Ancient Philosophers were of Opinion, that there was one
> Universal Intellectual Soul, the *Emanation of (the Great Mind) God,* cre-
> ated and diffused over the whole World, by whose general Virtue and Plastick
> Power, all things are generated and preserved, and the whole Frame of
> Nature continued in her uninterrupted Course . . . ; this the *Platonists* called
> *Animam Mundi,* and with them *Mercurius Trismegistus, Theophrastus, &c.*
> the *Stoicks* and the *Peripateticks* agree. *Zoroaster* styles it a *Catholick Invisible
> Fire: Virgil,* A *Mental Spirit,* actuating the Heavens, Earth, Seas and Stars.
> . . . So that our Poet has conformably seated this Universal Invigorating Spirit
> in the Sun, by the *Platonists* termed the Sphere of *Equality,* or of the *Soul of
> the World,* corresponding with the *Heart,* the *Vital Center of the Microcosm.*[76]

If Fludd was not Milton's source for this solar lore, he was certainly Hume's
source for this gloss:

> In like manner the Platonists did call the generall vertue, which did engen-
> der and preserve all things the *Animam mundi,* or *the soul of the world.* And
> to this their opinions, the *Arabick Astrologians* do seem to adhere: forasmuch
> as they did maintain, that every particular thing in the world hath his distinct
> and peculiar soul from this vivifying Spirit. To this opinion also *Mercurius*

Trismegistus, Theophrastus, Avicenna, Algazel, and as well all the Stoicks and Peripateticks, do seem wholly to consent or agree. Again, *Zoroaster* and *Heraclitus*, the *Ephesian*, conclude that the soul of the world is that catholick invisible fire, of which and by the action whereof, all things are generated and brought forth from puissance unto act. *Virgil*, that excellent Latine Poet, calleth it that mentall Spirit, which is infused through every joint and member of the world, whereby the whole Mass of it, namely the heaven and the earth, or spirit and body, are after an abstruse manner agitated and moved.[77]

Hume's gloss casts Milton as a Fluddian syncretist. But whereas Fludd is determined to show that all ancient sources converge in and confirm his world picture, Milton is consistently reluctant to make all theisms equal. Hume reproduces the same lines on the universal "mentall Spirit" from book 6 of the *Aeneid* that Fludd goes on to cite. He follows Fludd's *Mosaicall Philosophy* so closely that his emphasis, when he departs from the text, is striking. Fludd does not immediately associate the sun with the heart, "the *vital Center of the Microcosm*," but he often does elsewhere; the analogy is central to his cosmic system.[78] A literal reader of Psalm 19, he believed that if God put His tabernacle in the sun, "*the heart of heaven*," the Spirit resided there, and that His tabernacle in man was in the heart, in which the Spirit "moveth, as in this proper macrocosmicall Sunne in Systole, and Diastole namely, by contraction and dilation without ceasing, and sendeth his beames of life over all the whole frame of man, to illuminate, give life, and circular motion unto his spirit."[79] As penetrative as they are pervasive, these vital beams extend from the heart throughout and beyond the body.

Action or interaction between bodies varies according to their degree of natural likeness or spiritual affinity. "So we must surely confess," Fludd writes, "that where one spirit concurreth in Sympathy with another of the like nature, the power must be the greater, and the action performed at a larger distance."[80] Milton hyperbolizes this logic, so that Sin, as it were, overgoes Fludd. Whereas Fludd goes only so far as to claim that "where two do jointly affect by a Sympatheticall Union, there the action will spiritually be furthered at a far greater distance,"[81] Sin posits a "connatural force / Powerful at greatest distance." In a mode characteristic of Satan, one that might be called grammatical atheism, the comparative is raised up to a superlative. By maximizing the power of sympathy, Milton suggests, the occultist blasphemously minimizes "the Almighty Power" (1.44).

Milton does not immediately establish the basis of Sin's sympathy, but he subtly evokes her Satanic lineage. The word "connatural" denotes not only "equally natural to both," in Jonathan Richardson's gloss, but also more specifically "congenital, innate" (*OED* 1).[82] Having sprung out of Satan's head, Sin partook of his nature and perpetuated it, "familiar grown" (2.761). The "sympathy between things," Fludd writes, "will be so much the greater, and of more force, by how much nearer the spirits of the things, either present or dispersed, are in nature and consanguinity to one another."[83] Ontological proximity allows for sympathetic effects across great spatial divides. This claim was certainly not unique to Fludd. Francis Bacon, too, conceived of sympathy in terms of blood relation, though, characteristically, he called for further investigation of the phenomenon: "I would have it first throughly inquired, whether there be any Secret Passages of *Sympathy*, betweene *Persons* of *neare Bloud*; As *Parents, Children, Brothers, Sisters, Nurse-Children, Husbands, Wives*, &c."[84] Bacon goes on to relate his own "inward *Feeling*" of his father's death across the Channel and suggests that "concern" might provide as much of a basis for sympathy as consanguinity. He wonders "if a *Victorie* should be won, or lost, in *Remote Parts*, whether is there not some *Sense* thereof, in the *People* whom it concerneth" and then goes on to tell a story about Pius V, who had an occult sense of the Christians' victory over the Turks at the battle of Lepanto in 1571. "It is true," Bacon writes, "that *Victorie* had a *Sympathy* with his *Spirit*; For it was merely his *Worke*, to conclude that *League*."[85] Sin's mystical response to Satan's victory in Eden can thus be seen to have a double basis in the logic of occult speculation—a logic, Milton does not let us forget, that led to our defeat.

Milton makes the link between sympathy and consanguinity emphatic when the triumphant Satan is greeted by "his offspring dear" at the brink of Chaos, the site of a joyous reunion for hell's first family. Sin both repeats and refines her earlier speculation:

> O Parent, these are thy magnific deeds,
> Thy Trophies, which thou view'st as not thine own,
> Thou art thir Author and prime Architect:
> For I no sooner in my Heart divin'd,
> My Heart, which by a secret harmonie
> Still moves with thine, join'd in connexion sweet,
> That thou on Earth hadst prosper'd, which thy looks
> Now also evidence, but straight I felt
> Though distant from thee Worlds between, yet felt
> That I must after thee with this thy Son;
> Such fatal consequence unites us three.

> (10.354–364)

Here is Hume's mystical heart, corresponding to the sun, in Fluddian terms, as "the *vital Center of the Microcosm*."[86] Redescribing the sympathy, or "secret amity," she has felt as "a secret harmonie," Sin suggests a quasi-musical relation based on parallel pulsation, which Milton's use of ploce reinforces; the repetition of "my Heart" enacts a double rhythmic contraction, the same iambic "systole."[87] Sin goes on to claim that this cardiac sympathy has been continuous, presumably from birth, and in so doing she effectively weighs in on a seventeenth-century embryological debate. Her opening vocative, like her description of Death as "thy Son," underlines the genetic connection. One of the achievements of William Harvey's treatise on embryology, *Anatomical Exercitations Concerning the Generation of Living Creatures* (trans., 1653), was to establish the relative independence of the fetus from the mother. He did so, in part, by arguing that when the mother dies during delivery the baby's heart continues to beat. The fetal heart, "the Vital principle, and first particle," is powerfully autonomous: "But most certain it is, that those Arteries are not moved by the virtue or operation of the Mothers, but of his own proper *Heart*: For they keep a distinct time and pawze, from the Mothers *pulse*."[88] Sin's birth, of course, seems more Hesiodic than Harveian; springing from Satan's head, she is formed not in utero but in a more mythical matrix.[89] And yet the two share a strong physical bond, a single pulse; they retain a "sweet connexion" originating in the heart. Sin's emphasis falls on the occultness of the connection.

Sin appeals to something very much like Frazer's "Law of Contact or Contagion" in his famous discussion of "Sympathetic Magic" in *The Golden Bough*: "Things which have once been in contact with each other continue to act on each other at a distance after the physical contact has been severed,"[90] or as Bacon put it some three centuries earlier, "There is a *Sympathy* of *Individuals*: That is, that in *Things*, or the *Parts* of *Things*, that have beene once *Contiguous*, or *Entire*, there should remaine a *Transmission* of *Vertue* from the One to the Other."[91] Forming an entirety until the moment of her birth, "till on the left side op'ning wide" (2.755), Sin and Satan remain connected by means of the "virtue" transmitted from his heart to hers. Sin's phrase from book 2 curiously anticipates Adam's strongly cardiological account of the birth of Eve, of the Creator "Who stooping op'nd my left side, and took / From thence a Rib, with cordial spirits warme, / And Life-blood streaming fresh" (8.465–467). Hume comments that here Milton follows "the common Opinion, that the Heart inclines more to the left than right Side in Human Bodies, because its Pulsation is there felt." Hume derives "cordial" from "*Cor*, Latin, the Heart, the seat and spring of Life," so that the "cordial spirits" refer to "quick and active Spirits, proceeding from the Heart, and passing through it, with the Blood, Lifes Crimson Fiery Floud."[92] But whereas for the first couple—at least before the Fall—this connection is significant primarily for its metaphysical implications, it remains on a literal, physical,

and magical plane for Sin and Satan. Sin's natural connection to Satan leads
not to "conversation," the ideal mode of relation first celebrated in the *Doctrine*,
but to "intercourse" (10.260), physical passage. The construction of her bridge
of asphaltic slime reveals the extent to which she has lost, or failed to capture,
the spirit of sympathy. Unlike the Spirit conglobing like things to like, Sin and
Death impose their own brute necessity on matter: "what they met / Solid or
slimie, as in raging Sea / Tost up and down, together crowded drove / From each
side shoaling towards the mouth of Hell" (10.285–288). This act of creation is
not sympathetic but stochastic, a kind of anti-marvel of unintelligent design.
Death goes on to declare, "Alike is Hell, or Paradise, or Heaven" (10.598); this is
a travesty of the idea of cosmic sympathy. Death cannot imagine sympathy,
only benighted identity; the paratactic construction suggests not conjunction
but "crowding," the nihilistic collapse of all distinction and difference. For
Satan, Sin, and Death, compassion has devolved into mere collaboration and
conspiracy.

   The case with Adam and Eve is emphatically and instructively different.
Before Eve's birth, we recall, Adam justifies his request for a fit consort by
appealing to a basic human need for "Collateral love, and deerest amitie"
(8.426). In a wonderfully subtle note, Hume glosses "collateral" as "side by side"
and compares Adam's account of the immediate aftermath of Eve's birth from
book 4: "to give thee being I lent / Out of my side to thee, neerest my heart /
Substantial Life, to have thee by my side / Henceforth an individual solace dear"
(483–486).[93] Adam translates "Out of my side" into "by my side," not canceling
out the physical sense but expanding it. Unlike Sin's repetition of "my heart,"
which establishes a static relationship, Adam's repetition of "my side" is transfor-
mative, turning a scheme into a trope. The "secret amity" pulsing between Sin
and Satan is a demonic parody of the "deerest amitie" uniting Adam and Eve.[94]
This latter sympathy is not "secret" or occult. Rather, it proceeds from Adam's
understanding of the order of creation, according to which God's creatures seek
"to participate / All rational delight" (8.390–391). It is a matter of reason, not
speculation, a matter of will, not force; God satisfies Adam's "hearts desire" only
after Adam has demonstrated that he can "judge of fit and meet" (8.451, 448).

   As we have seen in our discussion of book 4, Milton represents sympathy as
a natural instinct to connect, the moral valence of which depends on how the
subject chooses to interpret it and to act on it; in other words, sympathy is not
necessarily "narcissistic" or demonic but becomes so when the sympathizer
neglects or turns against God and reason. This is precisely what Adam does
at the Fall, and Milton uses Sin's irrational and atheistic account of sympathy
to underline the point. Sin's statement "For Death from Sin no power can

separate" disturbingly echoes the language of the marriage ceremony; no one and nothing can put asunder what sympathy has joined together. God has been displaced and replaced by the "power" of sympathy. Echoing Death's appeal to "Fate and inclination strong" (10.265), Sin evokes a pagan Trinity: "Such fatal consequence unites us three." Here fate is not God's "what I will" (7.173) but rather Sin's false substitute for God. For Sin, fate and sympathy are allied as binding forces, determining her activity and position in space. The object of Milton's critique is not sympathy per se, but rather an occult view of it that reduces free and rational subjects to enchanted objects, "th' upright heart and pure" (1.18) to a mere magnet.[95]

THE OCCULT FALL

In *De Doctrina Christiana* Milton strings out the sins of Adam: he fell because "he was faithless, ungrateful, disobedient, greedy, uxorious" (6:383). In *Paradise Lost* Milton suggests a radically alternative cause of the Fall, one to which Sin, as we have seen, gives a name: sympathy. Sin's speculation on her sympathetic connection with Satan recapitulates Adam's resolution to fall with Eve, but more broadly it reveals the extent to which Milton conceives of the Fall as the nonfatal consequence of occult mentalities. In his temptation of Eve Satan attributes an occult quality to the fruit, a kind of *virtus scientifica*, which makes all qualities manifest—except, suspiciously, itself.[96] Apostrophizing the "Wisdom-giving Plant," he proclaims, "Now I feel thy Power / Within me cleere, not onely to discerne / Things in thir Causes, but to trace the wayes / Of highest Agents" (9.680–683). Satan—ever a close reader of the poem in which he figures as a major character—parodies and profanes the poet's aim to "justifie the wayes of God" (1.26); he attempts to persuade Eve that, having eaten the fruit, she, too, can understand the causes of all things on earth and in heaven. Karen Edwards likens Satan here to "the nostrum-mongering *ciarlatani* of the late Renaissance," and Eve is duped, adopting his mystical view of the fruit when, as a "budding natural philosopher," she "ought to have pitted her experiential knowledge more polemically against Satan's."[97] Eve blindly accepts that the fruit has an occult "vertue to make wise" (9.778) and idolatrously holds it up as "the Cure of all" (9.776), a conceit with Paracelsian associations.[98] Fludd suggests that "spirituall Mummy," which is mystically extracted out of bodies, "may be esteemed as a *Panacaea* or catholick medicine, to preserve health."[99] Yet far from preserving health, the fruit brings not just "distemper" (9.887) but death. Throughout his narrative of Eve's fall Milton shows the morbid intertwining of occultism and atheism.

For Adam it is not the apple, the "Fruit Divine" (9.776), that takes the place of God, but Eve herself, or rather his image in her. Adam has what Bacon calls an "inward feeling" of Eve's fall: "Yet oft his heart, divine of something ill, / Misgave him; hee the faultring measure felt" (9.845–846). The verb "felt" ensures that the pun in "faultring" is keenly felt. Sin and Satan's sympathetic pulse sounds in precise counterpoint to Adam's arrhythmia. Not yet fallen, Adam feels Eve's defeat at a distance, whereas, always already damned, Sin feels Satan's victory "though distant . . . Worlds between." When he and Eve come together, Adam's fault is to move from divination to determination, to mystify sympathy with what amounts to sophistry, however tender and heartfelt:

> How can I live without thee, how forgoe
> Thy sweet Converse and Love so dearly joyn'd,
> To live again in these wilde Woods forlorn?
> Should God create another Eve, and I
> Another Rib afford, yet loss of thee
> Would never from my heart; no no, I feel
> The Link of Nature draw me: Flesh of Flesh,
> Bone of my Bone thou art, and from thy State
> Mine never shall be parted, bliss or woe.
>
> (9.908–916)

Here it is we who feel the "faultring measure" ("no no"), as Adam "feels" what Sin "feels" one book later, occult sympathy. And like Sin he appears to make the same point twice:

> However I with thee have fixt my Lot,
> Certain to undergoe like doom, if Death
> Consort with thee, Death is to mee as Life;
> So forcible within my heart I feel
> The Bond of Nature draw me to my owne,
> My own in thee, for what thou art is mine;
> Our State cannot be severd, we are one,
> One Flesh; to loose thee were to loose my self.
>
> (9.952–959)

In the introduction to the *Doctrine*, Milton allegorizes Custom as "a meer face" lacking substance "until by secret inclination, shee accorporat her selfe with error" (2:223). Moved by the "secret inclination" of sympathy, Adam insists on "accorporating" himself with Eve; they will fall as one fallen body. Although Eve's birth required Adam to sacrifice "cordial spirits," her presence fills him with "The spirit of love" (8.466, 477). Adam's "cordial spirits" are sublimed and reclaimed in his doctrine of marriage, supplementing the account in Genesis to solidify the point Milton made again and again in the divorce tracts—that the conjunction of body without spirit means nothing, nothing but sin and suffering: "And they shall be one Flesh, one Heart, one Soule" (8.499). Adam omits the crucial third term of his own marriage doctrine, returning to Genesis as a fleshly literalist. Eve reinforces his sophistical, self-justifying rhetoric: "*Adam,* from whose deare side I boast me sprung, / And gladly of our Union heare thee speak, / One Heart, one Soul in both" (9.965–967). Eve supplies the missing term, but not as a meaningful correction. Showing herself to be still under Satan's attractive influence, she reduces the holy doctrine of *henosis* to a mere rhetorical formula, falsely glamorizing their disobedience as "one Guilt, one Crime" (9.971). She speaks of soul, but her emphasis, like Adam's, like Sin's one book later, falls on physical connection, Adam's "deare side." They are, as she puts it, "linkt in Love so deare" (9.970)—a phrase that echoes Adam's misguidedly romantic appeal to the "Link of Nature."

In his classic reading of these two passages, which he deemed "in many respects the two most important passages in *Paradise Lost,*" A. J. A. Waldock imagined a Milton caught between a sublime insight into Adam's feelings and "the thesis in the background"—that is, between the sense of romantic love and the fact of mortal sin.[100] Turner renewed this critical strain, similarly insisting on the irresistible pathos of the two passages: "It may be that the omission of 'soul' from this version of 'flesh of my flesh' is significant, but to stress Adam's carnality is to reduce the complexity of our response. The entire process of unfallen sexuality, the vast momentum of the idyllic books, flows through these lines, and our sympathies must run with this tide."[101] Just as Adam sympathizes with Eve, so we sympathize with Adam; Milton, that is, not only makes sympathy the cause of Adam's fall but also makes his fall sympathetic.[102] Yet the danger of both sympathies—indeed, of sympathy itself—for Milton is suggested by Turner's very construction ("our sympathies *must run with this tide*"; my emphasis), that in the strong current of emotion will and reason will get lost at sea. As we shall see in the next chapter, Milton foregrounds the ambivalence of sympathetic response in book 11, when Adam is no longer the subject of a pathetic drama but rather the spectator of one. Burrow provides a compelling warrant for readerly sympathy here beyond what Waldock claims to be the "truth" of Adam's feelings: Adam "falls for subtly regenerate reasons, reasons which grow from the main sources of what is good in the poem. God is on the brink of becoming one flesh with man; and it is from a sense of the practical consequences of being one flesh with Eve that Adam falls."[103] As the Father says to the Son, "Thir Nature also to thy Nature joyn" (3.282), but whereas the Son promises to "Freely put off" his heavenly glory (3.240), Adam, in asserting a consubstantial sympathy of the flesh, speaks the language of necessity.

Milton reinforces the relationship between fall and redemption by setting "accorporation" against Incarnation. But Adam's appeal to the "Link of Nature," like that still severer appeal to the "Bond of Nature," also deepens the sense in which he is distorting both his own and Milton's ideal of matrimony.[104] Commenting on Genesis 5:23 in *Tetrachordon*, Milton writes, "*Adam* . . . in these words does not establish an indissoluble bond of marriage in the carnal ligaments of flesh and bones, for if he did, it would belong only to himself in the literall sense" (2:602), and in his commentary on the next verse, Milton denies that a man must leave his family "to link himself inseparably with the meer carcass of a Mariage" (2:603). For Milton, physical inseparability is a dangerous and errant fiction, what he calls "a sluggish and underfoot Philosophy" (2:606). In spite of his moving case, Adam is in danger of draining the spiritual significance of "collateral." In the separation colloquy at the beginning of book 9, Adam reflects, "Why shouldst not thou like sense within thee feel / When I am present" (315–316). As the colloquy as a whole suggests, sympathy is not incompatible with, and does not preclude, difference; Adam and Eve are connected, but also distinct beings, possessing discrete points of view and habits of mind. Seemingly disturbed by difference, by dividuality, so to speak, Adam goes on to err in redefining sympathy as a law of identity, of sameness. The sympathy to which he appeals is revealingly suggestive of specularity. The repetition of the phrase "my own" conveys the extent of Adam's fixation on his own physical form. The Argument to book 9 attributes Adam's fall to "vehemence of love," which economically conveys his subordination of reason—the force of the etymon *mens*—to passion. I would refer it back to Eve's "sympathie and love," since Adam's justification is a blameful, rather than an innocent, "self-theme," to recall Cavendish's phrase. Unlike the newborn Eve, however, Adam has already had the benefit of Raphael's instruction on the great chain of being. Appearing to play the part of Neoplatonic tutor,[105] Raphael taught him in book 8 to direct his mind above and beyond his corporeal tie to Eve, to subordinate body to soul, passion to love, physical love to spiritual love:

> What higher in her societie thou findst
> Attractive, human, rational, love still;
> In loving thou dost well, in passion not,
> Wherein true Love consists not; love refines
> The thoughts, and heart enlarges, hath his seat
> In Reason, and is judicious, is the scale
> By which to heav'nly Love thou maist ascend.
>
> (8.586–592)

Raphael strongly demotes attraction, putting it first, and lowest, in a significant set of graded adjectives: "Attractive, human, rational." Having just made the point that the sense of touch has also been "voutsaf't / To Cattel and each Beast" (8.581–582), Raphael relates the attractive to animal instincts, lower than the human, and lower still than the "rational," the best part of human nature.[106] Raphael does not reject attraction; he just downgrades it. The "subliming" by "gradual scale" he had described as the divine tendency of all matter in book 5 is here emphatically predicated of "Reason." Satan promises the same ascent in a fraction of the time, but the "enlargement" of heart Raphael describes as the result of true and pious love is crucially different from the "dilated Spirits, ampler Heart" Eve boasts of to Adam after her fall (9.876). Waldock quotes the last two of Raphael's lines in support of his claim that Adam falls "through true love," but to collapse the distinction between love and attraction is to simplify Milton's account.[107]

By asserting the power of the "link" or "bond" of nature to "draw" him—the verb is repeated—Adam reinscribes the domestic within the sphere of the occult. In his *Magiae naturalis*, Della Porta, having described "the Antipathy and Sympathy of things," follows Ficino in founding magic on the sympathetic bond of nature: "For the parts of this huge world, like the limbs and members of one living creature, do all depend upon one Author, and are knit together by the bond of one Nature . . . [and] by reason that they are linked in one common bond, therefore they have love in common; and by force of this common love, there is amongst them a common attraction, or tilling of one of them to the other. And this indeed is Magick."[108] Raphael, in effect, disenchants this world-view, proceeding not from love to attraction, as Della Porta does, but rather in the opposite direction. For Milton, the greater the emphasis on attraction in the whole, the greater the risk of abridging, even abrogating, the freedom of the parts. Whereas love "hath his seat / In Reason," attraction is mindless, objectifying, a matter of mere force. On the verge of falling, Adam disowns all rational agency and effectively returns attraction to the privileged place it has in occult philosophy. And yet for Adam to mystify his love is also to express it. In this sense, the quality of Adam's sympathy seems profoundly different from Sin's— the echo also distorts the source—but Milton does not, I think, leave Adam's sin "in the background."

Immediately after the Fall, Adam's ad hoc philosophy of attraction is put into shameful practice. Sympathy has lapsed into contagion: "So said he, and forbore not glance or toy / Of amorous intent, well understood / Of *Eve*, whose Eye darted contagious Fire" (9.1034–1036). In Fluddian terms, their lust represents a "spiritual poison": "one blear-ey'd person, by darting his infectious beams for relief at a reasonable distance, becommeth a flame. . . . Wherefore as spirits are by union joined together and multiplied, like oyle added unto oyle, so doth the infectious flame increase, and feed equally upon them both."[109] It is only when Satan hurries back to hell to trumpet his success to his devilish audience that the full pathophysiology of sympathy becomes clear—in gory, Ovidian detail.[110] Milton again associates sin and suffering with a contagion of the eye:

> They saw, but other sight instead, a crowd
> Of ugly Serpents; horror on them fell,
> And horrid sympathie; for what they saw,
> They felt themselvs now changing; down thir arms,
> Down fell both Spear and Shield, down they as fast,
> And the dire hiss renew'd, and the dire form
> Catcht by Contagion, like in punishment,
> As in thir crime.
>
> (10.538–545)

An ophidian epidemic breaks out in hell, spreading in an instant, infecting all. The devils' likeness, in sin, in substance, only increases their susceptibility to "horrid sympathie." As in Eve's narrative in book 4, Milton uses the figures ploce and polyptoton to convey a sympathetic relation that is no more than reflexive—"saw" and "sight," "horror" and "horrid," "fell," "down," and "dire." But, as the emphasis on fallenness suggests, this new "contagious" sympathy is categorically different from Eve's. It is as virulent as hers is innocent, and, like the ashes the serpents chew over and over again, it is bitterly ironic: "like in punishment, / As in thir crime."

This is the final appearance of "sympathy" in the poem, its downward trajectory, like the rebel angels', complete. Yet it is precisely at the point at which it seems the most demonic that Milton reminds us that sympathy is, in its origin, divine. As Sin and Death gleefully, greedily ravage Paradise, imperiling not only "whatever thing" they find (10.605) but also the very theodicy itself, God explains that He "call'd and drew them thither / . . . to lick up the draff and filth" following from the Fall (10.629–630). The action of Sin and Death, we learn, is not primarily destructive but detergent. What Sin called "sympathie" was, in fact, God's "calling."[111] He, not Satan's magnetic heart, "drew" her. God thus provides a definitive response to Sin's mystical and mystifying speculation on "whatever draws me on." Conjecture yields to revelation. God reveals a power vastly superior to the "connatural force" surmised by Sin, one that brings like to like—in this case, Sin to sin—and one that will ultimately defeat Sin and Death with "one sling" (10.633). In His words, answered by heavenly songs of praise, occultism no less than atheism is gloriously confuted.

Yet the catastrophe of the Fall remains a terrible cosmic fact. Merely two books after having narrated the birth of the sympathetic universe, Milton begins the tragic tale of its expiration.[112] The sympathetic responsiveness of the earth to the Fall movingly conveys a sense of what has been and what will be no more:

> Earth trembl'd from her entrails, as again
> In pangs, and Nature gave a second groan,
> Skie lowr'd and muttering Thunder, som sad drops
> Wept at compleating of the mortal Sin
> Original; while *Adam* took no thought,
> Eating his fill, nor *Eve* to iterate
> Her former trespass fear'd, the more to soothe
> Him with her lov'd societie, that now
> As with new Wine intoxicated both
> They swim in mirth, and fansie that they feel
> Divinitie with them breeding wings
> Wherewith to scorne the Earth.
>
> (9.1000–1011)

Adam and Eve's sympathy is not with each other here, however much they pretend to "lov'd societie," not with the world, but with Sin, who, around this very moment, herself feels "Wings growing" (10.244). As their "mortal Sin" is completed, so is their disjunction from nature.[113] Whatever sympathetic structure can be said to inhere in the cosmos Adam and Eve have known is dissolved in noon's atonal nocturne, and they are oblivious to it, drowning in base sensory experience, taking "no thought." The mournful effect Milton creates is of sympathy lapsing into pathetic fallacy: "Skie lowr'd and muttering Thunder."[114] After the Fall, we get, in a sense, Romantic poetry. In the absence of a Pythagoras, any larger conjunction between man and nature will have to be, from this point forward, an act of reading and writing. With its elaborate allusions and analogies, Fludd's philosophy was just such a reconstitutive act. And yet within Eden, contrary to the "signs of woe" nature sends out after Eve's fall (9.783), all is not lost. If Paradise is to be regained, it will be found not in nature but in human nature.

4

PARADISE LOST AND THE HUMAN FACE OF SYMPATHY

In his crabbed but incisive life of Milton, Johnson writes of *Paradise Lost*, "Splendid passages, containing lessons of morality, or precepts of prudence, occur seldom. Such is the original formation of this poem, that as it admits no human manners till the Fall, it can give little assistance to human conduct."[1] Although I dissent from his claim that the poem lacks didactic content, I would like to draw from Johnson's words what I take to be a powerful insight: that the story of *Paradise Lost* after the Fall is "human manners" and "human conduct."[2] In the final three books Milton undertakes an intensive exploration of moral philosophy, which is to say of the tripartite discipline—as it was organized in the Aristotelian-Scholastic tradition—composed of ethics, economics, and politics.[3] In *Of Education*, Milton designates the three parts by the following phrases: ethics concerns "personall duty," economics "houshold matters," and politics knowledge of "the beginning, end, and reasons of politicall societies" (2:397, 398). Whereas at the Fall Adam treats sympathy primarily as a physical problem, appealing, as Sin does, to the magical "Chains" binding heart to heart, after the Fall Milton represents sympathy primarily as a moral problem.

In the last chapter I followed the darkening aura of the term "sympathy" from the 1630s to the 1660s and correlated it with Milton's growing disenchantment with mystical philosophy. To return to Robert Thyer's eighteenth-century scholium on the passage in which Sin and Satan celebrate at a distance in book 10—"The modern philosopher may perhaps take offense at this now exploded notion"—we might say that Milton introduces an occult "notion" of sympathy so that God can "explode" it. Theologically, then, Milton approaches and approximates the position of Thyer's "modern philosopher"; his critique of occult sympathy gives the lie to Thyer's distinction between the modern philosopher and the naïve poet. The disappearance of "sympathy" from the epic after the devils' "horrid" descent can be taken as further evidence of Milton's deceptive philosophical modernity. Milton casts off a term that, with its associations of magic and mystery, had been corrupted by the occultists. Yet having associated it with sin and with Sin, having quite literally demonized the name, Milton does not ultimately "explode" sympathy in *Paradise Lost* but rather works toward a redeemed and rationalized conception of it in the fallen world. In so doing, he calls the meaning, not the name, effectively ceding "sympathy" to the occultists, so as to construct an ideal of intimate interrelation without the aura of enchantment. Far from giving up on the concept, Milton made it a central problem of fallen human experience.

In this chapter I argue that in the last three books of *Paradise Lost* Milton theorizes a new coherence within human relations that could no longer be understood to inhere in the world. Human sympathy, he suggests, remedies and in part redeems the loss of universal sympathy. In so doing, it significantly contributes to and reinforces Milton's theodicy. In the first section I analyze the reconciliation scene between Adam and Eve in book 10, in which Milton rehabilitates the moral ideal of the divorce tracts. In the aftermath of the Fall, his moral concept of sympathy is no longer tied to and grounded in a sympathetic worldview on which he depended to justify a radical new argument about divorce, but which he could neither fully rationalize nor embrace. At the end of the epic a moral concept of sympathy does not serve the argument so much as it *becomes* the argument. Milton liberates human sympathy from the constraints of a deterministic nature and predicates it of what he refers to in *Of Education* as "*Proairesis*," moral choice (2:396). The reconciliation of Adam and Eve in book 10 hinges on the ability of the fallen couple to sympathize with each other. In his draft of "Adam Unparadized," Milton projected the reconciliation in strongly nonaffective terms. Here is his account of what became book 10: "Adam then & Eve returne accuse one another but especially Adam layes the blame to his wife, is stubborn in his offence Justice appeares reason with him convinces him the chorus admonisheth Adam, & bids him beware by Lucifers example of impenitence" (8:560). In the epic Milton eventually wrote reconciliation was a matter not of external persuasion but of internal passion and action, of intersubjectivity. In his Paradise, conversation and communication— in the rich sense in which Milton understood both—have a connective power that compensates for the disconnection of the world. Adam and Eve respond to each other in a way that ultimately restores their connection both to each other and to God.

In the next section of the chapter I analyze Adam's various responses to Michael's theatrical presentation of future biblical history in book 11. Milton moves sympathy further into the realm of moral philosophy by extending his purview from the family to the individual. Adam receives an intensive ethical education in sympathy under the tutelage of Michael, who inculcates an ideal of sympathy based on moral temperance and poised between narcissism and overidentification. Adam strives to find a rational middle ground between closeness and distance. Satan's fallen experience of sympathy, I go on to show, provides an instructive counterpoint to Adam's. Whereas Satan converts the emotional stuff of sympathy into a seductive, and destructive, rhetoric, Adam must learn to submit emotion to reason and to discern the righteous course of action. In the following two sections I examine Milton's reflections on and representations of sympathy in the political sphere—first in two works of controversial prose from the 1640s, *Of Reformation* (1641) and *The Tenure of Kings and Magistrates* (1649), and then in book 12 of *Paradise Lost*. Milton ultimately suggests that a sympathetic polity is a possibility in the fallen world, but a fleeting and uncertain one. In the epic his emphasis falls on the ordering potential of domestic and personal harmony. In the concluding section of the chapter I return to Thyer's view of the "modern philosopher" and make a case that the moral turn which defines the closing books of *Paradise Lost* provides a basis for Milton's own claim to philosophical modernity. Whereas in the seventeenth century mechanical philosophers like Digby, Descartes, and Charleton, as we have seen, claimed that sympathy and occult qualities could be reconceived in terms of matter and motion and thereby integrated into a new-philosophical system, Milton came to terms with sympathy in a different way; for him, the significance of sympathy was ultimately to be found not in mechanisms but in morals. Highlighting a significant allusion to *Paradise Lost* by Thyer's contemporary David Hume (1711–1776), I suggest that a momentous achievement of Milton's epic was to ground and to guide a major emphasis of eighteenth-century moral philosophy.

COMMISERATION AND POSTLAPSARIAN ECONOMICS

I began my discussion of book 10 in the previous chapter by noting that the Argument previews three instances of affective interaction, the Son's "pity" in covering up the fallen couple, Sin and Death's "wondrous sympathie," and Eve's "condolement" with the suffering Adam. The last of these, in echoing the first, functions as a redemptive corrective to the second—and so, by extension, to what it echoes, the occult sympathy that Adam insists on at the Fall. At the beginning of book 10, the Son, "pittying" Adam and Eve's nakedness, lowers himself to clothe them, "As when he wash'd his servants feet" (211, 215). The Son, as Michael Lieb has argued, represents in the epic "the embodiment of the possible in its sublimest form."[4] Divine love becomes the model of human love, and, as it were, vice versa. The Son's act of pity goes some way toward closing the "distance" that opens up between "Man" and "Heav'n" as a consequence of the Fall (9.9, 7, 8), and Eve then works to close the distance between man and woman.

The breakdown of the sympathetic universe, the tragic sense of "distance and distaste" (9.9), becomes ever more apparent in book 10. The baneful sympathetic contagion that linked fallen Adam and Eve to the literally fallen devils-as-serpents occurs on a macrocosmic level, ruining the sympathy of the whole: "These changes in the Heav'ns, though slow, produc'd / Like change on Sea and Land, sideral blast, / Vapour, and Mist, and Exhalation hot, / Corrupt and Pestilent" (10.692–695). The word "blast," harsh and cacophonous, functions as a grim token of the Fall. "O Fairest flower no sooner blown but blasted" (1), begins Milton's early poem "On the Death of a Fair Infant Dying of a Cough." The words "flower," "blown," and "blasted" are formally linked, but the cognation ironically heightens the sense of death and destruction. The "sideral blast" in book 10 is situated between two other instances achieving the same dark effect: "the blasted Starrs lookt wan" (10.412), and "*Boreas* and *Coecias* and *Argestes* loud / And *Thrascias* rend the Woods and Seas upturn; / With adverse blast up-turns them from the South / *Notus* and *Afer*" (10.699–702). The "rending of the woods" distantly recalls the disturbance and departure of the woodland deities in the *Nativity Ode*. The heavy parataxis of the last passage here and the lines surrounding it produces the effect of spreading infection, a kind of global pandemic, "Catcht by Contagion." Antipathy now rules the sky, north "adverse" to south. Then it spreads to God's creatures:

> Thus began
> Outrage from liveless things; but Discord first,
> Daughter of Sin, among th' irrational,
> Death introduc'd through fierce antipathie:
> Beast now with Beast gan war, and Fowle with Fowle,
> And Fish with Fish; to graze the Herb all leaving,
> Devourd each other; nor stood much in awe
> Of Man, but fled him, or with count'nance grim
> Glar'd on him passing: these were from without
> The growing miseries, which *Adam* saw
> Alreadie in part, though hid in gloomiest shade,

To sorrow abandond, but worse felt within,
And in a troubl'd Sea of passion tost,
Thus to disburd'n sought with sad complaint.

(10.706–719)

Milton's reference to "liveless things" suggests a draining out of the "vital vertue infus'd" at the Creation. The new pervasiveness of "fierce antipathie" is conveyed by the sequence of "Beast," "Fowle," and "Fish," or earth, air, and water; the "war" comprises all creatures, all elements, all places. The poet's repeated use of "with" is antiphrastic; suggestive of the "sym-" of sympathy, it refers in fact to the "anti-" of antipathy. Expressing his desire for a true sympathizer, Adam had commented in book 8 that "the brute / Cannot be human consort; they rejoyce / Each with thir kinde, Lion with Lioness" (391–393). What was "rejoycing" before the Fall has turned into rapacity, and if Adam was dissatisfied with his relationship with the lower creatures before, now he has reason to be despondent about it; they are not sympathetically drawn to him and Eve as they were, "About them frisking" (4.340), but menacingly repelled. Adam retreats to the darkness and darkly reflects. Never before has speech been instrumentalized in this way; the continuous soundtrack of Eden has stopped, never to continue again. Fowler refers to what follows as the "first of all human Complaints."[5]

Milton establishes "misery," like "blast," as a new fallen keyword. Alone, powerless to stop the "growing miseries," Adam can only watch as the world falls apart around him. "O miserable of happie!" (10.720), he begins, going on to worry that death will not be a coup de grâce, "Bereaving sense, but endless miserie" (10.810). Passion leads him to irrational extremes:

Thus *Adam* to himself lamented loud
Through the still Night, not now, as ere man fell,
Wholesom and cool, and mild, but with black Air
Accompanied, with damps and dreadful gloom,
Which to his evil Conscience represented
All things with double terror.

(10.845–850)

It is not only the air that has been corrupted but also Adam's experience of it. The smooth, rhythmic iambs "and cool, and mild," suggestive of prelapsarian concord, give way to the dark, disruptive spondee "black Air." Milton's use of "Accompanied" here is grimly ironic. As in the mind of Marvell's Mower, a gulf has opened up between subject and object; Adam's misery outstrips the world's by a factor of two, throwing off what had been, "ere man fell," a balanced equation.

Now when Adam communicates with nature, the effect is of apostrophe—a figure premised on the reality and recognition of distance—rather than direct address: "O Woods, O Fountains, Hillocks, Dales and Bowrs, / With other echo late I taught your Shades / To answer, and resound farr other Song" (10.860–862). Adam echoes his own account of his birth in book 8: "Ye Hills and Dales, ye Rivers, Woods, and Plaines, / And ye that live and move, fair Creatures, tell, / Tell, if ye saw, how came I thus, how here?" (275–277). The "desympathizing" effect of the Fall registers in the shift from the more intimate "Ye" to the vocative "O," but Adam's postlapsarian words also remind us of where the earlier speech ends: "when answer none return'd, / On a green shadie Bank profuse of Flours / Pensive I sate me down" (8.285–287). Adam had to discipline, to "teach," an uncertainly sympathetic nature to sympathize with him; now his "double terror" heightens his disjunction from nature, his inability to relate to the natural world as he once could.

When nature fails to answer him a second time, Adam does not sit and fall asleep in her comforting lap; rather, it is a sitting Eve who answers, trying both to comfort him and to find comfort herself. Unlike the fleeing beasts, Eve seeks Adam out: "Desolate where she sate, approaching nigh, / Soft words to his fierce passion she assay'd" (10.864–865). But Adam is too fixated on his own misery to find comfort. He resists the therapy of her speech. Instead he answers her with fierce words, lashing out with one misogynistic commonplace after another, denying her exalted essence: "all was but a shew / Rather than solid vertu, all but a Rib / Crooked by nature, bent, as now appears, / More to the part sinister from me drawn" (10.883–886).[6] In yielding to his "fierce passion," however, Adam degrades himself; he has become subject to the "fierce antipathie" that brings war to the animal kingdom. Antipathy has spread from the "irrational" (10.708) to the rational. Raphael had explained in book 8 that it was fierce—in the root sense of "feral"—passion "for which cause / Among the Beasts no Mate for thee was found" (593–594). Eve is capable of refining, and therefore of refined, passion. In reducing her to a superfluous appendage, Adam bitterly revises his account of her birth in that same book, where he had explained the physiological basis of their love; his rib, flowing with "cordial spirits warme, / And Life-blood streaming fresh" (8.465–467), is touched by his heart. Now fallen, Adam appears unable even to conceive of a sympathetic relationship between man and woman. The significant phrase he uses is "straight conjunction" (10.898), which ironically suggests the physical connection he had insisted on to justify his fall; now, it seems, he really is stuck with her. Having appealed to the "link of nature" (9.914), he is now "linkt and Wedlock-bound / To a fell Adversarie" (10.905–906). If only Milton had managed to persuade his countrymen that in such a state divorce was not only permissible but also advisable, Adam would have had a way out of his bind, but bound within the marriage, Adam abandons all hope—in a phrase immediately suggestive of the divorce tracts—of "houshold peace" (10.908).[7]

By emphasizing the error and excess of Adam's ways here, however, Milton is not, it seems to me, using the space of the epic to take up an old case. The narrative frame exposes Adam's attack as a distortion, since Eve immediately seeks out not only his presence but also "His peace" (10.913). She does not turn away from him as he has turned away from her. Eve prostrates herself and clasps Adam's feet, imitating the Son and establishing a nonoccult physical connection on a new plane. At the center of the Fall, and its aftermath in Sin, the heart is also the seat of restitution and reconciliation. Eve pleads with her estranged husband: "Forsake me not thus, *Adam*, witness Heav'n / What love sincere, and reverence in my heart / I beare thee" (10.914–916). She is no longer Satan's disciple aspiring to Godhead, "his faire / Inchanting Daughter" (10.352–353), as Milton refers to Sin, but God's penitent. Eve's speech is an elaborate mea culpa: "On me exercise not / Thy hatred for this miserie befall'n, / On me alreadie lost, mee then thy self / More miserable" (10.927–930), "Mee mee onely just object of his ire" (10.936). The hammering effect of the personal pronouns in these lines suggests that, having forsworn sinful pride, Eve has perhaps gone too far in the other direction. But the ultimate effect of her speech is to suggest that she has been listening to the poem. The elaborate network of echoes, with a double source in 1 Samuel and *Aeneid* 9, has been noted by Broadbent and Fowler.[8] The poem's own model of merciful martyrdom is again the Son, who in book 3 appeals to the Father, "Behold mee then, mee for him, life for life / I offer, on mee let thine anger fall" (236). Adam then echoes the Son in his complaint, where self-sacrifice is replaced by a combination of self-pity and self-loathing: "On mee, mee onely, as the sourse and spring / Of all corruption, all the blame lights due" (10.832–833). Whereas Adam assumes all blame in despair, Eve does so to relieve his despair, thus proving herself the truer imitator.[9]

Eve's acceptance of blame does not, of course, have the world-historical significance of the Son's. Adam, indeed, goes on to refuse it. But within the dimly emerging world of fallen humanity, the significance of Eve's response is profound:

> She ended weeping, and her lowlie plight,
> Immovable till peace obtain'd from fault
> Acknowledg'd and deplor'd, in *Adam* wraught
> Commiseration; soon his heart relented
> Towards her, his life so late and sole delight.

(10.937–941)

Tillyard refers to this moment as "the crisis of *Paradise Lost*."[10] Estranged, Adam and Eve are here reconciled.[11] The reconciliation is enacted in the poet's tortuous syntax. If "Immovable" modifies Adam rather than "her lowlie plight," which I take to be the more compelling reading, Milton uses what he elsewhere refers to as a "bold *Hyperbaton*" to create maximal poetic distance between Eve ("She") and Adam (1:708). Then after the "working" of commiseration Milton brings his pronouns together, "her, his."[12] The individual phonemes of the phrases "life so late" and "sole delight" merge to form a symbolic unity. Eve's misery has at once become Adam's, his hers; their miseries have become one. The Fall brought with it "Miserie / Deaths Harbinger" (9.12–13), and here it is "Commiseration"—a word without the magical associations of "sympathy"— that ushers in a new life together for the fallen couple.[13] Their merging leads not to double misery, as Adam has experienced "double terror," but ultimately to one peace. The disjunction from nature that Adam has just bemoaned is reme- died at this moment neither by joining nature, as he does in book 8, nor by insisting on a "straight conjunction" with Eve, but rather by conversing with her, in Milton's rich sense of the word. Adam's sympathy with Eve here is not specular but newly collateral. Sin, to extend Lieb's comment, might well instan- tiate the passible in its most debased form, but, as we have seen, at the Fall Adam himself becomes the embodiment of an errant passibility by reducing love to mere attraction. The fallen couple enter into this new union voluntarily, not as two magnetized objects, but rather as two fragile subjects; the Father's word is "frail" (3.180). Milton is careful to show that the new bond between Adam and Eve partakes of both reason and emotion; it is disenchanted, bearing no relation to what Pico called "the *iugges* of the magicians."[14] The inward motion of commiseration is occasioned by Eve's "lowlie plight," which I think should be read as an ellipsis for "Adam's perception of, or reflection on, her lowly plight." This mental assimilation of her case in turn occasions an emotional response: "soon his heart relented." We do not witness a mystical heart pulsing here so much as a gradual moral process unfolding. If there is a sense of passivity, and of necessity, in the construction "in *Adam* wraught / Commiseration," the subsequent clause undercuts it. In showing both action and reaction, Milton attempts a precise mimesis of postlapsarian emotional experience.

The story of Adam and Eve in book 10 is a story of imitation, reparation, and relapse before regeneration. The fallen couple must lift each other out of despair. Just as Eve has "besaught / His peace" (10.912–913), so Adam now addresses her with "peaceful words" (10.946); we witness an exchange of affec- tive positions. He will not let her bear judgment alone, recasting common misery as mutual love. Adam moves from enmity to amity: "But rise, let us no more contend, nor blame / Each other, blam'd enough elsewhere, but strive / In offices of Love, how we might light'n / Each others burden in our share of woe" (10.958–961). Eve's return to Adam's physical plane is a token of the togetherness he urges. Moved by his plea, she "recovers heart," but her recovery is only partial. Instead of embracing his solution, Eve contemplates absolute dissolution. As she works through her argument in favor of committing suicide, the word "misery" sounds a kind of death knell. In her distempered state Eve, divinely hailed as "Mother of human Race" (4.475), imagines a very different kind of family planning, seeking "to prevent / The Race unblest" (10.987–988). By the end of her speech Eve has in effect distorted her divine semblance, her face "di'd . . . with pale" (10.1009). She is less like the Son than like Satan at the beginning of book 4, when "passion dimm'd his face / Thrice chang'd with pale, ire, envie and despair" (114–115).

Adam, "nothing sway'd" (10.1010), returns to God now not by being moved by Eve but by not being moved. He counters her "vehement despair" with the "better hopes" of "his more attentive minde" (10.1011), a phrase that itself counters the etymological sense of "vehement." The reconciliation of the fallen couple depends as much on the mind as it does on the heart. Adam looks beyond Eve's pale face to find in her "somthing more sublime / And excellent" (10.1014–1015). He then remembers the *protevangelium*, the promise that their seed shall bruise the serpent's head in what Georgia Christopher has called the "*instant de passage* from despair to faith."[15] But, again, although this moment leads directly to penitence and prayer, Milton seems to be insisting not so much on a moment as on a process. Adam counsels against "impatience" (10.1044), recalling both divine judgment and divine mercy: "How much more, if we pray him, will his ear / Be open, and his heart to pitie incline" (10.1060–1061). Adam has once again opened his ear, echoing the Son echoing the Father: "but much more to pitie incline" (3.402). The dynamic of rising and falling, raising and lowering, in this scene finds its climax when Adam and Eve fall prostrate before the Lord, "Repairing where he judg'd them" (10.1099). This prostration, modeled first by Eve, redeems demonic proneness. In an image of common piety and collateral amity, the fallen couple imitate the Son together. They sympathize not reflexively but mindfully, not in misery but in contrition: "So spake our Father penitent, nor *Eve* / Felt less remorse" (10.1097–1098). The double negative reinforces the sense in which Adam and Eve now find themselves on common ground. In penitence Eve is not "less" but equal.

The significance of Eve's role in the process of regeneration is subtly reinforced in the opening lines of book 11, where her lapsarian heart, like Adam's, is softened by grace. Again the miraculous succeeds and supersedes the magical:

Thus they in lowliest plight repentant stood
Praying, for from the Mercie-seat above
Prevenient Grace descending had remov'd
The stonie from thir hearts, & made new flesh
Regenerate grow instead, that sighs now breath'd
Unutterable, which the Spirit of prayer
Inspir'd, and wing'd for Heav'n with speedier flight
Then loudest Oratorie.

(11.1–8)

It was Eve's "lowlie plight" that softened Adam's heart and allowed him to commiserate, and now "in lowliest plight," the fallen couple are transformed together.[16] Whereas Satan, unregenerately hardening his heart, falls ever further from God, here Adam and Eve move closer to Him. The phrase "loudest Oratorie" suggests a pointed contrast to Eve's "Soft words" (10.865), which, after "Adam to himself lamented loud" (10.845), begin the movement of reconciliation that culminates in regeneration. The "black Air" surrounding Adam earlier in book 10 becomes at the end the medium, "the Air / Frequenting" (10.1102–1103), through which their sighs rise heavenward. The movement of reconciliation depends not on Satanic "motion," not on forcible oration and persuasion, but rather on conversation and communication, a true rhetoric of the heart. When Adam sees that their prayers have been accepted, Eve looks out rather than up, reminding him of their labor in the fields, as he has reminded her in the previous book. Milton suggests that Eve has reformed her concept of work in the light of the reformation of her heart. She speaks of working together, not separately, as before the Fall. Adam has poignantly declared, "My labour will sustain me" (10.1056), but it is equally clear by now that they will sustain each other. The reunion of Adam and Eve is not a return to a prior union; the Fall cannot be rolled back. But in the wake of the breakdown of the sympathetic universe, the fallen couple reestablish coherence on the level of the personal. This new bond of sympathy is nonbinding and, so to speak, nonnetworked; it is no longer part of a universal system, no longer given but made. After the Fall, Adam and Eve must find coherence not beyond but within.

COMPASSION AND POSTLAPSARIAN ETHICS

Adam and Eve's reconciliation should be seen not only as the conclusion to a narrative that begins with their separation at the beginning of book 9 but also as the beginning of an intensive moral-philosophical exploration of sympathy in the fallen world. In book 11 Milton extends that exploration from economics—that is, domestic relations — to ethics. Adam must now reconcile himself to the sins that his sin has brought into the world, interacting at a temporal distance with his fallen descendants. Before Adam and Eve begin their labor, Michael arrives, amid nature's dark signs, and stops them in their tracks. The announcement of the expulsion creates a new crisis for the reconciled couple, one that, as if to test their new fallen intimacy, they must face in large part separately. Eve's absence during most of the final two books of the poem is conspicuous, but although this history is largely suppressed, in the end, as Maureen Quilligan argues, "we have Eve's assertion that the drama has all been hers."[17] In book 11 Adam adopts the role of student, but is above all a spectator to the drama of biblical history. Sympathy, Michael teaches him, is a matter not only of fellow feeling but also of "personall duty" (2:397), to recall Milton's gloss on ethics. Milton represents sympathy as an ethical trial, one that tests the individual's ability to reason and reflect in the midst of heightened emotional experience. As Milton shows in book 10, human sympathy functions as a powerful, compensatory principle of order in the fallen world, but its very power, in blurring the boundary between self and other, also imperils the freedom and integrity of the individual.

Michael's task in the final two books of the poem is in part to reinforce boundaries. He leads Adam up Eden's highest hill, corrects his fallen vision, and proceeds to show him a series of harrowing scenes. Having commiserated with Eve, Adam must now reflect on "miserable Mankind" (11.500). When Michael introduces him to the "many shapes / Of Death" (11.467–468), Adam gives in to his overflowing emotions:

> Sight so deform what heart of Rock could long
> Drie-ey'd behold? *Adam* could not, but wept,
> Though not of Woman born; compassion quell'd
> His best of Man, and gave him up to tears
> A space, till firmer thoughts restraind excess.

> (11.494–498)

It is something of a critical commonplace that Michael's scenes approximate tragic drama. Just as Adam has experienced "terror and horror," so he now experiences "pity" — Aristotle's "tragic passions."[18] But if Adam's "compassion" represents Aristotle's *eleos* or *philanthrōpia*, Milton does not simply prescribe it. Milton's representation of sympathy in the final books of the poem, I would argue, is far more complex and nuanced than a straightforward Aristotelian reading can account for and convey. Milton is not only evoking Aristotle's discussion of tragedy but also employing what David Marshall has referred to, in an eighteenth-century context, as "the figure of theater." In his discussion of

The Theory of Moral Sentiments, Marshall writes, "for Adam Smith, moral philosophy has entered the theater."[19] If less explicitly, I propose, for Milton moral philosophy enters the theater in book 11. He uses the structural model of the theater to analyze both the ethics and the dynamics of sympathy. Theatricality is a significant manifestation of the new relationship to reality that the Fall imposes on humankind. In this sense, Michael's biblical drama not only projects postlapsarian reality but also allegorizes it. After the Fall, the external world becomes a spectacle, and the spectatorial position that Adam occupies for the duration of Michael's performance has become, in effect, his new natural condition. What matters in particular for Adam now is how he responds to what he sees. Milton stages response as the crux of the ethical life.

Adam's response to Michael's "deform" spectacle is to suffer with those he sees suffering. The effect of the narrator's rhetorical question is to valorize this response, even to divinize it. The "heart of Rock" immediately recalls the working of grace in Adam and Eve at the beginning of the book, when "The stonie from thir hearts" is removed (11.4). Softened by grace, Adam melts. Yet the Shakespearean language that follows emphasizes not the divine but the human; although he did not have a mammalian birth, Adam acts like one woman-born. By weeping, moreover, he acts like a woman, in a starkly gendered image of sympathetic response that, as we saw in the Introduction, Shakespeare developed and complicated in *The Tempest*. Here in the space of four lines Adam's response is approved and then, with a stock put-down, seemingly reproved.[20] The sacred icon of equality that ends book 10 gives way here to a topos of sexual inequality; man is to woman as reason is to emotion. To a significantly greater extent than was the case with his earlier "commiseration," Adam does not seem to be in control of his "compassion." Fellow feeling appears again to be "working" in him. But here the mechanics of sympathy assumes a greater urgency, as if Adam were in danger of falling again.

The tension between the beginning of the passage and the end, between a more complex view of the sexes and a proverbial one, registers Milton's ambivalence about the force of sympathy in human experience. So strong is sympathetic response that the sympathizer is in danger of sympathizing past the point of his or her ability to stop; there is no clear line between weeping and drowning.[21] Milton conveys the effect of sympathy without end by not end-stopping after the phrase "and gave him up to tears." The complement beginning the next line prepares for Milton's characteristically rationalist solution; the phrase "A space" completes the clause and, in effect, brings Adam's compassion to completion. The units of fallen time—"*soon* his heart relented" (10.940; my emphasis)— give us the space within which to react to, or act on, our subrational impulses.

Reason, Milton insists, must check emotion. Adam's compassion attests to his humanity in the best sense of the word; it is not in and of itself a lapse, but the extremity of it is. The crucial word is "excess." Once he loses himself in compassion, he loses his "best of man," which can be taken as a metonymy for reason. Milton suggests a significant distinction between hardness of heart and firmness of mind, the "firmer thoughts" with which the mind "restrains" the heart. The self in Milton's metaphysics has a structural integrity. Satan is his ultimate example of the degraded, protean self: from angel to devil to "meaner angel" to cormorant to toad back to devil to mist to serpent back to devil back to serpent, Satan embraces instability, but he is also cursed by it, since the only self that really matters to him is the luminous one that he has lost.[22]

Adam's softening in book 11 recalls Satan's "melting" before Adam and Eve in book 4—both scenes represent the fallen experience of sympathy, and I want to treat the scene here as a significant counterpoint to the one in book 4. In *Tetrachordon* Milton affirms the law of Moses in allowing divorce for hardheartedness, which he defines in its primary sense as "the imperfection and decay of man from original righteousnesse." Milton accuses those who would abolish this Mosaic allowance of hypocrisy: "If they bee such enemies to hardnes of heart, although this groundlesse rigor proclaims it to be in themselves, they may yet learne, or consider that hardnesse of heart hath a twofould acception in the Gospel." Divorce was instituted to protect the fallen from the effects of the Fall, from "intolerable wrong and servitude above the patience of man to beare" (2:661). But although Adam suffers hardness of heart as a condition of his disobedience, he does not suffer from it in the "second signification" of the word as Milton construes it, "a stubborne resolution to doe evil" (2:662). The narrative of Satan is the narrative of this second type, of the *hardening* of heart. Adam can remedy, if not reverse, his fallenness through reason and mindful action. He is free to harden his heart to Eve but chooses to feel for her and with her. So choosing, he is also effectively choosing God; moving closer to her, he moves closer to Him.

Satan chooses not to act on sympathy but to act against it. During his passionate soliloquy at the beginning of book 4, Satan, unlike Adam six books later, refuses to "relent": "O then at last relent: is there no place / Left for Repentance, none for Pardon left? / None left but by submission" (79–81). Like Marlowe's Faustus, Satan manages to persuade himself that repentance is futile; evil has become his good. The description of Eden's atmosphere evokes Satan without naming him; the pure air of Paradise "to the heart inspires / Vernal delight and joy, able to drive / All sadness but despair" (4.154–156). And yet in spite of his ruined heart the spectacle of Adam and Eve seems to move him, indeed to soften him:

O Hell! what doe mine eyes with grief behold,
Into our room of bliss thus high advanc't
Creatures of other mould, earth-born perhaps,
Not Spirits, yet to heav'nly Spirits bright
Little inferior; whom my thoughts pursue
With wonder, and could love, so lively shines
In them Divine resemblance, and such grace
The hand that formd them on thir shape hath pourd.
Ah gentle pair, yee little think how nigh
Your change approaches, when all these delights
Will vanish and deliver ye to woe,
More woe, the more your taste is now of joy;
Happie, but for so happie ill secur'd
Long to continue, and this high seat your Heav'n
Ill fenc't for Heav'n to keep out such a foe
As now is enterd; yet no purpos'd foe
To you whom I could pittie thus forlorne
Though I unpittied: League with you I seek,
And mutual amitie so streight, so close,
That I with you must dwell, or you with me
Henceforth; my dwelling haply may not please
Like this fair Paradise, your sense, yet such
Accept your Makers work; he gave it me,
Which I as freely give. . . . .
. . . .
And should I at your harmless innocence
Melt, as I doe, yet public reason just,
Honour and Empire with revenge enlarg'd,
By conquering this new World, compels me now
To do what else though damnd I should abhorre.
    So spake the Fiend, and with necessitie,
The Tyrants plea, excus'd his devilish deeds.

                                   (4.358–381, 388–394)

Satan opens somewhere between apostrophe and expletive; he is keenly aware
of the distance between Eden and hell, between the unfallen couple and
himself, and he curses that distance. More important, he wants to remove it.
Having experienced a range of passions and then expelled them, or so he thinks,
Satan here is in the uncomfortable position of receiving an unwanted guest
whom he has already bidden adieu. Milton's point is that just as Satan can never
really leave hell, so he can never really leave his passions; the only "calme" he

enjoys is "outward" (4.120). In this case what he calls "love," then "pittie," then "mutual amitie"—this last closest to the sympathy of the divorce tracts, but "straitened"—moves him toward Adam and Eve. Satan's emotion carries the promise, or the threat, of intimacy, but not of the sort that he can accept. He uses language as a mode of stoic discipline; the conditional tense is meant to condition his drive toward Adam and Eve: "could love," "could pittie," "should . . . / Melt." Satan redescribes emotional connection, in a process with which we are already familiar, as physical closeness: "League with you I seek, / And mutual amitie so streight, so close, / That I with you must dwell, or you with me." He translates the couple's "happie nuptial League" (4.339) into a three-way "League," suggestive of his occult anti-Trinity with Sin and Death. On Satan's tongue the word "League" assumes its root sense of ligature, of binding. He imagines something like, but also worse than, the "strait conjunction" to which Adam bitterly refers, because his leagues never have the sanction, or blessing, of marriage. Satan can bear neither to participate in nor to be excluded from the "happie pair" (4.534).

Satan's *lapsus linguae*, "I with you . . . , or you with me," is enormously telling; it reveals his dangerous desire both for the happy pair and for Eden even as it suggests that, if he gets what he says he wants, the three of them will be so close together that it will be impossible to tell who is dwelling with whom. Satan's confusion here is analogous to Eve's later in book 4; Milton dramatizes the way in which an instinctual sympathetic drive confuses the boundaries of self, of subject and object. But instead of merging with the unfallen couple, Satan casts himself, as Burrow has shown, as a *pius* Aeneas, subordinating pity to *pietas*, rejecting *amor* for Roma.[23] Only at the end of his speech does Satan acknowledge his feeling for the first couple: "And should I at your harmless innocence / Melt, as I doe, yet public reason just. . . ." He slips out of the conditional for three syllables, and yet everything else in his speech works against his passion, the distraction of the etymological tautology "harmless innocence" (only a sophist such as he could conceive of a *harmful* innocence), the parenthetical phrase, the adversative "yet," the immediate shift from private to "public." But the poet is here working against Satan; the enjambment of "Melt" places emphasis precisely where Satan is trying to bury it. Lest we mistake his appeal to the public good, we learn that his is the "Tyrants plea." In spite of the antimonarchic resonance of this phrase, or perhaps in addition to it, Satan reveals himself to be his own tyrant, forcing his inner life into submission. Milton, in other words, is evoking not only the historical monarchy of the Stuarts but also the philosophical monarchy of the Stoics.[24] When Satan speaks again, he discovers in himself "neither joy nor love, but fierce desire" (4.509), which both recalls Eve's "vain desire" at the pool (4.466) and anticipates Adam's "fierce passion" in book 10. Satan succeeds in oppressing love and sympathy, but he cannot subdue his anarchic rage and envy. He can be neither fully stoic nor fully sympathetic. At the end of the book, exposed for the envious enemy he is, Satan mocks the "practis'd distances" of the obedient angels (4.945), but in a strong sense he has been the one—throughout book 4—practicing distance. Moved to sympathize, he chooses to harden his heart.[25]

Satan's imperfect stoic kingship condemns him to chronic self-tyranny. In book 9 we see him continually on the verge of melting and continually screwing up his "stubborne resolution to doe evil," to recall Milton's second definition of hardheartedness: "Thus he resolv'd, but first from inward griefe / His bursting passion into plaints thus pour'd" (9.97–98). Satan's hardened heart deliquesces before our eyes; his passion, "bursting" and "pouring," undoes the firmness of his resolve. He suppresses his new feelings again by distancing them grammatically—"With what delight could I have walkt thee round" (9.114)— and then by recasting sympathy as common misery: "Nor hope to be my self less miserable / By what I seek, but others to make such / As I, though thereby worse to me redound" (9.126–128). As Marlowe's Mephistopheles, one of Satan's literary ancestors, puts it, "*Solamen miseris, socios habuisse doloris*" (1.5.42).[26] This is the same sinful logic that Satan had used in hell; in the first words spoken in the poem, Satan gasps at Beëlzebub's dimmed visage:

> If he whom mutual league,
> United thoughts and counsels, equal hope
> And hazard in the Glorious Enterprize,
> Joynd with me once, now misery hath joynd
> In equal ruin.
>
> (1.87–91)

Satan is not commiserating here so much as drawing up an equation, straining to give his hellish plight an epic grandeur. He levels all difference and distinction until it is convenient for him not to: "The lower still I fall, onely Supream / In miserie" (4.91–92). Satan uses his misery strategically, but Adam and especially Eve continue to foil his strategy, inverting his negative passions, "disarm[ing]" his "enmitie" (9.465), and moving him back toward the "mutual amitie" that he has tried to dismiss: "Thoughts, whither have ye led me, with what sweet / Compulsion thus transported to forget / What hither brought us, hate, not love" (9.473–475). Satan's emphasis on the necessity of his love gives the lie to his earlier, pseudo-republican claim for the necessity of his hate. Milton insists that, in spite of God's foreknowledge, Satan is not compelled to bring about the Fall; though fallen, he still has the capacity for good, for love and sympathy. The determination is his own.

Satan's temptation of Eve depends on a new and enormously powerful technique of emotional displacement. He banishes love from his heart—or, as he would have it, his mind—and fixes it on his tongue. He turns feeling into acting, passion into pathos, in the rhetorician's sense:

> She scarse had said, though brief, when now more bold
> The Tempter, but with shew of Zeale and Love
> To Man, and indignation at his wrong,
> New part puts on, and as to passion mov'd,
> Fluctuats disturbd, yet comely and in act
> Rais'd, as of som great matter to begin.
> As when of old som Orator renound
> In *Athens* or free *Rome*, where Eloquence
> Flourishd, since mute, to som great cause addrest,
> Stood in himself collected, while each part,
> Motion, each act won audience ere the tongue,
> Sometimes in highth began, as no delay
> Of Preface brooking through his Zeal of Right.
> So standing, moving, or to highth upgrown
> The Tempter all impassiond thus began.
>
> (9.664–678)

As he proceeds to the climax of his temptation, Satan at last masters his feelings for "man" by using them against man; love has become "shew of Zeale and Love." The theatrical diction—"part," "act"—reinforces the art and artificiality of this new love. Condemned by his own fallenness to a spectatorial relation to Adam and Eve, Satan attempts to reverse that relation, insisting on himself as a spectacle. He no longer wavers like Faustus; instead, he "fluctuates" like Cicero. No longer moved by Eve, he moves her; Milton's use of polyptoton ("mov'd" . . . "Motion" . . . "moving") underlines the rhetorical function of *movere*. In spite of his logical, or seemingly logical, arguments, it is clear that Satan is appealing to Eve's heart rather than to her mind. References to his potent cardiology frame his seduction, from the exordium—"So gloz'd the Tempter, and his Proem tun'd; / Into the Heart of *Eve* his words made way" (9.549–550)—to the peroration—"He ended, and his words replete with guile / Into her heart too easie entrance won" (9.733–734). Satan's rhetorical strategy is to sympathize with Eve and at the same time to insist that the universe sympathizes with her, too. Once she begins to see herself as universal, the Fall is only

a matter of plucking and eating. "Thee all things living gaze on," Satan blan-
dishes before proclaiming Eve "universally admir'd" (9.539, 542). He recreates
the scenario of the dream Eve narrates at the beginning of book 5, refining the
strategy he used there. The moon shines, Satan had claimed, "in vain, / If none
regard; Heav'n wakes with all his eyes, / Whom to behold but thee, Natures
desire" (5.43–45). Although Satan cleverly recalls the point Adam makes to Eve
one book earlier, that man has "the regard of Heav'n on all his waies" (4.620), he
directly contradicts Adam's subsequent point about the stars: "These then,
though unbeheld in deep of night, / Shine not in vain, nor think, though men
were none, / That heav'n would want spectators, God want praise" (4.674–676).[27]
Construing sympathy as mere solipsism, Satan misses, in effect, the second half
of Adam's lecture.

In book 9 Satan's seductive idolization of Eve reaches its apotheosis. She is,
he says, "of right declar'd / Sovran of Creatures, universal Dame" (9.611–612).
Satan's oratory is certainly loud here, but it is also exquisitely controlled. He does
not himself proclaim Eve "universal Dame," which would be a dubiously
authoritative and suspiciously de facto proclamation; instead he uses the passive
participle: she is "of right declar'd," ingeniously suggesting both "that which is
right or correct" and a fictitious pseudo-legal "right," in either case puffing up the
authority of his false claim.[28] Satan artfully balances the high seriousness of that
claim with an affected modesty topos—"Mee thus, though importune perhaps"
(9.610). When he needs to drive home the point that the "taste" of the fruit is not
"mortal," he uses a flattering epithet to bolster a weak argument: "Queen of this
Universe, doe not believe / Those rigid threats of Death" (9.684–685). Satan
succeeds in returning Eve to the pool, to the state of perfect self-regard and
self-absorption she enjoyed in innocence, but now she has her own developed
intellect and the tuition of God and Adam to guide her. Having learned her
place in the scale of being, she should have the presence of mind to see through
Satan's get-divine-quick scheme, but instead she takes his word, arrogating to
herself a sovereignty reserved for God alone.

By transforming a seemingly instinctive sympathy into a rhetoric of sympathy,
Satan not only reduces the order of nature to a theatrical "part" but also, in
winning Eve's soul, brings about its collapse. The circular harmony of the
universe binding Eve to all things—not, as he would have it, the other way
around—becomes, in an instant, an irresistibly seductive trope, what John
Spencer, as we saw in the Introduction, dismissed as "a conceit as dear to some
Ancient and Modern Writers as their very eyes."[29] After the Fall, Milton suggests,
cosmic sympathy becomes a cosmic conceit, a rhetorical topos and tool. So
dear is it to Eve, so enchanting is its fatal charm, that she loses sight of God. Her

worldview becomes Satan's, and the world is lost. Milton would recall and revise this rhetoric of natural sympathy in *Paradise Regained*, where Satan tempts the Son by appealing to and manipulating the sympathetic effects of "all the Elements" (2.334).[30] But, unlike Eve, the Son, possessing and proclaiming a higher power, remains unpersuaded. In book 11 of *Paradise Lost*, Adam breaks from the Satanic model. He experiences sympathy, in all of its fallen complexity and ambivalence, but he does not exploit it, as Satan does beginning in book 4. In both instances Milton expresses his anxiety that strong emotion, "melting," has the power to dissolve the rational structure of the self—that sympathy is, in a phrase he used elsewhere of another virtue, "a liquid thing" (1:842).[31] In his "compassion" scene in book 11, and throughout the final books, Adam must not only, as Michael puts it, "be confirmd" (11.355) but also confirm himself; he must actively firm up his mind without hardening his heart.

If compassion threatens to turn Adam into a kind of caricature of Eve, blurring the line between the sexes, his lack of consideration threatens to return him to the Fall. In the next scene that Michael presents to him, Adam's descendants appear to be enjoying a postlapsarian paradise:

> The Men though grave, ey'd them, and let thir eyes
> Rove without rein, till in the amorous Net
> Fast caught, they lik'd, and each his liking chose;
> And now of love they treat till th' Eevning star
> Loves Harbinger appeerd; then all in heat
> They light the Nuptial Torch, and bid invoke
> *Hymen*, then first to marriage Rites invok't;
> With Feast and Musick all the Tents resound.
> Such happy interview and fair event
> Of love and youth not lost, Songs, Garlands, Flours,
> And charming Symphonies attach'd the heart
> Of *Adam*, soon enclin'd to admit delight,
> The bent of Nature.
>
>   (11.585–597)

Having dramatized the danger of losing oneself in grief, here Milton dramatizes the danger of losing oneself in "delight." Adam's sympathy with the feasters causes the poem momentarily to regress. We are again at the scene of the Fall, and Adam is again putting nature before God and insisting on the magical pull of his heart-strings. The idea of Adam's "attach'd . . . heart" represents a disturbing physics at odds with the mechanics of his regeneration. By describing Adam's sympathy as a quasi-physical "attachment," Milton creates not only an image of the Fall but also an image of the sympathy that leads to the Fall; "The bent of Nature" hearkens back to "the bond of Nature." Adam's error in this scene is again one of false identification. Overeager "to admit delight," he identifies with his own kind, with their "love and youth not lost," with their "Songs, Garlands, Flours." He sees what he wants to see, a pseudo-Edenic mirage. Desire supersedes judgment. Adam's misguided "bent" enables him to fantasize about "youth not lost" when he has just learned that, like all human beings, he must outlive his youth.

Adam's "bent" not only recalls his earlier "bond" but also echoes the initial description of his descendants. There Milton sets out an ideal of philosophical inquiry: "Just men they seemd, and all thir study bent / To worship God aright, and know his works / Not hid" (11.577–579). Unlike the occultists who claimed, as Fludd put it, to be "conversant in the Mysteries of God and nature," violating God's privacy, and prying into His secrets, these first physicists strove to "know his works / Not hid." Rather than following the "bent of Nature," they "bent" their minds to God. But, charmed by female luxury, as Adam was by fallen Eve, they turn from the philosophical to the physical. This implicit critique of an occult philosophy, in the literal sense of one that claims to make manifest what God has left concealed, reinforces Raphael's affirmation of God's refusal to "divulge / His secrets to be scann'd by them who ought / Rather admire" (8.73–75).[32] The "admiration" of the feasters here quickly becomes misplaced. Their "Nuptial Torch" is a pale imitation of the first couple's "bridal Lamp" (8.520). The singers' song is neither angelic nor Pythagorean. It is a Circean enchantment, as seductive as the music of Satan's oratory, and like Eve, like the pious students of God, Adam loses his heart to the "charming Symphonies." The phrase ironically echoes the angels in book 3:

> Then Crown'd again thir gold'n Harps they took,
> Harps ever tun'd, that glittering by thir side
> Like Quivers hung, and with Praeamble sweet
> Of charming symphonie they introduce
> Their sacred Song, and waken raptures high;
> No voice exempt, no voice but well could joine
> Melodious part, such concord is in Heav'n.

(365–371)

The angels sing the exaltation of the Son, whereas the feasters bring on the degradation of man. This "charming symphonie" represents an ideal of reverence and "rapture," of measured participation rather than self-seeking indulgence "without rein." In book 11 the musical sense of "charming" is contaminated with the magical sense; as it is not in heaven, an aura of the occult hovers over Adam's response to the scene on earth.

Michael's role in book 11 is to advocate a balance in morals that no longer obtains in physics. He attempts to inculcate into Adam an ethics of temperance, or what he refers to as "The rule of not too much, by temperance taught" (11.531). Having learned this lesson, Adam would not have found virtue in his descendants' "roving without rein," but he approves of their passion because he identifies with it. "True opener of mine eyes, prime Angel blest," Adam exclaims, "Much better seems this Vision," and, as he sums up the fallen drama before him, "Here Nature seems fulfilld in all her ends" (11.598–599, 602). As his double use of "seems" suggests, Adam mistakes appearance for reality, for "truth." However "purg'd" his "visual Nerve" may be (11.415), his moral vision remains flawed. Michael teaches Adam to look beyond false appearances, to distinguish lust from love, and to observe moderation in all things.

Michael's lesson is also a lesson about sympathy. He warns Adam against sympathizing solely on the basis of the bent of nature. Adam cannot let desire be his guide; he cannot, like the wicked race he sees "Unmindful of thir Maker" (11.611), forget the true image of God. Michael corrects Adam by reminding him of his divine resemblance; he has been "Created . . . to nobler end / Holie and pure, conformitie divine" (11.605–606). His form conforms to God's, and so should his character. Instead Adam puts his own image before God's. His narcissistic investment in the prelapsarian image causes him to misread what turns out to be an image of the Fall. When Michael interprets the scene for what it is, Adam does not gush as before: "O pittie and shame, that they who to live well / Enterd so faire, should turn aside to tread / Paths indirect" (11.629–631). Adam has dis-identified; he has regained aesthetic as well as moral distance. With Adam's movement from "compassion" to "pittie" in mind, we might consider Hannah Arendt's severe but suggestive distinction: "Pity, because it is not stricken in the flesh and keeps its sentimental distance, can succeed where compassion always will fail."[33] Having overcome his fixation on the flesh, Adam bends his mind back to the teachings of the Spirit. As Milton's domestic theory appears to fall degraded in the seductresses of book 11, he makes a high ethical point about seeing beyond semblance, about balancing closeness with distance. In a newly imbalanced world, the process of moral equilibration is a painfully inexact science, a matter, Milton suggests, of ongoing trial and error.

THE SYMPATHETIC BODY POLITIC

Antipathy in the domestic sphere, as Milton suggested in the divorce tracts, leads to antipathy in the civil sphere. This causal link is dramatized in book 11. Michael's next "Scene" is one of "Concours in Arms, fierce Faces threatning

Warr," of "bloody Fray," of "factious opposition," all of which, Michael explains to Adam, is the "product / Of those ill mated Marriages thou saw'st" (11.637, 641, 651, 664, 683–684). Milton constructs a vision of political antipathy that results from domestic error and originates in the physical and ethical ill of intemperance. In *Of Education*, we recall, he identified politics, the third part of moral philosophy, with the knowledge of "the beginning, end, and reasons of politicall societies"; politics, then, becomes a proper subject in the epic when Milton represents "politicall societies," of which there are principally three: the devils' in hell, God and the angels' in heaven, and Adam's descendants' on earth, which, given the scope of Michael's vision, ultimately encompasses every political society from first to last. Before focusing on the third of these, which necessarily reflects back on the other two, I want to examine Milton's representations of a sympathetic body politic in two of his prose works from the 1640s, *Of Reformation* (1641) and *The Tenure of Kings and Magistrates* (1649), which will enable us to understand more clearly Milton's representation of sympathy in the political sphere in the final two books of *Paradise Lost*.[34] For Milton, the Fall made the idea of a lasting and thoroughgoing political sympathy deeply problematic. Such a sympathy emerges in the prose as an ideal, linked more to hope than to belief, a condition more of the past and the future than of the present, a prospect to be envisioned, a telos to be worked toward. What might be called the optative status of political sympathy in his thought registers in the rhetorical asperities and adjustments in the two tracts. By the end of the 1640s Milton had high hopes for the establishment of a republic, a mode of political organization predicated not on rigid hierarchical subordination but rather on the harmonious interaction of the various parts of the polity. In this sense, Milton's view of sympathy and his view of republicanism shared an underlying logic, but the relationship between the two, as we shall see, was uncertain and complex.[35]

In *Of Reformation*, his first antiprelatical tract, Milton makes strategic use of two central topoi of political and ecclesiastical organization in classical and Christian thought, Menenius Agrippa's fable of the belly and Paul's figure of the body in 1 Corinthians 12, both of which rely on conceptions of sympathy, of interconnected parts forming a coherent whole. Of the moment of Milton's antiprelatical tracts, from the summer of 1641 to the spring of 1642, David Norbrook writes, "it was in defence of the church as part of the traditional body politic that a new party of constitutional royalists began to emerge," whereas Milton's "emphasis is mainly on the evils of the system he wants to destroy, on a hierarchy in which power is handed down from above," which necessitates "a full and clinical surgery to be performed on the body politic."[36] But although Milton's rhetoric in *Of Reformation* is on the whole strongly negative and vituperative, he does express hope for a positive reformation that would bring the English church more in line with the primitive church. Looking back to the age of Cyprian, Milton writes, "Then did the Spirit of unity and meeknesse inspire, and animate every joynt, and sinew of the mysticall body" (1:547). Milton conceives of the ancient body ecclesiastic as thoroughly sympathetic and raises the prospect that it can be so again. In his allusion to 1 Corinthians 12 here, Milton puts particular emphasis on the sympathetic communion of members, which holds on the deeper anatomic level of "every joynt, and sinew."[37]

Milton's view of "the mysticall body" is illuminated in *De Doctrina Christiana*, in which he cites 1 Corinthians 12 to support the idea that "[f]rom this communion which we have with Christ there arises the mutual communion of his members which, in the Apostles' Creed, is called THE COMMUNION OF SAINTS": "I Cor. xii. 12, 13: *as the body is one, and has many members; and as all those members of the body, which is one, are many, but it is still one body; so it is with Christ. For through one spirit we are all baptized into one body, both Jews and Greeks, both slaves and freemen: and we have all drunk into one spirit,* and xii. 27: *you are the body of Christ, and each of you a member*" (6:499). The communion among the members of Christ's body produces "that mystic body, THE INVISIBLE CHURCH," and, as Milton goes on to explain, "The body of Christ is mystically one, so it follows that the communion of his members must be mystic. It need not be subject to spatial considerations: it includes people from many remote countries, and from all ages since the creation of the world" (6:499, 500). The communion of the members of Christ's body represents a mystical—rather than occult—action at a distance, both spatial and temporal. In this passage Milton does not emphasize the hierarchical idea of Christ as head so much as a widely inclusive, horizontally conceived fellowship of members. The hierarchical idea is explicit not in 1 Corinthians but in Colossians, where, as Ernest Best claims, Paul "worked out the precise nature of the relationship between Christ and the Church."[38] The indefiniteness of that relationship in 1 Corinthians was to the advantage of those who would appeal to the organic analogy to make an antihierarchical point.

For Milton's early nonconformist allies, united in opposition to Bishop Joseph Hall's defense of episcopacy, the Pauline trope was a natural tactical tool—though, indeed, the organic analogy was so open to various rhetorical uses and ideological interpretations that it seemingly could be made to suit anyone's needs.[39] In a sermon preached before the House of Commons in December 1641, Edmund Calamy referred to "the consideration of the great breaches that are in Church and State" as a "bucket to draw the water of teares withal" and, with a war-torn Germany in mind, lamented, "It is a signe that we are not true members of the body of Christ, because we have no more fellow-feeling of the miseries of the same body. A dead member hath no sense of its own misery, or of the bodies distemper. If wee be living members, we will simpathize with the calamities of Gods people."[40] In a work published in 1642, Alexander Grosse also contrasted the living member and the dead: "Our Sympathy with the Churches afflictions should perswade us to this, we must apprehend the calamity which resteth upon the Church, as resting upon our owne persons: *If one member* (saith Saint *Paul*) *doe suffer, all the members suffereth with it.* A dead member indeed hath no sympathy with the rest; but the living member hath a fellow-feeling, a quicke and exquisite sence within, when any of the members are pained or hazarded."[41] Here Grosse proceeds from the suffering of the whole to the suffering of the parts; the suffering of the church perforce entails the suffering of its members. In a rousing Pauline appeal later in his sermon, Calamy exclaims, "We are all of one nation, of one body, one flesh, one Church. There is a Nationall Communion, a Morall Communion, a Politicall Communion, a Spirituall Communion amongst us. I may adde, There is a Communion in misery. We are all in the same condemnation. Let us labour to pitty one another, and to turn one another."[42] Calamy's strategic repetition of "Communion" emphasizes the idea of sympathy in every mode and on every level of human organization. In his well-known sermon *Meroz Cursed,* preached before the House of Commons in February 1642, Stephen Marshall asserted, "All our blessednesse *stands* or *falls* with the blessednesse of the Church. The Church is such a corporation or mysticall body, as hath in it all the properties of a naturall bodie wherein no members can be happy in an abstracted sense, but as parts conjoyned with the whole: because every part hath besides the neare relation to the whole, a subsistency in it." Marshall implores his audience not to turn away from the church but to respond passionately to it: "And indeed, there neither is nor can be, any more certaine or infallible signe of a living member of Christs body, and of our communion with Jesus Christ in his holy Spirit, that Spirit which dwels and acts in his whole mysticall body, then this, to sympathize with the Church, to suffer in the sufferings of it, to rejoyce in the consolations of it and to preferre the good of it, before that of our owne soules."[43] By the time he wrote *The Tenure of Kings and Magistrates,* Milton had put a new hermeneutic spin on the biblical example of Meroz, and Marshall and his fellow Presbyterian backsliders had become not so much allies as adversaries. But at the beginning of the decade Milton's view of a sympathetic body politic was necessarily less constrained.

Nevertheless, in *Of Reformation* Milton places his emphasis less on the sympathy of the body politic than on its disease and corruption. The characteristic tone, and approach, is that of the religio-political surgeon: "Seeing therfore the perillous, and confused estate into which we are faln, and that to the certain knowledge of all men through the irreligious pride and hatefull Tyranny of Prelats ... if we will now resolve to settle affairs ... we must first of all begin roundly to cashier, and cut away from the publick body the noysom, and diseased tumor of Prelacie, and come from Schisme to *unity* with our neighbour Reformed sister Churches" (1:598). This statement immediately recalls Milton's inventive rendering of the fable of the belly, to which I now turn: "Upon a time the Body summon'd all the Members to meet in the Guild for the common good (as *Aesops* Chronicles averre many stranger Accidents) the head by right takes the first seat, and next to it a huge and monstrous Wen little lesse then the Head it selfe, growing to it by a narrower excrescency" (1:583). In evoking the Short Parliament and the bishops in the House of Lords, figured by the "huge and monstrous Wen," Milton adapts the ancient fable to his own purposes; it "has little in common with the classical matrix," Annabel Patterson comments, "except its legendary comic tone."[44]

In Livy's telling, the fable underlines the significance of *concordia*—the word appears twice in the space of some twenty lines—and opposes it to *seditio*. Livy sets the idea of the sympathetic body politic against one that is, as it were, dismembered: "In the days when man's members did not all agree amongst themselves [omnia in unum consentiant], as is now the case, but had each its own ideas and a voice of its own, the other parts thought it unfair that they should have . . . the labour of providing everything for the belly."[45] The concord of the whole depends on the consent of the parts. Seneca, too, in appealing to the organic analogy, emphasized the sympathy of the members: "As all the members of the body are in harmony one with another [omnia inter se membra consentiunt] because it is to the advantage of the whole, so mankind should spare the individual man, because all are born for a life of fellowship, and society can be kept unharmed only by the mutual protection and love [amore] of its parts."[46] According to this view of sympathy, injuring a single human being injures the whole of which he or she is a part. For Seneca's contemporary Paul, it is the Spirit of Christ, not a generalized *pneuma*, that guarantees the sympathy of the whole.

Milton subtly collates the fable of the belly and the figure of the *corpus mysticum* when he writes that the Wen "thought it for the honour of the Body, that such dignities and rich indowments should be decreed him, as did adorne, and set out the noblest Members" (1:583). This sentiment is precisely antithetical to Paul's approach, which undermines the idea of a hierarchy of members and specifically undermines a hierarchical idea of honor: "And those *members* of the body, which we think to be less honourable, upon these we bestow more abundant honour" (1 Cor. 12:23). Insisting on aristocratic privilege, the Wen produces a travesty of the Pauline sentiment that if "one member be honoured, all the members rejoice with it." The members of Milton's body politic are not rejoicing but suffering. Then, as his narrative continues, "a wise and learned Philosopher"—ostensibly a figure of the author—intervenes in the dispute and denies that the Wen is a member of the body at all, much less a highly "honourable" one; the Wen is, rather, "a swolne Tumor," "a bottle of vitious and harden'd excrements," "a heape of hard, and loathsome uncleannes," and "to the head a foul disfigurment and burden" needing to be "cut . . . off" (1:583, 584). As Janel Mueller has shown, Milton's use of "Wen" recalls that by William Prynne in his *Lord Bishops, None of the Lords Bishops*, which appeared in 1640.[47] "But the Prelates (will some say) are by the Laws of the Land *authorized*, and so *incorporated* into the Body of the *State*," Prynne writes, "So as 'tis no easie matter to make this Separation. 'Tis true indeed, that an old *inbred malignant humour*, or *incorporated Wenne* (as *Junius* calls the *Popedome*, and *Hierarchie*) is not easily removed from the Body. But to your *comfort* most Noble Physitians the Wenne hath of its own accord started out of his place, So as it is but closing it up, that it returne not."[48] By extending Junius's figure, applied to "the *Popedome*," to the prelaty, Prynne and then Milton effectively extend the Reformation, taking it further in space and time. Milton denies that the bishops "are by the Laws of the Land *authorized*," and the vehemence, even violence, of his response to this constitutional crisis is underlined by comparison; whereas Prynne's wen will, it seems, simply fall off, Milton's needs to be "cut off." Barbara Lewalski comments that in *Of Reformation* Milton uses "a fiery scornful rhetoric closer to William Prynne than to Smectymnuus," but, in this case at least, Milton appears to out-Prynne Prynne.[49]

Emphasizing an excrescence on the body rather than a "rebellion" within it, Milton focuses less on the sympathetic interaction of parts, the idea that, when healthy, the "instruments" of the body are "mutually participate," as Shakespeare's Menenius Agrippa puts it in *Coriolanus* (1.1.102, 104). But the idea of a sympathetic body politic does gain momentum toward the end of the tract. Appealing again to the organic analogy, Milton observes that "the elements or humors in Mans Body" are not "exactly *homogeneall*," and so "the best founded Commonwealths, and least barbarous have aym'd at a certaine mixture and temperament, partaking the severall vertues of each other State, that each part drawing to it selfe may keep up a steddy, and eev'n uprightnesse in common" (1:599). In spite of the fact that Milton retains an allegiance to monarchism in *Of Reformation*, Norbrook detects "a republicanizing inflection" in this passage;

Milton, he argues, "sees the state not as a descending hierarchy but as a dynamic interaction of component parts which share a common interest. This is a commonwealth in which all the parts are subordinated to the whole rather than the body's being subordinated to the monarchical head. The parts are seen in terms of functions rather than individuals."[50] Especially interpreted along the Pauline lines of 1 Corinthians 12, a physiology of sympathy readily naturalizes a republican politics.

At the end of the treatise, Milton returns to the scriptural passage in imagining a better alternative to the corrupt system—really no system at all, in the true sense—which he heatedly denounces, asking, "Were it such an incurable mischiefe to make a little triall, what all this would doe to the flourishing and growing up of *Christs* mysticall body? As rather to use every poore shift, and if that serve not, to threaten uproare and combustion, and shake the brand of Civill Discord?" (1:612). Through rational reformation, the body politic, Milton suggests, can be as thoroughly sympathetic, as thoroughly concordant, as it once was. Confident that "our Ecclesiall, and Politicall choyses may consent and sort as well together without any rupture in the STATE, as Christians, and Freeholders," Milton turns finally to God, whom he implores to be "mov'd with pitty at the afflicted state of this our shaken *Monarchy*, that now lies labouring under her throwes, and struggling against the grudges of more dreaded Calamities" and, in sum, to "unite us intirely" (1:600, 614, 615). The sympathy of the body politic requires religious and political change on the part of its members, but it also requires the sympathy of God.

Given that the prime motivation of *The Tenure of Kings and Magistrates* was to justify the decapitation of the body politic, one could imagine a rehearsal of the rhetorical strategies of *Of Reformation* with the head now taking the place of the wen. The Pauline appeal to "a dynamic interaction of component parts which share a common interest," to recall Norbrook's characterization, would appear to have been more urgent and apposite than ever. But as Milton's political theory evolved in line with his experience of the Civil Wars, the organic analogy, with its authoritative premise of physiological truth, came to serve his antiregicidal opponents far better than it did him. Without a head, the human body was merely a lifeless trunk; to kill the king, then, was to kill the body politic. Accordingly, Milton developed a new set of rhetorical strategies, foremost among which, as Victoria Kahn argues, was the use of "the ethical logic of metaphor." By suggesting that "kingship was itself simply a metaphor," Milton employed a logic that was utterly inimical to that of the organic analogy, which takes physical presence as its very ground.[51] He argues that "the power of Kings and Magistrates is nothing else, but what is only derivative, transferr'd and committed to them in trust from the People, to the Common good of them all, in whom the power yet remaines fundamentally" (3:202). Conceived organically and analogically, the head's power is not "derivative" but constitutive, an unconditional fact of nature; the "relation" between head and body is not one that the body can "take away" (3:230) without, in effect, taking itself away along with it. When Milton evokes the organic analogy at one point in the *Tenure*, it comes as an afterthought, one in which the head and body are offensively, and nonsensically, apart. Allowing for the moment the idea of hereditary right, he asks, "what can be more just and legal . . . then that a King for crimes proportional, should forfet all his title and inheritance to the people: unless the people must be thought created all for him, he not for them, and they all in one body inferior to him single, which were a kinde of treason against the dignitie of mankind to affirm" (3:203–204). Milton wrests the charge of treason from his accusers and reconceives it on a deeper, more fundamental level. The organic analogy seems here less to expand and unite than to reduce and divide; it follows a logic of "inferior" and superior, high and low.

The model of government that Milton establishes in the *Tenure* is contractual and contingent. He supports that model with a natural-historical narrative. After the Fall, human beings "agreed by common league to bind each other from mutual injury, and joyntly to defend themselves against any that gave disturbance or opposition to such agreement. Hence came Citties, Townes and Common-wealths. And because no faith in all was found sufficiently binding, they saw it needfull to ordaine som authoritie, that might restrain by force and punishment what was violated against peace and common right. This autoritie and power of self-defence and preservation being originally and naturally in every one of them, and unitedly in them all, for ease, for order, and least each man should be his own partial Judge, they communicated and deriv'd either to one, whom for the eminence of his wisdom and integritie they chose above the rest, or to more then one whom they thought of equal deserving: the first was call'd a King; the other Magistrates" (3:199). Because this system proved vulnerable to tyranny, "the Law was set above the Magistrate," or king, and "if the King or Magistrate prov'd unfaithfull to his trust, the people would be disingag'd" (3:200). There is no necessary, organic relation between the ruler and the people. The ruler rules not by birthright but by merit. The power of the ruler is not naturally his; rather, power is "communicated" to him by the people, who possess it "unitedly." Milton effectively reinstates a sense of organicism here but pointedly separates it from kingship, which is merely a function, a consensual construct.

Milton's shrinking away from the organic analogy did not entail a rejection of sympathy as a guiding social and political principle. His valorization of sympathy in the *Tenure* emerges first negatively. Of the Presbyterian backsliders who claimed a fellow feeling with the suffering king, Milton writes, "certainly if we consider who and what they are, on a suddain grown so pitifull, wee may conclude, thir pitty can be no true, and Christian commiseration, but either levitie and shallowness of minde, or else a carnal admiring of that worldly pomp and greatness, from whence they see him fall'n; or rather lastly a dissembl'd and seditious pity, fain'd of industry to begett new discord" (3:193). To a reader of *Paradise Lost*, the third interpretation sounds strikingly Satanic. In Milton's analysis here, a "true, and Christian commiseration" cannot be produced by, or coexist with, cognitive or moral error. It must be morally true and rationally grounded. In *Eikonoklastes* (1649) Milton similarly accused Charles of "fain'd" sympathy.[52] Of the rebellion in Ireland he writes of the king, "He would be thought to commiserat the sad effects of that Rebellion, and to lament that *the teares and blood spilt there did not quench the sparks of our civil* discord heer. But who began these dissentions . . . to hinder and put back the releif of those distressed Protestants, which undoubtedly had it not bin then put back might have sav'd many streames of teares and that blood wherof he seems heer so sadly to bewaile the spilling" (3:480). Given that he was the direct cause of the suffering about which he commiserates, his commiseration is hardly "Christian." In reality, Charles, like Satan, is hardhearted: "But whom God hard'ns, them also he blinds" (3:516). So blinded, he is not capable of true sympathy. To read the *Tenure* forward onto the epic, Adam is in danger of becoming an errant Presbyterian in book 11, sympathizing with his sinful descendants before recognizing their sins. Michael serves, so to speak, to Christianize Adam's commiseration, to ensure that it is not marred and falsified by erroneous perception and interpretation.

Later in the *Tenure* Milton advances a more positive, and comprehensive, view of sympathy. Sympathy now appears far more stable and far less vulnerable to false approximation:

Who knows not that there is a mutual bond of amity and brother-hood between man and man over all the World, neither is it the English Sea that can sever us from that duty and relation: a straiter bond yet there is between fellow-subjects, neighbours, and friends; But when any of these doe one to another so as hostility could doe no worse, what doth the Law decree less against them, then op'n enemies and invaders? or if the Law be not present, or too weake, what doth it warrant us to less then single defence, or civil warr? and from that time forward the Law of civil defensive warr differs nothing from the Law of forren hostility. Nor is it distance of place that makes enmitie, but enmity that makes distance. He therfore that keeps peace with me, neer or remote, of whatsoever Nation, is to mee as farr as all civil and human offices an Englishman and a neighbour. (3:214–215).

Driving this passage is the idea that Charles, by virtue of his misdeeds, has become more truly foreign than a foreigner, but one wonders if Milton is guilty of a bit of political-theoretical backsliding here, embracing the very Pauline logic that his broader argument necessitates rejecting. Some pages later he will insist not on the transcendental nature of "relation" but on its contingency and separability (3:230–231). Here relation is "mystified"; Milton posits the reality of global interaction at a distance. But if one could make a case for a lapse in the logic of his argumentation at this point in the *Tenure*, one could also point to differences between this account of political sympathy and the Pauline account; there is no analogy here, no appeal to physiology. Moreover, and much to the point, there is no superintendent figure here, no king, no father. Milton emphasizes not paternity or patriarchy but "brother-hood," a universal, horizontal relation. In so doing, he projects a kind of universal republic.

A decade later, Milton strained to apply this vision of political sympathy even to his own countrymen, from whom he felt increasingly alienated as they sought reversion—regression, as he would have it—to monarchy and to a body politic in which the members were slaves to a tyrannical head. Nevertheless, there are intimations of organicism in Milton's final republican appeal before the Restoration, *The Readie and Easie Way to Establish a Free Commonwealth* (1660). He diagnoses the desire for restoration as "a strange degenerate contagion suddenly spread among us fitted and prepar'd for new slaverie" (7:422), and, far more emphatically, he writes of a reformed education system, "This would soon spread much more knowledge and civilitie, yea religion through all the parts of the land, by communicating the natural heat of government and culture more distributively to all extreme parts, which now lie numm and neglected, would soon make the whole nation more industrious, more ingenuous at home, more potent, more honorable abroad" (7:460). Milton imagines here a *regenerate* "contagion," a positive sympathetic "communication." As John Rogers suggests, he "conjures an image drawn directly from the radical physiology of a monist such as Francis Glisson," as if the nation were suffering from a severe case of rickets that a sympathetic reorganization of government could soon cure.[53] Yet this recrudescence of organicism does not, on balance, overturn Milton's major emphasis in *The Readie and Easie Way* on the error and disease of backsliding. The idea of the sympathetic body politic ultimately yields to the idea of the pathological body politic, the "degenerate contagion" spreading from top to bottom, head to toe.[54]

CONCORD AND POSTLAPSARIAN POLITICS

With the prose of the 1640s in mind, Michael Schoenfeldt writes, "In *Paradise Lost*, Milton completes the turn away from the nation as a significant unit of social or political organization. Indeed, it is only in the founding of Hell that Milton attends at all to the issue of a nation in his epic." Although I agree with Schoenfeldt's account of the "trajectory of a physiological politics" in Milton, I do not agree that Milton's attention to "the issue of a nation" is limited to his account of hell; the nation is of intense concern to him in his account of future biblical history in book 12—the word and its inflections appear sixteen times in the book. Moreover, Schoenfeldt's claim that Milton narrows his focus to "the one just man in a world of woe, isolated from any notion of a meaningful political community," does, I think, warrant some important qualification.[55] In the final book of the epic Milton excludes the idea of a sympathetic body politic, but he does not exclude the idea of a sympathetic "political community." He represents political sympathy as a postlapsarian reality, but one that is decidedly fragile and fleeting. Relative to the domestic and ethical conceptions of sympathy that we have analyzed, the political conception gets little rhetorical and narrative highlighting. Milton ultimately privileges the individual and the couple over the polity. But to leave out the polity is to discount the comprehensiveness of Milton's moral-philosophical vision of sympathy and to diminish his emphasis on the challenge of sympathy in the postlapsarian world.

A broader political sympathy is notably absent from Michael's dramatic rendering of antediluvian history. His scenes fall into the pattern set by Abdiel in book 5, according to which the virtuous individual stands alone among a multitude of dissentious sinners. Enoch alone opposes "factious opposition," and then Noah, confronted by the dissolute and their "civil Broiles," engages with them in their "Assemblies" and tries to convert them, "But all in vain" (11.718, 722, 726). Noah and his small number of human and animal companions are alone saved from "A World devote to universal rack" (11.821). In book 12, however, Michael gives Adam an account of the first sympathetic polity on earth, formed by Noah's descendants. It is characteristic of Milton's approach in the final book that this political sympathy is narratively, if not temporally, short-lived. The Noachidae

> Shal spend thir dayes in joy unblam'd, and dwell
> Long time in peace by Families and Tribes
> Under paternal rule; till one shall rise
> Of proud ambitious heart, who not content

With fair equalitie, fraternal state,
Will arrogate Dominion undeserv'd
Over his brethren, and quite dispossess
Concord and law of Nature from the Earth.

(12.22–29)

Patterson describes the rise of Nimrod as "a second Fall of Man."[56] Indeed, here Milton draws from the same lexicon of universal sympathy from which he drew prior to his account of the first Fall, when "Natures concord" prevailed (6.311). "Concord," as Spitzer shows, is a particularly complex and resonant word: "Due to a particular coincidence not extant in Greek, there was in Latin a radical *cord-* susceptible to two interpretations: it could be connected not only with *cor, cordis* 'heart' (which was the original meaning), but also with *chorda,* 'string,' the Latin loan word from *chorde*; thus *concordia* could suggest either 'an agreement of hearts, peace, order' (*concord-ia*) or a 'harmony of strings, world harmony' (**con-chord-ia*). Thus psychological harmony and musical harmony (and disharmony: *disc(h)ordia*) were ensconced in one word of poetic ambivalence which allowed for a kind of metaphysical punning."[57] A poet on whom such lexical density was never lost, Milton activates the root sense of "concord" by referring to Nimrod's "proud ambitious heart." By acting on the tyrannical stirrings of his own heart, Nimrod undoes a broad, sympathetic "agreement of hearts." So Milton extends the cardiological discourse of sin that we have followed throughout the epic.

Milton's reference to "paternal rule" is not in the service of a Filmerian ideology naturalizing kingship by analogy with fatherhood, as Milton's swift transition from "paternal" to "fraternal"—a republican keyword—suggests.[58] "Paternal" has the ring of the factual, whereas Milton's ideological emphasis falls on "fraternal," linked to "equalitie" and more powerfully still to "fair," which, by virtue of syntactic proximity, emerges as a kind of folk etymon of "*fra*-ternal." The "state" of Noah's descendants is a kind of brotherly commonwealth.[59] This lateral, familial arrangement produces, but does not guarantee, "concord." In the *Tenure* Milton opposes Charles, "an old and perfet enemy" who operates "by sowing discord," to those who "are still seeking to live at peace with . . . brotherly accord" (3:239). For Milton, true political concord cannot coexist with kingship insofar as kings are necessarily "exalted to that dignitie above thir Brethren" (3:198). The phrase alludes to Deuteronomy, to which Milton goes on to refer directly: "That his heart be not lifted up above his brethren" (Deut. 17:20). With his "proud, ambitious heart," Nimrod does precisely this, raising himself above his brethren and disrupting the sympathy of the political whole.

In *The Readie and Easie Way* the phrases "exalted above thir brethren," "elevated above thir brethren," and "presume or take upon him to be a king and lord over his brethren" pile up in the space of a few pages (7:424, 425, 429). Liberty and equality depend, for Milton, on fraternity. Adam is in no danger of sympathizing with Nimrod; he is "fatherly displeas'd" (12.63). Although he is the first father, he pointedly affirms the brotherly ideal: "O execrable Son so to aspire / Above his Brethren, to himself assuming / Authoritie usurpt, from God not giv'n" (12.64–66). The Deuteronomic phrase is emphatic at the beginning of the line; Milton underlines the hierarchical force of the preposition in order to underline Nimrod's sin.

Nimrod is the first and model tyrant in "regarding neither Law nor the common good," and in ruling "onely for himself and his faction" (3:212). Discord, as we have seen, has already divided the animal kingdom into predator and prey, and Nimrod divides the human race: "Hunting (and Men not Beasts shall be his game) / With Warr and hostile snare such as refuse / Subjection to his Empire tyrannous" (12.30–32). The enjambment of "Subjection" produces the same effect as the enjambment of "Above," but in the opposite direction; Nimrod needs to be above others and needs others to be below him, the root force of the preposition *sub-*. As Michael goes on to explain, "Hee with a crew, whom like Ambition joyns / With him or under him to tyrannize" (12.38–39). Like Satan's faction, Nimrod's is bound by a sympathy more apparent than real. The shift in prepositions is crucial and recapitulates the narrator's account of Satan's crew: "cruel his eye, but cast / Signs of remorse and passion to behold / The fellows of his crime, the followers rather" (1.604–606). Devilish fellowship is a mere illusion; the real arrangement is that of a tyrannical leader and his "followers." Ambition, or the "proud ambitious heart," is inconsistent with sympathy insofar as it always tends toward supremacy.

Milton had made the link between Nimrod and Charles in *Eikonoklastes*. "And yet the Bishops could have told him," he writes, "that *Nimrod*, the first that hunted after Faction is reputed, by ancient Tradition, the first that founded Monarchy; whence it appeares that to hunt after Faction is more properly the Kings Game" (3:466).[60] But the metaphorical use to which Milton put Nimrod's construction of the Tower of Babel in *The Readie and Easie Way* complicates the association: "And what will they at best say of us and of the whole *English* name, but scoffingly, as of that foolish builder, mentiond by our Saviour, who began to build a tower, and was not able to finish it. Where is this goodly tower of a Commonwealth, which the English boasted they would build to over-shadow kings, and be another *Rome* in the west? The foundation indeed they laid gallantly; but fell into a wors confusion, not of tongues, but of factions, then those at the tower of *Babel*" (7:422–423).[61] The object of critique in book 12 is broader than a single tyrant; it is tyranny and factionalism more generally. Milton suggests that Nimrod's story is another version of Satan's. The building of the Tower of Babel is typologically a rebuilding of Pandemonium. But whereas Satan and his crew succeed, Nimrod and his fail. Milton's bitter irony is that men who form factions are no better than devils—and maybe even worse. His image of infernal politics makes this point more explicit: "O shame to men! Devil with Devil damn'd / Firm concord holds, men onely disagree / Of Creatures rational" (2.496–498). Milton goes on to suggest that human society might be less discordant if we considered that we already have "hellish foes anow"; such a perspective "might induce us to accord" (2.504, 503). The devils' sympathy may be no more than a strategic and temporary consent—not true *concord-ia*—but men scarcely achieve even that. In the years before the Restoration Milton had had high hopes that the hearts of his countrymen would *ac-cord*. As this passage intimates, all hope is not lost, but it is tempting to hear in it the voice of the frustrated and embittered republican, who, like Cavendish, though across the political spectrum, found it hard to fathom that a race of men blessed by God with reason could act so unreasonably—and so found it hard to sympathize with them.

Nimrod's rebellion ruins the political sympathy of Noah's descendants, but the discord he brings does not banish concord permanently from the earth. Milton's next vision of political sympathy follows Michael's account of the deliverance of the Jews from Egypt. The primary antagonist is now not Nimrod and his "proud ambitious heart" but Pharaoh and his "stubborn heart . . . still as Ice / More hard'nd after thaw" (12.193–194), another major biblical model that Milton had used against Charles. Milton saw true concord in the primitive republicanism of the Hebrew tribes, what he referred to in *Of Reformation* as the "ancient Republick of the Jews" (1:574). Moses frees his people to a form of government that preserves and protects their freedom:

> the Race elect
> Safe towards *Canaan* from the shoar advance
> Through the wilde Desert, not the readiest way,
> Least entring on the *Canaanite* allarmd
> Warr terrifie them inexpert, and feare
> Return them back to *Egypt*, choosing rather
> Inglorious life with servitude; for life
> To noble and ignoble is more sweet
> Untraind in Armes, where rashness leads not on.
> This also they shall gain by thir delay

> In the wide Wilderness, there they shall found
> Thir government, and thir great Senate choose
> Through the twelve Tribes, to rule by Laws ordaind.
>
> (12.214–226)

In the phrase "not the readiest way" readers have not failed to hear an echo of the title to Milton's late defense of the commonwealth,[62] where he likened his countrymen's backsliding to the Israelites' returning to Egypt: "But I trust I shall have spoken perswasion to abundance of sensible and ingenuous men: to som perhaps whom God may raise of these stones to become children of reviving libertie; and may reclaim, though they seem now chusing them a captain back for *Egypt*, to bethink themselves a little and consider whether they are rushing" (7:463). Again and again Milton insists that political organization, like political action, must be rational—and not magical. In Milton's interpretation, Charles operated by a kind of Satanic magic, and Milton's project in *Eikonoklastes* was, as its core, a project of political disenchantment. He set out to dispel the false sympathetic magic of royalty. "And were that true, which is most fals," he writes, "that all Kings are the Lords Anointed, it were yet absurd to think that the Anointment of God, should be as it were a charme against Law" (3:586). For Milton, the "Law" cannot be "charmed." Only Christ, the Son of God, is the truly anointed; He alone was "Anointed universal king" (3.317). The king of England merely followed around "his own Bratt *Superstition*" (3:526). *Eikon Basilike* was a kind of charmed book, produced to win its readers over to the side of the king while his sins suddenly vanished into thin air.[63] Of Charles's service to Ireland and to Scotland, and his neglect of England, Milton writes, "and yet so many sober Englishmen not sufficiently awake to consider this, like men inchanted with the *Circaean* cup of servitude, will not be held back from running thir own heads into the Yoke of Bondage" (3:488). If the cup is servitude, the cupbearer is the king. His victims are "inchanted with these popular institutes of Tyranny," and those "whom perhaps ignorance without malice, or some error, less then fatal, hath for the time misledd, on this side Sorcery or obduration, may find the grace and good guidance to bethink themselves, and recover" (3:601). As this peroration suggests, the Circean monarch's spell can be broken by a return to God and godly reason. In his account of "the Race elect" in *Paradise Lost* this rationalism informs Milton's emphasis on patience and choice. God might well have "elected" the nation of Abraham and Moses, but they themselves "choose" to delay and to govern themselves as a peace-loving republic; the verb appears twice, the second time with line-ending emphasis, and the absence of end-stopping reinforces the sense of freedom. Milton cites "the supreme councel of seaventie, call'd the *Sanhedrim*, founded by *Moses*" as the first of the "greatest and noblest Commonwealths" (7:436).[64]

Milton's primary emphasis falls on choice in this passage, but he also highlights the significance of "Tribes." Behind its primary referent, "the twelve divisions of the people of Israel" (*OED* 1), lies a deeper sense of original order. Milton locates his first model polity not in history but in nature. The organizational behavior of the ant provides him with a first image of primitive republicanism, as opposed to Filmer's primitive monarchism:

> First crept
> The Parsimonious Emmet, provident
> Of future, in small room large heart enclos'd,
> Pattern of just equalitie perhaps
> Hereafter, join'd in her popular Tribes
> Of Commonaltie.
>
> (7.484–489)

Like his account of Nimrod, Milton's characterization of the "Parsimonious," or careful, ant has been the focus of considerable critical attention since Christopher Hill referred to it in his discussion of the politics of *Paradise Lost*.[65] The ant's status as "an ideologeme of Milton's programme" has led critics to put particular weight behind the words "perhaps"—a politic and defensive hedge—and "Hereafter"—a marker of future possibility.[66] In *The Readie and Easie Way* Milton was more direct in his ideological recruitment of the ant: "*Go to the Ant, thou sluggard*, saith *Solomon*; *consider her waies, and be wise; which having no prince, ruler, or lord, provides her meat in the summer, and gathers her food in the harvest*, which evidently shews us, that they who think the nation undon without a king, though they look grave or haughtie, have not so much true spirit and understanding in them as a pismire: neither are these diligent creatures hence concluded to live in lawless anarchie, or that commended, but are set the examples to imprudent and ungovernd men, of a frugal and self-governing democratie or Commonwealth; safer and more thriving in the joint providence and counsel of many industrious equals, then under the single domination of one imperious Lord" (7:427).[67] Indeed, as the example of Nimrod shows, it was monarchic tyranny that led to "lawless anarchie." By contrast, the ants, like the ancient Hebrews, resist factiousness and belligerence by means of fraternal providence. Milton privileges multiple virtues here, summed up by the phrase "the joint providence and counsel of many industrious equals." Against "domination" he promotes "equality."

Before the formation of "the twelve Tribes" (12.226), Noah's descendants "dwell / Long time in peace by Families and Tribes" (12.22–23), and long before the Flood, before even the creation of man, the ants dwell in their "popular Tribes." The term is common to all three of our examples illustrating sympathetic politics in the epic; for Milton it suggests a primitive, harmonious organizational structure, opposed to faction and natural to God's creation — Eve refers to the "Tribes" of flowers that she has cultivated and arranged in Eden (11.279). And yet the very fact that the tribe is primarily a postlapsarian structure forestalls the conclusion that Milton consigned the ideal polity to the unregainable paradise of the past. The analogy between the "great Senate" of the Israelites and the "Senat" that Milton proposes in *The Readie and Easie Way* suggests that a primitive political greatness might well be recovered — so long as the English imitate not only the "large heart" of the emmet but also the loving image of God.[68] Here again is Milton's radical *cord-*; in this instance, the phrase denotes less "kindly feeling" (*OED* 10b) than "spirit" (11) and "understanding" (12). In Cavendish's ultimately irenic "*Moral Tale of the* Ant *and the* Bee," in which she concludes, "But by this we may perceive, it is not such and such *kinds of Government*, but such and such *ways of Governing*, that make a Commonwealth flourish," she gives the ant's heart a sentimental interpretation: "Nor is it the bigness of the Heart that makes a Creature good-natur'd; for these little Creatures, although they have little Hearts, yet they have great Generosity, Compassion, and Charity to each other."[69] In *The Readie and Easie Way* Milton imagines something curiously like a commonwealth of ants, of men who "are not elevated above thir brethren; live soberly in thir families, walk the streets as other men" (7:425). Such men relate to one another as sympathetic equals.

In the epic the promise of the "great Senate" of the "twelve Tribes" is fulfilled, but, through the wide-angle lens with which Michael shows Adam human history, their success and sympathy are just as fleeting as those of Noah's descendants. So Milton solidifies our sense of a tragic pattern, which can be summed up as a period of concord broken when "dissension springs" (12.353). "Meanwhile they in thir earthly *Canaan* plac't," Michael explains, "Long time shall dwell and prosper, but when sins / National interrupt thir public peace" (12.315–317), God brings "enemies" to interrupt their amity. Milton's phrasing recalls that used to describe the Noachidae: "and dwell / Long time in peace by Families and Tribes." Next to the "eternal Paradise of rest" (12.314) that Michael prefigures for Adam, a "long time" is but a short time, and the sympathy of the godly polity seems like the briefest of triumphs.

As Michael's synoptic biblical drama draws to a close, Milton finally suggests that a universal sympathy is to be found not in the distant past but rather in the distant future. Michael narrates an alchemical apocalypse, in which God will raise

From the conflagrant mass, purg'd and refin'd,
New Heav'ns, new Earth, Ages of endless date
Founded in righteousness and peace and love,
To bring forth fruits Joy and eternal Bliss.

(12.547–551)

The collocation "peace and love" appears six times in the *Doctrine*; it names "the inward knot of mariage" and the sympathetic side of the "twofold Seminary or stock in nature, from whence are deriv'd the issues of love and hatred distinctly flowing through the whole masse of created things" (2:269, 272). But at the end of time, after the divine alchemist has sublimed "the whole masse of created things," sympathy reigns unitary and supreme.[70] At the promised end, "God shall be All in All" (3.341). This Pauline language, echoing 1 Corinthians 15:28, suggests a total and thoroughgoing participation. The sympathy of the whole ruined at the Fall returns after the conflagration.[71] For Fludd, we recall, universal sympathy was a continuously active phenomenon that depended on the universal spirit. His touchstone was not 1 Corinthians 15:28 but 1 Corinthians 12:6: "And there are diversities of operations, but it is the same God which worketh all in all." This Pauline claim, repeated dozens of times in *Mosaicall Philosophy*, underwrites Fludd's argument for universal sympathy as a present reality.[72] When Fludd does look ahead to the end of time, he imagines a magnetic rather than alchemical process. The "vivifying spirit" instills in every creature

> the faculty, to eschew with an irascible and antipatheticall disdain, that which unto it is contrary either in order or nature, or both: untill the time be accomplished, in which after he is exalted, he shall expell all contrariety and discord out of this world, by making a sympatheticall union amongst all things, which also St. Paul *doth argue in these words:* . . . *that God may be all in all. Whereby it is evident, that the catholick Magneticall virtue, which resideth in God's eternall Spirit, shall at the last be exalted after, his glorious victory, and draw all things unto him, and all things shall be one in him, and he in them, and consequently all Discord and Hatred being banished and laid apart, Love, Peace, and Unity, shall erect the perpetuall and never-dying Trophy of this hallowed Victory.*[73]

At the end of time antipathy is ended, and "a sympatheticall union amongst all things" prevails. But given Fludd's emphasis on sympathy not "at the last" but in the present, "this hallowed Victory," seen from a Miltonic perspective, seems less hallowed and less victorious. In Milton's fallen world, sympathy is partial, a provisional achievement, and what Fludd calls "antipatheticall disdain" is not protective but destructive. Before the final end, Paul's participatory logic is most clearly evoked in Abdiel's contest with Satan. Of the Son, Abdiel maintains, "since he the Head / One of our number thus reduc't becomes, / His Laws our Laws, all honour to him done / Returns our own" (5.842–845). Abdiel's conception of the celestial polity is organic and sympathetic.[74] Schoenfeldt establishes that Milton appeals to the idea of the body politic only in heaven, the only realm ruled by a true king and "Head."[75] For Milton, in Nigel Smith's summation, the "general paradigm" is "monarchist in heaven, republican on earth."[76] But, as we have seen, Milton's representation of political sympathy on earth in book 12 is equivocal and only flickeringly positive. The bright light of unified truth comes only when the Lord is "ampler known . . . , / Last in the Clouds from Heav'n to be reveald / In glory of the Father" (12.544–546).

At the very end of *Paradise Lost* Milton shifts from the political back to the domestic sphere.[77] This turn is in one sense dictated by his subject, but it is also prompted, I think, by the poet's "Wearied" political vision. I do not see him experiencing defeat here so much as reexperiencing a recent triumph, his conception of sympathy in Adam and Eve. This sympathy is not universal but particular; it is, so to speak, geographically specific, even as the fallen couple's "place of rest" remains undetermined. It is a matter of moments, of cases, of gestures. Adam and Eve exit from the poem "Both in one Faith unanimous though sad" (12.603). This phrase recalls their state after praying in book 4: "This said unanimous, and other Rites / Observing none, but adoration pure / Which God likes best, into thir inmost bowre / Handed they went" (4.736–739). Their sympathy here is not a matter of timing, and the sense of difference is emphatic when we set the unfallen couple's ingress at this moment in contrast to the fallen couple's exit from Paradise, "hand in hand" (12.648). Milton's insistence on Adam and Eve's "unanimity" also recalls the state of the angels before the War in Heaven, when they "wont to meet / So oft in Festivals of joy and love / Unanimous, as sons of one great Sire" (6.93–95). In the exaltation of the Son, it was unanimity that the Father prescribed: "Under his great Vice-gerent Reign abide / United as one individual Soule / For ever happie" (5.609–611). Satan, of course, could abide no such thing. The poet visibly and audibly enacts the idea of unity here; the sequence of words "United . . . one individual . . ." produces an emphatic pleonasm, heightened by the swift triple echo of the first syllable of "Under."[78] In "United as one individual Soule" Milton gives a diagrammatic definition of "unanimous." The variation of terms tending to the same semantic end conveys the sense of a dynamic unity, which is to be opposed to what Milton referred to in *Areopagitica* as "obedient unanimity" (2:545), the product of mindless conformity and authoritarian necessity.

Adam and Eve are not unanimous in the end in the way they were unanimous in the beginning. The product of mindful conversation, their unanimity fulfills the ideal of the marriage ceremony that Adam had literalized and physicalized at the Fall: "And they shall be one Flesh, one Heart, one Soule" (8.499); the third term has now been restored, if more mutedly. Adam and Eve are married to each other but divorced from the world, to which they will have to establish a new relationship. They are alone together. We see in that final scene the angels working in concert, but we do not get an image of universal sympathy; the image, rather, is emphatically local. The sadness the fallen couple expresses is just; it is not misery. Unlike Eve's in book 10 and Adam's in book 11, these last tears do not overflow. As they leave Eden, Adam and Eve sympathize because they have actively chosen to do so. Milton's point is clear: sympathy also is choice.

MILTON AND THE "MODERN PHILOSOPHER"

Having reached the end of our discussion of Milton, I want to return a final time to Thyer's distinction between Milton the poet and the "modern philosopher," and to make a final claim that the two should be seen in significant conjunction rather than opposition. In *A Treatise of Human Nature* (1739–1740), Thyer's contemporary David Hume both defined *"modern philosophy,"* which was to proceed "only from the solid, permanent, and consistent principles of the imagination," and set out to embody it.[79] In rigorously analyzing human nature, Hume identified sympathy at its very core:

> Whatever other passions we may be actuated by; pride, ambition, avarice, curiosity, revenge or lust; the soul or animating principle of them all is sympathy; nor wou'd they have any force, were we to abstract entirely from the thoughts and sentiments of others. Let all the powers and elements of nature conspire to serve and obey one man: Let the sun rise and set at his command: The sea and rivers roll as he pleases, and the earth furnish spontaneously whatever may be useful or agreeable to him: He will still be miserable, till you give him some one person at least, with whom he may share his happiness, and whose esteem and friendship he may enjoy.[80]

Some twenty years later, in his *Natural History of Religion*, Hume referred more directly to the text underlying this passage: "*Adam*, rising at once, in paradise, and in the full perfection of his faculties, would naturally, as represented by *Milton*, be astonished at the glorious appearances of nature, the heavens, the air, the earth, his own organs and members; and would be led to ask, whence this wonderful scene arose."[81] This is a paraphrase of Adam's first memory, recounted in book 8 of *Paradise Lost*, and precedes by some two hundred lines his appeal to "Collateral love, and deerest amitie." Adam expresses his natural theism and then proceeds to express his natural sympathy. Having recognized a presence above him, Adam goes on to seek one next to him. More than a half-century after Milton's death, his location of sympathy at the center of the moral life of humankind provided Hume with a crucial, authorizing exemplum. The commitments and conclusions of Milton's poetic anthropology both prefigured and partly configured those of what Hume called "the science of MAN."[82]

Milton was not, of course, a modern philosopher in Hume's sense. Whereas Milton conceived universal sympathy as a prelapsarian reality, if an uncertain one, Hume conceived it as a premodern fiction. The prelapsarian world that Milton described comes close to what Hume called the "*poetical* fiction of the *golden age*," when "avarice, ambition, cruelty, selfishness, were never heard of: Cordial affection, compassion, sympathy, were the only movements with which the mind was yet acquainted." This "*poetical* fiction," Hume argued, was "of a piece" with "the *philosophical* fiction of the *state of nature*," in which "a perpetual war of all against all was the result of men's untamed selfishness and barbarity."[83] At opposite extremes, both concepts, the Hesiodic or the Ovidian and the Hobbesian, were equally untrue. For Hume, as we shall see in the final chapter, there was no original, overarching order, except in the mind. Where Milton saw loss, Hume saw merely absence, and where Milton emphasized diachronic change, Hume emphasized psychological error. But even if Milton's Eden was a "*poetical* fiction," it powerfully captured and conveyed something that Hume found essentially true about human nature: we are constantly and connaturally "actuated" by sympathy. For Hume, sympathy functions as a principle of moral coherence in a "modern" philosophical system from which all totalizing principles have been excluded and exploded. Milton preceded Hume, I want to suggest, in proposing that human sympathy provided a compensatory idea of order in a world in which order could not be, or could no longer be, assumed as a universal ontological fact. In his project of developing a moral science, in his influence on Shaftesbury, Hutcheson, and Mandeville, among others, Hobbes contributed far more to the development of Hume's philosophy than Milton did. But Hobbes, too, was a kind of poet in Hume's eyes; he had imagined a great "anthropomachy" at the dawn of human time. If he was closer to Hobbes's method, then, Hume was closer to Milton's matter.

In his implicit critique of the occult science of sympathy in books 9 and 10 of *Paradise Lost,* and in his moral-philosophical analysis of sympathy more generally in the final three books, Milton not only anticipates Thyer's "modern philosopher," if not Hume's, but also establishes his own kind of philosophical modernity.[84] In the plot of *Paradise Lost* Milton provides us with a historical allegory of sympathy in the seventeenth century: as Adam and Eve pass from a state of innocence to a state of experience, the order of things ceases to be external and universal and is reestablished on an internal, moral level. Sympathy ceases to be an enchanted principle of things and is reconceived as a rational principle of persons. The Miltonic project of disenchanting sympathy finds its ultimate fulfillment, one might say, in the moral philosophy of Hume. But historical change—"real" rather than "allegoric," to borrow Satan's distinction from *Paradise Regained*—is not so simple or straightforward. The magic of sympathy did not just disappear. As we shall see in the next chapter, it found new life in a new paradise, "happier farr."

5

"MORAL MAGICK": CAMBRIDGE PLATONISM AND THE THIRD EARL OF SHAFTESBURY

Around the turn of the nineteenth century, Anna Seward reflected on the critical depreciation—already long-standing—of the final books of *Paradise Lost*: "What should we think of a critic who was to declare that those, so much less poetical books, had dissolved the enchantment of that work?"[1] We should think this critic, it might be answered, right in at least one sense, if not the intended one. Through book 9 and the middle of book 10 Milton shows the ruinous effects of attraction and magical thinking, and then, in the "less poetical books," he shows the reparative effects of love and rational thinking. Purged of occultism, human sympathy becomes a principle of coherence that compensates for the loss of universal sympathy. In this dynamic of competing and compensatory orders, we can see a poetic precedent for that at the center of Hume's antimystical moral philosophy. But to proceed from Milton directly to Hume, as we did at the end of the previous chapter, is to risk exaggerating the extent to which a magical view of the world was simply and swiftly "dissolved." Over the course of the century between the death of Milton and the death of Hume, sympathy emerged as a key topic, and a keyword, in moral-philosophical discussions at the same time that it was gradually disappearing from the mainstream of natural philosophy. Yet, as it became a subject of primarily moral—and aesthetic—consideration, sympathy retained its aura of enchantment. As it was increasingly located within human nature, the magical associations of sympathy persisted; within its more limited sphere of activity, sympathy carried with it traces of the Neoplatonic, natural-magical, and occultist traditions in which it had figured so significantly. At the turn of the eighteenth century, Richard Steele forcibly expressed this fusion of the moral and the magical:

"The Eternal God . . . presses us by Natural Society to a close Union with each other, which is methinks, a sort of enlargement of our very selves when we run into the Ideas, Sensations and Concerns of our Brethren: by this Force of their make, Men are insensibly hurried into each other, and by a secret charm we Lament with the Unfortunate, and rejoyce with the Glad."[2] One might detect the presence of Locke in the reference to "Sensations," the impact of Grotius, Pufendorf, and Cumberland in the emphasis on "Natural Society," as well as the voice of Paul in the echo of Romans 12:15, but in Steele's phrase "secret charm" a more mystical tradition registers. The long-standing association between sympathy and magic endured, and human sympathy continued to bear the "secret charm" of its cosmic counterpart.

In making a case for the enduring enchantment of sympathy, I demonstrate in this chapter the significant connection between the magical worldviews of the Cambridge Platonists—especially Ralph Cudworth (1617–1688), Henry More, and Benjamin Whichcote (1609–1683)—and the moral and aesthetic worldview of the third Earl of Shaftesbury (1671–1713). For both, sympathy functioned as a crucial conceptual stay against the disenchantment and, to use Shaftesbury's own term, "distraction" of the world. In reading Shaftesbury and the Cambridge Platonists, we find ourselves in a distinctly different world from Milton's, where the fact of climacteric change and the imperative of rational containment are almost everywhere apparent. In Shaftesbury's bright and tranquil settings in particular, "The catastrophe of that original pair," his summation of *Paradise Lost*, seems to have been no catastrophe at all. He evokes neither the fallen world into which Adam and Eve make their way at the end of the epic, nor its prelapsarian state; he seems to insist, rather, on a nonlapsarian world. In *The Moralists*, the philosophical dialogue at the center of his principal work, *Characteristicks of Men, Manners, Opinions, Times* (1st ed., 1711), Shaftesbury gives his audience a vision of a present paradise unlost, even unlosable. The sympathy of the whole remains, in all of its ravishing beauty.

Shaftesbury represents a critical transitional figure in the more expansive and more inclusive history of sympathy for which I have been making a case. More consistently and comprehensively than his philosophical precursors, Shaftesbury made a claim for sympathy as the binding force of the moral and social spheres. In the first decades of the eighteenth century there was a significant cultural synergy between this claim and those frequently made in the *Spectator*, the *Guardian*, and the *Tatler* for what Addison summed up by the term "Good-nature."[3] And yet what has not been sufficiently recognized is the extent to which Shaftesbury elevated human sympathy as an organizing principle of moral life within a totalizing sympathetic framework, one in which the part existed in necessary relation to a universal, mystical whole. This synecdochal scheme has tended to be referred to Shaftesbury's development of a philosophical aesthetics, but it was also a fundamental principle of Shaftesbury's natural philosophy, which built significantly on earlier natural and natural-magical traditions. Long understood to be a central figure in the history of sensibility, Shaftesbury has been read almost exclusively in one direction—forward—as if his writing about sympathy were merely the means to a future moral end.[4] It is time to approach him differently. In the case of Shaftesbury the historiographic tendency to treat sympathy as if it had two separate lives, one in the spheres of natural philosophy and natural magic and the other in the spheres of moral philosophy and aesthetics, is particularly glaring and particularly distorting of his larger philosophical project. To recognize Shaftesbury's achievement and the multivalent forms of Shaftesburian sympathy we need to see him not at the beginning of a historical movement, nor at the end, but as a particularly important presence in a broader, more complex history that goes back to Stoic and Neoplatonic cosmology as well as forward to later eighteenth-century literature and moral philosophy. In studying Shaftesburian sympathy from this integrative perspective, we are able to recover the totalizing aspiration of his philosophy, his commitment to a philosophy of nature as well as of human nature, which tends to get lost when he is treated narrowly as a "British moralist." In seventeenth-century literary and intellectual culture, I have been arguing, the discursive fields of sympathy were not starkly divided but rather overlapped in complex and constructive ways; this fruitful crossover did not simply cease at the turn of the eighteenth century.

No less than the work of Digby, Cavendish, and Milton, *Characteristicks* should be understood as a sustained and varied attempt to come to terms with sympathy—as a force of human nature, as a fact of cosmic order—one that was responsive to, and informed by, contemporary philosophical, political, and religious debates. Shaftesbury's project of coming to terms with sympathy, in its particular emphasis on the good, the beautiful, and the sublime, is strikingly new, but it is also importantly continuous with and in dialogue with forms and figures of the philosophical past. Shaftesbury inherited from the Cambridge Platonists a syncretizing rather than a segregating habit of mind, according to which any idea of moral coherence needed to be fitted into a broader natural scheme. He drew from More, Cudworth, and Whichcote not only a positive view of human nature but also an enchanted view of the world. Up until the end of the 1680s, More and Cudworth energetically promoted a magical, vitalist worldview of which sympathy was a central organizing principle. As with Shaftesbury, my motive in focusing on the Cambridge Platonists is in part corrective. Reacting against what he perceived as an overemphasis on Shaftesbury, R. S. Crane, as we have seen, looked further back to the "anti-Puritan, anti-Stoic, and anti-Hobbesian divines of the Latitudinarian school" in constructing his genealogy of sensibility. Crane identified Benjamin Whichcote as "an early pioneer" of this "movement," and, indeed, Whichcote opposed the stern Calvinism of his first tutor at Emmanuel College, Cambridge, Anthony Tuckney, and exhorted others to "detest and reject that doctrine which saith, that God made man *in a state of war*."[5] Whichcote's man, rather, was "the mildest creature under heaven"; in his natural state he was "most *Tender* and compassionate" and could not "by *true* Religion be made Fierce and Cruel."[6] In making morality natural, and in making morality the essence of religion, Whichcote propounded an irenic, "reconciling" Christianity in a time of division and war.[7] But the positive view of human nature shared by the Cambridge Platonists needs to be understood in a wider intellectual context—that is, beyond the Latitudinarian theology that Crane made his exclusive focus. As More and Cudworth in particular emphasized, the ethical and the physical were inextricable; they were part of the same "system," in the sense of the title of Cudworth's summa, *The True Intellectual System of the Universe* (1678). The divide that existed between Cavendish's view of the natural world, predicated on a comprehensive vitalist materialism, and her view of the social world, driven by an ambivalent Hobbesian pessimism, did not obtain in the vitalist, spiritualist scheme of the Cambridge Platonists, which was far less negatively affected and informed by the social and political crisis of the mid-century.

More clearly and determinedly than Cavendish's, the anti-Hobbesianism of the Cambridge Platonists was part of a broader anti-Epicureanism, an opposition to a thoroughgoing mechanistic worldview that made dispersion and disconnection the "natural" state of things on every level of reality. As Cudworth wrote of the mechanists, "They make a kind of Dead and Wooden World, as it were a Carved Statue, that hath nothing neither *Vital* nor *Magical* at all in it."[8] More and Cudworth insisted on a vital, magical world founded on a principle of sympathetic connection. If everything connected, so too did humankind, and to suggest otherwise was to oppose God and nature. In examining the natural and moral philosophies of the Cambridge Platonists, we gain a clearer sense of the close and highly significant relationship between the advancement of Epicurean physics in the seventeenth century and a new emphasis on sympathy as a principle of physical and ethical coherence—a relationship that the chaos of the Civil Wars made especially charged. For More and Cudworth the idea of sympathy was at the core not only of their promotion of Platonism but also of their opposition to Epicureanism; both used it as a rhetorical-conceptual tool in an effort to weaken and uproot a mechanical philosophy conceived along Epicurean lines and to advocate peace, love, and harmony in church and society.

Shaftesbury carried forward this anti-Epicurean strain, and it functioned similarly as a driving force of his philosophy. In rejecting the dry and detached approach of the natural philosopher, however, he transfigured the Stoic-Platonic worldview according to a new aesthetic orientation. In *Characteristicks*, universal sympathy begins to seem less like a principle of coherence than a principle of composition. Shaftesbury gives his readers the world *als Kunstwerk*. His version of a sympathetic worldview comes together and comes across in a markedly different way from More's and Cudworth's. The direction has changed; it seems no longer the case that a universal natural sympathy is setting the terms for a moral, social sympathy, but vice versa. While retaining an idea of order on the level of the whole, Shaftesbury shifted the primary locus of coherence to society. This shift went hand in hand with a systematic rethinking of philosophical discourse. Moving away from the hyperformal philosophical "system," the academic treatise with its remote particulars and interminable longueurs, Shaftesbury pursued a new decorum along gentlemanly lines; his elevation of sociability necessitated a more sociable form and, indeed, a more sociable variety of forms. In Gadamer's formulation, Shaftesbury was concerned with "the attitude of the man who understands a joke and tells one because he is aware of a deeper union with his interlocutor."[9] Conversation was as fundamental to Shaftesbury's thought as it was to Cavendish's and Milton's, but in Shaftesbury's case it was less an object of abstraction; as an idea and an ideal, it remained grounded in everyday social practice, a worldly discourse sustained by sympathetic interlocutors. For Cavendish, as we have seen, polite conversation was often no more than a form of violence fashionably veiled; for Shaftesbury, by contrast, it was a mode of communication whose "conventions," as Lawrence E. Klein has argued, "implied the values of freedom, equality, activity, pleasure, and restraint"—the core of a Whig "cultural ideology" that emerged after 1688.[10] Shaftesbury suggested that the social and moral life of humankind, which had been increasingly neglected by natural philosophy, depended on the communication and circulation of the passions. But in turning away from a certain form and character of natural philosophy, he did not turn away from natural philosophy altogether, which constituted an essential part of an overall understanding of the world. Shaftesbury's achievement was in part to make the enchanted world of More and Cudworth "conversable."

I begin this chapter by examining More's and Cudworth's conceptions and representations of the universe. In their natural-philosophical writing, we find evidence not of the widening "disenchantment of the world" but of an explicit and committed enchantment. Emphasizing ancient sources, More and Cudworth represented a sympathetic worldview as both classically pure and fundamentally sacred. In asserting the reality of a thoroughgoing magical sympathy in the world, they aimed on one hand to distance themselves from Paracelsian "enthusiasts," who disowned all reason in the reckless pursuit of private fancies, and on the other to confute Epicurean atheists, who saw the world not as a mystical unity but as a fortuitous configuration of warring atoms. More and Cudworth did not wholly reject the mechanical philosophy, but they expressed serious doubt that it could account for everything in the universe. In its denial of a spiritually charged reality, they emphasized, materialism courted atheism. In the next section, I examine More's and Cudworth's conceptions and representations of morality. Both insisted on a total order that subsumed the physical as well as the ethical. A concept of human sympathy emerges in their writing as a logical consequence of their natural-philosophical commitments and as a moral consequence of their theological commitments. More's and Cudworth's anti-Epicureanism assumed the form of an insistence on the real nature of morality and on the existence of a fundamental sympathy among human beings, who were not atomistically scattered but essentially interconnected. As the universe is mystically one, so too, they claimed, is society.

From the intellectual milieu of Cambridge Platonism I turn to that of Shaftesbury in the following three sections of the chapter, suggesting that we cannot fully understand the latter without carefully attending to the former. Shaftesbury's intellectual ties to the Cambridge Platonists have received critical attention, but the complex and significant relationship between Shaftesbury's natural and moral conceptions of sympathy, a crucial legacy of Cambridge Platonism, has not.[11] Previous accounts of Shaftesburian sympathy, more glancing than searching, have tended to focus on his moral worldview to the exclusion of his natural worldview, an approach that obscures his aim to unite physics, ethics, and aesthetics under a single philosophical banner. Shaftesbury gained from More, Cudworth, and Whichcote not only an idea of human nature as fundamentally good but also an idea of the natural world as vitally and magically united. In the first section devoted to Shaftesbury, I analyze his representation of sympathy as a process of what he called "*moral Magick*," a phrase that is importantly emblematic of his broader philosophical approach and achievement. Shaftesbury placed a new emphasis on the moral valence and value of sympathy while perpetuating an older aura of enchantment. This moral emphasis merged with a new aesthetic emphasis; acting on a natural propensity to sympathize with others was both good and beautiful. The generous sympathizer was a moral artist. The work of art was, at base, an act of generous sympathy. In its idealizing mode, Shaftesbury's philosophy comes to seem like an anagram in which every permutation of the constituent elements yields a perfect synonym.

But not least because of his commitment to bringing philosophy "to the world," to making it relevant to and reflective of the real experiences of men (and of men in particular), Shaftesbury also recognized that sympathy was not always as it was in the master's workshop or on the gentleman's estate—that it had a darker and more dangerous aspect. Unlike More and Cudworth, whose moral vision was focused on the "eternal and immutable," Shaftesbury also confronted sympathy as a problem in the here and now, one that, as we have seen in the cases of Digby, Cavendish, and Milton, was bound up with a recognition of sympathy's power. In *Characteristicks* Shaftesbury suggests that the process of affective communication is so powerful and pervasive that it accounts for not only the pleasures of associating with friends and family but also the dangers of forming factions, waging wars, and succumbing to religious fanaticism. He struggles to reconcile his anti-Hobbesian claim for the naturalness of kind affection, which promotes the idea of a universal social sympathy, with a more empirical survey of a volatile and heterogeneous society. In the next section I shift from Shaftesbury's view of society to his view of the cosmos, the former subsumed by the latter in a totalizing scheme, an organic "system." Whereas Digby and others, as we have seen, aimed to preserve a sympathetic worldview through mechanization, Shaftesbury aimed to *conserve* it, in the artistic sense, through aestheticization. Sympathy was a principle not only of order but also of beauty, to which a mechanistic understanding of things was antithetical. But if the case of Digby and his powder of sympathy ultimately revealed the weakening ontological status of sympathy as a universal principle, the case of Shaftesbury yields an analogous result from the very different vantage point of what might be called a philosophical success. Although he insisted on the reality of an overarching external order, Shaftesbury's internalization of sympathy, his treatment of it in psychological and aesthetic terms, could not but in the end cast that reality into doubt. This problem emerges particularly clearly in *The Moralists*, which is, among other things, a dialogue and debate about the very existence of a sympathetic universe. In a complex, hybrid form, a dialogue embedded in a letter, Shaftesbury puts the Stoic and the Platonic traditions in conversation with the Academic and the Pyrrhonian. At a moment of narrative climax, the former overcome the latter, but the victory is not definitive, nor, Shaftesbury seems to imply, can it be at this time. The ontological certainty of the Cambridge Platonists must now be won; it has become a matter of persuasion and probability. The universal sympathy of

things is no longer immediate but now subject to psychology, a matter of sensation and perception, and it has become subject to plot, to variable narrative
conditions. *The Moralists*, to which I devote an extended reading at the end of
the chapter, ultimately exposes the contingency and constructedness of a sympathetic worldview. But in registering the claims of skepticism and empiricism,
Shaftesbury also suggests how that worldview might survive—in the process of
sympathy itself.

MORE, CUDWORTH, AND THE ANTI-EPICUREAN COSMOS

The term "Cambridge Platonists" is always in danger of overstating the social
and intellectual uniformity of those to whom it is applied—as if it were a club
with strict requirements for membership—and of overstating the place and
importance of Platonic traditions in their thought. To take just one example,
Aristotle is a crucial, foundational source in *The True Intellectual System*.[12] It
remains true, however, that More, Cudworth, and Whichcote were, if not single-
minded Platonists, "very philosophically and platonically given"—a phrase that
More applied to the Quaker George Keith in a letter to Lady Anne Conway.[13]
Whichcote became a fellow of Emmanuel College, Cambridge, in 1633, and
over the next decade or so his teaching had a formative effect on Cudworth and
John Smith (1618–1652), both Emmanuel undergraduates. As Gilbert Burnet
wrote of Whichcote, "He set young students much on reading the ancient
Philosophers, chiefly *Plato, Tully*, and *Plotin*, and on considering the Christian
religion as a doctrine sent from God, both to elevate and sweeten humane
nature, in which he was a great example, as well as a wise and kind instructer."[14]
Like Milton, More was a student at Christ's College, Cambridge, and it was
there that, "'having begun to read now the *Platonick* Writers, *Marsilius Ficinus*,
Plotinus himself, *Mercurius Tismegistus*,'" as he explained, he found a new intellectual direction.[15] Among the Cambridge Platonists, More and Cudworth
expressed the strongest commitment to the idea of a general sympathy, and,
under a broadly Platonic influence, both conceived of it in magical terms. For
More and Cudworth, a magical view of things was not to be rejected or rationalized but purged and purified; it was always already rational. Their approach to a
sympathetic worldview was not mechanizing but spiritualizing on one hand and
classicizing on the other, both of which functioned to remove impurities, so to
speak. Like Digby—and, in a very different mode, Milton—More and Cudworth
aimed to free sympathy of its Paracelsian associations, but, unlike Digby and
Milton, they did not attempt to sever the tie between sympathy and magic; rather,

they sought to strengthen it by removing more recent cultural accretions and revealing its ancient purity. This classicizing approach to a sympathetic world-view ultimately set the stage, as we shall see, for Shaftesbury's aestheticizing approach, which preserved but reoriented an emphasis on Platonic mysticism—one far less ambivalent than Cavendish's. More and Cudworth bequeathed to Shaftesbury not only a mystical idea of sympathy but also the strategic recourse to that idea as part of a vitalist, spiritualist opposition to Epicureanism. Sympathy was at the core of More's and Cudworth's anti-Epicurean worldviews.

Like the Florentine Platonists, More and Cudworth went back *ad fontes* to support their claim that magic was not opposed to religion but deeply harmonious with it, even in some sense identical to it.[16] As Cudworth explained in *The True Intellectual System*—which, though it was not published until 1678, was long in the making and appears to have been completed by 1671—Zoroaster's magic "is defined to have been nothing else, but . . . *The Worship of the Gods*," and, he goes on, "as *Magick* is commonly conceived to be founded in a certain *Vital Sympathy* that is in the Universe, so did these ancient Persian *Magi*, and Chaldeans (as *Psellus* tells us) suppose . . . *that there was a Sympathy, betwixt the Superiour and Inferiour Beings*; but it seems, the only way at first by them approved, of attracting the Influence and Assistance of those Superior Invisible Powers, was by *Piety, Devotion*, and *Religious Rites*." Only later did this "*Theurgical Magick*" fall away from its sacred origins and become "*downright Sorcery* and *Witchcraft*; the only thing which is now vulgarly called *Magick*."[17] At the beginning sympathy, magic, and religion were all, in effect, one. More and Cudworth propounded an elite, intellectual view of magic that did not cross religion but rather aimed to strengthen its foundations. As More in particular argued, Paracelsianism, by contrast, gave magic a bad name. It took irrational liberties with an ancient truth. The urgency of More's opposition to it can be understood in terms of his own passionate support of a magical worldview; too close to the Paracelsians for comfort in a sense, More responded with vehement denunciation and dissociation.

This response is plainly in view in More's well-known debate with Thomas Vaughan (1621–1666), whom he accuses of going too far with his magical, animistic cosmology.[18] In the observations on Vaughan's writings appended to *Enthusiasmus Triumphatus* (1656), More's early strategy is to tar Vaughan with associations of Catholicism. Of Vaughan's *Anthroposophia Theomagica*, he writes, "Me thinks I smell a Gunpowder-plot," and suggests that Vaughan's cabal, the Rosicrucian Brotherhood, "might . . . be received with like solemnity that those Apostles at *Rome*, the Cardinals."[19] More's principal charge is that while the "grand fault" of the Aristotelians "is that they do not say the World is

Animate," Vaughan's is "far greater" in that he "gives so ridiculous unproportionable account of that Tenet." By means of the "meer vagrant imaginations seated in [his] own subsultorious & skip-jack phansie," Vaughan turns the mundane animal into a monster. Recalling Bacon's critique of natural magic from decades earlier, More claims that Vaughan is "a clicker at the slightest shadows of similitude" and a "pretty Parabolist."[20] For More, Vaughan's pseudonym was ironically antiphrastic; he was nowhere near the truth: "I say, *Philalethes,* The Sunne being the heart of the world, according to those that be more discreetly fantasticall (consult Dr. *Fludd,* thou art but a bad chip of that block) it was to be expected, if thou wouldst have the Flux and Reflux to be the Pulse, that it should come from the Sun, that is reputed the heart of the world; but it comes from the Moon." As we have seen, in his commentary on *Paradise Lost* Patrick Hume, too, associated the sun-heart analogy with Fludd. Vaughan, according to More, does not have the good sense even to follow the less outrageous conceits of other enthusiasts like Fludd; the phrase "discreetly fantasticall" is tartly oxymoronic. More again claims the Baconian mantle in declaring that "in the *Homologi termini* of similitudes, there ought to be something in some sort peculiar and restrained, or else it is flat, ridiculous, and non-sense." Similitudes lend themselves to enthusiastic overreaching, and so it is especially important that they be subjected to rational oversight. That More is speaking against the "pretty parabolist" as a fellow Parabolist becomes clear when More advertises his own "*Philosophicall Poems,*" in which "the intelligent Reader may understand, how far, and in what sense any sober *Platonist* will allow the world to be an *Animal.*"[21] Rather than a "sober Platonist," as More declared himself to be, Vaughan was an enthusiastic Fluddian.[22]

More promoted a Platonic worldview purged of Paracelsian or Fluddian fancy. In a burst of what seems itself to be enthusiasm in *Enthusiasmus Triumphatus* he condemns "the rampant and delirious Fancies of that great boaster of Europe *Paracelsus,* whose unbridled imagination and bold and confident obtrusion of his uncouth and supine inventions upon the world has . . . given occasion to the wildest Philosophicall Enthusiasmes that ever was broached by any either Christian or Heathen." More is not, he points out, accusing Paracelsus of atheism, but he does assert the threat to Christianity posed by Paracelsus's position on astrology, his making the stars "such knowing, powerfull, and compassionate spectatours of humane affairs," which does "damage . . . to the authority of our blessed Saviour his miracles."[23] In this respect, Paracelsus's view of sympathy went beyond More's. Cudworth approached Paracelsianism more soberly than More. Rather than pathologizing it, he historicized it, if loosely and self-confirmingly. Cudworth explains that Heraclitus bequeathed his idea of a dual, vertical order not only to

Zeno and his Stoic followers but also to Hippocrates, and, "Lastly, as the Latter *Platonists* and *Peripateticks* have unanimously followed their Masters herein, whose *Vegetative Soul* also is no other than a *Plastick Nature*; so the *Chymists* and *Paracelsians* insist much upon the same thing, and seem rather to have carried the Notion on further, in the Bodies of Animals, where they call it by a new name of their own, the *Archeus*."[24] In the phrase "seem to have carried the Notion on further" there is an undertone of criticism, but Cudworth's point is principally that the Paracelsian notion of "the *Archeus*" and his own notion of a plastic nature represent distinct branches of the same broad theistic genealogy.[25] In spite of their distancing and critical responses to Paracelsianism, both More and Cudworth were allied with "the *Chymists* and *Paracelsians*" in their vitalism and spiritualism.

More and Cudworth held in common with Paracelsus a guiding belief in sympathy as a fundamental organizing principle of life. Although Paracelsus and Fludd both looked back to antiquity in formulating their philosophical commitments, More believed that, under the influence of a "wild" enthusiasm, they had lost touch with the ancient wisdom. Setting their philosophical extravagances aside, he posited, we recall, a "*Magick Sympathy* . . . seated in the Unity of the Spirit of the World," one that accounted for "not onely the *Sympathy of parts* in one particular Subject, but of different and distant Subjects." The efficacy of sympathetic cures could ultimately be referred to the notion, as "*Plotinus* sayes, that the World is . . . *the grand* Magus or *Enchanter*."[26] Cudworth gave the genealogy of his sympathetic worldview in *The True Intellectual System*: he privileges the "Corporeal Theism" of Heraclitus and Zeno, "which supposes the whole World to be one *Animal*."[27] The two basic tenets of "the right *Heraclitick* and *Zenonian Cabbala*" are these: "First, that there was an *Animalish, Sentient* and *Intellectual Nature*, or a *Conscious Soul* and *Mind*, that presided over the whole World . . . ; Secondly, that this *Sentient* and *Intellectual Nature*, or *Corporeal Soul* and *Mind* of the Universe, did contain also under it, or within it, as the inferiour part of it, a certain *Plastick Nature* or *Spermatick Principle* which was properly the *Fate of all things*."[28] Cudworth's "Plastick Nature" mediates between highest and lowest, and he goes on to assert that "the Plastick nature . . . must be concluded to act *Fatally, Magically* and *Sympathetically*." To clarify this triad of adverbs, Cudworth turns to Plotinus. He cites and then glosses the passage in the *Enneads* (4.4.40) where Plotinus, himself looking back to Empedocles, describes the efficacy of magic in terms of *sympatheia*:

> The true *Magick* is the Friendship and Discord that is in the Universe; and again Magick is said to be founded . . . *In the Sympathy and Variety of diverse Powers conspiring together into one Animal.* Of which Passages, though the

Cambridge Platonism and Shaftesbury

Principal meaning seem to be this, that the ground of Magical Fascination, is one *Vital Unitive Principle* in the Universe; yet they imply also, that there is a certain *Vital Energy*, not in the way of *Knowledge* and *Fancy*, *Will* and *Animal Appetite*, but *Fatally Sympathetical* and *Magical*. As indeed that Mutual *Sympathy* which we have constant Experience of, betwixt our *Soul* and our *Body*, (being not a Material and Mechanical, but Vital thing) may be called also *Magical*.[29]

Cudworth's claim for a fundamental, magical sympathy is emphatic here. His "Plastick Nature" is analogous to More's "*Spirit of Nature* or *Inferiour Soul of the World*," which, we recall, More defined as "*pervading the whole Matter of the Universe, and exercising a plastical power therein*" and "*raising such Phaenomena in the World . . . as cannot be resolved into meer Mechanical powers*."[30] The terms "plastical" and "vital" carry the ideological burden of opposing the "merely" mechanical. Like Cudworth, More insisted that his principle was necessary: "This *Spirit of the World* has Faculties that work not by Election, but fatally or naturally."[31] Supporting this idea of a "fatal" nature Cudworth cites William Harvey's claim that nature acts "*secundum Leges*" or, as he later puts it himself, "according to *Laws* and *Commands*, prescribed to it by a *Perfect Intellect*, and imprest upon it."[32] John Henry has explained this insistence on natural necessity in the broader terms of a providential theology requiring that God act "in accordance with the moral demands placed upon Him by His own goodness and in accordance with the essential relationships inherent in the nature of things."[33] Plastic Nature and the Spirit of Nature function in part to guarantee the best possible world under the perfectly rational providence of God.

In putting forward his theory of plastic nature—which came to make a strong impression on Shaftesbury—Cudworth did not outright reject mechanism, but he denied its explanatory all-sufficiency.[34] As he explains, "the *Mechanick Powers* are not rejected, but taken in, so far as they could comply serviceably with the *Intellectual Model and Platform*," but the "One *Understanding* and *Intending Cause* . . . when either those *Mechanick Powers* fall short, or the *Stubborn Necessity* of *Matter* proves uncompliant, does over-rule the same, and supply the Defects thereof, by that which is *Vital*." Translated into literary terms, this theory suggests the climactic descent of a *deus ex machina*, or, rather, a kind of *deus super machinam*. Against the atheistic potential of an exclusively mechanistic conception of the world, Cudworth's account preserves a clear space for the divine. At the same time, the theory of plastic nature preserves God's majesty by not compelling Him to do the menial labor of a servant. Cudworth's underlying objection to a thoroughgoing mechanistic view of the world was that it necessarily denied the fundamental truth of the universal and divine sympathy produced by his plastic nature. Plastic nature "doth reconcile the *Contrarieties* and *Enmities* of Particular things, and bring them into one *General Harmony* in the *Whole*"; it "makes all things . . . to conspire every where, and agree together into one Harmony."[35] For More and Cudworth, a thoroughgoing mechanism constituted not a "new philosophy" but rather, as More put it, "those old cast rags of *Epicurus* his School, the *Exuvious Effluxes* of things."[36] It was no more than, in Cudworth's phrase, "Atheism openly Swaggering, under the glorious Appearance of Wisdom and Philosophy." The urgency and fervency of More's and Cudworth's responses to the mechanical philosophy reflect the enormously high stakes of contemporary natural-philosophy debate, which bore directly on the very foundations of religion—the belief in God and His role in the world. Cudworth explains that he was "obliged" to direct his "First and Principal Assault upon the *Atomick Atheism* . . . because it is that alone which publickly confronts the World, and like that proud *Uncircumcised Philistine*, openly *defies the Hosts of the Living God*."[37] The currency of and intellectual force behind Epicureanism required an elaborate and emphatic response. In a prefatory address to the reader in his *Explanation of the Grand Mystery of Godliness* (1660), More sets his own response in an intellectual-autobiographical context:

> I saw that other abhorred monster, Atheisme, *proudly strutting with a lofty gate and impudent forehead, boasting himself the onely genuine offspring of true Wisdome and Philosophy, namely of that which makes* Matter *alone the Substance of all things in the world. This misshapen Creature was first nour- ished up in the stie of* Epicurus, *and fancied it self afterward grown more tall and stout by further strength it seemed to have received from some new Principles of the* French Philosophy *misinterpreted and perverted by certain impure and unskilful pens.*
>
> *Which unexpected confidence of those blind boasters made me with all anxiety and care imaginable search into* the power of Matter and mere Mechanical motion, *and consider how far they might go of themselves in the production of the* Phaenomena *of the World. . . . I must confess I did as much admire* Des-Cartes *Philosophy as I did despise the* Epicurean, *who has carried on the power of Matter for the production of the* Phaenomena *of Nature. . . .*
>
> *This made me peruse his Writings with still more and more diligence: and the more I read, the more I admired his Wit; but at last grew the more con- firmed* That it was utterly impossible that *Matter* should be the onely essen- tial Principle of things.[38]

Here More represents anti-Epicureanism as the organizing impulse of his intel- lectual life. He opposes his own Baconian industry—"made me with all anxiety and care imaginable search into the power of Matter," "made me peruse his

Writings with still more and more diligence"—to his opponents' dangerous and deceptive bluster. He proceeds from his contempt of Epicurus's philosophy to his admiration of Descartes's and finally to his realization that the two philosophies were in the sense that mattered most one and the same—materialist atheism. In denying the providential ordering of the one true God, the Epicurean worldview was, in effect, antisympathetic.

Central to More's and Cudworth's opposition to Epicureanism was its physical premise of disconnection. The world they saw and defended was not "a mere *Congeries* of disunited Matter, or Aggregation of Divided Atoms," but a harmonious whole, magically united.[39] Without "*Divine Causality*," the world could be no more than "a mere *Heap* of *Dust*, Fortuitously agitated, or a *Dead Cadaverous* thing, that hath no *Signatures* of *Mind* and *Understanding*, *Counsel* and *Wisdom* at all upon it; nor indeed any other *Vitality* acting in it." This figuration of the Epicurean universe resonates with Cavendish's. And, like Cavendish, Cudworth pointedly associates Epicureanism with violence. Drawing on his prodigious verbal resources, he describes the fortuitous motions of the Epicureans' "*Infinite Atoms* of different sizes and figures, devoid of all Life and Sense," which thus have nothing in common, their "mutual *Occursions* and *Rencounters* . . . , their *Plagae*, their Stroaks and Dashings against one another, their Reflexions and Repercussions, their Cohesions, Implexions, and Entanglements, as also their Scattered Dispersions and Divulsions." With their heterogeneous, unmusical terminations, the nouns pile up here like "a mere *Heap*," mimicking the "confused *Chaos*" of the Epicureans' "Omnifarious Particles."[40] The Epicurean universe, Cudworth emphasizes, is essentially "Scattered." Such a "*Congeries of Lifeless and Souless things*" could not produce a "conspiration" of all things. For the Cambridge Platonists, the universe was essentially "conspiring," in the pneumatic root sense of "breathing with or together"; it was bound together by a single spirit. Against the "Cartesian Philosophy" Cudworth maintained that, "though it boast of Salving all the *Corporeal Phaenomena*, by mere *Fortuitous Mechanism*, and without any *Final* or *Mental Causality*, yet it gives no Accompt at all of that which is the Grandest *of all Phaenomena*, . . . *The Orderly Regularity and Harmony of the Mundane System*." For More and Cudworth, Cartesianism directly undermined theism, and essential to theism, as he understood it, was a belief not only in design but also in harmony. Cudworth makes the same point elsewhere in *The True Intellectual System*: Descartes has "quite disarmed the World, of that grand Argument for a Deity, taken from the *Regular Frame* and *Harmony of the Universe*."[41] The universe was above all a system; it was a symphonic, sympathetic unity, a vital, magical whole. The principle of sympathy was critical to More and Cudworth's opposition to a rising or resurgent

Epicureanism; it was a principle that could be used to "salve the phenomena" and, at least in part, to solve the crisis of coherence facing contemporary natural philosophy. As that crisis had enormously significant implications for religion, so, too, did it for ethics. A physics of disconnection went hand in hand with an ethics of disconnection, and here, too, the principle of sympathy could be invoked for response and restitution.

"ETERNAL AND IMMUTABLE MORALITY"

More's and Cudworth's magical worldviews were necessarily also moral worldviews. The sympathy binding the world together also bound society, heart to heart, soul to soul. Morality was essential to, and participated in, the "true intellectual system of the universe." The insistence of More and Cudworth on the real nature of morality followed from an antivoluntaristic theological stance.[42] Whichcote was a crucial model here, asserting that goodness was "determined, not by the Arbitrary pleasure of him that has Power over us; but by the Nature and Reason of Things"; there are, he claimed, "Primitive Rules of Moral good and evil," which "carry Reason with them, so immutable; that no time can abolish."[43] This aphorism comes close to the title of Cudworth's principal work of moral philosophy, A *Treatise Concerning Eternal and Immutable Morality*, which was not published until 1731. Behind the fact of posthumous publication lies a minor controversy that ultimately suggests the harmony between Cudworth's ethics and More's. Cudworth had long been planning to write "'concerning *Good and Evil*, or *natural Ethicks*,'" as he explained to John Worthington in 1665. That year More informed him that "'he had begun a discourse on the same argument,'" but when he heard that Cudworth was planning to finish his discourse, he happily offered to "'desist, and throw his into a corner.'"[44] As time passed, however, and Cudworth's treatise remained unfinished, More apparently retrieved his own and, like the "timely-happy spirit" he was, promptly finished it. More's *Enchiridion Ethicum* was published in 1667, and an English translation by Edward Southwell appeared under the title *An Account of Virtue* in 1690.

But even though Cudworth's *Treatise* did not appear until nearly a half century after his death, its core commitments were evident in *The True Intellectual System*. In the preface to *The True Intellectual System* he introduces his corrective view of God, who is to be understood as "not meer Arbitrary Will Omnipotent, Decreeing, Doing, and Necessitating all Actions, Evil as well as Good; but Essentially Moral, Good and Just."[45] Cudworth found support for the identification of God with goodness in Plato, who, in Cudworth's reading, conceived of virtue as "An Assimilation to the Deity" and of "Justice and Honesty" as "Nature and Perfection," which "descend downward to us from the Deity." As goodness was in Plato, so *"Love* or *Charity"* was the "Highest Perfection of Intellectual Beings" in the Bible, and love for Cudworth is "the Source, Life and Soul of all Morality."[46] Combining the two traditions, he also suggests that voluntarism is no better than Epicurean atheism: "The Deity is not to be conceived, as meer Arbitrariness, Humour, or Irrational Will and Appetite Omnipotent, (which would indeed be but Omnipotent Chance) but as an Overflowing Fountain of Love and Goodness, Justly and Wisely dispensing it self, and Omnipotently reaching all things." Cudworth takes pains to assert divine omnipotence, anticipating the voluntarist's objection by denying that the Deity is "Bound or Obliged to do the Best, in any way of Servility"; rather, the Deity does the best "only by the Perfection of its own Nature, which it cannot possibly deviate from, no more than Ungod it self."[47] God acts according to His perfection and lovingly communicates that perfection to us.

Cudworth's most passionate emphasis on divine love comes in the sermon he preached before the House of Commons in March 1647, at which time he was securely ensconced in academic life at Cambridge. Unlike those of Milton and Cavendish, Cudworth's and More's experiences of the Civil Wars produced no clear fissures in their thought and work. In the unity of their systems there was a broader message of cultural unity—in opposition to political and religious dissent. In the sermon Cudworth directs the members of his audience to forsake *"the Spirit of this World,"* lest they "have no true *Sympathy* with God and Christ, no *fellowship* at all with them."[48] Cudworth appeals instead to the Christian world spirit. *"Let us keep the unity of the Spirit in the bond of peace,"* he urges along with "the *Apostle*"; "Let this soft and silken Knot of *Love,* tie our Hearts together; though our Heads and Apprehensions cannot meet, as indeed they never will, but always stand at some distance off from one another." This appeal strikes a traditional note of Christian charity, but it is informed by Cudworth's magical view of the world, his belief in action and attraction at a distance. Love produces a sympathy of hearts in spite of the nonconformity of minds. The appeal is also informed by Cudworth's conciliatory view of the tumult of the times; his parenthetical phrase "as indeed they never will" functions to distance, even to transcend, the immediate significance of war. If "Heads and Apprehensions" are not "meeting," it is not because of what is going on outside the mind but rather consequent to the nature of the mind itself. The answer, then, is to be found not in outward consensus but rather in inward compassion, the "meeting" of sympathy. Wedded to truth, love "will draw men on with a sweet violence, whether they will or no"; it is "the sweet Harmony of souls," "That which reconciles the jarring Principles of the World, and makes them all chime together! That which melts mens Hearts into one another!"[49] Elsewhere Cudworth passionately denounced the idea "That our selves should be but a *Congeries* of *Atoms*"; here, in the hortatory mode, he imagines a community of hearts, "melting" into one.[50] Cudworth's reference to "sweet violence," a kind of Platonic oxymoron, uniting people "whether they will or no," anticipates the idiom of Barrow's sermons; in both cases, and in both moments, the goal of bringing disparate and dissenting individuals into communion effectively entails the sacrifice of the individual will, a psychological center of conflict to be circumvented in the interest of a greater "Harmony." The involuntary, automatic quality of this process is understood not in terms of Epicurean force but in terms of Platonic magic. In Cudworth's sermon human sympathy follows from the "strong *Magick* of Nature," which "pulls and draws every thing continually, to that place which is suitable to it," and thus while all goodness rises heavenward, "Hell wheresoever it is, will by strong *Sympathy* pull in all sinne, and *Magnetically* draw it to it self."[51] This natural-magical use of the term "*Sympathy*" tinges the later moral-theological reference to "true *Sympathy* with God and Christ." In this instance Cudworth provides an enchanted version of the Aristotelian conception of natural place, which enforces a mystical sense of the order of things. The day after Denzil Holles responded to a petition from disgruntled members of the New Model Army by declaring them "enemies to the state," Cudworth's message was that we should all be friends; our natural place was not apart, much less at war, but together, in harmony.[52] The world may be harsh and discordant, but if we "expresse this sweet harmonious Affection, in these jarring times," Cudworth promises, we "may tune the World at last, into better Musick."[53] The expression of love will bring his countrymen back into their natural state of sympathy. The deep belief in the natural moral contexture of the world that Cudworth inherited from Whichcote carried with it, in a moment of devastating human conflict, an optimism about not only human nature but also human relation.

The universal communication of divine goodness and love meant that all things were vitally connected both naturally and morally. The moralization of sympathy was both logically and spiritually consistent with More's and Cudworth's philosophical principles. The magical sympathy that united all things in the natural world naturally united all persons in the moral world. This deep consistency, which begins to be evident in the sermon, can be seen more clearly by collating two passages from the Cudworth manuscripts, most likely written in the 1660s or '70s. In the first Cudworth defines natural magic and develops his idea of plastic nature:

There is a ntrall Magick much talkt of by wch things may be done in nature otherwise y^n by ordinary physicall & mechanicall causes & at a greater distance such as appeares in ye use of ye vulnerary unguent or sympatheticall powder wch Magick is defined to be ye attraction of one Body by another at distance by a certain cognation of nature and community of one spirit or Soul whereby distant . . . parts of it are all so united so as to be . . . but members of one & ye same Animall, whether there be any such common mundane Spirit that can be a Foundation for such sympatheticall operations or no we will not . . . inquire. But it is out of question y^t there is one divine intellectual Spirit preciding over ye whole universe in wch all rational Beings are as it were knit together wch is either all of it or else ye lower part sympatheticall.[54]

Here Cudworth opposes the kind of mechanistic account of the "vulnerary unguent or sympatheticall powder" that, as we saw in the first chapter, Digby put forward and carefully elaborated. Whereas Digby aimed to disenchant sympathy in the interest of a more rigorous account of the cure, Cudworth embraces a magical view of it, and whereas Digby was determined to uphold the Aristotelian prohibition against action at a distance, Cudworth seems untroubled and unconstrained by it. Like More, he understands sympathetic cures not in mechanistic but in animistic terms, an exemplary instance of the vital ensoulment of the world. He doubts that "ordinary physicall & mechanicall causes" can account for all phenomena in the universe. In the second passage Cudworth's vision of universal "community" assumes a moral, social dimension:

There is a certain universality of being, whereby a man cant apprehend himself as a being standing by itself cut off, separated, & disjoynted from all other beings, whose good being private, is as it were opposite to ye good of other beings but looks upon himself as a member livingly united to ye whole sistem of all Intellectual beings, as one animal, & is concerned in ye good & welfare of all besides himself, there is a certain communicativenesse of nature, y^t makes us all concerned in ye good of one another, a principle of common simpathy in every one, y^t makes every one to have another being besides his own private selfish particularity whereby he rises above it, & is in a manner all; as parents & Children seem to make up a totum.[55]

The common emphasis of both passages is community, reinforced by the organic analogy, the idea that distant parts form a unified whole like "members of one & ye same Animall." The natural state of human beings is social and communicative; however physically distant we may be, we naturally interact with and attract one another. The negative construction at the beginning of the second passage points in the direction of Hobbes, who theorized from the premise of "every one having his private designes"; his concept of "Systemes" — "any numbers of men joyned in one Interest" — was not natural and ideal but convenient and contingent.[56] Hobbes was the latest adopter of an ancient and pernicious creed that Epicurus had made fashionable. To deny the true intellectual system of the universe, as Hobbes did, was to deny the true God. And to remove all morality from nature, all goodness and charity, as Hobbes did, was to turn human beings into mere atoms.[57] In his account of the *"Atheistick Atomology Lately Revived"* in *The True Intellectual System*, Cudworth accuses him, "our *Leucippus* and *Democritus*," of "necessarily excluding, besides *Incorporeal Substance* and *Immortality of Souls*, a *Deity* and *Natural Morality*; as also making all Actions and Events, *Materially* and *Mechanically necessary*." It was Hobbes's "wretched *Ill-natured Maxim* . . . That there is . . . No *Natural Charity*, but that . . . All benevolence ariseth onely, from Imbecillity and Fear. . . . So that all that is now called *Love* and *Friendship* amongst Men, is according to these really nothing, but either a *crouching* under *Anothers Power, whom they cannot Resist*; or else . . . *a certain kind of Merchandizing for Utilities*." For Cudworth, nothing so fundamental as morality was merely contingent or "crouching"; it was inherent and participated in a broader ontological coherence. If it was true, as Scripture made plain, "That *God is Love*," it was true that love was natural to His creatures, that a *"Natural Charity* and *Benevolence"* prevailed among humankind. Hobbes and his followers were allied with the Calvinists in their deeply negative view of human nature. The Hobbists established the "Foundation" of their ethics and politics "in the *Villainizing* of *Humane Nature*; as that which has not so much as any the least *Seeds*, either of *Politicalness*, or *Ethicalness* at all in it; nothing of *Equity* and *Philanthropy*; (there being no other *Charity* or *Benevolence* any where according to them, save what resulteth from *Fear, Imbecillity*, and *Indigency*) nothing of *Publick* and *Common Concern*, but all *Private* and *Selfish*."[58] When the Calvinists looked within the human soul, they saw the "villainy" of sin; when the Hobbists did so, they saw the "villainy" of selfishness. Both denied the fundamental truth of sympathy. Against the negatives of his opponents Cudworth counters with a copious effusion of positives: *"Equity," "Philanthropy," "Charity," "Benevolence,"* and *"Publick* and *Common Concern."*

Here, too, Whichcote blazed a trail for Cudworth to follow. To recall Gilbert Burnet's tribute, Whichcote taught and preached in order "to elevate and sweeten humane nature." But central to what Whichcote's students and admirers gained from him was the idea that human nature was essentially elevated and sweet. "There is much of GOD in *Man*," Whichcote insisted, and

"Man *as Man*, is Averse to what is Evil, and Wicked: for *Evil* is Unnatural, and *Good* is Connatural to Man."[59] This was precisely the opposite of "the *Villainizing* of *Humane Nature*." It is in our nature to be good, Whichcote preached. In his *Enchiridion Ethicum*, More supported this view by asserting that "Virtue is natural to human Nature, and born as a Twin therewith"; by insisting, "against the *Stoicks*," that the passions "are not only good, but singularly needful to the perfecting of human life"; and, most originally, by positing in human nature what he calls a *"Boniform Faculty."*[60] This faculty, More explains, "enables us to distinguish not only what is simply and absolutely the best, but to relish it," and it "is the most elevated and most divine Faculty of the Soul, and seems to supply the same place in it, as the essential Good of the *Platonicks*, is said to do in the Deity."[61] More thus identifies a specific means of connection between human beings in God. "Boniformity" is next to what More and Whichcote called "deiformity."

Whichcote emphasized not only that we possess goodness in common with God but also that this common possession unites us; the better we are, the more we benefit others. "Man, as a *sociable* Creature," Whichcote wrote, "is made for Converse with those that are his Equals; to receive from them, and to Communicate to them; to be the Better for them, and to make them the Better for him."[62] This universal communication of goodness is the very antithesis of the Hobbist's individual assertion of appetite and interest. From the Hobbist's rejection of natural morality, Cudworth reasoned, "it follows, that Nature absolutely *Dissociates* and *Segregates* men from one another, by reason of the *Inconsistency* of those *Appetites* of theirs, that are all Carried out only to *Private Good*, and Consequently that every man is by *Nature*, in a *State of War and Hostility*, against every man."[63] The reality of society gave the lie to Hobbes's political theory, his belief in, as John Farrell puts it, "not unity *of* but unity *against*."[64] Rather, it was "plain, that . . . there must of necessity be some *Natural* Bond or *Vinculum* to hold them together," which "Bond or *Vinculum* can be no other, than *Natural Justice*; and something of a *Common* and *Publick*, of a *Cementing* and *Conglutinating Nature*, in all Rational Beings; the Original of both which, is from the Deity."[65] As sympathy is the "Bond" of nature, so, too, it is the bond of society. Cudworth's emphasis on human sympathy is conveyed by a remarkably drawn-out noun phrase here, "something of a *Common* and *Publick*, of a *Cementing* and *Conglutinating Nature*." The sequence "*Common* . . . *Cementing* . . . *Conglutinating*" produces a crescendo effect that amplifies his claim for human connectedness. And in the indefinite "something" Cudworth preserves a sense of the mystery of sympathy, the sense that what draws us together defies precise expression, partaking as it does of the "original" divine magic.

In the project of naturalizing human affection and sympathy, the bond between parents and children provided More and Cudworth with a seemingly definitive, irrefutable example as well as a clear etiological point. It could be held up as the source of and model for all human sympathy. Digby had reasoned similarly, but insofar as he moralized the sympathy between parents and children, he tended to see deformity where More and Cudworth saw deiformity. "Among the Sorts or Species of *Love*," More writes, "there is principally to be considered; not only *Devotion* and *Complacency*, but what the *Greeks* call *Storge* (which is that strong Intercourse of Filial Parental Sympathy, that is founded in the Bowels of Nature.)"[66] Recognizing the need for clarification, Southwell exceeds the translator's office here; More's sentence stops right after "*Storge*." More does go on in the chapter to associate the Greek term with "genitos," but Southwell evidently took it upon himself to make More's point more strongly for him; the sympathy between parents and children is a fundamental fact of nature. The first time More uses the term *storgē* he refers to it as "nobilis illa *Amoris* species," or "that noble and natural sort of *Love*," and opposes it to "illa *Odii*, quae *Antipathia*."[67] From the point of view of historical semantics, it might be suggested that for More "antipathy" was a term that lent itself to moralization more easily than "sympathy," which figured so prominently in his natural philosophy, whereas, some twenty-five years later, Southwell inserted the word "sympathy" with the apparent expectation that it would illuminate More's moral discourse. In terms of the argument itself, that More uses *storgē* in its narrower, quasi-technical sense *after* introducing it in a more general and expansive sense subtly suggests his larger aim of naturalizing and generalizing love and sympathy.

Cudworth's claim in his manuscripts that "parents & Children seem to make up a totum" serves the same authorizing function, if far more elliptically, as More's appeal to *storgē* does. Nowhere is the reality of "a principle of common simpathy" more universally evident than in the home. Cudworth's insistence on a "*Publick* and *Common Concern*" in human nature flowed naturally and logically from his insistence on the "cognation of nature and community of one spirit or Soul" in the universe as a whole. Behind his "principle of common simpathy" is the idea of the "one *Whole*," the vital, magical *totum* which parents and children represent in epitome—and which was central to Cudworth's conception of the *prisca theologia*. The same principle accounts for the "vital Union" between body and body, body and soul, and, in the broadest sense, being and being.[68] As the universe is one, so are we one; moral, social, and political unity recapitulates cosmic unity. There is "*One Spirit*," "one Common Life," "One Supreme God," and "*One Supreme Good*."[69] This physico-ethical vision of sympathetic unity and community, broadly shared among the Cambridge Platonists, made a significant impression on those who came under their influence, whether as students, readers, or correspondents. That influence can be detected in a range of works in a variety of forms, from the moral philosophy of Thomas Traherne to the natural philosophy of Lady Anne Conway to the poetry of John Norris. But it is Shaftesbury's *Characteristicks*, comprising a remarkable variety of forms in itself, that most clearly reveals the lasting significance of Cambridge Platonism in the history of sympathy.

SHAFTESBURY AND THE CHARM OF SYMPATHY

Against the eternalizing backdrop of *The Moralists*, the philosophical dialogue that he placed at the center of his *Characteristicks of Men, Manners, Opinions, Times*, Shaftesbury at one curious point refers to *"the Intellectual System of the Universe"* and then to his own *"Fair* INQUIRY."[70] Both Shaftesbury and the "pious and learned" Cudworth were *"fair Authors"* who had been received unfairly. Shaftesbury's sense of opposition, as both agent and victim, was deep-rooted; his grandfather, the first earl, demonized as Dryden's "false Achitophel," was at the center of the Exclusion Crisis and the emergence of the Whigs, whose cause, having been little advanced by the second earl, was expected to be taken up by the third. In part toward that end, the first earl arranged for Locke to take charge of his grandson's education, and Locke's tutorials began in the early 1680s. After a Continental tour, in 1689 Shaftesbury returned to England, where he lived the sociable life that he soon began to theorize and idealize. He befriended, among others, Damaris Masham, Cudworth's daughter, who shared a close connection to Locke and who perhaps drew Shaftesbury closer to her father's work. Cudworth's philosophy might well have been impolite by Shaftesbury's standards—one imagines Shaftesbury thumbing through the massive folio with a mixture of approval and distaste— but it was not impious.[71] Shaftesbury saw in the work of the Cambridge Platonists a dense mass of piety and principle in need of sublimation, of socialization. In the preface to his edition of Whichcote's sermons, published in 1698, Shaftesbury writes, *"The unpolish'd Style, and Phrase of our Author, who drew more from a College than a Court; and who was more used to School-Learning, and the Language of an University, than to the Conversation of the fashionable World, may possibly but ill recommend his Sense to the Generality of Readers."*[72] Shaftesbury would reach the "generality of readers" conversably, in precisely the way he implies Whichcote could not. Where Cudworth cited, Shaftesbury recited—the final phrase of the subtitle to *The Moralists* is "A RECITAL of certain Conversations on *Natural* and *Moral* Subjects."

For Shaftesbury conversation is a moral and social ideal as well as an organizing formal and stylistic principle. As with Cavendish, whose unusual status as a woman philosopher made her particularly attuned to the question of how (not to mention if) her works would be read and received, there was a social motive behind the formal and generic variety of the works that Shaftesbury brought together in *Characteristicks*, a sympathetic aim to adapt not only form to matter but also both to the reader's taste and temperament. With the development of a wider and more diverse reading public, that kind of adaptation became both more necessary and more complicated. In varying the forms and genres of his work, while keeping them all "conversational," Shaftesbury was maintaining the connection between author and audience, a relationship that in his work assumed a new emphasis and significance.[73] Shaftesbury's cultivation of, and inquiry into, this relationship served to reinforce his larger argument about the moral value of human connection, but it also reflected some of the complexities and instabilities of that argument. In aiming to engage the reader, Shaftesbury faced the question not only of how to go about doing so but also of whom to engage. In that most obviously sociable part of the book, the preface, Shaftesbury distanced himself from *"all* Prefatory *or* Dedicatory *Discourse,"* immediately marking out a tension between a demanding and distasteful readership conditioned by current publishing norms, a group suggested by the phrase *"Friend to* PREFACES," and a gentlemanly audience of friends in the absolute sense (1:xxi). This latter audience was to be approached tastefully; its sympathies were to be taken into account, but not to the point of "effeminate" pandering, what Shaftesbury dismissed as "all this pretty Amour and Intercourse of Caresses between the Author and Reader" (1:125). Totaling 895 text-heavy pages of formal philosophical prose, the analytic contents alone running to some eighty pages, Cudworth's *True Intellectual System* extended no friendship to the reader, gentlemanly or otherwise; it embodied no recognition of the reader as reader, one mind engaging with another in experiential time and textual space. Cudworth reasoned with his readers but did not sympathize with them, and in this sense *The True Intellectual System* was, from Shaftesbury's perspective, an antisocial work. It lacked precisely the kind of decorum that was at the center of Shaftesbury's attempt to reform philosophical writing: Cudworth had made a strong case for *"Publick* and *Common Concern"* as a fundamental human quality in a work that in its formal nature seemed to show a profound lack of "public and common concern" for his audience.

But in developing his own "sense," Shaftesbury depended significantly on those of the Cambridge Platonists. They represented and participated in the first of the two philosophical traditions that Shaftesbury identified in a letter to

Pierre Coste: "the Civil, Social, Theistic," which "maintained that Society, Right, and, wrong was founded in Nature," and which included the Socratic, "the old Academic, the Peripatetic, and Stoic"; Hobbes represented the second tradition, "the Contrary," or the atheistic, which "derived in reality from Democritus, and pass[ed] into the Cyrenaic and Epicurean."[74] In something like the Cudworthian genealogical mode, Shaftesbury defined his philosophical identity against Epicureanism. But what is characteristically Shaftesburian here is the conception of philosophy in dialogic and dialectical terms. Shaftesbury eventually consigned Locke to the "Contrary" tradition as well, for, in his opposition to innate principles, Locke "struck at all Fundamentals, threw all *Order* and *Virtue* out of the World."[75] Shaftesbury saw the contemporary debate over innate principles as a misguided matter of Aristotelian shadow-boxing and ultimately to be beside the point; for him, the question was really "whether the Passion or Affection towards Society . . . was natural and came of it self."[76] To this question his philosophical writings constituted an enthusiastic and extensive, if not definitive, answer in the affirmative.

More insistently and influentially than his "platonically given" predecessors, Shaftesbury conceived of sympathy as a principle of connection founded in human nature, one that underlay not only ethics but also aesthetics, politics, and physics, all of which he understood to be of a piece—philosophy *tout court*. He shared with and inherited from the Cambridge Platonists a belief in a fundamental and overarching coherence, a universal system, maintained against Epicurean fortuity and chaos. "Nothing indeed can be more melancholy," Shaftesbury wrote, "than the Thought of living in a distracted Universe, from whence many Ills may be suspected, and where there is nothing good or lovely which presents it-self" (2:40). The word "distracted" denotes "agitated, disturbed," but suggests also the older, literal sense of "drawn apart, rent asunder," the natural state of the Epicurean cosmos (*OED* 2, 1). In insisting that the world remained magically alive and magically connected, Shaftesbury resisted the idea of a "dis-attracted" universe. Cudworth, we recall, deplored the mechanists' "Dead and Wooden World, as it were a Carved Statue, that hath nothing neither *Vital* nor *Magical* at all in it." Shaftesbury followed him in defending a vital, magical worldview. But the differences between his emphasis and Cudworth's are notable and instructive. For Shaftesbury the moral concern has become primary, and it is intimately bound to the aesthetic; "good" is paired with "lovely." Even as he perpetuated an enchanted idea of nature, the sympathetic worldview that Shaftesbury projected was not that of Cudworth and More but rather an aestheticized version of theirs. In Shaftesbury's writing the sympathetic universe has become a kind of beautiful artifact, a living statue. Shaftesbury did not, like Milton, ultimately retroject or reject a sympathetic worldview; instead, he restored it, presenting to his reader a new sympathetic world *picture*.

Whereas in the interest of reason and religion Milton sought to disenchant human relations, Shaftesbury followed the Cambridge Platonists' classicizing lead in conceiving human relations as part of a broader cosmic dynamics that was magical at its core. Shaftesbury's early and active engagement with Whichcote was crucial in this respect. Having two manuscript volumes of Whichcote's sermons in his possession, he decided to publish twelve of the sermons.[77] The publication enabled him to reflect on recent history and to assert his own religious and moral allegiances. Whichcote makes his entrance into Shaftesbury's preface as a kind of biblical prophet, empowered by God to restore "*the Principle of Good-nature*" that the Hobbists, the atheists, the Calvinists, and the "Mercenary" Christians have "*exploded.*"[78] Although Shaftesbury recognizes the opposition to Hobbes on the part of "all the eminent and worthy Divines of the Church of *England*," he suggests that "the Correction of his Moral Principles" has not gone far enough. As he explains, Hobbes, "reckoning up the Passions, or Affections, by which Men are held together in Society, . . . forgot to mention Kindness, Friendship, Sociableness, Love of Company and Converse, Natural Affection, or any thing of this kind; I say *Forgot*, because I can scarcely think so ill of any Man, as that he has not by experience found any of these Affections in himself, and consequently, that he believes none of them to be in others." Hobbes has not refuted the naturalness of kind affection; in the welter of the mid-century, it must have just slipped his mind. This rhetorical response, a logical extension of Shaftesbury's claim that "Natural Affection" has "*Ground and Foundation in Meer* NATURE," would be repeated and expanded in *Characteristicks*. For Shaftesbury, Whichcote was "the Preacher of Good-nature," the divine antitype and antidote to Hobbes, the philosopher of ill nature; he returned religion to its true essence, which was not calculation but "*Love.*"[79] "*Universal Charity,*" Whichcote had preached, "is a Thing Final in Religion."[80]

In his more formal introduction of Whichcote in the preface, Shaftesbury emphasizes Whichcote's magical, moral conception of sympathy. He introduces Whichcote in Whichcote's own words, with a quotation from a sermon on Ephesians 4:31–32: "Whatsoever (*says he*) some have said; *Man's Nature* is not so untoward a Thing (unless it be abused) but that there is a secret *Sympathy* in Human Nature, with Vertue and Honesty; which gives a Man an Interest even in bad Men."[81] We are naturally virtuous, to the point that even the acquired vices of others do not shut us off from them. As Whichcote expresses it earlier in the passage from which Shaftesbury quotes, "There is in Man, a secret *Genius* to Humanity; a *Bias* that inclines him to a Regard for all of his own Kind."[82] We are mysteriously drawn to our fellow creatures. In the seventeenth century the collocation "secret *Sympathy*" was firmly established in the discourse of natural magic. "There be many *Things*," Bacon writes, "that worke upon the *Spirits* of *Man*, by *Secret Sympathy*, and *Antipathy*"—his example is "The *Vertues* of *Pretious Stones*." Sylvester's Du Bartas refers to "the secret Sympathy . . . / Betwixt the bright Sun and the Marigold." Discussing the modern "discovery" of magnetic communication, George Hakewill describes the needles' "secret Sympathie." Thomas Browne, we recall, locates "the secret Sympathies of things" in the Paracelsian "*Archidoxes*."[83] Whichcote, by contrast, posits an "occult" sympathy specifically in human nature, an affinity for goodness that interests all in all. As iron is drawn to the lodestone, so we are naturally drawn to the good.[84] Parallels to Whichcote's conception of a magical sympathy between human nature and goodness can be found in John Smith's *Select Discourses* (1660) and Norris's *Theory and Regulation of Love* (1688).[85] In the latter, Norris appeals to an analogy between the natural and the moral that would become a crucial, authorizing move for eighteenth-century moral philosophers, as we shall see in the next chapter. He claims that a "radical *Complacency* and Connaturality of the Soul towards good (which I call her *Moral Gravity*) is nothing else but that first Alteration or Impression which is made upon her by the streaming influences of the Great and Supreme Magnet, God, continually acting upon her, and attracting her by his active and powerfull Charms."[86] Here the divine, the moral, the natural, and the natural-magical are all effectively put into systematic relation. The magical inflection of what Shaftesbury called "human Sympathy" becomes clearer and more explicable in the light of his positive engagement with Whichcote and those who were similarly "very philosophically and platonically given." In highlighting Whichcote's assertion of "a secret *Sympathy* in Human Nature," Shaftesbury provides us with a significant point of connection to his own.

I want now to turn directly to *Characteristicks* and to examine Shaftesbury's representations of "human Sympathy" as a principle of moral and social coherence. *An Inquiry Concerning Virtue, or Merit*, the first of the "treatises" in *Characteristicks* published separately, in 1699, is in large part a philosophical treatment of the passions. Emphasizing human flourishing and what he refers to as "natural affection," Shaftesbury sets out a new approach to a subject of intense interest in the seventeenth century. In the work immediately preceding the *Inquiry, Soliloquy: or, Advice to an Author*, Shaftesbury animadverts against those—like Descartes, Digby, and Charleton—who have "treated formally of *the Passions*, in a way of *natural Philosophy*" (1:180). His antimechanistic bias becomes more evident when he likens the natural-philosophical approach to the passions to that of a person who steps into a watchmaker's shop and inquires about the various parts of the watch "without examining what the real Use was of such an Instrument; or by what Movements its *End* was best attain'd." By the same token, if a philosopher chose only to consider "what Effects each Passion wrought upon the Body; what change of Aspect or Feature they produc'd; and in what different manner they affected the Limbs and Muscles; this might possibly qualify him to give Advice to an Anatomist or a Limner, but not to *Mankind* or to *Himself*: Since according to this Survey he consider'd not the real Operation or Energy of his Subject, nor contemplated the *Man*, as *real* Man, and as a human Agent; but as a *Watch* or common *Machine*" (1:181). Shaftesbury's use of the hedge "might possibly" is a subtle dig; the natural pathologist hardly even succeeds on his own terms. The mechanization of the passions, meanwhile, has effectively alienated philosophy from its primary aim, the enlightenment of "*real* Man." It has failed to provide humanity with anything of fundamental concern to itself. To this "super-speculative Philosophy" Shaftesbury opposes and prefers "a more practical sort, which relates chiefly to our Acquaintance, Friendship, and good Correspondence with *our-selves*." Rather than contriving intricate mechanisms, one does far better simply to look and converse within, to "soliloquize," and this more practical pursuit promotes not only self-knowledge but also a deeper understanding of humankind, "the Knowledg of *human Nature*" (1:183). Thus Shaftesbury provides both the warrant for and the transition into the *Inquiry*; he adds a footnote to the phrase "the INQUIRY after my Passions" referring the reader to his "INQUIRY, *viz.* Treatise IV. of these Volumes" (1:183). In so doing, Shaftesbury suggests that, in spite of their formal differences, on a deeper logical level the more conversational *Advice to an Author* and the more traditionally philosophical *Inquiry* share an underlying sympathy.

Shaftesbury argues in the *Inquiry* that virtue is founded on affection, which he analyzes into three types, of which human sympathy represents the ideal. He identifies "THE NATURAL AFFECTIONS" as those that "are founded in Love, Complacency, Good-will, and in a Sympathy with the Kind or Species." They "lead to the Good of THE PUBLICK," whereas "*Self-affections*," a sort of middle term, "lead only to the Good of THE PRIVATE," and "*unnatural Affections*" lead to the good of neither (2:57, 50). When we attend to and cultivate the natural affections, he argues, we are not only good but also happy. The idea of "a Sympathy with the Kind or Species" is crucial to what Stephen Darwall refers to as Shaftesbury's "other-directed" ethics.[87] Both virtue and happiness depend on a general social sympathy, "An *Enjoyment of Good by Communication: A receiving it, as it were by Reflection, or by way of Participation in the Good of others*" (2:62). Carrying forward the spirit of the Cambridge Platonists,

Shaftesbury conceives of this process in magical terms. Society is produced by the magic and power of sympathy. Of "the social Pleasures" he concludes, "Thus the CHARM of kind Affection is superior to all other Pleasure: since it has the power of drawing from every other Appetite or Inclination. And thus in the Case of Love to the Offspring, and a thousand other Instances, *the Charm* is found to operate so strongly on the Temper, as, in the midst of other Temptations, to render it susceptible of this Passion alone; which remains as the *Master-Pleasure* and *Conqueror* of the rest" (2:60). "Charm," with its deep sense of incantation and enchantment, is a crucial keyword in Shaftesbury's philosophy. Its importance and centrality can be suggested by an entry in the marvelously idiosyncratic and discursive index that Shaftesbury compiled for *Characteristicks*—"Charm *of Nature, in Moral Objects. See* Nature, Beauty, Harmony, Taste" (3:259)—as well as by his summary of the work as a whole: "IT HAS been the main Scope and principal End of these Volumes, 'To assert the Reality of a BEAUTY and CHARM in *moral* as well as *natural* Subjects'" (3:185). For him, charm is not only a kind of perceived grace but also a mystical reality. In a passage from the second treatise, *Sensus Communis: An Essay on the Freedom of Wit and Humour*, Shaftesbury expands the hendiadys "*close Sympathy* and *conspiring Virtue*" with the phrase "*confederating Charm*" (1:71). There is a magic by which we are drawn to one another and take pleasure in one another's company. "So insinuating are these Pleasures of Sympathy, and so widely diffus'd thro' our whole Lives," Shaftesbury reflects, "that there is hardly such a thing as Satisfaction or Contentment, of which they make not an essential part" (2:62). He makes a strong claim here for the centrality of sympathy in human experience. Wherever we go, whatever we do, sympathy "conquers" us, and we joy in falling under its sway, because it is a "*Master-Pleasure.*"

In Shaftesbury's emphasis on the power of sympathy and "kind Affection" we can recognize Foucault's master form of similitude, but with a new sphere of activity, mobilizing not so much "the things of the world" as the persons and passions of society.[88] Shaftesbury's sociocultural interpretation of Hobbes attests ultimately not only to the naturalness of sympathy but also to its prevailing force. Of those who, like Hobbes, "are so jealous of every religious or moral Principle," he writes, "Whatever *Savages* they may appear in Philosophy, they are in their common Capacity as *Civil* Persons, as one can wish. Their free communicating of their Principles may witness for them. 'Tis the height of Sociableness to be thus friendly and communicative" (1:57). So charmed by the sociability that he would deny to man in the state of nature, Hobbes cannot keep his principles to himself; he sociably shares his claim for unsociability. In this sense, publication, the formalizing of communication, represents the height of sociability; it is

fundamentally an act of "Sympathy with the Kind or Species." As Shaftesbury
elaborates, "What shou'd we say to one of these *Anti-zealots*, who, in the Zeal of
such a cool Philosophy, shou'd assure us faithfully, 'That we were the most
mistaken Men in the world, to imagine there was any such thing as natural
Faith or Justice? . . . That there was no such thing in reality as *Virtue*; no
Principle of Order in things above, or below; no secret *Charm* or Force of
Nature, by which every-one was made to operate willingly or unwillingly towards
publick Good.'" The answer is self-evident: "Is not this the very *Charm* it-self?
Is not the Gentleman at this instant under the power of it? . . . 'Tis not fit we
shou'd know that *by Nature* we are all *Wolves*. Is it possible that one who has
really discover'd himself such, shou'd take pains to communicate such a
Discovery?" (1:58–59). Hobbes is the example that proves the rule; he both puts
it to the test and confirms its validity. The fact of Hobbes's "communication," an
emphatic term that reinforces the tenor of the discussion as a whole, functions
as a knock-down argument against his own Epicurean principles. In denying it
publicly and communicating it negatively, Hobbes ends up demonstrating the
reality of a "secret *Charm* or Force of Nature, by which every-one was made to
operate willingly or unwillingly towards publick Good"—a formulation that
very much recalls Whichcote's. Even Hobbes, its most "wolfish" enemy, cannot
escape its power; the "secret *Charm*" of sympathy conquers all. By appealing to
an idea of magic, Shaftesbury follows the Cambridge Platonists in making what
is presented as an irrefutable argument against Epicureanism; the magic of
sympathy is a "reality" in society and in the world, not in and of itself a theory
but prior to theory and opinion, and independent of the will. It is essential to the
contexture of things. As we shall see, however, from a skeptical perspective the
strength of this claim covers up a troubling logical weakness.[89]

Shaftesbury's discussion of Hobbes helps to prepare for an aesthetic turn and
serves to strengthen his claim that sympathy enchants all forms of "communication," whether social or literary—a distinction that dissolves in his analysis. The
exchange of affection occurs not only between those in society but also between
artist and audience:

> Of all other Beautys which *Virtuosos* pursue, *Poets* celebrate, *Musicians* sing,
> and *Architects* or *Artists*, of whatever kind, describe or form; the most delight-
> ful, the most engaging and pathetick, is that which is drawn from real *Life*,
> and from the *Passions*. Nothing affects the Heart like that which is purely
> *from it-self*, and *of its own nature*. . . . This Lesson of Philosophy, even a
> Romance, a Poem, or a Play may teach us; whilst the fabulous Author leads
> us with such pleasure thro' the Labyrinth of the Affections, and interests us,
> whether we will or no, in the Passions of his Heroes and Heroines:

Like a Mage, he tortures, enrages, soothes, fills us with false terrors.

Let Poets, or the Men of Harmony, deny, if they can, this Force of *Nature*, or withstand this *moral Magick*. They, for their parts, carry a double portion of this Charm about 'em. For in the first place, the very Passion which inspires 'em, is it-self *the Love of Numbers, Decency and Proportion*; and this too, not in a narrow sense, or after a *selfish* way, (for who of them composes for *him-self?*) but in a friendly social View; for the Pleasure and Good of others; even down to Posterity, and future Ages. And in the next place, 'tis evident in these Performers, that their chief Theme and Subject, that which raises the Genius the most, and by which they so effectually move others, is purely *Manners*, and the *moral Part*. (1:85)

Here the moral and the aesthetic fully interpenetrate.[90] The *"Love of Numbers, Decency and Proportion"* goes hand in hand with kind affection for others, "a friendly social View." The true poet is, as Shaftesbury writes in the next treatise, a "moral Artist, who can thus imitate the Creator, and is thus knowing in the inward Form and Structure of his Fellow-Creature" (1:129). Morality and beauty are so closely connected because both depend on "inward Form." Nature is the ground of both. The true poet is a sympathetic and sympathizing force: "Like that Sovereign Artist or universal Plastick Nature, he forms *a Whole*, coherent and proportion'd in it-self, with due Subjection and Subordinacy of constituent Parts" (1:129).[91] Given that he elsewhere cites Cudworth's terms *"Pneumatophobia"* and *"Hylomania"* explicitly (3:42, 43), Shaftesbury's reference to "universal Plastick Nature" here can be heard as a distinct echo of *The True Intellectual System* and its central theoretical construct. The artistic sense of "plastic" as forming or "shaping" raw materials (*OED* 1a), secondary in Cudworth's account, has become the primary sense in Shaftesbury's. Shaftesbury insists here on the aesthetic *totum*, which recapitulates in miniature the sympathetic "coherence" and "proportion" of the cosmos as a whole. The creation of art is a powerful and transcendental act of sympathy; in creating, the artist sympathizes not only with his immediate audience but also with all future audiences. The immortality of art entails the immortality of sympathy. Sympathy acts not only at a spatial distance but at a temporal distance as well. Though it, too, must be rooted in sympathetic feeling, bad art, Shaftesbury implies, is that which is not "drawn from real *Life*, and from the *Passions*." The same goes for bad philosophy; this was the basis of his critique of the new philosophies. Mimesis and affectivity are presented as the conditions for a powerful sympathy between artist and audience, so powerful that, as we see again, the will of the reader is short-circuited and taken out of the equation; the author "interests us, whether we will or no." This "interest" leads inevitably to a kind of elation, so that the sacrifice of internal control is amply compensated by the experience of aesthetic pleasure. As Shaftesbury observes later in *Characteristicks*, "when by mere Illusion, as in *a Tragedy*, the Passions of this kind are skilfully excited in us; we prefer the Entertainment to any other of equal duration. We find by our-selves, that the moving our Passions in this mournful way, the engaging them in behalf of Merit and Worth, and the exerting whatever we have of social Affection, and human Sympathy, is of the highest Delight" (2:61–62). Aesthetic appreciation is moral experience; the reference to "Merit and Worth" is essential to Shaftesbury's larger point. The gerunds, "the moving . . . , the engaging . . . , and the exerting," emphasize the powerful and dynamic nature of sympathy. Passion answers passion as lute answers lute, in a process that Shaftesbury significantly refers to as "*moral Magick.*" This phrase epitomizes the Shaftesburian project of re-enchantment through a strategy of translation and redistribution. Like the plastic artist he celebrates, Shaftesbury reshapes the magical concept of sympathy he inherited from the Cambridge Platonists so that it answers a new commitment to and emphasis on the moral and aesthetic spheres. Although he quotes Horace, Shaftesbury is reconceiving magic in a distinctively modern way; his magician does not "wed earth to heaven," in Pico's phrase, but rather weds passion to passion, artist to audience, reader to character, spectator to personage, and, more generally, person to person.[92]

On the whole Shaftesbury's attitude toward historical and practical magic is critical; he aimed not only to moralize and aestheticize magic but also to update it in accordance with his sociable ideal. The "old" magic is not, as in Cudworth's account, allied to theism but adverse to it. To the order and design of the theists Shaftesbury opposes not only "the *Chaos* and *Atoms* of the ATHEISTS" but also "the *Magick* and *Daemons* of the POLYTHEISTS" (2:189). In *The Moralists*, to which I return in greater detail in the next section, the skeptical character Philocles concedes, "I shall now no longer be in danger of imagining either *Magick* or *Superstition* in the case; since you invoke no other POWER than that single ONE, which seems so natural" (2:205). Magic emerges as a theological error, with both ancient and modern manifestations. Shaftesbury is similarly contemptuous of folk magic, those "Parish-Tales, and gossiping Storys of *Imps*, *Goblins*, and *Demoniacal Pranks*, invented to fright Children, or make Practice for common Exorcists, and *Cunning-Men*! For by that Name, you know, Country People are us'd to call those Dealers in Mystery, who are thought to *conjure in an honest way*, and foil the Devil at his own Weapon" (1:93). The dismissive tone is that of the urbane aristocrat, and the interpolated "you know" suggests that Shaftesbury is addressing a sympathetic audience. His critique of Paracelsianism, in its coolness, suggests the passage of time, and the change of political circumstances, since the publication of More's *Enthusiasmus Triumphatus*. Whereas Pico and Ficino imagined the mage as a model of internal order and discipline, Shaftesbury imagines the Paracelsian as a deceiver and charlatan. He tells of a prisoner—identified by Leibniz as Francis Mercurius Van Helmont, son of Joan Baptista Van Helmont and close friend of Lady Anne Conway[93]—who "was one of those whom in this Age we usually call *Philosophers*, a Successor of PARACELSUS, and a Master in the occult Sciences. But as to *Moral* Science, or any thing relating to *Self-converse*, he was a mere Novice" (1:178). Rather than following Shaftesbury's prescribed method of soliloquy, the Paracelsian set about making all the various sounds he could by "various Collisions of the Mouth, and Operations of the active Tongue upon the passive Gum or Palat." After he was released, he wrote up his findings in a treatise and "esteem'd himself the only Master of Voice and Language on the account of this his *radical* Science, and *fundamental Knowledg* of Sounds," but those who sought to learn from him, Shaftesbury weighs in, "wou'd, I believe, have found themselves considerably deluded" (1:179). The Paracelsian's learning is not without value, but for Shaftesbury it is not true philosophy, because it does not concern the moral life of humankind. Distinguishing "*Moral* Science" from "the occult Sciences," he recalls the fusion and harmony of the two in the idea of "*moral Magick*," according to which the artist's work does not "delude" others but excites and edifies them. Shaftesbury dismisses Paracelsianism as a kind of technical irrelevance. The true magic takes place within.

It is in this sense that Shaftesbury reconceives and recovers the idea of enthusiasm.[94] "Whether in fact there be any real *Enchantment*, any Influence of *Stars*, any Power of *Daemons* or of foreign Natures over our own Minds," he writes in *Miscellany II*—one of five "miscellanies" that Shaftesbury used to elaborate on and in certain cases to defend the arguments of the earlier treatises—"is thought questionable by many. Some there are who assert the Negative, and endeavour to solve the Appearances of this kind by the natural Operation of our Passions, and the common Course of outward Things. For my own part, I cannot but at this present apprehend a kind of *Enchantment* or *Magick* in that which we call ENTHUSIASM" (3:19). Shaftesbury resists the modern skeptical logic of disenchantment in favor of a new internalized and aestheticized conception of magic, one that emphasizes not "foreign Natures" but inward nature. He acknowledges "that, in Religion, the ENTHUSIASM which works by *Love*, is subject to many strange Irregularitys; and that which works by *Fear*, to many monstrous and horrible Superstitions," but he nevertheless maintains that "ENTHUSIASM is, in it-self, a very natural *honest* Passion; and has properly nothing for its Object but what is *Good* and *Honest*" (3:24–25). In fact,

"VIRTUE it-self" is "no other than a noble *Enthusiasm* justly directed" (3:22). True enthusiasm is not demonic possession but sublime inspiration. At base it is not, in More's terms, "a misconceit of being *inspired*," much less a "mischievous Disease."[95] Rather, it is what moves the poet to move an audience, and being, like sympathy, "wonderfully powerful and extensive" (1:34), it is what moves everyone to embrace and communicate the good.

Yet in the course of reclaiming enthusiasm and assimilating it to his moral and aesthetic ideals, Shaftesbury exposes a more unsightly face of sympathy, one that cannot be easily mapped onto the utopian social vision projected by his ethics. The "many strange Irregularitys" and the "many monstrous and horrible Superstitions" associated with enthusiasm suggest an alternative vision of society still marked by the sectarian conflicts and chaos of the Civil Wars and their aftermath. Here we return to one of the central challenges of a philosophical commitment to sympathy, a version of which we have already worked through in the case of Cavendish. To the extent that the theorist of sympathy recognized and represented empirical reality, there would always be a gap between experienced particulars and the part conceived in abstract, ideal, and purely relational terms. Another way to put this problem is that, positioned against the unsociable mode of academic philosophy, Shaftesbury's mimetic commitment to representing social experience as it "really" was—variable, desultory, "irregular"—came into conflict with his moral and aesthetic commitment to picturing the world as it ideally was—immutable, orderly, harmonious.[96] He attempted to resolve this conflict partly by substituting the term "natural," in effect, for the term "ideal." In other words, society was in its nature as his ethics described it, and to the extent that it was irregular, it had deviated from its natural state. Disorder was simply a misdirection or falling away.

Shaftesbury's *Letter Concerning Enthusiasm*, published separately in 1708, was occasioned by an outbreak of "irregular," what might be called dysfunctionally sympathetic activity in London after the arrival two years earlier of millenarian French Protestants, who claimed the power of prophecy. Early on in the *Letter* Shaftesbury associates sympathy with what he calls "the Contagion of Enthusiasm" (1:10), pathological language that, as we have seen, Digby used to depreciate the communication of emotion. Given Shaftesbury's decision to place the *Letter* first in *Characteristicks*, a reader's initial sense of sympathy is of a volatile and morally ambiguous phenomenon—not yet an ideal virtue contained by the structural model of the system. Telling the mythical story of Pan, Shaftesbury observes, "One may with good reason call every Passion *Panick* which is rais'd in a Multitude, and convey'd by Aspect, or as it were by Contact or Sympathy (1:10)." Sympathy emerges here as a dangerous, demagogic force.

When the multitude is under the spell of such a passion, "especially where Religion had had to do," a mass pathology results: "In this state their very Looks are infectious. The Fury flies from Face to Face: and the Disease is no sooner seen than caught. They who in a better Situation of Mind have beheld a Multitude under the power of this Passion, have own'd that they saw in the Countenances of Men something more ghastly and terrible than at other times is express'd on the most passionate occasion. Such force has Society in ill, as well as in good Passions: and so much stronger any Affection is for being *social* and *communicative*" (1:11). Shaftesbury will go on to theorize society as a beautiful system, but here it is a mob of "ghastly and terrible" faces, a fertile breeding ground for infection and "Disease." Our natural relation to all humankind promotes virtue and happiness, but also vice and corruption. Communication becomes "Contagion," Shaftesbury suggests, when the medium is unnatural or "ill" affection. In a footnote he keys this passage to one in the next treatise where he makes a claim for the naturalness of "*Herding*" (1:69). He goes on to write, "For my own part, methinks, this *herding* Principle, and *associating* Inclination, is seen so *natural* and strong in most Men, that one might readily affirm, 'twas even from the Violence of this Passion that so much Disorder arose in the general Society of Mankind" (1:70). Sympathy unites society but also divides it, as in the case of faction, conspiracy, or war. The "very Spirit of *Faction*," Shaftesbury reflects, "for the greatest part, seems to be no other than the Abuse or Irregularity of that *social Love*, and *common Affection*, which is natural to Mankind" (1:72). The difference between "a Lover of Mankind" and "a Ravager" is nothing more than "a small mis-guidance of the Affection" (1:71). Here again Shaftesbury's emphasis falls on the power of sympathy, but in revealing its dark side, he ultimately runs the risk of undermining his subsequent claim for sympathy as a fundamental virtue, a universal principle of human goodness.

Shaftesbury aims to reconcile theory and reality by suggesting that the irregular can be made regular, or rather can return to regularity, if it is properly "treated," to use the medical language of the *Letter*. Confronting the problem of "ill" or "misguided" affection, Shaftesbury conceives two principal modes of response, which are introduced in the *Letter* and in effect split off and grow organically into the second and third treatises; "wit and humour" and "soliloquy" function to manage the enthusiastic passions and their negative sympathetic power. Looking to the classical past, Shaftesbury notes the social benefit of the philosopher's liberty "to use all the Force of Wit and Raillery against" what he calls "the Superstition and Enthusiasm of the Times" (1:12). Against the literary enthusiasm or "the florid and over-sanguine Humour of the *high Style*," the "*Comick* Genius was apply'd, as a kind of *Caustick*" (1:154). True wit does not trivialize serious matters; it sets reasonable boundaries for them. "We shall grow better *Reasoners*," Shaftesbury writes hopefully of his own age, "by reasoning pleasantly" (1:50). At the same time, "looking into our-selves" has the potential to "do us wondrous service, in rectifying our Errors in Religion." Even when "Men find . . . no prepossessing *Panick* which bewitches 'em," they are still susceptible to the panics of others, but "the knowledg of our Passions in their very Seeds, the measuring well the Growth and Progress of Enthusiasm, and the judging rightly of its natural Force, and what command it has over our very Senses, may teach us to oppose more successfully those Delusions which come arm'd with the specious Pretext of moral Certainty, and *Matter of Fact*" (1:27). In a spirit more Socratic than Stoic, Shaftesbury suggests that the passions should be not eliminated but calculated, "measured" and "judged."[97] In the *Inquiry* he implies that the Stoic pursuit of apathy is futile: "Let Indolence, Indifference, or Insensibility, be study'd as an Art, or cultivated with the utmost Care; the Passions thus restrain'd will force their Prison, and in one way or other procure their Liberty, and find full Employment. They will be sure to create to themselves *unusual* and *unnatural* Exercise, where they are cut off from such as is *natural* and *good*" (2:77). Passion will out, and so better to direct it and to cultivate the "*natural* and *good*."

Shaftesbury's emphasis on introspection and introversion reflects the fact that the relationship between self and society is far more complicated than that of nesting "systems" organized in analogic relation to the whole. As in the case of Cavendish, the valorization and idealization of sympathy in the social sphere coincide with the development of a "self-theme," to use her term, that functions in part to manage and resolve the tensions of that sphere. Confounded by the risks and rigors of heightened intersubjectivity, the self seeks refuge in height-ened subjectivity. The other is subsumed by what might be called the interior interlocutor. "Company," Shaftesbury writes, "is an extreme Provocative to Fancy; and, like a hot Bed in Gardening, is apt to make our Imaginations sprout too fast. But by this anticipating Remedy of SOLILOQUY, we may effectually provide against the Inconvenience" (1:100). The record of Shaftesbury's own experience belies the straightforwardness of this prescription. During a period of intellectual and political retirement, he considered the threat of society to the self most deeply and extensively in the notebooks that he started keeping in the Netherlands in 1698.[98] He had been elected to Parliament in 1695, proceeding to immerse himself in the affairs of the House of Commons. During his three years there, the need to reconcile principle to party—however nebulously defined— the reputation of his family, relations within his family, and deteriorating health all combined to put considerable strain on him. Shaftesbury was under "constant criticism," according to Robert Voitle, "for his lack of party spirit"; moreover, the "political heir of the man regarded as the archfiend of all Whiggery by the Tories could hardly expect any gratitude when he sided with them, as his principles often led him to do; at the same time this behavior made the Whigs mistrust him, even when he agreed with them."⁹⁹ When Parliament was dissolved in 1698, rather than stand again, Shaftesbury went to Rotterdam and began to engage in an intensive process of self-conversation and soul-searching recorded in the notebooks. With quotation after quotation of Marcus Aurelius and Epictetus, the notebooks double as a kind of Stoic florilegium. Although his positive view of the passions ultimately set him at odds with the Stoics, their ideal of the armored, anchored self held a deep appeal for Shaftesbury; sympathy and stoicism remained in active dialogue in his mind. Troubled by the contagious effects of society, he wrote, "Resolve . . . Never to forget *Thy Self.*"¹⁰⁰ The power of sympathy threatens not only to blur the boundaries between self and others but, more dangerously still, to cast the self into oblivion. And yet Shaftesbury was quick to recognize that forgetting others in the interest of a fully protected self would deprive the subject of his essential humanity. Without friends, the self cannot function properly: "But, if I enter not affectionately & with Warmth into their Concerns; if I feel not, so as to be in some degree animated; with what Effect can I speak or act?" The absence of sympathy amounts to a kind of aphasia. Nowhere is the social under greater pressure in Shaftesbury's writings, and even here his assertion of kind affection is overarching. Human vitality depends on social interaction. The innermost circle of social relation animates the center and mediates between it and the wider sphere: "But if I have no Sympathy with my Friends; how shall I be sensible towards Society?" The goal Shaftesbury sets is not to root out sympathy altogether but to "Cut off Familiarity Inwardness & that Sympathy of a wrong kind" and to "Learn to be with Self; to talk with Self. Commune with thy own Heart."¹⁰¹ Here is his "soliloquent" ideal adumbrated—and derived from personal crisis.

Soliloquy and raillery are not, however, sufficient to manage "Sympathy of a wrong kind" when it has gone viral. When the panic becomes a pandemic, a political solution has to be reached, and Shaftesbury's recognition of the need for the magistrate to intervene represents a further recognition of the power of sympathy—and a preference for that power to be centrally, or at least selectively, managed. The intervention from the top, he comments, should be not violent or repressive or "caustic" but sympathetic: "The Magistrate, if he be any Artist, shou'd have a gentler hand; and instead of Causticks, Incisions, and Amputations, shou'd be using the softest Balms; and with a kind Sympathy entering into the Concern of the People, and taking, as it were, their Passion upon him, shou'd, when he has sooth'd and satisfy'd it, endeavour, by chearful ways, to divert and heal it" (1:11). The political artist is a sort of sympathetic healer. In tune with his own passions, he can receive the ill passions of the people without catching them, and in receiving them, he effectively neutralizes them by means of a corrective sympathy. The magistrate assumes the office of master sympathizer. The function of the magistrate allows Shaftesbury to harmonize a more exclusive and a more inclusive view of sympathy. The magistrate in effect represents an external counterpart to the internal function of soliloquy and ultimately a kind of fail-safe mechanism; he promises to return irregular passions to their natural state of regularity, especially when people are unable to "divert and heal" those passions themselves. In the end, Shaftesbury suggests that the solution to the problem of "Sympathy of a wrong kind" is sympathy of the right kind.

THE MORALISTS AND THE CONVERSATION OF THE WORLD

Shaftesbury's portrait of the sympathetic magistrate in the *Letter* leads into a characteristic encomium on classical culture and society. "Not only the Visionarys and Enthusiasts of all kinds were tolerated, your Lordship knows, by the Antients," Shaftesbury writes; "but on the other side, Philosophy had as free a course, and was permitted as a Ballance against Superstition. And whilst some Sects, such as the *Pythagorean* and latter *Platonick*, join'd in with the Superstition and Enthusiasm of the Times; the *Epicurean*, the *Academick*, and others, were allow'd to use all the Force of Wit and Raillery against it. And thus matters were happily balanc'd; Reason had fair Play; Learning and Science flourish'd. Wonderful was the Harmony and Temper which arose from all these Contrarietys" (1:12). This account reads remarkably like a sympathetic description of *The Moralists*, a dialogue between a representative of the "enthusiastic" sects and a representative of the contrary, "the *Epicurean*, the *Academick*, and others." In *The Moralists* Shaftesbury effectively translates this historical ideal into narrative terms, thereby recovering it for both the present and the future. A dialogically "balanc'd" society becomes a socially "balanc'd" dialogue. In turning to *The Moralists*, I want to shift my attention from Shaftesbury's representations of sympathy in the moral and aesthetic spheres to his representations of sympathy in the natural world.[102] For Shaftesbury the natural and the moral were as closely allied as the moral and the aesthetic; all three were adequated "systematically." He specifies in his subtitle that *The Moralists* treats both "*Natural* and *Moral* Subjects," and we recall that he identified "the main Scope and principal End" of *Characteristicks* to be the assertion of "the Reality of a BEAUTY and CHARM in *moral* as well as *natural* Subjects." The progress of my analysis follows the visual-spatial trajectory of *Characteristicks*; the movement from the *Letter* to *Sensus Communis* to *Advice to an Author* to the *Inquiry* to *The Moralists* involves an adjustment in the angle of vision from inward to outward. From the London stage of the French prophets we proceed by turns to the stage of the world, the outermost circle in which all others concenter.

Set in an idealized pastoral landscape, *The Moralists* relates on the face of it the "conversion" of Philocles from skepticism to an enthusiastic form of theism. Philocles's conversion is represented as a dynamic process in which his interlocutor and eventual tutor, Theocles—a clear *sprechende Name*—sympathetically communicates to him the divine enthusiasm that he has received from the external world. In *The Moralists*, the "*moral Magick*" described in *Sensus Communis* is enacted dialogically.[103] Shaftesbury thus actualizes the ideal of enthusiasm that he theorizes earlier in *Characteristicks*. In sympathizing with each other, the two speakers effectively mirror the social sympathy of all things. This greater sympathy, the sympathy of the whole, is a keynote of Theocles's fervid effusions at the climax of the dialogue; having heard that all things connect, Philocles sees and feels the connection at this point. On the whole, *The Moralists* functions to reassure a reader disenchanted by a mechanistic worldview that a vital coherence remains a cosmic reality. The natural world, Shaftesbury insists, still has "Charms in abundance" (2:110). And yet it is in the course of most passionately and most beautifully drawing his sympathetic world picture that Shaftesbury exposes its artificiality and instability. In giving skepticism a voice, he adumbrates a range of arguments against a universal idea of sympathy that Theocles cannot in the end satisfactorily answer. In this sense Hume did not need to bring skeptical arguments to *Characteristicks*—and we shall consider Hume's critique of Shaftesbury in the final chapter—he merely had to bring them *out* of it. If ultimately the skeptic's objections could not be refuted logically, and could only be transcended emotionally, the ontological foundation of a sympathetic worldview was no longer secure. From this perspective the dialogic form of *The Moralists* does not recapitulate and reinforce the idea of cosmic sympathy, whereby the two speakers come to agree on the subject of the agreement of the whole; rather, it shifts that idea from inaccessible, transcendental premise to contested, and therefore contestable, opinion.

These competing and seemingly incompatible accounts of the unity of the world translate into two competing and seemingly incompatible accounts of the unity of the work—a problem of which Shaftesbury was acutely aware. In *Miscellany V* he presents *The Moralists* as a more sociable version of the *Inquiry*.

"It conceals," he writes, "what is *scholastical*, under the appearance of a polite Work. It aspires to *Dialogue*, and carrys with it not only those poetick Features of the Pieces antiently call'd MIMES; but it attempts to unite the several Personages and Characters in ONE *Action*, or *Story*, within a determinate Compass of *Time*, regularly divided, and drawn into different and proportion'd *Scenes*" (3:175). By this account *The Moralists* "aspires" to be a perfect Aristotelian drama, and the unity of the "*Action*, or *Story*," comports decorously with Theocles's principal message. But by giving the work the subtitle "A *Philosophical Rhapsody*," Shaftesbury invited the reader to categorize *The Moralists* in an altogether different way, as a "literary work consisting of miscellaneous or disconnected pieces" (*OED* 2a), or, in Shaftesbury's own terms, a "mix'd kind of Work" (3:175n). Such a work is far more in keeping with the way of the railleur, who is skeptical and subversive of monolithic formations, and whose incisive wit has a divisive effect. *The Moralists* is thus divided between a classical ideal of form and a more naturalistic, mimetic idea, tending toward the miscellaneous. Shaftesbury had a moral commitment to both. "Hardly," he writes, "will it be objected to our MORALIST, (the Author of the *philosophick Dialogue* above) 'That the Personages who sustain the *sceptical* or *objecting Parts*, are over-tame and tractable in their Disposition.' Did I perceive any such foul dealing in his Piece; I shou'd scarce think it worthy of the Criticism here bestow'd," for if "DIALOGUE . . . be attempted . . . , the Partys shou'd appear *natural*, and *such as they really are*. If we *paint* at all; we shou'd endeavour to paint *like Life*, and draw Creatures as they are know-able, in their *proper* Shapes and better Features" (3:180). Ultimately, Shaftesbury sacrificed unity and coherence for the sake of realism on one hand and fairness on the other. A weaker Philocles might make for a more unified "*Story*," but it might also mean distortion and "foul dealing." Aristotelian formalism runs the risk of violating the gentlemanly code. The "fair" author does not sympathize with his hero only; in his generosity he extends his sympathy to all "Partys."

But if sympathy is in some sense the cause of intellectual and formal division in *The Moralists*, I will go on to argue that Shaftesbury also conceived it as a means of reconciliation and resolution. In the end he stages neither the victory of one philosophical position over the other nor the failure of the two to meet; rather, he suggests that the two must accommodate each other in a process of sympathetic "yielding." This more active mode of sympathy is akin to that "art" practiced by the magistrate; it is a process not of passively reflecting the affections and inclinations of others but of actively "entering into" them. Philocles is meant to feel the heat of Theocles's enthusiasm and temper his skepticism, and Theocles is meant to feel the chill of Philocles's skepticism and temper his enthusiasm. Making strategic use of the "mix'd" form of the work,

Shaftesbury shows how the two characters come to sympathize with and learn from each other. In so doing, he stakes a claim to a different, and more difficult, kind of unity.

Theocles stands in as Shaftesbury's most forceful and eloquent advocate for the Stoic-Platonic, anti-Epicurean worldview that the Cambridge Platonists had promoted so vigorously in their philosophical writing. If More and Cudworth went back to the ancients to find the sources of magic and sympathy, Shaftesbury characterizes Theocles as himself a kind of ancient, an avatar of the *prisca sapientia*. His enthusiasm, Philocles explains to Palemon, is "more after the pleasing Transports of those antient *Poets* you are often charm'd with, than after the fierce unsociable way of modern *Zealots*" (2:124). Theocles combines the sublime enthusiasm of the ancients with the better "sociable way" of the moderns; he is, as it were, a clubbable Cambridge Platonist. When Philocles first encounters him, Theocles is "with his belov'd *Mantuan* MUSE, roving in the Fields" (2:126). Theocles is not only reading Virgil but also in some sense channeling him. The moral magic between author and reader will be recapitulated between the two characters in dialogue: "The moment he saw me," Philocles relates, "his Book vanish'd, and he came with friendly haste to meet me" (2:126). Theocles is not, Shaftesbury makes clear, a solitary bookworm or reclusive scholar but rather a sociable and tasteful gentleman. The third part of *The Moralists*, which contains its rhapsodic climax, also begins in the mystical company of Virgil, as Theocles opposes the Epicurean account of "the sole Powers of CHAOS, and blind *Chance*" to the Virgilian vision of *"The active mind, infus'd thro' all the Space,"* which *"Unites and Mingles with the mighty Mass"* (2:192). Theocles's vision of the natural world thus assumes almost immediately a literary character; with his ancient poet taking the place of their ancient philosophers, Shaftesbury's aestheticization of More's and Cudworth's sort of sympathetic worldview is immediately apparent. Shaftesbury would have that worldview sing. "Here, PHILOCLES," Theocles promises, "we shall find our *sovereign Genius*; if we can charm the *Genius* of the Place . . . to inspire us with a truer Song of Nature, teach us some celestial Hymn, and make us feel Divinity present in these solemn Places of Retreat" (2:193). Combining the form of dialogue with "Song" and "Hymn," Shaftesbury both socializes and aestheticizes philosophical discourse; philosophy, of late "immured . . . (poor Lady!) in Colleges and Cells," and given voice only in the *"School-syllogism,"* as Philocles laments, is in *The Moralists* now free to "rove in the Fields" (2:105). The syllogism, Digby's model of sympathetic order, is here dismissed as a token of scholastic rigidity and irrelevance. Philocles's personification of philosophy is very much to the point; it is a tactic of socialization—such a dignified lady as she has no business in a monastic academy; she must be allowed society and conversation as well as fresh air and grand vistas. She must be "charming"— both in the weaker social sense and in the stronger magical sense. In Theocles's description of the dialogue's enchanted setting, Shaftesbury evokes the full semantic range of the Latin *carmen*—song, verse, and incantation. Theocles and Philocles "are come to the sacred Groves of the *Hamadryads*" and are in the presence of the "Rural Powers and Graces" (2:193). The genius is not "parting," as in Milton's *Nativity Ode*, but beckoning, and if the oracles are dumb, the nymphs are still "breathing spells." In the "conversable Woods," with their "temperate Climates," as Theocles proclaims, "no fierce Heats nor Colds annoy us" (2:219). There is no sign of Milton's "brandisht Sword of God" coming "to parch that temperate Clime" (*PL*, 12.633, 636). Shaftesbury gives his audience a sympathetic paradise in the present tense, a neo-Arcadian green world; the catastrophe of the Fall has been effectively written out of Shaftesbury's literary cosmos.

Through his rhapsodizing, Theocles sentimentalizes the ruling claim at the heart of *The Moralists* for "a *Universal* UNION, *Coherence*, or *Sympathizing* of Things" (2:203).[104] Shaftesbury wants to insist that universal sympathy can be not only felt but also understood, and its answerability to reason is a crucial and crushing blow to the Epicurean cause. The idea of universal sympathy is both sensible and intelligible. It is also, Theocles tries to assure Philocles, demonstrable. In a kind of Poussinesque tableau, the two characters take an "Evening-Walk in the Fields," as the "laborious Hinds" are "retiring," and Philocles, learned "in the nature of *Simples*," offers some words on the local flora (2:159). Theocles immediately sees an opportunity to challenge Philocles's skepticism: "How is it possible that with such Insight, and accurate Judgment in *the Particulars* of natural Beings and Operations, you shou'd no better judg of the Structure of Things *in general*, and of the Order and Frame of NATURE? . . . How therefore, shou'd you prove so ill *a Naturalist* in *this* WHOLE, and understand so little the Anatomy of *the World* and *Nature*, as not to discern the same Relation of Parts, the same Consistency and Uniformity in *the Universe*! . . . Can you induce yourself ever to believe or think, that where there are Parts so variously united, and conspiring fitly within themselves, *the Whole* it-self shou'd have neither Union nor Coherence?" (2:159–160). In claiming the universal and fundamental reality of sympathy, Theocles adopts an all-or-nothing approach; Philocles cannot logically assert that the anatomic parts of a particular plant are "variously united, and conspiring fitly within themselves" without accepting that such union and conspiration obtain in nature as a whole. To Theocles, Philocles is a kind of learned fool, an unnatural naturalist, who has failed to open his eyes and mind wide enough to the world. Universal sympathy is demonstrable because it is readily perceptible. As Theocles confidently affirms,

> All things in this World are *united*. For as the *Branch* is united with the *Tree*, so is the Tree immediately with the *Earth*, *Air*, and *Water*, which feed it. As much as the fertile *Mould* is fitted to the Tree, as much as the strong and upright Trunk of the *Oak* or *Elm* is fitted to the twining Branches of the *Vine* or *Ivy*; so much are the very *Leaves*, the *Seeds*, and *Fruits* of these Trees fitted to the various *Animals*: These again to one another, and to the *Elements* where they live. . . . Thus in contemplating all on Earth, we must of necessity view *All in One*, as holding to one common Stock. Thus too in the System of the bigger World. . . . And know, my ingenious Friend, that by this Survey you will be oblig'd to own the UNIVERSAL SYSTEM, and coherent Scheme of Things, to be establish'd on abundant Proof, capable of convincing any fair and just Contemplator of the Works of Nature. For scarce wou'd any-one, till he had well survey'd this Universal Scheme, believe *a Union* thus evidently demonstrable, by such numerous and powerful Instances of mutual Correspondency and Relation, from the minutest Ranks and Orders of Beings to the remotest Spheres. (2:162–163)

In Theocles's claim for all "holding to one common Stock" and for the one "UNIVERSAL SYSTEM" Shaftesbury is reciting Cudworth's keynote. Philocles does not at the moment accept this claim, Theocles reasons, only because his vision has been too narrowly focused. When one examines a tree, one sees branches united to the trunk and leaves united to branches, a clear and lovely "Sympathizing of Parts" (2:195). Looking out more widely, one sees that "the very *Leaves*, the *Seeds*, and *Fruits*" of the tree are "fitted to the various *Animals*," and one perceives the tree's sensitive dependence on "the *Earth*, *Air*, and *Water*, which feed it." The idea of universal sympathy, then, is not a philosophical abstraction but a natural logical induction. To conclude that there is no such principle at work in the world is absurdly to deny what is in plain sight. It is to go against "what is evident from *natural History*, *Fact*, and the plain *Course of Things*" (2:180).

Shaftesbury effectively defangs the anti-Epicurean worldview, whose menace registers everywhere in the urgent tone of Cudworth's *True Intellectual System*, by suggesting that it is less dangerous than simply nonsensical. How could one, surveying the world, "suppose that each of these compleat and perfect Systems were fram'd, and thus united in just Symmetry, and conspiring Order, either by the accidental blowing of the Winds, or rolling of the Sands?" (2:164). Given this "just Symmetry, and conspiring Order," the logical inference is that there is an underlying and overarching principle of mind and design "active" in the world.[105] The Epicurean premise of matter in "accidental" motion is simply not borne out by the evidence. "Epicurean Nature" is a kind of contradiction in terms; the nature we see and know cannot be recognized in their account, which "represents a very *Chaos*, and reduces us to [their] belov'd Atoms, Chance, and confusion" (2:156). The Epicurean "disparagement" of human nature summed up in the phrase "That he is *to Man a Wolf*" makes little sense to anyone who has observed that "*Wolves* are *to Wolves* very kind and loving Creatures" (2:180). Only a philosopher who theorized human nature "abstract-edly and apart from Government and Society" would "represent it under monstrous Visages of *Dragons, Leviathans*, and I know not what devouring Creatures" (2:180). Hobbes's is a nightmare vision of society, not an actual or accurate one. Social terror follows from egoistic error: "The whole Order of the Universe, elsewhere so firm, intire, and immoveable, is here o'erthrown and lost by this one View; in which we refer all things to our-selves: submitting the Interest of *the Whole* to the Good and Interest of so small *a Part*" (2:164). It should be obvious that such a partial "view," making the whole of reality in our own troubled image, is necessarily distorting. The Epicurean worldview is the narcissistic projection of the ill-affected man. For Shaftesbury, Epicureanism is an anti-empirical philosophy in the sense that it is completely out of touch with the natural world as human beings see, perceive, and experience it. Any true theory of natural philosophy should be aligned with the practice of natural history, with the knowledge gained by inquiring into and interacting with the forms and figures of the natural world.

Shaftesbury's discussion of the tree as a synecdochal figure of universal sympathy comes very close to a passage under the heading "Deity" in the note-books, one that is crucial to understanding the totalizing aspiration of Shaftesburian sympathy. In the passage he goes on to give a discursive defini-tion of the verb "sympathize," which as it unfolds encompasses the whole range of creation:

> *To sympathize*, what is it?—To feel together, or be united in one Sence or Feeling.—the Fibers of the Plant sympathize. the Members of the Animal sympathize. and do not the heavenly Bodyes sympathize? why not?— Because we are not consciouse of this feeling—No more are we consciouse of the Feeling or Sympathizing of the Plant: neither can we be consciouse of any other in the world besides that of our own. If, however, it be true that these others sympathize; then the World, & the heavenly Bodyes (more united, & more harmoniously conspiring together then either the Plant or Animal-Body) must also sympathize. If there be a sympathizing of the Whole,

there is one Perception, one Intelligence of the Whole. If that, then all things are perceiv'd by that Intelligence. If so, then there is one all-knowing, & all-intelligent Nature.[106]

Anticipating the plot of *The Moralists*, Shaftesbury proceeds from skepticism to theism, from the sympathizing of the part to the "sympathizing of the Whole." Sympathy emerges in this early, searching period of Shaftesbury's writing as the structural principle of design. That he is under a Stoic influence here is strongly suggested by the quotation from Marcus Aurelius's *Meditations* (4.27) with which his notes on "Deity" begin. Here is the paragraph in full, of which Shaftesbury used only the first part of the second sentence: "Either there is a well-arranged Order of things [kosmos], or a maze, indeed, but not without a plan [kosmos]. Or can a sort of order [kosmos] subsist in thee, while in the Universe there is no order [akosmia], and that too when all things, though separated and dispersed, are still in sympathetic connexion [sumpathōn]?"[107] Sympathy is what makes the cosmos a "cosmos" in the true sense, an orderly whole. Marcus's assertion of cosmic sympathy underwrites Shaftesbury's in the notebooks. The sources of *Characteristicks* are far more eclectic, but the Stoic influence continues to be widely felt.[108] In a footnote keyed to the phrase "ONE System" in *The Moralists* Shaftesbury includes five supporting quotations, one from Cicero, one from Lucan, two from Seneca, and, perhaps more surprisingly, one from Locke. The passage from Cicero's *De oratore* (3.19–21) pays tribute to Shaftesbury's predecessors' belief that "everything above and below is one and bound together by one force and one harmony of Nature [*una consensione naturae*]" (2:161). The passages from Seneca, excerpts from Epistle 95, reinforce the idea of a deeper relation between the universal and the social. The first, to which I referred in the previous chapter, invokes the organic analogy: "We are members of one great body." The second conveys the interdependence of the species or kind. Seneca likens "our fellowship" to a stone arch that would collapse if each stone did not support the other (2:161). As the universe is unified and interconnected, so is society. By the spread of his quotations Shaftesbury implies that the idea of cosmic unity and consent is not unique to Stoicism or to any other philosophical school; rather, it is common to that "civil, social, Theistic" tradition with which he identified himself—and which he felt Locke had ultimately betrayed. But the reference to Locke's *Essay*, which comes first in the sequence of authorities listed in the footnote, should be seen less as the sign of any kind of inconsistency in Shaftesbury's philosophical allegiances and more as evidence that Shaftesbury understood sympathy as a principle that was widely held and maintained fully in accordance with reason. Even in the formal, methodical, unrhapsodic system of Locke, the universal order of things is asserted as a given.

Once he is reassured that Philocles has been convinced of his sympathetic view of things by means of reason, Theocles is willing again to move him. "My Doubts," Philocles proclaims, "are vanish'd. MALICE and CHANCE (vain *Phantoms!*) have yielded to that *all-prevalent* WISDOM which you have establish'd. You are Conqueror in the cool way of *Reason*, and may with Honour now grow warm again in your *poetick* Vein" (2:205). Philocles's skepticism has been exorcised and "conquered." And because Theocles has won him over "in the cool way of *Reason*" the victory has been fair, both just and pleasing. Theocles, answering Philocles's call, stokes the fire of his enthusiasm. As the dialogue as a whole reaches a climax, Theocles hymns the sympathetic universe: "'O mighty GENIUS! Sole-animating and inspiring Power! Author and Subject of these Thoughts! Thy Influence is universal: and in all Things, thou art inmost . . . . The vital Principle is widely shar'd, and infinitely vary'd: dispers'd thro'out; nowhere extinct. All lives; and by Succession still revives'" (2:205). Addressing the one deity as "Thou who art *Original* SOUL, diffusive, vital in all, inspiriting *the Whole*" (2:207), Theocles has become fully himself, the true bearer of a true name. We hear in this extended passage the vitalism and spiritualism of the Cambridge Platonists transformed into a "rapturous Strain" (2:207).

Theocles's rhapsody has a powerful sympathetic effect on Philocles. The erstwhile skeptic, "the cold indifferent PHILOCLES," experiences an infusion of sublime emotion. The heat of enthusiasm passes from Theocles to Philocles as if by contagion, but this is surely "sympathy of the right kind." Philocles catches Theocles's word "GENIUS" and recites it back to him: "Your *Genius*, the *Genius* of the Place, and the GREAT GENIUS have at last prevail'd. I shall no longer resist the Passion growing in me for Things of a *natural* kind" (2:220). Philocles goes on, "From this time forward . . . I shall no more have reason to fear those *Beautys* which strike a sort of *Melancholy*, like the Places we have nam'd, or like these solemn *Groves*. No more shall I avoid the moving Accents of *soft Musick*, or fly from the *enchanting Features* of the fairest *human Face*" (2:221). The magic of nature, of figure, has seized Philocles's heart. He confesses himself "*a Proselyte*" (2:223). In Shaftesbury's account of Philocles's conversion, skepticism emerges as a matter of "resistance" and "fear." Like Epicureanism, it seems here not a valid philosophical position so much as a local or internal disorder, a kind of blockage, sublimated into the form of philosophy. The sound mind does not discriminate among philosophical schools; perceiving one true nature, sympathetically connected, it embraces the one true philosophy, the true intellectual system of the universe.

Up to this point I have treated *The Moralists* as a straightforward conversion narrative: Philocles is skeptical; Theocles reasons with him and challenges his skepticism; Theocles rhapsodizes and overcomes his skepticism; Philocles is no longer skeptical but sympathetic and enthusiastic. But there are significant inconsistencies with this account. Soon after declaring his conversion, Philocles quickly finds that all is not as clear as it had seemed. As he says to Theocles, "The Matter, I must confess, is still mysterious" (2:221). Theocles goes on to ask Philocles, "May I bring this yet a little nearer? And will you follow me once more?" (2:222). These questions have the effect of calling into doubt the sympathetic connection just formed between the two speakers. When Theocles proceeds to instruct him in the appreciation of "these terrestrial Beautys, and whatever has the appearance of Excellence, and is able to attract," the spell of enthusiasm is broken: "Hold! hold!" Philocles interrupts; "you take this in too high a Key, above my reach. If you wou'd have me accompany you, pray lower this Strain a little; and talk in a more familiar way" (2:225). Suddenly it appears that the two interlocutors have fallen out of sympathy, out of sync; there is a discrepancy in conversational registers. Philocles and Theocles are no longer meeting on a higher plane of enthusiasm but simply failing to connect. They are not back to square one exactly, but there has been a kind of regression, which complicates the sense of a linear, progressive conversion narrative. That narrative is reasserted and reinforced when Theocles shifts to the declarative summary mode: "THUS, PHILOCLES, (continu'd he, after a short Pause) thus have I presum'd to treat of *Beauty* before so great a Judg, and such a skilful Admirer as your-self. For taking rise from Nature's Beauty, which transported me, I gladly ventur'd further in the Chase; and have accompany'd you in search of Beauty, as it relates to us, and makes our highest *Good*, in its sincere and natural Enjoyment" (2:238). Theocles here effectively redescribes the genre of the work as a philosophical quest romance, two eager adventurers "in search of Beauty."[109] But soon thereafter Philocles fills the "short Pause" preceding Theocles's confident and authoritative "THUS" with renewed doubt, and a more uncertain mode of dialogue returns. As he sees Theocles "going down the Hill," descending from their top of speculation, Philocles is thrust into internal crisis. He encourages Theocles to slow down, to exit "more gradually" from "both the *Woods*, and that Philosophy which he confin'd to 'em," for, as he explains, "as much convinc'd as I was, and as great a Convert to his Doctrine, my Danger still, I own'd to him, was very great: and I foresaw that when the Charm of these Places, and his Company was ceas'd, I shou'd be apt to release, and weakly yield to that too powerful Charm, *the World*" (2:239). Theocles's claim for the transcendental order, beauty, and enchantment of the cosmos, Philocles's response suggests, may be no more than contingent and contextual, specific to "these Places" and to "his Company." What happens in these woods may stay in these woods.

The world is suddenly subject to *"the World,"* and here the narrative of *The Moralists* begins to seem more circular than linear. We are back at the beginning, where Philocles addresses Palemon as "the only well-bred Man who wou'd have taken the Fancy to talk Philosophy in such a Circle of good Company as we had round us yesterday, when we were in your Coach together, in *the Park*," and goes on to conclude that Palemon must have "an extravagant Passion for Philosophy, to quit so many Charms for it" (2:104–105). Shaftesbury provides a specific social context for *The Moralists*, one that, under Theocles's visionary guidance, Philocles will leave behind, relocating from *"the Park"* to *"the Woods,"* and adjusting his vision from "a Circle of good Company" to the outermost circle of the universe, from "the *fashionable* World" to the world as a whole. At the end of *The Moralists* that movement is reversed: "BY this time we found our-selves insensibly got home. Our *Philosophy* ended, and we return'd to the common Affairs of Life" (2:247). In this sense, the dialogic mode of *The Moralists* approaches not romance but pastoral, with its characteristic pattern of retreat and return, city-country-city. Yet that pattern is itself complicated by Shaftesbury's embedding of the dialogue, which, we recall, is related, or "recited," in a letter from Philocles to Palemon—hence the beginning of *The Moralists* takes place after the ending. The complex structure and chronology further undermine any stable sense of Philocles's conversion from skepticism. Before relating the dialogue, Philocles exclaims, "O . . . PALEMON! that it had been my fortune to have met you the other day, just at my Return out of the Country from *a Friend*, whose Conversation had in one day or *two* made such an Impression on me, that I shou'd have suted you to a Miracle. You wou'd have thought indeed that I had been cur'd of my *Scepticism* and Levity, so as never to have rally'd more, at that wild rate, on any Subject, much less on these which are so serious" (2:123). There is a subversive counterfactual force to the construction "You wou'd have thought indeed that I had been cur'd of my *Scepticism*." The suggestion is that Philocles's "cure," his conversion, not only has been transient but also might have been merely apparent—that is, it might not have really happened at all. In going on to praise Theocles, Philocles can be seen to undercut him instead: "Tho he had all of the *Enthusiast*, he had nothing of the *Bigot*. He heard every thing with Mildness and Delight; and bore with me when I treated all his Thoughts as visionary; and when, Sceptick-like, I unravel'd all his Systems" (2:124). This hardly sounds like a summary of a conversion narrative. Theocles emerges here not as the "Conqueror" but as a kind of good loser. Indeed, earlier in part I, Philocles defends the skeptical "way of Questioning and Doubting" to Palemon as an act of courage, which is unsettlingly similar to the way Theocles has defended his enthusiastic philosophy: "We are too lazy and effeminate and, withal a little too cowardly to dare *doubt*. The decisive way best becomes our Manners. It sutes as well with our Vices as with our Superstition: Which-ever we are fond of, is secur'd by it. . . . If, by means of our ill Morals, we are broken with Religion, 'tis the same Case still: We are as much afraid of *Doubting*. We must be sure to say, '*It cannot be*'; and ' *'tis Demonstrable*': for otherwise *Who knows?* And not to *know*, is to *yield!*'" (2:108). Having apparently been persuaded by Theocles "to dare believe," Philocles is here urging men "to dare *doubt*."

Philocles can be seen here not only as regressing to his earlier skeptical state but also as denouncing Theocles's "decisive way," his insistence that the unity and sympathy of things is "*Demonstrable*." Philocles's strictures on dogmatism echo—though precede in the order of narration—his most devastating critique of Theocles's sympathetic worldview:

> "For if DEITY be *now* really extant; if by any good Token it appears that there is *at this present* a universal Mind; 'twill easily be yielded there *ever* was one."—This is your argument.—You go (if I may say so) upon *Fact*, and wou'd prove that things *actually are* in such a state and condition, which if they really *were*, there wou'd indeed be no dispute left. Your UNION is your main Support. Yet how is it you prove this? What Demonstration have you given? What have you so much as offer'd at, beyond *bare Probability*? So far are you from *demonstrating* any thing, that if this uniting Scheme be the chief Argument for Deity, (as you tacitly allow) you seem rather to have demonstrated, "That the Case it-self is incapable of Demonstration." For, "How," say you, "can a narrow Mind see *All Things*?"—And yet if, in reality, It sees not *All*, It had as good see *Nothing*. The demonstrable part is still as far behind. For grant that this *All*, which lies within our view or knowledg, is orderly and united, as you suppose: this mighty *All* is a mere Point still, a very Nothing compar'd to what remains. (2:167–168)

In the passage from "Deity" in the notebooks, we recall, Shaftesbury had moved swiftly and smoothly from recognizing a skeptical problem—"and do not the heavenly Bodyes sympathize? why not?—Because we are not consciouse of this feeling—No more are we consciouse of the Feeling or Sympathizing of the Plant: neither can we be consciouse of any other in the world besides that of our own"—to providing an inductive solution—"If, however, it be true that these others sympathize; then the World, & the heavenly Bodyes (more united, &

more harmoniously conspiring together then either the Plant or Animal-Body)
must also sympathize." In Philocles's critique, the problem of our inability to
"be conscious of any other in the world besides that of our own" returns in full
force, and the inductive solution is exposed as "*bare Probability*," nowhere near
the standard of "Demonstration." The words that Philocles emphasizes effi-
ciently and effectively highlight the logical weaknesses of Theocles's account.
Theocles assumes that "*now*" necessarily implies "*ever*," that the subjunctive
"*were*" can be equated with the indicative "*actually are*," but Theocles's insistent "*All*" amounts in the end to "*Nothing.*" "This," Philocles offers by way of
conclusion, "is all I dare offer in opposition to your *Philosophy*" (2:168). This
seemingly modest, unemphasized "all" is corrosively ironic given the attack
that has preceded it. "All" that Philocles has "dared offer" by way of "opposition" threatens to reduce "all" of Theocles's argument about "this mighty *All*"
to "nothing." Theocles responds with no clear or direct refutation to this challenge, which sinks from view in the rarefied air of the dialogue's setting.

In Philocles's skeptical discourse we can begin to sense the "unraveling" of
the sympathetic worldview itself. Shaftesbury shared and carried forward More's
and Cudworth's claim for sympathetic order as a necessary and fundamental
reality, but in his aestheticization and "affectivization" of their Stoic-Platonic
worldviews he was ultimately submitting, and sacrificing, ontology to psychology.
In Theocles's climactic rhapsodies on the spiritual vitality of the cosmos, we
can see a line of descent from the Cambridge Platonists to Shaftesbury, but we
also sense a departure. In spite of Shaftesbury's reasonings—one might even say
because of them—universal sympathy has begun to seem less a matter of fact
than of feeling. More's and Cudworth's painstaking philosophical elaborations
of a sympathetic worldview conveyed a sense that universal sympathy was an
unquestioned and unquestionable reality, a premise of apodictic force. But in
Shaftesbury's sociable philosophy universal sympathy has come to seem like a
privileged perception. In this sense the exorcism of his old tutor is revealed to
have been partly a failure; the repressed Locke returns. Shaftesbury's emphasis
on what can be sensed and perceived both reflects and effects an attenuated
sense of universal presence. The more internally mediated universal sympathy
is said to be, the less externally fixed it seems to be. In response to Theocles's
first round of effusions, Philocles laments, "I only wish . . . that you had been a
little stronger in your Transport, to have proceeded as you began, without ever
minding me. For I was beginning to see Wonders in that *Nature* you taught me,
and was coming to know the Hand of your *divine Artificer*. But if you stop here,
I shall lose the Enjoyment of the pleasing Vision. And already I begin to find a
thousand Difficultys in fansying such a *Universal Genius* as you describe"

(2:195). The sympathetic worldview, Philocles's response suggests, may be no more than a "pleasing Vision," and an unstable one at that; it must be sustained by "Transport," and it is susceptible to "loss." Earlier in their dialogue, Theocles says to Philocles, "How little do you know the Extent and Power of *Good-nature*, and to what an heroick pitch a Soul may rise, which knows the thorow Force of it; and distributing it rightly, frames in it-self an equal, just, and universal Friendship!" (2:137). But the dialogue as a whole raises the suggestion that a "universal Friendship" can be "known" only when the soul has "risen" to "an heroick pitch," that the knowledge is contingent on the rise, on an elevated point of view. If so, "the Extent and Power" of sympathy seem significantly diminished. Philocles responds doubtfully: "As for a plain natural Love of *one single* Person in either Sex, I cou'd compass it, I thought, well enough; but this *complex universal* sort was beyond my reach. I cou'd love the Individual, but not the Species. This was too mysterious; too metaphysical an Object for me" (2:137). Here the mystical sympathy of the cosmos is soberly set against and reduced to the "plain natural Love of *one single* Person." Theocles goes on to argue, as we have seen, that "the universal system and coherent scheme of things" is "convincing" to "any fair and just Contemplator of the Works of Nature," but if even Philocles, who "is curious in the Works of Nature and has been let into a Knowledge of the animal and vegetable Worlds" (2:163), who has been admitted, so to speak, to the club of nature, struggles to extend his vision to the outermost circle of the universe, how then can Shaftesbury claim that his sympathetic worldview is natural and normative?

This is not the first time that the problem of perception has come up in *Characteristicks*. In *Sensus Communis* Shaftesbury recognizes the limits of "the Eye": "Universal Good, or the Interest of *the World in general* is a kind of remote philosophical Object. That *greater Community* falls not easily under the Eye. Nor is a National Interest, or that of a whole People, or Body Politick, so readily apprehended" (1:70). A sympathetic worldview seems to require perception that is either extraordinary or enhanced, or perhaps both. Shaftesbury goes on in the same discussion to reflect on the political challenge of perceiving the "remote"; the problem with imperial expansionism is the danger that "the Relation be less sensible, and in a manner lost, between the Magistrate and People, in a Body so unwieldy in its Limbs, and whose Members lie so remote from one another, and distant from the Head" (1:71). Shaftesbury's conception of the "Body Politick" in its ideal form is organic, but the more it is expanded, the more it becomes a kind of ungraspable visual field. Here we might say that Shaftesbury's aristocratic preference for what he calls "less Partys," his mascu-linist social exclusivism, trumps his theoretical construction of sympathy as a magical connective principle transcending space and time and, one might think, gender and class as well.[110] His psychological point about the limits of perception quickly slides into an ideological point about the habits and inclinations of gentlemen. As Shaftesbury asserts, "The most generous Spirits are the most combining" (1:71); "*herding*" becomes a mark of breeding, and conspiracy and combat are viewed as elite forms of "combination." It is in this sense that Julie Ellison has written that "Shaftesbury defines sympathy as a consequence of contestation and idealizes the community of debaters."[111]

On one hand, then, there is Theocles's claim that anyone who looks out into the world will own that it is a coherent, sympathetic whole; on the other hand, there is Philocles's counterclaim, reinforced by Shaftesbury himself earlier in *Characteristicks*, that the world as a whole is "too mysterious, too metaphysical an object" to be easily perceived. Theocles's perceptual idealism is, it might be objected, simply a glorified form of social elitism. As Michael Prince has observed, "The vantage the rhapsodist claims in imaginative terms is matched by the very real advantage he enjoys as the owner of a substantial landed estate."[112] A wide survey of the whole requires a position at the top, both socially and topographically. After his apparent conversion, Philocles makes a "confession": "I have hitherto been one of those Vulgar, who cou'd never relish *the Shades, the Rustick,* or *the Dissonancys* you talk of. I have never dreamt of such *Master-pieces* in NATURE. 'Twas my way to censure freely on the first view. But I perceive I am now oblig'd to go far in the pursuit of *Beauty*; which lies very absconded and deep: And if so, I am well assur'd that my *Enjoyments* hitherto have been very shallow" (2:224–225). The Platonic adept is indistinguishable here from the aristocratic aesthete, whose elevated status is both constituted and confirmed by his ability to "relish" and appreciate what the "Vulgar" cannot. The superficial "first view" is succeeded by a superior one, "far" and "deep." But, in spite of the claim for a "deep" reality, Shaftesbury's emphasis on the viewer and the viewed has the ultimate effect of making sympathy seem like a kind of surface effect, as if it were not a Platonic idea but a painterly one, no deeper than an image on canvas.

THE "*HEALING CAUSE*"

In attending to the harsher notes of Philocles's speech, which late in *The Moralists* tend to get lost in the sublime cadences of Theocles's rhapsodies, a reader is divided between two seemingly irreconcilable interpretations of the dialogue—that it resolves in conversion or that it dead-ends. But if the epistolary opening has the effect of calling into question whether or not Philocles has really been converted, it also functions to suggest an alternative kind of resolution, one that does not require a linear conversion narrative.[113] Philocles, as we have seen, defends the way of skepticism to Palemon, but, in interacting and conversing with him, Philocles also recognizes the limits of skepticism as a philosophical position. "Both were join'd together," Philocles relates, referring to "*Religion*" on one hand and "*Gallantry*" on the other, "in the Charge you made against me, when you saw I adher'd to nothing: but was now as ready to declaim against *the Fair*, as I had been before to plead their Cause, and defend the Moral of Lovers. This, you said, was my constant way in all Debates: I was as well pleas'd with the Reason on one side, as on the other: I never troubled my-self about the Success of the Argument, but laugh'd still, whatever way it went; and even when I convinc'd others, never seem'd as if I was convinc'd myself. I own'd to you, PALEMON, there was Truth enough in your Charge" (2:117). Philocles concedes that, taken to an extreme, skepticism approaches nihilism, an indiscriminate raillery detached from any kind of principle, "adhering to nothing." He goes on to call this "the worst sort of *Scepticism*, such as spar'd nothing; but overthrew all Principles, *Moral* and *Divine*" (2:118). Seeking "to compensate my *Sceptical* Misbehaviour," as he puts it, Philocles assures Palemon, "YOU shall find then . . . that it is possible for me to be serious; and that 'tis probable I am growing so, for good and all. Your Over-seriousness a-while since, at such an unseasonable time, may have driven me perhaps into a contrary Extreme, by opposition to your melancholy Humour" (2:119). The evidence for this "growth" is the long passage of "*Philosophical Enthusiasm*" that follows (2:119).

Philocles proceeds according to the very same inductive logic that he had earlier called into question, instructing Palemon to "rise to what is more general" and moving from "the Lineaments of a fair Face" to "a beautiful Society" and from "the Beauty of a Part" to "the Interest and Prosperity of *the Whole*" (2:120). The "aspiring Soul" will not content itself with a smaller circle but will instead seek something greater, "extending further its communicative Bounty" (2:120), and ultimately reorienting its vision from the design to the designer, "since without such a supreme Intelligence and providential Care, the distracted Universe must be condemn'd to suffer infinite Calamitys; 'tis here the generous Mind labours to discover that *healing Cause* by which the Interest of *the Whole* is securely establish'd, the Beauty of Things, and the universal Order happily sustain'd" (2:121). Hearing these cosmic effusions, Palemon is stupefied, asking, as Philocles relates, "what had befall'n me, that of a sudden I had thus chang'd my Character, and enter'd into Thoughts, which must certainly . . . have some Foundation in me, since I cou'd express them with such seeming Affection as I had done" (2:123). A skeptical reader might object that Philocles is simply doing what Horace instructed all poets to do, producing "Affection" within himself to produce affection in his audience, and thereby putting on a very convincing Theocles. But Philocles appears to "own" this affection as genuine and not merely generated for the sake of the occasion. He might not be "cur'd" of his skepticism, but he has glimpsed the *"healing Cause"* at the heart of things. He has not lost his "Inclination to SCEPTICISM" (2:117), but his view of the world has changed; his vision has widened. The rapture in the woods has ended, but it has stayed with him.

Shaftesbury idealizes a social milieu in which the extremes of human nature are not fully "cur'd"—an improbable outcome—but temporarily "healed," and the remedy he proposes is sympathy. We should recall in this context Shaftesbury's ideal magistrate, who, "with a kind Sympathy entering into the Concern of the People, and taking, as it were, their Passion upon him, shou'd, when he has sooth'd and satisfy'd it, endeavour, by cheerful ways, to divert and heal it." In hymning a sympathetic whole, Philocles produces a sympathetic echo of Theocles's rhapsody and reveals the lasting "healing" power of their sympathetic exchange. Philocles assumes the role of sympathetic tutor to Palemon that Theocles had served for him, and so a sympathetic chain has been established that Palemon in turn can "happily sustain." The dialogue achieves a more lasting kind of resolution by holding to a principle of sympathetic "compensa-tion," whereby each character sympathetically adjusts and accommodates his own views and inclinations to those of the other. Philocles appeals to this model of sympathetic accommodation, figured in musical terms, when he urges Theocles to "pray lower this Strain a little." This is sympathy not as contagious communication but rather as conscious "tuning," an active form of Shaftesburian politeness. The meeting of sympathy requires that the skeptic raise his strain to harmonize with the enthusiast, and that the enthusiast lower his strain to harmo-nize with the skeptic. This active process of sympathy as harmonization would receive its fullest and strongest formulation in Smith's *Theory of Moral Sentiments*, in which the "person principally concerned" is said to be able to "obtain" a "concord" of emotion "only . . . by lowering his passion to that pitch, in which the spectators are capable of going along with him."[114] Shaftesbury ultimately suggests that just as Philocles needs Theocles to keep him from falling into extreme skepticism, so Theocles needs Philocles to keep him from flying too high in "downright *Enthusiasm*" (2:123). In the midst of his rapture, Theocles interrupts himself: "O PHILOCLES, said he, 'tis well remember'd. I was growing too warm, I find; as well I might indeed, in this *hot* Element. . . . [I]n these high Flights, I might possibly have gone near to burn my Wings," to which Philocles responds, "Indeed . . . you might well expect the Fate of ICARUS, for your high-soaring. But this, indeed, was not what I fear'd. For you were got above Danger; and, with that devouring Element on your side, had master'd not only the *Sun* himself, but every thing which stood in your way. I was afraid it might, in the issue, run to what they tell us of a *universal Conflagration*; in which I knew not how it might go, possibly, with our GENIUS" (2:213). This is a deft bit of raillery; in reassuring Theocles that he will not suffer "the Fate of ICARUS," Philocles raises the possibility that a far worse fate, indeed a universal one, might be in the offing. Raillery functions in the dialogue as a kind of coolant, keeping the temperature from running too high. Without enthusiasm, the skeptic freezes, and without skepticism, the enthusiast burns. Sympathy produces and guarantees a dynamic equilibrium.

For Shaftesbury balance is a moral as well as aesthetic ideal. During his rhapsodic speech to Palemon, Philocles asserts, "'Tis . . . from this Order of inferior and superior Things, that we admire the World's Beauty, founded thus *on Contrarietys*: whilst from such various and disagreeing Principles, *a universal Concord* is establish'd. Thus in the several Orders of terrestrial Forms, *a Resignation* is requir'd, a Sacrifice and mutual yielding of Natures one to another" (2:121). In *The Moralists* as a whole Shaftesbury mirrors this "Sacrifice and mutual yielding of Natures one to another" on the level of character; the "Natures" of the skeptic and the enthusiast must "mutually yield one to another," and this sociable act of sympathy is carried forward and perpetuated in the communication between Philocles and Palemon. In embedding the dialogue within the form of a letter, which preserves it in narrative form, Shaftesbury suggests that although the light of enthusiasm dims, there will be continual access to it insofar as the narrative is shared and "recited" among sympathetic friends. Sympathy and sociability ensure that enthusiasm is an endlessly renewable resource. The climactic sympathetic connection between Theocles and Philocles is sustained not in the singular experience of rapture, which passes and fades, but rather in the sociable practice of cultivating and relating experiences of rapture. In *Advice to an Author* Shaftesbury argues that if a modern author were to write a dialogue "after the manner of our antient Authors," inevitably "a thousand Ridicules" would "aris[e] from the Manner, the Circumstances and Action it-self, compar'd with modern Breeding and Civility" (1:126). "THUS," he goes on to conclude, "*Dialogue* is at an end" (1:127). The epistolary frame of *The Moralists*, which allows for flexibility in the retelling, functions to mitigate this problem of imitation, decorum, and probability. If Shaftesbury regarded hybridization as a formal necessity, he made a philosophical virtue of it. The epistolary frame does not reflect the fact that "*Dialogue* is at an end"; rather, it suggests the possibility of dialogue *without end*, a potentially endless series of sympathetic acts, "compensations," "Sacrifices," and "mutual yieldings."

The Moralists keenly registers and reflects a contemporary crisis of genre. The inheritance of generic norms and conventions from antiquity raised the problem of accommodation to modern tastes; what was once acceptable and credible might well no longer be. Dialogue raised this problem, as did epic, which Shaftesbury also considered in *Advice to an Author*. In the second of two references to Milton in *Characteristicks*, Shaftesbury writes, "I shou'd be unwilling to examine rigorously the Performance of our great Poet, who sung so piously the *Fall of Man*" (1:221). This backhanded tribute to Milton is part of a larger critique of biblical-historical epic as necessarily falling short of its model. *Paradise Lost*, in limiting itself to what Shaftesbury calls "Matters . . . with such a resemblance of *Mythology*," succeeds poetically, whereas an epic centered on the "Lives and Characters" of the patriarchs and matriarchs would fail. Moreover, the "*Theology*, or THEOGONY, of *the Heathens* cou'd admit of such different Turns and figurative Expressions, as suted the Fancy and Judgment of each Philosopher or Poet," but such "Variation" can no longer be "admitted" (1:221). For Shaftesbury, then, as for many others in the eighteenth century, epic was a kind of dead end. Theocles can be credibly reading Virgil, but Shaftesbury cannot credibly write a Virgilian, much less a Miltonic, epic in his day and age; he can merely "recite" epic accents and tonalities and recreate an epic ambiance. And then there was chivalric romance: "I know not what *Faith* our valiant Ancestors may have had in the Storys of their Giants, their Dragons, and ST. GEORGE's. But for our *Faith* indeed, as well as our *Taste*, in this other way of reading; I must confess I can't consider it, without Astonishment" (1:211–212). The "Giants and Dragons" of romance were no more or less believable than Hobbes's leviathan. In *The Moralists* the traditional mode of pastoral seems merely quaint: "For in the manner I was now wrought up, 'twas as agreeable to me to hear him, in this kind of *Passion*, invoke his *Stars* and *Elements*, as to hear one of those amorous *Shepherds* complaining to his *Flock*, and making the Woods and Rocks resound the Name of *Her* whom he ador'd" (2:210). The singing, lovelorn shepherd is updated by the rhapsodizing, enthusiastic aesthete. Shaftesbury's response to the modern problem of genre was formal innovation, what Prince punningly refers to as "combining older forms into novel assemblages," in the process of which Shaftesbury came up with "a theoretical rationale for the practice of many early novelists," whereby "a digressive encounter with error, opinion, experience, phenomenal diversity" is set "within a progressive narrative leading to moral edification."[115] Shaftesbury's mixing of forms enabled him to provide his readers with a pleasing variety in accordance with modern tastes and reading habits, but also to achieve more complex and naturalistic moral effects.

The idea of sympathy holds out the promise of resolving not only the philosophical division that Shaftesbury stages in *The Moralists*, I want to suggest, but also the problem of the work's form. If the formal tension in *The Moralists* can in some sense be summed up by Philocles's phrase "VIRGIL or HORACE" (2:126), Shaftesbury ultimately alters that "or" to an "and" by appealing to a third term—Heraclitus. Shaftesbury's footnote to Philocles's account of the "mutual yielding of Natures one to another," with its insistence on "the World's Beauty, founded thus *on Contrarietys*" and on *"a universal Concord"* produced "from such various and disagreeing Principles," directs the reader to a footnote in *Miscellany* V, in which Shaftesbury justifies including a long passage from the "antient Peripatetick" work *On the Cosmos* on the basis of its "Sutableness . . . to what has been often advanc'd in the philosophical Parts of these Volumes, concerning the universal *Symmetry*, or Union of *the Whole*": "And perhaps Nature wants opposites too, and wants to make harmony out of them, not out of similars. . . . Art too seems to do this in imitation of nature. For painting, by combining the natures of black and white, yellow and red, makes its representations correspond with their types. Music, uniting sharp and grave notes, and long and short syllables, makes one harmony among different sounds. . . . This is the very point which was given forth by Heraclitus the Obscure, who said, 'combine wholes and parts, that which is dispersed and that which is united, that which makes discord and that which is in unison, and out of all comes one and out of one comes all'" (3:162n–163n). In its intimate association between nature and art one readily appreciates why Shaftesbury put such weight and emphasis on this pseudo-Aristotelian account. The elevation of what might be called a Heraclitean aesthetics, the idea of a harmony of discords, provides Shaftesbury with a way of claiming a deeper unity for *The Moralists* than that suggested by his ex post facto assimilation of the work to the ideal *mythos* of Aristotle's *Poetics*. If Philocles's strong and enduring skeptical maneuverings call into question the unified conversion narrative of which Theocles is the clear "Hero" (3:175n), they can also be seen to provide the *"Contrarietys"* and *"Dissonancys"* that are the essential precondition of a Heraclitean "harmony." "Fair" or "proper" dialogue, as Shaftesbury understood it, was not either "dispersed," as suggested by the term "rhapsody," or "united," as in Aristotelian drama or epic, but ultimately both; it was the formal embodiment of Heraclitus's dynamic combinatory model. For Shaftesbury, this model was central to the "dialogic" practice of classical culture; to recall the passage with which our discussion of *The Moralists* began: "And whilst some Sects, such as the *Pythagorean* and latter *Platonick*, join'd in with the Superstition and Enthusiasm of the Times; the *Epicurean*, the *Academick*, and others, were allow'd to use all the Force of Wit and Raillery against it. And thus matters were happily balanc'd; Reason had fair Play; Learning and Science flourish'd. Wonderful was the Harmony and Temper which arose from all these Contrarietys" (1:12). The form of *The Moralists* is "wonderful" in that it achieves "Harmony and Temper" not by excluding "Contrarietys" but by giving them "fair Play" and working through them.

Shaftesbury reinforced this formal idea by paragoning dialogue with painting. At the beginning of *The Moralists*, Philocles redescribes dialogue as "moral Painting, by way of *Dialogue*" (2:107). As in a painting, so in a dialogue formal tensions and oppositions are necessary to create a balanced and pleasing whole. As Shaftesbury puts it in *Sensus Communis*, "Proper Foils, and Contrarietys" ultimately "serve as Graces" in the "Limning" (1:86). "Mixing," to recall Shaftesbury's gloss on rhapsody as a form, does not destroy unity; rather, it raises it to a higher level. Here we should recall, too, Philocles's "confession" to having "been one of those Vulgar, who cou'd never relish *the Shades, the Rustick,* or *the Dissonancys* you talk of," and whose "way" was "to censure freely on the first view," but who now believes himself "oblig'd to go far in the pursuit of *Beauty*; which lies very absconded and deep" (2:224–225). The Heraclitean fragment preserved by Hippolytus in his *Refutation of All Heresies* is very much to the point here: "An unapparent connexion is stronger than an apparent one."[116] Shaftesbury effectively embraced this "obscure" principle as a matter of taste. To appreciate the "stronger" because "unapparent" unity of *The Moralists* requires a discriminating eye. And the same might be said of *Characteristicks* as a whole. Including *A Notion of the Historical Draught, or Tablature of the Judgment of Hercules. With a Letter concerning Design,* which constitutes two parts, the first appearing in the 1714 edition, the second in the full run of the 1732 edition, *Characteristicks* consists of a "letter"; an "essay"; a work of opinion, recommendation, or "advice"; an "inquiry"; a "philosophical rhapsody"; "miscellaneous reflections"; and a "notion," subsequently redescribed as "the forming of a *Project*" (3:243), to which is added another "letter." A work whose aim is in no small part to refute the Epicurean worldview ends up, in its seemingly fortuitous mixture of forms, ironically embodying it. A more imperfect decorum could hardly be imagined. But the Epicurean form of *Characteristicks* is only apparent; its rhapsodic heterogeneity "on the first view" might be reason for free and facile "censure," but its "deep" beauty is ultimately to be grasped in its complex "Dissonancys." An apparent antipathy is folded into a "stronger" sympathy.

There is some evidence, however, that Shaftesbury himself did not have full faith in the unity of his work, however conceived, that he recognized a gap between "aspiration" and achievement. This is precisely the kind of gap that complicates his account of sympathy throughout *Characteristicks*. Shaftesbury's various, multiform, and "dissonant" representations of sympathy ultimately reflect a widening uncertainty about the ontological unity and harmony of the whole. To whatever extent Philocles takes Theocles's part, his own cannot be fully evaded or denied; the sympathetic universe now casts a darker skeptical shadow. The philosophical resolution of *The Moralists* suggests, moreover, that the idea of universal sympathy now depends on a social sympathy to sustain it. It requires "recitation." The universal is subordinated to the social, which is granted a more immediate reality—hence the collocation "universal Friendship." It is in this sense that we can grasp Shaftesbury's significance as a transitional figure in the history of sympathy. He remained committed to an older view of the world but adapted it according to a new emphasis on society. He perpetuated the totalizing scheme of the Cambridge Platonists but reversed the coordinates. He insisted on the magic of sympathy but identified it primarily in moral terms. Shaftesbury's new aesthetic commitment worked against an older ontological claim for universal sympathy, but it also moved the sympathetic worldview in the direction of a cultural domain in which it was relatively insulated from the challenges of philosophical skepticism—literature. What Theocles's rhapsodies on the sympathy of the whole lacked in philosophical rigor they could make up for in poetic power. In this sense the poetic functioned as a means of compensation. If Shaftesbury could not fully persuade his readers that he was representing the world as it was, he could move them to see the world as they wanted it to be.

Shaftesbury's endeavor to "mix" philosophy and poetry, to be "*a* POET *in due form*" (3:175), to defend a sympathetic worldview in "number'd Prose," contributed significantly to the success of *Characteristicks*. By the end of the eighteenth century, thirteen editions had appeared in English.[117] Pierre Coste, Pierre Des Maizeaux, and Denis Diderot translated parts of *Characteristicks* into French, and German translations have been dated to 1738.[118] Among others, Leibniz, Goethe, Johann Gottfried von Herder, Gotthold Lessing, and Moses Mendelssohn all fell under Shaftesbury's spell, prompting Cassirer's claim that "the Platonism of Shaftesbury" nurtured and promoted the development of "the philosophy and aesthetics of German idealism."[119] In tracing the translation of Shaftesburianism from west to east, Cassirer omitted Shaftesbury's more immediate, and more ambivalent, reception in England, Scotland, and Ireland, a void that Isabel Rivers has admirably filled. Shaftesbury's "legacy," she has suggested, "was not so much a book as a language."[120] But Shaftesbury's legacy was also importantly a worldview, ancient as well as modern, magical as well as beautiful, centered on the moral, social principle of sympathy. That legacy is the subject of my final two chapters.

6

THE FUTURE OF SYMPATHY I:
THE POETRY OF THE WORLD

With Shaftesbury our study of sympathy has moved into the eighteenth century and into what could uncontroversially be called the "age of sympathy." Indeed, as one scholar has written, "Whether celebrated or charted by its political, economic, and social failings, since at least the 1940s it has been taken for granted in eighteenth-century studies that 'sympathy,' the ability to be affected by or to enter into the feelings of others, is the concept *par excellence* of the eighteenth century."[1] The argument that follows this claim does not challenge or attempt to unseat the assumption so much as reinterpret it. So defined by eighteenth centurists, sympathy has been approached from a number of angles and from a number of methodological perspectives—formalist, historicist, philosophical, psychological, sociological, economic and commercial, neurophysiological and medical, in terms of gender, in terms of genre, and the list could go on. But, in spite of this wealth of illuminating analysis, the treatment of sympathy in eighteenth-century studies continues to be limited by a limited concept of sympathy as a concept, the "taking for granted" that in the eighteenth century sympathy meant only one thing—"the ability to be affected by or to enter into the feelings of others." In focusing on the mind and body, on the subject and society, on the moral world, studies of sympathy in the eighteenth century have tended to overlook the natural world. The complex relationship that I have demonstrated in seventeenth-century literary and philosophical writing between natural and natural-magical conceptions of sympathy on one hand and moral, social, and psychological conceptions on the other persisted well into the eighteenth century; the balance undoubtedly shifted toward the latter, but the two remained in active conversation. Not least because of ongoing concern about the Epicurean threat, the idea of sympathy as an ordering principle of the whole, of the world beyond the world of society, remained a vital subject in eighteenth-century literary and philosophical writing.

In examining a select group of poems, dialogues, and treatises from the first half of the eighteenth century in this chapter and the next, I want to draw out some of the conclusions of the preceding chapters and suggest how we might connect two significant and recurrent topics in eighteenth-century studies that have generally been treated as independent and unrelated, the "rise" of sympathy on one hand and the end or "eclipse of analogy," in Blanford Parker's phrase, on the other.[2] We have considered R. S. Crane's seminal contribution to critical discussion of the former, and an important essay by Earl Wasserman, published in 1953, set the stakes for critical discussion of the latter. "The Elizabethan mind did not simply think analogically, it grasped truth in an intricate network of analogical relationships," Wasserman writes. "But by the end of the eighteenth century the loss of faith in the divine analogy prevented the high imagination from freely flying as she was wont of old." In the phrase the "Elizabethan mind" we can hear an allusion to Tillyard's "Elizabethan world picture," and Wasserman casually implies a continuity between the Tudor and Stuart mental worlds, taking as the historical starting points of his analysis the Platonism of Shaftesbury and the physico-theology of Thomas Burnet, both of which were structured analogically. Between the late seventeenth century and the end of the eighteenth Wasserman describes a period of epistemic "confusion," as analogy continued to be "the relational norm of image and value" but was cast into doubt: "Analogy was found to have an ontological foundation—or only an epistemological one. The epistemological analogy applies to the physical and divine orders—or only to human abstractions and divine attributes. And analogies are valid—or valid only because of man's necessary ignorance—or untrustworthy—or entirely false."[3] If we generally accept Wasserman's account—and subsequent studies by Parker, Michael Prince, and others of the fate of analogy, design, and other totalizing principles in the eighteenth century have broadly confirmed it—we can proceed to the schematic observation that during the same period in which an analogic understanding of the world was in decline, a sympathetic understanding of the individual and society was in the ascendant. I do not wish to claim that the former was simply the proximate cause of the latter, but I would like to argue, less reductively, that the two were significantly correlated—a correlation that is most clearly evident in Hume's *Treatise*, which I consider in the next chapter. It was Milton who enabled us to see how human sympathy could function as a means of compensation for the loss of a broader cosmic coherence. This

Miltonic insight, I suggest, can provide us with a model for understanding the ongoing relationship in the eighteenth century between natural and moral representations of sympathy. The increasing emphasis on sympathy as a fundamental virtue and as a natural source of social cohesion functioned in part to secure an idea of order that was increasingly uncertain and unstable on the level of the whole.

The workings of sympathy in society were so abundantly evident, as Shaftesbury and others after him repeatedly insisted, that if a belief in cosmic sympathy seemed more and more to require a leap of faith, such a leap was both less difficult and, given the sense of "fullness" now promised by the moral world, less necessary. The Cambridge Platonists, as we have seen, suffered no apparent "loss of faith"; human sympathy was simply a logical extension of universal sympathy, a system within a system. Shaftesbury aimed to keep that faith, but in a later, one might say Lockean, age, his recognition of the claims of empiricism and skepticism worked against it. He reinforced an uncertain claim for the ontological validity of a sympathetic worldview by making a less discreditable claim for its aesthetic beauty. And he made the wider ontological claim more probable by defining human nature in terms of a sympathetic affection of which there was ample empirical evidence in society. Calling attention precisely to such expressions of what she calls "sentimental self-evidence," Nancy Yousef has made a case for "a dynamic (if not quite dialectical) entwining of sympathy with skepticism" in eighteenth-century moral philosophy, according to which sentimentalist claims for the immediacy and transparency of sympathy functioned to bind an epistemological anxiety about the accessibility of other minds. But the extent of the emphasis and pressure placed on "sentimental self-evidence"—by Shaftesbury, Hutcheson, Hume, and others—needs to be understood in terms of a broader epistemological challenge, extending from other minds to what Shaftesbury called "Universal Mind." The idea of a natural, automatic, instantaneous sympathy recognizable in its effects, whether physiognomic or physiological, provided a reassuring sense of presence and coherence in the wake of a growing sense of doubt about the existence and intelligibility of an overarching order. Here the long-standing association between sympathy and magic suggested a way around an epistemological challenge. The problem of separate minds could be overcome by recourse to the mystical idea of interaction at a distance. Answerable to empirical demands, human sympathy represented an acceptable, believable kind of magic in a skeptical age.

In this chapter I advance my case for the enduring vitality of natural and magical conceptions of sympathy in the eighteenth century by examining the reception of Shaftesbury's worldview, and secondarily Milton's, in the work of two authors in particular, the moral philosopher David Fordyce (1711–1751) and the poet James Thomson (1700–1748). The Edenic paradise of Milton, which we explored in the third chapter, and the Arcadian paradise of Shaftesbury, which we explored in the previous chapter, both served as iconic and imaginatively potent means of preserving and perpetuating a sympathetic view of the world. Both Milton and Shaftesbury, widely read in the eighteenth century, understood and represented human sympathy as bearing an essential, if complex, relation to the order and coherence of the cosmos. Dustin Griffin has proposed that "the most pervasive and creative influence of *Paradise Lost* upon eighteenth-century poetry was not its Christianization of epic, or its diction and prosody, but its elaboration of a myth of the lost garden, somehow to be recovered." Griffin goes on to refer in passing to what he calls "philosophical optimists," citing Leibniz, Spinoza, and Bolingbroke as examples, who called into question the fact of loss.[4] Shaftesbury, whom Leibniz praised and admired, is a significant, even glaring, omission from this list. The paradise represented in *The Moralists* has not been "recovered"; as Shaftesbury's blending of ancient and modern, of the classical-mythological and the "fashionable," serves to suggest, it is as it always has been. For both Fordyce and Thomson, the idea of sympathy, closely associated with Shaftesburian enthusiasm and deeply infused with Shaftesburian mystery, was not limited to human nature but rather extended to nature as a whole; the sociable subject mirrored a sociable world.

Fordyce's and Thomson's Shaftesburianism depended in part on the dissemination of Shaftesbury's thought from England to Ireland and Scotland, of which the Irish politician Robert Molesworth (1656–1725) was an important driver. Born in Dublin, he made Shaftesbury's acquaintance in the late 1690s, when both were broadly allied with the "Country Whigs" in Parliament. They subsequently became friends and correspondents.[5] When Molesworth lost his seat in Parliament in 1722, nearly a decade after Shaftesbury's death, he retired and formed an intellectual circle in Dublin devoted in part to Shaftesbury's thought. Molesworth reached out to Scottish universities, and, as Rivers argues, "The most important of the means by which Shaftesburian thought was diffused from the 1720s onwards was moral philosophy teaching at Scottish universities." Moreover, "because of the different kinds of publication in which this teaching was incorporated—published lecture courses, books based on lectures given years earlier, educational manifestos, student handbooks, classics textbooks—its influence was felt far beyond the confines of these universities and in England as well as in Scotland."[6] Fordyce taught moral philosophy at Marischal College, Aberdeen, and Thomson likely received his introduction to Shaftesbury when he was a student at the University of Edinburgh. Fordyce and Thomson both generally adopted Shaftesbury's aestheticized version of an anti-Epicurean worldview, and, in the case of Thomson, Shaftesbury's poeticization of nature was logically extended into the form of poetry itself. Shaftesburianism lent itself increasingly, to adapt Foucault's phrase, to a poetry of the world. In composing *The Seasons* (1730), a long poem in blank verse, Thomson looked back to Milton's Eden, translating the idea of universal sympathy from the lost prelapsarian past to an idealizing seasonal present. But in developing what Johnson called a poem "of a new kind," Thomson ultimately carried forward not Milton's vision of a diachronic break between physical and ethical orders but Shaftesbury's vision of an essential and transcendental bond between the two.

The project of advancing a sympathetic worldview in the eighteenth century meant not only reciting and updating those of the past but also confronting and containing the challenge of skepticism. In *The Moralists* Shaftesbury endeavored to meet that challenge in part by developing a mixed form in which the skeptic was shown to accommodate himself to a universal idea of sympathy as an antidote to the nihilistic tendency of his own skepticism. Shaftesbury worked around the charge that universal sympathy was not philosophically demonstrable in part by suggesting that it was heuristically valuable, even necessary. If Shaftesbury's adaptation of philosophical dialogue functioned to counter skepticism by "shifting concern from metaphysics to education,"[7] Fordyce's took that strategy to its logical extreme, producing a series of dialogues *about* education. In his *Dialogues Concerning Education* (1745–1748), Fordyce effectively made Shaftesbury's secondary "concern" his primary subject. "Dialogue IX," the closest in form and content to *The Moralists*, concludes not with the principal characters returning to the disenchanted world of society but rather with them remaining in the enchanted ambience of an ideal academy. Through dialogic discussion Fordyce mounts a philosophical defense of a sympathetic worldview, but his emphasis is not on its demonstrability so much as on its suitability for improving and expanding young minds. Fordyce ultimately suggests, then, that a sympathetic worldview is not a unique and privileged perception but one that can be broadly secured as a matter of instruction, habituation, and cultivation. In this sense he uses Lockean principles as a mode of philosophical reinforcement, redescribing a potential weakness as a potential strength. Yet in looking ahead to the future, and in focusing on the potential rather than the real, Fordyce ends up encouraging the sense that a sympathetic worldview may be no more than a utopian fiction. He manages that doubt in part by capitalizing on the resources of the form he inherited from Shaftesbury; the achieved sympathy of the participants in the dialogue serves to establish a sense of active presence in the social sphere that cannot be experienced in the same way and to the same extent in the world beyond it.

From Fordyce's recital and revision of Shaftesburian dialogue in the first section of the chapter I proceed to Thomson and the subject of Shaftesburian poetry. The translation of a sympathetic worldview from philosophical argumentation to literary expression functioned broadly to shelter that worldview from the shearing force of skepticism. Insofar as the survival of a sympathetic worldview seemed increasingly to depend on heightened experience and heightened expression, the Shaftesburian poet could create and control such a climate free from the constraints of metaphysical rigor.[8] *The Seasons* is an intensely thermostatic poem. My reading is centered on Thomson's representation of sympathy as a general, mystical force, received from the natural world and then communicated from the individual to what he calls "Social Friends." If the poetic was less vulnerable to the challenge of skepticism, however, it was increasingly subject to a new challenge—empiricism. The Thomsonian process of "moral magic," I argue, works to counteract the entropic tendency of the poem's empirical commitment to the particular. Thomson's various assertions that the natural world is a unified, sympathetic whole come into conflict with the effects of his descriptive practice, which yields a vision of nature as an overwhelming accumulation of items and images taken in by a frantic visual apparatus working endless, and potentially fruitless, overtime. *The Seasons* exposes the threat empiricism poses to a sympathetic worldview, which, in its Stoic and Platonic roots, is essentially antiparticularist.[9] In this sense the empiricist challenge is analogous to the Epicurean, grounded in a particulate theory of matter. From the uncertainty of the eye Thomson effectively seeks refuge in the steadily pulsing warmth of the heart. Shaftesbury provided Thomson with a sentimentalist bulwark against encroaching metaphysical and epistemological concerns. In the Shaftesburian mode, Thomson establishes an idea of order by enlisting the natural in the service of the moral, so that the natural world, which in its minutiae threatens to isolate and alienate the subject, emerges at the same time as a site and source of moral and social cohesion. The section concludes with a brief treatment of the Shaftesburian poem *Concord*, which turns on an analogous arrangement of the natural and the moral.

In the final section of the chapter, I show how Fordyce and Thomson wedded Newtonianism to Shaftesburianism in part to reinforce the universalist aspiration of Shaftesburian ethics. The appeal to Newtonian physics to support a claim for ethical coherence was a frequent and significant authorizing move in the first half of the eighteenth century. Newtonianism provided an authoritative response to a skeptical challenge to a sympathetic worldview. It not only suggested that sympathy was a universal force in the moral world analogous to gravity in the natural world but also functioned to strengthen a Shaftesburian claim that sympathy was the overarching principle of both. And yet in spite of the reinforcement that Newtonianism provided, or promised to provide, to moral philosophy, there remained a strong sense that the kind of sympathetic worldview that Shaftesbury inherited and adapted from the Cambridge Platonists was increasingly out of place in philosophical discourse, and at home in the affectively and imaginatively freer form of poetry.

FORDYCE'S "SECRET AND AMAZING SYMPATHY" AND SHAFTESBURIAN DIALOGUE

"Hath *Sophron* forgot those chaste, simple, and withal sublime Dialogues, of that illustrious Nobleman Lord *Shaftesbury*, which revive with such Lustre the old *Platonic Mimes*, and present us with many Things, elegant in Conversation, profound in Philosophy, and amiable in Life? Did he never catch the Spirit of Enthusiasm they breathe, and turn a downright Love of that Nature which is so sweetly painted there? I know his Heart is too tender to have resisted such Enchantment."[10] As if the form of the work in which they are contained did not do so already, these lines make it abundantly clear that their author, David Fordyce, most certainly did not "forget" Shaftesbury's "chaste, simple, and withal sublime Dialogues." Fordyce's *Dialogues Concerning Education*, the first volume published in 1745, the second in 1748, consists of twenty dialogues that promote not only Shaftesbury's commitment to a sympathetic form but also his version of a sympathetic worldview.[11] In their unmistakable sympathy with *The Moralists*, Fordyce's dialogues attest to Shaftesbury's success in practicing the "moral magic" that he described; having "caught" it as if by contagion, Fordyce attempts to "breathe" the same "Spirit of Enthusiasm" into his readers as Shaftesbury. That the *Dialogues* went through five editions by 1768 suggests that Fordyce, too, succeeded in this aim. Born near Aberdeen, he attended Marischal College, where he trained for a career in the ministry. But his career took a different path; nine years after receiving his B.D., he was appointed in 1742 to a position as professor of moral philosophy at Marischal, where he exerted a significant influence; his *Elements of Moral Philosophy* (1754), the fruit of his teaching there, also appeared in multiple editions in the second half of the century. A turning point in Fordyce's intellectual life came during a trip to England in 1737–1738, when he visited the academy of Philip Doddridge (1702–1751). Doddridge, the scion of a nonconformist minister, attended a dissenting academy and then proceeded to establish his own in

Northampton in 1730. Doddridge's academy, with its aversion to dogmatism and commitment to intellectual freedom, provided Fordyce with a model for a new educational ideal, which he elaborated in Shaftesburian terms in the *Dialogues*. By means of its sympathetic recital of a sociable form, the work as a whole promotes the Shaftesburian virtue of social sympathy as well as the Shaftesburian vision of sympathy as a thoroughgoing principle of the natural and moral worlds. It endeavors to enhance Shaftesbury's claim for the diffusiveness of sympathy in society as well as Shaftesbury's attempt to counter skepticism about the presence of sympathy in the universe.

The setting for Fordyce's *Dialogues* is an idealized academy run by Euphranor, a Doddridgean figure who shows "not the Authority of the Master . . . so much, as the real Concern and Benevolence of the Friend" (1:14). The work is narrated by Simplicius, who begins by describing an early morning "Stage-Coach" journey in the direction of the academy. The five people in the coach—"an honest Country Gentleman" and his wife, a "grave elderly Gentleman" and his ward, a "young Lady in all the Bloom of Life," and Simplicius—function as a kind of epitome of society. Fordyce combines the pastoral model of retreat—"We were observing the agreeable Verdure of the Fields and delightful Freshness of the Air at a distance from the Smoke of the Town"—and something like a Shaftesburian psychology experiment, which serves both to test and to confirm the naturalness of human sympathy. As the passengers move out into the country, and the sun begins to brighten, Simplicius narrates, "Our Recovery out of Darkness gave us a visible Increase of Spirits, and the chearful Aspect of human Faces, from which we had been, for a while, secluded, made us more sociable and better affected to one another" (1:3, 2). Just as night yields to day, so unfamiliarity yields to sociability; the latter process is made to seem just as natural and automatic as the former. Simplicius goes on to observe that "the young Lady's Sentiments had a peculiar Beauty in them" and that she "had had a refined Education under the Eye and Care of her Guardian" (1:5). This observation reinforces not only Shaftesbury's alignment of ethics and aesthetics but also his predication of both on "refined Education." In a note to *Advice to an Author* Shaftesbury deplored the modern state of education: "It seems indeed somewhat improbable, that according to modern Erudition, and as Science is now distributed, our ingenious and noble Youths shou'd obtain the full advantage of a just and liberal Education, by uniting the *Scholar*-part with that of the real *Gentleman* and *Man of Breeding*. Academys for Exercises, so useful to the Publick, and essential in the Formation of a genteel and liberal Character, are unfortunately neglected. Letters are indeed banish'd, I know not where, in distant Cloisters. . . . The sprightly Arts and Sciences are sever'd from *Philosophy*, which consequently must grow dronish, insipid, pedantick, useless, and directly opposite to the real Knowledg and Practice of the World and Mankind" (*Character.*, 1:205n). Shaftesbury's insistent critique of contemporary philosophy could be partly boiled down to a critique of contemporary education. Taking a cue from Doddridge's academy, Fordyce imagined and described precisely the kind of education that would "unite" the "*Scholar*-part with that of the real *Gentleman*"; Euphranor's academy functions to reunite the "sprightly Arts and Sciences" with "*Philosophy.*" Like Theocles's estate in *The Moralists*, the academy, likened to the "Muses Seat," is topographically suited to wide, sympathetic views. It is situated "on a rising Ground, whence we have a fine Prospect of the Windings of the River, the contiguous Valley, the green Fields and surrounding Mountains" (1:9). And like Theocles and his interlocutors, the students are not cloistered scholars but sociable philosophical adventurers. Fordyce's account of Simplicius's arrival captures the utopianism of the work as a whole: "When I first entered this Mansion of the Muses, I was very agreeably surprized with the Sight of so many young Gentlemen, some of them of Rank and Fortune, who were come hither from all Quarters to imbibe the Principles of Science and Virtue, in order to qualify them for the Service of their Friends and Country. They received me as a new Guest, with that Affection and Sincerity, which becomes the Votaries of the Muses" (1:10). The students' response fuses classical *xenia* and Shaftesburian "Affection and Sincerity." Fordyce's utopianism extends from number to class or "Rank"—the students "are trained . . . for being sober, honest, and beneficent Creatures, in any Rank or Station of Life, in which Providence may place them" (1:30)—and ultimately to gender, as Cleora's "*Plan of* Female Education" in "Dialogue XIV" suggests. In this sense Fordyce is not only "reciting" Shaftesburian dialogue but also widening its social purview.

Throughout Fordyce remains deeply committed to the underlying Shaftesburian "spirit." Sophron, Simplicius's initial connection to the academy, "has naturally a rich Vein of Fancy"—he is, in other words, a natural enthusiast—and "his Knowledge is not hoarded up by him as an useless Treasure, but he can, with an admirable Dexterity, apply the Experience of ancient and modern Times to the Use of Life and Entertainment of Company" (1:13). He is learned but not remote; his "Dexterity" allows him to synthesize "Knowledge" and "Experience" toward a pleasing, sociable end. Euphranor takes this synthetic dexterity to the highest level: "To a profound Skill in Philosophy and the Mathematics he joins an elegant Taste in the classic Writers" (1:15). Euphranor is not Doddridge so much as a kind of Shaftesburian bust of Doddridge. In a classicizing mode, Sophron characterizes the "Genius of our Society" as "the most free and philosophical that can be; and we are taught more in the way of Conversation than in a formal didactic manner" (1:19). The academy allows for maximal colloquy and soliloquy, in Shaftesbury's sense. The students "feel none of the Restraints or Biass of Systems," one of Shaftesbury's bugbears, and they aspire to be a perfect image of "the *old Academy*," of the ancient philosophers' "Suspense of Judgment, of their Freedom of Enquiry, that Patience of Debate and Contradiction, that Caution not to be deceived, and that noble Facility of confessing and retracting, when one has been in the wrong" (1:21). Fordyce imitates the Shaftesburian decorum whereby an idealization of a "dialogic" culture and society is accommodated to, and reinforced by, dialogic form. In focusing on and modeling education, however, Fordyce suggests how the classical dialogic ideal of society might be not only formally approximated but also actually *formed*. The students at the academy learn to challenge and to contradict but also to yield and to sympathize, all of which are essential to the formation of a balanced and harmonious society. For Fordyce an education in the classics is above all an education in sympathy; the instructor, as Sophron explains, "interests us in the most distant Scenes of Action: so that while a *Demosthenes* thunders, or a *Cicero* charms, or a *Livy* paints, we enter into the Characters of Men, and Interests of Nations, we take part with the Actors, sift their Counsels, share their Fortunes, and, in a manner, *live o'er* the busy Scene" (1:23). In Fordyce's theatrical diction the distance in time between classical author and modern reader is reduced to the distance in space between actor and spectator. Thus study does not obstruct or interfere with the "social and public Spirit" enshrined by the academy (1:32); it nourishes and sustains it.

Having described the Shaftesburian framing of Fordyce's *Dialogues*, I want now to focus my attention on "Dialogue IX," the most conspicuously Shaftesburian of the twenty dialogues as a whole in that it hews most closely to *The Moralists*. "Dialogue IX" is described in the contents as follows: "A *philosophical* Rhapsody *concerning the Being and Providence of* GOD. *Observations of the Club on it. The Use and Advantage of the Study of Nature in Education*" (1:iv). The extension of Shaftesbury's subtitle can be seen as analogous to the use of the adjectives "chaste, simple, and withal sublime" in Fordyce's characterization of the "Dialogues, of that illustrious Nobleman Lord *Shaftesbury*"; both register and serve to refute an abiding criticism of Shaftesbury, who, in giving skepticism and atheism ample airtime, and in analyzing morality apart from religion, left himself open to charges of impiety.[12] The "Club" refers to "the *Philosophical* Club" to which Simplicius has been generously admitted, and which consists of Eugenio, a kind of Shaftesburian aristocrat, who, "Heir to a considerable Estate," is "naturally gay and sprightly" and emphatically sympathetic—"he studies to mould himself so thoroughly into the Sentiments of his Company, and accommodates himself with such an easy Condescension to their Humour" (1:56)—Constant, who "is of an even, steady Temper, has an acute Understanding, and ready, tho' dry Elocution; is deeply versed in *mathematical*, and has, at the same time, a strong Turn for *moral* and *political* Knowledge" (1:58), and Hiero, a clear descendant of Shaftesbury's

Theocles, "a Youth of a serious and devout Turn . . . who will improve the slightest
Occasion to hint some religious Sentiment," who "minds but little the Distinctions
that prevail among Christians," and who "studies to imbibe the very Spirit of the
divinest Moralists, ancient and modern; so that you would think the Soul of a *Plato*,
or *Antoninus*, were transfused into him" (1:60). Fordyce casts Hiero not only in the
mold of Theocles but also in the tradition of the Cambridge Platonists. Indeed,
toward the end of the last of Fordyce's dialogues, Hiero admiringly refers to "the
manly and exalted Writings of *Cudworth*, *Smith*, and *Whichcot*," among other
"noble Worthies and Moralists," and suggests, "When we are touched by the Flame
of those heroic Spirits, and feel the noble Contagion of Sentiment and Passion
which they spread, our Minds will then naturally . . . burst forth in heaven-taught
Strains of Piety and Adoration" (2:461, 462). Hiero endeavors to communicate the
same "noble Contagion of Sentiment and Passion" that the Cambridge Platonists
have communicated to him.

　　Fordyce's aim to defend Shaftesbury's sympathetic worldview and at the same
time to minimize and mitigate the skeptical challenge to it is particularly evident
in "Dialogue IX." The first step Fordyce takes toward the latter end is, in effect,
to remove the voice of the skeptic from the dialogue; none of the four members
of the philosophical club has Philocles's "Inclination to SCEPTICISM" (*Character.*,
2:117). But Fordyce is sympathetic to Shaftesbury's opinion that silencing or cari-
caturing the voice of opposition violates the principle of fairness. Although none
of his four characters embraces skepticism as a defining position, Fordyce allows
each of them to experience and express doubt as a matter of course. Indeed, as
Sophron explains in "Dialogue I," "The grand Principle by which we profess to
be governed in our Enquiries, is to doubt till we are convinced" (1:21). Fordyce
thus contains skepticism by institutionalizing it on one hand and implying on
the other that it leads inexorably to "conviction"; skepticism is not a resistance
to belief but an initial stage in the process of coming to belief.

　　The structure of "Dialogue IX" similarly functions to counter doubt. Rather
than placing Hiero's rhapsody toward the end of the dialogue, as Shaftesbury had
done with Theocles's, Fordyce places it toward the beginning. Rather than retracing
Shaftesbury's narrative trajectory from reasoning to rhapsodizing, then, Fordyce
proceeds in the reverse order, thereby strengthening the claim for the rationality of
a sympathetic worldview and undercutting the potential objection that universal
sympathy is no more than a fleeting enthusiastic fiction. "Dialogue IX" begins with
Simplicius walking out into a Shaftesburian landscape, where, as he explains, the
"blooming and various Aspects of Nature" inspire "a *mystical* sort of Admiration"
and "Rapture" (1:235). The naturalness of an enthusiastic response to nature is thus
initially presented as a given. Simplicius goes on to find Hiero in the midst of

"philosophic Effusions" and immediately decides to transcribe the "Rhapsody," which begins, "'—IT must be so. Else why such Harmony in their Operations, and Constancy in their Effects? Can Beings concur in Efficacy, which never united in Design, without some common Band of Confederacy, or combining Cause? Can Chance be the Parent of *Uniformity* which never fails, or Fate give birth to infinite *Variety*? The several Parts of this material Frame, how distant soever in Situation, and different in their Matter and Composition, do yet operate continually on each other, and concur, by some mighty, though invisible Influence'" (1:237). Here Fordyce reproduces Shaftesbury's emphasis on design and sympathy, the "common Band of Confederacy, or combining Cause," the mystical interaction at a distance of things, which "yet operate continually on each other," as well as Shaftesbury's anti-Epicureanism; the negative keywords are "Chance" and "Fate." Nature is "'*one* conspiring *Whole*,'" and the various parts of the universe make up a "'common System'" (1:239). This is precisely the Cudworthian idiom that Shaftesbury himself had recited. Hiero follows Theocles's inductive, "aesthetic" logic, proceeding from part to whole, design to designer: "'Through what an ascending Scale of Being and Beauty, am I led, to recognize a governing Nature, or universal Mind'" (1:240). The passive construction makes induction seem less like a dubious philosophical leap than an automatic natural progression.

From the natural Hiero proceeds breathlessly to the moral, and here we can clearly see Fordyce perpetuating Shaftesbury's ideal, "systematic" model, setting the ideas of human sympathy and universal sympathy in the relation of part to whole. "'It was Thou, O Parent of Love,'" he apostrophizes, "'who taughtest the human Face to charm with such expressive Sweetness, and ordained'st the Passions to vibrate from Heart to Heart, with Harmony so responsive; by those endearing Bands linking him with the Partners of his Nature in friendly and enchanting Union'" (1:244–245). Fordyce subjoins an "enchanted" idea of human nature to an enchanted idea of nature as a whole. Making use of the figure of resonance, a crucial topos, as we have seen, in the natural-magical tradition, he echoes Shaftesbury's platonizing language to convey the idea of "*moral Magick*." That idea is an important and recurrent one in the *Dialogues*. In "Dialogue XI," which is devoted to the heuristic value of fable, the musical analogy returns. "Our Hearts, like musical Strings, feel every Vibration which is made on those of others; so that they beat to each other's Pleasures and Pains," Fordyce writes. "So powerful is this Instinct, that we love to indulge the social Sympathy, even where it gives us Pain." Our readiness to participate in others' suffering as well as the sense of approbation that accompanies our fellow-feeling yet again demonstrates the "power" of sympathy. "Nature," Fordyce writes in "Dialogue XV," "in order to maintain a friendly Harmony among individual Minds, has touched them with a secret and amazing Sympathy, between the Affections of one Man and those of another. In Consequence of this, and of that expressive Eloquence which is couched in the Human Countenance and Gesture, those Affections run with an instantaneous Glance from Eye to Eye, and the same Movements are conveyed from one Heart to another, by the slightest Touch upon either" (2:175). The ease and instantaneity of affective communication give it its aura of magic; for Fordyce, as for Shaftesbury, there is "a secret and amazing Sympathy" in human nature or, as he refers to it in a subsequent dialogue, a "secret, but quick and powerful Sympathy" (2:371). That "secret Sympathy" is not limited to "human nature"; rather, it extends to all of nature and defines the whole as a "common System."

Hiero's rhapsody on the sympathy of the whole, like Theocles's, is "recited." Simplicius reads his transcript to Sophron, Eugenio, Constant, and Hiero, but rather than an immediate sympathetic communication of enthusiasm, Fordyce proceeds to a moment of doubt. "I MUCH doubt, Gentlemen," Hiero says, "that the Rhapsodist is not a little obliged to the Reciter, for the Distinctness and Coherence of the Rhapsody. I am afraid the Heat of an extempore Transport would scarce have produced a piece of Reasoning, which seems to hang together" (1:247). Voiced by the work's ultimate believer, a mitigating tactic in and of itself, Hiero's doubt is quickly answered, as Sophron expresses his confidence that "a beautiful and well-connected Rhapsody" is eminently achievable "during that sudden Glow of Fancy" (1:247). This expression of confidence in the idea of "a beautiful and well-connected Rhapsody" is translated into an expression of confidence in the idea of a beautiful and well-connected world—a point to which we shall return. As the discussion of Hiero's rhapsody plays out, Fordyce creates the effect of collating *The Moralists* with *A Letter Concerning Enthusiasm*. The less enthusiastic Eugenio argues that an occasional fit of madness is harmless so long as we remain capable of returning to "our sober Senses," and, moreover, he suggests, "By giving vent to the frantic Humour in philosophic Ravings, or poetic Sallies, which have been often thought allied to Phrenzy, we shall, I imagine, sooner discuss the Fewel of the Distemper, and be in less danger of growing delirious in our ordinary Commerce, and at the expence of others" (1:250). Sophron is hesitant to endorse this quasi-homeopathic approach to madness and claims instead that if we are to give way to fancy or frenzy, "the Beauties of Nature" should be what moves us to it; they inspire "that noble Enthusiasm"—the phrase is unmistakably Shaftesburian—that hardly needs "checking" (1:251, 252). Eugenio, hesitating in turn, proceeds to deliver nothing less than an elegy for the disenchantment of the world:

> I frankly confess, that I can look at Nature in all her Bloom, and dressed out, if you will, in every Charm that can be supposed to allure the Eye, without

falling into those Extasies my worthy Friends talk of, or growing a distracted Lover of the beauteous Dame. Was Nature animated now, as she was in ancient Times, with Deities and Graces, were the Woods now inhabited by *Dryads* and *Hamadryads*, and had one a Chance to meet a sweet light-footed Nymph at every other Fountain or the End of a Walk, I do not question but I should grow a warm Admirer of Nature; and might, perhaps, make an Elopement too in a Morning, to spend an Hour or so with one of those fair Divinities; but ever since our rigid, cold Philosophy, and levelling Theology, have banished those Powers and Graces, and dis-peopled the Groves and Meadows of their gay Inhabitants, I look at Nature with the Eyes of a Philosopher, rather than a Lover; and, like a disenchanted Knight, imagine myself in perfect Solitude in a Desert. (1:253)

For Eugenio, the genius has parted, and the nymphs are past mourning; they are long gone.[13] Nature has lost its soul, its charm. The heavy change is not a function or consequence of time so much as of "our rigid, cold Philosophy, and levelling Theology"—familiar Shaftesburian targets. "Cold" philosophy is inimical to the heat of enthusiasm. Narrow thought precludes expansive feeling. This is arguably the strongest skeptical challenge to a sympathetic worldview presented in "Dialogue IX," but it is considerably and conspicuously weaker than Philocles's objection in *The Moralists*. Fordyce makes Eugenio not a voice of skepticism so much as a *victim* of skepticism. The problem is not that nature is no longer "enchanted" but that certain philosophers have made it seem so.

Fordyce strengthens his case by having not the enthusiast respond but the "cold Philosopher," the impartial mathematician. Constant's response is to challenge Eugenio's hard-and-fast distinction between the "Philosopher" and the "Lover." "But though the World of the Ancients may have better suited the Taste of a Lover or a Poet," he says, "yet I cannot help thinking that, to a true Philosopher, the Universe, unpeopled as it is of those imaginary Inhabitants, will appear more beautiful and august, than when the whole Council of the Gods assembled on the Top of *Ida*." Nor is the beauty that of a barren landscape. Modernity, Fordyce suggests, need not mean a loss of plenitude; in fact, replacing the mythical with the real, it holds out the promise of a superior ontology: "If indeed *Eugenio* does, as he pretends, look upon the Universe with the Eyes of a Philosopher, he will find it peopled with infinitely greater Swarms of Inhabitants, than it was thought to be in ancient Times," and "he will discern an admirable Subordination of the different Ranks of Creatures to each other, and of all to the Good of the universal System," so that every part of that system will "daily astonish him with new Discoveries of the supreme Wisdom and Beneficence of the Almighty Geometrician" (1:254, 255). From a certain philosophical perspective, the world is "a Desart," but from the "true" one, it continues to have "Charms in abundance." In representing and defending a still-enchanted world, Shaftesbury showed a way out of the modern bind, according to which philosophical enlightenment was set at odds with, and came at the cost of, poetic feeling. "Reciting" the Shaftesburian worldview, Fordyce attempts to reassure his audience that they can have both.

Fordyce also recites Shaftesbury's climactic conversion. Eugenio, in the role of Philocles, confesses, "I begin to understand a little of *Sophron's* Philosophy. I have often felt Places and Things infectious. Why then may not particular Aspects of Nature be catching too? If the Infection be so delightful withal, as you, Gentlemen, have represented it, I am resolved to put myself in a proper Posture for being seized with it" (1:265). Eugenio has become susceptible to the "Contagion" of enthusiasm, and Hiero responds, "I perceive . . . *Eugenio* will in due time grow a Proselyte to this mystical Philosophy" (1:265). Here again we see Fordyce's tactic of blunting the skeptical thrust of *The Moralists*. Rather than narrating Philocles's conversion and subsequent falling away, Fordyce defers Eugenio's conversion to a point beyond the confines of the dialogue; it is a future prospect and therefore not subject to evanescence or regression. It is enough that Eugenio is "resolved" to be converted. "Dialogue IX" ends with a return to Fordyce's guiding concern: education. This emphasis has the effect of sweeping away difficult and destabilizing questions about the ontological status of the order of nature and centering the conversation on how a "taste for nature" is "to be acquired" (1:261). Hiero concludes by making, in effect, a curricular recommendation. If, "before they are hurried into the World," the "Minds" of "our Youth" could be "seasoned with the Love of Nature," he urges, if they could be "engaged in those natural Investigations, which may be best pursued in the Country; such as observing the Growth and Propagation of Plants, the Generation, Instincts, Passions, and Oeconomies of Birds, Insects, and other Animals . . . ; I am convinced it would not only employ them in a Sphere of very rational Activity, but likewise open a Scene of immense Delight for their Entertainment. This would give a Refinement and Dignity to their Taste, and . . . would inure them to Contemplation, and prepare them for entering into the more active Stations of Life with less Hazard than they commonly do" (1:266, 267). The question shifts from whether or not a "Universal Mind" exists to how best to "season" young "Minds" to appreciate its effects; the inductive leap is taken for granted. If not everyone grasps the sympathy of the whole, it is not because it may be a fiction of the mind but rather because everyone has not learned how, or been habituated, to see it. Fordyce effectively circles back to ontology through psychology; regardless of whether or not one has the opportunity or leisure time to "converse frequently with Nature," in his academic utopia everyone sees the same sympathetic nature, and that kind of ideal perceptual consensus naturally leads to the conclusion that the consent of the whole is stable and secure.

But it is in the insistent utopianism of "Dialogue IX" that an anxiety about the reality of a larger external order registers most strongly.[14] Fordyce's response is not only to shift the focus to education but also to establish two more immediate, "healing" ideas of order. The first is literary and aesthetic and bears a distinctive Shaftesburian trace. The brief debate among the group about whether the "Coherence of the Rhapsody" is a result of the creative art of the rhapsodist or the sympathetic collaboration of the "Reciter" in "giv[ing] Shapeliness and Proportion to the whole" (1:248) is not about the resolution so much as about the unquestioned premise behind the debate that the rhapsody is a model of coherence in and of itself. The second is moral and social and helps us to understand more clearly why philosophical dialogue was such a vital form in a skeptical age; it gave the skeptic a voice, gave the hero—or "Hiero"—the chance to win him over, and ultimately produced a model of a society ideally balanced between challenge and affirmation, reason and affect. Reflecting on the *"Philosophical* Club" before he has become a part of it, Simplicius confidently asserts that, among "a Set of ingenious Men," "the Discourse must be managed with Life and Spirit, while they are animated by each other's Presence, and feel the joint Influence of mutual Aspect, Voice, Gesture, and every friendly Emotion" (1:65). By virtue of sympathy, the "Set" provides a sense of "Presence" that mitigates the need for and doubt about the reality of a universal presence. The "Life and Spirit" of the cosmos that the Cambridge Platonists took for granted has been transferred to, and is reassuringly recreated in, the "Club." The inductive claim is there—indeed, Sophron insists that "every Club is a Picture of the Academy in Miniature" (1:70), a microcosm of the macrocosm that is meant to function itself as a microcosm of *the* macrocosm— but it is hedged by the sentimentalist one. The core of Fordyce's confidence is in the ordering potential of society and the sympathetic feeling of "ingenious Men." The lingering doubt about the charms of the natural world as a whole is effectively cured by a utopian optimism about the charms of the social world.

THOMSON'S "HAPPY WORLD," MILTON, AND SHAFTESBURIAN POETRY

When in Fordyce's "Dialogue IX" Hiero gushes that "every social and sympathizing Mind" enters deeply into the natural world when it is exposed to the sun and the elements, he goes on to quote a passage of poetry. Hiero is evidently not only a passionate observer but also a passionate reader:

The Progress of the Mind in such a Situation, is charmingly painted by our admirable Poet, in these sublime Lines, which I can never read without feeling some degree of that Rapture which must have fired his Mind when he wrote them.

> ———*Contentment walks*
> *The sunny Glade, and feels an inward Bliss*
> *Spring o'er his Mind, beyond the Power of Kings*
> *To purchase. Pure Serenity apace*
> *Induces Thought, and Contemplation still.*
> *By swift Degrees the Love of Nature works,*
> *And warms the Bosom; till at last sublim'd*
> *To Rapture, and enthusiastic Heat,*
> *We feel the present* DEITY, *and taste*
> *The Joy of* GOD *to see a happy World.* (1:258–259)

The "admirable Poet" is James Thomson, and the work is *The Seasons*, which appeared in 1730. Thomson's introduction to Shaftesbury's thought likely came at the University of Edinburgh, where he matriculated in 1715. Thomson owned a copy of the 1732 edition of *Characteristicks*, but his familiarity almost certainly predated the acquisition.[15] If, as has been claimed, Thomson is the author of the poem "The Works, and Wonders, of Almighty Power," which appeared in *The Plain Dealer* in 1724, that familiarity was more like intimacy; the poem is a rough versification of several passages from *The Moralists*.[16] Attributed to an anonymous youth, it hearkens back in its presentation to the "Poetick Rhapsody" published by "A Young Oxford-Scholar," which appeared in 1709, the same year in which *The Moralists* was first published, and which Alfred Owen Aldridge refers to as "the first of many suggestions that the style of *The Moralists* resembles blank verse."[17] In evoking the wide classical sense of *carmen*, we recall, Shaftesbury himself called attention to the poetic nature of Theocles's rhapsodizing, its "number'd Prose"; the genius loci of *The Moralists* is also a muse, to be invoked "to inspire" and incite "a truer Song of Nature" and a "celestial Hymn" (*Character.*, 2:193). For Shaftesbury, number is deeper than meter; like harmony and proportion, it is a fundamental aesthetic truth. Theocles's theistic "argument" is a poem in the true sense; it is, so to speak, self-numbering. The recital of a poetic world is a poem—whether it is versified or not. *The Moralists* inspired poetry not only because it claimed in part to be poetic but also because, on a deeper level, it poeticized the world. Shaftesbury taught his readers how to be poets; by contemplating nature, he suggested, they would be inspired to sing of nature. In the same way one becomes a true theist one becomes a true poet.

Some pages after the quotation from *The Seasons* in "Dialogue IX," Thomson is explicitly mentioned and paired with Shaftesbury. When Constant reflects on Eugenio's prospective conversion, he imagines the proselyte no longer in search of elegant ladies, as has been his wont, but rather "with a Book in his Hand, a *Shaftesbury* perhaps, or a *Thomson*, our excellent *philosophical* Poet, in some unfrequented Field or Lane, throwing out philosophic Rhapsodies, and solemnly invoking the Genius of the Place to favour his Retreat and inspire his Meditations" (1:264). Fordyce thus suggests a double route to rhapsody—by contemplating the works of nature and by contemplating the works of Shaftesbury and Thomson. This suggestion follows Shaftesbury's own in *The Moralists* when Theocles is introduced "with his belov'd *Mantuan* MUSE, roving in the Fields." In imagining Eugenio "with a Book in his Hand," and in having Simplicius begin "Dialogue IX" by quoting "*Shakespear*" on "the Face of Nature" (1:235), Fordyce recites Shaftesbury's literary version of a sympathetic worldview. Now, however, three decades after Shaftesbury's death, the enthusiast's enchiridion is not Virgil but Shaftesbury himself. The aspiring Shaftesburian poet need not look back so far; Shaftesbury and Thomson will, along with "the Genius of the Place," inspire his song.

Fordyce's Thomson is a poet of rhapsody and enthusiasm.[18] In his life of Thomson, Johnson reinforced this view by suggesting that Thomson's "descriptions of extended scenes and general effects bring before us the whole magnificence of Nature" and that he "imparts to us so much of his own enthusiasm, that our thoughts expand with his imagery and kindle with his sentiments." But Johnson recognized another dimension of Thomson's poetic, a heightened attention to "the minute," emphasizing the organ that has long been the focus of Thomson criticism—the eye. Thomson saw the natural world, as Johnson puts it, with an "eye that distinguishes, in every thing presented to its view, whatever there is on which imagination can delight to be detained."[19] This Thomson is a poet not of enthusiasm but of empiricism, of the "literal," in Parker's formulation, of phenomenal Lockean objects. Johnson paid tribute to Thomson's excellence as a poet by claiming that *The Seasons* gave its readers both "the minute" and "the vast," a novel synthesis that startled its first readers but "by degrees gained upon the publick; and one edition was very speedily succeeded by another."[20] But in praising Thomson and thus accounting for the popularity of the poem, Johnson ends up smoothing over a deep and persistent tension in it, the tension between what might be called representing "every thing" and representing "everything." The unity that is philosophically granted to the natural world and formally reinforced by the poem's balanced quadripartite structure is constantly threatened by an empirical practice that produces a sense of endless particularity, a particularity that cannot but exceed the capacity of the "eye that distinguishes." The whole becomes ungraspable, uncontainable. Extreme empiricism effectively reduces a sympathetic worldview to an Epicurean one, a superabundance of distinct observable things, as if matter in motion were coming to rest in still life. In looking back to Milton as well, Thomson extracted the sympathetic nature of the world before the Fall and then all but subtracted the Fall itself. Yet even a turn away from the Presbyterian theology of his youth could not bring back the Miltonic whole.[21] Confronting similar challenges, Shaftesbury, I suggest, proved more helpful to Thomson. The question of the extent of Shaftesbury's influence on Thomson has been debated by modern critics since C. A. Moore's strong claim for it appeared in 1916.[22] Weighing in on that more general question is beyond the scope of my discussion of *The Seasons*, but in focusing on Thomson's representation of sympathy as a mystical force, I will argue for a significant Shaftesburian inheritance.[23] The Shaftesburian dynamics of Thomsonian sympathy produces an idea of order that functions as a counterweight to the radically disorganizing tendency of Thomson's empiricism. Rather than a vast, packed, static expanse inviting and simultaneously resisting inventory, Shaftesbury provides Thomson with an active, communicative nature that does not overwhelm the eye but rather greatly increases its perceptual power. To contain the inexhaustible "excursiveness," to use one of his favored terms, of the empirical-poetic mode, Thomson develops a teleological moral pattern that begins with nature, proceeds to enthusiasm, and ends in sympathy. The problem of the eye is resolved in part through an appeal to the heart.

The Seasons opens, in effect, in the Edenic books of *Paradise Lost*. In the initial narrative movement from winter into spring, the first of the seasons depicted, Thomson asserts a harmonious, paradisal whole, but his distance from Milton is immediately apparent in his optical emphasis and in his overt interrelation of the natural and the moral. To "the cherish'd eye," which enables the gift of perception, "Nature all / Is blooming, and benevolent, like [the Countess of Hartford]," and the "Sower" places his grain "Into the faithful Bosom of the Ground."[24] Value flows freely between the natural and moral worlds. Whereas Milton associates the Edenic eye with the tortured fallen voyeurism of Satan, Thomson redescribes it in terms of what provides, rather than what excludes. Along with the flora, the eye, too, is "blooming," opening out. "Th' expansive Atmosphere" of springtime is "full of Life and vivifying Soul" (*Sp.*, 28, 29). Thomson creates the effect of having closely studied books 4 and 7 of Milton's epic, with their celebration of a sympathetic and vitalistic nature, their especially dynamic and "vivified" blank verse, and having discarded the rest. He picks up Milton's account in book 7 of the natural world sympathetically springing to life but mystifies it by moving the Creator to the background: "At once, array'd / In all the Colours of the flushing Year, / By Nature's swift and secret-working Hand, / The Garden glows" (*Sp.*, 95–98). Thomson's emphasis on "swiftness," furthered by parallel participles, echoes Milton's, and the "glow" of the garden reinforces the sense of an organic whole. An overarching sympathy gloriously prevails in what Thomson sums up as "consenting SPRING" (*Sp.*, 1168).

And yet as Thomson proceeds from "blooming Nature" to "every Bud that blows" (*Sp.*, 473), the whole begins to get lost. Assertion is challenged by description. As the ocular epithets pile up, a sense of the instability of things intrudes:

AT length the finish'd Garden to the View
Its Vistas opens, and its Alleys green.
Snatch'd thro' the verdant Maze, the hurried Eye
Distracted wanders; now the bowery Walk
Of Covert close, where scarce a Speck of Day
Falls on the lengthen'd Gloom, protracted, sweeps;
Now meets the bending Sky, the River now,
Dimpling along, the breezy-ruffled Lake.

(*Sp.*, 516–523)

The eye has become "hurried." The violent effect of "Snatch'd" at the front of its line breaks up the Miltonic harmony, and the repetition of "now" conveys a sense not of presence so much as of jerky, scattershot succession. Thomson's use of enjambment here suggests less "sense variously drawn out," to recall Milton's note on "The Verse," than sense "hurriedly," hastily, "sweeping" out. The internal rhyme of "Distracted" and "protracted" is itself distracting to the readerly eye. Profusion gives way to distraction and confusion. The unity suggested by "View" is initially divided by "Vistas," and then dissolves into minute, decreasingly numerable particulars, "Specks," "Dimples" of river, "ruffles" of lake.

The tension between Thomson's holism and this kind of particularism emerges continually in *The Seasons*. The dimples and ruffles of water in *Spring* become, in effect, "the filmy Threads / Of Dew" in *Autumn* (1211–1212) and the "Flakes" of snow that "Fall broad, and wide, and fast" in *Winter* (230–231), or wintry frost, "Myriads of little Salts, or hook'd, or shap'd / Like double Wedges" (*Wi.*, 718–719). In *Summer* especially, the longest of the seasons by some four hundred lines, the sense of a graspable whole, both formal and physical, is threatened at almost every turn by the insistent claim, and atomizing effect, of the minute.[25] Nature's "numerous Kinds" teem, "Evading even the microscopic

Eye" (*Su.*, 287, 288).[26] In the space of ten lines Thomson observes "subterranean Cells, / Where searching Sun-Beams scarce can find a Way," the "Forest-Boughs, / That dance unnumber'd to the playful Breeze," the "nameless Nations . . . / Of evanescent Insects," the "Millions" that "stray" in the midst of "the floating Verdure" (*Su.*, 294–295, 299–300, 302–303, 305). The positive "numerous" swiftly becomes the negative "unnumber'd" and "nameless," as Thomson elaborates on the insufficiency of "even the microscopic Eye." Thomson's famous survey of "the Wonders of the *torrid Zone*" (*Su.*, 632) yields a geographic part that does not lend itself to inductive or synecdochal extension to a cosmic whole. There "Plains immense / Lie stretch'd below, interminable Meads, / And vast Savannahs, where the wandering Eye, / Unfixt, is in a verdant Ocean lost" (*Su.*, 690–693). The "immense" poses as great and overwhelming a challenge to the eye as the minute. The whole itself seems increasingly "Unfixt." A holistic view of things defies "the straining Eye," which is preoccupied with "th' imperfect Surfaces of Things," a phrase that aptly suggests the problem of reconciling a sympathetic worldview to a sensationalist, empiricist one; rather than a unified whole, the latter tends to produce "one swimming Scene, / Uncertain if beheld" (*Su.*, 1689, 1688, 1692–1693). Empiricism threatens to reduce the order of things to "th' imperfect Surfaces of Things." In response to a widening "uncertainty" about the order of the whole, the epic catalogue, backed by a secure ontology, becomes the empirical inventory, which, if it can be likened to still life, at its least orderly suggests an overturned dustbin. "Confus'd above," Thomson writes in *Autumn*, "Glasses and Bottles, Pipes and Gazetteers, / As if the Table even itself was drunk," make up "a wet broken Scene" (557–559, 560). If for Milton the problem is fallenness, for Thomson it is "brokénness," a world broken up, and down, into images and "scenes." The phrase "broken Scene" also appears in *Summer* (589), and both hearken back to Thomson's reference in *Spring* to "a broken World" (318). This world seems the very antithesis of the "happy World" that Fordyce associated with Thomson.

Thomson addresses and redresses the problem of brokenness by developing an idea of moral coherence that depends on, but ultimately detaches from, the natural world. He appeals to the magic of sympathy, which involves a mystical conversation between the natural world and the subject and then between the subject and the moral world. Thomson's major mode of conceiving this double conversation is in terms of infusion and diffusion.[27] From the profusion of nature the subject receives an infusion of spirit and diffuses it to all humankind. Sympathy is thus a kind of mystical aura, a breeze that always blows in the right direction. The pattern of infusion and diffusion is a recurrent structure in *The Seasons*. Its ultimate effect is to interiorize narrative, inscribing it on the level of the passions. The verse paragraph from which Fordyce quotes in "Dialogue IX" begins, "STILL let my Song a nobler Note assume, / And sing th' infusive Force of Spring on Man" (*Sp.*, 867–868). We receive the influence of the natural world and are animated by it. Those whom this "Force" does not affect, "ye sordid Sons of Earth, / Hard, and unfeeling of Another's Woe," are sent away, whereas those who feel, who sympathize, are called together and welcomed in: "But come, ye generous Minds, in whose wide Thought, / Of all his Works, CREATIVE BOUNTY burns, / With warmest Beam" (*Sp.*, 875–876, 878–880). Thought widens in response to the sublime profusion of its object. Sympathy has the power to overcome the limits of ordinary vision.

For Thomson, responsiveness to nature goes hand in hand with responsiveness to humankind. To be unsympathetic, or "unfeeling of Another's Woe," is to cut oneself off from the world and the spirit diffused throughout it. In *Summer* Thomson again opposes the selfish and the "sordid" to "the generous still-improving Mind, / That gives the hopeless Heart to sing for Joy, / Diffusing kind Beneficence around" (1637, 1641–1643). Here the movement outward is more explicit. Enthusiasm is not an end in and of itself; it moves the enthusiast to communicate his feeling to others. The process is more mystical than the word "Beneficence" suggests. Thomson is imagining something far more abstract and atmospheric than a good deed; he is imagining something approximating Shaftesbury's idea of moral magic, an invisible but powerful transmission of goodness through a rarefied medium. Earlier in *Summer* Thomson depicts an unnamed man taking a walk after the heat of day has passed, "him who lonely loves / To seek the distant Hills, and there converse / With Nature; there to harmonize his Heart." Having received an infusion of vital energy from "the distant Hills," he returns to society, "in pathetic Song to breathe around / The Harmony to others[,] Social Friends, / Attun'd to happy Unison of Soul" (*Su.*, 1380–1382, 1383–1385). Here diffusion is figured as exhalation. The "pathetic Song" is taken in by a sympathetic audience, "Social Friends"—an emphatic tautology—whose souls resonate. The "broken Scene" presented to the eye is reunited and resolved in the "Harmony" of the "Heart," a verbal pairing that enacts the very idea of harmony itself.

This moral pattern is adjusted season by season but underlies the whole and functions to unify it. The lack of fixity and certainty associated with the eye is remedied by a deep confidence in the heart. The "lonely" nature lover in *Summer* finds a counterpart in the "sickled Swain" of *Autumn*:

When Autumn's yellow Luster gilds the World,
And tempts the sickled Swain into the Field,

Seiz'd by the general Joy, his Heart distends
With gentle Throws; and, thro' the tepid Gleams
Deep-musing, then he *best* exerts his Song.

(*Au.*, 1322–1326)

The emphatic use of "Seiz'd" here might be compared to that of "Snatch'd" in
the passage we considered in *Spring*, but a similar metrical effect defines two very
different subjective experiences, that of the "hurried Eye" versus that of the
"Heart" that "distends," one of Thomson's many synonyms for the act of diffusion.
The counterpart to "th' infusive Force of Spring" in *Autumn* is "the POWER / Of
PHILOSOPHIC MELANCHOLY" (*Au.*, 1004–1005). The pattern is essentially repeated:

O'er all the Soul his sacred Influence breathes;
Inflames Imagination; thro' the Breast
Infuses every Tenderness; and far
Beyond dim Earth exalts the swelling Thought.

(*Au.*, 1010–1013)

The sequence "Influence . . . Inflames . . . Infuses" underlines the inward
movement, and then the movement outward, "the swelling Thought," follows.
The sequence of prepositions, syntactically heightened, reinforces the pattern:
"O'er . . . / . . . thro' . . . / . . . / Beyond." As the verse paragraph continues,
Thomson moves, as before, from the natural world to the moral:

Devotion rais'd
To Rapture, and divine Astonishment;
The Love of Nature unconfin'd, and, chief,
Of human Race; the large ambitious Wish,
To make them blest; the Sigh for suffering Worth,
Lost in Obscurity, the noble Scorn,
Of Tyrant-Pride; the fearless great Resolve;
The Wonder which the dying Patriot draws,
Inspiring Glory thro' remotest Time;
Th' awaken'd Throb for Virtue, and for Fame;
The Sympathies of Love, and Friendship dear;
With all the *social Offspring of the Heart.*

(*Au.*, 1018–1029)

The accumulation of noun phrases in this passage produces a sublime "throb-
bing" effect. "Rapture, and divine Astonishment" are enacted enumeratively, but
the effect is quite different from that of objects piling up in inventory, the "confusion" of "Glasses and Bottles, Pipes and Gazetteers." The "large ambitious Wish"

is a characteristic figure of diffusiveness, and Thomson's approach to politics here is just as diffuse as his approach to ethics; the "Tyrant" is "Pride"—Thomsonian personification is at base a mode of diffusion—and in "the dying Patriot" we are to contemplate not a person so much as a broad idea, a spirit acting at a distance, "Inspiring Glory thro' remotest Time."[28] *The Seasons* aims to spread its Whig nationalism in the same way it spreads its sentimentalist ethics—by sympathy.[29]

Thomson locates "The Sympathies of Love, and Friendship dear" at the climax and conclusion of his minidrama of "PHILOSOPHIC MELANCHOLY," the genesis of which can ultimately be traced back to his reading of Milton's *Il Penseroso*.[30] But the phrase itself is an allusion to *Paradise Lost* and the hymn to "wedded Love," elevating "Relations dear, and all the Charities / Of Father, Son, and Brother" (4.756–757).[31] Francis Hutcheson (1694–1746), too, had referred to this passage in his *Inquiry into the Original of Our Ideas of Beauty and Virtue* (1725), a work that established him as Shaftesbury's chief philosophical successor. Calling into question the force of our natural benevolence, Hutcheson imagines that even if we had been victimized by a group of villains, we would still ultimately prefer that "they should recover the ordinary Affections of Men, become Kind, Compassionate, and Friendly; contrive Laws, Constitutions, Governments, Propertys; and form an honest happy Society, with Marriages, and 'Relations dear, and all the Charities / Of Father, Son, and Brother.'"[32] But whereas Hutcheson follows Milton's sense, emphasizing the natural goodness of familial "relations," Thomson transforms it. In effect, he subjects Milton's idea to his own principle of expansion and diffusion. Thomson moves from familial relations to all social relations. The allusion neatly sums up Thomsonian sympathy as a dual inheritance—a revision of Milton on one hand and a recital of Shaftesbury on the other. In substituting "Sympathies" for "Charities," Thomson also diffuses Milton's piety. The son of a Presbyterian minister and a candidate for the Presbyterian ministry himself, Thomson, in the words of his biographer, "became theologically liberal to the point of deism."[33] Milton's solid theism, we might say, has become Thomson's vaporous deism.

With Thomson's theological liberalism came an openness to perfectibilism. Not everyone sympathized, not everyone opened his heart to nature and humankind; there were the "sordid Sons of Earth, / hard, and unfeeling of Another's Woe," the "Sons of Interest," opposed to "Virtue" (*Su.*, 1391). When Thomson describes the Fall in *Spring*—"BUT now those white unblemish'd Minutes, whence / The fabling Poets took their golden Age, / Are found no more amid these iron Times" (272–274)—he represents its effects primarily in emotional terms; he makes apathy, antipathy, and a lack of sympathy the major signs of fallenness. In our fallen state we do not sympathize with "another's Joy" but meanly envy it. We are consumed by "The partial Thought, a listless Unconcern, / Cold, and averting from our Neighbour's Good" (*Sp.*, 284, 301–302). We think only of ourselves, and our partiality deprives us of vital energy; we receive nothing and communicate nothing. The result is hardheartedness. Thomson's account of the heart's hardening seems less biblical, or Miltonic, than Shaftesburian: "At last, extinct each social Feeling, fell / And joyless Inhumanity pervades, / And petrifies the Heart" (*Sp.*, 305–307). The pun "Feeling, fell," evoking "Fall," is Miltonic, but the emphasis on "social Feeling" suggests Shaftesbury's moral landscape, not Milton's. In situating his account of the Fall early in the poem, Thomson denies it the narrative centrality that it had in Milton's epic, its climactic weight, its tragic immediacy. Thomson thus allows the narrative of recovery and redemption far greater scope. The "Sons of Interest" are not necessarily constrained by their own interest; they are capable of becoming "Social Friends." Thomson's affective Fall is not irrevocable. If "fond Man" properly considered society, he writes in *Winter*, "The conscious Heart of Charity would warm, / And her wide Wish Benevolence dilate; / The social Tear would rise, the social Sigh" (348, 354–356). By an inward adjustment, even the most self-interested can participate in the magic of sympathy, what Thomson elsewhere describes as "Friendship heighten'd by the mutual Wish, / Th' enchanting Hope, and sympathetic Glow" (*Su.*, 1180–1181). The familiar rise in temperature produces a sublime "dilation." The movement outward here precedes a marvelous movement upward; unlike natural tears, "social" ones "rise." They are sublimed. The transition from "social Tear" to "social Sigh" enacts a kind of quasi-chemical state change, so that sympathy diffuses more widely into social space. Even in the coldest of winters—as it does from season to season—human sympathy produces a reliable "warmth."

The final two lines of *The Seasons*, "The Storms of WINTRY TIME will quickly pass, / And one unbounded SPRING encircle All" (*Wi.*, 1068–1069), can be seen to evoke Milton's lines from book 4—"Universal *Pan* / Knit with the *Graces* and the *Hours* in dance / Led on th' Eternal Spring." Thomson's closure, which produces a narrative form of circularity that reinforces the seasonal idea of cyclicality, need not point in the direction of a unity after time because that unity, "a *perfect Whole* / Uniting" (*Wi.*, 1047–1048), exists in time. He thus concludes with an emphatic assertion of order on the level of the whole, but the certainty that spring will follow winter cannot so easily be conflated with the certainty that spring will "encircle All." Earlier in the final verse paragraph Thomson writes, "VIRTUE sole survives, / Immortal, never-failing Friend of Man" (*Wi.*, 1039–1040). The difference in tense, present versus future ("survives" versus "will . . . pass, / And . . . encircle"), is significant and revealing. It is ultimately in "never-failing" virtue, rather than in the promise and prospect of a universal vernal unity, that the core of Thomson's confidence resides. His faith in what can be felt functions to manage and mitigate his doubt about what can be seen and known. When all else fails, including the perceptual power of the eye, the virtuous heart "survives." For Thomson, human sympathy can be counted on in a way that the order of the whole, with its countless, uncountable particulars, cannot. The unity and friendship of "Man" ultimately emerges as the ground and first principle of order.

The phrase "Friend of Man" makes a crucial appearance earlier in *The Seasons*, where it refers not to "VIRTUE" but to Shaftesbury himself, whom Thomson holds up as virtue's great embodiment and advocate. With its heated accumulation of clauses, the portrait achieves an enthusiastic effect:

> The generous ASHLEY thine, the Friend of Man;
> Who scann'd his Nature with a Brother's Eye,
> His Weakness prompt to shade, to raise his Aim,
> To touch the finer Movements of the Mind,
> And with the *moral Beauty* charm the Heart.
>
> <div align="right">(<i>Su.</i>, 1551–1555)</div>

The italicization of the phrase *"moral Beauty"* suggests emphasis, but also something like quotation. In his index Shaftesbury has separate references to *"Moral Beauty," "Moral Beauty and Deformity,"* and *"Beauty of Sentiments, Character, Mind"* (*Character.*, 3:257). In a characteristic statement, he asserts "the *natural* Affection of all Mankind towards moral Beauty and Perfection" (*Character.*, 1:174). Thomson makes the interfusion of the moral and the aesthetic Shaftesbury's signal achievement. But there is a subtler effect here to which I want to call attention, the movement from the "Eye" to "the Heart." This is, I have been suggesting, one of the defining movements of *The Seasons*, establishing an idea of order that offsets its empiricist tendency to move endlessly outward from thing to thing and place to place. In the commotion and confusion of *Summer*, the poet at one point observes, "MUCH yet remains unsung" (1092). This is the problem of the empiricist poem, whose infinite matter stretches and soon exceeds the capacity of the poet to contain it in song. But by establishing a teleological moral pattern that "never fails" to reach the sympathetic heart, Thomson works to resolve the formal as well as philosophical problem of "MUCH" or too-muchness. A moral order fixed in the heart compensates for an "Unfixt" and "Uncertain" whole dependent on a mutable, fallible eye.

The Seasons significantly preserved and perpetuated Shaftesbury's representation of sympathy as a mystical principle of moral order. The number of subscriptions for the 1730 edition of the poem reached upward of four hundred, and the 1744 edition was even more widely known, especially abroad.[34] The recital of

Shaftesburian sympathy came to be one of the characteristic gestures of the Shaftesburian "school of literature," in the phrase of the 1778 edition of the *Biographia Britannica*.[35] To conclude this section I will briefly examine one such gesture in the poem *Concord*, composed in 1751 and attributed to Shaftesbury's nephew James Harris (1709–1780), which further exemplifies the natural-to-moral pattern that we have been tracing. Although he did not know his uncle, Harris had a strong connection to him through the fourth earl, who was two years his junior, and with whom he collaborated on a reverent portrait of Shaftesbury that appeared in *A General Dictionary, Historical and Critical* (1734).[36] *Concord* begins with a broad appeal to cosmic sympathy, described in the Argument as the *"General Sympathy of all Things"* and framed in a neat chiasmus: "CONGE-NIAL THINGS TO THINGS CONGENIAL TEND: / So Rivulets their little Waters join, / To form one River's greater Stream," and "Earth to Earth down goes; and upwards flies / To Fires ethereal."[37] The assertion of the attraction of like to like, like the survey of the elements, is thoroughly traditional, but Harris wants to infuse his subject matter with life. And so he applies the Shaftesburian-Thomsonian vapor-izer: "Yet not here / Confin'd the sacred Sympathy, but wide / Thro' *Plant* and *Animal* diffusely spread."[38] The addition of "sacred" to "Sympathy" produces a kind of deistic hypallage. The enjambment of the second of these lines mimics widening in poetic space, and the phrase "diffusely spread," with its intensifying adverb, gets line-ending emphasis. Like Thomson, Harris follows the spread of sympathy from nature to man:

> Hence Man, ally'd to all, in all things meets
> Congenial Being, Effluence of Mind.
> And as the tuneful String spontaneous sounds
> In Answer to its kindred Note; so He
> The secret Harmony within him feels,
> When aught of Beauty offers.[39]

The word "Effluence" does important diffusive duty here, and the presence of Shaftesbury is keenly felt in the aura of "secrecy," in the use of the familiar musical analogy, which establishes a natural sympathy with the beautiful. Harris goes on to describe the response of the human mind to music or "what the Sculptor graves, the Painter paints" in terms of "Rapture." There is a sublime joy in contemplating works of art as well as works of nature, the "verdant Plains" or the "Ocean's mighty Vastness," but the greatest of these is sympathy:

> Yet chief by far,
> Chief is Man's Joy, when, mixt with human Kind,
> He feels Affection melt the social Heart;

Feels Friendship, Love, and all the Charities
Of Father, Son, and Brother. Here the pure,
Sincere Congenial, free from all Alloy,
With Bliss he recognizes. For to Man
What dearer is than Man?[40]

The Miltonic "Charities" are ultimately subsumed by the Shaftesburian-Thomsonian "social Heart." Again Milton's sentiment is effectively diffused; what matters most is not "Father, Son, and Brother" but general "Man." The emphasis and energy of Harris's poem are concentrated here, not in the world as a whole, but in the world of man. The order of the whole is to be accepted less as philosophical truth than as poetic convention. The introduction of the physical elements establishes balance primarily on the level of the poetic line. But the attenuation of physical presence, we see again, is counterbalanced by the heightening of moral and social presence. The sympathy between "Man" and "Man" is expressed in the form of a rhetorical question not because it is in doubt but because it is not. Like Thomson's, Harris's confidence in human sympathy functions to secure an idea of order in human nature that has come to seem increasingly uncertain and unavailable in nature as a whole. The widening emphasis on "Relations dear," in the expanded Miltonic sense, in the first half of the eighteenth century needs to be understood in part as a recognition of and response to a widening crisis of faith among the intellectual elite about the fixity and intelligibility of sympathetic relations in the universe. As his relation to the whole came increasingly into doubt, man's relation to man became increasingly "dear."

SYMPATHY AND MORAL NEWTONIANISM

A major response, I have been arguing, to an increasing intellectual uncertainty about the idea of universal sympathy was a heightened confidence in human sympathy as an ordering principle. Social presence was effectively tasked with supplying a cosmic absence. In the final section of this chapter I want to call attention to an important, alternative kind of response, one that worked in tandem with the first—an emphasis on and appeal to Newtonian law. If skepticism and empiricism functioned to call into question the reality of a perfect, coherent whole, Newtonianism provided an apparently definitive and irrefutable account of its reality. In the preface to his summa, *The Principles of Moral and Christian Philosophy* (1740), George Turnbull (1698–1748), who arrived at the University of Edinburgh four years before Thomson and went on to lecture on moral philosophy at Marischal College—some two decades before Fordyce—calls for a poet to "*sing those wonderful harmonies and beauties of*

nature which have been lately discovered by searching into her order and admin-
istration; and the praises of that Divine *man to whom we are principally beholden*
for all these momentous discoveries."[41] Turnbull here pays tribute to the saintly
Newton, who, "*by unraveling the deepest mysteries of nature,*" had "*effectually*
discomfited Atheism and Superstition" and dispelled "*all the gloomy horrors*
which naturally sprout from the frightful notion of a fatherless world and blind
chance, or, which is yet more terrible, the opinion of a malignant administration."
Where the Epicureans saw only "*blind chance,*" Newton revealed divine design
and order. Turnbull affirmed not only Newton's "*momentous discoveries*" but
also the method by which he came by them.[42] He made the famous conclusion
to the *Opticks* one of his two epigraphs: "And if natural Philosophy in all its
Parts, by pursuing this Method, shall at length be perfected, the Bounds of
Moral Philosophy will also be enlarged." For the drawing together of the natural
and moral worlds moral philosophers could claim Newton's own authority. As
in the natural world, so in the moral world the moral philosopher could make
"*momentous discoveries*" by means of what Newton called "Experiments and
Observations."[43] Newton's theory of gravitation gave the old analogy between
physical and ethical order a new scientific basis.[44] In that analogy sympathy,
extended from the natural world to the moral, could be not only reauthorized
but also reuniversalized. The project of enlisting sympathy into the service of a
"moral Newtonianism," in Elie Halévy's significant phrase, found its ultimate
fulfillment in Smith's *Theory of Moral Sentiments*.[45] As James Wodrow wrote in
the early nineteenth century, Smith's *Theory* "founded on sympathy" was "a
very ingenious attempt to account for the principal phenomena in the moral
world from this one general principle, like that of gravity in the natural world."[46]
Following the Newtonian method, Smith "ingeniously" established sympathy
as the gravity of the moral world.

Before returning to Turnbull's preface and his appeal to Newtonian poetry, I
want to consider some versions of the Newtonian analogy to shed further light on
sympathy's complex relationship to the poetic and the scientific in the first half
of the eighteenth century. The Shaftesburian inheritance, it might be suggested,
went in two major directions during this period: toward the scientific, corresponding to a conception of sympathy as an empirical fact, and toward the poetic,
corresponding to a conception of sympathy as a mystical force. In the practice of
moral Newtonianism these two tracks significantly overlapped. The Newtonian
analogy promised to strengthen and enhance the scientific status of sympathy
and, at the same time, to add philosophical weight to a Shaftesburian poetry of
the world. In the main body of his *Principles* Turnbull elaborates and reinforces
his claim for the fundamental nature of society by "comparing the uniting,

benevolent principle in our nature to attraction in the material system." In drawing the Newtonian analogy, he acknowledges his debt to "an excellent paper in the *Guardian* to this purpose."[47] The "paper" is undoubtedly the one dated 5 August 1713, in which George Berkeley (1685–1753) carefully elaborated the analogy:

> FROM the Contemplation of the Order, Motion and Cohesion of Natural Bodies, Philosophers are now agreed, that there is a mutual Attraction between the most distant Parts at least of this Solar System. All those Bodies that revolve round the Sun are drawn towards each other and towards the Sun, by some secret, uniform and never-ceasing Principle. . . . And as the larger Systems of the Universe are held together by this Cause, so likewise the particular Globes derive their Cohesion and Consistence from it.
>
> NOW if we carry our Thoughts from the Corporeal to the Moral World, we may observe in the Spirits or Minds of Men, a like Principle of Attraction, whereby they are drawn together into Communities, Clubs, Families, Friendships, and all the various Species of society. . . .
>
> AND as the attractive Power in Bodies is the most universal Principle which produceth innumerable Effects, and is a Key to explain the various *Phaenomena* of Nature; so the corresponding Social Appetite in Humane Souls is the great Spring and Source of moral Actions. This it is that inclines each Individual to an Intercourse with his Species, and models every one to that Behaviour which best suits with the Common Well-being. Hence that Sympathy in our Nature, whereby we feel the Pains and Joys of our Fellow-creatures.[48]

Sympathy attests to a common benevolence, "that reciprocal Attraction in the Minds of Men," "that diffusive Sense of Humanity so unaccountable to the selfish Man who is untouch'd with it, and is, indeed, a sort of Monster." Berkeley emphasizes not only the universality of his moral principle but also its primacy. Moral attraction "is not the Result of Education, Law or Fashion; but is a Principle originally engrafted in the very first Formation of the Soul by the Author of our Nature."[49] A decade later in the *Inquiry*, Hutcheson similarly asserted the independence of the "Disposition to Compassion" from "Custom, Education, or Instruction." Hutcheson makes this point at the end of the section in which he draws the same universalizing analogy: "The universal Benevolence toward all Men, we may compare to that Principle of Gravitation, which perhaps extends to all Bodys in the Universe; but . . . increases as the Distance is diminish'd, and is strongest when Bodys come to touch each other."[50] Shaftesburian ethics here receives the sanction and support of Newtonian physics. Whereas Hutcheson took the side of Shaftesbury against Bernard Mandeville (1670–1733), Berkeley condemned both as "minute philosophers" in *Alciphron* (1st ed., 1732), in which the genre of philosophical dialogue was used not, as by Fordyce, to show a recitative sympathy with Shaftesbury, but rather to deliver a pointed rebuke.⁵¹ As these passages suggest, however, Berkeley and Hutcheson had Newton in common. Although Berkeley objected to the irreligion and irrationality of the moral-aesthetic system that Hutcheson inherited from Shaftesbury, his organic conception of the whole in the *Guardian* essay does not radically differ from theirs. At the beginning of the essay, Berkeley writes, "Iғ we consider the whole Scope of the Creation that lies within our View, the Moral and Intellectual, as well as the Natural and Corporeal, we shall perceive throughout a certain Correspondence of the Parts, a Similitude of Operation, and Unity of Design."⁵² The correspondence between natural and moral attraction was underwritten by the fundamental correspondence of the whole.⁵³

As we have seen, Fordyce emphasized the sympathetic dynamics of association and education in part as a hedge against an uncertain cosmic ontology, but he also aimed to shore up that ontology by appealing to Newtonian law. In Hiero's rapture at the beginning of "Dialogue IX," the Newtonian world becomes the object of Shaftesburian enthusiasm:

> "What Wonders are performed by that simple Engine, the Power of Gravitation or Attraction, by which the huge Machinery of Nature is linked in inviolable Union, and the vast Worlds of Matter continue suspended and balanced in perfect Equilibrium! . . . To it we owe our Tides, which keep the immense Collection of the Waters continually fresh and wholesome; and the Ascent of the nourishing Juices to the Tops of the highest Trees. To it we are indebted for the Force of our Pumps, the Vigour of our Machines, and the indissoluble Cohesion of Bodies. In this wonder-working Power, I recognize thy Being, and universal Providence; a Power which penetrates the Essence and inmost Particles of Bodies, combines the remotest Objects in mutual Sympathy and Concord; and, operating by unmechanic Forces, produces the most perfect Mechanism of a World!"⁵⁴

In Fordyce's anaphoric use of "To it," rhapsody becomes litany. But the invocation of Newton also functions to provide support for the claim made subsequently in the dialogue that Hiero's rhapsody on the sympathetic whole, and rhapsody in general, is not a mere fit of passion; it can be the harmonious product of a rational mind. For Fordyce, Newtonianism is not a threat to an older sympathetic worldview; in its assertion of "unmechanic Forces," it sublimely reinforces it. Newton projected not a cold and empty world but a warm and providential one. In his *Poem Sacred to the Memory of Sir Isaac Newton*, which first appeared in 1727, Thomson proceeds from "Nature's general Sympathy" to "the boundless hand of PROVIDENCE / Wide-working thro' this universal Frame" and thence to the philosopher whose vision made both eminently clearer: Newton "by the mingling / Of *Gravitation* and *Projection* saw / The whole in silent Harmony revolve."[55] Thomson went on to put the analogy between natural and moral attraction into poetic practice. In *Liberty* (1735–1736), celebrating "UNBOUNDED LOVE / Effus'd," he writes of a *"moral Gravitation*, rushing prone / To press the *public Good.*"[56] Here the Shaftesburian point comes across in Newtonian terms. As Alan McKillop writes of Thomson and his age, the "Newtonian principle of gravitation was . . . simply the most cogent form of unity in variety; it was given a central position not merely because of its precision and economy but because of the aesthetic, moral, philosophical, and religious associations to which it lent itself." Over time, however, "gravitation came to be regarded as a purely mechanistic principle, and the world view developed from Newtonian physics excluded human values."[57] The worldview developed from Shaftesburian ethics, by contrast, was subject to no such exclusion.

For Turnbull, to return to his preface, poetry held out the promise of bringing Newtonianism and Shaftesburianism together in a single, sublime world picture. Soon after celebrating Newton, he includes a message and a challenge to a *"certain poet,"* most likely Thomson. Given that Turnbull openly acknowledges his debts to other writers, including Shaftesbury—whom he praises for his *"complete system of* Moral Philosophy *demonstrated in the strictest manner"* and defends against the charge of atheism—his refusal to name Thomson, if indeed he had Thomson in mind, seems puzzling.[58] The poet, Turnbull claims, *"is universally confessed to have shewn a most extraordinary genius for descriptive poetry in some of his works, and in all of them a heart deeply impregnated with the warmest love of virtue and mankind,"* and, Turnbull goes on, *"if he chances to cast his eye on this* Preface, *as his friendship to me will naturally induce him to do upon whatever bears my name,"* Turnbull would have him *"set about a work so greatly wanting, and which must gain him immortal honour."*[59] Although he does not name the poet, Turnbull provides him with a significant epithet: he is to be *"a* Counter-lucretius."[60] Was *The Seasons* not the "Counter-lucretian" epic that Turnbull had in mind? Could the 1744 edition, with its widened loco-descriptive reach, be in some small part an answer to Turnbull's *"call"*?

But the puzzle of Turnbull's address to Thomson is ultimately far less important than the claim Turnbull is making in his preface for poetry in general. In acknowledging his debt to Pope, who provided him with the second of his two epigraphs, Turnbull defends the enterprise of philosophical poetry: *"I have often felt,* that principles, precepts or maxims, written in such *harmonious* verse, both strike the reason more strongly at first, and are more easily retained by it afterwards." This defense, emphasizing the force and the mnemonic function of poetry, is unremarkable, but in posing the rhetorical question "AND *what is susceptible of poetical charms, if the beautiful order, and the immense magnificence of nature in all her works be not?*" Turnbull is suggesting a new claim about the sympathy, the congeniality, between poetry and the Newtonian world.[61] He is suggesting that the best defense of a sympathetic worldview against the "*blind chance*" of the Lucretians and Epicureans might now be not in the kind of philosophical discourse that he is himself producing but through the medium of poetry. Why? Because poetry, more than philosophical prose, moved the passions, and universal sympathy was now more to be felt than known, and because poetry could supply an uncertainly enchanted nature with its own "*charms.*" At the end of *The True Intellectual System* Cudworth acknowledged Lucretius's elegance as a poet but condemned him for giving his readers "*Poetick Flourish* . . . without any *Philosophick Truth.*"[62] Whereas in the eyes of his critics Shaftesbury had simply mistaken the first for the second, in the eyes of his admirers he had suggested a sublime way to unite and to communicate both. Turnbull's preface helps us to see that, in the face of skeptical and empirical challenges, a sympathetic worldview continued to have a vital psychological and cultural function—to "counter" Lucretianism and to promote a consoling order. Yet, decades after the publication of Cudworth's pious summa, the mode and medium of projection have changed. "*Poetick Flourish*" is no longer a problem; it is now the solution.

THE FUTURE OF SYMPATHY II: HUME AND THE AFTERLIFE OF SHAFTESBURIANISM

David Hume's *Treatise of Human Nature* (1739–1740) represents the first full-fledged moral and psychological theory of sympathy in British philosophy, and it has accordingly received extensive attention in eighteenth-century studies, often serving as a starting point for literary-historical inquiries into sympathy and sensibility.[1] But such inquiries, even when they have uncovered the complexity and ambivalence of Hume's account of sympathy, have generally proceeded from a narrow and partial view of his philosophical commitments. Hume's sentimentalist ethics has tended to be emphasized at the expense of his skeptical metaphysics, so that the Hume who made sympathy "the basis of social harmony," in Janet Todd's phrase, has been split off from the Hume who "threw a dark shadow of doubt over the entire subject" of analogy, in Wasserman's.[2] In formal terms this split could be described as one between the Hume of the second and third books of the *Treatise*, "Of the Passions" and "Of Morals," and the Hume of the first, "Of the Understanding," which has been relatively neglected in treatments of Humean sympathy.[3] In the previous chapter I argued that Fordyce and Thomson appealed to a moral idea of sympathy as a way of securing a sense of presence and coherence that a totalizing natural idea of sympathy, unsettled by skepticism and empiricism, could no longer be counted on to provide. I want to extend that argument in this chapter and to show further how our study of sympathy in the seventeenth century as a conversation between natural and moral subjects can expand our understanding of formations of sympathy in the eighteenth, for which Hume's is a critical case.

Hume's critique of sympathy as a principle of the whole, governing the totality of subjects and objects, heaven and earth, represents the culmination of a native line of philosophical critique going back to Bacon and continuing with Hobbes, Boyle, and others. More elaborately than these predecessors Hume objected to the anthropomorphism implied by a universal concept of sympathy, which attributed sense and feeling to things incapable of either, and to the "fallacy of induction" on which it was founded.[4] In famously determining "to introduce the experimental Method of Reasoning into MORAL SUBJECTS," as stated on the title page of the *Treatise*, Hume removed sympathy from the whole, which could not be the object of proper reasoning, and located it definitively in the mind, where he claimed it could be. Whereas Shaftesbury, and his followers, enthusiastically rhapsodized about sympathy as a universal power, Hume coolly analyzed it as a psychological mechanism—and so significantly accelerated the gradual process of psychologization that we observed in chapter 5. For Hume, Shaftesbury's enthusiastic philosophy was guided by fiction; true philosophy, by contrast, rested on fact. In the *Treatise* sympathy emerges as the guiding fact of Hume's "science of man," one that is continually experienced and observed. It is not only a constant of moral experience, he concludes, but also the basis of moral judgment. In this conclusion we can see Hume attempting to resolve the ongoing crisis of coherence that we have observed in various forms and from various angles in the seventeenth century. Hume came to terms with sympathy not by positing or repositioning a "true intellectual system of the universe," in which the moral and the natural were essentially aligned, but by rigorously limiting the scope of sympathy and locating it at the center of moral life. Human sympathy fills the void of order created by his explosion of all totalizing principles. Whereas in *Paradise Lost*, as we saw in chapter 4, Milton produced a narrative of compensation, in the *Treatise* Hume provides a logic of compensation. In arguing that we can never know how things ultimately connect, he assures us that we can know how people do. A psychology of connection supersedes an ontology of connection; the refutation of the latter clears the way for the assertion of the former.

In the first section of the chapter I analyze this compensatory dynamic in the *Treatise* and establish a link between Hume's critique of the sympathetic worldview as conceived by Shaftesbury and by the "antient philosophy," and Hume's advancement of sympathy as the connective principle of society. In his late *Dialogues Concerning Natural Religion* (1779), this critique of what the skeptical character Philo calls "the coherence and apparent Sympathy in all the parts of this world," and the anti-Epicurean position that depended on it, received its fullest and most damaging articulation. Coming after Shaftesbury and Fordyce, Hume's revision of philosophical dialogue produces no real climax, no real consensus; it is not the sympathetic worldview that is dialogically revealed and reinforced but rather its "tottering foundation."⁵ I go on to argue that Hume's social-psychological analysis of sympathy in the *Treatise* functions to establish a more secure and stable foundation in human nature and human relations. In the next section I shift from Hume's reception of Shaftesbury's metaphysics to his reception of Shaftesbury's ethics. Although he rejected the metaphysical backdrop, the painterly manner, and the mystical airs, Hume ultimately shared with, and to some extent drew from, Shaftesbury a claim for the force and significance of sympathy in society. He effectively "recited" Shaftesbury's insights into the power of sympathy and the ambivalence of its effects, which ranged from peace to panic, order to disorder. But whereas Shaftesbury endeavored to enchant human relations, Hume, employing the kind of systematic philosophical method that Shaftesbury dismissed, endeavored to "anatomize" and rationalize human relations. The result of that rationalization was not a sympathetic worldview but a new science of sympathy.

In Hume's "modern" philosophy, the aura of enchantment perceptibly dims. As I observe in the final section, that sense of disenchantment widens in Adam Smith's *Theory of Moral Sentiments* (1759). In modifying and qualifying Hume's account of sympathy, Smith (1723–1790) adopted Hume's factual approach and aimed to advance his project of a moral science founded on sympathy. I discuss Smith's moral philosophy only briefly before turning to Samuel Jackson Pratt (1749–1814), a lesser-known admirer of Hume's whose poem *Sympathy* went through multiple editions in 1781. Although Hume held up sympathy as a principle of social and moral order that could supply the place of the "uncertain and useless" principle of transcendental induction that he had exploded, Pratt's poem suggests a lingering attachment to Shaftesburian warmth in a cold Humean climate.⁶ *Sympathy* both recognizes the priority of the mind and reveals a desire for connection beyond it. The reality of total sympathetic connectedness insisted on by the Cambridge Platonists and others has become, in effect, a wish fulfillment, and poetry, we see again, becomes the medium in which that wish can be fulfilled. As the case of Pratt suggests, a significant danger of constructing a narrowly philosophical history of sympathy that begins with Shaftesbury and proceeds to Hutcheson, Hume, and Smith is that such a history lends itself readily to a limited and monolithic Weberian interpretation, a rising narrative of *Rationalisierung*. As sympathy became increasingly the focus of philosophical analysis, it was increasingly subject to rational containment. But by recognizing the deep and long-lasting relationship between sympathy and magic, and by shifting our attention from the philosophical to the literary, we can see that, in spite of the emergence of a new analytic of sympathy, it remained a principle in defiance, and in excess, of the rational, a power beyond the reach of reason.

HUME AND THE NEW SCIENCE OF SYMPATHY

Although the *Treatise* was first published anonymously, Hume identified himself in the introduction with an eminent group of names, outlining a philosophical-historical tradition. As Bacon is his point of origin, he begins with the Baconian critique of philosophical method with which Digby, too, aligned himself: "Amidst all this bustle 'tis not reason, which carries the prize, but eloquence," and so the true philosopher must be militant; he must be like "the men at arms, who manage the pike and the sword," rather than like "the trumpeters, drummers, and musicians of the army."[7] Bacon led the charge in natural philosophy, and Hume promises to continue it in moral philosophy: "And as the science of man is the only solid foundation for the other sciences, so the only solid foundation we can give to this science itself must be laid on experience and observation. 'Tis no astonishing reflection to consider, that the application of experimental philosophy to moral subjects should come after that to natural at the distance of above a whole century; since we find in fact, that there was about the same interval betwixt the origins of these sciences; and that reckoning from THALES to SOCRATES, the space of time is nearly equal to that betwixt my Lord BACON and some late philosophers in *England*, who have begun to put the science of man on a new footing." In a footnote he specifies these "late philosophers": "Mr. *Locke*, my Lord *Shaftsbury*, Dr. *Mandeville*, Mr. *Hutchinson*, Dr. *Butler*, &c."[8] Of these names, only two appear again in the *Treatise*, Locke's and Shaftesbury's. Shaftesbury's ontology was a crucial negative to Hume's project, but, independent of that ontology, as we shall see, Shaftesbury's ethics became a crucial positive. Whereas Shaftesbury aimed to conserve a sympathetic worldview, Hume sought to expose it as nothing more than a castle in the air. Having refuted and repudiated a universal idea of sympathy, which depended on an unphilosophical inductive leap, Hume reestablished sympathy on the level of the moral and of the psychological. Characterized as a readily observable fact, human sympathy was a principle of coherence capable of passing skepticism's test and so of restoring for the part the order removed from the whole.

In 1726, the year after he left the University of Edinburgh without graduating, Hume procured a copy of the third edition of *Characteristicks* (1723).[9] He appears to have admired what he later called "the sublimity of SHAFTESBURY," but in his essay "Of Superstition and Enthusiasm," Hume adopts a predominantly negative stance toward "the summit of enthusiasm," where "every whimsy is consecrated" and "the imagination swells with great, but confused conceptions."[10] Shaftesbury's rehabilitation of enthusiasm seems nowhere in evidence here, and if "great, but confused conceptions" are suggestive of sublimity, Hume in no way valorizes them. Hume's emphasis in the *Treatise* on "experience and observation"—on what he calls more expansively at the end of the introduction "a cautious observation of human life," as it manifests itself "in the common course of the world, by men's behaviour in company, in affairs, and in their pleasures"—comes into contrast with the Shaftesburian emphasis on *heightened* experience—an emphasis that, as we have seen, Fordyce and Thomson extended.[11] For Hume, in the heat of enthusiasm, confusion, not clarity, came. His second explicit reference to Shaftesbury occurs in the first book of the *Treatise* while he is criticizing "our propension to confound identity with relation," one "so great, that we are apt to imagine something unknown and mysterious, connecting the parts, beside their relation." Hume adds in a footnote, "If the reader is desirous to see how a great genius may be influenc'd by these seemingly trivial principles of the imagination, as well as the mere vulgar, let him read my Lord *Shaftsbury's* reasonings concerning the uniting principle of the universe, and the identity of plants and animals. See his *Moralists*: or, *Philosophical rhapsody*." In a consideration of the whole, it was improper, Hume goes on, to "add a *sympathy* of parts to their *common end*, and suppose that they bear to each other, the reciprocal relation of cause and effect in all their actions and operations."[12] For Hume, Shaftesbury's cosmic "reasonings" amounted less to a system than to a phantom. Shaftesbury did not discover "the uniting principle of the universe"; rather, he imagined it. Shaftesbury's assertion of "a *Universal* UNION, *Coherence*, or *Sympathizing* of Things" was no more than an errant fiction; universal sympathy was always already a figment of the imagination. The magic of sympathy did not inhere in the universe; rather, it was inserted there by a misguided mind, fantasizing "something unknown and mysterious." In the space of a footnote, Hume undertakes the disenchantment of the Shaftesburian world. Whereas Fordyce presented the disenchanted view only to try to refute it, Hume treats disenchantment as a factual reality. In locating the mystery within, he removes it from without. And in exploding the very foundation of Shaftesbury's philosophy, the idea of a universal, mystical coherence that was Shaftesbury's major inheritance from the Cambridge Platonists, Hume perhaps recognized that only an epithet as florid as "great genius" could salvage their philosophical relationship.

Though he identified Shaftesbury with the moderns in the introduction to the *Treatise*, Hume's critique of his worldview effectively consigned Shaftesbury to the ancients. Previous treatments of Humean sympathy have not recognized the significant relationship between Hume's analysis of the universal sympathy of the ancients and his modern analysis of psychological sympathy, which has been the nearly exclusive focus.[13] In book I, "Of the Understanding," "sympathy" appears for the first time in the work in a section entitled "Of the antient philosophy."[14] For Hume, the "antient philosophy," for which the Peripatetic stands in as a synecdoche, does not reveal an ancient cosmic wisdom but rather constitutes a massive case study in psychological error: "I am persuaded, there might be several useful discoveries made from a criticism of the fictions of the antient philosophy, concerning *substances, and substantial forms, and accidents, and occult qualities*; which, however unreasonable and capricious, have a very intimate connexion with the principles of human nature." The section concludes with an indictment of sympathy:

> But among all the instances, wherein the Peripatetics have shewn they were guided by every trivial propensity of the imagination, no one is more remarkable than their *sympathies, antipathies, and horrors of a vacuum.* There is a very remarkable inclination in human nature, to bestow on external objects the same emotions, which it observes in itself; and to find every where those ideas, which are most present to it. This inclination, 'tis true, is suppress'd by a little reflection, and only takes place in children, poets, and the antient philosophers. It appears in children, by their desire of beating the stones, which hurt them: In poets, by their readiness to personify every thing: And in the antient philosophers, by these fictions of sympathy and antipathy. We must pardon children, because of their age; poets, because they profess to follow implicitly the suggestions of their fancy: But what excuse shall we find to justify our philosophers in so signal a weakness?[15]

As Shaftesbury was "influenc'd by these seemingly trivial principles of the imagination," so the ancients "were guided by every trivial propensity of the imagination." Shaftesbury is a late addition to Hume's "children, poets, and . . . antient philosophers," a crew of imaginers more motley than Shakespeare's lunatics, lovers, and poets. The Peripatetics in Hume's account are, in effect, children who never grew up, accidental poets. They fail to make a distinction between human nature and the natural world; they mistake projection for perception and apprehension. Emotion is a distinctively human possession, a quality of subjects, not "external objects." Hume here follows Hobbes and Boyle in critiquing the scholastic tendency to conflate subjects and objects, but he differs from them in focusing less on the error than on the psychological "principles" and "propensities" underlying it. Hume does not simply dismiss Shaftesbury's conception of the world; he diagnoses it. The implication that Shaftesbury would have escaped Hume's critical attention if he had simply called himself a poet is a further, if subtle, suggestion that, however much it influenced other philosophers, Shaftesbury's philosophy was increasingly viewed as more consistent and congenial with the canons of poetry than with those of philosophy. For Hume, a sympathetic worldview properly belonged to the realm of art.

Hume developed his critique of a philosophical conception of universal sympathy most fully in his *Dialogues Concerning Natural Religion*, published posthumously, according to his wishes, by his nephew in 1779.[16] In the form in which he would have most naturally looked back to Shaftesbury—philosophical dialogue—Hume pointedly veered away from him. His *Dialogues* serves to debunk the "uniting" and totalizing logic on which *Characteristicks* was founded. In seemingly Shaftesburian fashion, the dialogues do not unfold "live" but are recounted to a mostly absent auditor. The narrator, Pamphilus, must thus reassure Hermippus that he has carefully remembered the participants' arguments and promises that he "shall not omit or confound any considerable Part of them in the Recital."[17] In the *Dialogues*, however, the Shaftesburian term "Recital" has none of its resonant Shaftesburian sense. The pastoral paradigm is abandoned, and Hume begins not in an Arcadian landscape conducive to rhapsodies on the sympathetic beauty and coherence of the whole but in "*Cleanthes*'s Library," from which the natural world is effectively shut out.[18] Hume's structural innovation was to turn philosophical dialogue into "trialogue," as the conversation unfolds among the skeptic Philo, the theist Cleanthes, and the fideist Demea, whose "introduction," as Prince argues, "transforms what had been the higher principle of adjudication—the third term—into the fallible character of the dogmatist, thus destroying the paradigmatic structure of religious dialogue," according to which the theist "converts" the skeptic or atheist by means of his protagonistic position and superior argumentation.[19] Hume does not show the skeptic and the theist ultimately coming together in a sympathetic process of mutual accommodation, as Shaftesbury had done. Hume's Philo represents a far more corrosive force than Shaftesbury's Philocles. The morphological and metrical parallelism of Shaftesbury's names, it might be observed, is a subtle suggestion of the prevailing sympathy between Theocles and Philocles; by apocope, Hume cancels that effect—"Philo," "Cleanthes," and "Demea" do not match up, and the sense of sympathy among them is less a matter of mystical communication than of constantly shifting rhetorical and strategic alignments, a matter of what Demea calls "Alliance."[20]

In Hume's *Dialogues* a universal sympathy is not revealed for the sake of rapture and devotion, as in *The Moralists*, but merely hypothesized for the sake of exposure and explosion. Philo temporarily adopts and naturalizes the Stoic-Platonic worldview in order to point up the artifice of Cleanthes's argument from design. "Now if we survey the Universe, so far as it falls under our Knowledge," Philo begins, with a qualification that is very much to his point, "it bears a great Ressemblance to an animal or organiz'd Body, and seems actuated with a like Principle of Life and Motion. . . . The closest Sympathy is perceiv'd throughout the entire System: And each Part or Member, in performing its proper Offices, operates both to its own Preservation and to that of the Whole. The World, therefore, I infer, is an Animal, and the Deity is the SOUL of the World, actuating it, and actuated by it."[21] Philo argues that this "Opinion, which . . . was maintain'd by almost all the Theists of Antiquity," appears truer than Cleanthes's "modern Theory" about the universe as a great machine only to make the point that both are fundamentally false.[22] As Philo plays out the cosmogonic logic of the ancient theory, Demea makes his point for him in the next part of the *Dialogues*: "But what wild, arbitrary Suppositions are these? What *Data* have you for such extraordinary Conclusions? And is the slight, imaginary Ressemblance of the World to a Vegetable or an Animal sufficient to establish the same Inference with regard to both? Objects, which are in general so widely different; ought they to be a Standard for each other?" Demea "catches" Philo's sentiment in a burst of what might be called anti-enthusiasm. Philo then fixes on Demea's keyword "*Data*": "I have still asserted, that we have no *Data* to establish any System of Cosmogony. Our Experience, so imperfect in itself, and so limited both in Extent and Duration, can afford us no probable Conjecture concerning the Whole of things."[23] Shaftesbury's "Method of Reasoning" was akin to Cleanthes's: "What we see in the Parts, we may infer in the Whole." But for Hume the part can never properly be "a Rule for the Whole."[24] In the final part of the *Dialogues*, by which point a vexed Demea has left the conversation—in a gesture that seems antithetical to the sociable ethic built into the form of philosophical dialogue as Shaftesbury conceived it— Hume returns to the idea of universal sympathy. Again it is the skeptic Philo who voices it:

> I ask the Theist, if he does not allow, that there is a great and immeasurable, because incomprehensible, Difference between the *human* and the *divine* mind: The more pious he is, the more readily will he assent to the Affirmative, and the more will he be dispos'd to magnify the Difference. . . . I next turn to the Atheist . . . ; and I ask him, whether, from the coherence and apparent Sympathy in all the parts of this world, there be not a certain degree of anal- ogy among all the operations of Nature, in every situation and in every age; whether the rotting of a Turnip, the generation of an animal, and the struc- ture of human thought be not energies that probably bear some remote anal- ogy to each other: It is impossible he can deny it: He will readily acknowledge it. Having obtain'd this Concession, I push him still farther in his retreat; and I ask him, if it be not probable, that the Principle which first arrang'd, and

still maintains order in this universe, bears not also some remote inconceivable analogy to the other operations of Nature, and among the rest to the Oeconomy of human Mind and Thought. However reluctant, he must give his Assent. Where then, cry I to both these Antagonists, is the Subject of your dispute: The Theist allows, that the original Intelligence is very different from human reason: The Atheist allows, that the original Principle of Order bears some remote Analogy to it. Will you quarrel, Gentlemen, about the degrees, and enter into a controversy, which admits not of any precise meaning, nor consequently of any determination?[25]

This is a devastating treatment of the idea of "Sympathy in all the parts of this world." Hume reduces the sympathetic worldview to a series of forced and far-fetched analogies. The collocation of "the rotting of a Turnip, the generation of an animal, and the structure of human thought" reduces what Foucault called "the vast syntax of the world" to a jumble of absurdity. Hume undoes not only Stoic-Platonic ontology but also, in effect, Shaftesburian aesthetics; Shaftesbury's beautiful branching tree has become Hume's rotten turnip. Hume chips away at a robust ontological conception of analogy phrase by phrase: "a certain degree of analogy," "some remote analogy," "some remote inconceivable analogy," and again "some remote Analogy." Merely "apparent," universal sympathy is neither a secure premise nor a satisfactory solution. Given its totalizing terms and aims, Hume suggests, Shaftesburian dialogue cannot but reach a dead end.

Shaftesbury's sympathetic whole is, in the final analysis, a false induction.[26] If the whole is mysterious, it is so only to the extent of our ignorance of it and its inaccessibility to us. As Hume writes in the final paragraph of *The Natural History of Religion*, which first appeared as one of *Four Dissertations*, published in 1757, "The whole is a riddle, an aenigma, an inexplicable mystery. Doubt, uncertainty, suspence of judgment appear the only result of our most accurate scrutiny, concerning this subject."[27] The "science of man," by contrast, was a subject about which, Hume claimed, certain judgments could be made.[28] In the second book of the *Treatise* Hume argues that human sympathy "is an object of the plainest experience, and depends not on any hypothesis of philosophy."[29] His theory, therefore, rests on an endless stream of "*Data.*" He invites his reader "to take a general survey of the universe, and observe the force of sympathy thro' the whole animal creation, and the easy communication of sentiments from one thinking being to another. In all creatures, that prey not upon others, and are not agitated with violent passions, there appears a remarkable desire of company, which associates them together, without any advantages they can ever propose to reap from their union. This is still more conspicuous in man, as being the creature of the universe, who has the most ardent desire of society, and is fitted for it by the most advantages. We can form no wish, which has not a reference to society."[30] Hume uses the same language in the *Dialogues*, but this "survey of the universe," unlike Philo's, yields a proper and reasonable conclusion; it is factual rather than rhetorical, because the whole here is really a part, one of which we have constant experience, "the whole animal creation." Hume makes no claim for a mystical, all-binding sympathy. The social does not, as in Shaftesbury and his followers, point to the cosmic, and vice versa. Sympathy is "the soul" of the social world alone.

In the *Treatise* the all-encompassing sympathy of Shaftesbury and of the ancients, critiqued and cast off in the first book, and Hume's own modern concept, developed in the second and third books, are structurally segregated, but they are dynamically related. At base, Hume conceives of sympathy as the transfer of emotions or inclinations. In the conception that he rejects, the transfer is imaginary rather than actual; a person transmits his or her own sentiments to a thing—whether a magnet, say, or the world—and supposes in error that it actually possesses them. Properly conceived, sympathy occurs only between "thinking beings." As Hume writes in the *Enquiry Concerning the Principles of Morals*, "There are a numerous set of passions and sentiments, of which thinking rational beings are, by the original constitution of nature, the only proper objects: and though the very same qualities be transferred to an insensible, inanimate being, they will excite not the same sentiments. The beneficial qualities of herbs and minerals are, indeed, sometimes called their *virtues*; but this is an effect of the caprice of language, which ought not to be regarded in reasoning."[31] Just as Hume sought to narrow the sphere of sympathy, so he sought to narrow the sphere of "virtue," to make it the subject of proper, modern moral inquiry. Accordingly, he centered his reasoning on the transfer of sentiments from one rational being to another. In the *Treatise* Hume begins his account of "the nature of *sympathy*" with a grand and sweeping claim:

> No quality of human nature is more remarkable, both in itself and in its consequences, than that propensity we have to sympathize with others, and to receive by communication their inclinations and sentiments, however different from, or even contrary to our own. This is not only conspicuous in children, who implicitly embrace every opinion propos'd to them; but also in men of the greatest judgment and understanding, who find it very difficult to follow their own reason or inclination, in opposition to that of their friends and daily companions.[32]

In Hume's psychology the minds of children are as receptive as they are projective. Whereas we grow out of, make art out of, or "suppress" the one "very remarkable inclination in human nature," that is, "to bestow on external objects the same emotions, which it observes in itself," we live out our lives acting on, or being acted on by, the true inclination of human sympathy. Hume applies the principles of his foregoing analysis "of the understanding" to account for the process of sympathy: "'Tis indeed evident, that when we sympathize with the passions and sentiments of others, these movements appear at first in *our* mind as mere ideas, and are conceiv'd to belong to another person, as we conceive any other matter of fact. 'Tis also evident, that the ideas of the affections of others are converted into the very impressions they represent, and that the passions arise in conformity to the images we form of them." For Hume, the experience of sympathy depends on, and confirms the fundamental truth of, relation. Our lively ideas of others' passions and the ease with which they are converted into "the very impressions they represent" depend on the relations of resemblance and conti-guity; we are so similar to other human beings and are often so close to them — in space, "blood," or "acquaintance" — that we readily sympathize with them.[33]

In identifying sympathy as the crucial dynamic of human nature, and in insisting on our fundamental relatedness to others, Hume founds in society the coherence that he has removed from the universe. Although he quibbled with Hume's account of sympathy in his *Essays on the Principles of Morality and Natural Religion* (1st ed., 1751), Henry Home, Lord Kames (1696–1782), ultimately reinforced it in referring to the "eminent principle of sympathy" as "the cement of human society"; sympathy, he boldly asserts, "connects persons in society by ties stronger than those of blood."[34] In the social sphere, the *"sympathy* of parts" that can only be imagined in the world at large is everywhere experienced and observed. The extraordinary weight that Hume places on the presence of human sympathy needs to be understood as a response to an absence that he himself in part had created. His evacuation of order on the level of the whole goes hand in hand with his establishment of order on the level of society. Having dispensed with the order of things, Hume philosophically embraces the connection of "persons in society." His insistent doubt about the former is remedied by his insistent — one might even say enthusiastic — confidence in the latter. Humean sympathy functions to hold together a narrower sphere set adrift from the inaccessible All.

HUME, SHAFTESBURY, AND THE POWER OF SYMPATHY

Hume's emphasis on the fundamentally social nature of humankind, his absolute claim that "we can form no wish, which has not a reference to society," suggests that, even as he dismissed Shaftesbury's view of the world, he drew from his view of society.[35] Whereas Hume rejected Shaftesbury's metaphysics, he accepted key elements of his ethics. Detached from its universal ontological foundation, Shaftesbury's ethics could stand on its own. Like Shaftesbury, Hume regarded Hobbes's "selfish system of morals" as fundamentally unnatural. Making self-love the driving force of human nature required an act of contortion or, indeed, of quasi-alchemical transmutation. Hume's expression of this point is a variation of Hutcheson's claim that the Hobbist "will rather twist Self-Love into a thousand Shapes, than allow any other Principle of Approbation than Interest."[36] "An Epicurean or a Hobbist readily allows," Hume writes, "that there is such a thing as friendship in the world, without hypocrisy or disguise; though he may attempt, by a philosophical chymistry, to resolve the elements of this passion, if I may so speak, into those of another, and explain every affection to be self-love, twisted and moulded, by a particular turn of imagination, into a variety of appearances."[37] Those who suspect that Hobbes and his ilk "cannot possibly feel the true sentiments of benevolence" will turn out to have been "very much mistaken," and in this sense Hobbes's system was belied by his own example—a point, we recall, that Shaftesbury made as well.[38] For Hume, sympathy, not self-love, is the true first principle, and maintaining otherwise is nothing but a misguided philosophical labor resulting from a fundamental misreading of the data. Our natural sympathy with others is plainly and universally evident.

In Hume's claim for the power and pervasiveness of human sympathy, we can see his reception of Shaftesbury most clearly and concretely. Soon after asserting in the *Inquiry* that "*the* CHARM *of kind Affection is superior to all other* Pleasure: since it has the power of drawing from every other Appetite or Inclination," Shaftesbury makes the claim for the communicative and diffusive nature of sympathy that made such a strong impression on Thomson: "It will be consider'd how many the Pleasures are, of *sharing Contentment and Delight with others*; of receiving it in Fellowship and Company; and gathering it, in a manner, from the pleas'd and happy States of those around us, from accounts and relations of such Happinesses, from the very Countenances, Gestures, Voices and Sounds, even of Creatures foreign to our Kind, whose Signs of Joy and Contentment we can anyway discern. So insinuating are these Pleasures of Sympathy, and so widely diffus'd thro' our whole Lives, that there is hardly such a thing as Satisfaction or Contentment, of which they make not an essential part" (*Character.*, 2:62). Hume recalls, and condenses, this passage in asserting near the end of the third book of the *Treatise* that the "principle of sympathy is of so powerful and insinuating a nature, that it enters into most of our sentiments and passions."[39] He has earlier insisted on "the force of sympathy thro' the whole animal creation," and the collocation "the force of sympathy" is a recurrent one in the *Treatise*.[40] In the *Enquiry Concerning the Principles of Morals*

Hume deemphasized the term "sympathy," frequently preferring "humanity," but the sense of power and force is undiminished: "Have we any difficulty to comprehend the force of humanity and benevolence? Or to conceive, that the very aspect of happiness, joy, prosperity, gives pleasure; that of pain, suffering, sorrow, communicates uneasiness?"[41] In going on to illustrate his point about the diffusiveness of sympathy, his claim that "the benevolent concern for others is diffused, in a greater or less degree, over all men, and is the same in all," Hume uses the example of the theater:

> In general, it is certain, that, wherever we go, whatever we reflect on or converse about, everything still presents us with the view of human happiness or misery, and excites in our breast a sympathetic movement of pleasure or uneasiness. In our serious occupations, in our careless amusements, this principle still exerts its active energy.
>
> A man who enters the theatre, is immediately struck with the view of so great a multitude, participating of one common amusement; and experiences, from their very aspect, a superior sensibility or disposition of being affected with every sentiment, which he shares with his fellow-creatures. . . .
>
> Every movement of the theatre, by a skilful poet, is communicated, as it were by magic, to the spectators; who weep, tremble, resent, rejoice, and are inflamed with all the variety of passions, which actuate the several personages of the drama.[42]

Here, after all, is Shaftesbury's *"moral Magick."* The poet achieves his effects by managing and directing the "active energy" of sympathy. The spectators run the gamut of sympathetic emotions communicated by the actors, who themselves have been "actuated" by the emotions communicated by the poet or playwright. What seems a "common amusement" is really common experience organized and particularized. We are constant spectators of one another and constantly present spectacles to one another. Social relation activates—and is ever reactivating— the magic of sympathy. Even in the cool climate of Hume's modern philosophy, we see here, the ancient associations of sympathy leave a mystical Shaftesburian trace.

For Hume, as for Shaftesbury, passivity is a consequence of the power of sympathy. Sympathy appears to happen to us or to act on us; we "receive by communication" the affections of others, as Hume puts it in his initial account in the *Treatise*. Humean sympathy thus retains an association with contagion. "The passions are so contagious," he writes, "that they pass with the greatest facility from one person to another, and produce correspondent movements in all human breasts."[43] In the *Enquiry* Hume posits a "set of mental qualities, which, without any utility or any tendency to farther good, either of the community or of the possessor, diffuse a satisfaction on the beholders, and procure friendship and regard. Their immediate sensation, to the person possessed of them, is agreeable. Others enter into the same humour, and catch the sentiment, by a contagion or natural sympathy."[44] The epidemic here is one of "kindly emotion," and the patient is happy to be infected. Earlier in the *Enquiry* Hume cites the same passage on the contagious quality of emotion from the *Ars Poetica* that Digby made so central to his account of human sympathy: "The human countenance, says Horace, borrows smiles or tears from the human countenance."[45] In Hume's writing, "contagion" has not only a metaphorical sense, inimical to Digby's all-encompassing materialist approach, but also a meliorative one. For Digby, writing from a Stoic perspective, we recall, the power of sympathy was a problem; it threatened to short-circuit our recourse to reason, to subordinate the mind to the heart. For Hume, who unsettled the supremacy of reason, who cast doubt on "the magnanimous firmness of the philosophic sage," and who argued that the philosophy of Epictetus was "only a more refined system of selfishness," the power of sympathy was a crucial positive; without its "great influence" on us, sympathy could not be, as Hume concluded, "the chief source of moral distinctions."[46] Our approbation and disapprobation depend on our keen and continual impressions of the experience of others. If, "from a cold insensibility, or narrow selfishness of temper," a person "is unaffected with the images of human happiness or misery," Hume reasoned, "he must be equally indifferent to the images of vice and virtue." And yet such a person could hardly be said to exist; some sympathize more often or more tenderly than others, but "none are so entirely indifferent to the interest of their fellow-creatures."[47] Sympathy enables us to distinguish between what benefits society and what harms it. Digby, by contrast, regarded sympathy as no more than a source of moral confusion.

Yet Hume did recognize and reflect on the danger that sympathy posed to society, and here, too, he looked back to Shaftesbury. "Popular sedition, party zeal, a devoted obedience to factious leaders," Hume writes, "these are some of the most visible, though less laudable effects of this social sympathy in human nature."[48] Shaftesbury, we recall, considered "the very Spirit of *Faction*" simply "the Abuse or Irregularity of that *social Love*, and *common Affection*, which is natural to Mankind." Hume referred more directly to this passage from *Sensus Communis* in his essay "Of Some Remarkable Customs," where he borrows Shaftesbury's figure of "*Wheels within Wheels*," suggesting the tendency in human nature to "seek a narrower Sphere of Activity" in which to sympathize and confederate with others (*Character.*, 1:72).[49] Hume reached a conclusion about human nature similar to Shaftesbury's, but from a different social context;

Hume's experience of "particular clubs and companies" in Edinburgh above all vividly demonstrated the *"close Sympathy* and *conspiring Virtue."*[50] He seized on Shaftesbury's discussion of the formation of factions and parties as a source of further corroborative data. The "instances of popular tumults, seditions, factions, panics, and of all passions, which are shared with a multitude," confirm "the influence of society in exciting and supporting any emotion." Our happiness, Hume insisted, depends on this "influence," but—and here we can sense Shaftesbury's *Letter Concerning Enthusiasm* in the background—the same influence also leads to "the most ungovernable disorders."[51] The power of sympathy tends to the good of society, but it also has the potential to undermine it.

Hume's moralization of human sympathy, I have been suggesting, is to a significant extent consistent with Shaftesbury's, but to imply that Hume merely knocked the ontology out of Shaftesbury's scheme and adopted the rest wholesale is to distort the very core of Hume's moral project. Breaking away from what he perceived as the esoteric, scholastic irrelevancies of natural philosophy, Shaftesbury was not interested in developing a "science," even of human nature, or in conducting "careful and exact experiments."[52] As we have seen, he inveighed against the philosopher who undertook the kinds of inquiries into the passions that "might possibly qualify him to give Advice to an Anatomist or a Limner, but not to *Mankind* or to *Himself*" (*Character.*, 1:181). Hume, too, steered clear of a purely physiological analysis of the passions, but in spirit he identified with the anatomist.[53] In the final paragraph of the *Treatise* he writes, "The anatomist ought never to emulate the painter: nor in his accurate dissections and portraitures of the smaller parts of the human body, pretend to give his figures any graceful and engaging attitude or expression," but the anatomist, "however, is admirably fitted to give advice to a painter; and 'tis even impracticable to excel in the latter art, without the assistance of the former." Hume then goes on to conclude that "the most abstract speculations concerning human nature, however cold and unentertaining, become subservient to *practical morality.*"[54] Shaftesbury favored a different climate. Turning away from a "cold and unentertaining" philosophy, he preferred to paint his morals in the warmth of the Arcadian sun. Hume's decision to pursue "the most abstract speculations concerning human nature," which proved a commercially costly one, was rooted in his determination to give his moral philosophy a scientific status.[55] The result was an analysis of sympathy that was far more detailed and developed than Shaftesbury's. In his attempt to capture and clarify the mechanism of sympathy, Hume was in a sense closer to Digby than to Shaftesbury, but in the end Digby's natural-philosophical approach was taken over and significantly reconceived by the actual anatomists, by those working in the neurophysiological tradition of

Thomas Willis and others. In the opening section of his *Observations on Man* (1749), David Hartley (1705–1757) refers twice to the "Writings of Physicians and Anatomists," which provided a base of support for his "vibrational" account of *"the Pleasures and Pains of Sympathy."*[56]

Developing a "moral anatomy," Hume acknowledged a debt to his English predecessors but he also saw himself as producing something new, and here his treatment of and claim for sympathy were crucial. As the *Treatise* proceeds, Hume's account of sympathy becomes increasingly complex and ramified, even taxonomic. Whereas at first sympathy emerges as a principle of communication or contagion that is experienced passively, Hume goes on to specify "different kinds of sympathy," including a far more active one.[57] In his discussion of pity, which he defines as "a sympathy with pain," he writes, "When a person of merit falls into what is vulgarly esteem'd a great misfortune, we form a notion of his condition; and carrying our fancy from the cause to the usual effect, first conceive a lively idea of his sorrow, and then feel an impression of it, entirely overlooking that greatness of mind, which elevates him above such emotions, or only considering it so far as to encrease our admiration, love and tenderness for him."[58] Here Hume's emphasis shifts from emotional susceptibility to imaginative activity; note his use of the verb "conceive," in contrast to "receive," the verb that stands out from his initial discussion of sympathy. This shift sets up Hume's subsequent distinction between "limited" and "extensive sympathy." In extensive sympathy, the imagination assumes a broad, creative power.[59] Ultimately the more Hume emphasizes conscious mental activity, the less magical sympathy begins to seem—and the more remote from Shaftesbury's *"moral Magick."* Even when Hume seems to be reciting Shaftesbury—"Every movement of the theatre, by a skilful poet, is communicated, as it were by magic, to the spectators"—we sense the relative disenchantment. Whereas Shaftesbury was seeking to widen the sphere of magic by aestheticizing it, Hume is merely using it as a convenient point of reference. Hume's "as it were" subtly measures the distance between the *Enquiry* and Cudworth's *True Intellectual System*, where the magic of sympathy was vitally real. Shaftesbury, as we have seen, endeavored to preserve that vitality by various means. Even as Hume widely recognized the "force of sympathy," however, in his philosophy the Shaftesburian endeavor largely lost its charm.

For Hume, the anti-Epicureanism that provided such a strong motive to the preservation and perpetuation of a magical, vitalist worldview, which the Cambridge Platonists and their followers and Shaftesbury and his followers held in common, was founded on a false premise. In the *Enquiry Concerning Human Understanding*, which first appeared under the title *Philosophical Essays*

Concerning Human Understanding (1748), "Epicurus" rehearses the argument of the anti-Epicureans, who "paint, in the most magnificent colours, the order, beauty, and wise arrangement of the universe; and then ask, if such a glorious display of intelligence could proceed from the fortuitous concourse of atoms."[60] This was the very kind of poetic "painting" that Turnbull called for, as we saw in the previous chapter. But in their painting the anti-Epicureans "forget, that this superlative intelligence and benevolence are entirely imaginary, or, at least, without any foundation in reason."[61] Entertaining the Epicurean hypothesis about the universe in the *Dialogues*, Philo asks, "Is it not possible that it may settle at last, so as not to lose its Motion and active Force (for that we have suppos'd inherent in it) yet so as to preserve an Uniformity of Appearance, amidst the continual Motion and Fluctuation of its Parts?"[62] Hume suggests that the sympathy and design of the whole are no more than the fanciful figures the anti-Epicureans have imposed on a "Uniformity of Appearance" that *could* proceed from a fortuitous concourse of atoms. At the same time, he maintains that this metaphysical debate does not involve or impinge on "the security of good morals, or the peace and order of society."[63] In Hume's philosophical writing we see the breakup of the all-embracing, all-related conceptual "system"—with its idealizing, harmonious coordination of physics, ethics, and divinity—that the Cambridge Platonists bequeathed to Shaftesbury. In spite of the philosophizing and "painting" of Shaftesbury and the Shaftesburians, as Hume puts it, "*Epicurus*'s old Questions are yet unanswer'd."[64]

FACTS AND FAIRY SCENES

By the time that *The Theory of Moral Sentiments* appeared in 1759, Adam Smith had known Hume for about a decade. Smith seems to have been accused of reading Hume's irreligious *Treatise* at Oxford in the 1740s, and he proceeded to extend Hume's commitment to a "science of man" while at the same time he restored sympathy to the central place in that science it had had in the *Treatise* and lost in the *Enquiry Concerning the Principles of Morals*.[65] Sympathy is the central fact on which Smith's moral theory is founded. "That we often derive sorrow from the sorrow of others," Smith writes, echoing Hume, in the opening paragraph of the *Theory*, "is a matter of fact too obvious to require any instances to prove it."[66] Smith then goes on to take a Humean empirical approach to refine Hume's account of sympathy. The refinement is particularly evident when he adapts Hume's musical analogy—the analogy that, as we have seen, was called on to do so much philosophical work in the previous century. At the beginning of the third part of the third book of the *Treatise*, Hume begins "considering a-new the nature and force of *sympathy*." "The minds of all men are similar in their feelings and operations," he writes, "nor can any one be actuated by any affection, of which all others are not, in some degree susceptible. As in strings equally wound up, the motion of one communicates itself to the rest; so all the affections readily pass from one person to another, and beget correspondent movements in every human creature."[67] The appeal to resonance here is not made as part of a larger claim for cosmic truth but rather is meant merely to illuminate the matter at hand; the analogy is not an ontological key but a "heuristic tool."[68] Hume balances "motion" with "movements"; the idea of "communication" applies to both vibrations and affections.

Smith recalls this passage early in the *Theory*. Of the object of sympathy, or "the person principally concerned," Smith writes,

> He longs for that relief which nothing can afford him but the entire concord of the affections of the spectator with his own. To see the emotions of their hearts, in every respect, beat time to his own, in the violent and disagreeable passions, constitutes his sole consolation. But he can only hope to obtain this by lowering his passion to that pitch, in which the spectators are capable of going along with him. He must flatten, if I may be allowed to say so, the sharpness of its natural tone, in order to reduce it to harmony and concord with the emotions of those who are about him. What they feel, will, indeed, always be, in some respects, different from what he feels, and compassion can never be exactly the same with original sorrow; because the secret consciousness that the change of situations, from which the sympathetic sentiment arises, is but imaginary, not only lowers it in degree, but, in some measure, varies it in kind, and gives it a quite different modification. These two sentiments, however, may, it is evident, have such a correspondence with one another, as is sufficient for the harmony of society. Though they will never be unisons, they may be concords, and this is all that is wanted or required.[69]

For Smith, the "strings" of our minds cannot be "equally wound up," as in Hume's account; passion differs from vibration because it is subject to mind, the "secret consciousness" that necessarily modifies it.[70] Whereas Hume had claimed that the converted impression of the spectator "acquires such a degree of force and vivacity as to become the very passion itself," Smith insists that "mankind, though naturally sympathetic, never conceive, for what has befallen another, that degree of passion which naturally animates the person principally concerned."[71] When Smith looks back to Hume's Horatian account of sympathetic contagion, he revises it subtly, but significantly: "The passions, upon some occasions, may seem to be transfused from one man to another, instanta-neously, and antecedent to any knowledge of what excited them in the person principally concerned. Grief and joy, for example, strongly expressed in the look and gestures of any one, at once affect the spectator with some degree of a like painful or agreeable emotion. A smiling face is, to every body that sees it, a cheerful object; as a sorrowful countenance, on the other hand, is a melancholy one."[72] Smith carefully qualifies Hume's account: "*may seem* to be transfused," "*with some degree* of a like painful or agreeable emotion" (my emphases). Because of the reality of human uniqueness, there can be no perfect echo or reflection of "original" emotion, and so we engage in a process of mutual accommodation—a process that, as we have seen, Shaftesbury appealed to in order to resolve the philosophical tensions of *The Moralists*. We strive to harmo-nize with others, and the harmonies that we produce, however imperfect, produce a larger harmony, "the harmony of society."[73] Smith effectively replaces Humean "unison" with the more active and accurate notion of "concord." In revising Hume's account, in applying Hume's own principles of "*mitigated* scepticism" to it, one might say, Smith was attempting to move Hume's theory of sympathy further in the direction of the scientific.[74]

Smith was undoubtedly Hume's most important and influential follower, and Smith's account of sympathy has been variously and fruitfully explicated. In closing I want to turn to the work of a far less obvious, and far less influential, follower of Hume's, Samuel Jackson Pratt. Pratt became a preacher, then an actor, then a writer. In 1777, the year after Hume's death, he wrote *An Apology for the Life and Writings of David Hume*. In the prefatory letter he quotes Smith's assessment of Hume "'as approaching as nearly to the idea of a perfectly wise and virtuous man, as perhaps the nature of human frailty will permit'" and specifies the "object" of his work as "a confirmation of that assertion, as well as a philo-sophical plea for the justice on which it is founded."[75] Pratt proceeds as if what he is doing is risky and anticipates how it will be received "in this suspicious age"; readers will expect his apology "to be either abstruse, or difficult, or else dangerous, and deistical."[76] But, he assures them, it is none of these. Hume emerges from Pratt's apology as the ultimate antihypocrite, one who maintained perfect "consistency" in his life and in all of his writings. But Pratt also wants to canonize Hume as a consummate moralist. "It is impossible for the sentiments of the elegant Tillotson, or the orthodox Addison," he writes, "to be more the champions of every part of conduct, which tends to the welfare of the social world, than those sentiments which are to be collected from Hume." It is hard to imagine that this assertion would have won general assent. When Pratt repeats this claim, he barely tempers his enthusiasm: "It hath, generally, been thought that, our author carried this mental geography, as he calls it, too far into the realms of scepticism, and into the abstruse, bewildering deserts of uncheurful metaphysics. Yet, however ardent he was in speculations of this abstract and diffi-cult nature, no one will deny, that he drew the form of virtue, upon all occasions, as the most lovely and estimable of all objects."[77] In identifying with the anato-mist rather than with the painter, however, Hume himself acknowledged that "drawing" the form of virtue was not his chief aim. In a letter to Hutcheson from 1739 he appealed to this distinction in responding to one of Hutcheson's objec-tions to what would soon be published as the third book of the *Treatise*: "What affected me most in your Remarks is your observing, that there wants a certain Warmth in the Cause of Virtue, which, you think, all good Men wou'd relish, & cou'd not displease amidst abstract Enquirys."[78] Pratt endeavored to assert the "Warmth" that Hutcheson found lacking. But to do so was, in effect, to replace Hume's scalpel with Shaftesbury's brush. The natural climate of Humean philos-ophy, as we have seen, was cool by comparison with the Shaftesburian.

In 1781, four years after his *Apology* appeared, Pratt published a poem entitled *Sympathy; or, A Sketch of the Social Passion*, which went through five editions that year. The poem bears no mention of Hume, and, indeed, the mise-en-scène provided in the introduction evokes no writer more than Shaftesbury. Rivers contends that "the crucial decades for Shaftesbury's popularity were the 1720s to the 1750s" and that "by the time of the 1773 Baskerville edition, the last edition of the century published in the British Isles, Shaftesbury's popularity was fading,"[79] but Pratt's poem suggests that Shaftesburianism still retained a vital warmth. The poet has come to a villa to see a friend, who is not there: "The fairest productions of animated nature were before him. They occupied the same spot. He was seated in the midst of them. His heart dilated. If, as seems to be admitted, a virtuous enthusiasm be necessary to the proper enjoyment of such scenery, the Critic of Nature will hardly know how to be offended, should he find, that here and there have been indulged effusions, which, if closely examined when the mind is cold, may be found not altogether in strict connec-tion."[80] With its Shaftesburian milieu and Shaftesburian performance of "virtuous enthusiasm," Pratt's poem aims to imbue Humean sympathy with the warmth that Hutcheson missed—and that Pratt could not provide discursively on Hume's behalf in the *Apology*. It was the "cold reasoner," Pratt wrote, who tried to "disprove / These varied powers of sympathetic love"; Pratt's Hume did the very opposite, but his reasoning was cold nevertheless.[81]

Sympathy, Pratt concedes, may lose some of its charm "if closely examined when the mind is cold." But he asks his reader to sympathize with him. If the

poem lacks the consistency that he so admired in Hume's works, Pratt should
be forgiven, for he has done all "in the cause of Benevolence."[82] If the poem
strikes the cold mind as in need of an editor, Pratt should be indulged, for,
"zealous to prove the powers of Universal Sympathy, the writer felt the sollici-
tudes of an author, united with those of a philanthropist. Of course, the idea of
obliterating what had any chance of cementing the social affections was too
painful to be adopted."[83] The painter requires, and receives, a license unavailable to the anatomist. The sense of Shaftesburian enchantment settles on the
reader almost immediately:

> And yet to touch me various powers combine,
> Here summer revels with a warmth divine;
> The bloomy season every charm supplies,
> From earth's rich harvest crown'd with cloudless skies.[84]

Pratt's warm world has "Charms in abundance." The heavens touch the earth,
and both "touch" the speaker-poet. The indefinite appeal to "various powers"
furthers an idea of mystical participation. Like Shaftesbury, Pratt universalizes
the social and socializes the universal:

> Instinct, or Sympathy, or what you will,
> The social principle is active still;
> Of every element it glows the soul,
> Touches, pervades, and animates the whole;
> Floats in the gale, surrounds earth's wide domain,
> Ascends with fire, and dives into the main.[85]

The old elements—air, earth / fire, water—come together here in a cosmological conceit, as Pratt's couplets assume a particularly Popean quality. Whereas
in his introduction Pratt can be seen to conform to Humean bounds in
"sketching" the "Sympathetic Principle" as influencing "the whole animal
creation,"[86] here he shows a Shaftesburian enthusiasm in extending sympathy
more broadly and absolutely to "the whole." Pratt's emphasis on enchantment
reinforces the link to Shaftesburian tradition: "Oh power of powers, whose
magic thus can draw / Earth, air, and ocean, by one central law." The "sacred
force of heav'n-born Sympathy" extends "Above, below," and even the "sordid,"
a Thomsonian keyword, cannot deny that force: "Spite of your little selves,
when virtue charms, / To nature true, the social passion warms."[87] Virtue has an
irresistible "charm" that operates on the world as a whole.

And yet elsewhere in *Sympathy* Pratt locates that magic within. In giving
priority to "fancy," he takes a more Humean approach to sympathy:

> Whence then the gloom that gathers in the sky?
> Whence the warm tear now starting to the eye?
> Whence then th' apparent change when friends depart?
> 'Tis FANCY striking on the feeling heart:
> 'Tis varied Fancy, whose aetherial wand
> Bids plastic nature move to her command:
> Oh should I follow where *she* leads the way,
> What magic meteors to her touch would play![88]

Here Pratt describes the mind conjuring matter. It is not "plastic nature," as in Cudworth's system, that wields the "aetherial wand" but "varied Fancy."[89] The sympathy between the speaker and the natural world is not real, only "apparent." He earlier refers to the "shrubs and bow'rs" around him as "fix'd productions of th' unconscious plain," which "no gentle sympathies can know, / But as the planter bends them learn to grow." Sympathy in this case is not inherent but artificial, cultivated. It is also a product of art: "As poets sing, thus Fancy takes her range, / Whose fairy fables can the system change." In and of itself, the "system" is "unconscious." When a poet dies, we imagine the weeping of the muses and the "solemn dirge" of the raven, but in reality there is no such change. In a striking expression of disenchantment, Pratt writes, "Yet separate facts from fairy scenes like these, / Nature, we find, still keeps her first decrees."[90] Suddenly the temperature has dropped. In this moment of unwonted coolness, the factual bias of Hume and Smith makes its presence felt.

Just as quickly, however, Pratt makes an about-face. The speaker experiences a kind of antiskeptical recoil: "But, is it Fancy ALL! what, no reserve? / From one dull point can nature never swerve? / Is change of seasons all the change she knows?" In his reluctance to accept the immutability and insensibility of nature, the speaker turns from the mind and the eye to the heart, a consoling and compensatory movement that I have suggested was central to the organization of Thomson's *Seasons*:

> Say, is it Fancy's vision works the charm,
> When these blest objects lose their power to warm?
> Ah! no; from other sources springs the smart,
> Its source is here, hard pressing on my heart.
> Yes, 'tis the heart which rules the roving eye,
> And turns a gloomy to a cloudless sky;
> The soft magician governs every scene,
> Blossoms the rock, or desolates the green.[91]

A more general magic is reinstated as a matter of feeling rather than of fancy. The sonic effects of the sequence "here, hard . . . heart" are emphatic. But even as Pratt goes on to suggest that "truth herself destroys the bloom of May, / When death or fortune tears a friend away,"[92] the "source" remains within; the truth is ultimately inward.

At the end of *Sympathy*, Pratt's speaker leaves the charming setting of his "effusions," as Philocles and Theocles do at the end of *The Moralists*. He mourns the absence of his dear friend and hopes that somehow his feeling words will be conveyed "by SYMPATHY."[93] It is this absence that generates the poem, but the poem generates the sense of a much larger absence. What Pratt conveys in the end is less the reality of a universal sympathy than a yearning for it, both psychological and spiritual, a yearning in a world of "facts" for "fairy scenes." The cold, factual approach of Hume and Smith, the poem suggests, leaves something to be desired—a desire that perhaps only poetry itself, with its "power to warm," can now fulfill. As magic was increasingly located in the mind, the poetic functioned to return it to the world—if to a world of its own making.

The world-making power of art, establishing by means of the imagination a new coherence, has long been recognized as a guiding theme of the Romantics. Art and "the imaginative faculty which produces art," in M. H. Abrams's classic formulation, came to be "the reconciling and unifying agencies in a disintegrating mental and social world of alien and warring fragments."[94] Considering the long-term fortunes of analogy, Wasserman similarly emphasizes the Romantic drive toward unification or reunification: "The divine analogy remained for the eighteenth century the relational norm of image and value, and when it finally collapsed through over-much probing, it was obvious to the Romantic that his first task was to put the two worlds together again."[95] More recently David Quint, with Goethe's *Faust* in mind, has referred to the Romantics' quest to renew the "romance of the world."[96] Yet the new romance, set against enlightened philosophies "sheathd in dismal steel," as Blake would have it, could not be the same as the old. The Romantics' inspiriting of the old mystical sympathies—one thinks especially of Coleridge's fascination with occultist and Platonic traditions—is a subject that warrants far more attention than it can receive here, but it is my hope that the present book might shine new light on it.

In its various turns and equivocations, Pratt's *Sympathy* offers us an instructive insight into the history of its titular subject, a history defined, as we have seen over the course of this book, by perpetual contest—between the movements of enchantment and disenchantment, mystification and rationalization, universalization and specification, enthusiastic idealization and wistful realization, heightened expression and cool exposition. We have followed these complex movements from Digby's philosophical and theological discourses to Hume's, from Cavendish's utopian fictions to Fordyce's, from Milton's cosmological poetry to Thomson's, from More's and Cudworth's philosophical systems to Shaftesbury's philosophical rhapsodies. In so doing, we have seen how variously and ambivalently sympathy has been represented, and we have seen that those variations and ambivalences do not settle into a simple dichotomy between the natural and cosmic on one hand and the moral and social on the other, between a sixteenth-century episteme or Elizabethan world picture on one hand and an eighteenth-century culture of sensibility on the other. In illuminating representations of sympathy at the intersection of physics and ethics, I have treated sympathy as a principle of dynamics, implicated over time in an intellectually and ideologically significant interplay of orders. This interplay has not yet received sufficient attention in critical studies of eighteenth-century literary and philosophical writing, where the legacy of historiographic isolation remains. "From Hutcheson in the 1720s to Wordsworth in the 1790s," Sean Gaston has written, "there is an incessant call for sympathy to be at the heart of morality and an unending confession of the insufficiency of sympathy. This continual need to imagine, idealize, and describe what is lacking suggests that we need to re-examine the eighteenth century as a century in *search* of sympathy."[97] This is a point well taken, but, as I have tried to demonstrate, the "search" for sympathy did not begin in the 1720s, nor was it limited to the domain of morals. Sympathy was sought in the self and society, but also in the stars and spheres, in matter as well as spirit, in the distilling house as well as the drawing room. The "unending confession of the insufficiency of sympathy" in the eighteenth century needs to be understood in the broader intellectual and historical context of a search for sympathy in the world—and a widening doubt about finding it.

When Pratt's speaker declares, "All, SYMPATHY, is thine," he is, one might say, simply giving voice to the zeitgeist, but behind this expression lies a doubt and concern about what is his, about where the subject stands in relation to the world.[98] This eighteenth-century concern, I have argued, has deep roots in the intellectual debates of the seventeenth century, roots that must be uncovered if we are to gain a fuller historical and rhetorical understanding of sympathy. Against pressing doubt, Pratt asserted an emphatic all: "This then is clear, while human kind exist, / The social principle must still subsist, / In strict dependency of one on all."[99] This is a poetic claim that brooks no opposition, countering doubt with clarity and necessity. The "social principle" of sympathy, as fundamental to the species as life itself, has been made to bear the weight of the world.

CODA: HAWTHORNE'S DIGBY AND MARY SHELLEY'S MILTON

At the age of thirteen, Victor Frankenstein comes upon "a volume of the works of Cornelius Agrippa," and, allured by its "wonderful facts," he proceeds "to procure the whole works of this author, and afterwards of Paracelsus and Albertus Magnus."[1] As Frankenstein's autobiographical narrative proceeds, a subtle but pointed contrast emerges between these works and the academic "discourse" of "potassium and boron, of sulphates and oxyds" he receives at the University of Ingolstadt, mere "terms" that are meaningless to him (23). Frankenstein cannot understand them because he has missed the professor's preparatory lectures, but Mary Shelley's broader suggestion here is that the nuts and bolts of modern chemistry have no charm, and produce no wonder, in and of themselves. The same group of occultists appears in Nathaniel Hawthorne's story "The Birth-mark." As Aylmer attempts to remove the "Crimson Hand" from Georgiana's cheek, she passes part of the time looking at his books, "the works of the philosophers of the middle ages, such as Albertus Magnus, Cornelius Agrippa, Paracelsus, and the famous friar who created the prophetic Brazen Head."[2] For Shelley and Hawthorne, the occultist tradition has entered into what might be called the scientist's library. But it is not inert, not merely historical. Acting primarily on the imagination, the occultist tradition provides not instruction so much as aspiration. It represents a vital—but morally perilous—alternative to a technical and trivial-seeming modern science that has divorced knowledge from power.

Over the course of the seventeenth and eighteenth centuries, as we have seen, the magic of sympathy increasingly found a cultural refuge in the aesthetic sphere. By way of conclusion I want to extend this narrative of enchantment to the nineteenth century. Shelley and Hawthorne have figured prominently in critical discussions of sympathy over the past three decades, and the general practice has been to set the two authors' representations of sympathy in the context of eighteenth- and nineteenth-century social, intellectual, and aesthetic developments. I will argue that Shelley and Hawthorne actively engaged not only with earlier natural and magical traditions of sympathy but also, and more specifically, with the conceptions of sympathy of two of the seventeenth-century authors central to this book, Milton and Digby. As a principle of mystical connection, sympathy has not simply disappeared, or reappeared as a matter of nostalgia; rather, it emerges as a vital force at the center of Shelley's *Frankenstein* (1st ed., 1818) and Hawthorne's *Scarlet Letter* (1850). The two novels sharply expose the inadequacy of the disenchantment narrative for the history of sympathy and serve to reinforce the claim that, long after the ages of Ficino and Fludd, sympathy retained the aura of the magical.

At the beginning of "The Birth-mark," the narrator explains that Aylmer, "a man of science—an eminent proficient in every branch of natural philosophy," has recently fallen in love. He has, Hawthorne writes, "made experience of a spiritual affinity, more attractive than any chemical one."[3] Having experimented with the affinities of matter, Aylmer comes to experience an emotional or "spiritual" affinity with another human being. In *Frankenstein* Shelley similarly appeals to different registers and valences of "attraction." As Walton writes of his journey to the North Pole in the opening letter of the novel's outermost narrative frame, "I may there discover the wondrous power which attracts the needle" (7). In his pursuit of the secret of magnetic attraction, however, Walton keenly experiences an absence of human sympathy. "I have no friend, Margaret," he laments to his sister; "when I am glowing with the enthusiasm of success, there will be none to participate my joy. . . . I desire the company of a man who could sympathize with me; whose eyes would reply to mine" (10). The arrival of Frankenstein fulfills that desire: "For my own part, I begin to love him as a brother; and his constant and deep grief fills me with sympathy and compassion. He must have been a noble creature in his better days, being even now in wreck so attractive and amiable" (15). However diminished and debilitated Frankenstein may now be, he remains a vital source of "attraction." Seeking "the wondrous power which attracts the needle," Walton discovers "the wondrous power" that attracts *him*; he is sympathetically drawn to Frankenstein, and in the idea of eyes "replying" to one another, as if magnetically, Shelley immediately establishes a more mystical idea of sympathy. In effect, she transforms a phrase that appeared in her father's novel *Caleb Williams*—"There was a magnetical sympathy between me and my master"—into a guiding conceit.[4] In developing that conceit, Shelley looked to and drew from *Paradise Lost*, energetically engaging with Milton's complex representation of sympathy as a principle of "genetic" connection. But whereas Milton goes on to redeem the mystical, physical conception of sympathy that binds Adam to Eve at the Fall and Satan to Sin and Death, Shelley narrates no such redemption, ultimately suggesting that Frankenstein and his creature have nothing more than a mystical connection. The truer moral bond that Adam and Eve develop in the aftermath of the Fall never develops between Shelley's primary couple. Although language presents itself to the creature as a means of establishing such a bond, his newfound linguistic and rhetorical expertise fails to produce anything deeper or more lasting than a transitory feeling of connection. Shelley's emphasis is finally on the failure of sympathy.

Just as Shelley looked back to Milton in her representation of sympathy as a potentially occult force, so, I argue, Hawthorne looked back to Digby, named in *The Scarlet Letter* as a kind of alter ego to his "man of science," Roger Chillingworth. The plot of the novel turns on the idea of sympathetic action at a distance. Seemingly localized in the letter itself, sympathy powerfully connects Hester Prynne and Arthur Dimmesdale, and both to the mystery of sin. Hawthorne subordinates a secret and secretive science of sympathy, associated with and practiced by Chillingworth, to an open ethic of sympathy, which Hester and Dimmesdale share at the novel's climax. And yet, as Hawthorne ultimately suggests, the two sympathies are not so easily distinguished and set apart. However rationalized and moralized, sympathy, we see, remains a principle of enchantment, of occult dynamics. The intertwining of the moral and the magical in *The Scarlet Letter* provides us with one final warrant for thinking of the history of sympathy in terms of integration rather than isolation.

Critics have put forward a variety of possible sources for Shelley's sustained inquiry into and emphasis on human sympathy in *Frankenstein*. David Marshall has asserted that "Rousseau is the theoretician of sympathy who most significantly informs Mary Shelley's investigation"; Janis Caldwell has made a case for Shelley's engagement with "Romantic theories of physiologic sympathy"; and Jeanne Britton has argued that *Frankenstein* "brings Smith's sympathy firmly into the genre of the novel."[5] Marshall's focus on Rousseau is driven in part by a polemical impulse. "It has been generally accepted," he writes, "that *Frankenstein* is deeply informed by Mary Shelley's reading of Milton. I will argue that the figure of Rousseau is an even more pervasive and significant presence in the novel."[6] I do not see much to be gained by tallying points; it is by now clear that on a metatextual level *Frankenstein* is inhabited by a variety of "significant presences." But it seems to me worthwhile to reassert the presence of Milton for two reasons: first, because Shelley also used Milton to explore the topic on which Marshall claims Rousseau was especially important to her—sympathy—and, second, because Milton provided Shelley with a conceptual bridge between the "principles of Agrippa," which Frankenstein in his philosophical experience deems "entirely exploded," and the "modern" principles of theorists like Adam Smith.

I have emphasized the word "attractive" in Walton's reflection on Frankenstein—"He must have been a noble creature in his better days, being even now in wreck so attractive and amiable"—but the central term here is "creature," a keyword in the novel that highlights both the act of creation at its core and the central relationship established by that act, between Frankenstein and his creature. In *Paradise Lost*, we recall, Milton represents sympathy as essentially "creaturely"; it is an affective connection originating in the act and fact of creation. The creature appeals to Frankenstein for sympathy on the basis of creaturely connection: "You, my creator, detest and spurn me, thy creature, to whom thou art bound by ties only dissoluble by the annihilation of one of us" (65). At the same time that Shelley is prefiguring the novel's end here, she is also appealing to a logic analogous to Adam's in his justification of falling with Eve. The ontological "ties" between creator and creature should, the latter reasons, enforce emotional ties. "Remember," he remonstrates with Frankenstein, "that I am thy creature: I ought to be thy Adam; but I am rather the fallen angel, whom thou drivest from joy for no misdeed. Every where I see bliss, from which I alone am irrevocably excluded" (66). Whereas the creature believes he should have the relationship with Frankenstein that Adam has with God, Frankenstein has turned him into a solitary Satan through, he insists, no fault of his own. The creature turns to art to establish a sympathetic connection that he claims does exist in nature, or, rather, did exist until his creator severed it. "Let your compassion be moved," the creature implores, "and do not disdain me. Listen to my tale: when you have heard that, abandon or commiserate me" (66–67). He attributes to narrative in particular and language in general a positive sympathizing power. Yet his narrative itself reinforces his claim for a sympathy deeper than, and prior to, language. The creature's program of distance learning courtesy of the De Lacey family includes, among other things, a lesson about creaturely connectedness, "how the father doated on the smiles of the infant . . . ; how all the life and cares of the mother were wrapt up in the precious charge; how the mind of youth expanded and gained knowledge; of brother, sister, and all the various relationships which bind one human being to another in mutual bonds" (81). This last phrase significantly alludes to Milton's "Relations dear, and all the Charities / Of Father, Son, and Brother," which, as we have seen, became a kind of locus classicus in the eighteenth century. The creature considers himself cruelly and unnaturally deprived of "Relations dear."

The creature's discovery of a copy of *Paradise Lost* establishes the verisimilitude of such an allusion and reinforces its point. As he explains, "I often referred the several situations, as their similarity struck me, to my own. Like Adam, I was created apparently united by no link to any other being in existence; but his state was far different from mine in every other respect. He had come forth from the hands of God a perfect creature, happy and prosperous, guarded by the especial care of his Creator. . . . Many times I considered Satan as the fitter emblem of my condition; for often, like him, when I viewed the bliss of my protectors, the bitter gall of envy rose within me" (87). Through readerly sympathy the creature becomes more fully aware of the creaturely sympathy that he has been unjustly denied, as if he were the protagonist of an atheodical version of *Paradise Lost*. The creature's use of "apparently" in the phrase "created apparently united by no link to any other being in existence" is critical; he is insisting that he has a strong and immediate "link" to Frankenstein and that he deserves "the especial care" of his own creator. The creature's sympathetic identification with Satan only intensifies when the De Lacey family rejects him. Having read book 4 of *Paradise Lost*, he proceeds to reenact it. His bitter experience "Of sympathie and love" is not Eve's—"'but how was I terrified,'" he reflects, "'when I viewed myself in a transparent pool!'" (76)—but Satan's. Like Satan, the creature curses his lack of connection to the world outside him: "'Oh! What a miserable night I passed! the cold stars shone in mockery, and the bare trees waved their branches above me; now and then a sweet voice of a bird burst forth amidst the universal stillness. All, save I, were at rest or in enjoyment: I, like the arch fiend, bore a hell within me; and finding myself unsympathized with, wished to tear up the trees, spread havoc and destruction around me, and then to have sat down and enjoyed the ruin'" (92). He is like Satan drawn to "pittie thus forlorne / Though [he] unpittied" (*PL*, 4.374–375).

But just as Milton provides the creature with a means of expressing his suffering, so he also provides him with a way out of it. Before running afoul of the De Laceys, the creature occasionally permitted himself, as he puts it, "'to ramble in the fields of Paradise, and dared to fancy amiable and lovely creatures sympathizing with my feelings and cheering my gloom; their angelic countenances breathed smiles of consolation. But it was all a dream: no Eve soothed my sorrows, or shared my thoughts; I was alone. I remembered Adam's supplication to his Creator; but where was mine? he had abandoned me, and, in the bitterness of my heart, I cursed him'" (88). Here the creature refers directly to Adam's appeal to God for a "human consort" based on his expressed need for

"Collateral love, and deerest amitie" (*PL*, 8.392, 426). Given Frankenstein's abandonment of him, the creature has been deprived of the opportunity to express his own need for creaturely sympathy. In the presence of his creator, he effectively repeats Adam's appeal to God, entreating Frankenstein, " 'You must create a female for me, with whom I can live in the interchange of those sympathies necessary for my being' " (98). The creature's appeal to sympathy produces sympathy in Frankenstein, but not of the deep, durable kind that the creature believes to be his due. Shelley suggests that language can go only so far. "His words had a strange effect upon me," Frankenstein relates; "I compassionated him, and sometimes felt a wish to console him; but when I looked upon him, when I saw the filthy mass that moved and talked, my heart sickened, and my feelings were altered to those of horror and hatred. I tried to stifle these sensations; I thought, that as I could not sympathize with him, I had no right to withhold the small portion of happiness which was yet in my power to bestow" (99–100). Frankenstein's "compassion" is fleeting and fugitive; the sympathy that the creature desperately desires, he concludes, is beyond his capacity.

And yet, even as Frankenstein denies it, he and the creature share a deeper, more mystical sympathy, which Shelley carefully develops. "There can be no community between you and me," Frankenstein tells the creature, but there remains a "magnetical sympathy" between them. It is in this sense that Shelley evokes not only the sympathetic connection between God and Adam in Milton's epic but also that among Satan, Sin, and Death. In conceiving of the birth and animation of the creature, in other words, Shelley looked not only to the electrical experiments of Galvani and Aldini but also to the allegorical experiments of Milton. Like animal magnetism, electricity did not supersede sympathy as a mystical principle but in effect supported and sustained it—indeed, Mesmer advanced the magnetic theory that Van Helmont had used to account for the action of the weapon salve.[7] Like Death, Shelley's creature is a "Sin-born Monster" (*PL*, 10.596), and, like Sin, he is born without a mother. Investigating the deep and complex relationship between sympathy and gender, Shelley suggests that Frankenstein's counter-evolutionary exclusion of the mother in the process of reproduction bears materially on the problem of sympathy in the novel, for both creature and creator. As Anne Mellor has argued, "Mother Nature," disregarded and misused by Frankenstein, "fights back"; she "prevents him from creating a 'normal' creature by denying him the maternal instinct or the emotional capacity for empathy."[8]

In his unholy anti-Trinity, Milton provided Shelley with a striking vision not only of unnatural creation but also of a "connatural" sympathy more magical than moral, one that ultimately sets an occult physics of connection against a positive ethics of connection.⁹ Anticipating Frankenstein, Satan essentially abandons his creature, leaving nature to run its course in the absence of nurture, to the extent that Milton must stage a grim recognition scene to prevent the family romance from devolving into a Greek tragedy. In Shelley's novel, Frankenstein and the creature interact at both a physical and a textual distance. Frankenstein is mystically informed of the murder of his brother: "The figure passed me quickly, and I lost it in the gloom. Nothing in human shape could have destroyed that fair child. *He* was the murderer!" (48). This moment is suggestive of that when Adam "divines" Eve's fall, but the creature is less like Eve here than like Sin and Death. When he exclaims, " 'I, like the arch fiend, bore a hell within me; and finding myself unsympathized with, wished to tear up the trees, spread havoc and destruction around me, and then to have sat down and enjoyed the ruin,' " the creature approaches the "situation" of Sin and Death after the Fall, who seek "to destroy," to "waste and havoc yonder World" (*PL*, 10.611, 617). In the phrase "bore a hell within me," he is echoing both Milton and his creator's own echo of Milton. With William's death and the arrest of Justine in mind, Frankenstein laments, "Anguish and despair had penetrated into the core of my heart; I bore a hell within me, which nothing could extinguish" (57). The text of Milton's epic becomes itself a means of expressing the secret sympathy between Frankenstein and the creature. Shelley uses her own narrative to further this effect. To take just a single example, Frankenstein relates, "My abhorrence of this fiend cannot be conceived. When I thought of him, I gnashed my teeth" (60). However much he may "abhor" the creature, he is mystically drawn to him here, communicating with him at a distance. After Frankenstein abandons his project of making a female companion, the creature "gnashed his teeth in the impotence of anger" (116). It is as though creature and creator share a single sympathetic mind.

At the end of the novel, creature and creator reunite, but only, as the former predicted, when one of them has been "annihilated." Again Shelley sets the artful manipulation and solicitation of sympathy against the ideal of a natural, noncontingent sympathy, as desirable as it is elusive. Confronting the creature, Walton is "at first touched by the expressions of his misery," but the creature conclusively declares, "No sympathy may I ever find" (154). He holds open only the dimmest hope of a creaturely sympathy beyond life, addressing his dead creator, "and if yet, in some mode unknown to me, thou hast not yet ceased to think and feel . . . , " and looking ahead to that time when his "spirit will sleep in peace; or if it thinks, it will not surely think thus" (156). The novel's closing phrase, "darkness and distance," an alliterative pairing suggestive of Milton's "distance and distaste," can be seen to sum up its representation of the failure of sympathy. By the end of the novel, Shelley has alluded to nearly all the major moments and modes of sympathy in Milton's epic, but she ultimately expresses a more pessimistic view of it, as if we are all longing for a prelapsarian state of sympathetic connectedness and looking for it, again and again, in vain. For all of its power, sympathy cannot in the end transcend the distance that matters most.

In the early American novel *The Power of Sympathy* (1789), whose title alone can be seen to constitute a kind of implicit rebuke to Foucault, William Hill Brown established a tragic conflict between emotional and physical, or biological, connection, drawing sympathy into the orbit of incest.[10] Like Shelley after him, Brown found in *Paradise Lost* an authoritative model for a more magical idea of sympathy, one that was inexorably bound up with tragedy. As Harriot writes to Harrington, the lover who is revealed to be her brother, "ALLIED by birth, and in mind, and similar in age—and in thought still more intimately connected, the sympathy which bound our souls together, at first sight, is less extraordinary. Shall we any longer wonder at its irresistible impulse?—Shall we strive to oppose the *link of nature* that draws us to each other?"[11] As any attentive reader of Milton would recognize at this moment, hearing Adam's deterministic appeal to mystical attraction, the path of "irresistible impulse" led to disaster.

Milton's importance to early American culture has been well established, but in developing his own complex conception of sympathy, Hawthorne turned less to Milton than to another seventeenth-century British writer as a significant model—Digby. Hawthorne referred directly to Digby in his biographical sketch of Roger Chillingworth, the principal antagonist of *The Scarlet Letter*. "His first entry on the scene," he writes, "few people could tell whence, dropping down, as it were, out of the sky, or starting from the nether earth, had an aspect of mystery, which was easily heightened to the miraculous. He was now known to be a man of skill; it was observed that he gathered herbs, and the blossoms of wild-flowers, and dug up roots and plucked off twigs from the forest-trees, like one acquainted with hidden virtues in what was valueless to common eyes. He was heard to speak of Sir Kenelm Digby, and other famous men,—whose scientific attainments were esteemed hardly less than supernatural,—as having been his correspondents or associates."[12] Chillingworth's affinity with Digby is established earlier in the novel when Hawthorne narrates his "first entry on the scene." Introduced as "a man of skill in all Christian modes of physical science," a kind of Digbeian virtuoso, Chillingworth defines his particular brand of physic as a combination of the naturalistic and the alchemical: "'My old studies in alchemy,' observed he, 'and my sojourn, for above a year past, among a people well versed in the kindly properties of simples, have made a better physician of me than many that claim the medical degree'" (96, 97). He goes on, "'I have learned many new secrets in the wilderness, and here is one of them,—a recipe that an Indian taught me, in requital of some lessons of my own, that were as old as Paracelsus'" (98). Of the few suggestions in Hawthorne's works that he had a specific knowledge of Digby's, this one is especially compelling.[13] Hawthorne here evokes Digby's "genealogie of the Powder of Sympathy" in *A Late Discourse*, where Digby relates that he learned the "secret" of the powder from "a religious *Carmelite*, that came from the *Indies*, and *Persia* to *Florence*" after he had had the "opportunity to do an important courtesie to the said Fryer"; it was this "courtesie" on Digby's part "which induced him to discover unto me his secret."[14] Paracelsus, we recall, was often associated with sympathetic cures in the sixteenth and seventeenth centuries, and Hawthorne appears to echo both Digby's identification of an "Indian" source and, more strikingly, Digby's claim to have learned the "secret" by virtue of what Hawthorne calls "requital." Hawthorne intimates a strong mystical "association" between Chillingworth and Digby.

In his reading of *The Scarlet Letter*, Gordon Hutner identifies what he calls "a rhetoric of secrecy," but, in the course of developing that reading, he leaves out the complex *history* of secrecy.[15] Hutner observes that the "conjunction" of the terms "secret" and "sympathy" is "habitual in Hawthorne's prose," but, as we have seen, that conjunction had a long and eventful history before the age of Hawthorne. Linking sympathy to "a Romantic ideal of communication," Hutner traces Hawthorne's emphasis on sympathy back to "his college instruction in the eighteenth-century Scottish philosophers," and, indeed, there is a record of Hawthorne's having checked out a copy of Smith's *Theory of Moral Sentiments* from the Salem Athenaeum in 1827.[16] The tendency in critical treatments of Hawthornean sympathy has been to associate it on one hand with Smith's moral philosophy and on the other with what Robert Levine refers to as "contemporaneous formations of sympathy," especially those produced in, and in response to, a politically charged culture of reform in mid-nineteenth-century America.[17] But Hawthorne's deep interest in history, both regional and global, should alert us to the need for a more expansive genealogy. In a reading attentive to contemporaneous medical culture, Taylor Stoehr has suggested that Chillingworth "anachronistically borrows homoeopathic techniques to treat both body and soul of his patient Arthur Dimmesdale," but there is no need to resort to "anachronism" here.[18] In explicitly referring to Digby and alluding to his account of sympathy powder, Hawthorne is suggesting that Chillingworth is skilled in the mystical art of *sympathy*. Although he wishes to inflict no further punishment on Hester and Pearl, Chillingworth explains, he is desperately determined to avenge himself on the child's father: "'I shall seek this man, as I have sought truth in books; as I have sought gold in alchemy. There is a sympathy that will make me conscious of him. I shall see him tremble. I shall feel myself shudder, suddenly and unawares. Sooner or later, he must needs be mine!'" (100–101). Chillingworth conceives of his target as a kind of base metal, the lead on which he will work his alchemical magic, and he believes the father's identity will be revealed to him by virtue of sympathetic "contagion," the transfer of a somatic state at a distance. In asking Hester to keep his own identity concealed from the community, Chillingworth enforces on her a "secret bond" that she instinctively resists, at least in part because it puts her in a position analogous to that of his would-be patient.

Incapable of an open, affectionate moral sympathy, Chillingworth can enter into the minds and hearts of others only secretly and magically. Hawthorne keenly develops the irony that he who makes use of sympathy in one sense has no use for it in another.[19] For Hawthorne, Digby represents the man of *unfeeling*. Punning on his own name—a characteristic mode of Hawthornean allegoresis—Chillingworth admits, "'The world had been so cheerless! My heart was a habitation large enough for many guests, but lonely and chill, and without a household fire'" (100). As for Aylmer, so for Chillingworth there is an antithetical relationship between the idea of a domestic "fire" and a chemical one; what he cannot kindle in the "household" he burns and distills in the laboratory. Once he had taken up residence with Dimmesdale, the narrator relates, Chillingworth "arranged his study and laboratory; not such as a modern man of science would reckon even tolerably complete, but provided with a distilling apparatus, and the means of compounding drugs and chemicals, which the practiced alchemist knew well how to turn to purpose" (148). And so the mystical "practice" of spiritual alchemy begins. Hawthorne represents in spatial terms the process of secret, sympathetic interchange, or "intercourse" (160), that is simultaneously occurring on the spiritual level: "With such commodiousness of situation, these two learned persons sat themselves down, each in his own domain, yet familiarly passing from one apartment to the other, and bestowing a mutual and not incurious inspection into one another's business" (148). As Chillingworth mystically penetrates into the interior life of Dimmesdale, so the patient has an occult insight into the physician. In the case of Dimmesdale, Hawthorne appeals to a neurophysiological concept of sympathy: "Mr. Dimmesdale, whose sensibility of nerve often produced the effect of spiritual intuition, would vaguely become aware that something inimical to his peace had thrust itself into relation with him. But old Roger Chillingworth, too, had perceptions that were almost intuitive; and when the minister threw his startled eyes towards him, there the physician sat; his kind, watchful, sympathizing, but never intrusive friend" (151).

The word "sympathizing" is ironically ambivalent here. In an expression that would be at home in a wide range of seventeenth-century texts, not least Marvell's "Dialogue between the Soul and the Body," Chillingworth goes on to attribute Dimmesdale's mysterious condition to a "strange sympathy betwixt soul and body" (158). The sympathy between Chillingworth and Dimmesdale is itself "strange," a matter of occult communication and interaction.

Sympathetic action at a distance is a driving principle of *The Scarlet Letter*. Over the course of the novel, Hawthorne maps out a complex of sympathetic interactions in multiple directions. The scarlet letter enables Hester to sympathize at a wide distance. As the narrator explains, "It now and then appeared to Hester,—if altogether fancy, it was nevertheless too potent to be resisted,—she felt or fancied, then, that the scarlet letter had endowed her with a new sense. She shuddered to believe, yet could not help believing, that it gave her a sympathetic knowledge of the hidden sin in other hearts" (110–111). The sympathetic "sense" that Chillingworth has gained from his studies Hester has gained from her sins. "Sometimes," Hawthorne writes, "the red infamy upon her breast would give a sympathetic throb, as she passed near a venerable minister or magistrate, the model of piety and justice," whereas at other times "the electric thrill would give her warning,—'Behold, Hester, here is a companion!'" (111). Puritan New England is full of the secret sharers of sin; piety and hypocrisy are inseparably twinned. This passage recalls Hawthorne's "Young Goodman Brown," in which the title character enters into the forest and comes upon a "witch-meeting" in which many of the town worthies participate. The minister cries out, "'By the sympathy of your human hearts for sin, ye shall scent out all the places—whether in church, bed-chamber, street, field, or forest—where crime has been committed. . . . It shall be yours to penetrate, in every bosom, the deep mystery of sin.'"[20] But the passage has a more immediate textual sympathy with one later in *The Scarlet Letter*, when Hawthorne describes a "burden" weighing on Dimmesdale that "gave him sympathies so intimate with the sinful brotherhood of mankind; so that his heart vibrated in unison with theirs, and received their pain into itself, and sent its own throb of pain through a thousand other hearts, in gushes of sad, persuasive eloquence" (163). Hawthorne describes an occult process of moral resonance. In a discussion of *The Marble Faun*, Emily Budick has characterized Hawthornean sympathy as "passive, quiet, like art itself," but here Hawthorne's emphasis is on the reverberating power of sympathy.[21] Partaking of her sin, Dimmesdale has a more particular sympathy with Hester, and she with him. Hester is said to move Dimmesdale, "instinctively exercising a magnetic power over a spirit so shattered and subdued" (214). On Dimmesdale's own breast, on "that spot, in very truth, there was, and there had long been, the gnawing and poisonous tooth of bodily pain" (168). Like the body and the soul, Hester and Dimmesdale are in secret dialogue.

Hawthorne puts sympathy in a more clearly positive light in two principal scenes, by which he suggests, however provisionally, something like the triumph of the protagonists' nature over the antagonist's art. The first scene takes place at night, the second in the light of day. In the seeming secrecy of darkness, Dimmesdale ascends the scaffold on which Hester has been shamed, and soon thereafter she appears with Pearl. After inviting them to join him, Dimmesdale touches Pearl's hand, and a vital, sympathetic reaction occurs: "The moment that he did so, there came what seemed a tumultuous rush of new life, other life than his own, pouring like a torrent into his heart, and hurrying through all his veins, as if the mother and the child were communicating their vital warmth to his half-torpid system. The three formed an electric chain" (172). The sympathy between mother and child was, as we have seen, a matter of long-standing philosophical speculation, and here, in a newer galvanic idiom, Hawthorne has the father complete the circuit. But it is soon broken when Dimmesdale refuses Pearl's request to re-form their "electric chain" in "the daylight of this world" (173). The idea of "a meeting-point of sympathy" is both reliteralized and redeemed when Hester, Pearl, and Dimmesdale meet in daylight in the forest.[22] The public eye is absent, but there is nevertheless a new openness and transparency in their "magic circle" (220). Hester reveals the secret of Chillingworth's identity, and Dimmesdale realizes that on some level he has been aware of it all along: "'I did know it! Was not the secret told me in the natural recoil of my heart, at the first sight of him, and as often as I have seen him since?'" (211). As the scene in the forest unfolds, this idea of a secret sympathy gives way to one more openly and truly heartfelt. Hawthorne adds a chapter to Dimmesdale's extraordinary saint's, or martyr's, life: "to this poor pilgrim, on his dreary and desert path, faint, sick, miserable, there appeared a glimpse of human affection and sympathy, a new life, and a true one, in exchange for the heavy doom which he was now expiating" (218). The adjective "human" has an emphatic force here. Hester and Dimmesdale regain a full humanity at this moment. He does not ask so much as announce, "'Do I feel joy again?'" (219).

Hawthorne expresses the power of this new sympathy by extending it to the forest as a whole. Nature sympathizes with the couple in their woe and then in their sudden joy: "And, as if the gloom of the earth and sky had been but the effluence of these two mortal hearts, it vanished with their sorrow. All at once, as with a sudden smile of heaven, forth burst the sunshine, pouring a very flood into the obscure forest, gladdening each green leaf, transmuting the yellow fallen ones to gold. . . . The course of the little brook might be traced by its merry gleam afar into the wood's heart of mystery, which had become a mystery of joy" (220). Chillingworth's dark alchemical art has been itself "transmuted" into a natural process, of illumination and aurification. Hawthorne comments, "Such was the sympathy of Nature—that wild, heathen Nature of the forest, never subjugated by human law, nor illumined by higher truth—with the bliss of these two spirits!" (220). The forest is similarly responsive to Pearl; it becomes her "playmate" (221). The birds and animals all embrace her. She adorns herself with flowers that offer themselves to her and so becomes "a nymph-child, or an infant dryad, or what-ever else was in closest sympathy with the antique wood" (222). The sympathetic meeting of the novel's true family bends the arrow of time backward; they are transported to a time and place of original and absolute connectedness.[23]

In the midst of this rhapsody, however, Hawthorne also gives us a sign that sympathy might not have the power he has ascribed to it, a power that those of the historical period in which the novel is set might have found easier to credit: "A wolf, it is said,—but here the tale has surely lapsed into the improbable,—came up, and smelt of Pearl's robe, and offered his savage head to be patted by her hand. The truth seems to be, however, that the mother-forest, and these wild things which it nourished, all recognized a kindred wildness in the human child" (222). This is a rather complex narratorial move. It is as if, in his enthusiasm, Hawthorne finds himself overreaching and retreats—a movement, which I observed particularly in Milton's *Nativity Ode*, highlighting the crucial and recurrent tension in the history of sympathy between desire and reality. Hawthorne seems to experience a paroxysm of ambivalence, establishing distance twice in proximity, passing from the parenthetical "it is said" to the more elabo-rately parenthetical "but here the tale has surely lapsed into the improbable." Yet even as he pulls back from the extreme verge of imagined sympathetic response, Hawthorne puts forward an alternative account that is hardly more "probable." The pattern of overreaching and retreat is repeated on a more minute level in the phrase "The truth seems to be." In the terms of Pratt's *Sympathy*, Hawthorne, in the course of painting his "fairy scene" in the forest, has an uncomfortable brush with "fact." The enchantment is framed as an aesthetic embellishment. When she sees Pearl in her floral state, Hester muses, "'It is as if one of the fairies, whom we left in our dear old England, had decked her out to meet us'" (223). This recalls a passage earlier in the novel, when Pearl is similarly associated with fairyland. Mr. Wilson asks her, "'Dost know thy cate-chism? Or art thou one of those naughty elfs or fairies, whom we thought to have left behind us, with other relics of Papistry, in merry old England?'" (132). Both of these passages suggest what Walsham refers to as the "rhetoric of 'disen-chantment,'" and Hawthorne goes out of his way to expose it as a hypocritical

falsehood. His Puritan world teems with suggestions and manifestations of the
supernatural. The New Englanders who claim that when they left England they
left magic and superstition—and Catholicism—behind are the very same ones
who spread the rumor that the scarlet letter "was not mere scarlet cloth, tinged in
an earthly dye-pot, but was red-hot with infernal fire, and could be seen glowing
all alight, whenever Hester Prynne walked abroad in the night-time" (112). But if
the Puritans are hypocritical, Hawthorne's contemporaries, his audience, are
skeptical; theirs is not an enchanted worldview but a probabilistic one. Hawthorne
locates magic in the historical past and subjects it to modern standards of aesthetic
judgment.

Or so the truth seems to be. In Hawthorne's keen interest in not only the
theory but also the history of sympathy, and in his multiform, multivalent representations of it, we can see a determined resistance to the disenchantment of the
world. After relating the supernatural fancies of "the vulgar" about the scarlet
letter, Hawthorne adds, "And we must needs say, it seared Hester's bosom so
deeply, that perhaps there was more truth in the rumor than our modern incredulity may be inclined to admit" (112). In his modern desire for the supernatural,
Hawthorne challenges "modern incredulity." In the introductory portion of *The
Scarlet Letter*, "The Custom-House," set in his own age, Hawthorne tells the
tale of his discovery of the scarlet letter in a dusty corner. He finds in the midst
of a "mysterious package" what he indifferently calls "a certain affair of fine red
cloth, much worn and faded." He proceeds to put it on his breast, and, as he
relates, "I experienced a sensation not altogether physical, yet almost so, as of
burning heat; and as if the letter were not of red cloth, but red-hot iron." He
reflects, "Certainly, there was some deep meaning in it, most worthy of interpretation, and which, as it were, streamed forth from this mystic symbol, subtly
communicating itself to my sensibilities, but evading the analysis of my mind"
(62). The Puritans did not leave the magical and the mystical behind in England,
and, Hawthorne suggests, neither did their descendants leave them behind in
the Puritan age. The magic and the mystery transcend both time and space.
The scarlet letter is a "curious relic" of interest to the "local antiquarian," but
Hawthorne wants us to understand that it is also much more, a "mystic symbol,"
a site and source of enduring power, its meaning "subtly communicating itself"
to those who come into its sphere of activity. The power of the scarlet letter is
the power of sympathy. It cannot be effaced or forgotten.

NOTES

INTRODUCTION

1. Shakespeare, *The Tempest*, 3.2.136. Quotations of Shakespeare's poems and plays follow *The Riverside Shakespeare*. All subsequent references are to this edition and will be given parenthetically in the text.
2. On Prospero's magic, see especially Mowat, "Prospero, Agrippa"; Orgel, ed., *The Tempest*, 20–22; and Mebane, *Renaissance Magic*, 174–199.
3. Like the correspondence between Lear's madness and the storm in act 3, this is a version of a Renaissance commonplace. See Nohrnberg, *Analogy*, 784. On the commonplace, see Foucault, *Order of Things*, 22–23.
4. Lucretius, *De rerum natura* 2.1–4. If Shakespeare turned to Florio's Montaigne for Gonzalo's speech on "th' commonwealth" in act 2, he might well have had Montaigne in mind in composing Miranda's lines in act 1. In *"Of profit and honestie,"* Montaigne cites the first two lines of the second book of *De rerum natura* in the context of discussing "compassion": "for in the midst of compassion, we inwardly feele a kinde of bitter-sweete-pricking of malicious delight, to see others suffer; and children feele it also: *Suave mari magno turbantibus aequora ventis, / E terra magnum alterius spectare laborem.*" Florio, *Essayes*, 475. Miranda's "I have suffered / With those that I saw suffer" is suggestive of Florio's "see others suffer." But Shakespeare seems to be exalting Miranda's virtue by subtracting Lucretius's and Montaigne's emphasis on the "bitter-sweete-pricking of malicious delight." On the subsequent importance of the passage from Lucretius, see Hathaway, "Lucretian 'Return upon Ourselves.'"
5. On Miranda's sympathy, see also James, "Dido's Ear," 367–370.
6. *Oxford English Dictionary*, s.v. "sympathy," 3b. All subsequent references to the OED will be given parenthetically in the text by definition number.
7. See, among other studies, Marshall, *Surprising Effects of Sympathy*; Barnes, *States of Sympathy*; Stern, *Plight of Feeling*; Jaffe, *Scenes of Sympathy*; Rai, *Rule of Sympathy*; Gottlieb, *Feeling British*; Ablow, *Marriage of Minds*; and Chandler, *Archaeology of Sympathy*. James's "Dido's Ear" is a notable exception, but in gesturing toward "a

prehistory for the problem of sympathy familiar in eighteenth-century moral philosophy" (361), and in limiting her inquiry to the theater and theatricality, James passes over
the problem of sympathy familiar in seventeenth-century natural philosophy and natural magic—a problem that Shakespeare actively dramatized. Engaged in a project of
historiographic revision parallel to mine, Mary Floyd-Wilson has more recently called
attention to the early modern "theater's staging of occult phenomena in everyday life."
Focusing on a group of plays that "repeatedly stage the question of whether women
have a privileged access to nature's secrets but also whether women's bodies possess
and transmit hidden, occult properties," she illuminates the deep and complex relationship between sympathy and gender in the age of Shakespeare. Floyd-Wilson,
Occult Knowledge, 24. I discuss another exception, Victoria Kahn's work on romance
in the 1650s, later in the Introduction.

8. Skinner, "Meaning and Understanding," 34, 35.
9. Skinner, "Reply to My Critics," 283.
10. On the complexity of the distinction between *res* and *verba*, and its embeddedness
    in both classical rhetorical theory and Aristotelian linguistic theory, see Vickers,
    "'Words and Things,'" 287–335.
11. Spitzer, *Essays in Historical Semantics*, 1.
12. See Williams, *Keywords*.
13. Shakespeare does use the word elsewhere, usually in the sense of "agreement, accord,
    harmony, consonance" (*OED* 2). We might wonder about the fact that most of his uses
    appear before 1600. Especially suggestive among the early instances are those in *Titus
    Andronicus* and *The Rape of Lucrece*. After the violation of Lavinia, Titus strains to sym-
    pathize with her—"Or shall we cut away our hands like thine? / Or shall we bite our
    tongues, and in dumb shows / Pass the remainder of our hateful days?"—before bemoan-
    ing to the gathered members of his family, "O, what a sympathy of woe is this" (3.1.130–
    132, 148). In the phrase "sympathy of woe" Shakespeare in effect tropes the word's
    etymology. Sympathy and woe, indeed, are guiding concerns in *Titus*, from Tamora's
    early plea for pity to Lavinia's parallel plea in act 2 to the peculiar fly scene in act 3 and
    Marcus's dark allusion to Romans 12:15, "To weep with them that weep doth ease some
    deal, / But sorrow flouted at is double death" (3.1.244–245), to his desperate lamentation
    in act 4, "O heavens, can you hear a good man groan / And not relent, or not compassion
    him?" (4.1.123–124), to Aemilius's feeling words toward the end of act 5, "My heart is not
    compact of flint nor steel / Nor can I utter all our bitter grief, / But floods of tears will
    drown my oratory, / And break my utt'rance, even in the time / When it should move ye
    to attend me most, / And force you to commiseration" (5.3.88–93). On sympathy and
    consent in *The Rape of Lucrece*, see Arkin, "'That Map.'" The directions of influence
    and the chronology itself are hard to pin down, but I would speculate that wider interest
    in the word "sympathy" was generated by the appearance of Josuah Sylvester's transla-
    tions of Du Bartas starting from 1590. A significant number of English uses of "sympa-
    thy" and its variants before that time appear in translations of French texts. The French
    sympathie is recorded as early as the fifteenth century. The *OED*'s earliest recorded use,
    in the Latinate form "sympathia," is from 1567. "Sympathia" appeared thirty years earlier
    in Elyot's Latin-English dictionary. Elyot, *Dictionary of Syr Thomas Eliot*, Bb3r.

14. Marshall, *Surprising Effects of Sympathy*, 3–4.
15. Ablow, *Marriage of Minds*, 8.
16. For examples of such groupings of terms, see James, "Dido's Ear," 371–372; and Staines, "Compassion in the Public Sphere," 92.
17. Konstan, *Pity Transformed*, 106.
18. See McNamer, *Affective Meditation*.
19. Sharpe, *Remapping Early Modern England*, 43.
20. Hippocrates, *Nutriment* 23; Hippocrates, *Ancient Medicine*, 350–351.
21. Lapidge, "Stoic Cosmology," 176. On Zeno, see Long, "Astrology: Arguments Pro and Contra," 167; and Couliano, *Eros and Magic*, 112. On *sympatheia* in ancient thought, see Weidlich, "Sympathie in der antiken Litteratur"; Stemplinger, *Sympathieglaube und Sympathiekuren*, 6–32; Röhr, *Okkulte Kraftbegriff*, 34–76; and Richter, *Theorie der Sympathie*. For the association of sympathy with "primitive mentalities" in nineteenth- and twentieth-century anthropology, see especially Frazer, *Golden Bough*; Lévy-Bruhl, *How Natives Think*; and Cornford, *From Religion to Philosophy*, 139–142. For critical accounts of Frazer's concept of "sympathetic magic," see Mauss, *General Theory of Magic*, 14–17, 121–126; and Tambiah, *Magic, Science, Religion*, 51–54. For Lévy-Bruhl's influence on Hélène Metzger's contributions to the historiography of early modern science, see Golinski, "Hélène Metzger." For an anthropologically framed study of sympathy in the early pastoral tradition, see Dick, "Ancient Pastoral"; and the response in Rosenmeyer, *Green Cabinet*, 247–250. The subject of sympathy and pastoral could constitute a study in its own right; I have chosen not to make it a focus of the present one. An extension of this project would also involve integrating the more recent insights of ecocriticism in early modern studies.
22. Stanley, *History of Philosophy*, pt. 8, 103.
23. On the early history of microcosmism, see Allers, "Microcosmus," 337–343, 357; and Barkan, *Nature's Work of Art*, 8–60.
24. See, for example, Laurand, "Sympathie universelle," 517–535.
25. Cicero, *De natura deorum* 2.7; Cicero, *Nature of the Gods*, 142–143.
26. Cicero, *De divinatione* 2.14; Cicero, *Divination*, 406–407, 408–409. I have slightly modified the Loeb translation here.
27. On Cicero, divination, and the link to Posidonius, see Luck, "On Cicero, *De Fato* 5"; and Brunt, "Philosophy and Religion."
28. Garani, *Empedocles "Redivivus,"* 238n78. Epicurus, *Epistola ad Herodotum* 48, 50, 52, 53, 64.
29. Edelstein, "Greek Medicine," in *Ancient Medicine*, 234n95.
30. Theophrastus, *Caus. Pl.* 3.10.4; *Concerning Odours*, 62–63. On Theophrastus's relationship to the "root-cutters," see Lloyd, *Science, Folklore and Ideology*, 120–126. On Androtion, the root-cutters, and the idea of sympathy, see Kingsley, *Ancient Philosophy*, 299.
31. Gordon, "Imagining Greek and Roman Magic," 233, 234.
32. On the importance of antipathy in the pseudo-Democritean tradition, see Gordon, "*Quaedam Veritatis Umbrae*," 136, 139. On "Empedocles the magician" and the connection to Bolus, see Kingsley, *Ancient Philosophy*, 298–299. On Empedocles's model, see Solmsen, "Love and Strife."

33. More, *Immortality of the Soul*, 279.
34. On Plotinus, see Richter, *Theorie der Sympathie*, 227–241; and Graf, "Theories of Magic," 93–104. On Synesius, see Couliano, *Eros and Magic*, 113–117. On Iamblichus, see Wallis, *Neoplatonism*, 121–122. On Proclus, see Copenhaver, "Hermes Trismegistus," 84–87. In spite of the various differences among them, Wallis claims that "it was common ground for all Neoplatonists that the sympathy linking all parts of the sensible cosmos enabled the magician to draw power from the celestial spheres" (*Neoplatonism*, 107).
35. Plotinus, *Enneads* 4.40; Plotinus, *Enneads*, 4:260–261.
36. On the link to Stoicism, see Graeser, *Plotinus and the Stoics*, 68–69; and Wallis, *Neoplatonism*, 25, 70–71. On the connection to the pseudo-Democritean tradition, see Gordon, "Imagining Greek and Roman Magic," 229. On the debt to Plato, see Graeser, *Plotinus and the Stoics*, 69–72; and Graf, "Theories of Magic," 103–104.
37. Copenhaver, "Magic," 518. On the subject of Renaissance magic more generally, see in particular Walker, *Spiritual and Demonic Magic*; Yates, *Giordano Bruno*; Couliano, *Eros and Magic*; Copenhaver, "Astrology and Magic"; Copenhaver, "Natural Magic"; and Zambelli, *White Magic, Black Magic*. On the *prisca theologia*, see Yates, *Giordano Bruno*, 14–19; Walker, *Ancient Theology*; and Mulsow, "Ambiguities."
38. Ficino, *Commentary on Plato's "Symposium*," 127; Ficino, *Marsilio Ficino's Commentary*, 91.
39. Copenhaver, "How to Do Magic," 137.
40. Ficino, *Three Books on Life*, 384–387. On Ficino's magic more generally, see especially Walker, *Spiritual and Demonic Magic*, 30–59; and Couliano, *Eros and Magic*, 130–143.
41. Zambelli, *White Magic, Black Magic*, 2.
42. Pico della Mirandola, "Oration," in Cassirer, Kristeller, and Randall, eds., *Renaissance Philosophy of Man*, 248–249; Garin, ed., *De Hominis Dignitate*, 152. On Pico's magic more generally, see especially Rabin, "Pico on Magic."
43. Pico, "Oration," in Cassirer, Kristeller, and Randall, eds., *Renaissance Philosophy of Man*, 247.
44. Cassirer, "Giovanni Pico della Mirandola," 52. For a critical challenge to Cassirer's interpretation of Pico, see Craven, *Giovanni Pico della Mirandola*, 12–14.
45. On Agrippa and occultism, see Nauert, *Agrippa*; Zambelli, "Magic and Radical Reformation"; and Copenhaver, "Magic," 519–526.
46. Agrippa, *Three Books*, 568; Agrippa, *De incertudine*, in *Opera*, 2:90.
47. Agrippa, *Three Books*, 74; Agrippa, *De occulta philosophia*, in *Opera*, 1:66.
48. Paracelsus, *Philosophia ad Athenienses*, in *Sämtliche Werke*, 13:409.
49. Webster, *Paracelsus*, 132, 143. On Paracelsus's medical and philosophical thought, see also Pagel, *Paracelsus*.
50. Cassirer, *Individual and the Cosmos*, 150. On Cardano, see Grafton, *Cardano's Cosmos*, esp. 156–177. On Telesio, see Walker, *Spiritual and Demonic Magic*, 189–192; Mulsow, *Frühneuzeitliche Selbsterhaltung*; and Giglioni, "First of the Moderns." On Della Porta, see Eamon, *Science and the Secrets of Nature*, 210–233; and Piccari, *Giovan Battista Della Porta*, esp. 47–71. On Campanella, see Walker, *Spiritual and Demonic Magic*, 203–236; and Headley, *Tommaso Campanella*, esp. 64–69.

51. On Bacon's complex relationship to natural-magical and natural-philosophical traditions, see Rossi, *Francis Bacon*; Walker, "Francis Bacon and *Spiritus*"; Rees, "Francis Bacon's Semi-Paracelsian Cosmology"; Gaukroger, *Francis Bacon*, 166–220; and Henry, *Knowledge Is Power*, 42–81.

52. Gilbert, *De Magnete*, 209–210; Mottelay, trans., *De Magnete*, 310–311. I have slightly modified Mottelay's translation. On Bacon's relationship to Gilbert, see Boas, "Bacon and Gilbert"; and Rees, "Unpublished Manuscript," 383–386.

53. Bacon, *New Organon*, 146; Spedding et al., *Works*, 1:280.

54. Bacon, *Philosophical Studies*, 180, 181.

55. Bacon, *New Organon*, 217; Spedding et al., *Works*, 1:361.

56. Bacon, *Instauratio Magna*, 196, 197.

57. Bacon, *Natural and Experimental History*, 49; Spedding et al., *Works*, 2:81.

58. On the significance of this work, see Rees, "Unpublished Manuscript," 377–412. On its eclecticism, see Gaukroger, *Francis Bacon*, 28–36.

59. Bacon, *Sylva Sylvarum*, 126.

60. Ibid., 245, 247. On Della Porta as Bacon's principal source in *Sylva*, see Rees, "Unpublished Manuscript," 389; and Gaukroger, *Francis Bacon*, 33.

61. Rees, "Unpublished Manuscript," 387.

62. Boyle, *Discourse of Things*, 58.

63. Boyle, *Some Considerations*, 68–69.

64. On the polemical drive of Boyle's science, see Shapin and Schaffer, *Leviathan and the Air-Pump*, 155–224; and Shapin, *Social History of Truth*, 126–192.

65. Boyle, *Reflections*, 25–26.

66. Spencer, *Discourse concerning Prodigies*, 66–68. On Spencer's argument and the immediate context, see Burns, " 'Our Lot Is Fallen.' "

67. Spencer, *Discourse concerning Prodigies*, 68.

68. Ibid., 68, 69–70.

69. Donne, *Complete English Poems*, lines 68–69. Subsequent references to Donne's poetry will follow this edition, with line numbers given parenthetically in the text.

70. On the relationship between the metaphysical conceit and the analogical worldview, see Mazzeo, "Metaphysical Poetry," 228–230. On Donne's poem, see especially Nohrnberg, *Analogy*, 784–786.

71. Foucault, *Order of Things*, 132.

72. In using the indefinite article, I mean to convey my understanding that there was no such thing as "*the* sympathetic worldview" at any particular point in time shared equally by all. Indeed, a significant goal of this book is to suggest the plurality of sympathetic views of the world in the seventeenth century. But I am aware that my use of the term "worldview" carries the risk of implied homogeneity on one hand and perceived anachronism on the other. On the history and theory of "worldview" and "world picture," see Heidegger, "Age of the World Picture," in *Essays*; and Koerner, "Hieronymus Bosch's World Picture."

73. For a useful summary of Foucault's argument and its reception, see Gutting, *Michel Foucault's Archaeology*, 139–226. On critical responses, see Maclean, "Process of Intellectual Change." On Foucault's limited reading and his overemphasis on the occult tradition, see Maclean, "Foucault's Renaissance Episteme," 149–166. For a claim that

Foucault misreads that tradition, see Copenhaver, "Did Science Have a Renaissance?" For the critique of irruption in particular, see, for example, Jay, *Downcast Eyes*, 403; and Freedberg, *Eye of the Lynx*, 4.

74. Foucault, *Order of Things*, 23.

75. Ibid., 25, 28. On conceptions of the signature, see Bianchi, *Signatura Rerum*; and Agamben, *Signature of All Things*, 33–80.

76. Foucault, *Order of Things*, 17, 24, 25.

77. Ibid., 50, 51.

78. Ibid., 49. For a modern analogue, see Nabokov, "Signs and Symbols," in *Stories*, 598–603. Nabokov uses Herman Brink's idea of "referential mania" as the generating principle of the fiction.

79. Foucault, *Order of Things*, xiv. Foucault blunts his own emphasis by pointing out that the new modalities of the classical age constitute "a general phenomenon in seventeenth-century culture—a more general one than the particular fortunes of Cartesianism" (56).

80. Boas, "Establishment of the Mechanical Philosophy," 422.

81. See especially Hutchison, "What Happened to Occult Qualities"; Millen, "Manifestation of Occult Qualities"; Henry, "Occult Qualities"; and Copenhaver, "Occultist Tradition." In this context, "occult" is a Scholastic term of art. In the present book, I generally use it in the sense in which it appears in Agrippa's title *De occulta philosophia*: "Of or relating to magic, alchemy, astrology, theosophy, or other practical arts held to involved agencies of a secret or mysterious nature; of the nature of such an art" (*OED* 1b).

82. Charleton, *Physiologia*, 341.

83. Descartes, *Principles of Philosophy*, 275; *Principia Philosophiae*, in *Oeuvres de Descartes*, 8:314–315.

84. Charleton, *Physiologia*, 343.

85. Ibid., 344.

86. On the history of sensibility, see especially Crane, "Suggestions," in *Essays*; Humphreys, "'Friend of Mankind'"; Tuveson, "Importance of Shaftesbury"; Fiering, "Irresistible Compassion"; De Bruyn, "Latitudinarianism"; Todd, *Sensibility*; Barker-Benfield, *Culture of Sensibility*; Van Sant, *Eighteenth-Century Sensibility*; and Goring, *Rhetoric of Sensibility*.

87. Crane, "Suggestions," in *Essays*, 1:213. For a characteristic response to Crane, see Keymer, "Sentimental Fiction," 577–578. For a more critical account, one that I think overstates the extent to which Crane has been refuted, see Gaston, "Impossibility of Sympathy," 132–134.

88. For More and Cumberland, see Fiering, "Irresistible Compassion," 198–200. For Barrow, to whom I return in chapter 2, see Crane, "Suggestions," in *Essays*, 1:194, 205–206. For Cudworth, see Herdt, "Rise of Sympathy," 370–374.

89. Where there have been suggestions of sympathy's earlier life, there has been minimal exploration; see, for example, De Bruyn, "Latitudinarianism," 355–356, 368; Fiering, *Moral Philosophy*, 164; Herdt, "Rise of Sympathy," 372, 376–377; Caldwell, *Literature and Medicine*, 30–31; and Lamb, *Evolution of Sympathy*, 47–49. On the moralization of the discourse of magnetism, see Fara, *Sympathetic Attractions*, 190–193.

90. See Van Engen, "Puritanism"; and Gaston, "Impossibility of Sympathy."

91. See also Hebrews 4:15. On nonscriptural uses of *sympatheia* in a human, social context, by Plutarch, Soranus, and others, see Burkert, "Zum altgriechischen Mitleidsbegriff," 63–66; Lloyd, *Science, Folklore and Ideology*, 178–181; and Konstan, *Pity Transformed*, 58, 63.

92. On Aesop and the harmony between politic and ecclesiastic bodies, see Hicks, "Body Political."

93. On the Pauline analogy and the Stoic connection, see Conzelmann, *Commentary*, 211–214; and Lee, *Paul, the Stoics*.

94. Meeks, *First Urban Christians*, 89–90.

95. On the body politic and the organic analogy, see Tillyard, *Elizabethan World Picture*; Barkan, *Nature's Work of Art*, 61–115; Harris, *Foreign Bodies*; Sharpe, *Remapping Early Modern England*, 38–123; and Schoenfeldt, "Reading Bodies."

96. Harris, *Foreign Bodies*, 32.

97. Averell, *Mervailous Combat of Contrarieties*, D1r, D2v. For the claim that Averell's appeal to sympathy is Paracelsian, see Harris, *Foreign Bodies*, 41–42.

98. Forset, *Comparative Discourse*, 27–28.

99. Sharpe, *Remapping Early Modern England*, 111.

100. On FitzGeffry and the crisis at sea, see Duffin, *Faction and Faith*, 41–57, 134–143.

101. FitzGeffry, *Compassion towards Captives*, 41–42.

102. Ibid., 24.

103. Diogenes, *Lives* 1.24; Theon of Smyrna, *Expos.* (ed. Hiller, 51); Aristotle, *Problems* 7.1.

104. Fracastoro, *De sympathia et antipathia*, A2v, A3v.

105. On Fracastoro's natural philosophy, see Peruzzi, "Antioccultismo e filosofia naturale"; and Pearce, "Nature and Supernature."

106. Charleton, *Physiologia*, 348.

107. Grotius, *Rights of War and Peace*, 83–84; Grotius, *De jure belli ac pacis*, Prolegomena, *5v. On Grotius and the idea of natural sociability, see Tuck, *Natural Right Theories*, 58–81; and Schneewind, *Invention of Autonomy*, 66–73.

108. Hirschman, *Passions and the Interests*, 20.

109. Ibid., 47.

110. Kahn, "Reinventing Romance," 658–659.

111. Rousseau, "Nerves, Spirits, Fibres."

112. Willis, *Dr. Willis's Practice of Physick*, 114. On Willis and the nervous system, see Meier, "'Sympathy' as a Concept"; and Frank, "Thomas Willis and His Circle."

113. See Lawrence, "Nervous System and Society"; Mullan, *Sentiment and Sociability*; and Van Sant, *Eighteenth-Century Sensibility*. For a broader perspective on the science of sensibility, see Riskin, *Science in the Age of Sensibility*; and Gaukroger, *Collapse of Mechanism*, 387–420. Foucault pairs sympathy and sensibility in *Madness and Civilization*, where, in the context of eighteenth-century medical discourse, he writes, "The entire female body is riddled by obscure but strangely direct paths of sympathy; it is always in an immediate complicity with itself, to the point of forming a kind of absolutely privileged site for the sympathies; from one extremity of its organic space to the other, it encloses a perpetual possibility of hysteria." Foucault, *Madness and Civilization*, 153–154. Similarly addressing the diseased body, he refers

at the beginning of *The Birth of the Clinic* to "the old theory of sympathies," which "spoke a vocabulary of correspondences, vicinities, and homologies." Foucault, *Birth of the Clinic*, 3. But ultimately the subjects of cosmic sympathy and somatic sympathy, the "old theory of sympathies" and the newer one of "obscure but strangely direct paths of sympathy," remain fundamentally divided in Foucault's work. On the whole, one might say that Foucault thinks of sympathy primarily in transcendental spatial terms—the historical is secondary.

114. Rousseau, "Nerves, Spirits, Fibres," 145. On Locke and Willis, see also Wright, "Locke, Willis."

115. Rousseau, "Nerves, Spirits, Fibres," 150, 139.

116. Willis, *Dr. Willis's Practice of Physick*, 115.

117. Pagel, *Van Helmont*, 59. On Willis and Van Helmont, see ibid., 79–87; and Meier, "'Sympathy,'" esp. 98–103. Willis, Meier argues, "probably took the equation of sense and sympathy from a very similar passage in Van Helmont's treatise on sympathetic cures" (103). On Galen's conception of sympathy, see Siegel, *Galen's System of Physiology*, 360–382.

118. On Paracelsus's use of the term "archeus," see Pagel, *Paracelsus*, 105–112. On Van Helmont's use, see Pagel, *Van Helmont*, 96–102.

119. Willis, *Dr. Willis's Practice of Physick*, 104.

120. Dryden and Davenant, *The Tempest*, in *Works of John Dryden*, lines 17–26.

121. On the phrase and its alleged Schillerian source, see Lehmann, *Entzauberung der Welt*, 9–20. On Weber's concept of disenchantment, see Cascardi, *Subject of Modernity*, 16–49; Breyer, "Magie, Zauber, Entzauberung"; Gane, *Max Weber and Postmodern Theory*, 15–49; and Kippenberg, *Discovering Religious History*, 155–174.

122. Weber, *Protestant Ethic*, 105.

123. Ibid., 117.

124. Thomas, *Religion and the Decline*, 279, 665.

125. Ibid., 661. Taylor, *Secular Age*, 27.

126. On the reception of Thomas's work, see Macfarlane, "Civility"; and Walsham, "Reformation," 498–499.

127. On Weberian disenchantment and the history of science, see Daston, "Nature of Nature."

128. Webster, *From Paracelsus to Newton*, 3.

129. Ibid., 11.

130. On Newton, see, for example, Dobbs, *Janus Faces of Genius*; and Gouk, *Music, Science*, 224–257. On Boyle, see Principe, *Aspiring Adept*; Hunter, *Robert Boyle*, 93–118, 223–224; and Hunter, *Boyle*, 179–194.

131. Hunter, *Robert Boyle*, 244.

132. See Henry, "Fragmentation of Renaissance Occultism."

133. Webster, "Paracelsus, Paracelsianism," 15.

134. Thomas, *Religion and the Decline*, 227; Webster, *From Paracelsus to Newton*, 64.

135. Kassell, "Secrets Revealed," 61, 63.

136. Eamon, *Science and the Secrets of Nature*, 9.

137. Scribner, "Reformation, Popular Magic," 476, 493, 492.

138. Ibid., 484, 490, 491.
139. Walsham, *Reformation of the Landscape*, 336.
140. Walsham, "Reformation," 508, 512.
141. Ibid., 522, 526, 527.
142. Ibid., 528. For studies that have given more prominence to change, see Van Ruler, "Minds, Forms, and Spirits"; and Cameron, *Enchanted Europe*. Cameron's methodology differs from Scribner's in its focus, or re-focus, on theological sources; see *Enchanted Europe*, 12–14.
143. Weber, *From Max Weber*, 155.
144. See Taylor, *Secular Age*, 5–7.
145. Spitzer, *Essays*, 184, 300.
146. Horkheimer and Adorno, *Dialectic of Enlightenment*, 7.
147. Harrington, *Reenchanted Science*, xv.
148. Ibid., xvi.
149. Cudworth, *True Intellectual System*, 663.
150. Bennett, *Enchantment of Modern Life*, 62.
151. Weber, *From Max Weber*, 342.
152. Foucault, *Order of Things*, 44.
153. Ibid., 50, 49.
154. Adorno, *Minima Moralia*, 222. On art and enchantment, see also Adorno, *Aesthetic Theory*, 45–61. For a critical account of the disenchantment narrative in the context of the history of the visual arts, see Wood, *Forgery, Replica, Fiction*, 71–84.
155. Walsham, "Reformation," 518. On the "cultural repackaging" of magic into art and literature, see also Porter, "Witchcraft and Magic," 245–250; and During, *Modern Enchantments*. On magic, poetry, and the imagination in the late eighteenth and nineteenth centuries, see Taylor, *Magic and English Romanticism*.
156. Latour, *We Have Never Been*, 115.

CHAPTER 1. SIR KENELM DIGBY AND THE MATTER OF SYMPATHY

1. Butler, *Hudibras*, 35.
2. Butler, *Hudibras . . . with Several Additions and Annotations*, 197. For the claim that Orsin is modeled on Sir Gilbert Talbot rather than Digby, see Hedrick, "Romancing the Salve," 183n78. But the tradition of associating Orsin with Digby predates Digby's twentieth-century readers; see Butler, *Hudibras . . . With Large Annotations*, 1:119.
3. Hutson, ed., *Sir Kenelm Digby's Powder of Sympathy*, xiv. On Digby's life and learning, see in particular Petersson, *Sir Kenelm Digby*; Henry, "Atomism and Eschatology"; Janacek, "Catholic Natural Philosophy"; and Henry, "Sir Kenelm Digby."
4. Fara, *Sympathetic Attractions*, 150.
5. Foucault, *Order of Things*, 67.
6. For bibliographic information I have consulted Keynes, *Bibliography of Sir Thomas Browne*.
7. On Paracelsus's influence and legacy, especially in England, see Rattansi, "Paracelsus"; Debus, *English Paracelsians*; Webster, "Alchemical and Paracelsian Medicine"; and

Trevor-Roper, "Paracelsian Movement." For a wider perspective, see Pumfrey, "Spagyric Art."

8. Paracelsus's recipe appears in the 1656 English edition of the *Archidoxes*, but not in the 1660 edition.

9. Paracelsus, *Archidoxes of Magic*, 117; Paracelsus, *Archidoxis magicae*, in *Sämtliche Werke*, 14:448.

10. On sympathy and the microcosm-macrocosm analogy in Paracelsus's thought, see Pagel, *Paracelsus*, 50–72; and Webster, *Paracelsus*, 142–156.

11. Paracelsus, *Archidoxes of Magic*, 117.

12. Ibid., 118.

13. Charleton, *Physiologia*, 381. On action at a distance as a recurrent concern in the history of science, see Hesse, *Forces and Fields*; and Hesse, "Action at a Distance."

14. Mairhofer, *De principiis discernendi*, D3v.

15. Libavius, *Tractatus duo physici*.

16. Porta, *Natural Magick*, 228.

17. Van Helmont, *Ternary of Paradoxes*, 1.

18. Thorndike, *History of Magic*, 7:504.

19. Charleton, *Physiologia*, 380.

20. On Van Helmont's defense of the weapon salve and its consequences, see Pagel, *Van Helmont*, 8–13.

21. On the contest among Goclenius, Roberti, and Van Helmont, and the Jesuit response to sympathetic cures, see Ziller-Camenietzki, "Jesuits and Alchemy"; and Waddell, "Perversion of Nature."

22. On the Fludd-Foster debate, see Debus, "Robert Fludd." On Fludd *agonistes* more generally, see Huffman, *Robert Fludd*, 50–71.

23. Foster, *Hoplocrisma-spongus*, A3v.

24. Ibid., A3v, A3r.

25. Fludd, *Doctor Fludds Answer*, 130.

26. On Fludd and his local and international contexts, see Pagel, "Religious Motives," 266–288; Debus, *English Paracelsians*, 105–127; Westman, "Nature, Art, and Psyche"; Huffman, *Robert Fludd*; Barbour, *Literature and Religious Culture*, 181–185; Kassell, "Magic, Alchemy"; and Schmidt-Biggemann, "Robert Fludd's Kabbalistic Cosmos."

27. Fludd, *Doctor Fludds Answer*, 62, 65.

28. Ibid., 95.

29. On resonance in early modern thought, see Gouk, *Music, Science*, 169–170, 181, 189, 238, 268–269. By the seventeenth century, it had already become a topos.

30. Foucault, *Order of Things*, 18. On mystical analogy and ontology, see Vickers, "On the Function of Analogy"; and Vickers, "Analogy versus Identity."

31. Fludd, *Doctor Fludds Answer*, 140.

32. Ibid., 98–99.

33. Foster, *Hoplocrisma-spongus*, 5.

34. Ibid., 6, 7, 9, 34.

35. Ibid., 26, 27, 28–29, 30.

36. On the devil's power and early modern demonology, see Clark, "Scientific Status of Demonology"; and Clark, *Thinking with Demons*, 151–178. Fludd's *argumentum ad sympathiam* is presented as an alternative to a demonic explanation of the cure.

37. Foster, *Hoplocrisma-spongus*, 21.

38. Ibid., 26.

39. Besides those between Goclenius and Roberti, and Fludd and Foster, a third pamphlet war broke out between Papin and Isaac Cattier in 1651; see Thorndike, *History of Magic*, 7:503–505. For a broader survey of the weapon-salve controversy in France, see Ziller-Camenietzki, "Poudre de Madame."

40. Webster, *Paracelsus*, 162, 157.

41. Fludd, *Doctor Fludds Answer*, 135–136. On Paracelsus and the Magi, see Webster, *Paracelsus*, 65–69.

42. In the *Bibliotheca Digbeiana*, there is a record of *"Foster* of the Magical Art by Weapon-salve" (108). On Digby's treatise, see especially Petersson, *Sir Kenelm Digby*, 259–274; Dobbs, "Studies"; Gilman, "Arts of Sympathy"; and Hedrick, "Romancing the Salve." Gilman's discussion of Digby, which reaches some similar conclusions about Digby's ties to the old world picture, is part of a larger inquiry into the social and cultural circulation around the Earl of Arundel in the 1630s. Hedrick understands Digby's claim to be the "intellectual retailer" ("Romancing the Salve," 164) of the cure in the broader light of his interest in showing fealty to the Stuarts at a critical juncture.

43. Digby, *Late Discourse*, 3. All subsequent references to Digby's treatise will be cited parenthetically in the text by page number.

44. Dobbs, "Studies," 6.

45. Digby, *Two Treatises*, 332.

46. Hobbes, *Leviathan*, 468. See also Galileo, *Dialogue*, 410.

47. Boyle, *Some Considerations*, 68.

48. Locke, *Essay*, 512.

49. Bacon, *Advancement of Learning*, 143. On Bacon's view of the imagination, see Park, "Bacon's 'Enchanted Glass.'"

50. Hedrick, "Romancing the Salve," 162; see also 169–171, 180–183.

51. Fuller, *History of the Worthies*, 79; quoted in Debus, *English Paracelsians*, 106.

52. Clericuzio, *Elements, Principles and Corpuscles*, vii. See also Clucas, "Atomism of the Cavendish Circle," 256–259.

53. Gilman, "Arts of Sympathy," 276.

54. Clericuzio, *Elements, Principles and Corpuscles*, 9. On Sennert's matter theory, see Newman, *Atoms and Alchemy*, 85–153.

55. On the rhetoric of atomistic analysis, see Jones, "Rhetoric of Science."

56. *Diary of John Evelyn*, ed. De Beer, 3:49.

57. Le Fèvre, *Compendious Body of Chymistry*, 14.

58. Digby is credited with the first use of the verb "corporify" (*OED* 1), from *Two Treatises*.

59. Le Fèvre, *Compendious Body of Chymistry*, 13–14, 14.

60. Dobbs, "Studies," 24.

61. More, *Immortality of the Soul*, 456.

62. Ibid., 450, 218. On More's complex relationship to Descartes and Cartesianism, see Gabbey, "Philosophia Cartesiana Triumphata"; and Cottingham, "Force, Motion and Causality."

63. More, *Immortality of the Soul*, 217, 221.

64. Ibid., 453, 454, 455.

65. Ibid., 456–457, 452.

66. Glanvill, *Vanity of Dogmatizing*, 207.

67. Ibid., 208.

68. Boyle, *Certain Physiological Essays*, 91–92.

69. On the cultural significance of credit in the early modern period, see Shapin, *Social History of Truth*, 238–242.

70. Boyle, *Certain Physiological Essays*, 227, 232.

71. See Anstey and Principe, "John Locke."

72. Dobbs, who traces the use of English vitriol "as an ordinary chemical medication" back to the 1610s, undermines Digby's claim to originality: "Digby's function in the history of the use of this powder . . . would seem to be one of advertisement rather than of discovery" ("Studies," 7). For the full "case against Digby," see Hedrick, "Romancing the Salve," 167–172, 180–183.

73. Hartman, *Choice Collection*, 271.

74. Glanvill, *Vanity of Dogmatizing*, 208.

75. Dobbs, "Studies," 8.

76. Thorndike, *History of Magic*, 7:505.

77. On "registration" as "a particular term of art," see Shapin, *Social History of Truth*, 303.

78. For Paracelsus's derivation of magic from the East, see Braun, ed., *Paracelse: De la magie*, 102.

79. Bacon, *Sylva Sylvarum*, 264.

80. Cajori, *Sir Isaac Newton's Mathematical Principles*, 547; quoted in Henry, "Occult Qualities," 358. On Glanvill, see ibid., 359.

81. Glanvill, *Scepsis Scientifica*, 151.

82. Shadwell, *The Virtuoso*, 3.3.92.

83. See Houghton, "English Virtuoso," 61, 69.

84. Porta, *Natural Magick*, 51.

85. On the topic, see King, *Philosophy of Medicine*, 152–181; Zambelli, "L'immaginazione e il suo potere"; Huet, *Monstrous Imagination*, 1–78; and Daston and Park, *Wonders*, 339–343. On the importance of the imagination in occultist thought, see Pagel, *Paracelsus*, 111–112, 121–125, 300–301; Schott, "'Invisible Diseases'"; and Kavey, "Building Blocks."

86. On the Baconian paradox of recruiting the imagination while repudiating it, see Park, "Bacon's 'Enchanted Glass.'"

87. On the link between the maternal imagination and artistic creation, see Huet, *Monstrous Imagination*, 7, 24–27.

88. Horace, *Ars poetica* 102–103; Horace, *Art of Poetry*, 458–459.

89. Horace, *Ars poetica* 101–102; Horace, *Art of Poetry*, 458–459.

90. On the older view, see Maclean, *Renaissance Notion of Woman*, 28–46. On the gendered female imagination and the "imaginationist" controversy in the eighteenth century, see Boucé, "Imagination, Pregnant Women"; Wilson, "'Out of Sight'"; and Cody, *Birthing the Nation*, 120–151.

91. On the multivalence of "contagion," see Healy, *Fictions of Disease*, 40–43. On the relationship between sympathy and contagion in the work of Fracastoro, see Nutton, "Reception of Fracastoro's Theory." The 1584 edition of Fracastoro's *Opera Omnia* appears in the *Bibliotheca Digbeiana* (39).

92. Bacon, *Sylva Sylvarum*, 242–243. Bacon, too, notes the *"Infective"* quality of melancholy and joy (251), but Digby deviates from him significantly in his rejection of action at a distance; Bacon maintains that "All *Operations* by *Transmission* of *Spirits, and Imagination*, have this, That they *Worke* at *Distance*, and not at *Touch*" (244).

93. Malebranche, *Search after Truth*, 119, 122. On this part of the work, see Lennon, "Contagious Communication."

94. Digby, *Two Treatises*, 335.

95. Ibid., 381.

96. Horace, *Ars poetica* 99, 101, 104; Horace, *Art of Poetry*, 458–459.

97. Digby, *Two Treatises*, 377.

98. See Petersson, *Sir Kenelm Digby*, 163–175; and Wise, *Sir Thomas Browne's "Religio Medici*," 57–121.

99. Digby, *Observations*, 92.

100. Browne, *Religio Medici*, 57; Willey, *English Moralists*, 195.

101. Browne, *Religio Medici*, 72, 77–78.

102. Ibid., 70.

103. Ibid., 30.

104. Ibid., 74, 79, 44.

105. On Brownean charity, and its links to Stoicism, see Barbour, *Literature and Religious Culture*, 200–203; and Preston, *Thomas Browne*, 68–72, 80–81. On "the charitable-sociable ideal" more generally in this period, see Barbour, *English Epicures and Stoics*, 158–239.

106. Browne, *Religio Medici*, 81.

107. Digby, *Observations*, 96–97.

108. Healey, trans., *Epictetus His Manuall*, 27–28.

109. Epictetus, *Encheiridion* 16. Long, *Epictetus*, 253.

110. Seneca, *De clementia* 2.6.3, 4.

111. Senault, *Use of Passions*, 506. On Senault's work, see especially Levi, *French Moralists*, 213–233.

112. Senault, *Use of Passions*, 506, 507, 508.

113. Browne, *Christian Morals*, in *Works*, 1:274, 284.

114. Digby, *Observations*, 93–94.

115. Ibid., 2–3.

116. Digby, *Sr. Kenelme Digbyes Honour*, A3r–A4v.

117. On Digby's emphasis on the soul, see Henry, "Atomism and Eschatology," 223–227; and Shuger, "Laudian Idiot," 46–55.

118. Digby, *Discourse Concerning Infallibility*, 117–118.
119. *Encyclopédie*, 15:740.
120. Barckley, *Felicitie of Man*, 6.
121. Digby, *Discourse Concerning Infallibility*, 112.

CHAPTER 2. THE "SELF-THEMES" OF MARGARET CAVENDISH
AND THOMAS HOBBES

1. *Collection of Letters*, 65.
2. *Bibliotheca Digbeiana*, 83.
3. On Cavendish's natural philosophy, see especially James, "Philosophical Innovations"; O'Neill, ed., *Margaret Cavendish: Observations*, xxi–xxxv; Detlefsen, "Atomism, Monism, and Causation"; and Sarasohn, *Natural Philosophy of Margaret Cavendish*.
4. On the social milieu, see Whitaker, *Mad Madge*, 84–106; and Smith, "French Philosophy and English Politics." On the scientific milieu, see Clucas, "Atomism of the Cavendish Circle," 247–273. Cavendish's response to the debate about sympathetic cures, with which Digby was closely identified, can be only partially extrapolated. In *Poems, and Fancies* she associates them with "*Juglers, Mountebanks, and Gypsies*": these last "delude many; as *Sympathy Powder, Viper Wine, Love Powder, Cramp Rings, crosse Knots, raking up the ashes on St Agnes Eve*, laying *Bride-cake* under their heads, and many the like" (Cavendish, *Poems, and Fancies*, 210). Sympathy powder is here rejected as one bit of superstitious quackery among many. Later, after a careful reading of Van Helmont's *Of the Magnetick Cure of Wounds*, and perhaps under the influence of Digby's treatise, she takes the cure more seriously but remains skeptical: "I believe all those remedies will not so often cure, as fail of cure, like as the Sympathetical Powder" (Cavendish, *Philosophical Letters*, 389). This expression of doubt is not dissimilar to Bacon's and Boyle's.
5. Of Cavendish's contemporaries, Joseph Glanvill took her philosophy perhaps most seriously. On the relationship between Cavendish and Glanvill, see Broad, "Margaret Cavendish and Joseph Glanvill."
6. Cavendish, *Poems, and Fancies*, 196.
7. See ibid., 5, 6–7, 9–10, 12. On Cavendish's poetry, see Chalmers, "'Flattering Division.'"
8. On the development of Cavendish's natural philosophy, see Clucas, "Atomism of the Cavendish Circle"; Stevenson, "Mechanist-Vitalist Soul"; and the response to both in Detlefsen, "Atomism, Monism, and Causation."
9. Cavendish, *Philosophical Letters*, 297.
10. Boyle, "Fame, Virtue, and Government," 281, 271–272. Especially given the attention she pays to Cavendish's *Orations*, I think that Boyle underplays the significance of rhetoric in Cavendish's moral thought. For the suggestion that Cavendish's moral philosophy has an Epicurean tinge, see Sarasohn, *Natural Philosophy of Margaret Cavendish*, 86.
11. On the relationship between the physical and the moral in Hobbes, see Verdon, "On the Laws"; and Sarasohn, "Motion and Morality."
12. For a different kind of challenge, see Starr, "Aphra Behn."

13. For an alternative treatment of Cavendish and "discourse," conceived much more broadly than I have here, see Robinson, "Figurative Matter."

14. Cavendish, *Sociable Letters*, C2r. All subsequent references to this work will be cited parenthetically in the text by page number. On the form and genre of *Sociable Letters*, see especially Barnes, "Restoration of Royalist Form"; Fitzmaurice, *Familiar Letter*, 175–188; Rees, *Margaret Cavendish*, 175–176; and Schneider, *Culture of Epistolarity*, 266–267.

15. See Whyman, *Sociability and Power*, 87–109.

16. Perry, *First Duchess of Newcastle*, 251. For additional suggestions about Cavendish's place in the history of the novel, see Rees. *Margaret Cavendish*, 88; and MacCarthy, *Female Pen*, 137–138.

17. For the persistent critical linkage of sympathy and eighteenth-century fiction, see, for example, Gallagher, *Nobody's Story*, 166–174; and Britton, "Translating Sympathy." On earlier epistolary traditions and the movement of the passions, see especially Jardine, *Reading Shakespeare Historically*, 78–97; and Eden, *Renaissance Rediscovery of Intimacy*, 5–72.

18. Sarasohn, *Natural Philosophy of Margaret Cavendish*, 19.

19. Cavendish, *Philosophical Letters*, 278.

20. Cavendish, *Playes*, 224.

21. The irony of the title is echoed in the title to Cavendish's play *The Sociable Companions; or, The Female Wits*, in *Plays, never before Printed*. On the shifting meaning of the word "sociable" and its importance to Cavendish, see Masten, "Material Cavendish," 64–66.

22. Hobbes, *Leviathan*, 91.

23. This is not to say Stoicism. In imagining a world within, Cavendish was not managing complex emotions so much as creating a space for their free exchange. Although she advocates for patience and constancy in certain instances, I do not see Cavendish's "tactics of selfhood" as primarily Stoic; I borrow this phrase from Gordon Braden (*Renaissance Tragedy*, 26).

24. Cavendish, *Philosophical and Physical Opinions*, 439–440.

25. Ibid., 438, 439.

26. Cavendish, *Grounds of Natural Philosophy*, 159–160.

27. On Cavendish's conception of occasional causation, see O'Neill, ed., *Margaret Cavendish: Observations*, xxix–xxxv; Detlefsen, "Atomism, Monism, and Causation," 227–235; and Michaelian, "Margaret Cavendish's Epistemology," 45–48.

28. Cavendish, *Philosophical and Physical Opinions*, 442.

29. On Cavendish's interest in and engagement with Shakespeare, see Romack and Fitzmaurice, eds., *Cavendish and Shakespeare*.

30. Cavendish, *Worlds Olio*, 15.

31. Cavendish, *Philosophical Letters*, 216. On Cavendish's separation of theology and natural philosophy, paralleled by Hobbes's, see Detlefsen, "Margaret Cavendish."

32. On the significance of this volume, in terms of both genre and gender, see Sutherland, "Aspiring to the Rhetorical Tradition"; and Rees, *Margaret Cavendish*, 166–176. On the idea that Cavendish privileged private conversation over public oration, see Donawerth, "Conversation."

33. Horace, *Ars poetica* 101; Horace, *Art of Poetry*, 458–459.
34. For a parallel, if brief, expression of the idea of an "imaginative sympathy" produced through letter writing, see Schneider, "Affecting Correspondences," 33.
35. Cavendish, *Observations upon Experimental Philosophy*, A1r.
36. On the philosophical letter as a genre, see Sarasohn, "*Leviathan* and the Lady," 41–45.
37. Cavendish, *Philosophical Letters*, 297.
38. Ibid., 295.
39. Ibid., 291–292.
40. Cavendish, *Observations upon Experimental Philosophy*, 54.
41. On this critique, see Keller, "Producing Petty Gods"; Campbell, *Wonder and Science*, 213–218; Dear, "Philosophical Duchess"; and Sarasohn, *Natural Philosophy of Margaret Cavendish*, 149–172.
42. Cavendish, *Observations upon Experimental Philosophy*, 127.
43. Cavendish, *Philosophical Letters*, 31.
44. O'Neill asserts, but does not fully substantiate, the positive case: "The pervasiveness in nature of rational matter accounts for how all the parts of nature know how to change their configurations on the occasion of changes in distinct parts of nature with which they share an affinity or sympathy" (*Margaret Cavendish: Observations*, xxxii). For a similar suggestion, see James, "Philosophical Innovations," 237–238. On the dynamics of sympathy in Cavendish's natural philosophy, see also Robinson, "Figurative Matter," 74–80.
45. Cavendish, *Philosophical Letters*, 154, 155–156.
46. Cavendish, *Observations upon Experimental Philosophy*, 34.
47. Cavendish, *Philosophical Letters*, 23.
48. Ibid., 22.
49. Ibid., 490–491.
50. Cavendish, *Observations upon Experimental Philosophy*, 31.
51. Cavendish, *Worlds Olio*, 132.
52. On Cavendish and the question of feminism, see especially Gallagher, "Embracing the Absolute"; Chalmers, *Royalist Women Writers*, 28–55; Norbrook, "Women, the Republic of Letters," 223–240; and Dear, "Philosophical Duchess."
53. Cavendish, *Philosophical Letters*, 446.
54. Cavendish, *Philosophical and Physical Opinions*, 110.
55. Cavendish, *Worlds Olio*, 32.
56. *Letters Written*, 6.
57. Langbaine, *Account*, 390.
58. Lower, ed., *Lives*, 274–277.
59. Ibid., 282.
60. Cavendish, *Natures Picture[s]*, 140.
61. Cavendish, *Worlds Olio*, 58–59.
62. Cavendish, *Natures Picture[s]*, 140.
63. On the importance for Cavendish of privacy, retreat, and retirement, see Sanders, "'Closet Opened'"; and Chalmers, *Royalist Women Writers*, 128–148. On the significance of the domestic in Cavendish's writing, see Dodds, "Margaret Cavendish's Domestic Experiment."

64. Cavendish, *Grounds of Natural Philosophy*, 158, 160.

65. Lower, ed., *Lives*, 299.

66. Cavendish, *Grounds of Natural Philosophy*, 160, 75.

67. Ibid., 80.

68. Cavendish, *Blazing World*, 82.

69. Ibid., 100.

70. Ibid., 86, 90, 100.

71. Cavendish, *Observations upon Experimental Philosophy*, 19. On "Assaulted and Pursued Chastity," see Weitz, "Romantic Fiction."

72. Cavendish, *Observations upon Experimental Philosophy*, 34.

73. Cavendish, *Blazing World*, 101.

74. Ibid., 102.

75. Grant, *Margaret the First*, 167.

76. Cavendish, *Grounds of Natural Philosophy*, 21.

77. Cavendish, *Philosophical Letters*, 217.

78. On the "conversation of souls" as a central figure for Cavendish, see also Harris, *Untimely Matter*, 155–159.

79. Cavendish, *Worlds Olio*, 53.

80. On Henrietta Maria and the cult of Platonic love, see Veevers, *Images of Love*. On Cavendish's relationship to this culture and its influence on her work, see Battigelli, *Margaret Cavendish*, 11–38; and Chalmers, *Royalist Women Writers*, 40–51.

81. Howell, *Epistolae Ho-Elianae*, 202–203.

82. On this period in Cavendish's life, see Whitaker, *Mad Madge*, 47–63.

83. Cavendish, *Philosophical Letters*, 219.

84. Cavendish, *Worlds Olio*, 109.

85. For a different approach to Cavendish and the matter of Platonism, see Starr, "Cavendish, Aesthetics."

86. Cavendish, *Blazing World*, 46, 53, 64, 65.

87. Ibid., 92, 107, 108, 111, 121.

88. Ibid., 123.

89. Ibid., b*r.

90. Ibid., 97.

91. Cavendish, *Grounds of Natural Philosophy*, 21–22.

92. Gallagher, "Embracing the Absolute," 30. Harris, by contrast, argues for "a persistently dialogic strain throughout Cavendish's writing that qualifies her solipsism; she does not just subdivide internally but also finds traces of the other in herself, and vice versa" (*Untimely Matter*, 159). On the complexity of construing the self and intersubjectivity in Cavendish's writing, see also Wagner, "Romancing Multiplicity"; and Graham, "Intersubjectivity, Intertextuality." On Cavendish's predilection for "self-" compounds, see Fitzmaurice, *Familiar Letter*, 178.

93. Cavendish, *Natures Picture[s]*, A5v–r.

94. Cavendish, *Observations upon Experimental Philosophy*, 2nd ed., 62, 63.

95. In her not exactly tributary discussion of Cavendish, Virginia Woolf recognized "her sympathy with fairies and animals so true and tender." Woolf, *Common Reader*, 111–112. On Cavendish's sympathetic view of animals, see Broad, *Women Philosophers*, 50–55; Bowerbank, *Speaking for Nature*, 69–71; and Sarasohn, *Natural Philosophy of Margaret Cavendish*, 11–12.

96. On Hobbes's reception in the seventeenth century, see especially Parkin, *Taming the Leviathan*; and Goldie, "Reception of Hobbes."

97. On Barrow's homiletics, see Simon, "The Preacher."

98. See Crane, "Suggestions," in *Essays*, 1:203–210.

99. Barrow, *Of the Love of God*, 276–277.

100. Pope, *Life of the Right Reverend*, 132.

101. Ibid., 141, 142.

102. Barrow, *Of the Love of God*, 185–186.

103. Ibid., 186–187. Crane uses this passage as a central example ("Suggestions," in *Essays*, 1:206).

104. Parkin, *Taming the Leviathan*, 10.

105. Hobbes, *Leviathan*, 87, 88, 90, 41.

106. That Hobbes was truly a "psychological egoist," however defined, has been much debated. On the question, see especially Gert, "Hobbes and Psychological Egoism"; Raphael, *Hobbes*, 64–71; Sorell, *Hobbes*, 97–100; McClintock, "Meaning"; Malcolm, *Aspects of Hobbes*, 30–31; and Zagorin, *Hobbes and the Law*, 86, 99–112.

107. Clark, ed., "Brief Lives," 1:352.

108. Hobbes, *Leviathan*, 43. See also the earlier account of pity, composed in 1640, in Hobbes, *Elements of Law*, 53. For a comparison of Hobbes's accounts of pity, see Kemp, "Hobbes on Pity."

109. Aristotle, *Rhetoric* 2.8.1–16. Hobbes, *Briefe of the Art*, 93.

110. Aristotle, *Rhetoric* 2.8.13–14; Aristotle, *Rhetoric*, 228–229.

111. Butler, *Fifteen Sermons*, 81. On Hobbesian pity and Butler's critique, see Sorell, *Hobbes*, 97–98; and Curley, "Reflections on Hobbes," 171–173.

112. Barrow, *Of the Love of God*, 187, 220.

113. Descartes, "Passions of the Soul," in *Philosophical Writings*, 1:395; *Oeuvres de Descartes*, 11:470. On Descartes's conception of generosity, see Brown, *Descartes and the Passionate Mind*, 188–209.

114. Charleton, *Natural History of the Passions*, 129, 130, 131. On Descartes's theatrical conception of pity, see Kahn, "Happy Tears."

115. Charleton, *Natural History of the Passions*, B1r, BB2v, 148.

116. Barrow, *Of the Love of God*, 278.

117. Ibid., 291, 292.

118. Ibid., 285–286.

119. Ibid., 173, 155.

120. Sarasohn, *Natural Philosophy of Margaret Cavendish*, 190.

CHAPTER 3. MILTON AND THE LINK OF NATURE

1. On Miltonic sympathy in its generic context, see Burrow, *Epic Romance*, 244–289. Burrow traces a conceptual line from Homeric *eleos* to Virgilian *pietas* to the *pietà* and "pity" of Renaissance epic. I agree that Homer explores a phenomenon to which we would now give the name "sympathy," but I am uncomfortable with the methodological discrepancy in Burrow's history between his analyses of pity and sympathy. I do not believe that Milton conceives sympathy primarily in terms of "Homeric fellow-feeling" (278), nor do I believe that the history of sympathy is primarily a shadow history of epic. My approach to Miltonic sympathy is closer to, and indebted to, that of Goodman, "'Wasted Labor.'" Starting from Virgil's *Georgics*, Goodman relates the dynamics of work, both physical and emotional, to the emerging aesthetic sphere.
2. Quoted in Newton, ed., *Paradise Lost*, 2:231.
3. Cudworth, *True Intellectual System*, 175.
4. Hartman, "Adam on the Grass," in *Essays*, 132.
5. On Milton's sociolegal conception of consent in the *Doctrine*, which I do not address, see Halley, "Female Autonomy," 243–244; and Kahn, *Wayward Contracts*, 198–207.
6. References to Milton's prose are cited parenthetically in the text, by volume and page number, and follow the Yale *Complete Prose Works*. Citations of Milton's Latin follow the Columbia *Works of John Milton*. Citations of Milton's poetry, given parenthetically by line number, follow the editions of Revard, *John Milton: Complete Shorter Poems*, and Lewalski, *John Milton: Paradise Lost*.
7. Fallon, "Metaphysics," 70. See also Aers and Hodge, "'Rational Burning'"; Turner, *One Flesh*, 200; and Fallon, "Spur of Self-Concernment."
8. For points of connection and comparison between Milton and Cavendish, see Rogers, *Matter of Revolution*, 177–181; and Miller, *Engendering the Fall*, 136–167.
9. Hill, *Milton and the English Revolution*, 110.
10. Fludd, *Doctor Fludds Answer*, 41.
11. See Saurat, *Milton et le matérialisme*, 13–43; and Saurat, *Milton: Man and Thinker*, 248–267. The latter, with a revised discussion of Milton and Fludd, first appeared in 1925. See also Adams, *Milton and the Modern Critics*, 133; Hughes, *Ten Perspectives on Milton*, 87–94; Hill, *Milton and the English Revolution*, 34, 38–40, 110–111, 324–328; and Fallon, *Milton among the Philosophers*, 114–115.
12. On the challenge of associating Milton closely and specifically with contemporary natural philosophers, see Poole, "Milton and Science."
13. Burrow also attributes the Fall to sympathy (*Epic Romance*, 282–285), but to a different sympathy: "The Fall is brought about by the precursor—even the precondition—of the sympathy which runs from the Homeric poems through the innumerable forms of their successors: a moment when a man chooses to accept the mortal nature of his lady" (284). Michael Schoenfeldt very briefly discusses sympathy in relation to the Fall in "'Commotion Strange,'" 62.
14. Spitzer, *Classical and Christian Ideas*, 76.
15. Cicero, *De natura deorum* 2.6; Cicero, *Nature of the Gods*, 142–143.
16. Cicero, *De natura deorum* 3.11; Cicero, *Nature of the Gods*, 312–313.

17. Spitzer, *Classical and Christian Ideas*, 148, 150.
18. Ibid., 18, 148, 149, 150, 151.
19. On Milton's command of the conceit in this prolusion, see Hale, *Milton's Cambridge Latin*, 82–85.
20. For the claim that the *Nativity Ode* and the second prolusion are "in dialogue," see Quint, "Expectation and Prematurity," 195, 204–206. On the importance of harmony in the *Nativity Ode*, see Fawcett, "Orphic Singer." On song and music in Milton's 1645 *Poems* more broadly, see Mattison, "Sweet Imperfection."
21. On the speaker's yearning in the *Nativity Ode* and the poem's dramatic turn, see Halpern, "Great Instauration"; Revard, *Milton and the Tangles*, 82–83; and Quint, "Expectation and Prematurity," 206–214.
22. Seneca, *Naturales quaestiones* 2.6.2; Seneca, *Natural Questions*, 1:106–109.
23. Manilius, *Astronomica* 2.63–66; Manilius, *Astronomica*, 86–89.
24. In his reading of Milton's representation of the earth in *Paradise Lost*, DuRocher, it seems to me, overemphasizes the place of Roman Stoicism in the background. See DuRocher, "Wounded Earth."
25. On the methodological question, see Shumaker, "Literary Hermeticism."
26. Hill, *Milton and the English Revolution*, 110.
27. Yates, *Giordano Bruno*, 280.
28. Greene, "Enchanting Ravishments," 300.
29. Ibid., 322n11.
30. On the significance of the conjunction for Milton, see Herman, *Destabilizing Milton*, 43–59.
31. See Cable, "Coupling Logic"; Fish, "Wanting a Supplement"; and Turner, *One Flesh*, 188–229. For rhetorical approaches to the divorce tracts, see also Egan, "Rhetoric, Polemic, Mimetic"; Van den Berg, "Women, Children"; and Nichols, "Milton's Claim for Self."
32. Holland, trans., *Historie of the World*, pt. 2, 35.
33. On Milton's negotiation between monism and dualism in the divorce tracts, see Fallon, "Metaphysics," 70–77. Subsequent work on Milton's concepts of matter and substance has challenged the view that he evolved from a Platonically influenced dualist into a committed monist around the time that he started composing *Paradise Lost*. For the evolutionary view, see especially Fallon, *Milton among the Philosophers*, 79–110. Adding to the complexity of this critical debate is the problem of definition; the terms "monism" and "dualism" are susceptible of multiple and various interpretations. For the idea of a variously committed, or uncommitted, Milton, see Kolbrener, *Milton's Warring Angels*, 89–93, 136–139; Trubowitz, "Body Politics"; Donnelly, *Milton's Scriptural Reasoning*, 49–76; and Sugimura, "*Matter of Glorious Trial*."
34. Luxon, *Single Imperfection*, 57.
35. Friedman, "Divisions on a Ground," 206.
36. On Milton's reading of Genesis 2, see Nyquist, "Genesis of Gendered Subjectivity."
37. Patterson, "No Meer Amatorious Novel?" 99.
38. On medical and scientific language in the tract, see Svendsen, "Science and Structure."

39. On the appeal to, and of, determinism in the *Doctrine*, see Fallon, "Metaphysics," 78; and Kahn, "'Duty to Love,'" 91. For an argument that determinism is merely apparent in the *Doctrine*, see Nichols, "Milton's Claim," 205–208.

40. Spitzer, *Classical and Christian Ideas*, 9.

41. Quoted in Debus, *English Paracelsians*, 25.

42. For a different account of nature in these lines, see Tuve, *Images and Themes*, 48. As in her account of *Lycidas* (97–111), Tuve sees Milton's acceptance of universal sympathy as uncritical. My interpretation is closer to that of Nohrnberg (*Analogy*, 764–765). For a reading of the *Nativity Ode* that supports the idea of the poet as disenchanter, see Buhler, "Preventing Wizards."

43. The Lady's words echo Philomela's in Ovid, *Metamorphoses* 6.546–547: "si silvis clausa tenebor, / inplebo silvas et conscia saxa movebo." On the Lady's affinity to Philomela, see Duran, "Lady in Milton's *A Mask*." On unresponsiveness in *Comus*, see Orgel, "Case for Comus," 39–41.

44. French, ed., *Life Records*, 4:298, 320, 333, 360.

45. Empson, *Some Versions of Pastoral*, 157. On the merging of idyll and country-house poem in these lines, see Lewalski, *Rhetoric of Literary Forms*, 180–181.

46. Johnson, *Lives*, 1:239–240.

47. On Milton's poetic creation more broadly, see Curry, *Milton's Ontology*, 92–113; Lieb, *Dialectics of Creation*, 56–78; and Gallagher, "Creation in Genesis."

48. On the problem of "dregs" here, see Rogers, *Matter of Revolution*, 130–143; Sugimura, "*Matter of Glorious Trial*," 255–268; and Mascetti, "Satan and the 'Incompos'd' Visage," 42–45.

49. On "monist animism" in book 7, see McColley, *Poetry and Ecology*, 118–125.

50. On the "victory of creation over chaos," see Schwartz, *Remembering and Repeating*, 24–32. The chaological literature is vast, but for a helpful overview of the interpretive problems posed by Milton's Chaos, see Leonard, "Milton, Lucretius"; and, in the same volume, Rumrich, "Of Chaos and Nightingales."

51. Spitzer, *Classical and Christian Ideas*, 7.

52. Fowler, ed., *Milton: Paradise Lost*, 449n. See also Leonard, *Naming in Paradise*, 27–28.

53. On Adam's recognition of lack, see Grossman, "Rhetoric of Feminine Priority," 431.

54. Spitzer, *Classical and Christian Ideas*, 151.

55. Hartman, "Adam on the Grass," in *Essays*, 126–127.

56. Ibid., 126.

57. On the romance significance of these terms, see Parker, *Inescapable Romance*, 138–149.

58. Hartman, "Adam on the Grass," in *Essays*, 126, 132.

59. On this scene and the question of natural theology, see Edwards, *Milton and the Natural World*, 64–67.

60. See Burden, *Logical Epic*, 173.

61. See, for example, 8.254. On the significance of subject and object pronouns in this passage, see McChrystal, "Redeeming Eve," 499–501.

62. On Eve, Ovid, and Narcissus, see especially DuRocher, *Milton and Ovid*, 85–93; James, "Milton's Eve"; Guillory, "Milton, Narcissism, Gender," 202–208; Green, *Milton's Ovidian Eve*, 27–41; and Kilgour, *Milton and the Metamorphosis*, 203–209.

On the relevance of the Patristic tradition, see Parker, *Inescapable Romance*, 114–123. On the relevance of Ausonius's *Mosella*, see Poole, *Milton and the Idea*, 168–170.

63. Ovid, *Metamorphoses* 3.493. On Narcissus and Ovid's engagement with Platonism, see Kilgour, *Milton and the Metamorphosis*, 175–181.

64. On the question of coercion and subordination, see Froula, "When Eve Reads Milton"; Halley, "Female Autonomy," 247–248; Silver, *Imperfect Sense*, 318–319; Kahn, *Wayward Contracts*, 208–214; and Dobranski, "Seizures, Free Will." For a different reading, one that underlines the challenge of closeness and "conversation," see Levao, "'Among Unequals What Society,'" 90–95.

65. For readings of the scene that deny a vicious narcissism, see especially McColley, *Milton's Eve*, 74–85; Nyquist, "Genesis of Gendered Subjectivity," 119–122; Leonard, *Naming in Paradise*, 37–40; Martin, *Ruins of Allegory*, 268–269; Mintz, *Threshold Poetics*, 33–67; and Kilgour, *Milton and the Metamorphosis*, 209, 227–228. For a critique of the broader interpretive approach, see Edwards, "Resisting Representation."

66. Fowler, ed., *Milton: Paradise Lost*, 249n.

67. Turner, *One Flesh*, 260.

68. On the Ovidian character of this passage, see Knoespel, "Limits of Allegory," 81; and Kilgour, *Milton and the Metamorphosis*, 198–199.

69. On the idea of "a vector of maturation" here, see Kerrigan, *Sacred Complex*, 70. On Eve's coming to wisdom in book 4, see DiPasquale, "'Heav'n's Last Best Gift,'" 51–55.

70. Hesse, *Forces and Fields*, 69.

71. On the Aristotelian character of this passage, see Rumrich, *Matter of Glory*, 54–56.

72. For a concise account of Milton's opposition to secrecy, see Fleming, *Milton's Secrecy*, 6–13.

73. Fludd, *Mosaicall Philosophy*, 146.

74. Ibid., 170, 224.

75. Marjara, *Contemplation of Created Things*, 218. For a different reading, see Broadbent, *Some Graver Subject*, 166–168. On the Keplerian resonance of the sun's "Magnetic beam" (3.583), see Marjara, *Contemplation of Created Things*, 123–127. On Milton's solar lore more broadly, see Quint, "'Things Invisible,'" 257–263.

76. Hume, *Annotations*, 174.

77. Fludd, *Mosaicall Philosophy*, 145.

78. On the analogy, see Debus, *English Paracelsians*, 113–116.

79. Fludd, *Mosaicall Philosophy*, 64; Fludd, *Doctor Fludds Answer*, 66.

80. Fludd, *Mosaicall Philosophy*, 228.

81. Ibid.

82. Richardson, *Explanatory Notes*, 447.

83. Fludd, *Mosaicall Philosophy*, 196.

84. Bacon, *Sylva Sylvarum*, 261–262.

85. Ibid., 262.

86. Hume, *Annotations*, 174. I do not see Milton referring here primarily to the Galenic conception of the heart's attractive power *within* the body, on which see Harris, *Heart and the Vascular System*, 329, 369–373. For a different approach to the heart in *Paradise Lost*, see Erickson, *Language of the Heart*, 89–146.

87. The word "harmony" subtly emerges as the embedded solution to a kind of aural rebus: *heart* + *moves* + joined + *sweet*.

88. Harvey, *Anatomical Exercitations*, preface, 536. On the figurative significance of Harvey's biology, see Rogers, *Matter of Revolution*, 16–27; and Erickson, *Language of the Heart*, 61–88. For connections between Harvey and Fludd, see Debus, "Harvey and Fludd."

89. On the birth of Sin and contemporary obstetrics, see Schwartz, *Milton and Maternal Mortality*, 211–232.

90. Frazer, *Golden Bough*, 11.

91. Bacon, *Sylva Sylvarum*, 246.

92. Hume, *Annotations*, 238.

93. Ibid., 237.

94. Hartman claims that "Milton's picture of Sin and Death is . . . an exact travesty of *participation mystique*" ("Adam on the Grass," in *Essays*, 131).

95. For analogous claims about Milton's attitude toward alchemy, see Martin, "'What If the Sun,'" 244–245; and Duran, *Age of Milton*, 75–76. For a more extensive, if less critical, approach, see Abraham, "'Sounding Alchymie.'"

96. On the problem of *virtutes*, see Hutchison, "Dormitive Virtues." On the apple as a "magical container" of knowledge, see Lewis, *Preface*, 69. For a wide-ranging anthropological reading of the fruit, see Lieb, *Poetics of the Holy*, 89–118.

97. Edwards, *Milton and the Natural World*, 29, 21, 33.

98. On the link between "'magic tree' ideas" and Paracelsianism, see Poole, *Milton and the Idea*, 68–76, 185–186.

99. Fludd, *Mosaicall Philosophy*, 236.

100. Waldock, *"Paradise Lost" and Its Critics*, 46, 51. In descending order of vehemence, Waldock opposes Lewis's charge of "uxoriousness" (*Preface*, 126) and Tillyard's claim for "gregariousness" (*Milton*, 262). Lewis's Augustinian reading of the Fall, according to which Adam "did not believe what his wife said to him to be true, but yielded because of the social bond (*socialis necessitudo*) between them" (*Preface*, 68), suggests an important alternative source for Milton's emphasis on sympathy.

101. Turner, *One Flesh*, 298.

102. For an Aristotelian reading of Adam's fall, with the claim that "Adam's own pity and fear for Eve . . . invite our sympathetic identification with Adam," see Kahn, *Wayward Contracts*, 219–221.

103. Burrow, *Epic Romance*, 283.

104. My position here is close to Burden's (*Logical Epic*, 167).

105. For a challenge to the idea of Raphael's Neoplatonism, see Daniel, "Milton's Neo-Platonic Angel?"

106. On the significance of touch, and its connection to marriage and the hierarchy of the sexes, see Rogers, "Transported Touch."

107. Waldock, *"Paradise Lost" and Its Critics*, 52.

108. Porta, *Natural Magick*, 13.

109. Fludd, *Mosaicall Philosophy*, 292. Silver suggests that, at this moment, "Adam and Eve have become each other's fetish, not only in the sexual but also in the magical sense" (*Imperfect Sense*, 338).

110. On the connections to Ovid—and Lucan—in this scene, see DuRocher, *Milton and Ovid*, 119–130; Kerrigan, "Complicated Monsters"; and Kilgour, *Milton and the Metamorphosis*, 199–201. On the natural-historical significance, see Edwards, *Milton and the Natural World*, 85–98.

111. Lewis (*Preface*, 67) makes this point as well.

112. For a reading of Milton's Eden that deemphasizes the distinction between pre- and postlapsarian reality, see Piciotto, *Labors of Innocence*, 400–492. My view is closer to that of Poole: "For Milton, occasionally called a Baconian or a radical, the Fall not only damaged our ability to describe, but it cracked the frame of the cosmos. To this extent, no work embodies a more devastating, literally catastrophic vision of the Fall" (*Milton and the Idea*, 180).

113. On the wounding of the earth and the new divide between the human and the natural, see Hiltner, *Milton and Ecology*, 48–52, 125–134.

114. For the claim that Milton is achieving a particularly "Vergilian effect" in this scene, see Revard, "Vergil's *Georgics*," 275, 280n20. For Shumaker, Milton's "animizing expressions" imply a cosmic sentience that Milton carries over from "remote antiquity" (*Unpremeditated Verse*, 68). Shumaker's reading does not, I think, do full justice to the complexity and ambivalence of Milton's vitalist vision; ultimately there is little to distinguish Shumaker's Milton from, say, Campanella. For an explicit rejection of the idea of pathetic fallacy in this scene, see DuRocher, "Wounded Earth," 101.

CHAPTER 4. *PARADISE LOST* AND THE HUMAN FACE OF SYMPATHY

1. Johnson, *Lives*, 1:246–247.

2. Especially since the publication of Stanley Fish's *Surprised by Sin*, Johnson's assessment of the epic as generally uninstructive has seemed strongly countercurrent. On Milton's poem as "paideutic," see Radzinowicz, "Politics of *Paradise Lost*," 206; and Thickstun, *Milton's "Paradise Lost."*

3. On the traditions of moral philosophy that Milton inherited, see Kraye, "Moral Philosophy." For a broad characterization of Milton's conception of moral philosophy, see Fallon, "Milton and Literary Virtue."

4. Lieb, *Theological Milton*, 160.

5. Fowler, ed., *Milton: Paradise Lost*, 580n.

6. On the origination and assimilation of antifeminist discourse in this scene, see Miller, "Serpentine Eve," 59–64.

7. Burden suggests that instead of falling Adam should sue for divorce (*Logical Epic*, 168–171). For a rejoinder, see Leonard, *Naming in Paradise*, 213–221.

8. Broadbent, *Some Graver Subject*, 151–152; Fowler, ed., *Milton: Paradise Lost*, 585n. See also Wittington, "Vergil's Nisus."

9. On Eve as imitator, see Grossman, "*Authors to Themselves*," 158–161.

10. Tillyard, *Studies in Milton*, 40. Tillyard goes on to write, "The whole elaborate edifice has been staged to give all possible weight to a quite uncomplicated and commonplace trickle of pure human sympathy" (43). For a counterpoint, see Christopher, *Science of the Saints*, 163–174. I do not agree with Christopher, however, that the

burden of reconciliation falls on Adam. On "Milton's special sympathy for Eve" in this scene, see Ferry, "Milton's Creation of Eve," 127–130. On Eve as a "Homeric suppliant" and Adam's Achillean pity, see Revard, "Milton, Homer," 33.

11. Milton effectively revisited this scene, and this passage, in *Samson Agonistes*, where Dalila implores Samson, "And Love hath oft, well meaning, wrought much wo, / Yet always pity or pardon hath obtain'd. / Be not unlike all others, not austere / As thou art strong, inflexible as steel. / If thou in strength all mortals dost exceed, / In uncompassionate anger do not so" (813–818). In rewriting the scene, Milton reversed it: Samson and Dalila do not reconcile; Samson, unlike Adam, remains "uncompassionate" toward his estranged partner.

12. On the significance of "wrought," see Goodman, "'Wasted Labor,'" 432–434.

13. If, as Burrow suggests (*Epic Romance*, 282–283), Milton knew Joseph Beaumont's account of the Fall in *Psyche, or Loves Mysterie*, then we might see Milton revising Beaumont by supplementing his own version of the Fall with this scene. Note the use of "Commiseration" in Beaumont's lines: "But at last / Commiseration of his *Spous's* case / Grew to such strength in his too-tender Breast / That Pitty to himselfe it did displace" (*Psyche*, 94). In book 10 Milton imagines a redemptive "Commiseration."

14. Pico, "Oration," in Cassirer, Kristeller, and Randall, eds., *Renaissance Philosophy of Man*, 249.

15. Christopher, *Science of the Saints*, 167.

16. Goodman has also noted this echo ("'Wasted Labor,'" 433).

17. Quilligan, *Milton's Spenser*, 241.

18. Burden, *Logical Epic*, 191. On Milton's engagement with the conventions of tragedy in his epic, see also Steadman, *Epic and Tragic Structure*, esp. 33–40; and Lewalski, *Rhetoric of Literary Forms*, 220–253. On the idea of history as tragedy, see Loewenstein, *Milton and the Drama of History*, 94–101.

19. Marshall, *Figure of Theater*, 169.

20. On Adam and the question of gender in this scene, see Lehnhof, "Performing Masculinity," 74–75.

21. Cf. 11.757.

22. On the theme of "proteanism," see Giamatti, *Exile and Change*, 115–150.

23. Burrow, *Epic Romance*, 271–272.

24. On Milton's relationship to Stoic pathology, see Hughes, *Ten Perspectives on Milton*, 153–159; Shifflett, *Stoicism, Politics, and Literature*, 107–154 (with minimal discussion of *Paradise Lost*); and Schoenfeldt, "'Commotion Strange,'" 51–53.

25. On this theme, see Radzinowicz, "Eve and Dalila."

26. Marlowe, *Doctor Faustus*, 140. On Milton's Satan and Marlowe, see Forsyth, *Satanic Epic*, 152–155.

27. This use of "spectators" suggests that spectatorship is not an inherently fallen state. But whereas we might say that the spectatorial is a posture of appreciation and glorification before the Fall, after the Fall it is more imposed, and it is subject to the experience of exclusion and alienation.

28. On Milton and the matter of rights, see Patterson, "Rights Talk in Milton's Poetry."

29. Spencer, *Discourse concerning Prodigies*, 70.

30. On Satan's temptations and the "removal of the demonic from nature" in *Paradise Regained*, see Quint, "Disenchanted World."
31. For a very different reading of this phrase, see Fish, "Wanting a Supplement," 64.
32. On scientific pursuit and "forbidden knowledge" in the seventeenth century, see Eamon, *Science and the Secrets of Nature*, 291–300, 320–322.
33. Arendt, *On Revolution*, 84.
34. On the challenge of reading the political positions of Milton's revolutionary prose in relation to his poetry, see Patterson, "His Singing Robes."
35. On Milton and republicanism, see especially Dzelzainis, "Milton's Classical Republicanism"; Corns, "Milton and the Characteristics"; Norbrook, *Writing the English Republic*, 109–139, 182–212, 433–491; and Worden, *Literature and Politics*, 218–240. Of republicans, Worden argues, Milton "is never a doctrinaire one" (229).
36. Norbrook, *Writing the English Republic*, 110.
37. On the rhetorical complexity of this passage, see Cable, *Carnal Rhetoric*, 58–62.
38. Best, *One Body in Christ*, 96.
39. On the openness and adaptability of the analogy, see Sharpe, *Remapping Early Modern England*, 112; and Schoenfeldt, "Reading Bodies," 221–227.
40. Calamy, *Englands Looking-Glasse*, 32, 34.
41. Grosse, *Sweet and Soule-Perswading Inducements*, 358.
42. Calamy, *Englands Looking-Glasse*, 69.
43. Marshall, *Meroz Cursed*, 19, 28–29.
44. Patterson, *Fables of Power*, 128. Patterson sees the fable as "an image of the Long Parliament" (129), but here I accept the argument of Prior, "New Light on Milton's 'Fable,'" 397–398.
45. Livy, *Ab urbe condita* 2.32.9; Livy, *From the Founding*, 1:322–325.
46. Seneca, *De ira* 2.31; Seneca, *Moral Essays*, 1:236–237.
47. Mueller, "Embodying Glory."
48. Prynne, *Lord Bishops*, L1v–r.
49. Lewalski, *Life of John Milton*, 129.
50. Norbrook, *Writing the English Republic*, 113.
51. Kahn, *Wayward Contracts*, 128.
52. On Charles as an object of compassion, see Staines, "Compassion in the Public Sphere."
53. Rogers, *Matter of Revolution*, 138.
54. On the pathological body politic, see Harris, *Foreign Bodies*.
55. Schoenfeldt, "Reading Bodies," 235, 234, 236.
56. Patterson, *Reading between the Lines*, 255.
57. Spitzer, *Classical and Christian Ideas*, 84.
58. On Nimrod and republicanism, see Dzelzainis, "Politics of *Paradise Lost*," 566.
59. For similar characterizations of the polity of Noah's descendants, see Smith, "Civil War to Restoration," 262; and Radzinowicz, "Politics of *Paradise Lost*," 213.
60. See Patterson, *Reading between the Lines*, 252–256.
61. On the contemporary use of the Babel story, see Achinstein, *Milton and the Revolutionary Reader*, 83–88.

62. See, for example, Loewenstein, *Milton and the Drama of History*, 122–123; and Quint, *Epic and Empire*, 306–307.

63. On the king and his book as idols, see Lewalski, "Milton and Idolatry," 220–221. On the topical optics of *Eikonoklastes*, see Achinstein, *Milton and the Revolutionary Reader*, 136–176.

64. On the model of the Sanhedrin, see Brown, "Great Senates and Godly Education," 46–50.

65. Hill, *Milton and the English Revolution*, 408.

66. Patterson, ed., *John Milton*, 14. See also Patterson, *Milton's Words*, 200–202.

67. On Solomon as "good moral naturalist," see Radzinowicz, "Politics of *Paradise Lost*," 207–208.

68. On the analogy, see Loewenstein, *Milton and the Drama of History*, 123.

69. Cavendish, *Natures Picture[s]*, 286, 282.

70. For the claim that Milton employs alchemical language here, see Cummins, "Matter and Apocalyptic Transformations," 170–171.

71. On the question of whether or not this participation preserves the status of the individual, see Benet, " 'All in All' "; McColley, " 'All in All' "; and Cummins, "Matter and Apocalyptic Transformations," 171–172.

72. At one point Fludd tellingly alters the mood of 1 Corinthians 15:28, cited marginally: "And therefore the Scriptures aver in another place, that God is *omnia in omnibus, God is all in all*" (*Mosaicall Philosophy*, 45). The elided verb is transformed, as it were by attraction, in the translation; the subjunctive *sit* becomes the indicative *est*.

73. Fludd, *Mosaicall Philosophy*, 242–243.

74. On the political milieu of Milton's heaven more generally, see Lewalski, "*Paradise Lost* and Milton's Politics," 156–158.

75. Schoenfeldt, "Reading Bodies," 235–236. On the body politic and Milton's view of kingship, see also Trubowitz, "Body Politics."

76. Smith, "Civil War to Restoration," 263.

77. Milton returns to economics, but we might also say that he returns to gender politics; Michael's elevation of "unanimity" comes six lines after his description of Eve's "meek submission" (12.597). On this moment, see Wittreich, *Feminist Milton*, 106.

78. By paralleling "Under . . ." and "United . . . ," Milton creates the folk-etymological effect that the root of the preposition is the Latin participial stem *unit-*.

79. Hume, *Treatise of Human Nature*, 226.

80. Ibid., 363.

81. Hume, *Natural History of Religion*, 28.

82. Hume, *Treatise of Human Nature*, xv.

83. Hume, *Enquiries*, 189.

84. My emphasis on this moral turn, from the universal to the personal, can be seen to parallel Gordon Teskey's claim for Milton's modernity: "Milton is the last major poet in the European literary tradition for whom the act of creation is centered in God and the first in whom the act of creation begins to find its center in the human." But whereas I see in Milton primarily a rationalization of the magical, Teskey, engaging with Benjamin, sees technologization on one hand and poeticization on the other: "The mysterious effects that do survive in the account of Creation in book seven of

Paradise Lost survive, so to speak, as quotations, as wonders that have been enframed by a wholly technological outlook. Where, then, does the mystery go? It is transferred to the poet who creates. If God creates like a great scientist and engineer, according to reason, the poet's access to God's accomplishment becomes deeply invested with aura." Teskey, *Delirious Milton*, 5–6, 27.

CHAPTER 5. "MORAL MAGICK"

1. Seward, *Letters of Anna Seward*, 4:366. Quoted in Wittreich, *Feminist Milton*, 110.
2. Steele, *Christian Hero*, 87–88.
3. *Spectator*, 2:165. On this theme, see in particular *Spectator* nos. 169, 177, 273, 302, 351, 357, 397. On Addison's and Steele's dramatic engagement with the sentimental virtues, see Chandler, *Archaeology of Sympathy*, 218–223; Ellison, *Cato's Tears*, 48–62; and Hynes, "Richard Steele."
4. See, for example, Tuveson, "Importance of Shaftesbury"; Mullan, *Sentiment and Sociability*, 18–56; Starr, *Lyric Generations*, 72–100; Gottlieb, *Feeling British*, 28–30; and Yousef, "Feeling for Philosophy." A notable exception is Ellison, *Cato's Tears*, 23–47.
5. Crane, "Suggestions," in *Essays*, 1:203. Whichcote, *Works*, 4:213. On the Whichcote-Tuckney exchange, see Rivers, *Reason, Grace, and Sentiment*, 1:8–12, 53–54. On the "Puritan background" of the Cambridge Platonists and their opposition to Calvinism, see Cragg, ed., *Cambridge Platonists*, 7–11.
6. Whichcote, *Works*, 4:213; Whichcote, *Moral and Religious Aphorisms*, 136.
7. For a similar claim about More and Cudworth, see Rogers, "Other-Worldly Philosophers."
8. Cudworth, *True Intellectual System*, 148.
9. Gadamer, *Truth and Method*, 22.
10. Klein, "Enlightenment as Conversation," 158, 155.
11. On Shaftesbury and the Cambridge Platonists, see Cassirer, *Platonic Renaissance in England*, 157–202; Passmore, *Ralph Cudworth*, 96–100; and, more critically, Rivers, *Reason, Grace, and Sentiment*, 2:87–88, 129–132.
12. On the problem of identification, see Rogers, "Other-Worldly Philosophers," 4–6. On the complex relationship of More, Cudworth, and Whichcote to Platonism, see, for example, Henry, "Cambridge Platonist's Materialism"; and Scott, "Reason, Recollection."
13. Nicolson, ed., *Conway Letters*, 391.
14. Burnet, *Bishop Burnet's History*, 1:187.
15. Ward, *Life*, 12. On this period, see Crocker, *Henry More, 1614–1687*, 4–8.
16. On More, Cudworth, and magical traditions, see Webster, *From Paracelsus to Newton*, 68–71; and Hall, *Henry More*, 23–38.
17. Cudworth, *True Intellectual System*, 286.
18. On the polemic between More and Vaughan, see Burnham, "More-Vaughan Controversy"; Brann, "Conflict between Reason and Magic"; and Guinsburg, "Henry More, Thomas Vaughan."
19. More, *Enthusiasmus Triumphatus*, 70, 70–71.
20. Ibid., 73, 75, 195, 196.
21. Ibid., 204, 199, 205.

22. On More's critique and the problem of enthusiasm in the seventeenth century, see especially Williamson, "Restoration Revolt"; Heyd, "Reaction to Enthusiasm"; and Heyd, *"Be Sober and Reasonable,"* 1–164.

23. More, *Enthusiasmus Triumphatus*, 46, 48.

24. Cudworth, *True Intellectual System*, 153.

25. On Cudworth's "contemporary orientation" toward the ancients (148), see Hutton, "Some Thoughts."

26. More, *Immortality of the Soul*, 279, 221.

27. Cudworth, *True Intellectual System*, 136.

28. Ibid., 133, 153, 152.

29. Ibid., 161, 162.

30. More, *Immortality of the Soul*, 266, 450. On More's and Cudworth's conceptions of nature, see especially Hunter, "Seventeenth Century Doctrine"; Henry, "Medicine and Pneumatology"; Henry, "Henry More versus Robert Boyle"; Lotti, *Ralph Cudworth*; and Smith and Phemister, "Leibniz and the Cambridge Platonists."

31. More, *Immortality of the Soul*, 222.

32. Cudworth, *True Intellectual System*, 161, 172.

33. Henry, "Henry More versus Robert Boyle," 62. On intellectualist versus voluntarist theologies and "the voluntarism and science thesis," see also Henry, "Voluntarist Theology"; and Harrison, "Voluntarism and the Origins."

34. On More's and Cudworth's complex positions on the mechanical philosophy, see Gabbey, "Limits of Mechanism"; and Gabbey, "Cudworth, More."

35. Cudworth, *True Intellectual System*, 152, 167.

36. More, *Antidote against Atheisme*, 159.

37. Cudworth, *True Intellectual System*, 61, 146.

38. More, *Explanation of the Grand Mystery*, vii.

39. Cudworth, *True Intellectual System*, 341.

40. Ibid., 147, 98, 97, 98.

41. Ibid., 823, 175.

42. For a lucid exposition of this theological stance, see Gill, *British Moralists on Human Nature*, 20–23. On its complexity, see Herdt, "Affective Perfectionism."

43. Whichcote, *Moral and Religious Aphorisms*, 38–39, 112.

44. Cudworth, *True Intellectual System*, 2nd ed., xi.

45. Cudworth, *True Intellectual System*, A4r.

46. Ibid., 205.

47. Ibid., 874.

48. Cudworth, *Sermon*, 53.

49. Ibid., 64–65, 62–63, 60.

50. Cudworth, *True Intellectual System*, 663.

51. Cudworth, *Sermon*, 61, 50.

52. Kishlansky, *Monarchy Transformed*, 172.

53. Cudworth, *Sermon*, 61.

54. British Library, Add. MS 4980, 219. I have altered the metathesized *ni*. Cudworth's discussion of natural magic is also noted in Herdt, "Rise of Sympathy," 377.

55. British Library, Add. MS 4983, 83. On the "Cudworth manuscripts," see Passmore, *Ralph Cudworth*, 107–113. If Cudworth did not write this passage, as has been suggested, the author was a very exacting imitator of his style. Passmore's attribution of Add. MS 4983 to Cudworth can be supported on lexical grounds. Cudworth uses the collocation "Livingly united" in *The True Intellectual System* (307), and *totum* is a Cudworthian keyword. Passmore cites this passage to emphasize the "notion of 'system'" in Cudworth's philosophy (*Ralph Cudworth*, 71); he reads "lovingly united" rather than "livingly united."

56. Hobbes, *Leviathan*, 52–53, 155.

57. On Cudworth's response to Hobbes, see Zagorin, "Cudworth and Hobbes"; Zarka, "Critique de Hobbes"; and Parkin, *Taming the Leviathan*, 322–334.

58. Cudworth, *True Intellectual System*, 175, 662, 660, 890.

59. Whichcote, *Moral and Religious Aphorisms*, 38, 8.

60. More, *Account of Virtue*, 6, 34, 41.

61. Ibid., 6, 8.

62. Whichcote, *Moral and Religious Aphorisms*, 97.

63. Cudworth, *True Intellectual System*, 891.

64. Farrell, *Paranoia and Modernity*, 139.

65. Cudworth, *True Intellectual System*, 895, 896.

66. More, *Account of Virtue*, 61. On the historical idea and importance of *storgē*, see Fiering, "Irresistible Compassion," 197–198; and Rivers, *Reason, Grace, and Sentiment*, 2:123, 209–210.

67. More, *Enchiridion Ethicum*, 54, 42.

68. Cudworth, *Treatise*, 80.

69. Cudworth, *True Intellectual System*, 504, 132, 270, 540.

70. Shaftesbury, *Characteristicks*, 2:148. Subsequent quotations from *Characteristicks* will be cited parenthetically in the text by volume and page number.

71. On Shaftesbury, politeness, and philosophical endeavor, see Klein, *Shaftesbury*, esp. 3–23, 34–41, 111–119. For a response to Klein's "genealogy" of Shaftesburian politeness, see Ellison, *Cato's Tears*, 27–29.

72. [Shaftesbury], preface to *Select Sermons of Dr Whichcot*, A9r.

73. On Shaftesbury's construction of, and emphasis on, the author-reader relationship, see Marshall, *Figure of Theater*, 13–28.

74. P.R.O. 30/24/27/20, 2r. For a discussion of this analytical distinction, see Rivers, *Reason, Grace, and Sentiment*, 2:92–93.

75. [Shaftesbury], *Several Letters*, 39.

76. P.R.O. 30/24/27/23 (1), 4r.

77. See Voitle, *Third Earl of Shaftesbury*, 111–112.

78. [Shaftesbury], preface, A7r, A8v.

79. Ibid., A5v, A5v-r, A6v, A8r.

80. Whichcote, *Moral and Religious Aphorisms*, 97.

81. [Shaftesbury], preface, A8r.

82. Whichcote, *Select Sermons of Dr Whichcot*, 381.

83. Bacon, *Sylva Sylvarum*, 257; Sylvester, *Du Bartas His Devine Weekes*, 189; Hakewill, *Apologie*, 268; Browne, *Religio Medici*, 26.

84. This internalizing move, which Shaftesbury extends, can be seen to exemplify the broader ethical trend toward "subjectivization" that Charles Taylor has asserted in relation to Shaftesbury; see Taylor, *Sources of the Self*, 255–259.

85. See Smith, *Select Discourses*, 148, 333, 365.

86. Norris, *Theory*, 20.

87. Darwall, *British Moralists*, 194.

88. Foucault, *Order of Things*, 23.

89. From this perspective Hobbes is like the critic of psychoanalysis who, challenging the theory of repression as unprovable and untestable, is told that his challenge is in fact further confirmation of the theory; he is merely repressing the idea of repression.

90. On this connection, see Cassirer, *Platonic Renaissance in England*, 195–196; and Norton, *Beautiful Soul*, 27–28, 34–38.

91. On the significance of this passage in the history of philosophical aesthetics, see Cassirer, *Platonic Renaissance in England*, 166. On a parallel passage in Shaftesbury's *Plastics, or the Original Progress and Power of Designatory Art* (1712), see Prince, *Philosophical Dialogue*, 43–46.

92. Pico, "Oration," in Cassirer, Kristeller, and Randall, eds., *Renaissance Philosophy of Man*, 249. Shaftesbury's treatment of magic exemplifies his bent toward what Klein refers to as "the 'modernization' of antiquity" (*Shaftesbury*, 46).

93. Leibniz, *Philosophical Papers and Letters*, 631–632.

94. On Shaftesbury's approach to enthusiasm, see Klein, *Shaftesbury*, 160–169; Heyd, "*Be Sober and Reasonable*," 211–240; and Rosenberg, "'Accumulate! Accumulate!'" Heyd links the history of enthusiasm to the history of secularization, concluding in Weberian terms, "If by secularization one means the gradual decline of the Church and of the authority of the ecclesiastical establishment, then the enthusiasts themselves indeed contributed to this process. If, however, we take secularization to mean the 'disenchantment of the world,' the retreat of the supernatural dimension from human and natural affairs, then it is the reaction to enthusiasm of the clerical establishment which may be taken as an indication of this process. Indeed, Christian intellectuals, especially Protestant ones, in the early modern period rejected not only magical and demonological beliefs, but also the claims of enthusiasts to have direct access to the supernatural realm" ("*Be Sober and Reasonable*," 274–275). The example of Shaftesbury, I think, does not confirm this conclusion; it significantly complicates it. For a comment—likely prompted by Heyd's work—that comes closer to my view, see Klein, ed., *Characteristics*, xxxi.

95. More, *Enthusiasmus Triumphatus*, 2.

96. On the "ambiguity of sympathy in Shaftesbury's account," see also Mullan, *Sentiment and Sociability*, 29.

97. On Shaftesbury's elevation of Socrates and the Socratic, see Klein, *Shaftesbury*, 42–44, 107–111.

98. On the characterization of the self in the notebooks, see Marshall, *Figure of Theater*, 55–70; and Klein, *Shaftesbury*, 70–90.

99. Voitle, *Third Earl of Shaftesbury*, 77.

100. P.R.O. 30/24/27/10 (1), 30r.

101. Ibid., 33r, 36v, 89v.
102. On Shaftesbury's view of the natural world, see Brett, *Third Earl of Shaftesbury*, 62–74. There are moments in Cassirer's *Platonic Renaissance in England* where, as if by metempsychosis, Shaftesbury seems to become a sixteenth-century natural philosopher; just as Telesio and Della Porta conceive of the natural world in terms of "the 'fact' of universal sympathy" (*Individual and the Cosmos*, 150), so Shaftesbury turns, or returns, to "some form of natural sympathy . . . as a basis and first datum" (*Platonic Renaissance in England*, 195). One of the virtues of Cassirer's approach to Shaftesbury's writing, it seems to me, is that he recognizes the significance of older natural conceptions of sympathy in Shaftesbury's thought. But whereas most accounts of Shaftesbury emphasize the moral dimension of sympathy to the exclusion of the natural, Cassirer's strikes me as having the opposite deficiency. In claiming that "there is hardly a word said about Shaftesbury's preoccupation with moral philosophy," Norton does not, I think, do justice to Cassirer's account (*Beautiful Soul*, 27n30), but I agree that Cassirer's emphases lie elsewhere. Not surprisingly, given the context, Cassirer makes a stronger distinction between Shaftesbury and his philosophical predecessors in *Philosophy of the Enlightenment*, 84–85. It is almost as though Shaftesbury himself functions for Cassirer as a kind of Cassirer-esque "symbolic form." I have in mind Erwin Panofsky's use of Cassirer in *Perspective as Symbolic Form*. Of perspective Panofsky writes, "Indeed, it may even be characterized as (to extend Ernst Cassirer's felicitous term to the history of art) one of those 'symbolic forms' in which 'spiritual meaning is attached to a concrete, material sign and intrinsically given to this sign.' This is why it is essential to ask of artistic periods and regions not only whether they have perspective, but also which perspective they have" (*Perspective*, 40–41). For Cassirer, the Renaissance, the Enlightenment, and the Romantic period all have their Shaftesburies, as it were.
103. On Shaftesbury's self-conscious use of dialogue, see Prince, *Philosophical Dialogue*, 47–73.
104. For claims that Shaftesbury submitted rhapsody to a process of positive reconception analogous to that to which he submitted enthusiasm, see Rogers, "Aesthetics of Rhapsody"; and Terry, "Rhapsodical Manner."
105. On design, see Rivers, "'Galen's Muscles'"; Prince, "Eighteenth-Century Beauty Contest"; and Prince, "Preliminary Discourse," esp. 396–409.
106. P.R.O. 30/24/27/10 (1), 12r–13v.
107. Marcus Aurelius, *Meditations* 4.27; Marcus Aurelius, *Meditations*, 82–83.
108. On Shaftesbury's relationship to Stoicism, see Tiffany, "Shaftesbury as Stoic"; Klein, *Shaftesbury*, 60–61, 81–90; and Rivers, *Reason, Grace, and Sentiment*, 2:94–95.
109. In its first published form, *The Moralists* was given the subtitle "A Philosophical Adventure."
110. On Shaftesbury's charged relationship to gender, see especially Barker-Benfield, *Culture of Sensibility*, 105–118; and Ellison, *Cato's Tears*, 25–27, 46–47.
111. Ellison, *Cato's Tears*, 46.
112. Prince, *Philosophical Dialogue*, 52–53.
113. My interpretation of the formal resolution of *The Moralists* overlaps with Prince's (*Philosophical Dialogue*, 66–69). Although he does not describe it in terms of sympathy,

Prince offers a similar account of the dynamics between characters: "The skeptic, no less than the theist, is locked within a single, calcified view of his own identity. The situation of dialogic exchange, like the situation of letter-writing, however, requires that each participant to some extent abandon his existing conception of self and take on the role of the other" (*Philosophical Dialogue*, 68).

114. Smith, *Theory of Moral Sentiments*, 22.
115. Prince, *Philosophical Dialogue*, 69.
116. Kirk, Raven, and Schofield, eds., *Presocratic Philosophers*, 192.
117. See Alderman, "English Editions."
118. Rivers, *Reason, Grace, and Sentiment*, 2:96–97; Boyer, "Schleiermacher, Shaftesbury," 182.
119. Cassirer, *Platonic Renaissance in England*, 200.
120. Rivers, *Reason, Grace, and Sentiment*, 2:152.

CHAPTER 6. THE FUTURE OF SYMPATHY I

1. Gaston, "Impossibility of Sympathy," 129.
2. See Parker, *Triumph of Augustan Poetics*, 25–71.
3. Wasserman, "Nature Moralized," 67–68, 41, 57.
4. Griffin, *Regaining Paradise*, 104, 105.
5. See Voitle, *Third Earl of Shaftesbury*, 70–71.
6. Rivers, *Reason, Grace, and Sentiment*, 2:155, 179.
7. Prince, *Philosophical Dialogue*, 68.
8. For a similar comment about the "outmoded appeal to 'design'"—a comment that has influenced my thinking—see Prince, "Editing Shaftesbury's *Characteristicks*," 40.
9. On the influence of Lockean principles and the privileging of the part in Pope's *Essay on Man*, see McGann, *Poetics of Sensibility*, 15–16.
10. Fordyce, *Dialogues*, 1:391. Subsequent quotations of this work will be cited parenthetically by volume and page number.
11. On Fordyce and his educational project, see Jones, "Scottish Professoriate"; Wood, *Aberdeen Enlightenment*, 49–55; and Rivers, *Reason, Grace, and Sentiment*, 2:181–184.
12. On Shaftesbury and deism, see Rivers, *Reason, Grace, and Sentiment*, 2:7–84, 133.
13. On the "genius loci" topos in eighteenth- and nineteenth-century poetry, see Hartman, "Romantic Poetry," in *Essays*, 311–336.
14. On Fordyce's relation to analogy, see Wasserman, "Nature Moralized," 46–52.
15. Inglesfield, "Thomson and Shaftesbury," 71–72.
16. Drennon, "Source."
17. Aldridge, "Shaftesbury and the Deist Manifesto," 372.
18. On Thomsonian enthusiasm, see Irlam, *Elations*, 113–141.
19. Johnson, *Lives*, 4:268, 269.
20. Ibid., 4:252.
21. On Thomson's deep and complex relationship to Milton, see Griffin, *Regaining Paradise*, 179–202; and Reid, "Thomson's Poetry of Reverie."
22. For a sense of the debate, see Moore, "Shaftesbury and the Ethical Poets"; Cohen, *Unfolding*, 264–269; and Inglesfield, "Thomson and Shaftesbury."

23. On Thomson's concern with sympathy in the light of "lyric tensions," see Starr, *Lyric Generations*, 80. Starr draws a connection between Shaftesbury's hymnic style in *The Moralists* and Thomson's in *The Seasons*, both of which function to socialize—that is, in her reading, to absorb—the self. My interpretation of Thomsonian sympathy moves beyond the self and society to consider the broader tension in *The Seasons* between ontology and psychology.

24. Thomson, *Seasons, Sp.*, lines 89, 9–10, 44, 46. Subsequent quotations from *The Seasons* will be cited parenthetically in the text by season and line number.

25. On *Summer* as the work that "most perfectly embodies the ever expanding margins of the empirical project" (173), see Parker, *Triumph of Augustan Poetics*, 156–173.

26. For a detailed reading of this passage, and a contextualizing account of Thomson's "microscopic eye," see Goodman, *Georgic Modernity*, 56–66.

27. For the claim that Thomson's emphasis on "diffusion" is indebted to Milton, see Reid, "Thomson's Poetry of Reverie."

28. On personification, abstraction, and labor in *The Seasons*, see Williams, *Country and the City*, 68–71; and Goodman, *Georgic Modernity*, 38. On personification and the instability of ontological categories in the poem, see Keenleyside, "Personification for the People."

29. On Thomson, patriotism, and nationalism, see Griffin, *Patriotism and Poetry*, 74–97.

30. On Thomson's debt to *Il Penseroso*, see Griffin, *Regaining Paradise*, 184–188.

31. See Broadbent, "Shaftesbury's Horses of Instruction," 88.

32. Hutcheson, *Inquiry*, 106.

33. Sambrook, *James Thomson, 1700–1748*, 15.

34. My source here is James Sambrook's account of Thomson's life in the *Oxford Dictionary of National Biography*.

35. Kippis, *Biographia Britannica*, 4:264.

36. See Rivers, *Reason, Grace, and Sentiment*, 2:115–116.

37. [Harris], *Concord*, 5, 6. The poem is attributed to Harris in *The Poetical Calendar* (1763).

38. Ibid., 6.

39. Ibid., 8–9.

40. Ibid., 9.

41. Turnbull, *Principles*, 1:16.

42. Ibid. On Turnbull's Newtonianism and his use of the analogy between natural and moral philosophy, see Wood, "Science and the Pursuit," 130–137; and Wood, *Aberdeen Enlightenment*, 40–49.

43. Newton, *Opticks*, 381. On the use and significance of this passage, see Emerson, "Science and Moral Philosophy," 31–32.

44. On the "organic unity" of philosophy in Stoic theory, see Verbeke, "Ethics and Logic."

45. Halévy, *Growth of Philosophic Radicalism*, 6. On this topic, see Emerson, "Science and Moral Philosophy"; and Cremaschi, "L'Illuminismo scozzese." For a broader historical view, see Cohen, "Analysis of Interactions."

46. Quoted in Adam Smith, *Theory of Moral Sentiments*, 3.

47. Turnbull, *Principles*, 1:218.

48. *Guardian*, 2:152–154; Berkeley, *Works*, 7:225–227.
49. *Guardian*, 2:154.
50. Hutcheson, *Inquiry*, 161, 149.
51. On *Alciphron* and dialogic form, see Prince, *Philosophical Dialogue*, 107–135.
52. *Guardian*, 2:152.
53. On Berkeley and analogy, see Walmsley, *Rhetoric of Berkeley's Philosophy*, 160–172; and Prince, *Philosophical Dialogue*, 79–88.
54. Fordyce, *Dialogues*, 1:243.
55. Thomson, *Poem Sacred*, 6, 7.
56. Thomson, *Liberty, The Castle of Indolence*, part V, lines 223–224, 257–258.
57. McKillop, *Background of Thomson's "Seasons*," 31, 34.
58. Turnbull, *Principles*, 1:16, 13.
59. Ibid., 1:16–17.
60. Ibid., 1:16.
61. Ibid., 1:15, 17.
62. Cudworth, *True Intellectual System*, 876.

CHAPTER 7. THE FUTURE OF SYMPATHY II

1. See, for example, Gallagher, *Nobody's Story*, 166–174; and Keen, *Empathy and the Novel*, 42–44.
2. Todd, *Sensibility*, 27; Wasserman, "Nature Moralized," 57.
3. For an important exception to this trend, see Yousef, "Feeling for Philosophy," 621–622.
4. Prince borrows this phrase from Karl Popper; on its relevance to Hume, see Prince, *Philosophical Dialogue*, 144–149.
5. Hume, *Dialogues*, 195.
6. Hume, *Enquiries*, 142.
7. Hume, *Treatise of Human Nature*, xiv.
8. Ibid., xvi–xvii.
9. Mossner, *Life of David Hume*, 31.
10. Hume, *Essays*, 179, 74.
11. Hume, *Treatise of Human Nature*, xix.
12. Ibid., 254, 257.
13. On Hume's moral and psychological account of sympathy, see especially Mercer, *Sympathy and Ethics*; Jenkins, "Hume's Account of Sympathy"; Mullan, *Sentiment and Sociability*, 18–43; Árdal, *Passion and Value*, 41–59, 148–161; Herdt, *Religion and Faction*; and James, "Sympathy and Comparison." In an argument that has some resonance with mine, Herdt interprets Hume's moral emphasis on sympathy as part of a larger project of "displacing providence"; for Hume, she argues, "sympathy is enough to prod us out of self-interested concerns; we do not need divine threats or promises which end up entangling us even more hopelessly in self-interested pursuits." (*Religion and Faction*, 80).
14. Hume, *Treatise of Human Nature*, 224. *Pace*, for example, Herdt, *Religion and Faction*, 39; and Christensen, *Practicing Enlightenment*, 73.

15. Hume, *Treatise of Human Nature*, 219, 224–225.
16. On the complicated matter of publication, see Mossner, *Life of David Hume*, 592–593, 602–607.
17. Hume, *Dialogues*, 145.
18. Ibid.
19. Prince, *Philosophical Dialogue*, 139.
20. Hume, *Dialogues*, 243.
21. Ibid., 195–196.
22. Ibid., 196.
23. Ibid., 203, 203–204.
24. Ibid., 200, 169.
25. Ibid., 249.
26. On Hume's critique of induction in the *Dialogues* and the larger question of conclusiveness, see Prince, *Philosophical Dialogue*, 136–154; and Rivers, *Reason, Grace, and Sentiment*, 2:251–252, 276–279, 321–329.
27. Hume, *Dialogues*, 95.
28. On Hume's conception of, and commitment to, the scientific, see Jones, ed., *"Science of Man"*; Force, "Hume's Interest in Newton"; Barfoot, "Hume and the Culture of Science"; and Wood, "Hume, Reid."
29. Hume, *Treatise of Human Nature*, 319–320.
30. Ibid., 362–363.
31. Hume, *Enquiries*, 213n.
32. Hume, *Treatise of Human Nature*, 316.
33. Ibid., 319, 318.
34. Homes, *Essays*, 19, 20.
35. On Hume's relationship to Shaftesbury, see Rivers, *Reason, Grace, and Sentiment*, 2:241, 293; Mullan, *Sentiment and Sociability*, 26–29; Stewart, "Hume's Intellectual Development," 37–38; and Townsend, *Hume's Aesthetic Theory*, 12–46.
36. Hutcheson, *Inquiry*, 93. On Hume's ties to Hutcheson, see Moore, "Hume and Hutcheson."
37. Hume, *Enquiries*, 296–297.
38. Ibid., 296.
39. Hume, *Treatise of Human Nature*, 593.
40. Ibid., 363, 389, 575.
41. Hume, *Enquiries*, 220. On the representation of sympathy in the *Enquiry* and Hume's move away from associationism, see Herdt, *Religion and Faction*, 71–81.
42. Hume, *Enquiries*, 221–222. In arguing that "the case of the theater does not threaten Hume's model of sympathy because that model is fully theatrical," Christensen, it seems to me, overstates the case somewhat, as if he were reading Smith back on to Hume (*Practicing Enlightenment*, 71).
43. Hume, *Treatise of Human Nature*, 605.
44. Hume, *Enquiries*, 250–251.
45. Ibid., 220.
46. Hume, *Enquiries*, 40; Hume, *Treatise of Human Nature*, 618.

47. Hume, *Enquiries*, 225.
48. Ibid., 224. For a similar claim, see Mullan, *Sentiment and Sociability*, 28.
49. Hume, *Essays*, 370.
50. Hume, *Enquiries*, 281. On this dimension of Hume's social experience, see Sher, *Church and Society*, 59–62, 231–233; and Mullan, *Sentiment and Sociability*, 3–4.
51. Hume, *Enquiries*, 275.
52. Hume, *Treatise of Human Nature*, xvii.
53. My discussion is indebted here to Rivers, *Reason, Grace, and Sentiment*, 2:265–267.
54. Hume, *Treatise of Human Nature*, 620–621, 621.
55. On the commercial and intellectual reception of Hume's work, see Christensen, *Practicing Enlightenment*, 92–95; and Feiser, "Eighteenth-Century British Reviews."
56. Hartley, *Observations on Man*, 1:7, 8, 471. On Hartley, neuroanatomy, and the doctrine of vibrations, see Allen, *David Hartley on Human Nature*, 104–129.
57. Hume, *Treatise of Human Nature*, 387. On Hume's emphasis on mental activity, and his distinction between "limited" and "extensive" sympathy, see Radner, "Art of Sympathy," 196–199; Herdt, *Religion and Faction*, 42–49, 74–75; and Ainslie, "Sympathy and the Unity."
58. Hume, *Treatise of Human Nature*, 370. For a careful analysis of Hume's account of pity, see Herdt, *Religion and Faction*, 44–47. "Pity depends, in a great measure," Hume writes, "on the contiguity, and even sight of the object; which is a proof, that 'tis deriv'd from the imagination. Not to mention that women and children are most subject to pity, as being the most guided by that faculty. The same infirmity, which makes them faint at the sight of a naked sword, tho' in the hands of their best friend, makes them pity extremely those, whom they find in any grief or affliction" (*Treatise of Human Nature*, 370). The reference to the "naked sword" might possibly be an allusion to Digby's anecdote about King James's "strange antipathy . . . to a naked sword," mediated by Malebranche's citation of it in the second book of *De la recherche de la vérité*—an important continental source for Hume. On Hume's relationship to Malebranche, see James, "Sympathy and Comparison."
59. On the idea of the "sympathetic imagination" more generally in the eighteenth and nineteenth centuries, see Bate, *From Classic to Romantic*, 129–159; and Engell, *Creative Imagination*, 143–160.
60. Hume, *Enquiries*, 135.
61. Ibid., 137–138. On Hume's view of induction in the *Enquiry*, see Millican, "Hume's Sceptical Doubts."
62. Hume, *Dialogues*, 211.
63. Hume, *Enquiries*, 140.
64. Hume, *Dialogues*, 226.
65. Phillipson, *Adam Smith*, 65, 71. On Smith's account of sympathy, see especially Marshall, *Figure of Theater*, 167–192; Mullan, *Sentiment and Sociability*, 43–56; Ellison, *Cato's Tears*, 10–12; Griswold, *Adam Smith*, 76–125, 336–344; and Raphael, *Impartial Spectator*, 12–31. Smith's deep and long-standing engagement with Stoicism has been widely recognized; on its early phase, see Phillipson, *Adam Smith*, 19–23. Although I agree with Raphael and Macfie's claim that for Smith the notion of sympathy "was

intimately related to the Stoic outlook," their claim that the Stoics "applied the notion to society no less than to the physical universe, and used the Greek word *sympatheia* (in the sense of organic connection) of both" strikes me as dubious (Smith, *Theory*, 7). Given the Stoic premise of total continuity and connectedness, the idea of sympathy can be seen to apply to society in Stoic philosophy, but I do not agree that the Stoics standardly used *sympatheia* to refer to social connection. On the possible relationship between Stoic *sympatheia* and Smith's sympathy, see also Vivenza, *Adam Smith and the Classics*, 42, 44–46. In my reading, Smith no more than tentatively establishes a point of connection between the two in his account of the Stoic sage: "He enters, if I may say so, into the sentiments of that divine Being, and considers himself as an atom, a particle, of an immense and infinite system" (*Theory*, 276). Here Smith effectively assimilates the Stoic idea of "enter[ing] into the things that are done [eisduesthai . . . eis ta ginomena]" (Marcus Aurelius, *Meditations* 7.30) to his own idea of sympathy, the imaginative work "of the spectator to enter into the sentiments of the person principally concerned, and . . . of the person principally concerned, to bring down his emotions to what the spectator can go along with" (*Theory*, 23). On Marcus and the ethical implications of *sympatheia* (with particular reference to 9.9), see Laurand, "Sympathie universelle," 533–535.

66. Smith, *Theory*, 9.
67. Hume, *Treatise of Human Nature*, 575–576.
68. Vickers, "Analogy versus Identity," 95.
69. Smith, *Theory*, 22.
70. For Smith's technical account of resonance, see *Essays*, 213.
71. Hume, *Treatise of Human Nature*, 317; Smith, *Theory*, 21.
72. Smith, *Theory*, 11.
73. On harmony and beauty as driving concerns in Smith's *Theory*, see Griswald, *Adam Smith*, 109–112, 330–335.
74. Hume, *Enquiries*, 161. On Smith's commitment to the scientific, see Campbell, *Adam Smith's Science*, 25–64; Cremaschi, "Adam Smith: Sceptical Newtonianism"; Schliesser, "Wonder"; and Schliesser, "Some Principles."
75. Pratt, *Apology*, iv, v.
76. Ibid., x, x–xi.
77. Ibid., 71–72, 74–75.
78. Greig, *Letters of David Hume*, 32.
79. Rivers, *Reason, Grace, and Sentiment*, 2:103.
80. Pratt, *Sympathy*, vi.
81. Ibid., 39.
82. Ibid., vi, vii. On Pratt and the complexity of this topic, see Macey, "Amiable Deception."
83. Pratt, *Sympathy*, vi–vii.
84. Ibid., 2.
85. Ibid., 14.
86. Ibid., v.
87. Ibid., 45, 30, 32, 31.

88. Ibid., 7.
89. Pratt may well be echoing Pope's use of this phrase: "See plastic Nature working to this end, / The single atoms each to other tend, / Attract, attracted to, the next in place / Form'd and impell'd its neighbour to embrace" (*An Essay on Man*, Epistle III, lines 9–12).
90. Pratt, *Sympathy*, 5, 8, 9.
91. Ibid., 10, 12.
92. Ibid., 17.
93. Ibid., 48.
94. Abrams, *Natural Supernaturalism*, 212.
95. Wasserman, "Nature Moralized," 41.
96. Quint, "Disenchanted World," 193.
97. Gaston, "Impossibility of Sympathy," 145–146.
98. Pratt, *Sympathy*, 38. In a "zeitgeistlich" vein, Gottlieb argues that Pratt's poem "represents sympathy's apogee as a public discourse" and that its "popularity . . . attests to sympathy's contemporary currency as both explanation and motivation for society's harmonious functioning" (*Feeling British*, 49).
99. Pratt, *Sympathy*, 41.

CODA

1. Shelley, *Frankenstein*, 21, 22. All subsequent quotations of the novel will be cited parenthetically in the text by page number.
2. Hawthorne, *Selected Tales*, 261, 270.
3. Ibid., 259. On the idea of chemical "affinities," see Knight, "Sympathy, Attraction and Elective Affinity." On the Baconian origin of "elective affinity" in *Sylva Sylvarum*, see Dupré, *Passage to Modernity*, 72.
4. Godwin, *Caleb Williams*, 2:19. This phrase is also noted in Marshall, *Surprising Effects*, 201; and Fara, *Sympathetic Attractions*, 213. My interpretation of magnetic attraction in *Frankenstein* parallels Fara's in her brief discussion of the novel (*Sympathetic Attractions*, 213–214).
5. Marshall, *Surprising Effects*, 198–199; Caldwell, *Literature and Medicine*, 45; Britton, "Novelistic Sympathy," 8. In emphasizing the relationship of *Frankenstein* to "the sentimental tradition," James Chandler puts roughly equal weight on Rousseau and Smith; see Chandler, *Archaeology of Sympathy*, 243–246.
6. Marshall, *Surprising Effects*, 182. On Mary Shelley's relationship to Milton, see especially Lamb, "Mary Shelley's *Frankenstein*"; and Gilbert and Gubar, *Madwoman in the Attic*, 213–247.
7. On *Frankenstein*, the Shelleys, and contemporary natural philosophy, see Hindle, "Vital Matters"; Mellor, "*Frankenstein*: A Feminist Critique"; and Knellwolf and Goodall, eds., *Frankenstein's Science*. On mesmerism and animal magnetism, see Darnton, *Mesmerism and the End*; Porter, "Witchcraft and Magic," 250–254; and Fara, *Sympathetic Attractions*, 195–207.
8. Mellor, "Making a 'Monster,'" 19.

9. If, as Marshall suggests, "for Mary Shelley the figure of Rousseau was charged with all the valences of [a] perverse family romance" (*Surprising Effects*, 189), so were the figures of Milton's Satan, Sin, and Death.

10. On this work, see Barnes, *States of Sympathy*, 31–41; Stern, *Plight of Feeling*, 12–14, 22–29; and Chandler, "Placing *The Power of Sympathy*." Chandler's reading of Brown's novel leans heavily on Smith's account of sympathy.

11. Mulford, ed., *"Power of Sympathy*," 87.

12. Hawthorne, *Scarlet Letter*, 142–143. All further references to this work will be cited parenthetically in the text by page number.

13. Digby has been linked not only to *The Scarlet Letter* but also to "The Birth-mark" and "The Man of Adamant"; see Reid, *Yellow Ruff*, 93–95; Reid, "Hawthorne's Humanism"; and Gallagher, "Sir Kenelm Digby." Of arguably equally strong textual grounding is Reid's claim about "The Birth-mark": "One of Digby's experiments, reported to the Royal Society as *Vegetation of Plants*, included an attempt, exactly like Aylmer's, to revive such flowers as the rose and tulip from heaps of 'Ashes' to their 'Idaeal shapes' by applying 'gentle heat under any of them'" ("Hawthorne's Humanism," 340).

14. Digby, *A Late Discourse*, 14, 11, 12.

15. Hutner, *Secrets and Sympathy*, 34.

16. Ibid., 7, 11. See Kesselring, "Hawthorne's Reading," 67.

17. Levine, "Sympathy and Reform," 225. Levine's essay considers both of these "sources" of sympathy. On the connection between Hawthorne and Smith, see also Hunt, "*Scarlet Letter*"; and Barnes, *States of Sympathy*, 5–7. In its recognition of earlier intellectual traditions, the approach to Hawthornean sympathy most similar to mine is that of Male, "Hawthorne and the Concept." Citing Male, Hutner only briefly glances at "the quasi-medical doctrine Chillingworth practices," which he refers to as "primitive" (*Secrets and Sympathy*, 30, 31).

18. Stoehr, *Hawthorne's Mad Scientists*, 114.

19. On medical ethics in the eighteenth and nineteenth centuries, and the ideal of the sympathetic physician, see Haakonssen, *Medicine and Morals*.

20. Hawthorne, *Selected Tales*, 145.

21. Budick, "Perplexity, Sympathy," 233.

22. On the significance of this scene and Hawthorne's complex positioning of sympathy in relation to justice, see Thomas, "Love and Politics." The curious effect produced by the *Cambridge Companion to Nathaniel Hawthorne* is is that sympathy has, à la Foucault, assimilated the whole of its contents.

23. On Hawthorne's representation of a similar idea in *The Marble Faun*, see Dryden, *Nathaniel Hawthorne*, 128–129.

BIBLIOGRAPHY

PRIMARY SOURCES

Agrippa, Heinrich Cornelius. *De incertudine & vanitate scientiarum*. In *Opera cum appendici*. Hildesheim: Georg Olms, 1970.

———. *De occulta philosophia libri tres*. In *Opera cum appendici*. Hildesheim: Georg Olms, 1970.

———. *Three Books of Occult Philosophy*. London, 1651.

———. *Of the Vanitie and Uncertaintie of Artes and Sciences*. Translated by James Sanford. London, 1569.

Aristotle. *Problems*. Translated by W. S. Hett. Loeb Classical Library. 2 vols. Cambridge, MA: Harvard University Press, 1936–1937.

———. *Rhetoric*. Translated by J. H. Freese. Loeb Classical Library. Cambridge, MA: Harvard University Press, 1967.

Averell, William. *A Mervailous Combat of Contrarieties*. London, 1588.

Bacon, Francis. *The Advancement of Learning*. In *Francis Bacon*, edited by Brian Vickers. Oxford: Oxford University Press, 1996.

———. *The Natural and Experimental History of Winds, &c*. London, 1671.

———. *The New Organon*. Edited by Lisa Jardine and Michael Silverthorne. Cambridge: Cambridge University Press, 2000.

———. *The Oxford Francis Bacon: The Instauratio Magna: Last Writings*. Edited by Graham Rees. Oxford: Clarendon Press, 2000.

———. *The Oxford Francis Bacon: Philosophical Studies c. 1611–c. 1619*. Edited by Graham Rees. Oxford: Clarendon Press, 1996.

———. *Sylva Sylvarum, or A Naturall history in ten Centuries*. London, 1651.

———. *Works*. Edited by James Spedding, Robert Leslie Ellis, and Douglas Denon Heath. 14 vols. 1858–1874. Reprint, New York: Garrett Press, 1968.

Barckley, Richard. *The Felicitie of Man, or, His Summum Bonum*. 2nd ed. London, 1631.

Barrow, Isaac. *Of the Love of God and Our Neighbours, In Several Sermons*. London, 1680.

Beaumont, Joseph. *Psyche, or Loves Mysterie*. London, 1648.

Berkeley, George. *The Works of George Berkeley, Bishop of Cloyne*. Edited by A. A. Luce and T. E. Jessop. 9 vols. London: Thomas Nelson and Sons, 1948–1957.

Bibliotheca Digbeiana, sive Catalogus Librorum In variis Linguis Editorum, Quos post Kenelmum Digbeium. London, 1680.

Bond, Donald, ed. *The Spectator*. 5 vols. Oxford: Clarendon Press, 1965.

Boyle, Robert. *Certain Physiological Essays written at distant times, and on several occasions*. London, 1661.

——. *A Discourse of Things above Reason; Inquiring whether a philosopher should admit there are any such*. London, 1681.

——. *Reflections upon the Hypothesis of Alcali and Acidum*. London, 1675.

——. *Some Considerations touching the Usefulnesse of Experimental Naturall Philosophy*. Oxford, 1663.

Browne, Sir Thomas. *Christian Morals*. In *The Works of Sir Thomas Browne*, vol. 1, edited by Geoffrey Keynes. Chicago: University of Chicago Press, 1964.

——. *Religio Medici*. In *Sir Thomas Browne: Selected Writings*, edited by Sir Geoffrey Keynes. Chicago: University of Chicago Press, 1968.

Burnet, Gilbert. *Bishop Burnet's History of His Own Time*. 2 vols. London, 1724–1734.

Butler, Joseph. *Fifteen Sermons Preached at the Rolls Chapel*. London, 1726.

Butler, Samuel. *Hudibras*. Edited by John Wilders. Oxford: Clarendon Press, 1967.

——. *Hudibras. The First Part. Written In the Time of the Late Wars. Corrected and Amended with Several Additions and Annotations*. London, 1704.

——. *Hudibras, In Three Parts, Written in the Time of the Late Wars: Corrected and Amended. With Large Annotations . . . by Zachary Grey*. London, 1744.

Calamy, Edmund. *Englands Looking-Glasse, Presented in a Sermon Preached before the Honorable House of Commons*. London, 1642.

Cassirer, Ernst, Paul Oskar Kristeller, and John Herman Randall Jr., eds. and trans. *The Renaissance Philosophy of Man*. Chicago: University of Chicago Press, 1948.

Cavendish, Margaret. *CCXI Sociable Letters*. London, 1664.

——. *Grounds of Natural Philosophy*. London, 1668.

——. *Natures Picture[s]*. 2nd ed. London, 1671.

——. *Observations upon Experimental Philosophy. To which is Added, the Description of a New Blazing World*. London, 1666.

——. *Orations of Divers Sorts*. London, 1662.

——. *Philosophical and Physical Opinions*. London, 1655.

——. *Philosophical and Physical Opinions*. 2nd ed. London, 1663.

——. *Philosophical Letters: or, Modest Reflections upon some Opinions in Natural Philosophy*. London, 1664.

——. *Playes Written by the Thrice Noble, Illustrious and Excellent Princess*. London, 1662.

——. *Plays, never before Printed*. London, 1668.

——. *Poems, and Fancies*. London, 1653.

——. *The Worlds Olio*. London, 1655.

Charleton, Walter. *Natural History of the Passions*. London, 1674.

————. *Physiologia Epicuro-Gassendo-Charltoniana: or A Fabrick of Science Natural, Upon the Hypothesis of Atoms*. 1654. Reprint, New York: Johnson Reprint Corporation, 1966.

Cicero. *De Senectute, De Amicitia, De Divinatione*. Translated by William Armistead Falconer. Loeb Classical Library. Cambridge, MA: Harvard University Press, 1923.

————. *On the Nature of the Gods. Academics*. Translated by H. Rackham. Loeb Classical Library. Cambridge, MA: Harvard University Press, 1933.

Clark, Andrew, ed. *"Brief Lives," chiefly of Contemporaries, set down by John Aubrey, between the Years 1669 & 1696*. Oxford: Clarendon Press, 1898.

A Collection of Letters, Poems, etc. written to . . . the Duke and Duchess of Newcastle. London, 1678.

Cooper, Anthony Ashley, third Earl of Shaftesbury. *Characteristicks of Men, Manners, Opinions, Times*. 3 vols. Indianapolis: Liberty Fund, 2001.

[————]. Preface to *Select Sermons of Dr Whichcot*. London, 1698.

————. *Several Letters Written by a Noble Lord to a Young Man at the University*. London, 1716.

Cudworth, Ralph. *A Sermon Preached before the Honourable House of Commons*. Cambridge, 1647.

————. *A Treatise Concerning Eternal and Immutable Morality*. London, 1731.

————. *The True Intellectual System of the Universe*. London, 1678.

————. *The True Intellectual System of the Universe*. 2nd ed. London, 1743.

De Beer, E. S., ed. *The Diary of John Evelyn*. 6 vols. Oxford: Clarendon Press, 1955.

Descartes, René. *Oeuvres de Descartes*. Edited by Charles Adam and Paul Tannery. 11 vols. Paris: Librairie Philosophiques J. Vrin, 1964–1974.

————. *The Passions of the Soul*. In *The Philosophical Writings of Descartes*, translated by John Cottingham, Robert Stoothoff, and Dugald Murdoch. 3 vols. Cambridge: Cambridge University Press, 1984–1991.

————. *Principles of Philosophy*. Translated by Valentine Rodger Miller and Reese P. Miller. Dordrecht: D. Riedel, 1983.

Diderot, Denis, and Jean le Rond d'Alembert, eds. *Encyclopédie, ou dictionnaire raisonné des sciences, des arts, et des métiers*. Paris, 1765.

Digby, Sir Kenelm. *A Discourse Concerning Infallibility in Religion*. Paris, 1652.

————. *A Late Discourse made in a Solemne Assembly of Nobles and Learned Men at Montpellier in France . . . Touching the Cure of Wounds by the Powder of Sympathy*. London, 1658.

————. *Observations upon Religio Medici*. London, 1643.

————. *Sr. Kenelme Digbyes Honour Maintained. By a Most Couragious Combat Which He Fought with the Lord Mount Le Ros, Who by Base and Slanderous Words Reviled Our King*. London, 1641.

————. *Two Treatises. In the one of which, The Nature of Bodies; In the other, The Nature of Mans Soule*. 1644. Reprint, New York: Garland, 1978.

Diogenes Laertius. *Lives of the Eminent Philosophers*. Translated by R. D. Hicks. Loeb Classical Library. 2 vols. Cambridge, MA: Harvard University Press, 1925.

Donne, John. *The Complete English Poems*. Edited by A. J. Smith. London: Penguin, 1986.

Dryden, John, and Sir William Davenant. *The Tempest, or The Enchanted Island*. In vol. X of *The Works of John Dryden*, edited by Maximillian E. Novak and George R. Guffey. Berkeley: University of California Press, 1970.

Elyot, Sir Thomas. *The Dictionary of Syr Thomas Eliot knyght*. London, 1538.

Epictetus. *The Discourses, Fragments, Encheiridion*. Translated by W. A. Oldfather. Loeb Classical Library. Cambridge, MA: Harvard University Press, 1928.

——. *Epictetus His Manuall. And Cebes His Table. Out of the Greeke Originall*. Translated by John Healey. London, 1610.

Ficino, Marsilio. *Commentary on Plato's "Symposium" on Love*. Translated by Sears Jayne. Dallas: Spring, 1985.

——. *Marsilio Ficino's Commentary on Plato's "Symposium": The Text and a Translation*. Edited and translated by Sears Reynolds Jayne. Columbia: University of Missouri Press, 1944.

——. *Three Books on Life*. Edited and translated by Carol V. Kaske and John R. Clark. Binghamton, NY: Medieval & Renaissance Texts & Studies, 1989.

FitzGeffry, Charles. *Compassion towards Captives. Chiefly towards our Brethren and Country-men who are in miserable bondage in Barbarie*. Oxford, 1637.

Florio, John, trans. *The Essayes or Morall, Politike and Millitarie Discourses of Michaell de Montaigne*. London, 1603.

Fludd, Robert. *Doctor Fludds answer unto M. Foster: or, The squeesing of Parson Fosters sponge, ordained by him for the wiping away of the weapon-salve*. London, 1631.

——. *Mosaicall Philosophy: grounded upon the essentiall truth, or eternal sapience*. London, 1659.

Fordyce, David. *Dialogues Concerning Education*. 2 vols. London, 1745–1748.

Forset, Edward. *A Comparative Discourse of the Bodies Natural and Politique*. London, 1606.

Foster, William. *Hoplocrisma-spongus: or, A Sponge to wipe away the Weapon-Salve*. London, 1631.

Fracastoro, Girolamo. *De sympathia et antipathia rerum*. Venice, 1546.

French, Joseph Milton, ed. *The Life Records of John Milton*. 5 vols. New Brunswick, NJ: Rutgers University Press, 1949–1966.

Fuller, Thomas. *The History of the Worthies of England*. London, 1662.

Galilei, Galileo. *Dialogue Concerning the Two Chief World Systems*. Translated by Stillman Drake. 2nd ed. Berkeley: University of California Press, 1967.

Gilbert, William. *De Magnete*. Translated by P. Fleury Mottelay. New York: Dover, 1958.

——. *De Magnete, Magneticisque Corporibus, et De Magno Magnete Tellure*. London, 1600.

Glanvill, Joseph. *Scepsis Scientifica, or, Confest ignorance, the way to science in an essay of The vanity of dogmatizing, and confident opinion*. London, 1664.

——. *The Vanity of Dogmatizing: or, Confidence in Opinions*. London, 1661.

Godwin, William. *Things as They Are; or, The Adventures of Caleb Williams*. 3 vols. London, 1794.

Greig, J. Y. T., ed. *The Letters of David Hume*. Oxford: Clarendon Press, 1969.

Grosse, Alexander. *Sweet and Soule-Perswading Inducements Leading unto Christ.* London, 16[42].

Grotius, Hugo. *De Jure Belli ac Pacis Libri Tres.* Edited by James Brown Scott. Washington, DC: Carnegie Institution of Washington, 1913.

———. *The Rights of War and Peace.* Edited by Richard Tuck. Indianapolis: Liberty Fund, 2005.

The Guardian. 2 vols. London, 1714.

Hakewill, George. *An Apologie of the Power and Providence of God in the Government of the World.* Oxford, 1627.

[Harris, James]. *Concord.* London, 1751.

Hartley, David. *Observations on Man, His Frame, His Duty, and His Expectations.* 2 vols. London, 1749.

Hartman, George. *A Choice Collection of Rare Secrets and Experiments in Philosophy.* London, 1682.

Harvey, William. *Anatomical Exercitations Concerning the Generation of Living Creatures.* London, 1653.

Hawthorne, Nathaniel. *The Scarlet Letter: A Romance.* New York: Viking Penguin, 1983.

———. *Selected Tales and Sketches.* New York: Penguin Books, 1987.

Hippocrates. *Ancient Medicine. Airs, Waters, Places. Epidemics* 1 and 3. *The Oath. Precepts. Nutriment.* Translated by W. H. S. Jones. Loeb Classical Library. Cambridge, MA: Harvard University Press, 1923.

Hobbes, Thomas. *A Briefe of the Art of Rhetorique. Containing in substance all that Aristotle hath written in his Three Bookes of that Subject.* London, 1637.

———. *The Elements of Law.* Edited by J. C. A. Gaskin. Oxford: Oxford University Press, 1994.

———. *Leviathan.* Edited by Richard Tuck. Cambridge: Cambridge University Press, 1996.

Homes, Henry. *Essays on the Principles of Morality and Natural Religion.* Edited by Mary Catherine Moran. Indianapolis: Liberty Fund, 2005.

Horace. *Satires. Epistles. The Art of Poetry.* Translated by H. Rushton Fairclough. Loeb Classical Library. Cambridge, MA: Harvard University Press, 1929.

Howell, James. *Epistolae Ho-Elianae: Familiar Letters Domestic and Forren.* London, 1650.

Hume, David. *Enquiries concerning Human Understanding and concerning the Principles of Morals.* 3rd ed. Revised by P. H. Nidditch. Oxford: Clarendon Press, 1975.

———. *Essays, Moral, Political, and Literary.* Revised by Eugene F. Miller. Indianapolis: Liberty Fund, 1985.

———. *The Natural History of Religion [and] Dialogues Concerning Natural Religion.* Edited by A. Wayne Colver and John Vladimir Price. Oxford: Clarendon Press, 1976.

———. *A Treatise of Human Nature.* 2nd ed. Revised by P. H. Nidditch. Oxford: Clarendon Press, 1978.

Hume, Patrick. *Annotations on Milton's "Paradise Lost."* London, 1695.

Hutcheson, Francis. *An Inquiry into the Original of Our Ideas of Beauty and Virtue.* Revised by Wolfgang Leidhold. Indianapolis: Liberty Fund, 2008.

Johnson, Samuel. *The Lives of the Most Eminent English Poets. With Critical Observations of their Works.* 4 vols. London, 1790–1791.

Kippis, Andrew. *Biographia Britannica: or, The Lives of the Most Eminent Persons who Have Flourished in Great-Britain and Ireland.* 2nd ed. London, 1789.

Kirk, G. S., J. E. Raven, and M. Schofield, eds. *The Presocratic Philosophers.* 2nd ed. Cambridge: Cambridge University Press, 1983.

Langbaine, Gerard. *An Account of the English Dramatick Poets.* Oxford, 1691.

Le Fèvre, Nicaise. *A Compendious Body of Chymistry.* London, 1662.

Leibniz, Gottfried Wilhelm. *Philosophical Papers and Letters.* 2nd ed. Edited and translated by Leroy E. Loemker. Dordrecht: Kluwer, 1989.

Letters Written by Charles Lamb's "Princely Woman, the thrice Noble Margaret Newcastle." London: John Murray, 1909.

Libavius, Andreas. *Tractatus duo physici; prior de imposturia vulnerum per unguentum armarium sanatione Paracelsis usitata.* Frankfurt, 1594.

Livy. *From the Founding of the City, Books 1–2.* Translated by B. O. Foster. Loeb Classical Library. Cambridge, MA: Harvard University Press, 1952.

Locke, John. *An Essay Concerning Human Understanding.* Edited by Peter H. Nidditch. Oxford: Oxford University Press, 1975.

Lower, Mark Antony, ed. *The Lives of William Cavendishe, Duke of Newcastle, and of his wife, Margaret Duchess of Newcastle.* London: John Russell Smith, 1872.

Lucretius. *On the Nature of Things.* Translated by W. H. D. Rouse. Revised by Martin Ferguson Smith. Loeb Classical Library. Cambridge, MA: Harvard University Press, 1992.

Mairhofer, Matthias. *De principiis discernendi philosophiam veram reconditioremque a magia infami ac superstitiosa disputatio philosophica.* Ingolstadt, 1581.

Malebranche, Nicolas. *The Search after Truth.* Translated by Thomas M. Lennon and Paul J. Olscamp. Columbus: Ohio State University Press, 1980.

Manilius. *Astronomica.* Edited and translated by G. P. Goold. Loeb Classical Library. Cambridge, MA: Harvard University Press, 1977.

Marcus Aurelius. *Meditations.* Translated by C. R. Haines. Loeb Classical Library. Cambridge, MA: Harvard University Press, 1930.

Marlowe, Christopher. *Doctor Faustus: A- and B-texts (1604, 1616).* Edited by David Bevington and Eric Rasmussen. Manchester: Manchester University Press, 1993.

Marshall, Stephen. *Meroz Cursed, or A Sermon Preached to the Honourable House of Commons, At their Late Solemn Fast, Febr. 23. 1641.* London, 1642.

Milton, John. *Complete Prose Works of John Milton.* Edited by Don Wolfe et al. 8 vols. New Haven: Yale University Press, 1953–1982.

———. *John Milton: Complete Shorter Poems.* Edited by Stella P. Revard. Chichester, West Sussex: Wiley-Blackwell, 2009.

———. *John Milton: Paradise Lost.* Edited by Barbara K. Lewalski. Oxford: Blackwell, 2007.

———. *Milton: Paradise Lost.* Edited by Alastair Fowler. 2nd ed. London: Longman, 1997.

———. *The Works of John Milton.* Edited by Frank Patterson et al. 18 vols. New York: Columbia University Press, 1931–1938.

More, Henry. *An Account of Virtue: or Dr. Henry More's Abridgment of Morals.* London, 1690.

——. *An Antidote against Atheisme, or An Appeal to the Natural Faculties of the Minde of Man, Whether There Be Not a God*. London, 1653.

——. *Divine Dialogues, Containing sundry Disquisitions & Instructions Concerning the Attributes and Providence of God*. London, 1668.

——. *Enchiridion Ethicum, Praecipua Moralis Philosophiae Rudimenta Complectens*. London, 1667.

——. *Enthusiasmus Triumphatus, or, A Discourse of the Nature, Causes, Kinds, and Cure, of Enthusiasme*. London, 1656.

——. *An Explanation of the Grand Mystery of Godliness; or, A True and Faithfull Representation of the Everlasting Gospel*. London, 1660.

——. *The Immortality of the Soul, So Farre Forth as It Is Demonstrable from the Knowledge of Nature and the Light of Reason*. London, 1659.

Mulford, Carla, ed. *"The Power of Sympathy": William Hill Brown and "The Coquette": Hannah Webster Foster*. New York: Penguin Books, 1996.

Nabokov, Vladimir. *The Stories of Vladimir Nabokov*. New York: Knopf, 1995.

Newton, Sir Isaac. *Opticks*. 4th ed. London, 1730.

——. *Sir Isaac Newton's Mathematical Principles of Natural Philosophy and His System of the World*. Edited by Floran Cajori. Berkeley: University of California Press, 1946.

Newton, Thomas, ed. *Paradise Lost. A Poem in Twelve Books*. 2 vols. London, 1749.

Nicolson, Marjorie Hope, ed. *The Conway Letters: The Correspondence of Anne, Viscountess Conway, Henry More, and Their Friends, 1642–1684*. Revised by Sarah Hutton. Oxford: Clarendon Press, 1992.

Norris, John. *The Theory and Regulation of Love. A Moral Essay*. Oxford, 1688.

Ovid. *Metamorphoses*. Translated by Frank Justus Miller. Revised by G. P. Goold. Loeb Classical Library. 2 vols. Cambridge, MA: Harvard University Press, 1984.

Paracelsus. *The Archidoxes of Magic*. 1656. Reprint, London: Askin, 1975.

——. *Archidoxis magicae*. In vol. XIV of *Sämtliche Werke*, edited by Karl Sudhoff. Munich and Berlin: Oldenbourg, 1933.

——. *Paracelse: De la magie*. Edited and translated by Lucien Braun. Strasbourg: Presses Universitaires de Strasbourg, 1998.

——. *Paracelsus: Essential Readings*. Translated by Nicholas Goodrick-Clarke. Wellingborough, England: Crucible, 1990.

——. *Philosophia ad Athenienses*. In vol. XIII of *Sämtliche Werke*, edited by Karl Sudhoff. Munich and Berlin: Oldenbourg, 1931.

Pico della Mirandola, Giovanni. *De hominis dignitate heptaplus de ente et uno*. Edited by Eugenio Garin. Florence: Vallecchi Editore, 1942.

Pliny. *The Historie of the World: Commonly called, The Naturall Historie of C. Plinius Secundus*. Translated by Philemon Holland. 2nd ed. London, 1634.

Plotinus. *Enneads*. Translated by A. H. Armstrong. Loeb Classical Library. 6 vols. Cambridge, MA: Harvard University Press, 1966–1988.

Pope, Walter. *The Life of the Right Reverend Father in God Seth, Lord Bishop of Salisbury, and Chancellor of the Most Noble Order of the Garter. With a Brief Account of Bishop Wilkins, Mr. Lawrence Rooke, Dr. Isaac Barrow, Dr. Turberville, and Others*. London, 1697.

Porta, John Baptista. *Natural Magick.* 1658. Reprint, New York: Basic Books, 1957.

[Pratt, Samuel Jackson]. *An Apology for the Life and Writings of David Hume, Esq.* 2nd ed. London, 1777.

———. *Sympathy; or, A Sketch of the Social Passion.* 2nd ed. London, 1781.

Prynne, William. *Lord Bishops, None of the Lords Bishops. Or A Short Discourse, wherin is proved that prelaticall jurisdiction, is not of divine institution, but forbidden by Christ himselfe.* Amsterdam, 1640.

Richardson, Jonathan. *Explanatory Notes and Remarks on Milton's "Paradise Lost."* 1734. Reprint, New York: Garland, 1970.

Senault, J. F. *The Use of Passions.* Translated by Henry Carey, Earl of Monmouth. London, 1649.

Seneca. *Moral Essays.* Translated by John W. Basore. Loeb Classical Library. 3 vols. Cambridge, MA: Harvard University Press, 1928–1935.

———. *Natural Questions.* Translated by Thomas H. Corcoran. Loeb Classical Library. 2 vols. Cambridge, MA: Harvard University Press, 1971–1972.

Seward, Anna. *Letters of Anna Seward: Written Between the Years 1784 and 1807.* Edinburgh, 1811.

Shadwell, Thomas. *The Virtuoso.* Edited by Marjorie Hope Nicolson and David Stuart Rodes. Lincoln: University of Nebraska Press, 1966.

Shakespeare, William. *The Riverside Shakespeare.* Edited by G. Blakemore Evans et al. 2nd ed. Boston: Houghton Mifflin, 1997.

———. *The Tempest.* Edited by Stephen Orgel. Oxford: Clarendon Press, 1987.

Shelley, Mary. *Frankenstein: The 1818 Text.* Edited by J. Paul Hunter. New York: Norton, 1996.

Smith, Adam. *Essays on Philosophical Subjects.* Edited by W. P. D. Wightman and J. C. Bryce. Indianapolis: Liberty Fund, 1982.

———. *The Theory of Moral Sentiments.* Edited by D. D. Raphael and A. L. Macfie. Indianapolis: Liberty Fund, 1982.

Smith, John. *Select Discourses.* London, 1660.

Smith, Sir Thomas. *The Common-Welth of England, and Maner of Government Thereof.* London, 1589.

Spencer, John. *A Discourse concerning Prodigies: Wherein the Vanity of Presages by them is reprehended, and their true and proper Ends asserted and vindicated.* 2nd ed. London, 1665.

Stanley, Thomas. *The History of Philosophy, In Eight Parts.* London, 1656.

Steele, Richard. *The Christian Hero: An Argument Proving that No Principles but those of Religion Are Sufficient to Make a Great Man.* London, 1701.

Sylvester, Josuah, trans. *Du Bartas His Devine Weekes and Workes Translated.* London, 1611.

Theon of Smyrna. *Expositio rerum mathematicarum.* Edited by E. Hiller. Leipzig: B. G. Teubner, 1878.

Theophrastus. *De Causis Plantarum.* Translated by Benedict Einarson and George K. K. Link. Loeb Classical Library. 3 vols. Cambridge, MA: Harvard University Press, 1976–1990.

——. *Enquiry into Plants and Minor Works On Odours and Weather Signs*. Translated by Sir Arthur Hort. Loeb Classical Library. 2 vols. Cambridge, MA: Harvard University Press, 1916.

Thomson, James. *Liberty, The Castle of Indolence, and Other Poems*. Edited by James Sambrook. Oxford: Clarendon Press, 1986.

——. *A Poem Sacred to the Memory of Sir Isaac Newton*. 3rd ed. London, 1727.

——. *The Seasons*. Edited by James Sambrook. Oxford: Clarendon Press, 1981.

Turnbull, George. *The Principles of Moral and Christian Philosophy*. Edited by Alexander Broadie. 2 vols. Indianapolis: Liberty Fund, 2005.

Usener, Hermannus, ed. *Epicurea*. Rome: "L'Erma" di Bretschneider, 1963.

Van Helmont, Jean Baptiste. *A Ternary of Paradoxes*. Translated by Walter Charleton. London, 1649.

Ward, Richard. *The Life of the Learned and Pious Dr Henry More*. London, 1710.

Whichcote, Benjamin. *Moral and Religious Aphorisms*. Norwich, 1703.

——. *Select Sermons of Dr Whichcot*. London, 1698.

——. *The Works of the Learned Benjamin Whichcote*. Aberdeen, 1751.

Willis, Thomas. *Dr. Willis's Practice of Physick, Being the Whole Works of that Renowned and Famous Physician*. London, 1684.

SECONDARY SOURCES

Ablow, Rachel. *The Marriage of Minds: Reading Sympathy in the Victorian Marriage Plot*. Stanford: Stanford University Press, 2007.

Abraham, Lyndy. "Milton's *Paradise Lost* and 'The Sounding Alchymie.'" *Renaissance Studies* 12 (1998): 261–276.

Abrams, M. H. *Natural Supernaturalism: Tradition and Revolution in Romantic Literature*. New York: Norton, 1971.

Achinstein, Sharon. *Milton and the Revolutionary Reader*. Princeton: Princeton University Press, 1994.

Adams, Robert Martin. *Milton and the Modern Critics*. Ithaca: Cornell University Press, 1955.

Adorno, Theodor. *Aesthetic Theory*. Translated by Robert Hullot-Kentor. Minneapolis: University of Minnesota Press, 1997.

——. *Minima Moralia: Reflections on a Damaged Life*. Translated by E. F. N. Jephcott. London: Verso, 2005.

Aers, David, and Bob Hodge. "'Rational Burning': Milton on Sex and Marriage." *Milton Studies* 13 (1979): 3–18.

Agamben, Giorgio. *The Signature of All Things: On Method*. Translated by Luca D'Isanto and Kevin Attell. New York: Zone Books, 2009.

Ainslie, Donald. "Sympathy and the Unity of Hume's Idea of the Self." In *Persons and Passions: Essays in Honor of Annette Baier*, edited by Joyce Jenkins, Jennifer Whiting, and Christopher Williams, 143–174. Notre Dame: University of Notre Dame Press, 2005.

Alderman, William E. "English Editions of Shaftesbury's *Characteristics*." *Papers of the Bibliographical Society of America* 61 (1967): 315–334.

Aldridge, Alfred Owen. "Shaftesbury and the Deist Manifesto." *Transactions of the American Philosophical Society* 41 (1951): 297–385.

Allen, Richard C. *David Hartley on Human Nature*. Albany: State University of New York Press, 1999.

Allers, Rudolf. "Microcosmus: From Anaximandros to Paracelsus." *Traditio* 2 (1944): 319–407.

Ankers, Neil. "Paradigms and Politics: Hobbes and Cavendish Contrasted." In Clucas, ed., *Princely Brave Woman*, 242–254.

Anstey, Peter R., and Lawrence M. Principe. "John Locke and the Case of Anthony Ashley Cooper." *Early Science and Medicine* 16 (2011): 379–503.

Árdal, Páll S. *Passion and Value in Hume's "Treatise."* 2nd ed. Edinburgh: Edinburgh University Press, 1989.

Arendt, Hannah. *On Revolution*. New York: Viking, 1963.

Arkin, Samuel. "'That Map Which Deep Impression Bears': Lucrece and the Anatomy of Shakespeare's Sympathy." *Shakespeare Quarterly* 64 (2013): 349–371.

Armitage, David, Armand Himy, and Quentin Skinner, eds. *Milton and Republicanism*. Cambridge: Cambridge University Press, 1995.

Barbour, Reid. *English Epicures and Stoics: Ancient Legacies in Early Stuart Culture*. Amherst: University of Massachusetts Press, 1998.

———. *Literature and Religious Culture in Seventeenth-Century England*. Cambridge: Cambridge University Press, 2002.

Barfoot, Michael. "Hume and the Culture of Science in the Early Eighteenth Century." In Stewart, ed., *Studies in the Philosophy of the Scottish Enlightenment*, 151–190.

Barkan, Leonard. *Nature's Work of Art: The Human Body as Image of the World*. New Haven: Yale University Press, 1975.

Barker, Peter. "Stoic Contributions to Early Modern Science." In Osler, ed., *Atoms, Pneuma, and Tranquillity*, 135–154.

Barker, Peter, and Bernard R. Goldstein. "Is Seventeenth-Century Physics Indebted to the Stoics?" *Centaurus* 27 (1984): 148–164.

Barker-Benfield, G. J. *The Culture of Sensibility: Sex and Society in Eighteenth-Century Britain*. Chicago: University of Chicago Press, 1992.

Barnes, Diana. "Familiar Epistolary Philosophy: Margaret Cavendish's *Philosophical Letters* (1664)." *Parergon* 26 (2009): 39–64.

———. "The Restoration of Royalist Form in Margaret Cavendish's *Sociable Letters*." In *Women Writing, 1550–1750*, edited by Jo Wallwork and Paul Salzman, 201–214. Bundoora: Meridian, 2001.

Barnes, Elizabeth. *States of Sympathy: Seduction and Democracy in the American Novel*. New York: Columbia University Press, 1997.

Bate, Walter Jackson. *From Classic to Romantic: Premises of Taste in Eighteenth-Century England*. 1945. Reprint, New York: Harper Torchbooks, 1961.

Battigelli, Anna. *Margaret Cavendish and the Exiles of the Mind*. Lexington: University Press of Kentucky, 1988.

Benet, Diana Treviño. "'All in All': The Threat of Bliss." In Durham and Pruitt, eds., *"All in All,"* 48–67.

Bennett, Jane. *The Enchantment of Modern Life: Attachments, Crossings, and Ethics.* Princeton: Princeton University Press, 2001.

Best, Ernest. *One Body in Christ: A Study in the Relationship of the Church to Christ in the Epistles of the Apostle Paul.* London: S.P.C.K., 1955.

Bianchi, Massimo Luigi. *Signatura Rerum: Segni, magia e conoscenza da Paracelso a Leibniz.* Rome: Edizioni dell'Ateneo, 1987.

Boas, Marie. "Bacon and Gilbert." *Journal of the History of Ideas* 12 (1951): 466–467.

———. "The Establishment of the Mechanical Philosophy." *Osiris* 10 (1952): 412–541.

Boonin-Vail, David. *Thomas Hobbes and the Science of Moral Virtue.* Cambridge: Cambridge University Press, 1994.

Boucé, Paul-Gabriel. "Imagination, Pregnant Women, and Monsters, in Eighteenth-Century England and France." In *Sexual Underworlds of the Enlightenment*, edited by G. S. Rousseau and Roy Porter, 86–100. Chapel Hill: University of North Carolina Press, 1988.

Bowerbank, Sylvia. *Speaking for Nature: Women and Ecologies of Early Modern England.* Baltimore: Johns Hopkins University Press, 2004.

Boyer, Ernest, Jr. "Schleiermacher, Shaftesbury, and the German Enlightenment." *Harvard Theological Review* 96 (2003): 181–204.

Boyle, Deborah. "Fame, Virtue, and Government: Margaret Cavendish on Ethics and Politics." *Journal of the History of Ideas* 67 (2006): 251–290.

———. "Margaret Cavendish's Nonfeminist Natural Philosophy." *Configurations* 12 (2004): 195–227.

Braden, Gordon. *Renaissance Tragedy and the Senecan Tradition: Anger's Privilege.* New Haven: Yale University Press, 1985.

Brann, Noel L. "The Conflict between Reason and Magic in Seventeenth-Century England: A Case Study of the Vaughan-More Debate." *Huntington Library Quarterly* 43 (1980): 103–126.

Brett, R. L. *The Third Earl of Shaftesbury: A Study in Eighteenth-Century Literary Theory.* London: Hutchinson's University Library, 1951.

Breyer, Stefan. "Magie, Zauber, Entzauberung." In *Max Webers "Religionssystematik,"* edited by Hans G. Kippenberg and Martin Riesebrodt, 119–130. Tübingen: Mohr Siebeck, 2001.

Britton, Jeanne M. "Novelistic Sympathy in Mary Shelley's *Frankenstein*." *Studies in Romanticism* 48 (2009): 3–22.

———. "Translating Sympathy by the Letter: Henry Mackenzie, Sophie de Condorcet, and Adam Smith." *Eighteenth-Century Fiction* 22 (2009): 71–98.

Broad, Jacqueline. "Margaret Cavendish and Joseph Glanvill: Science, Religion, and Witchcraft." *Studies in History and Philosophy of Science* 38 (2007): 493–505.

———. *Women Philosophers of the Seventeenth Century.* Cambridge: Cambridge University Press, 2002.

Broadbent, J. B. "Shaftesbury's Horses of Instruction." In *The English Mind: Studies in the English Moralists Presented to Basil Willey*, edited by Hugh Sykes Davies and George Watson, 79–89. Cambridge: Cambridge University Press, 1964.

———. *Some Graver Subject: An Essay on "Paradise Lost."* New York: Schocken Books, 1960.

Brown, Cedric C. "Great Senates and Godly Education: Politics and Cultural Renewal in Some Pre- and Post-Revolutionary Texts of Milton." In Armitage, Himy, and Skinner, eds., *Milton and Republicanism*, 46–60.

Brown, Deborah J. *Descartes and the Passionate Mind.* Cambridge: Cambridge University Press, 2006.

Brunt, P. A. "Philosophy and Religion in the Late Republic." In *Philosophia Togata: Essays on Philosophy and Roman Society*, edited by Miriam Griffin and Jonathan Barnes, 174–198. Oxford: Clarendon Press, 1989.

Budick, Emily Miller. "Perplexity, Sympathy, and the Question of the Human: A Reading of *The Marble Faun*." In Millington, ed., *Cambridge Companion to Nathaniel Hawthorne*, 230–251.

Buhler, Stephen M. "Preventing Wizards: The Magi in Milton's Nativity Ode." *Journal of English and Germanic Philology* 96 (1997): 43–57.

Burden, Dennis H. *The Logical Epic: A Study of the Argument of "Paradise Lost."* Cambridge, MA: Harvard University Press, 1967.

Burkert, Walter. "Zum altgriechischen Mitleidsbegriff." Ph.D. diss., Friedrich-Alexander-Universität, 1955.

Burnham, Frederic B. "The More-Vaughan Controversy: The Revolt against Philosophical Enthusiasm." *Journal of the History of Ideas* 35 (1974): 33–49.

Burns, William E. "'Our Lot Is Fallen into an Age of Wonders': John Spencer and the Controversy over Prodigies in the Early Restoration." *Albion* 27 (1995): 237 252.

Burrow, Colin. *Epic Romance: Homer to Milton.* Oxford: Clarendon Press, 1993.

Cable, Lana. *Carnal Rhetoric: Milton's Iconoclasm and the Poetics of Desire.* Durham, NC: Duke University Press, 1995.

——. "Coupling Logic and Milton's Doctrine of Divorce." *Milton Studies* 15 (1981): 143–159.

Caldwell, Janis McLarren. *Literature and Medicine in Nineteenth-Century Britain: From Mary Shelley to George Eliot.* Cambridge: Cambridge University Press, 2004.

Cameron, Euan. *Enchanted Europe: Superstition, Reason, and Religion.* Oxford: Oxford University Press, 2010.

Campbell, Mary Baine. *Wonder and Science: Imagining Worlds in Early Modern Europe.* Ithaca: Cornell University Press, 1999.

Campbell, T. D. *Adam Smith's Science of Morals.* London: Allen & Unwin, 1971.

Cascardi, Anthony J. *The Subject of Modernity.* Cambridge: Cambridge University Press, 1992.

Cassirer, Ernst. "Giovanni Pico della Mirandola: A Study in the History of Renaissance Ideas." In *Renaissance Essays*, edited by Paul Oskar Kristeller and Philip P. Wiener, 11–60. New York: Harper Torchbooks, 1968.

——. *The Individual and the Cosmos in Renaissance Philosophy.* Translated by Mario Domandi. Philadelphia: University of Pennsylvania Press, 1972.

——. *The Philosophy of the Enlightenment.* Translated by Fritz C. A. Koelln and James P. Pettegrove. Boston: Beacon Press, 1955.

——. *The Platonic Renaissance in England.* Translated by James P. Pettegrove. 1953. Reprint, New York: Gordian Press, 1970.

Chalmers, Hero. "'Flattering Division': Margaret Cavendish's Poetics of Variety." In Cottegnies and Weitz, eds., *Authorial Conquests*, 123–144.

——. *Royalist Women Writers, 1650–1689*. Oxford: Clarendon Press, 2004.

Chandler, James. *An Archaeology of Sympathy: The Sentimental Mode in Literature and Cinema*. Chicago: University of Chicago Press, 2013.

——. "Placing *The Power of Sympathy*: Transatlantic Sentiments and the 'First American Novel.'" In *The Atlantic Enlightenment*, edited by Susan Manning and Francis D. Cogliano, 131–148. Aldershot: Ashgate, 2008.

Christensen, Jerome. *Practicing Enlightenment: Hume and the Formation of a Literary Career*. Madison: University of Wisconsin Press, 1987.

Christopher, Georgia B. *Milton and the Science of the Saints*. Princeton: Princeton University Press, 1982.

Clark, Stuart. "The Scientific Status of Demonology." In Vickers, ed., *Occult and Scientific Mentalities*, 351–374.

——. *Thinking with Demons: The Idea of Witchcraft in Early Modern Europe*. Oxford: Clarendon Press, 1997.

Clericuzio, Antonio. *Elements, Principles, and Corpuscles: A Study of Atomism and Chemistry in the Seventeenth Century*. Dordrecht: Kluwer, 2000.

Clucas, Stephen. "The Atomism of the Cavendish Circle: A Reappraisal." *Seventeenth Century* 9 (1994): 247–273.

——. "Poetic Atomism in Seventeenth-Century England: Henry More, Thomas Traherne and 'Scientific Imagination.'" *Renaissance Studies* 5 (1991): 327–340.

——, ed. *A Princely Brave Woman: Essays on Margaret Cavendish, Duchess of Newcastle*. Aldershot: Ashgate, 2003.

Cody, Lisa Forman. *Birthing the Nation: Sex, Science, and the Conception of Eighteenth-Century Britons*. Oxford: Oxford University Press, 2005.

Cohen, I. Bernard. "An Analysis of Interactions between the Natural Sciences and the Social Sciences." In *The Natural Sciences and the Social Sciences: Some Critical and Historical Perspectives*, edited by I. Bernard Cohen, 1–99. Dordrecht: Kluwer, 1994.

Cohen, Ralph. *The Unfolding of "The Seasons."* Baltimore: Johns Hopkins University Press, 1970.

Conzelmann, Hans. *A Commentary on the First Epistle to the Corinthians*. Translated by James W. Leitch. Philadelphia: Fortress Press, 1975.

Copenhaver, Brian P. "Astrology and Magic." In Schmitt and Skinner, eds., *Cambridge History of Renaissance Philosophy*, 264–300.

——. "Did Science Have a Renaissance?" *Isis* 85 (1992): 387–407.

——. "Hermes Trismegistus, Proclus, and the Question of a Philosophy of Magic in the Renaissance." In Merkel and Debus, eds., *Hermeticism and the Renaissance*, 79–110.

——. "How to Do Magic, and Why: Philosophical Prescriptions." In *The Cambridge Companion to Renaissance Philosophy*, edited by James Hankins, 137–170. Cambridge: Cambridge University Press, 2007.

——. "Magic." In *The Cambridge History of Science: Early Modern Science*, edited by Katharine Park and Lorraine Daston, 518–540. Cambridge: Cambridge University Press, 2006.

——. "Natural Magic, Hermetism, and Occultism in Early Modern Science." In *Reappraisals of the Scientific Revolution*, edited by David C. Lindberg and Robert S. Westman, 261–302. Cambridge: Cambridge University Press, 1990.

——. "The Occultist Tradition and Its Critics." In *The Cambridge History of Seventeenth-Century Philosophy*, edited by Daniel Garber and Michael Ayers, 454–512. Cambridge: Cambridge University Press, 1998.

Cornford, F. M. *From Religion to Philosophy: A Study in the Origins of Western Speculation*. London: Edward Arnold, 1912.

Corns, Thomas N. "Milton and the Characteristics of a Free Commonwealth." In Armitage, Himy, and Skinner, eds., *Milton and Republicanism*, 25–42.

Cottegnies, Line, and Nancy Weitz, eds. *Authorial Conquests: Essays on Genre in the Writings of Margaret Cavendish*. Madison, NJ: Fairleigh Dickinson University Press, 2003.

Cottingham, John. "Force, Motion and Causality: More's Critique of Descartes." In Rogers, Vienne, and Zarka, eds., *Cambridge Platonists in Philosophical Context*, 159–171.

Couliano, Ioan P. *Eros and Magic in the Renaissance*. Translated by Margaret Cook. Chicago: University of Chicago Press, 1987.

Cragg, Gerald R., ed. *The Cambridge Platonists*. New York: Oxford University Press, 1968.

Crane, R. S. *The Idea of the Humanities and Other Essays Critical and Historical*. 2 vols. Chicago: University of Chicago Press, 1967.

Craven, William G. *Giovanni Pico della Mirandola: Symbol of His Age*. Geneva: Droz, 1981.

Cremaschi, Sergio. "Adam Smith: Sceptical Newtonianism, Disenchanted Republicanism, and the Birth of Social Science." In *Knowledge and Politics: Case Studies in the Relationship between Epistemology and Political Philosophy*, edited by Marcelo Dascal and Ora Gruengard, 83–110. Boulder: Westview Press, 1989.

——. "L'Illuminismo scozzese e il newtonianismo morale." In *Passioni, interessi, convenzioni: Discussioni settecentesche su virtù e civiltà*, edited by Marco Geuna and Maria Luisa Pesante, 41–76. Milan: FrancoAngeli, 1992.

Crocker, Robert. *Henry More, 1614–1687: A Biography of the Cambridge Platonist*. Dordrecht: Kluwer, 2003.

Cummins, Juliet. "Matter and Apocalyptic Transformations in *Paradise Lost*." In *Milton and the Ends of Time*, edited by Juliet Cummins, 169–183. Cambridge: Cambridge University Press, 2003.

Curley, Edwin. "Reflections on Hobbes: Recent Work on His Moral and Political Philosophy." *Journal of Philosophical Research* 15 (1989–1990): 169–250.

Curry, Walter Clyde. *Milton's Ontology, Cosmogony and Physics*. Lexington: University of Kentucky Press, 1957.

Daniel, Clay. "Milton's Neo-Platonic Angel?" *Studies in English Literature* 44 (2004): 173–188.

Darnton, Robert. *Mesmerism and the End of the Enlightenment in France*. New York: Schocken Books, 1970.

Darwall, Stephen. *The British Moralists and the Internal "Ought": 1640–1740*. Cambridge: Cambridge University Press, 1995.

Daston, Lorraine. "The Nature of Nature in Early Modern Europe." *Configurations* 6 (1998): 149–172.

Daston, Lorraine, and Katharine Park. *Wonders and the Order of Nature, 1150–1750*. New York: Zone Books, 1998.

Dear, Peter. "A Philosophical Duchess: Understanding Margaret Cavendish and the Royal Society." In *Science, Literature and Rhetoric in Early Modern England*, edited by Juliet Cummins and David Burchell, 125–142. Aldershot: Ashgate, 2007.

De Bruyn, Frans. "Latitudinarianism and Its Importance as a Precursor of Sensibility." *Journal of English and Germanic Philology* 80 (1981): 349–368.

Debus, Allen G. *The English Paracelsians*. New York: Franklin Watts, 1966.

———. "Harvey and Fludd: The Irrational Factor in the Rational Science of the Seventeenth Century." *Journal of the History of Biology* 3 (1970): 81–105.

———. "Robert Fludd and the Use of Gilbert's *De Magnete* in the Weapon-Salve Controversy." *Journal of the History of Medicine* 19 (1964): 389–417.

Detlefsen, Karen. "Atomism, Monism, and Causation in the Natural Philosophy of Margaret Cavendish." In *Oxford Studies in Early Modern Philosophy*, edited by Daniel Garber and Steven Nadler, 3:199–240. Oxford: Clarendon Press, 2006.

———. "Margaret Cavendish on the Relation between God and World." *Philosophy Compass* 4 (2009): 421–438.

Dick, Bernard F. "Ancient Pastoral and the Pathetic Fallacy." *Comparative Literature* 20 (1968): 27–44.

DiPasquale, Theresa M. "'Heav'n's Last Best Gift': Eve and Wisdom in *Paradise Lost*." *Modern Philology* 95 (1997): 44–67.

Dobbs, B. J. T. *The Janus Faces of Genius: The Role of Alchemy in Newton's Thought*. Cambridge: Cambridge University Press, 1991.

———. "Studies in the Natural Philosophy of Sir Kenelm Digby." *Ambix* 18 (1971): 1–25.

Dobranski, Stephen B. "Seizures, Free Will, and Hand-Holding in *Paradise Lost*." In Tournu and Forsyth, eds., *Milton, Rights and Liberties*, 277–291.

Dodds, Lara. "Margaret Cavendish's Domestic Experiment." In *Genre and Women's Life Writing in Early Modern England*, edited by Michelle M. Dowd, Julie A. Eckers, and Laura Knoppers, 151–168. Abington: Ashgate, 2007.

Donawerth, Jane. "Conversation and the Boundaries of Public Discourse in Rhetorical Theory by Renaissance Women." *Rhetorica* 16 (1998): 181–199.

Donnelly, Phillip J. *Milton's Scriptural Reasoning: Narrative and Protestant Toleration*. Cambridge: Cambridge University Press, 2009.

Drennon, Herbert. "The Source of James Thomson's 'The Works and Wonders of Almighty Power.'" *Modern Philology* 32 (1934): 33–36.

Dryden, Edgar A. *Nathaniel Hawthorne: The Poetics of Enchantment*. Ithaca: Cornell University Press, 1977.

Duffin, Anne. *Faction and Faith: Politics and Religion of the Cornish Gentry before the Civil War*. Exeter: University of Exeter Press, 1996.

Dupré, Louis. *Passage to Modernity: An Essay in the Hermeneutics of Nature and Culture*. New Haven: Yale University Press, 1993.

Duran, Angelica. *The Age of Milton and the New Science*. Pittsburgh: Duquesne University Press, 2007.

———. "The Lady in Milton's *A Mask*: From Philomela to *luscinia magarhynchos*." *Essays in Arts and Sciences* 31 (2002): 45–63.

Durham, Charles W., and Kristin A. Pruitt, eds. "*All in All*": *Unity, Diversity and the Miltonic Perspective*. London: Associated Universities Press, 1999.

During, Simon. *Modern Enchantments: The Cultural Power of Secular Magic*. Cambridge, MA: Harvard University Press, 2002.

DuRocher, Richard J. *Milton and Ovid*. Ithaca: Cornell University Press, 1985.

———. "The Wounded Earth in *Paradise Lost*." *Studies in Philology* 93 (1996): 93–115.

Dzelzainis, Martin. "Milton's Classical Republicanism." In Armitage, Himy, and Skinner, eds., *Milton and Republicanism*, 3–24.

———. "The Politics of *Paradise Lost*." In *The Oxford Handbook of Milton*, edited by Nicholas McDowell and Nigel Smith, 547–570. Oxford: Oxford University Press, 2009.

Eamon, William. *Science and the Secrets of Nature: Books of Secrets in Medieval and Early Modern Culture*. Princeton: Princeton University Press, 1994.

Edelstein, Ludwig. *Ancient Medicine: Selected Papers of Ludwig Edelstein*. Edited by Owsei Temkin and C. Lillian Temkin. Baltimore: Johns Hopkins University Press, 1987.

Eden, Kathy. *The Renaissance Rediscovery of Intimacy*. Chicago: University of Chicago Press, 2012.

Edwards, Karen L. *Milton and the Natural World: Science and Poetry in "Paradise Lost."* Cambridge: Cambridge University Press, 1999.

———. "Resisting Representation: All about Milton's 'Eve.'" *Exemplaria* 9 (1997): 244–253.

Egan, James. "Rhetoric, Polemic, Mimetic: The Dialectic of Genres in *Tetrachordon* and *Colasterion*." *Milton Studies* 41 (2002): 117–138.

Ellison, Julie. *Cato's Tears and the Making of Anglo-American Emotion*. Chicago: University of Chicago Press, 1999.

Emerson, Roger L. "Science and Moral Philosophy in the Scottish Enlightenment." In Stewart, ed., *Studies in the Philosophy of the Scottish Enlightenment*, 11–36.

Empson, William. *Some Version of Pastoral: A Study of the Pastoral Form in Literature*. London: Chatto & Windus, 1935.

Engell, James. *The Creative Imagination: Enlightenment to Romanticism*. Cambridge, MA: Harvard University Press, 1981.

Erickson, Robert A. *The Language of the Heart, 1600–1750*. Philadelphia: University of Pennsylvania Press, 1997.

Fallon, Stephen M. "The Metaphysics of Milton's Divorce Tracts." In Loewenstein and Turner, eds., *Politics, Poetics, and Hermeneutics*, 69–84.

———. *Milton among the Philosophers: Poetry and Materialism in Seventeenth-Century England*. Ithaca: Cornell University Press, 1991.

———. "Milton and Literary Virtue." *Journal of Medieval and Early Modern Studies* 42 (2012): 181–200.

———. "The Spur of Self-Concernment: Milton in His Divorce Tracts." *Milton Studies* 38 (2000): 220–242.

Fara, Patricia. *Sympathetic Attractions: Magnetic Practices, Beliefs, and Symbolism in Eighteenth-Century England*. Princeton: Princeton University Press, 1996.

Farrell, John. *Paranoia and Modernity: Cervantes to Rousseau*. Ithaca: Cornell University Press, 2006.

Fawcett, Christina. "The Orphic Singer of Milton's Nativity Ode." *Studies in English Literature* 49 (2009): 105–120.

Feiser, James. "The Eighteenth-Century British Reviews of Hume's Writings." *Journal of the History of Ideas* 57 (1996): 645–657.

Ferry, Anne. "Milton's Creation of Eve." *Studies in English Literature* 28 (1988): 113–132.

Fiering, Norman S. "Irresistible Compassion: An Aspect of Eighteenth-Century Sympathy and Humanitarianism." *Journal of the History of Ideas* 37 (1976): 195–218.

———. *Moral Philosophy at Seventeenth-Century Harvard*. Chapel Hill: University of North Carolina Press, 1981.

Fish, Stanley. *Surprised by Sin: The Reader in "Paradise Lost."* Berkeley: University of California Press, 1967.

———. "Wanting a Supplement: The Question of Interpretation in Milton's Early Prose." In Loewenstein and Turner, eds., *Politics, Poetics, and Hermeneutics*, 41–68.

Fitzmaurice, Susan M. *The Familiar Letter in Early Modern English: A Pragmatic Approach*. Amsterdam: John Benjamins, 2002.

Fleming, James Dougal. *Milton's Secrecy and Philosophical Hermeneutics*. Aldershot: Ashgate, 2008.

Floyd-Wilson, Mary. *Occult Knowledge, Science, and Gender on the Shakespearean Stage*. Cambridge: Cambridge University Press, 2013.

Force, James E. "Hume's Interest in Newton and Science." *Hume Studies* 13 (1987): 166–216.

Forsyth, Neil. *The Satanic Epic*. Princeton: Princeton University Press, 2003.

Foucault, Michel. *The Birth of the Clinic: An Archaeology of Medical Perception*. Translated by A. M. Sheridan Smith. New York: Pantheon, 1973.

———. *Madness and Civilization: A History of Insanity in the Age of Reason*. Translated by Richard Howard. New York: Pantheon, 1965.

———. *The Order of Things: An Archaeology of the Human Sciences*. A translation of *Les mots et les choses*. New York: Pantheon, 1970.

Frank, Robert G., Jr. "Thomas Willis and His Circle: Brain and Mind in Seventeenth-Century Medicine." In *The Languages of Psyche: Mind and Body in Enlightenment Thought*, ed. G. S. Rousseau, 107–146. Berkeley: University of California Press, 1990.

Frazer, Sir James George. *The Golden Bough: A Study in Comparative Religion*. 2 vols. London: Macmillan, 1890.

———. *The Golden Bough: A Study in Magic and Religion*. New York: Macmillan, 1940.

Freedberg, David. *The Eye of the Lynx: Galileo, His Friends, and the Beginnings of Modern Natural History*. Chicago: University of Chicago Press, 2002.

Friedman, Donald M. "Divisions on a Ground: 'Sex' in *Paradise Lost*." In *Of Poetry and Politics: New Essays on Milton and His World*, edited by P. G. Stanwood, 201–212. Binghamton, NY: Medieval & Renaissance Texts & Studies, 1995.

Froula, Christine. "When Eve Reads Milton: Undoing the Canonical Economy." In *John Milton*, edited by Annabel Patterson, 142–164. London: Longman, 1992.

Gabbey, Alan. "Cudworth, More and the Mechanical Analogy." In Kroll, Ashcraft, and Zagorin, eds., *Philosophy, Science, and Religion in England*, 109–127.

——. "Henry More and the Limits of Mechanism." In Hutton, ed., *Henry More (1614–1687)*, 19–36.

——. "Philosophia Cartesiana Triumphata: Henry More (1646–1671)." In *Problems of Cartesianism*, edited by Thomas M. Lennon, John M. Nicholas, and John W. Davis, 171–250. Kingston: McGill-Queen's University Press, 1982.

Gadamer, Hans-Georg. *Truth and Method*. 2nd rev. ed. Translated by Joel Weinsheimer and Donald G. Marshall. London: Continuum, 2004.

Gallagher, Catherine. "Embracing the Absolute: The Politics of the Female Subject in Seventeenth-Century England." *Genders* 1 (1988): 24–39.

——. *Nobody's Story: The Vanishing Acts of Women Writers in the Marketplace, 1670–1820*. Berkeley: University of California Press, 1994.

Gallagher, Edward J. "Sir Kenelm Digby in Hawthorne's 'The Man of Adamant.'" *Notes and Queries* 17 (1970): 15–16.

Gallagher, Philip J. "Creation in Genesis and in *Paradise Lost*." *Milton Studies* 20 (1984): 163–204.

Gane, Nicholas. *Max Weber and Postmodern Theory: Rationalization versus Re-enchantment*. Houndmills, Basingstoke: Palgrave, 2002.

Garani, Myrto. *Empedocles "Redivivus": Poetry and Analogy in Lucretius*. New York: Routledge, 2007.

Gaston, Sean. "The Impossibility of Sympathy." *The Eighteenth Century* 51 (2010): 129–152.

Gaukroger, Stephen. *The Collapse of Mechanism and the Rise of Sensibility: Science and the Shaping of Modernity*. Oxford: Clarendon Press, 2010.

——. *Francis Bacon and the Transformations of Early-Modern Philosophy*. Cambridge: Cambridge University Press, 2001.

Gert, Bernard. "Hobbes and Psychological Egoism." *Journal of the History of Ideas* 28 (1967): 503–520.

Giamatti, A. Bartlett. *Exile and Change in Renaissance Literature*. New Haven: Yale University Press, 1984.

Giglioni, Guido. "The First of the Moderns or the Last of the Ancients? Bernardino Telesio on Nature and Sentience." *Bruniana & Campanelliana* 16 (2010): 69–87.

Gilbert, Sandra M., and Susan Gubar. *The Madwoman in the Attic: The Woman Writer and the Nineteenth-Century Literary Imagination*. 2nd ed. New Haven: Yale University Press, 2000.

Gill, Michael B. *The British Moralists on Human Nature and the Birth of Secular Ethics*. Cambridge: Cambridge University Press, 2006.

Gilman, Ernest B. "The Arts of Sympathy: Dr. Harvey, Sir Kenelm Digby, and the Arundel Circle." In Herman, ed., *Opening the Borders*, 265–298.

Goldie, Mark. "The Reception of Hobbes." In *The Cambridge History of Political Thought, 1450–1700*, edited by J. H. Burns, 589–615. Cambridge: Cambridge University Press, 1991.

Golinski, Jan. "Hélène Metzger and the Interpretation of Seventeenth-Century Chemistry." *History of Science* 25 (1987): 85–97.

Goodman, Kevis. *Georgic Modernity and British Romanticism: Poetry and the Mediation of History*. Cambridge: Cambridge University Press, 2004.

——. "'Wasted Labor'? Milton's Eve, the Poet's Work, and the Challenge of Sympathy." *English Literary History* 64 (1997): 415–446.

Gordon, Richard. "Imagining Greek and Roman Magic." In *Witchcraft and Magic in Europe: Ancient Greece and Rome*, edited by Bengt Ankarloo and Stuart Clark, 159–275. Philadelphia: University of Pennsylvania Press, 1999.

——. "*Quaedam Veritatis Umbrae*: Hellenistic Magic and Astrology." In *Conventional Values of the Hellenistic Greeks*, edited by Per Bilde, Troels Engberg-Pedersen, Lise Hannestad, and Jan Zahle, 128–158. Aarhus: Aarhus University Press, 1997.

Goring, Paul. *The Rhetoric of Sensibility in Eighteenth-Century Culture*. Cambridge: Cambridge University Press, 2005.

Gottlieb, Evan. *Feeling British: Sympathy and National Identity in Scottish and English Writing, 1707–1832*. Lewisburg: Bucknell University Press, 2007.

Gouk, Penelope. *Music, Science and Natural Magic in Seventeenth-Century England*. New Haven: Yale University Press, 1999.

Graeser, Andreas. *Plotinus and the Stoics: A Preliminary Study*. Leiden: Brill, 1972.

Graf, Fritz. "Theories of Magic in Antiquity." In *Magic and Ritual in the Ancient World*, edited by Paul Mirecki and Marvin Meyer, 93–104. Leiden: Brill, 2002.

Grafton, Anthony. *Cardano's Cosmos: The Worlds and Works of a Renaissance Astrologer*. Cambridge, MA: Harvard University Press, 1999.

Graham, Elspeth. "Intersubjectivity, Intertextuality, and Form in the Self-Writings of Margaret Cavendish." In *Genre and Women's Life Writing in Early Modern England*, edited by Michelle M. Dowd, Julie A. Eckers, and Laura Knoppers, 131–150. Abington: Ashgate, 2007.

Grant, Douglas. *Margaret the First: A Biography of Margaret Cavendish, Duchess of Newcastle, 1625–1673*. Toronto: University of Toronto Press, 1957.

Green, Mandy. *Milton's Ovidian Eve*. Burlington, VT: Ashgate, 2009.

Greene, Donald. "Latitudinarianism and Sensibility: The Genealogy of the 'Man of Feeling' Reconsidered." *Modern Philology* 75 (1977): 159–183.

Greene, Thomas M. "Enchanting Ravishments: Magic and Counter-Magic in *Comus*." In Herman, ed., *Opening the Borders*, 298–323.

Grell, Ole Peter, ed. *Paracelsus: The Man and His Reputation, His Ideas and Their Transformation*. Leiden: Brill, 1998.

Griffin, Dustin. *Patriotism and Poetry in Eighteenth-Century Britain*. Cambridge: Cambridge University Press, 2002.

——. *Regaining Paradise: Milton and the Eighteenth Century*. Cambridge: Cambridge University Press, 1986.

Griswold, Charles L., Jr. *Adam Smith and the Virtues of Enlightenment*. Cambridge: Cambridge University Press, 1999.

Grossman, Marshall. *"Authors to Themselves": Milton and the Revelation of History*. Cambridge: Cambridge University Press, 1987.

——. "The Rhetoric of Feminine Priority and the Ethics of Form in *Paradise Lost*." *English Literary Renaissance* 33 (2003): 424–443.

Guillory, John. "Milton, Narcissism, Gender: On the Genealogy of Male Self-Esteem." In *Critical Essays on John Milton*, edited by Christopher Kendrick, 165–193. New York: G. K. Hall, 1995.

Guinsburg, Arlene Miller. "Henry More, Thomas Vaughan and the Late Renaissance Magical Tradition." *Ambix* 27 (1980): 36–58.

Gutting, Gary. *Michel Foucault's Archaeology of Human Reason*. Cambridge: Cambridge University Press, 1989.

Haakonssen, Knud. *Natural Law and Moral Philosophy: From Grotius to the Scottish Enlightenment*. Cambridge: Cambridge University Press, 1996.

Haakonssen, Lisbeth. *Medicine and Morals in the Enlightenment: John Gregory, Thomas Percival and Benjamin Rush*. Amsterdam: Rodopi, 1997.

Hale, John K. *Milton's Cambridge Latin: Performing in the Genres, 1625–1632*. Tempe: Arizona Center for Medieval and Renaissance Studies, 2005.

Halévy, Elie. *The Growth of Philosophic Radicalism*. Translated by Mary Morris. Boston: Beacon Press, 1955.

Hall, A. Rupert. *Henry More and the Scientific Revolution*. 1990. Reprint, Cambridge: Cambridge University Press, 2002.

Halley, Janet E. "Female Autonomy in Milton's Sexual Politics." In *Milton and the Idea of Woman*, edited by Julia M. Walker, 230–253. Urbana: University of Illinois Press, 1988.

Halpern, Richard. "The Great Instauration: Imaginary Narratives in Milton's 'Nativity Ode.'" In Nyquist and Ferguson, eds., *Re-membering Milton*, 10–18.

Harrington, Anne. *Reenchanted Science: Holism in German Culture from Wilhelm II to Hitler*. Princeton: Princeton University Press, 1996.

Harris, C. R. S. *The Heart and the Vascular System in Ancient Greek Medicine: From Alcmaeon to Galen*. Oxford: Clarendon Press, 1973.

Harris, Jonathan Gil. *Foreign Bodies and the Body Politic: Discourses of Social Pathology in Early Modern England*. Cambridge: Cambridge University Press, 1998.

——. *Untimely Matter in the Time of Shakespeare*. Philadelphia: University of Pennsylvania Press, 2009.

Harrison, Peter. "Voluntarism and the Origins of Modern Science: A Reply to John Henry." *History of Science* 47 (2009): 223–231.

Hartman, Geoffrey H. *Beyond Formalism: Literary Essays 1958–1970*. New Haven: Yale University Press, 1970.

Hathaway, Baxter. "The Lucretian 'Return upon Ourselves' in Eighteenth-Century Theories of Tragedy." *PMLA* 62 (1947): 672–689.

Headley, John M. *Tommaso Campanella and the Transformation of the World*. Princeton: Princeton University Press, 1997.

Healy, Margaret. *Fictions of Disease in Early Modern England: Bodies, Plagues and Politics*. Basingstoke: Palgrave, 2001.

Hedrick, Elizabeth. "Romancing the Salve: Sir Kenelm Digby and the Powder of Sympathy." *British Journal for the History of Science* 41 (2008): 161–185.

Heidegger, Martin. *The Question Concerning Technology and Other Essays.* Translated by William Lovitt. New York: Harper & Row, 1977.

Henry, John. "Atomism and Eschatology: Catholicism and Natural Philosophy in the Interregnum." *British Journal for the History of Science* 15 (1982): 211–239.

———. "A Cambridge Platonist's Materialism: Henry More and the Concept of the Soul." *Journal of the Warburg and Courtauld Institutes* 49 (1986): 172–195.

———. "The Fragmentation of Renaissance Occultism and the Decline of Magic." *History of Science* 46 (2008): 1–48.

———. "Henry More versus Robert Boyle: The Spirit of Nature and the Nature of Providence." In Hutton, ed., *Henry More (1614–1687),* 55–75.

———. *Knowledge Is Power: How Magic, the Government and an Apocalyptic Vision Inspired Francis Bacon to Create Modern Science.* Cambridge: Icon Books, 2002.

———. "Medicine and Pneumatology: Henry More, Richard Baxter, and Francis Glisson's *Treatise on the Energetic Nature of Substance.*" *Medical History* 31 (1987): 15–40.

———. "Occult Qualities and the Experimental Philosophy: Active Principles in Pre-Newtonian Matter Theory." *History of Science* 24 (1986): 335–381.

———. "Sir Kenelm Digby, Recusant Philosopher." In *Insiders and Outsiders in Seventeenth-Century Philosophy,* edited by G. A. J. Rogers, Tom Sorell, and Jill Kraye, 43–75. New York: Routledge, 2010.

———. "Voluntarist Theology at the Origins of Modern Science: A Response to Peter Harrison." *History of Science* 47 (2009): 79–113.

Herdt, Jennifer A. "Affective Perfectionism: Community with God without Common Measure." In *New Essays on the History of Autonomy: A Collection Honoring J. B. Schneewind,* edited by Natalie Brender and Larry Krasnoff, 30–60. Cambridge: Cambridge University Press, 2004.

———. *Religion and Faction in Hume's Moral Philosophy.* Cambridge: Cambridge University Press, 1997.

———. "The Rise of Sympathy and the Question of Divine Suffering." *Journal of Religious Ethics* 29 (2001): 367–399.

Herman, Peter C. *Destabilizing Milton: "Paradise Lost" and the Poetics of Incertitude.* New York: Palgrave Macmillan, 2005.

———, ed. *Opening the Borders: Inclusivity in Early Modern Studies: Essays in Honor of James V. Mirollo.* London: Associated University Presses, 1999.

Hesse, Mary B. "Action at a Distance." In *The Concept of Matter in Modern Philosophy,* edited by Ernan McMullin, 372–392. Rev. ed. Notre Dame: University of Notre Dame Press, 1978.

———. *Forces and Fields: The Concept of Action at a Distance in the History of Physics.* New York: Philosophical Library, 1962.

Heyd, Michael. *"Be Sober and Reasonable": The Critique of Enthusiasm in the Seventeenth and Early Eighteenth Centuries.* Leiden: Brill, 1995.

———. "The Reaction to Enthusiasm in the Seventeenth Century: Towards an Integrative Approach." *Journal of Modern History* 53 (1981): 258–280.

Hicks, Ruth Ilsley. "The Body Political and the Body Ecclesiastical." *Journal of Bible and Religion* 31 (1963): 29–35.

Hill, Christopher. *Milton and the English Revolution*. London: Penguin, 1979.

Hiltner, Ken. *Milton and Ecology*. Cambridge: Cambridge University Press, 2003.

Hindle, Maurice. "Vital Matters: *Frankenstein* and Romantic Science." *Critical Survey* 2 (1990): 29–35.

Hirschman, Albert O. *The Passions and the Interests: Political Arguments for Capitalism before Its Triumph*. Princeton: Princeton University Press, 1977.

Horkheimer, Max, and Theodor W. Adorno. *Dialectic of Enlightenment: Philosophical Fragments*. Translated by Edmund Jephcott. Stanford: Stanford University Press, 2002.

Houghton, Walter E., Jr. "The English Virtuoso in the Seventeenth Century: Part I." *Journal of the History of Ideas* 3 (1942): 51–73.

Huet, Marie-Hélène. *Monstrous Imagination*. Cambridge, MA: Harvard University Press, 1993.

Huffman, William H. *Robert Fludd and the End of the Renaissance*. London: Routledge, 1988.

Hughes, Merritt Y. *Ten Perspectives on Milton*. New Haven: Yale University Press, 1965.

Humphreys, A. R. "'The Friend of Mankind' (1700–1760)—An Aspect of Eighteenth-Century Sensibility." *Review of English Studies* 24 (1948): 203–218.

Hunt, Lester H. "*The Scarlet Letter*: Hawthorne's Theory of Moral Sentiments." *Philosophy and Literature* 8 (1984): 75–88.

Hunter, Michael. *Boyle: Between God and Science*. New Haven: Yale University Press, 2009.

———. *Robert Boyle, 1627–1691: Scrupulosity and Science*. Woodbridge, U.K.: Boydell Press, 2000.

Hunter, William B., Jr. "The Seventeenth Century Doctrine of Plastic Nature." *Harvard Theological Review* 43 (1950): 197–213.

Hutchison, Keith. "Dormitive Virtues, Scholastic Qualities, and the New Philosophies." *History of Science* 29 (1991): 245–278.

———. "What Happened to Occult Qualities in the Scientific Revolution?" *Isis* 73 (1982): 233–253.

Hutner, Gordon. *Secrets and Sympathy: Forms of Disclosure in Hawthorne's Novels*. Athens: University of Georgia Press, 1988.

Hutson, K. Garth, ed. *Sir Kenelm Digby's Powder of Sympathy: An Unfinished Essay by Sir William Osler*. Los Angeles: Plantin Press, 1972.

Hutton, Sarah. *Anne Conway: A Woman Philosopher*. Cambridge: Cambridge University Press, 2004.

———. "In Dialogue with Thomas Hobbes: Margaret Cavendish's Natural Philosophy." *Women's Writing* 4 (1997): 421–432.

———, ed. *Henry More (1614–1687): Tercentenary Studies*. Dordrecht: Kluwer, 1990.

———. "Some Thoughts Concerning Ralph Cudworth." In *Studies on Locke: Sources, Contemporaries, and Legacy: In Honour of G. A. J. Rogers*, edited by Sarah Hutton and Paul Schuurman, 143–158. Dordrecht: Springer, 2008.

Hynes, Peter. "Richard Steele and the Genealogy of Sentimental Drama: A Reading of *The Conscious Lovers*." *Papers on Language and Literature* 40 (2004): 142–166.

Inglesfield, Robert. "Thomson and Shaftesbury." In *James Thomson: Essays for the Tercentenary*, edited by Richard Terry, 67–92. Liverpool: Liverpool University Press, 2000.

Irlam, Shaun. *Elations: The Poetics of Enthusiasm in Eighteenth-Century Britain*. Stanford: Stanford University Press, 1999.

Jaffe, Audrey. *Scenes of Sympathy: Identity and Representation in Victorian Fiction*. Ithaca: Cornell University Press, 2000.

James, Heather. "Dido's Ear: Tragedy and the Politics of Response." *Shakespeare Quarterly* 52 (2001): 360–382.

———. "Milton's Eve, the Romance Genre, and Ovid." *Comparative Literature* 45 (1993): 121–145.

James, Susan. *Passion and Action: The Emotions in Seventeenth-Century Philosophy*. Oxford: Clarendon Press, 1997.

———. "The Philosophical Innovations of Margaret Cavendish." *British Journal for the History of Philosophy* 7 (1999): 219–244.

———. "Sympathy and Comparison: Two Principles of Human Nature." In *Impressions of Hume*, edited by M. Frasca-Spada and P. J. E. Kail, 107–125. Oxford: Clarendon Press, 2005.

Janacek, Bruce. "Catholic Natural Philosophy: Alchemy and the Revivification of Sir Kenelm Digby." In *Rethinking the Scientific Revolution*, edited by Margaret J. Osler, 89–118. Cambridge: Cambridge University Press, 2000.

Jardine, Lisa. *Reading Shakespeare Historically*. London: Routledge, 1996.

Jay, Martin. *Downcast Eyes: The Denigration of Vision in Twentieth-Century French Thought*. Berkeley: University of California Press, 1993.

Jenkins, John J. "Hume's Account of Sympathy—Some Difficulties." In *Philosophers of the Scottish Enlightenment*, edited by V. Hope, 91–104. Edinburgh: Edinburgh University Press, 1984.

Jones, Peter. "The Scottish Professoriate and the Polite Academy, 1720–46." In *Wealth and Virtue: The Shaping of Political Economy in the Scottish Enlightenment*, edited by Istvan Hont and Michael Ignatieff, 89–119. Cambridge: Cambridge University Press, 1983.

———, ed. *The "Science of Man" in the Scottish Enlightenment: Hume, Reid and Their Contemporaries*. Edinburgh: Edinburgh University Press, 1989.

Jones, R. F. "The Rhetoric of Science in England of the Mid-Seventeenth Century." In *Restoration and Eighteenth-Century Literature*, edited by Carroll Camden, 5–24. Chicago: University of Chicago Press, 1963.

Kahn, Victoria. "'The Duty to Love': Passion and Obligation in Early Modern Political Theory." *Representations* 68 (1999): 84–107.

———. "Happy Tears: Baroque Politics in Descartes's *Passions de l'âme*." In *Politics and the Passions, 1500–1850*, edited by Victoria Kahn, Neil Saccamano, and Daniela Coli, 93–110. Princeton: Princeton University Press, 2006.

———. "Reinventing Romance, or the Surprising Effects of Sympathy." *Renaissance Quarterly* 55 (2002): 625–661.

———. *Wayward Contracts: The Crisis of Political Obligation in England, 1640–1674*. Princeton: Princeton University Press, 2004.

Kargon, Robert H. *Atomism in England from Hariot to Newton*. Oxford: Clarendon Press, 1966.

Kassell, Lauren. "Magic, Alchemy and the Medical Economy in Early Modern England: The Case of Robert Fludd's Magnetical Medicine." In *Medicine and the Market in England and Its Colonies, c. 1450–c. 1850*, edited by Mark S. R. Jenner and Patrick Wallis, 88–107. Basingstoke: Palgrave Macmillan, 2007.

———. "Secrets Revealed: Alchemical Books in Early-Modern England." *History of Science* 49 (2011): 61–88.

Kavey, Allison B. "Building Blocks: Imagination, Knowledge, and Passion in Agrippa von Nettesheim's *De Oculta Philosophia Libri Tres*." In *World-Building and the Early Modern Imagination*, edited by Allison B. Kavey, 35–58. New York: Palgrave Macmillan, 2010.

Keen, Suzanne. *Empathy and the Novel*. Oxford: Oxford University Press, 2007.

Keenleyside, Heather. "Personification for the People: On James Thomson's *The Seasons*." *English Literary History* 76 (2009): 447–472.

Keller, Eve. "Producing Petty Gods: Margaret Cavendish's Critique of Experimental Philosophy." *English Literary History* 64 (1997): 447–471.

Kemp, John. "Hobbes on Pity and Charity." In *Thomas Hobbes: His View of Man*, edited by J. G. van der Bend, 57–62. Amsterdam: Rodopi, 1982.

Kerrigan, William. "Complicated Monsters: Essence and Metamorphosis in Milton." *Texas Studies in Literature and Language* 46 (2004): 324–339.

———. *The Sacred Complex: On the Psychogenesis of "Paradise Lost."* Cambridge, MA: Harvard University Press, 1983.

Kesselring, Marion L. "Hawthorne's Reading, 1828–1850." *Bulletin of the New York Public Library* 53 (1949): 55–71.

Keymer, Thomas. "Sentimental Fiction: Ethics, Social Critique and Philanthropy." In Richetti, ed., *Cambridge History of English Literature, 1660–1780*, 572–601.

Keynes, Geoffrey. *A Bibliography of Sir Thomas Browne Kt. M.D.* 2nd ed. Oxford: Clarendon Press, 1968.

Kilgour, Maggie. *Milton and the Metamorphosis of Ovid*. Oxford: Oxford University Press, 2012.

King, Lester S. *The Philosophy of Medicine: The Early Eighteenth Century*. Cambridge, MA: Harvard University Press, 1978.

Kingsley, Peter. *Ancient Philosophy, Mystery, and Magic: Empedocles and Pythagorean Tradition*. Oxford: Clarendon Press, 1995.

Kippenberg, Hans G. *Discovering Religious History in the Modern Age*. Translated by Barbara Harshav. Princeton: Princeton University Press, 2002.

Kishlansky, Mark. *A Monarchy Transformed: Britain 1603–1714*. London: Penguin Books, 1996.

Klein, Lawrence E. *Shaftesbury and the Culture of Politeness: Moral Discourse and Cultural Politics in Early Eighteenth-Century England*. Cambridge: Cambridge University Press, 1994.

———. Introduction to *Characteristics of Men, Manners, Opinions, Times*, by Anthony Ashley Cooper, vii–xxxi. Edited by Lawrence E. Klein. Cambridge: Cambridge University Press, 1999.

———. "Enlightenment as Conversation." In *What's Left of Enlightenment? A Postmodern Question,* edited by Keith Michael Baker and Peter Hanns Reill, 148–166. Stanford: Stanford University Press, 2001.

Knellwolf, Christa, and Jane Goodall, eds. *Frankenstein's Science: Experimentation and Discovery in Romantic Culture, 1780–1830.* Aldershot: Ashgate, 2008.

Knight, David. "Sympathy, Attraction and Elective Affinity." *Bulletin de la Société d'Études Anglo-Américaines des XVIIe et XVIIIe Siècles* 56 (2003): 21–30.

Knoespel, Kenneth J. "The Limits of Allegory: Textual Expansion of Narcissus in *Paradise Lost.*" *Milton Studies* 22 (1986): 79–99.

Koerner, Joseph Leo. "Hieronymus Bosch's World Picture." In *Picturing Science, Picturing Art,* edited by Caroline A. Jones and Peter Galison, 297–323. New York: Routledge, 1998.

Kolbrener, William. *Milton's Warring Angels: A Study of Critical Engagements.* Cambridge: Cambridge University Press, 1997.

Konstan, David. *Pity Transformed.* London: Duckworth, 2001.

Kraye, Jill. "Moral Philosophy." In Schmitt and Skinner, eds., *Cambridge History of Renaissance Philosophy,* 303–386.

Kroll, Richard, Richard Ashcraft, and Perez Zagorin, eds. *Philosophy, Science, and Religion in England, 1640–1700.* Cambridge: Cambridge University Press, 1992.

Lamb, Jonathan. *The Evolution of Sympathy in the Long Eighteenth Century.* London: Pickering & Chatto, 2009.

Lamb, John B. "Mary Shelley's *Frankenstein* and Milton's Monstrous Myth." *Nineteenth-Century Literature* 47 (1992): 303–319.

Lapidge, Michael. "Stoic Cosmology." In *The Stoics,* edited by John M. Rist, 161–186. Berkeley: University of California Press, 1978.

Latour, Bruno. *We Have Never Been Modern.* Translated by Catherine Porter. Cambridge, MA: Harvard University Press, 1993.

Laurand, Valéry. "La sympathie universelle: union et séparation." *Revue de Métaphysique et de Morale* 48 (2005): 517–535.

Lawrence, Christopher. "The Nervous System and Society in the Scottish Enlightenment." In *Natural Order: Historical Studies of Scientific Culture,* edited by Barry Barnes and Steven Shapin, 19–40. London: Sage Publications, 1979.

Lee, Michelle V. *Paul, the Stoics, and the Body of Christ.* Cambridge: Cambridge University Press, 2006.

Lehmann, Hartmut. *Die Entzauberung der Welt: Studien zu Themen von Max Weber.* Göttingen: Wallstein, 2009.

Lehnhof, Kent R. "Performing Masculinity in *Paradise Lost.*" *Milton Studies* 50 (2009): 64–77.

Lennon, Thomas M. "The Contagious Communication of Strong Imaginations: History, Modernity, and Scepticism in the Philosophy of Malebranche." In *The Rise of Modern Philosophy: The Tension between the New and Traditional Philosophies from Machiavelli to Leibniz,* edited by Tom Sorell, 197–211. Oxford: Clarendon Press, 1993.

Leonard, John. "Milton, Lucretius, and 'the Void Profound of Unessential Night.'" In Pruitt and Durham, eds., *Living Texts,* 198–217.

———. *Naming in Paradise: Milton and the Language of Adam and Eve*. Oxford: Clarendon Press, 1990.

Levao, Ronald. "'Among Equals What Society': *Paradise Lost* and the Forms of Intimacy." *Modern Language Quarterly* 61 (2000): 79–107.

Levi, Anthony, S.J. *French Moralists: The Theory of the Passions, 1585–1649*. Oxford: Clarendon Press, 1964.

Levine, Robert S. "Sympathy and Reform in *The Blithedale Romance*." In Millington, ed., *Cambridge Companion to Nathaniel Hawthorne*, 207–229.

Lévy-Bruhl, Lucien. *How Natives Think*. Translated by Lilian A. Clarke. Princeton: Princeton University Press, 1985.

Lewalski, Barbara Kiefer. *The Life of John Milton: A Critical Biography*. Rev. ed. Cambridge, MA: Blackwell, 2003.

———. "Milton and Idolatry." *Studies in English Literature* 43 (2003): 213–232.

———. "*Paradise Lost* and Milton's Politics." *Milton Studies* 38 (2000): 141–168.

———. *"Paradise Lost" and the Rhetoric of Literary Forms*. Princeton: Princeton University Press, 1985.

Lewis, C. S. *A Preface to "Paradise Lost."* Oxford: Oxford University Press, 1942.

Lieb, Michael. *The Dialectics of Creation: Patterns of Birth & Regeneration in "Paradise Lost."* Amherst: University of Massachusetts Press, 1970.

———. *Poetics of the Holy: A Reading of "Paradise Lost."* Chapel Hill: University of North Carolina Press, 1981.

———. *Theological Milton: Deity, Discourse and Heresy in the Miltonic Canon*. Pittsburgh: Duquesne University Press, 2006.

Lindberg, D. C., and R. S. Westman, eds. *Reappraisals of the Scientific Revolution*. Cambridge: Cambridge University Press, 1990.

Lloyd, G. E. R. *Science, Folklore and Ideology: Studies in the Life Sciences in Ancient Greece*. Cambridge: Cambridge University Press, 1983.

Loewenstein, David. *Milton and the Drama of History: Historical Vision, Iconoclasm, and the Literary Imagination*. Cambridge: Cambridge University Press, 1990.

Loewenstein, David, and James Grantham Turner, eds. *Politics, Poetics, and Hermeneutics in Milton's Prose*. Cambridge: Cambridge University Press, 1990.

Long, A. A. "Astrology: Arguments Pro and Contra." In *Science and Speculation: Studies in Hellenistic Theory and Practice*, edited by Jonathan Barnes, Jacques Brunschwig, Myles Burnyeat, and Malcolm Schofield, 165–192. Cambridge: Cambridge University Press, 1982.

———. *Epictetus: A Stoic and Socratic Guide to Life*. Oxford: Oxford University Press, 2002.

Lotti, Brunello. *Ralph Cudworth e l'idea di natura plastica*. Udine: Campanotto, 2004.

Luck, Georg. "On Cicero, *De Fato* 5 and Related Passages." *American Journal of Philology* 99 (1978): 155–158.

Luxon, Thomas H. *Single Imperfection: Milton, Marriage and Friendship*. Pittsburgh: Duquesne University Press, 2005.

MacCarthy, B. G. *The Female Pen*. Oxford: Blackwell, 1946.

Macey, J. David, Jr. "Amiable Deception and Flaming Fancy: Samuel Jackson Pratt and the Literature(s) of Benevolence." *Philological Review* 27 (2001): 25–35.

Macfarlane, Alan. "Civility and the Decline of Magic." In *Civil Histories: Essays Presented to Sir Keith Thomas*, edited by Peter Burke, Brian Harrison, and Paul Slack, 145–159. Oxford: Oxford University Press, 2000.

Maclean, Ian. "Foucault's Renaissance Episteme Reassessed: An Aristotelian Counterblast." *Journal of the History of Ideas* 59 (1998): 149–166.

———. "The Process of Intellectual Change: A Post-Foucauldian Hypothesis." *Arcadia* 33 (1998): 169–181.

———. *The Renaissance Notion of Woman: A Study in the Fortunes of Scholasticism and Medical Science in European Intellectual Life*. Cambridge: Cambridge University Press, 1980.

Malcolm, Noel. *Aspects of Hobbes*. Oxford: Clarendon Press, 2002.

Male, Roy R., Jr. "Hawthorne and the Concept of Sympathy." *PMLA* 68 (1953): 138–149.

Marjara, Harinder Singh. *Contemplation of Created Things: Science in "Paradise Lost."* Toronto: University of Toronto Press, 1992.

Marshall, David. *The Figure of Theater: Shaftesbury, Defoe, Adam Smith, and George Eliot*. New York: Columbia University Press, 1986.

———. *The Surprising Effects of Sympathy: Marivaux, Diderot, Rousseau, and Mary Shelley*. Chicago: University of Chicago Press, 1988.

Martin, Catherine Gimelli. *The Ruins of Allegory: "Paradise Lost" and the Metamorphosis of Epic Convention*. Durham, NC: Duke University Press, 1998.

———. "'What If the Sun Be Centre to the World?': Milton's Epistemology, Cosmology, and Paradise of Fools Reconsidered." *Modern Philology* 99 (2001): 231–265.

Mascetti, Yaakov. "Satan and the 'Incompos'd' Visage of Chaos: Milton's Hermeneutic Indeterminacy." *Milton Studies* 50 (2009): 35–63.

Masten, Jeffrey. "Material Cavendish: Paper, Performance, 'Sociable Virginity.'" *Modern Language Quarterly* 65 (2004): 49–68.

Mattison, Andrew. "Sweet Imperfection: Milton and the Troubled Metaphor of Harmony." *Modern Philology* 106 (2009): 617–647.

Mauss, Marcel. *A General Theory of Magic*. Translated by Robert Brain. 1902. Reprint, London: Routledge, 2001.

Mazzeo, Joseph. "Metaphysical Poetry and the Poetry of Correspondence." *Journal of the History of Ideas* 14 (1953): 221–234.

McChrystal, Deirdre Keenan. "Redeeming Eve." *English Literary Renaissance* 23 (1993): 490–508.

McClintock, Thomas. "The Meaning of Hobbes's Egoistic Moral Philosophy." *Philosophia* 23 (1994): 247–263.

McColley, Diane Kelsey. "'All in All': The Individuality of Creatures in *Paradise Lost*." In Durham and Pruitt, eds., *"All in All,"* 29–41.

———. *Milton's Eve*. Urbana: University of Illinois Press, 1983.

———. *Poetry and Ecology in the Age of Milton and Marvell*. Aldershot: Ashgate, 2007.

McGann, Jerome. *The Poetics of Sensibility: A Revolution in Literary Style*. Oxford: Clarendon Press, 1996.

McKillop, Alan Dugald. *The Background of Thomson's "Seasons."* Hamden, CT: Archon Books, 1961.

McNamer, Sarah. *Affective Meditation and the Invention of Medieval Compassion.* Philadelphia: University of Pennsylvania Press, 2009.

Mebane, John S. *Renaissance Magic and the Return of the Golden Age: The Occult Tradition and Marlowe, Jonson, and Shakespeare.* Lincoln: University of Nebraska Press, 1989.

Meeks, Wayne A. *The First Urban Christians: The Social World of the Apostle Paul.* 2nd ed. New Haven: Yale University Press, 2003.

Meier, Richard Y. "'Sympathy' as a Concept in Early Neurophysiology." Ph.D. diss., University of Chicago, 1979.

———. "'Sympathy' in the Neurophysiology of Thomas Willis." *Clio Medica* 17 (1982): 95–111.

Mellor, Anne K. "*Frankenstein*: A Feminist Critique of Science." In *One Culture: Essays in Science and Literature,* edited by George Levine, 287–312. Madison: University of Wisconsin Press, 1987.

———. "Making a 'Monster': An Introduction to *Frankenstein.*" In *The Cambridge Companion to Mary Shelley,* edited by Esther Schor, 9–25. Cambridge: Cambridge University Press, 2003.

Mercer, Philip. *Sympathy and Ethics: A Study of the Relationship between Sympathy and Morality with Special Reference to Hume's "Treatise."* Oxford: Clarendon Press, 1972.

Merchant, Carolyn. *The Death of Nature: Women, Ecology and the Scientific Revolution.* New York: Harper & Row, 1983.

Merkel, Ingrid, and Allen G. Debus, eds. *Hermeticism and the Renaissance: Intellectual History and the Occult in Early Modern Europe.* Washington, DC: Folger Books, 1988.

Michaelian, Kourken. "Margaret Cavendish's Epistemology." *British Journal for the History of Philosophy* 17 (2009): 31–53.

Millen, Ron. "The Manifestation of Occult Qualities in the Scientific Revolution." In *Religion, Science, and Worldview,* edited by Margaret H. Osler and Paul Lawrence Farber, 185–216. Cambridge: Cambridge University Press, 1985.

Miller, Shannon. *Engendering the Fall: John Milton and Seventeenth-Century Women Writers.* Philadelphia: University of Pennsylvania Press, 2008.

———. "Serpentine Eve: Milton and the Seventeenth-Century Debate Over Women." *Milton Quarterly* 42 (2008): 44–68.

Millican, Peter. "Hume's Sceptical Doubts concerning Induction." In *Reading Hume on Human Understanding,* edited by Peter Millican, 107–173. Oxford: Oxford University Press, 2002.

Millington, Richard H., ed. *The Cambridge Companion to Nathaniel Hawthorne.* Cambridge: Cambridge University Press, 2004.

Mintz, Samuel I. *The Hunting of Leviathan: Seventeenth-Century Reactions to the Materialism and Moral Philosophy of Thomas Hobbes.* Cambridge: Cambridge University Press, 1962.

Mintz, Susannah B. *Threshold Poetics: Milton and Intersubjectivity.* Newark: University of Delaware Press, 2003.

Moore, C. A. "Shaftesbury and the Ethical Poets in England, 1700–1760." *PMLA* 31 (1916): 264–325.

Moore, James. "Hume and Hutcheson." In *Hume and Hume's Connexions*, edited by M. A. Stewart and John P. Wright, 23–57. University Park: Pennsylvania State University Press, 1994.

Mossner, Ernest Campbell. *The Life of David Hume.* 2nd ed. Oxford: Clarendon Press, 1980.

Mowat, Barbara A. "Prospero, Agrippa, and Hocus Pocus." *English Literary Renaissance* 11 (1981): 281–303.

Mueller, Janel. "Embodying Glory: The Apocalyptic Strain in Milton's *Of Reformation.*" In Loewenstein and Turner, eds., *Politics, Poetics, and Hermeneutics,* 9–41.

Mullan, John. *Sentiment and Sociability: The Language of Feeling in the Eighteenth Century.* Oxford: Clarendon Press, 1988.

Mulsow, Martin. "Ambiguities of the *Prisca Sapientia* in Late Renaissance Humanism." *Journal of the History of Ideas* 65 (2004): 1–13.

——. *Frühneuzeitliche Selbsterhaltung: Telesio und die Naturphilosophie der Renaissance.* Tübingen: Max Niemeyer, 1998.

Nauert, Charles G. *Agrippa and the Crisis of Renaissance Thought.* Urbana: University of Illinois Press, 1965.

Newman, William R. *Atoms and Alchemy: Chymistry and the Experimental Origins of the Scientific Revolution.* Chicago: University of Chicago Press, 2006.

Nichols, Jennifer L. "Milton's Claim for Self and Freedom in the Divorce Tracts." *Milton Studies* 49 (2009): 192–211.

Nohrnberg, James. *The Analogy of "The Faerie Queene."* Princeton: Princeton University Press, 1976.

Norbrook, David. "Margaret Cavendish and Lucy Hutchinson: Identity, Ideology, and Politics." *In-Between* 9 (2000): 179–203.

——. "Women, the Republic of Letters, and the Public Sphere in the Mid-Seventeenth Century." *Criticism* 46 (2004): 223–240.

——. *Writing the English Republic: Poetry, Rhetoric and Politics, 1627–1660.* Cambridge: Cambridge University Press, 1999.

Norton, Robert E. *The Beautiful Soul: Aesthetic Morality in the Eighteenth Century.* Ithaca: Cornell University Press, 1995.

Nutton, Vivian. "The Reception of Fracastoro's Theory of Contagion: The Seed that Fell among Thorns?" *Osiris,* 2nd ser., 6 (1990): 196–234.

Nyquist, Mary. "The Genesis of Gendered Subjectivity in the Divorce Tracts and *Paradise Lost.*" In Nyquist and Ferguson, eds., *Re-membering Milton,* 99–127.

Nyquist, Mary, and Margaret W. Ferguson, eds. *Re-membering Milton: Essays on the Texts and Traditions.* London: Methuen, 1988.

O'Neill, Eileen. Introduction to *Observations upon Experimental Philosophy*, by Margaret Cavendish, x–xxxvi. Edited by Eileen O'Neill. Cambridge: Cambridge University Press, 2001.

Orgel, Stephen. "The Case for Comus." *Representations* 81 (2003): 31–45.

Osler, Margaret J., ed. *Atoms, Pneuma, and Tranquillity: Epicurean and Stoic Themes in European Thought.* Cambridge: Cambridge University Press, 1991.

Pagel, Walter. *Joan Baptista Van Helmont: Reformer of Science and Medicine*. Cambridge: Cambridge University Press, 1982.

——. *Paracelsus: An Introduction to Philosophical Medicine in the Era of the Renaissance*. Rev. ed. Basel: Karger, 1982.

——. "Religious Motives in the Medical Biology of the Seventeenth Century." *Bulletin of the Institute of the History of Medicine* 3 (1935): 97–128, 213–231, 265–312.

Panofsky, Erwin. *Perspective as Symbolic Form*. Translated by Christopher S. Wood. New York: Zone Books, 1997.

Park, Katharine. "Bacon's 'Enchanted Glass.' " *Isis* 75 (1984): 290–302.

Parker, Blanford. *The Triumph of Augustan Poetics: English Literary Culture from Butler to Johnson*. Cambridge: Cambridge University Press, 1998.

Parker, Patricia A. *Inescapable Romance: Studies in the Poetics of a Mode*. Princeton: Princeton University Press, 1979.

Parkin, Jon. *Taming the Leviathan: The Reception of the Political and Religious Ideas of Thomas Hobbes in England, 1640–1700*. Cambridge: Cambridge University Press, 2007.

Passmore, John. *Ralph Cudworth: An Interpretation*. Cambridge: Cambridge University Press, 1951.

Paster, Gail Kern, Katherine Rowe, and Mary Floyd-Wilson, eds. *Reading the Early Modern Passions: Essays in the Cultural History of Emotion*. Philadelphia: University of Pennsylvania Press, 2004.

Patterson, Annabel. *Fables of Power: Aesopian Writing and Political History*. Durham, NC: Duke University Press, 1991.

——. "His Singing Robes." *Milton Studies* 48 (2008): 178–194.

——, ed. *John Milton*. London: Longman, 1992.

——. *Milton's Words*. Oxford: Oxford University Press, 2009.

——. "No Meer Amatorious Novel?" In Loewenstein and Turner, eds., *Politics, Poetics, and Hermeneutics*, 85–102.

——. *Reading between the Lines*. Madison: University of Wisconsin Press, 1993.

——. "Why Is There No Rights Talk in Milton's Poetry?" In Tournu and Forsyth, eds., *Milton, Rights and Liberties*, 197–209.

Pearce, Spencer. "Nature and Supernature in the Dialogues of Girolamo Fracastoro." *Sixteenth Century Journal* 27 (1996): 111–132.

Perry, Henry Ten Eyck. *The First Duchess of Newcastle and Her Husband as Figures in Literary History*. Boston: Ginn, 1918.

Peruzzi, Enrico. "Antioccultismo e filosofia naturale nel *De sympathia et antipathia rerum* di Girolamo Fracastoro." *Atti e Memorie dell'Accademia Toscana di Scienze e Lettere La Colombaria* 45 (1980): 41–131.

Petersson, R. T. *Sir Kenelm Digby: The Ornament of England, 1603–1665*. Cambridge, MA: Harvard University Press, 1956.

Phillipson, Nicholas. *Adam Smith: An Enlightened Life*. New Haven: Yale University Press, 2010.

Piccari, Paolo. *Giovan Battista Della Porta: Il filosofo, il retore, lo scienzato*. Milan: FrancoAngeli, 2007.

Picciotto, Joanna. *Labors of Innocence in Early Modern England*. Cambridge, MA: Harvard University Press, 2010.

Poole, William. *Milton and the Idea of the Fall*. Cambridge: Cambridge University Press, 2005.

———. "Milton and Science: A Caveat." *Milton Quarterly* 38 (2004): 18–34.

Popkin, Richard H. "The Spiritualistic Cosmologies of Henry More and Anne Conway." In Hutton, ed., *Henry More (1614–1687)*, 97–114.

Porter, Roy. "Witchcraft and Magic in Enlightenment, Romantic and Liberal Thought." In *Witchcraft and Magic in Europe: The Eighteenth and Nineteenth Centuries*, edited by Bengt Ankarloo and Stuart Clark, 191–274. Philadelphia: University of Pennsylvania Press, 1999.

Preston, Claire. *Thomas Browne and the Writing of Early Modern Science*. Cambridge: Cambridge University Press, 2005.

Prince, Michael B. "Editing Shaftesbury's *Characteristicks*." *Essays in Criticism* 54 (2004): 38–59.

———. "The Eighteenth-Century Beauty Contest." *Modern Language Quarterly* 55 (1994): 251–279.

———. *Philosophical Dialogue in the British Enlightenment: Theology, Aesthetics, and the Novel*. Cambridge: Cambridge University Press, 1996.

———. "A Preliminary Discourse on Philosophy and Literature." In Richetti, ed., *Cambridge History of English Literature, 1660–1780*, 391–422.

Principe, Lawrence. *The Aspiring Adept: Robert Boyle and His Alchemical Quest*. Princeton: Princeton University Press, 1998.

Prior, Charles W. A. "New Light on Milton's 'Fable of the Wen.'" *Notes and Queries* 54 (2007): 395–400.

Pruitt, Kristin A., and Charles W. Durham, eds. *Living Texts: Interpreting Milton*. London: Associated University Presses, 2000.

Pumfrey, Stephen. "The Spagyric Art; Or, The Impossible Work of Separating Pure from Impure Paracelsianism: A Historiographical Analysis." In Grell, ed., *Paracelsus: The Man and His Reputation*, 21–51.

Quilligan, Maureen. *Milton's Spenser: The Politics of Reading*. Ithaca: Cornell University Press, 1983.

Quint, David. "The Disenchanted World of *Paradise Regained*." *Huntington Library Quarterly* 76 (2013): 181–194.

———. *Epic and Empire: Politics and Generic Form from Virgil to Milton*. Princeton: Princeton University Press, 1993.

———. "Expectation and Prematurity in Milton's *Nativity Ode*." *Modern Philology* 97 (1999): 195–206.

———. "'Things Invisible to Mortal Sight': Light, Vision, and the Unity of Book 3 of *Paradise Lost*." *Modern Language Quarterly* 71 (2010): 229–269.

Rabin, Sheila. "Pico on Magic and Astrology." In *Pico della Mirandola: New Essays*, edited by M. V. Dougherty, 152–178. Cambridge: Cambridge University Press, 2008.

Radner, John B. "The Art of Sympathy in Eighteenth-Century British Moral Thought." In *Studies in Eighteenth-Century Culture*, edited by Roseann Runte, 189–210. Madison: University of Wisconsin Press, 1979.

Radzinowicz, Mary Ann. "Eve and Dalila." In *Reason and the Imagination: Studies in the History of Ideas, 1600–1800*, edited by Joseph Mazzeo, 155–181. New York: Columbia University Press, 1962.

———. "The Politics of *Paradise Lost*." In *Politics of Discourse: The Literature and History of Seventeenth-Century England*, edited by Kevin Sharpe and Steven N. Zwicker, 204–229. Berkeley: University of California Press, 1987.

Rai, Amit S. *Rule of Sympathy: Sentiment, Race, and Power, 1750–1850*. New York: Palgrave, 2002.

Raphael, D. D. *Hobbes: Morals and Politics*. London: Allen & Unwin, 1977.

———. *The Impartial Spectator: Adam Smith's Moral Philosophy*. Oxford: Clarendon Press, 2007.

Rattansi, P. M. "Paracelsus and the Puritan Revolution." *Ambix* 11 (1963): 24–32.

Rees, Emma L. E. *Margaret Cavendish: Gender, Genre, Exile*. Manchester: Manchester University Press, 2003.

Rees, Graham. "Francis Bacon's Semi-Paracelsian Cosmology." *Ambix* 22 (1975): 81–101.

———. "An Unpublished Manuscript by Francis Bacon: *Sylva Sylvarum* Drafts and Other Working Notes." *Annals of Science* 38 (1981): 377–412.

Reid, Alfred S. "Hawthorne's Humanism: 'The Birthmark' and Sir Kenelm Digby." *American Literature* 38 (1966): 337–351.

———. *The Yellow Ruff and "The Scarlet Letter": A Source of Hawthorne's Novel*. Gainesville: University of Florida Press, 1955.

Reid, David. "Thomson's Poetry of Reverie and Milton." *Studies in English Literature* 43 (2003): 667–682.

Revard, Stella P. "Milton, Homer, and the Anger of Adam." *Milton Studies* 41 (2002): 18–62.

———. *Milton and the Tangles of Neaera's Hair*. Columbia: University of Missouri Press, 1997.

———. "Vergil's *Georgics* and *Paradise Lost*." In *Vergil at 2000: Commemorative Essays on the Poet and His Influence*, edited by John D. Bernard, 259–280. New York: AMS, 1986.

Richetti, John, ed. *The Cambridge History of English Literature, 1660–1780*. Cambridge: Cambridge University Press, 2005

Richter, Jürgen. *Die Theorie der Sympathie*. Frankfurt am Main: Peter Lang, 1996.

Riskin, Jessica. *Science in the Age of Sensibility: The Sentimental Empiricists of the French Enlightenment*. Chicago: University of Chicago Press, 2002.

Rivers, Isabel. "'Galen's Muscles': Wilkins, Hume, and the Educational Use of the Argument from Design." *Historical Journal* 36 (1993): 577–597.

———. *Shaftesbury to Hume*. Vol. II of *Reason, Grace, and Sentiment: A Study of the Language of Religion and Ethics in England, 1660–1780*. Cambridge: Cambridge University Press, 2000.

———. *Whichcote to Wesley*. Vol. I of *Reason, Grace, and Sentiment: A Study of the Language of Religion and Ethics in England, 1660–1780*. Cambridge: Cambridge University Press, 1991.

Robinson, Leni Katherine. "A Figurative Matter: Continuities between Margaret Cavendish's Theory of Discourse and Her Natural Philosophy." Ph.D. diss., University of British Columbia, 2009. https://circle.ubc.ca/handle/2429/17451.

Rogers, G. A. J. "The Other-Worldly Philosophers and the Real World: The Cambridge Platonists, Theology and Politics." In Rogers, Vienne, and Zarka, eds., *Cambridge Platonists in Philosophical Context*, 3–16.

Rogers, G. A. J., J. M. Vienne, and Y. C. Zarka, eds. *The Cambridge Platonists in Philosophical Context: Politics, Metaphysics and Religion.* Dordrecht: Kluwer, 1997.

Rogers, John. *The Matter of Revolution: Science, Poetry, and Politics in the Age of Milton.* Ithaca: Cornell University Press, 1996.

——. "Transported Touch: The Fruit of Marriage in *Paradise Lost.*" In *Milton and Gender*, edited by Catherine Gimelli Martin, 115–132. Cambridge: Cambridge University Press, 2004.

Rogers, Pat. "Shaftesbury and the Aesthetics of Rhapsody." *British Journal of Aesthetics* 12 (1972): 244–257.

Röhr, Julius. *Der okkulte Kraftbegriff im Altertum* (*Philologus*, Supplementband 17.1). Leipzig: Dieterich, 1923.

Romack, Katherine, and James Fitzmaurice, eds. *Cavendish and Shakespeare, Interconnections.* Aldershot: Ashgate, 2006.

Rosenberg, Jordana. "'Accumulate! Accumulate! That is Moses and the Prophets!': Secularism, Historicism, and the Critique of Enthusiasm." *Eighteenth Century* 51 (2010): 471–490.

Rosenmeyer, Thomas G. *The Green Cabinet: Theocritus and the European Pastoral Lyric.* Berkeley: University of California Press, 1969.

Ross, Ian Simpson. *The Life of Adam Smith.* Oxford: Clarendon Press, 1995.

Rossi, Paolo. *Francis Bacon: From Magic to Science.* Translated by Sacha Rabinovitch. London: Routledge & Kegan Paul, 1968.

Rousseau, G. S. "Nerves, Spirits, Fibres: Towards Defining the Origins of Sensibility." In *Studies in the Eighteenth Century III*, edited by R. F. Brissenden and J. C. Eade, 137–157. Canberra: Australian National University Press, 1976.

Rumrich, John. "Of Chaos and Nightingales." In Pruitt and Durham, eds., *Living Texts*, 218–227.

——. *Matter of Glory: A New Preface to "Paradise Lost."* Pittsburgh: University of Pittsburgh Press, 1987.

Sambrook, James. *James Thomson, 1700–1748: A Life.* Oxford: Clarendon Press, 1991.

Sanders, Julie. "'The Closet Opened': A Reconstruction of 'Private' Space in the Writings of Margaret Cavendish." In Clucas, ed., *Princely Brave Woman*, 127–140.

Sarasohn, Lisa. "Leviathan and the Lady: Cavendish's Critique of Hobbes in the *Philosophical Letters.*" In Cottegnies and Weitz, eds., *Authorial Conquests*, 40–58.

——. "Motion and Morality: Pierre Gassendi, Thomas Hobbes and the Mechanical World View." *Journal of the History of Ideas* 46 (1985): 363–379.

——. *The Natural Philosophy of Margaret Cavendish: Reason and Fancy during the Scientific Revolution.* Baltimore: Johns Hopkins University Press, 2010.

Saurat, Denis. *Milton: Man and Thinker.* London: J. M. Dent & Sons, 1944.

——. *Milton et le matérialisme Chrétien en Angleterre.* Paris: Rieder, 1928.

Schliesser, Eric. "Wonder in the Face of Scientific Revolutions: Adam Smith on Newton's 'Proof' of Copernicanism." *British Journal for the History of Philosophy* 13 (2005): 697–732.

——. "Some Principles of Adam Smith's Newtonian Methods in the *Wealth of Nations.*" *Research in the History of Economic Thought and Methodology* 23 (2005): 33–74.

Schmidt-Biggemann, Wilhelm. "Robert Fludd's Kabbalistic Cosmos." Translated by Geoff Dumbreck and Douglas Hedley. In *Platonism at the Origins of Modernity: Studies on Platonism and Early Modern Philosophy,* edited by Douglas Hedley and Sarah Hutton, 75–92. Dordrecht: Springer, 2008.

Schmitt, Charles B., and Quentin Skinner, eds. *The Cambridge History of Renaissance Philosophy.* Cambridge: Cambridge University Press, 1988.

Schneewind, J. B. *The Invention of Autonomy: A History of Modern Moral Philosophy.* Cambridge: Cambridge University Press, 1998.

Schneider, Gary. "Affecting Correspondences: Body, Behavior, and the Textualization of Emotion in Early Modern English Letters." *Prose Studies* 23 (2000): 31–62.

——. *The Culture of Epistolarity: Vernacular Letters and Letter Writing in Early Modern England, 1500–1700.* Newark: University of Delaware Press, 2005.

Schoenfeldt, Michael C. "'Commotion Strange': Passion in *Paradise Lost.*" In Paster, Rowe, and Floyd-Wilson, eds., *Reading the Early Modern Passions,* 43–67.

——. "Reading Bodies." In *Reading, Society and Politics in Early Modern England,* edited by Kevin Sharpe and Steven N. Zwicker, 214–243. Cambridge: Cambridge University Press, 2003.

Schott, Heinz. "'Invisible Diseases'—Imagination and Magnetism: Paracelsus and the Consequences." In Grell, ed., *Paracelsus: The Man and His Reputation,* 309–321.

Schwartz, Louis. *Milton and Maternal Mortality.* Cambridge: Cambridge University Press, 2009.

Schwartz, Regina M. *Remembering and Repeating: Biblical Creation in "Paradise Lost."* Cambridge: Cambridge University Press, 1988.

Scott, Dominic. "Reason, Recollection and the Cambridge Platonists." In *Platonism and the English Imagination,* edited by Anna Baldwin and Sarah Hutton, 139–150. Cambridge: Cambridge University Press, 1994.

Scribner, Robert W. "The Reformation, Popular Magic, and the 'Disenchantment of the World.'" *Journal of Interdisciplinary History* 23 (1993): 475–494.

Shapin, Steven. *A Social History of Truth: Civility and Science in Seventeenth-Century England.* Chicago: University of Chicago Press, 1994.

Shapin, Steven, and Simon Schaffer. *Leviathan and the Air-Pump: Hobbes, Boyle, and the Experimental Life.* Princeton: Princeton University Press, 1985.

Sharpe, Kevin. *Remapping Early Modern England: The Culture of Seventeenth-Century Politics.* Cambridge: Cambridge University Press, 2000.

Sher, Richard B. *Church and Society in the Scottish Enlightenment: The Moderate Literati of Edinburgh.* Princeton: Princeton University Press, 1985.

Shifflett, Andrew. *Stoicism, Politics, and Literature in the Age of Milton: War and Peace Reconciled.* Cambridge: Cambridge University Press, 1998.

Shuger, Debora. "The Laudian Idiot." In *Sir Thomas Browne: The World Proposed*, edited by Reid Barbour and Claire Preston, 46–55. Oxford: Oxford University Press, 2008.

Shumaker, Wayne. "Literary Hermeticism: Some Test Cases." In Merkel and Debus, eds., *Hermeticism and the Renaissance*, 293–301.

———. *Unpremeditated Verse: Feeling and Perception in "Paradise Lost."* Princeton: Princeton University Press, 1967.

Siegel, Rudolph E. *Galen's System of Physiology and Medicine: An Analysis of His Doctrines and Observations on Bloodflow, Respiration, Humors and Internal Diseases.* Basel: Karger, 1968.

Silver, Victoria. *Imperfect Sense: The Predicament of Milton's Irony.* Princeton: Princeton University Press, 2001.

Simon, Irène. "The Preacher." In *Before Newton: The Life and Times of Isaac Barrow*, edited by Mordechai Feingold, 303–332. Cambridge: Cambridge University Press, 1990.

Skinner, Quentin. "Meaning and Understanding in the History of Ideas." In *Meaning and Context: Quentin Skinner and His Critics*, edited by James Tully, 29–67. Princeton: Princeton University Press, 1988.

———. "A Reply to My Critics." In *Meaning and Context: Quentin Skinner and His Critics*, edited by James Tully, 231–288. Princeton: Princeton University Press, 1988.

Smith, Charles Kay. "French Philosophy and English Politics in Interregnum Poetry." In *The Stuart Court and Europe: Essays in Politics and Political Culture*, edited by R. Malcolm Smuts, 188–200. Cambridge: Cambridge University Press, 1996.

Smith, Justin E. H., and Pauline Phemister. "Leibniz and the Cambridge Platonists: The Debate over Plastic Natures." In *Leibniz and the English-Speaking World*, edited by Pauline Phemister and Stuart Brown, 95–110. Dordrecht: Springer, 2007.

Smith, Nigel. "*Paradise Lost* from Civil War to Restoration." In *The Cambridge Companion to Writing of the English Revolution*, edited by N. H. Keeble, 251–267. Cambridge: Cambridge University Press, 2001.

Solmsen, Friedrich. "Love and Strife in Empedocles' Cosmology." *Phronesis* 10 (1965): 109–148.

Sorell, Tom. *Hobbes.* London: Routledge & Kegan Paul, 1986.

Spitzer, Leo. *Classical and Christian Ideas of World Harmony: Prolegomena to an Interpretation of the Word "Stimmung."* Edited by Anna Granville Hatcher. Baltimore: Johns Hopkins University Press, 1963.

———. *Essays in Historical Semantics.* New York: S. F. Vanni, 1948.

Staines, John. "Compassion in the Public Sphere of Milton and King Charles." In Paster, Rowe, and Floyd-Wilson, eds., *Reading the Early Modern Passions*, 89–110.

Starr, G. A. "Aphra Behn and the Genealogy of the Man of Feeling." *Modern Philology* 87 (1990): 362–372.

Starr, G. Gabrielle. "Cavendish, Aesthetics, and the Anti-Platonic Line." *Eighteenth-Century Studies* 39 (2006): 295–308.

———. *Lyric Generations: Poetry and the Novel in the Long Eighteenth Century*. Baltimore: Johns Hopkins University Press, 2004.

Steadman, John M. *Epic and Tragic Structure in "Paradise Lost."* Chicago: University of Chicago Press, 1976.

Stemplinger, Eduard. *Sympathieglaube und Sympathiekuren in Altertum und Neuzeit*. Munich: Gmelin, 1919.

Stern, Julia A. *The Plight of Feeling: Sympathy and Dissent in the Early American Novel*. Chicago: University of Chicago Press, 1997.

Stevenson, Jay. "The Mechanist-Vitalist Soul of Margaret Cavendish." *Studies in English Literature* 36 (1996): 527–543.

Stewart, M. A. "Hume's Intellectual Development." In *Impressions of Hume*, edited M. Frasca-Spada and P. J. E. Kail, 11–58. Oxford: Clarendon Press, 2005.

———, ed. *Studies in the Philosophy of the Scottish Enlightenment*. Oxford: Clarendon Press, 1990.

Stoehr, Taylor. *Hawthorne's Mad Scientists: Pseudoscience and Social Science in Nineteenth-Century Life and Letters*. Hamden, CT: Archon Books, 1978.

Sugimura, N. K. *"Matter of Glorious Trial": Spiritual and Material Substance in "Paradise Lost."* New Haven: Yale University Press, 2009.

Sutherland, Christine Mason. "Aspiring to the Rhetorical Tradition: A Study of Margaret Cavendish." In *Listening to Their Voices: The Rhetorical Activities of Historical Women*, edited by Molly Meijer Wertheimer, 255–271. Columbia: University of South Carolina Press, 1997.

Svendsen, Kester. "Science and Structure in Milton's *Doctrine of Divorce*." *PMLA* 67 (1952): 435–445.

Tambiah, Stanley Jeyaraja. *Magic, Science, Religion, and the Scope of Rationality*. Cambridge: Cambridge University Press, 1990.

Taylor, Anya. *Magic and English Romanticism*. Athens: University of Georgia Press, 1979.

Taylor, Charles. *A Secular Age*. Cambridge, MA: Harvard University Press, 2007.

———. *Sources of the Self: The Making of the Modern Identity*. Cambridge, MA: Harvard University Press, 1989.

Terry, Richard. "The Rhapsodical Manner in the Eighteenth Century." *Modern Language Review* 87 (1992): 273–285.

Teskey, Gordon. *Delirious Milton: The Fate of the Poet in Modernity*. Cambridge, MA: Harvard University Press, 2006.

Thickstun, Margaret Olofson. *Milton's "Paradise Lost": Moral Education*. New York: Palgrave Macmillan, 2007.

Thomas, Brook. "Love and Politics, Sympathy and Justice in *The Scarlet Letter*." In Millington, ed., *Cambridge Companion to Nathaniel Hawthorne*, 162–185.

Thomas, Keith. *Religion and the Decline of Magic: Studies in Popular Beliefs in Sixteenth- and Seventeenth-Century England*. 1971. Reprint, New York: Oxford University Press, 1997.

Thorndike, Lynn. *A History of Magic and Experimental Science*. 8 vols. New York: Columbia University Press, 1923–1958.

Tiffany, Esther A. "Shaftesbury as Stoic." *PMLA* 38 (1923): 642–684.

Tillyard, E. M. W. *The Elizabethan World Picture*. London: Chatto and Windus, 1943.

———. *Milton*. London: Chatto and Windus, 1949.

———. *Studies in Milton*. London: Chatto and Windus, 1955.

Todd, Janet M. *Sensibility: An Introduction*. London: Methuen, 1986.

Tournu, Christophe, and Neil Forsyth, eds. *Milton, Rights and Liberties*. Bern: Peter Lang, 2005.

Townsend, Dabney. *Hume's Aesthetic Theory: Taste and Sentiment*. London: Routledge, 2001.

Trevor-Roper, Hugh. "The Paracelsian Movement." In *Renaissance Essays*. Chicago: University of Chicago Press, 1985.

Trubowitz, Rachel J. "Body Politics in *Paradise Lost*." *PMLA* 121 (2006): 388–404.

Tuck, Richard. *Natural Right Theories: Their Origin and Development*. Cambridge: Cambridge University Press, 1979.

Turner, James Grantham. *One Flesh: Paradisal Marriage and Sexual Relations in the Age of Milton*. Oxford: Clarendon Press, 1993.

Tuve, Rosemond. *Images and Themes in Five Poems by Milton*. Cambridge, MA: Harvard University Press, 1957.

Tuveson, Ernest. "The Importance of Shaftesbury." *English Literary History* 20 (1953): 267–299.

———. "The Origins of the 'Moral Sense.'" *Huntington Library Quarterly* 11 (1948): 241–259.

Van den Berg, Sara. "Women, Children, and the Rhetoric of Milton's Divorce Tracts." *Early Modern Literary Studies* 10 (2004): 1–13. http://purl.oclc.org/emls/10–1/bergmilt.htm.

Van Engen, Abram. "Puritanism and the Power of Sympathy." *Early American Literature* 45 (2010): 533–564.

Van Ruler, Han. "Minds, Forms, and Spirits: The Nature of Cartesian Disenchantment." *Journal of the History of Ideas* 61 (2000): 381–395.

Van Sant, Ann Jessie. *Eighteenth-Century Sensibility and the Novel: The Senses in Social Context*. Cambridge: Cambridge University Press, 1993.

Veevers, Erica. *Images of Love and Religion: Queen Henrietta Maria and Court Entertainments*. Cambridge: Cambridge University Press, 1989.

Verbeke, Gerard. "Ethics and Logic in Stoicism." In Osler, ed., *Atoms, Pneuma, and Tranquillity*, 11–24.

Verdon, Michel. "On the Laws of Physical and Human Nature: Hobbes's Physical and Social Cosmologies." *Journal of the History of Ideas* 43 (1982): 653–663.

Vickers, Brian. "Analogy versus Identity: The Rejection of Occult Symbolism, 1580–1680." In Vickers, ed., *Occult and Scientific Mentalities*, 95–164.

———. "On the Function of Analogy in the Occult." In Merkel and Debus, eds., *Hermeticism and the Renaissance*, 265–292.

———, ed. *Occult and Scientific Mentalities in the Renaissance*. Cambridge: Cambridge University Press, 1984.

———. "'Words and Things'—or 'Words, Concepts, and Things'? Rhetorical and Linguistic Categories in the Renaissance." In *Res et Verba in der Renaissance*, edited by Eckhard Kessler and Ian Maclean, 287–335. Wiesbaden: Harrassowitz in Kommission, 2002.

Vivenza, Gloria. *Adam Smith and the Classics: The Classical Heritage in Adam Smith's Thought*. Oxford: Oxford University Press, 2001.

Voitle, Robert. *The Third Earl of Shaftesbury, 1671–1713*. Baton Rouge: Louisiana State University Press, 1984.

Waddell, Mark A. "The Perversion of Nature: Johannes Baptista Van Helmont, the Society of Jesus, and the Magnetic Cure of Wounds." *Canadian Journal of History* 38 (2003): 179–197.

Wagner, Geraldine. "Romancing Multiplicity: Female Subjectivity and the Body Divisible in Margaret Cavendish's *Blazing World*." *Early Modern Literary Studies* 9 (2003): 1–59. http://purl.oclc.org/emls/09–1/wagnblaz.htm.

Waldock, A. J. A. *"Paradise Lost" and Its Critics*. Cambridge: Cambridge University Press, 1962.

Walker, D. P. *The Ancient Theology: Studies in Christian Platonism from the Fifteenth to the Eighteenth Century*. Ithaca: Cornell University Press, 1972.

——. "Francis Bacon and *Spiritus*." In *Science, Medicine, and Society in the Renaissance: Essays to Honor Walter Pagel*, edited by Allen G. Debus, 121–130. Vol. 2. New York: Science History Publications, 1972.

——. *Spiritual and Demonic Magic from Ficino to Campanella*. 1958. Reprint, University Park: Pennsylvania State University Press, 2000.

Wallis, R. T. *Neoplatonism*. 2nd ed. Indianapolis: Hackett, 1995.

Walmsley, Peter. *The Rhetoric of Berkeley's Philosophy*. Cambridge: Cambridge University Press, 1990.

Walsham, Alexandra. "The Reformation and 'The Disenchantment of the World' Reassessed." *Historical Journal* 51 (2008): 497–528.

——. *The Reformation of the Landscape: Religion, Identity, and Memory in Early Modern Britain and Ireland*. Oxford: Oxford University Press, 2011.

Wasserman, Earl R. "Nature Moralized: The Divine Analogy in the Eighteenth Century." *English Literary History* 20 (1953): 39–76.

Weber, Max. *From Max Weber: Essays in Sociology*. Edited and translated by H. H. Gerth and C. Wright Mills. New York: Oxford University Press, 1958.

——. *The Protestant Ethic and the Spirit of Capitalism*. Translated by Talcott Parsons. London: Routledge, 1992.

Webster, Charles. "Alchemical and Paracelsian Medicine." In *Health, Medicine and Mortality in the Sixteenth Century*, edited by Charles Webster, 301–334. Cambridge: Cambridge University Press, 1979.

——. *From Paracelsus to Newton: Magic and the Making of Modern Science*. Cambridge: Cambridge University Press, 1982.

——. *Paracelsus: Medicine, Magic and Mission at the End of Time*. New Haven: Yale University Press, 2008.

——. "Paracelsus, Paracelsianism, and the Secularization of the Worldview." *Science in Context* 15 (2002): 9–27.

Weidlich, Theodor. "Die Sympathie in der antiken Litteratur." In *Programm des Karls-Gymnasiums in Stuttgart*. Stuttgart: K. Hofbuchdruckerei Carl Liebich, 1894.

Weitz, Nancy. "Romantic Fiction, Moral Anxiety, and Social Capital in Cavendish's 'Assaulted and Pursued Chastity.'" In Cottegnies and Weitz, eds., *Authorial Conquests*, 145–160.

Westman, Robert S. "Nature, Art, and Psyche: Jung, Pauli, and the Kepler-Fludd Polemic." In Vickers, ed., *Occult and Scientific Mentalities*, 177–229.

Whitaker, Katie. *Mad Madge: Margaret Cavendish, Duchess of Newcastle, Royalist, Writer, and Romantic.* London: Chatto & Windus, 2003.

Whyman, Susan E. *Sociability and Power in Late-Stuart England: The Cultural World of the Verneys, 1660–1720.* Oxford: Oxford University Press, 1999.

Willey, Basil. *The English Moralists.* London: Chatto & Windus, 1964.

Williams, Raymond. *The Country and the City.* New York: Oxford University Press, 1973.

———. *Keywords: A Vocabulary of Culture and Society.* Rev. ed. New York: Oxford University Press, 1985.

Williamson, George. "The Restoration Revolt against Enthusiasm." *Studies in Philology* 30 (1933): 571–603.

Wilson, Philip K. "'Out of Sight, Out of Mind?': The Daniel Turner-James Blondel Dispute over the Power of the Maternal Imagination." *Annals of Science* 49 (1992): 63–85.

Wise, James N. *Sir Thomas Browne's "Religio Medici" and Two Seventeenth-Century Critics.* Columbia: University of Missouri Press, 1973.

Wittington, Leah. "Vergil's Nisus and the Language of Self-Sacrifice in *Paradise Lost.*" *Modern Philology* 107 (2010): 588–606.

Wittreich, Joseph. *Feminist Milton.* Ithaca: Cornell University Press, 1987.

Wood, Christopher S. *Forgery, Replica, Fiction: Temporalities of German Renaissance Art.* Chicago: University of Chicago Press, 2008.

Wood, Paul B. *The Aberdeen Enlightenment: The Arts Curriculum in the Eighteenth Century.* Aberdeen: Aberdeen University Press, 1993.

———. "Hume, Reid and the Science of the Mind." In *Hume and Hume's Connexions*, edited by M. A. Stewart and John P. Wright, 119–139. University Park: Pennsylvania State University Press, 1994.

———. "Science and the Pursuit of Virtue in the Aberdeen Enlightenment." In Stewart, ed., *Studies in the Philosophy of the Scottish Enlightenment*, 127–149.

Woolf, Virginia. *The Common Reader.* New York: Harcourt, Brace, 1925.

Worden, Blair. *Literature and Politics in Cromwellian England: John Milton, Andrew Marvell, Marchamont Nedham.* Oxford: Oxford University Press, 2007.

Wright, John P. "Locke, Willis, and the Seventeenth-Century Epicurean Soul." In Osler, ed., *Atoms, Pneuma, and Tranquillity*, 239–258.

Yates, Frances A. *Giordano Bruno and the Hermetic Tradition.* Chicago: University of Chicago Press, 1964.

Yousef, Nancy. "Feeling for Philosophy: Shaftesbury and the Limits of Sentimental Certainty." *English Literary History* 78 (2011): 609–632.

Zagorin, Perez. "Cudworth and Hobbes on Is and Ought." In Kroll, Ashcraft, and Zagorin, eds., *Philosophy, Science, and Religion in England*, 128–150.

———. *Hobbes and the Law of Nature.* Princeton: Princeton University Press, 2009.

Zambelli, Paola. "L'immaginazione e il suo potere: Da al-Kindi, al-Farabi e Avicenna al Medioevo latino e al Rinascimento." In *Orientalische Kultur und Europäisches Mittelalter*, edited by Albert Zimmermann and Ingrid Craemer-Ruegenberg, 188–206. Berlin: De Gruyter, 1985.

———. "Magic and Radical Reformation in Agrippa of Nettesheim." *Journal of the Warburg and Courtauld Institutes* 39 (1976): 69–103.

———. *White Magic, Black Magic in the European Renaissance: From Ficino, Pico, Della Porta to Trithemius, Agrippa, Bruno.* Leiden: Brill, 2007.

Zarka, Yves-Charles. "Critique de Hobbes et fondement de la morale chez Cudworth." In Rogers, Vienne, and Zarka, eds., *Cambridge Platonists in Philosophical Context*, 39–52.

Ziller-Camenietzki, Carlos. "Jesuits and Alchemy in the Early Seventeenth Century: Father Johannes Roberti and the Weapon-Salve Controversy." *Ambix* 48 (2001): 83–101.

———. "La Poudre de Madame: La Trajectoire de la Guérison Magnétique des Blessures en France." *Dix-Septième Siècle* 211 (2001–2002): 285–305.

INDEX

Ablow, Rachel, 5
Abrams, M. H., 311
action at a distance: Cavendish and, 72, 74, 80–81, 99; concept of, 4; Cudworth and, 215; Fludd and, 144; in *Frankenstein*, 319; in *Paradise Lost*, 110, 141–49; psychological/social, 24, 63, 67, 72, 74, 80–81, 99; in *The Scarlet Letter*, 315, 322–23; of sympathetic cures, 33, 43, 50, 56; in sympathetic universe, 42
Adam: and ethics, 165–76; Eve's relationship with, 134–41, 161–65, 194–95; and the Fall, 149–55; Frankenstein and, 315–20; and human sympathy, 113, 131; order of nature discovered by, 130–31; reconciliation of Eve with, 157, 163–65; sins of, 149; sympathy between Eve and, 150–55; and universal/natural sympathy, 112, 127–28
Addison, Joseph, 305
Adorno, Theodor, 31, 32
aesthetics. *See* art, literature, and aesthetics
affection, 224, 250
Agrippa, Menenius, 20, 177
Agrippa von Nettesheim, Heinrich Cornelius, 10, 313, 316
Albertus Magnus, 313
alchemy, 29, 320–22. *See also* magic
Aldini, Giovanni, 318
Aldridge, Alfred Owen, 272
Alexander of Aphrodisias, 6

analogy: declining significance of, in eighteenth-century thought, 257; Hume's critique of, 297
Androtion, 7
animals: antipathy demonstrated by, 45; political analogy using, 191–92; sympathy demonstrated by, 45, 105
anima mundi, 13, 53, 144
animism, 8, 11, 13–15, 44
anthropomorphism, 290
anti-Epicureanism, 31, 86, 96, 201–2, 210–12, 221, 237–40, 260, 267, 284, 288, 305. *See also* Epicurus and Epicureanism
antipathy: Bacon's conception of, 12; Cavendish's conception of, 70, 85, 88–89; in the civil sphere, 176; Foucault on, 17; in Greek world view, 7; mechanistic explanation of, 45–46; Milton's conception of, 122–24; scientific approach to, 19; in social relations, 88–91; theoretical difficulties presented by, 74
apathy, 39, 232, 279
Archidoxis magica (pseudo-Paracelsian treatise), 40
Arendt, Hannah, 176
argument *in utrumque partem*, 79
Aristotle and Aristotelians: on action at a distance, 40, 43, 142, 144; anti-Pythagoreanism of, 115; authority of, 38; critiques of, 206–7; Digby as follower of, 37, 39, 47; epistemology of, 18; on pity, 106;